The Waite Group's
Microsoft® C
Bible

Nabajyoti Barkakati

HOWARD W. SAMS & COMPANY

A Division of Macmillan, Inc.
4300 West 62nd Street
Indianapolis, Indiana 46268 USA

To Leha, Ivy, and Emily

International Standard Book Number: 0-672-22620-0
Library of Congress Catalog Card Number: 88-61544

From The Waite Group, Inc.:
Development Editor: *Mitchell Waite*
Editorial Director: *James Stockford*
Content Editor: *Harry Henderson*
Technical Reviewer: *John Ferguson*
Managing Editor: *Scott Calamar*

From Howard W. Sams & Company:
Acquisitions Editor: *James S. Hill*
Development Editor: *James Rounds*
Manuscript Editor: *Don MacLaren, BooksCraft, Inc., Indianapolis*
Keyboarder: *Lee Hubbard*
Designer: *Glenn Santner*
Illustrator: *T. R. Emrick*
Cover Illustrator: *Kevin Caddell*
Indexer: *Ted Laux*
Compositor: *Shepard Poorman Communications Corp.*

Printed in the United States of America

Contents

III. Data Processing 187

IV. Files and I/O 375

V. Graphics 659

Preface

Microsoft C is a huge product, loaded with features, tools, aids, extensions, and manuals that no one book could ever fully describe. One of Microsoft C's greatest values is its huge library of C function calls. With its 370 routines, requiring almost 1,000 manual pages to cover (counting the C language reference and the library reference), the Microsoft C library lets you do everything from calculating an arc sine to drawing a pie chart to performing a quicksort of an array of strings.

Much of this power remains untapped, however. The manuals provided by Microsoft are *so* extensive that they are hard to use for ready reference, yet not detailed enough to use for learning. Their emphasis is on providing an "official" description of every function and feature. My approach, on the other hand, is to write as a programmer for programmers, to put the information you need at your fingertips while at the same time providing you with the background, context, and practical tips you need to master the C library.

Frankly, I wrote *The Waite Group's Microsoft C Bible* because *I* wanted such a book at my elbow when I wrote my next big C program. This book is based on The Waite Group's "bible" model, which has been successful in both the MS-DOS and UNIX worlds. My goal was to make a reference book that would be handy for looking up functions and would provide a clear and concise tutorial.

The Waite Group's Microsoft C Bible describes each of the 370 functions in the Microsoft C library. Practical, real-world MS-DOS-based examples are provided for each function. The routines are divided into functional categories, with an intermediate-level tutorial preceding each category, followed by the reference entries in alphabetical order. Additionally, this book features:

▶ Two "quick start" tutorials: one is a refresher course on the basic elements of the C language and one is on running the Microsoft C compiler, including a survey of its main features and options

- ▶ Tutorials that detail how the functions in each category are related, how to pick the right function to do a given job, and cautions to observe
- ▶ Complete ANSI prototypes for each function—a feature not found in the Microsoft manuals
- ▶ More extensive (and, I hope, more interesting) program examples than those in the Microsoft manuals
- ▶ Tables that provide helpful, MS-DOS-specific information
- ▶ Check boxes that tell you at a glance whether a given function is compatible with earlier releases of the Microsoft C compiler, the new ANSI draft standard, the System V UNIX library, QuickC, and Turbo C
- ▶ Quick access to any function through two "jump tables," one in alphabetical order and one grouped by functional category
- ▶ Suggestions for further reading on C in general, aspects of programming, and algorithms used by particular functions

Your use of this book can grow as your programming ability does. If you are new to programming, you can use this book as a learning resource, together with a good C primer such as those suggested in the *Further Reading* for the first tutorial. By reading the tutorials in order, you can ensure that you grasp all of the key ideas of C, move beyond the coverage of a "beginner's" book, and get a feel for the practical considerations involved in each area of programming. As you start to write programs you can study the various groups of functions in detail.

If you are an experienced programmer in languages other than C, this book can give you a fast start to learning C because its survey of C is complete but not condescending. Since you already know what programs have to do, you can quickly find out how they do it with Microsoft C. And if you are an experienced C programmer, you can jump to the second tutorial, quickly master the compiler, and then survey the functional areas to find out how Microsoft C deals with your areas of interest. This book will also help you port your applications to Microsoft C by enabling you to find equivalent functions quickly.

I hope you will be pleased with the convenience and utility of this book. If you have questions or suggestions, or would like to contribute to a future revision, please contact The Waite Group, 100 Shoreline Highway, Suite 285, Mill Valley, CA 94941.

Acknowledgments

From the author:

I am grateful to Mitchell Waite for providing me with the opportunity to write this book and for his guidance throughout the project. I would like to thank Harry Henderson for his thorough editing, helpful suggestions, and thoughtful comments. Finally, a project of this magnitude requires the support of family and friends. This book would not be possible without the love and inspiration of my wife Leha and my daughters Ivy and Emily. Thanks for being there!

Nabajyoti Barkakati

From Mitchell Waite:

Every once in a great while a writer comes to us who is so special that we must stop and acknowledge how lucky we are to have met him or her. I first met Naba Barkakati when he wrote a chapter on serial communications for *The Waite Group's MS-DOS Papers*. His chapter was especially lucid and had absolutely great illustrations (something unusual for computer book authors). What really shocked us was that he delivered the chapter early (unheard of in this industry)! Obviously, we needed this author. From that start, Naba has gone on to write what we think is the most comprehensive C reference book available.

I would like to take this opportunity to thank Naba for his commitment to this massive project (well over 1,200 manuscript pages, 370 program examples, and 100 tables) and for his diligence and sensitivity to the subject. This is truly his magnum opus.

I would like to thank Harry Henderson, editor of The Waite Group's UNIX and C series, for his meticulous editing, his ideas for example programs, and his sincere letters to the author. I would like to thank Jim Stockford for his valuable feedback on the page design and, along with Scott Calamar, for helping us to visualize and attain the right feeling for the cover art.

I would like to thank all the folks at Microsoft Corporation who have helped make this book possible, especially Greg Lobdell, Languages Group Project Manager, who provided constant updates of the beta versions of the Microsoft C compiler and continuing support to our author.

Finally, I give my thanks to the people behind the scenes at Howard W. Sams, who took our manuscript and turned it into a marketable product that we are all proud of: to Jim Hill for his faith in the idea for a user-friendly C reference book; to Wendy Ford for skillfully managing a most complex production job; to Kevin Caddell for the book's great cover painting; to Jim Rounds for casting off this back-breaker of a manuscript; to Glenn Santner for bringing the vision of the cover to the artists; to Don Herrington for coordinating the manuscript; to Don MacLaren for editing the manuscript; to Jim Irizarry and his sales team for moving our titles into the book stores in ever increasing quantities; to Damon Davis and Tom Surber for steering Howard W. Sams so wisely over the years; and to all the other people at Howard W. Sams who in one way or another were involved with making *The Waite Group's Microsoft C Bible* a success.

Mitchell Waite

Trademarks

All terms mentioned in this book that are known to be trademarks or service marks are listed below. In addition, terms suspected of being trademarks or service marks have been appropriately capitalized. Howard W. Sams & Co. cannot attest to the accuracy of this information. Use of a term in this book should not be regarded as affecting the validity of any trademark or service mark.

IBM, IBM PC, IBM AT, IBM XT, and OS/2 are registered trademarks of International Business Machines Corporation.

Codeview debugging program, Microsoft, MS-DOS, and QuickC are registered trademarks of Microsoft Corporation.

Turbo C is a registered trademark of Borland International.

UNIX is a registered trademark of Bell Laboratories.

WordStar is a registered trademark of Micropro International Corporation.

Introduction

Overall Organization

The book is organized into the following parts.

PART I: THE C LANGUAGE AND MICROSOFT C
This part is a refresher on C and the features of Microsoft C suitable for beginning and intermediate C programmers. Chapter 1, "Overview of the C Language," provides a succinct discussion of the C programming language including references to the proposed ANSI extensions. You can skip this section if you are already familiar with C. Chapter 2, "Microsoft C 5.1 Compiler Features and Options," discusses keywords and features of C programming that are specific to Microsoft C 5.1. For example, we describe the memory models offered by Microsoft C and keywords such as *interrupt* that are new to Microsoft C 5.0 and 5.1, and we detail the command-line options for the compiler program, CL.

PART II: PROCESS CONTROL AND MEMORY MANAGEMENT
Part II begins the tutorials and reference pages on the functions in the Microsoft C library. The common theme in this part is the management of processes, communication between functions, and memory management. This part includes the following categories of functions:

3. Process control
4. Variable-length argument lists
5. Memory allocation and management
6. Buffer manipulation

PART III: DATA PROCESSING
This part covers the routines that process, convert, calculate, and handle data. Such tasks as mathematical computations, searching, and sorting are discussed here. This part includes the categories:

7. Data conversion routines

8. Math routines

9. Character classification and conversion

10. String comparison and manipulation

11. Searching and sorting

12. Time routines

PART IV: FILES AND I/O Part IV focusses on routines that manipulate files and perform Input and Output (I/O) operations. The MS-DOS and BIOS interface routines are covered in Chapter 16, "System Calls." These categories are included:

13. File manipulation

14. Directory manipulation

15. Input and output routines

16. System calls

PART V: GRAPHICS The three chapters in this part describe the graphics routines introduced in Microsoft C 5.0. Chapter 17, "Graphics Modes, Coordinates, and Attributes," includes all the preliminary information you need to get started with graphics programming. Among the routines discussed are those that set colors, line styles, and fill masks and those that enable you to determine the status of parameters maintained internally by the graphics library. Chapter 18, "Drawing and Animation," covers the objects you can draw with the graphics routines, including point, line, rectangle, ellipse, arc, and pie. We also discuss how to perform animation. Chapter 19, "Combining Graphics and Text," describes the text output routines and tells you how to control the appearance of text on the screen and confine text to a window.

Chapter Organization

Beginning with Chapter 3, each chapter begins with a tutorial on the category of routines being discussed in that section. Each tutorial establishes the concepts necessary to understand and use that category of routines. In each category the routines are catalogued alphabetically and also grouped according to the tasks they perform. The tutorials show how the functions in a group are related, and details their similarities and differences so you will know which of many similarly-named functions is appropriate for a given situation. They show you how to use the functions to perform commonly needed programming tasks and in many cases offer suggestions for further reading.

The tutorial is followed by the reference entries for the functions in that category, arranged alphabetically. The reference entries provide a structured guide to the purpose, syntax, and usage of the function and contain an example call and example program using the function. Here's how each reference entry is presented:

| | | The name of the function |

_getfillmask

COMPATIBILITY	MSC 3	MSC 4	MSC 5	QC	TC	ANSI	UNIX V
			▲	▲	getfillpattern		

PURPOSE Use _getfillmask to retrieve the 8 bytes that define the current 8×8 mask used by the routines _floodfill, _rectangle, _ellipse, and _pie that fill an area with the current color. (See the description of _setfillmask for an explanation of how the fill mask is used.)

SYNTAX `unsigned char far * far _getfillmask(unsigned char far *fillmask);`

`unsigned char far *fillmask;` 8×8 bit pattern that determines how the filled area looks

EXAMPLE CALL `p_mask = _getfillmask(current_mask);`

INCLUDES `#include <graph.h>` For function declaration

DESCRIPTION The _getfillmask function is used to retrieve the 8×8 pattern of bits that serves as the current mask to be used by the routines _floodfill, _rectangle, _ellipse, and _pie to fill an area with the current color.

The fill pattern is returned in eight characters whose address is provided to _getfillmask in the argument fillmask. The reference page on _setfillmask explains how to interpret the fill mask.

COMMON USES This function gets and saves the current fill mask so that the mask can be restored to its original value before exiting a graphics routine.

RETURNS If no mask is present, _getfillmask returns a NULL.

COMMENTS If you switch fill masks in a graphics routine, it is a good idea first to use _getfillmask to retrieve the current mask so that you can restore the mask to normal before returning from the routine.

SEE ALSO _setfillmask To define a new fill mask

EXAMPLE Write a C program to obtain the current fill mask by using the _getfillmask function. Then alter the mask and verify that this has indeed happened by calling _getfillmask again.

```
#include <stdio.h>
#include <graph.h>
#define RED 4      /* Color number 4 is red */
/* Define a fill mask */
unsigned char fillmask[8] =
     { 1, 3, 7, 0xf, 0x1f, 0x3f, 0x7f, 0xff },
     oldmask[8];  /* Placeholder for old fill mask */
```

Left-column annotations:

- The name of the function
- A bullet appears when the function is available. For Turbo C, the name of the compatible function is shown
- Short description of where function is used
- Full ANSI prototype. Shows argument declarations also
- Shows how function is used
- Lists include files needed by the function
- How the function works and how you should use it
- Situations in which the function is helpful
- The value returned by the function if any
- Special notes that might help you avoid mistakes and use the function effectively
- Related functions and how they are related
- One or more complete example programs illustrating how function is used

About the Author

Nabajyoti Barkakati works as an electronics engineer for a well-known research laboratory. He began his programming career in 1975 and he has worked extensively with FORTRAN, C, and several assembly languages. An avid programmer still, he is primarily interested in developing communications and graphics software on the IBM PC and Macintosh. He has a Ph.D. in electrical engineering from the University of Maryland at College Park.

I The C Language and Microsoft C

- ► Overview of the C Language
- ► Microsoft C 5.1 Compiler Features and Options

Introduction

The composition of C—a sparse core with a large support library—makes it an ideal language for developing software on the IBM PC. The core offers a good selection of data types and control structures while all additional tasks, including input and output (I/O), graphics, math computations, and access to peripheral devices are relegated to a library of functions. This access to all parts of the system enables you to harness the system's full potential.

Many C compilers are available for use with PCs, but with such utilities as MAKE for automating recompilations and with the CodeView symbolic debugger with full-screen user interface Microsoft C offers one of the best environments for program development. The 5.0 version introduced in 1987 improves an already-good product. The library has been enhanced with many more routines, most notably for system calls (for accessing DOS and BIOS services) and for graphics. The Quick C integrated programming environment provides new ease of use. The language implementation conforms to the proposed ANSI standard for C and the library is also compatible now with UNIX System V. In 1988 a new version, Microsoft C 5.1, was introduced. This update provides support for the OS/2 operating system. With it, you can build both OS/2 "protected" mode and "real" mode (which is the same as DOS 3.x) applications. Overall, the changes from version 5.0 to 5.1 are minor, especially those in the run-time library, the primary topic of this book.

This book is designed to help you use the Microsoft C 5.1 compiler to its fullest potential. We focus on the library because it is the library which gives a C compiler its personality. The concepts that unify each group of related functions are presented in a *tutorial* section followed by individual *reference* pages on each member function.

This chapter constitutes a refresher course on C, including a list of reading material on C and programming on the IBM PC. Chapter 2 summarizes features specific to Microsoft C 5.1 and describes the compiler and the linker that you use to build your programs. In the following discussion of the basic features of C, we will point out how the proposed draft ANSI standard for C affects a particular feature. For your convenience, these notes are marked with the symbol: ⌐AN⌐SI⌐

Structure of a C Program

As shown in Figure 1-1, a file containing a C program consists of preprocessor directives, declarations of variables and functions, a *main* function, the body of the *main* function, and other functions. The body of each function, including *main*, contains expressions and statements.

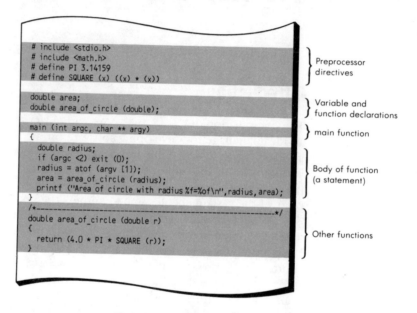

```
# include <stdio.h>
# include <math.h>
# define PI 3.14159
# define SQUARE (x) ((x) * (x))
```
} Preprocessor directives

```
double area;
double area_of_circle (double);
```
} Variable and function declarations

```
main (int argc, char ** argv)
{
```
} main function

```
    double radius;
    if (argc <2) exit (0);
    radius = atof (argv [1]);
    area = area_of_circle (radius);
    printf ("Area of circle with radius %f=%of\n",radius,area);
}
```
} Body of function (a statement)

```
/*_____*/
double area_of_circle (double r)
{
    return (4.0 * PI * SQUARE (r));
}
```
} Other functions

Figure 1-1. *Structure of a C program*

The "preprocessor" is a facility unique to C. As its name implies, it processes the source file before the compilation begins. The preprocessor performs several important tasks such as incorporating the contents of another file into the C program (the *#include* directive) and replacing one string pattern in the program with another (the *#define* directive).

"Declarations" state which variables and functions will be used in the program and what type of data will be used by each. Declarations outside the body of the functions are *global*, that is, they are available to any functions, including code in other source files. Variables and functions from other files used by functions in this file are also declared: these declarations are "external." Variables "local" to a function are declared within the body of the function. Declaring a variable also informs the compiler to allocate storage for that variable. Storage is not allocated, however, for variables referenced from other files.

The "body of a function" contains declarations that are local to that function and statements and expressions that implement the procedure being performed by that function. The "statements" control the flow of execution and use the values provided by expressions. An "expression" is a combination of operators, variables, and function calls that result in a single value. An expression is always part of a statement.

Preprocessor Directives

The preprocessor processes the source text of a program file and acts on commands, called "preprocessor directives," embedded in the text. These directives begin with the character **#**. Usually the compiler automatically invokes the preprocessor before beginning compilation, but in Microsoft C 5.1, you can invoke the preprocessor alone by using the /E or /EP options. The preprocessor provides three important services that enable users to make their programs modular, more easily readable, and easier to customize for different computer systems: including the contents of a file into their C program (file inclusion), replacing one string with another (token replacement and macro processing), and compiling selected portions of a program (conditional compilation).

FILE INCLUSION The ability to include files provides for modularity. Declarations that are used repeatedly can be held in a file and included where needed using *#include*, which can be used in three formats:

```
#include <stdio.h>
#include "local.h"
#include "c:\test\specific.h"
```

The first and the most common format asks the preprocessor to read in the named file, in this case a standard C header file, *stdio.h*, from the default include directory. In Microsoft C, the default directory is specified either by the environment variable INCLUDE or by the compiler option /I. The next two forms of the directive each specify the exact pathname of the file to be included. In the example, the preprocessor will first try to locate *local.h* in the directory in which the source code resides, whereas the search for *specific.h* occurs in the directory \test of drive *c*.

Search Rules for Header Files

The preprocessor in Microsoft C 5.1 searches up to three sets of directories for a file to be included: the current working directory, the directories specified with the compiler option /I, and the directories listed in the INCLUDE environment variable. The order in which these directories are searched depends on the format of the file name in the *#include* directive.

⟨*filename*⟩   First search the directories specified with the /I compiler option, then the directories listed in the INCLUDE environment variable.

"*filename*"   First search the current working directory, then the directories given with the /I compiler option and finally, the list in the INCLUDE environment.

"*c:\ . . . \filename*"   Look for the file in the specified directory only.

Token Replacement and Macro Processing

One common use of the preprocessor is to replace all occurrences of a "string" (or "token") with another, for example, to define a symbolic name for a numerical constant. This greatly improves the readability of the source code. The *#define* directive is used for this purpose. This directive can be used in two forms, one of which takes optional parameters. Here is an example:

```
#define PI         3.14159
#define SQUARE(x) ((x)*(x))
```

The first *#define* directive simply stipulates that the string *3.14159* be substituted at every occurrence of the string *PI* in the source file. The second line defines a macro with one parameter. A "macro" can have arguments or parameters just as a function does. In this case, if you use *SQUARE(2)* in your code, it becomes *((2)*(2))* after the preprocessor has performed the replacement. This macro is the equivalent of a function that squares its arguments. By the way, notice the number of parentheses in the definition of *SQUARE(x)*. They are absolutely necessary. To understand why, consider what happens when we define *SQUARE(x)* simply as *x*x*. Suppose you use the macro in the form *SQUARE(y+z)* to square the sum of two variables *y* and *z*. After the preprocessor makes the replacements, the macro reduces to *y+z*y+z* which is certainly not what you want. With the definition shown earlier, the macro would have generated *((y+z)*(y+z))* which gives the correct result. Use parentheses liberally when defining macros with arguments that could possibly be ambiguous.

⌐AN⌐
⌐SI⌐
TOKEN PASTING
AND STRING-IZING
OPERATORS

The ANSI proposal includes two new preprocessor operators that are supported by Microsoft C 5.1. The first one, called the "token-pasting" operator, enables you to join one token to another to create a third token. Here is an example:

```
#define MSC4 4
#define MSC5 5
#define version(x) MSC##x
```

When the preprocessor replaces *version(5)*, it first gets the string *MSC##5* which, upon interpretation of the "token-pasting" operator, reduces to the token *MSC5*. The preprocessor finds that this token is defined to be *5* and uses it as the replacement for the macro *version(5)*.

The "string-izing" operator makes a string out of an operand with a *#* prefix. It does this by putting the operand in quotes. For example, if you defined and used a macro *value_now* as

```
#define value_now(x)  printf(#x" = %d\n", x)
    :
    :
value_now(counter);
```

the preprocessor generates the statement

```
printf("counter"" = %d\n", counter);
```

as the replacement. Since the ANSI proposal also stipulates that adjacent strings will be concatenated, this becomes equivalent to

```
printf("counter = %d\n", counter);
```

which illustrates when the "string-izing operator" is useful.

Conditional Compilation

This feature lets you control which parts of a source file get compiled, under which conditions. This capability enables you to maintain a single set of source files that can be compiled with different compilers and in different environments. Other forms of customization are also possible; for example, you may decide to insert *printf* statements for debugging that are compiled only if a symbol named DEBUG is defined.

The directives *#if, #elif, #else* and *#endif* are the primary means of conditionally excluding portions of text from use by the compiler. The *#ifdef* and *#ifndef* directives, special cases of the *#if* directive, are used more widely than the other conditional directives. The typical use of these directives is of the form:

```
    :
    :
#ifdef DEBUG
    printf("Count = %d\n", count);
#endif
    :
    :
#if defined(MSC)
```

```
   #include <graph.h>
#elif defined(TURBOC)
   #include <graphics.h>
#endif
```

The first fragment shows the use of *#ifdef* to compile a *printf* statement only if the symbol DEBUG is defined. This can be done by using the /D option at compile time. The second fragment of code shows how you can include a different header file depending on which symbol, MSC or TURBOC, is defined.

Other Preprocessor Directives

There are several other preprocessor directives meant for miscellaneous tasks. For example, the *#undef* directive can be used to undo the current definition of a symbol. Using *#undef DEBUG* removes the definition of *DEBUG*, for instance.

The Microsoft C compiler maintains two predefined preprocessor symbols, _ _FILE_ _ and _ _LINE_ _. The first refers to the current input file name and the latter refers to the current line number being processed by the compiler. You can use the *#line* directive to change their values. For example, *#line 20 "myprog.c"* causes the line number maintained by the compiler to be reset to 20 and the file name to be changed to *myprog.c*. This feature is useful when you write a translator that takes an input file in a *language* of your design (let us call it MY4GL, for "my 4th-generation language") and generates a C source file. When working with the source file, you can insert *#line* directives to refer to the file name of the MY4GL file and the line number that you are translating and use the _ _FILE_ _ and the _ _LINE_ _ symbols in reporting errors. That way, the printed error messages make sense because they refer to the line numbers in the original MY4GL file. With version 5.1, Microsoft has added further means to control compilation through predefined processor symbols. (See our discussion in Chapter 2 and Table 2-4.)

The *#pragma* is another special-purpose directive that you can use to instruct the C compiler to turn on or off certain features. Pragmas vary from one compiler to another. Here is a list of pragmas supported by the Microsoft C compiler. Pragmas introduced with version 5.1 are so indicated. These new pragmas deal with formatting source listings and placing comments in the object file generated by the compiler.

#pragma alloc_text(text_segment, function1, function2 . . .)   Places the far functions (function1, function2 . . .) in *text_segment*—where the compiled code (the *code segment*) resides. This is useful for organizing the memory layout of code.

#pragma check_stack(on) or #pragma check_stack(off)   Turns on or off the generation of stack-checking code. (Also see compiler option /Gs.)

#pragma comment (commenttype, [commentstring]) (version 5.1)   Places a comment record of type *commenttype* in the object file. The optional parameter *commentstring* is used to add additional information to comment records. The following comment record types are supported:

Record	Description
compiler	Places the name and the version number of the compiler in a comment record. The *commentstring* parameter is not needed. The linker ignores this comment record.
exestr	Places the string specified by *commentstring* in a comment record. The linker copies this string into the executable file. This comment can be used to add a version number or copyright information to an executable file.
lib	Places the *commentstring* into a library search comment record. The linker searches the named library to resolve external references. The parameter *commentstring* should be the name of a library, including, if necessary, the complete pathname.
user	Places the *commentstring* into a general comment record that is ignored by the linker.

#pragma data_seg([segmentname]) (version 5.1)   When present, *segmentname* is used as the name of the data segment to be loaded by any subsequent function that will load its own data segment (see the *_loadds* reference pages for more information). If the parameter *segmentname* is missing, the compiler uses the segment name specified with the /ND option. If the /ND option is also absent, DGROUP is used.

#pragma function(name1, name2 . . .)   Tells the compiler to generate function calls instead of using the intrinsic forms of the functions (*name1, name2 . . .).* Using the *"intrinsic"* form implies placing the code of the function in-line, giving faster execution because function calls increase program size.

#pragma intrinsic (name1, name2 . . .)   Tells the compiler to use the intrinsic form of functions called "name1, name2. . . . "

#pragma linesize([numchars]) (version 5.1)   Tells the compiler the line size to use when generating source listings. The value of *numchars* should be between 79 and 132. If you do not specify *numchars*, the value given by the /Sl option is used. If the /Sl option is not used, the line size defaults to 79 characters.

#pragma loop_opt(on) or #pragma loop_opt(off)   Turns on or off loop optimizing. Also controllable by compiler option /O.

#pragma message(messagestring) (version 5.1)   Tells the compiler to display the string *messagestring* as it processes the line with this pragma.

#pragma pack(1) or #pragma pack(2) or #pragma pack(4)   Specifies the byte boundary for packing members of C structures. (Also see compiler option /Zp.)

#pragma page([numpages]) (version 5.1)   Asks the compiler to generate form feeds in the source listing at the line where this pragma appears. The number of form feeds is specified by the parameter *numpages* which must be between 1 and 127. If *numpages* is missing, a default value of 1 is used.

#pragma pagesize([numlines]) (version 5.1)   Specifies the number of lines per page for source listings. The parameter *numlines* must be between 15 and 255. When *numlines* is absent, the value specified with the command line option /Sp is used. If the /Sp option is also missing, a default value of 63 lines per page is used.

#pragma same_seg(variable1, variable2 . . .)   Directs the compiler to assume that the external far variables named *variable1, variable2 . . .* are all in the same segment. Use option /ND when compiling the modules where the variables are actually defined.

#pragma skip([numlines]) (version 5.1)   Directs the compiler to skip *numlines* (a value between 1 and 127) lines in the source listing. If *numlines* is not specified, 1 line is skipped.

#pragma subtitle(subtitlestring) (version 5.1)   Tells the compiler to use the string *subtitlestring* as the subtitle for the rest of the pages in the source listing. The subtitle appears below the title on each page of the listing.

#pragma title(titlestring) (version 5.1)   Tells the compiler to use the string *titlestring* as the title for the rest of the pages in the source listing. The title appears in the upper left hand corner of each listing page.

Comments

A comment is an explanatory statement that is not part of the program code itself, but serves to document the operation of the program: /* marks a comment's beginning and */ marks its end. For example:

```
int score;  /* player's total score */
```

This comment explains the use of the variable *score*, which is declared here. A comment can appear on multiple lines as well:

```
/* comment line one */
/* comment line two */
```

Or, as an alternative style:

```
/* comment line one
   comment line two */
```

Microsoft C 5.1 provides a new way to indicate comments: by starting them with a pair of slashes (//). This means anything from the // to the end of the line is a comment. For example:

```
printf("%c", name);  // the rest of this line is a comment
```

or

```
prinft("%s", msgstr);
// All of this line is a comment
```

Since this feature is nonstandard, you may want to avoid using it. After all, the standard C comments are easy to use, and the single-line comments provide no added functionality to your program.

Declarations in C

All variables and functions must be declared before use. The declaration of a variable specifies the "visibility" and the "lifetime" of the variable, its "type," and, where allowed, its initial value. The declaration of a function specifies its "visibility" as well as the type of value it returns.

DATA TYPES IN C   There are four basic data types in C: *char, int, float,* and *double.* The *char* and *int* are for storing characters and integers, and *float* and *double* are for floating-point numbers. The storage sizes for the floating-point types depend on the convention used to represent floating-point numbers in binary form. Microsoft C uses the Institute of Electrical and Electronics Engineers (IEEE) format, for floating-point numbers. A *char* takes a single byte while an *int* is the same size as a word on the underlying machine (for instance, 2 bytes on the IBM PC—and in Microsoft C—and 4 bytes on a DEC VAX). Here are some declarations using the basic types:

```
char    c;
int     count, i, j;
float   a, b;
double  x, y, z;
```

The basic data types can be expanded into a much larger set with the use of the *long, short*, and *unsigned* qualifiers as prefixes. The *long* and the *short* qualifiers are size modifiers. For example, a *long int* is 4 bytes long in Microsoft C, capable of holding a much larger value than an *int.* In Chapter 2 (in Table 2-1) we list the sizes of data types in Microsoft C and the range of values that each type can store. The *unsigned* qualifier is for *int* and *char* types only. Normally, each holds negative as well as positive values; this is the default *signed* form of these variable types. With the *unsigned* qualifier, you tell the compiler that the variable will hold positive values only, which allows the variable to hold maximum values twice as large as signed ones. Here is a fragment of C code showing the use of the qualifiers.

```
unsigned char  c;
short i, j, small_int;   /* Shorthand for "short int" */
long large_int;          /* Shorthand for "long int"  */
unsigned count;          /* Shorthand for "unsigned int" */
unsigned short ui, uj;
```

```
unsigned long   ul;

long double     xlarge;
```

Note that when the *long, short,* and *unsigned* qualifiers are used with *int* types, you can drop the *int* from the declaration. Also, among the floating-point types, only *double* takes the *long* qualifier.

NEW DATA TYPE: ENUM

The proposed ANSI C standard introduces the type *enum*, which holds one integer value from a fixed set of named integer constants. An *enum* variable can be used anywhere an *int* type is used. The *enum* type can be used in such a situation as:

```
enum boolean {false = 0, true = 1, no = 0, yes = 1, off = 0, on = 1};
enum boolean flag = off;
```

The example shows several properties of *enum*. The first line defines *boolean* to be an enumerated type. The list within the braces shows the constants that are valid values of a *enum boolean* variable. Each constant can be initialized to a value of your choice and several constants can use the same value. In our example, we have chosen the constants *false, no* and *off* to be 0 and *true, yes* and *on* to be 1. The second line shows the declaration of an enumerated variable of type *boolean*. Its name is *flag* and it is initially set to *off*. Note that *enum* does not introduce a new basic data type; it simply improves the readability of your programs.

The *long double* is another type of floating-point variable specified in the ANSI standard. Some older compilers recognize ·the type *long float*, which is no longer valid under the proposed standard.

ARRAYS

An "array" is a convenient way to organize a large number of identical data items. You can declare arrays of any type of data item, including structures and types defined by the *typedef* statement. Arrays can be single- or multidimensional. For example,

```
char    str[81];
int     id[100];
double  x[40], a[5][10];
:
str[0] = 'A';   /* Set the first character in str to 'A' */
id[99] = -1;    /* The last element in array id is -1    */
a[4][9] = x[1]; /* Copy an element of x into another in a */
```

declares a character string, *str*, capable of holding 81 characters, an array of 100 integers named *id*, an array of 40 double variables *x*, and a 5×10 two-dimensional array of doubles, *a*. Using the syntax of the last three lines any element in an array can be referenced. Notice that while the dimension of an array shows the actual number of items, the index goes up from 0. So an array with 100 elements can have indices ranging from 0 to 99. Also, strings in C are

always terminated by a byte containing a 0 (a "null character" denoted by \0).
Thus, in our example, *str* can only hold 80 characters because the last space
will be occupied by a null. A two-dimensional array represents a "matrix,"
such as a spreadsheet. Think of a *[5][10]* as a spreadsheet with 5 rows and 10
columns, capable of holding up to 50 elements. Since memory is not laid out
like a spreadsheet, the actual storage is done by laying out one row after another in memory. In the notation shown above, the second dimension denotes the number of columns, or the number of elements along a row.
Because C stores a matrix by row, it always needs the second dimension in
the declaration of a matrix.

POINTERS   A "pointer" is a variable that can hold the address of an object that can be
either a variable or a function. If *px* is a pointer to an integer, you would declare and use it as

```
int *px, x;
:
px = &x;
```

The compiler will allocate storage space for an integer *x* and a *pointer to the
integer px*. The number of bytes necessary to hold the address will depend
on the machine's addressing scheme. Of course, you should not use *px* until
it contains the address of a valid object. The last line shows *px* being initialized to the address of the integer variable *x* (The *&* operator extracts the address of *x*). Following this, you can refer to the value of *x* with **px* ("the
contents of the object whose address is in *px* ").

Pointers are useful in many situations. Consider, for example, dynamic
allocation of memory. In C you can request a chunk of memory—enough to
hold, say, 100 integers. Once the memory is reserved, you get back the starting address of the block. Since this address is the only way to reach that memory block, you must store it in a variable capable of holding the address of an
integer, so you need a pointer to an integer. If you used *px* for this purpose,
how could you access the integers in that block of memory? You would treat
it like an "array" of 100 integers with the name *px*. So the last element in the
array is referenced as

```
px[99]
```

which is equivalent to

```
*(px+99)
```

Similarly, the compiler treats the name of an array as a pointer to the first
element of the array (element 0). The difference between the name of an array
and a pointer variable is that the first is a "constant" lacking explicit storage
necessary to hold the address of the array's first element, whereas the latter is
actually a "storage bin" capable of holding the address of any data of a specific type.

Neither an array nor a function can be returned by a function. To circumvent this, you can give the address of the array or the function that you want as the return value. (We will discuss *pointers to functions* in a later section.)

STRUCTURES AND UNIONS

When organizing any type of data, it is preferable to group items in a way that makes sense. For example, when storing the names and addresses of acquaintances, we treat the name and the address of each person as a single data record. In C you can organize your data in this manner with "structures." The definition of a structure to hold names, addresses, and some other information might look like:

```
struct financial;
{
    double        annual_income;
    double        life_insurance;
    double        net_worth;
    unsigned char investment_strategy;
};


struct client_info
{
    char            name[80];
    char            company[80];
    char            mailstop[20];
    char            street[80];
    char            city[40];
    char            state[40];
    unsigned int    zipcode;
    struct financial details;
};


struct client_info client[100];
```

This is the data base of an investment counselor. First we define a structure called *financial* that contains information about the client's financial situation. Each of the data fields in the *financial* structure, such as *annual_income* and *life_insurance*, is called a "member" of the structure. Next we define the structure *client_info* that contains the name and address of the client as well as the *financial* structure embedded in it. The last line declares a 100-element array called *client* in which each element is a structure of type *client_info*. (The fields of a structure are accessed by the "member selection" operator, which we will discuss later.)

"Unions" are declared like structures, but they are used when you want to view the same data item in different ways. The header file *dos.b* in Microsoft C library includes an example. Each of the 8086 registers AX, BX, CX and DX is 16 bits in size, but each can also be thought of as two 8-bit registers; for example, the 16-bit AX comprises the 8-bit registers AH and AL.

To use one storage area for these registers, but to refer to them in either manner, we first declare a structure, WORDREGS, containing the 16-bit registers:

```
struct WORDREGS
{
    unsigned int ax;
    unsigned int bx;
    unsigned int cx;
    unsigned int dx;
    unsigned int si;
    unsigned int di;
    unsigned int cflag;
};
```

Then we define another structure, BYTEREGS, using symbols for the 8-bit registers:

```
struct BYTEREGS
{
    unsigned char al, ah;
    unsigned char bl, bh;
    unsigned char cl, ch;
    unsigned char dl, dh;
};
```

Now a "union" of the two structures enables us to refer either to WORDREGS or BYTEREGS, accessing the registers as 16-bit or as 8-bit entities. The union that overlays the two structures is defined as:

```
union REGS
{
    struct WORDREGS x;
    struct BYTEREGS h;
};
```

Now if we declare *union REGS reg1* in the program, we can access the AH register using the name *reg1.h.ah*, and a reference such as *reg1.x.ax* gets the 16-bit AX register.

NAMING YOUR OWN DATA TYPES

Using the *typedef* facility, you can define names for your own data types. Here are some examples:

```
typedef unsigned char byte;
typedef struct POINT
{
    short x;
    short y;
} POINT;
```

```
typedef POINT *P_POINT;   /* Defines P_POINT as pointer to POINT */

byte    flag;
POINT   a, b;
P_POINT p_a = &a;
```

We have defined *byte*, POINT, and P_POINT as synonyms for other data types. The last three lines show the use of the new data types. Note that we first defined POINT and then used it in the definition of P_POINT. In this way, you can use *typedef* to declare complex data types.

Visibility and Lifetime of Variables

The "visibility" or the "scope" of a variable tells you which source file (also called a "module") of your program can use the variable without declaring it. For example, all variables that are declared outside the body of functions are global in nature; any module can use them. On the other hand, declarations within the function's body define variables that are visible only inside that function. Take, for example, the code:

```
:
int current_object_id;
:
:
main()
{
    int id;
    :
    :
    id = create_object();
    :
}
int create_object()
{
    int id;
    :
    :
    if(current_object_id == 0) ...
    :
    return(id);
}
```

The variable *current_object_id* is declared before any of the functions (including *main*), so it is visible in the entire source file. On the other hand, the variable *id* is local to *main( )* and to *create_object( )*. Each function has its own copy of *id*. Changes made to one copy do not affect any of the others.

The variable *current_object_id* is not only visible in its source file, it can even be referenced from any other file with the declaration

```
extern int current_object_id;
```

This is how global variables are used in C. Since the variable may be accessed at any time during the execution of the program, these variables are allocated storage for the life of the program and are said to have global "lifetimes."

The qualifier *static* also declares variables with global lifetimes, but it restricts the visibility of variables to a single source file. For example, you could define the variable *current_object_id* as

```
static int current_object_id = 0;
```

in a file and use it within the file without altering its globally visible counterpart with the same name. In other words, you have a separate storage location for the copy of *current_object_id* that is visible only in the file in which it is declared.

When a variable, such as *id* in our example, is defined within the body of a function, its storage remains allocated as long as that function is active. Such variables are said to have local lifetimes. You can also declare variables with local lifetimes by using the reserved words *auto* and *register*. Variables declared inside a function are by default of type *auto*. The *register* storage specifier is a hint to the compiler to place that variable in a register, if possible. You can use the *register* qualifier only for variables of type *int* or for pointers that can be stored in the same number of bytes as an *int*. Table 1-1 summarizes the information on the visibility and lifetime of declarations in C.

Table 1-1. *Scope and Lifetime of C Declarations*

Where Declared	Keyword	Visibility	Lifetime
Before all functions in a file (may be initialized here)	None	Entire file plus other files where variable is declared extern	Until program ends (global)
Before all functions in a file (cannot be initialized here)	extern	Entire file plus other files where variable is declared	Global
Before all functions in a file	static	Only in that file	Global
Inside a function	None or auto	Only in that function	Until function returns
Inside a function	register	Only in that function	Until function returns
Inside a function	static	Only in that function	Global

NEW KEYWORDS: CONST AND VOLATILE

Two new keywords, *const* and *volatile*, are part of the proposed ANSI standard C. You can use *const* as a modifier in a declaration to tell the compiler that the particular data object must not be modified by the program. This means the compiler must not generate code that might alter the contents of the location where that data item is stored. On the other hand, *volatile* specifies that the value of a variable may be changed by factors beyond the control of the program. You can use both keywords on a single data item to mean that while the item must not be modified by your program, it may be altered by some other process. The *const* and *volatile* keywords always modify the item immediately to their right. The information provided by *const* and the *volatile* helps the compiler optimize the code it generates. For example, if you declare and initialize the variable *x* as

```
const int x = 1024;
```

the compiler need not generate code to load the value of *x* from memory. Instead it can use the value 1024 wherever *x* is used. However, if you add *volatile*:

```
volatile const int x = 1024;
```

the compiler cannot optimize away any reference to *x* because its contents might be changed by an external process. This can happen when you declare a pointer to an I/O port or video memory in order to access them from your program.

FUNCTION DECLARATIONS

A function declaration tells the compiler the type of value the function returns and the number and type of arguments it takes. Most of us are used to declaring functions only when they return something other than an *int*. For example, a typical declaration would be

```
char *locate_char();
```

This changes under the proposed ANSI standard for C.

PROTOTYPES

The introduction of *function prototypes* is probably the most significant feature of ANSI C. It requires you to declare the formal parameters that a function takes as well as the return value. If our sample function *locate_char( )* takes a string and an integer as an argument, the ANSI-style prototype for this function is

```
char *locate_char(char *, int);
```

with the formal argument list shown with the type of each parameter only. You may include an identifier for each formal parameter, such as

```
char *locate_char(char *str, int c);
```

HOWARD W. SAMS & COMPANY

Bookmark

DEAR VALUED CUSTOMER:

Howard W. Sams & Company is dedicated to bringing you timely and authoritative books for your personal and professional library. Our goal is to provide you with excellent technical books written by the most qualified authors. You can assist us in this endeavor by checking the box next to your particular areas of interest.

We appreciate your comments and will use the information to provide you with a more comprehensive selection of titles.

Thank you,

Vice President, Book Publishing
Howard W. Sams & Company

COMPUTER TITLES:

Hardware
- ☐ Apple 140
- ☐ Macintosh I01
- ☐ Commodore I10
- ☐ IBM & Compatibles I14

Business Applications
- ☐ Word Processing J01
- ☐ Data Base J04
- ☐ Spreadsheets J02

Operating Systems
- ☐ MS-DOS K05
- ☐ OS/2 K10
- ☐ CP/M K01
- ☐ UNIX K03

ELECTRONICS TITLES:
- ☐ Amateur Radio T01
- ☐ Audio T03
- ☐ Basic Electronics T20
- ☐ Basic Electricity T21
- ☐ Electronics Design T12
- ☐ Electronics Projects T04
- ☐ Satellites T09

Programming Languages
- ☐ C L03
- ☐ Pascal L05
- ☐ Prolog L12
- ☐ Assembly L01
- ☐ BASIC L02
- ☐ HyperTalk L14

Troubleshooting & Repair
- ☐ Computers S05
- ☐ Peripherals S10

Other
- ☐ Communications/Networking M03
- ☐ AI/Expert Systems T18

- ☐ Instrumentation T05
- ☐ Digital Electronics T11

Troubleshooting & Repair
- ☐ Audio S11
- ☐ Television S04
- ☐ VCR S01
- ☐ Compact Disc S02
- ☐ Automotive S06
- ☐ Microwave Oven S03

Other interests or comments: _____

_____

Name _____

Title _____

Company _____

Address _____

City _____

State/Zip _____

Daytime Telephone No. _____

A Division of Macmillan, Inc.
4300 West 62nd Street Indianapolis, Indiana 46268

22620

Bookmark

fff

HOWARD W. SAMS & COMPANY

BUSINESS REPLY CARD

FIRST CLASS   PERMIT NO. 1076   INDIANAPOLIS, IND.

POSTAGE WILL BE PAID BY ADDRESSEE

HOWARD W. SAMS & CO.
ATTN: Public Relations Department
P.O. BOX 7092
Indianapolis, IN 46209-9921

HOWARD W. SAMS & COMPANY

Dept. DM
4300 West 62nd Street
Indianapolis, IN 46268-2589

In this case, the prototype can look exactly like the first line in the definition of the function, except that in the prototype you terminate the line with a semicolon.

What is the purpose of the prototype? It is mainly there to help the compiler check function arguments and to let it generate code that uses a faster mechanism to return from functions. Since the prototype tells the compiler the exact number and type of arguments to expect, it can catch any mistakes you might make when calling a function, such as passing the wrong number of arguments (when the function takes a fixed number of arguments), or passing the wrong type of argument to a function.

Prototypes also allow the C compiler to use a calling convention different from the usual one used by C. (See the tutorial in Part IV for a discussion of the ordinary argument-passing mechanism used by C.) The non-C convention, used by all other languages, involves placing the arguments on the stack in the order that they appear in the function call. In this case, the function knows the exact number of arguments placed on the stack and can clean up the stack with a single 8086 assembly language statement of the form *RET* ⟨*n*⟩ where ⟨*n*⟩ refers to the number of bytes to be discarded from the stack before returning. The usual C calling convention places arguments in the reverse order and does not require a fixed number of arguments in each call. Since the function does not know the number of arguments on the stack, only the calling program can clean up the stack by adjusting the stack pointer (SP). This is normally done with the assembly language instruction *ADD SP,*⟨*n*⟩. Not only is this instruction slower than *RET* ⟨*n*⟩ but it also makes the program larger because the *ADD SP,*⟨*n*⟩ instruction appears wherever a function is called. By the way, Microsoft C provides the keyword *cdecl* which, when appearing in a function declaration, specifies that the C calling convention must be used for that function.

What do you do when a function does not return anything or when it does not accept any parameters? To answer this, we have to describe a new data type that is part of the ANSI C proposal.

THE TYPE VOID

The ANSI standard adds to C the type *void*, which is useful for declaring functions and for describing pointers that can point to any type of data. If a function does not return anything, say the *exit* function in the library, it can be declared as

```
void exit(int);
```

If a function does not accept formal parameters, its list of arguments can be represented by the word *void*:

```
int getchar(void);
```

The use of a pointer to a *void* as a data type is appropriate for functions that manipulate contiguous arrays of bytes ("buffers") in memory. For example, when you request a certain number of bytes from the memory allocation routine *malloc*, you can use these locations to store any data that fits the space. In this case, the address of the first location of the allocated block of memory is returned as a pointer to a variable of type *void* with

```
void *malloc(size_t size);
```

as the prototype. By the way, *size_t* is a new standard data type in ANSI C. Microsoft C uses *typedef* to define *size_t* as an alias for *unsigned int*. Most library routines that require the size of a data item use the *size_t* type. The *sizeof* operator also returns a value of type *size_t* in ANSI C.

Expressions in C

An expression in C is a combination of variables, function calls, and operators with the result a single value. For example,

```
(strlen(my_string) * sizeof(char) + 1)
```

is an expression, which yields a value of type *size_t*, involving a function call, *strlen(my_string)*, and the operators *sizeof*, a multiplication (*) and an addition (+).

Since operators are at the heart of expressions, let us summarize the operators available in C. We do this in Table 1-2, where each operator is shown with an example and a short explanation of its usage.

Table 1-2. *Operators in C*

Operator	Name	Example	Explanation
		Arithmetic Operators	
*	Multiplication	x*y	Multiply x and y
/	Division	x/y	Divide x by y
%	Modulo	x%y	Divide remainder of x by y
+	Addition	x+y	Add x and y
−	Subtraction	x−y	Subract y from x
+ +	Increment	x+ +	Increment x after use
− −	Decrement	− −x	Decrement x before use
−	Negation	−x	Negate the value of x
		Relational and Logical Operators	
⟩	Greater than	x⟩y	1 if x exceeds y, else 0
⟩ =	Greater than or equal to	x⟩ = y	1 if x is greater than or equal to y, else 0
⟨	Less than	x⟨y	1 if y exceeds x, else 0

Table 1-2. *(cont.)*

Operator	Name	Example	Explanation

Relational and Logical Operators

Operator	Name	Example	Explanation
⟨ =	Less than or equal to	x⟨ = y	1 if x is less than or equal to y, else 0
= =	Equal to	x = = y	1 if x equals y, else 0
! =	Not equal to	x! = y	1 if x and y unequal, else 0
!	Logical NOT	!x	1 if x is 0, else 0
&&	Logical AND	x&&y	0 if either x or y is 0
¦ ¦	Logical OR	x¦ ¦y	0 if both x and y are 0

Assignment Operators

Operator	Name	Example	Explanation
=	Assignment	x = y;	put value of y into x
0 =	Compound assignment	x 0 = y;	equivalent to x = x 0 y; where 0 is one of the operators: + − * / % ⟨⟨ ⟩⟩ & ^ ¦

Data Access and Size Operators

Operator	Name	Example	Explanation
[ ]	Array element	x[0]	first element of array x
.	Member selection	s.x	member x in structure s
→	Member selection	p→x	member named x in a structure that p points to
*	Indirection	*p	contents of location whose address is in p
&	Address of	&x	address of x
sizeof	Size in bytes	sizeof(x)	size of x in bytes

Bitwise Operators

Operator	Name	Example	Explanation
~	Bitwise complement	~ X	flip 1 bits to 0 and 0 bits to 1
&	Bitwise AND	x&y	bitwise AND of x and y
¦	Bitwise OR	x¦y	bitwise OR of x and y
^	Bitwise exclusive OR	x^y	value with 1s at bits where corresponding bits of x and y differ
⟨⟨	Left shift	x ⟨⟨ 4	x shifted to the left by 4 bit positions
⟩⟩	Right shift	x ⟩⟩ 4	x shifted to the right by 4 bit positions

Miscellaneous Operators

Operator	Name	Example	Explanation
( )	Function	malloc(10)	call malloc with argument 10
(type)	Type cast	(double)i	i converted to a double
? :	Conditional	x1 ? x2 : x3	if x1 is not 0, x2 is evaluated, else x3 is evaluated
,	Sequential evaluation	i + +, j + +	first increment i, then increment j

Operator Precedence

Typically, you use several operands and operators in many statements of your program. For example, if you write

```
*ptr[2]
```

is the result the value to which ptr[2] points, or is it the third element from the location whose address is in *ptr*? To determine this, you need to know the order in which operators are applied. This is specified by operators' *precedence*, which is summarized in Table 1-3. Operators with highest precedence—those which are applied first—are shown first. The order in which operators at the same level get evaluated (associativity) is also shown. If you consult the table, you will find that the [] operator has precedence over the * operator. So in our example, ptr[2] will be evaluated first and then the "indirection" operator applied, resulting in the value whose address is in ptr[2].

Table 1-3. *Operator Precedence and Associativity in C*

Operator type	Operators	Associativity
Expression	( ) [ ] . →	Left to right
Unary	– ~ ! * & + + – – sizeof (type)	Right to left
Multiplicative	* / %	Left to right
Additive	+ –	Left to right
Shift	⟨⟨ ⟩⟩	Left to right
Relational (inequality)	⟨ ⟨ = ⟩ ⟩ =	Left to right
Relational (equality)	= = ! =	Left to right
Bitwise AND	&	Left to right
Bitwise XOR	^	Left to right
Bitwise OR	¦	Left to right
Logical AND	&&	Left to right
Logical OR	¦ ¦	Left to right
Conditional	? :	Right to left
Assignment	= *= /= %= += –= ⟨⟨= ⟩⟩= &= ¦= ^=	Right to left
Sequential Evaluation	,	Left to right

Statements in C

Statements control the flow of execution of a C program. A "statement" consists of keywords, expressions, and other statements. Each statement ends with a semicolon. Here are some simple C statements:

```
;          /* a null statement */
x = y = 2;
```

```
x++;
if(y > 0) x /= y;
```

The body of a function that is enclosed in a pair of braces ({ . . . }) is considered a single statement. Known as "blocks," such compound statements can have local variable declarations and statements.

Here is a summary of C statements, in terms of keywords.

---

assignment statement	Assigns a value of the expression on the right-hand side to the variable on the left-hand side of the equality (=).
Example:	`pages = 800;`

---

break;	Ends the innermost do, for, switch, or while statement in which it appears.

Example:	`while(i > 0)`
	`{`
	`    if(i < 10) break; /* Loop ends when i < 10`
	`*/`
	`}`

---

continue;	Begins the next iteration of the innermost do, for, or while statement in which it appears, skipping the loop body.

Example:	`for (1=0; i < 100; i++)`
	`{`
	`    if(i == 50) continue; /* Loop skipped for`
	`i=50 */`
	`}`

---

do-while loop	Executes a block of statements until the expression in the while statement fails.

Example:	`do    /* Copy y to x until i exceeds 10 */`
	`{`
	`    x[i] = y[i];`
	`} while (++i < 10)`

---

for loop	For (*expr1*; *expr2*; *expr3*) ⟨*statements*⟩ Evaluates *expr1* once. The ⟨*statements*⟩ are executed as long as *expr2* is true (nonzero). After each pass through the loop, *expr3* is evaluated. Loop stops when *expr2* becomes false (0).
Example:	`for (i=0, sum=0; i < 11; i++) sum += i;` `/* Computes sum of integers 0 through 10 */`

---

goto statement	Transfers control to statement designated LABEL.
Example:	`if(i == 0) goto L1;`

```
         a = x[i];
    L1: x[i] = c;
```

if statement	if (*expr1*) *statement1* else *statement2* executes *statement1* if *expr1* is nonzero. Otherwise *expr2* is executed. The else clause is optional.
| **Example:** | ```
if (y !=0)
    x /= y;
else
    x = 0;
``` |

Null statement	Indicates, with a solitary semicolon, that nothing happens. Used, for example, when all processing is to be done in the loop expressions rather than the body of the loop.
| **Example:** | ```
for (i=0; str[i] != '\0'; i++)
    ;  /* Null statement */
``` |

return	Stops executing the current function and returns control to the calling function. A single value can be passed back.
| **Example:** | ```
return (answer);
``` |

| **switch** | ```
switch (expr)
{
    case value1: statement_block_1
    case value2: statement_block_2
    :

    :
    default: statement_default
}
``` |

If *expr* evaluates to *value1*, *statement_block_1* is executed. If it is equal to *value2*, *statement_2* is executed. If the value does not match any of the case statements, control passes to the block *statement_default*. Each statement block typically ends with a break statement.

| **Example:** | ```
switch (interrupt_id)
{
    case MDMSTATUS:   s_ms();
                      break;
    case TXREGEMPTY:  s_trmty();
                      break;
    case RXDATAREADY: s_rda();
                      break;
    case RLINESTATUS: s_rls();
                      break;
    default:
``` |
```

while loop	while *(expr) statement_block* The *statement_block* is executed repeatedly as long as *expr* evaluates to a nonzero value.

Example:	```while (i >= 0) /* Copy one string onto another */```
	```{```
	``` str1[i] = str2[i];```
	``` i--;```
	```}```

Function Definitions

The building blocks of C programs, *functions* are independent collections of declarations and statements you mix and match to create stand-alone applications in C. Each C program has at least one function: the *main* function. The library supplied with the Microsoft C compiler consists mainly of functions (in addition to quite a few macros). For the most part, developing software in C is a matter of writing functions.

COMPLEX RETURN TYPES FOR FUNCTIONS The definition of a C function starts with the type of value returned by the function; the function's name; and, in parentheses, the list of arguments the function accepts. For example, a function *getmax* that returns the larger of two *double* variables can be declared as:

```
double getmax( double a, double b)
{
    if ( a >= b)
        return (a);
    else
        return (b);
}
```

If you wanted the definition of this function to be localized to the source file in which it appears, you could use the keyword *static* as a prefix on the line declaring *getmax*. Without *static*, the function would be visible outside the source file.

Sometimes you need to return more complicated data types from your function. Normally these would be pointers to one data type or another, but a structure might be returned too, because the proposed ANSI C standard allows this. When declaring complex return types, you can use the *typedef* statement to your advantage. Suppose you want to write a function that accepts a pointer to an array of three double variables and its return value is of the same type. In notation cryptic enough to confuse even an expert, the function that we call *process3double* can be declared as

```
double (*process3double(double (*)[3]))[3];        /* Prototype */
:
:
double (*process3double(double (*x)[3]))[3]         /* Definition */
{
     return (x);
}
```

On the other hand, with a judicious use of *typedef* s you can rewrite the example as

```
typedef double DBL3[3];    /* DBL3 will mean array of 3 doubles */
typedef DBL3    *PDBL3;    /* PDBL3 will mean pointer to DBL3    */
PDBL3           process3double(PDBL3);              /* Prototype */
:
:
PDBL3 process3double(PDBL3 x)                       /* Definition */
{
     return (x);
}
```

The first approach takes less space, but the second method is certainly more readable than the first.

POINTERS TO
FUNCTIONS

A function cannot return an array or another function directly. Also, an array cannot have functions among its elements. This is not a problem because you can always use pointers to functions in places where functions themselves are not allowed. Declaring a pointer to a function is similar to declaring a pointer to a variable. For example, you can declare a pointer to a function that accepts two *int* arguments and returns an *int* as

```
int (*p_func)(int, int)
```

Once *p_func* is initialized to point to the appropriate function, its invocation will look like the declaration above:

```
z = (*p_func)(x, y);
```

Again, the *typedef* keyword can come to your rescue when you have to declare something complicated, say an array of 5 functions, each like the *process3double* function of our earlier example. Using *typedef*, the declaration will be as simple as

```
/* First define a synonym for a pointer to this function */
typedef PDBL3  (*P_F_PDBL3)(PDBL3);

/* Now declare the array of functions */
```

```
P_F_DBL3    funclist[5];

funclist[0] = process3double;
```

In this example, we even initialized the first element of the array *funclist* to the function *process3double*, which we defined in our previous example.

Further Reading

If you are beginning to learn C on an IBM PC, Lafore's book[1] is an ideal place to start. An alternative is the best-selling introduction to the C language by Waite, Prata, and Martin[2]; it is based on UNIX C. You can follow up with the more advanced guide by Prata[3].

Once you feel comfortable with C, there are several resources that can help you learn more about using C effectively on the IBM PC. The books by Hansen[4], Biggerstaff[5], Campbell[6], and Rochkind[7] develop libraries of functions that show you how to use the DOS and BIOS services for file input/output (I/O) and fast screen updates.

If you wish to program the serial communications port or the graphics cards directly, another Campbell book[8] has all you need to know to access the serial port and Johnson's book[9] shows examples of graphics programming for the EGA. The text by Lafore also shows how to program the graphics adapters.

On the MS-DOS front, Duncan[10] and Angermeyer and Jaeger[11] can advise you of the various services available. Another recent book by the Waite Group[12] is a collection of essays, each of which illustrates a specific aspect of the PC and MS-DOS. This can be a valuable source for ideas for your programs.

For information on the IBM PC and the PC-AT, the popular book by Norton[13] and the one by Smith[14] can provide all the information you need to get started.

1. Robert Lafore, The Waite Group, *Microsoft C Programming for the IBM,* Howard W. Sams & Company, Indianapolis, IN, 1987, 681 pages.

2. Mitchell Waite, Stephen Prata and Donald Martin, The Waite Group, *C Primer Plus*, Revised Edition, Howard W. Sams & Company, Indianapolis, IN, 1987, 531 pages.

3. Stephen Prata, The Waite Group, *Advanced C Primer++*, Howard W. Sams & Company, Indianapolis, IN, 1986, 502 pages.

4. Augie Hansen, *Proficient C*, Microsoft Press, Redmond, WA, 1987, 492 pages.

5. Ted J. Biggerstaff, *Systems Software Tools*, Prentice-Hall, Englewood Cliffs, NJ, 1986, 317 pages.

6. Joe Campbell, *Crafting Tools for the IBM PCs*, Prentice-Hall, Englewood Cliffs, NJ, 1986, 434 pages.

7. Marc J. Rochkind, *Advanced C Programming for Displays*, Prentice-Hall, Englewood Cliffs, NJ, 1988, 331 pages.

8. Joe Campbell, *C Programmer's Guide to Serial Communications*, Howard W. Sams & Company, Indianapolis, IN, 1987, 655 pages.

9. Nelson Johnson, *Advanced Graphics in C*, Osborne McGraw-Hill, Berkeley, CA, 1987, 670 pages.

10. Ray Duncan, *Advanced MS-DOS*, Microsoft Press, Redmond, WA, 1986, 468 pages.

11. John Angermeyer and Kevin Jaeger, The Waite Group, *MS-DOS Developer's Guide*, Howard W. Sams & Company, Indianapolis, IN, 1987, 440 pages.

12. The Waite Group, Ed., *MS-DOS Papers*, Howard W. Sams & Company, Indianapolis, IN, 1988, 608 pages.

13. Peter Norton, *The Peter Norton Programmer's Guide to the IBM PC*, Microsoft Press, Redmond, WA, 1985, 426 pages.

14. James T. Smith, *The IBM PC AT Programmer's Guide*, Prentice-Hall, New York, NY, 1986, 277 pages.

2 *Microsoft C 5.1 Compiler Features and Options*

Implementation Notes

In this chapter we discuss some of the features of Microsoft C 5.1 related to the 8086 microprocessor, including storage size of variables in Microsoft C, the concept of "memory models" that arise in 8086 microprocessors, special purpose keywords, global variables, and certain preprocessor constants defined by Microsoft C.

STORAGE SIZE OF DATA ITEMS Table 2-1 shows the basic data types in Microsoft C 5.1, their storage sizes, and the range of values they can hold.

Table 2-1. *Data Types and Sizes in Microsoft C*

Type Name	Storage Size	Range of Values
char	1 byte	− 128 to 127
int	2 bytes	− 32768 to 32767
short	2 bytes	− 32768 to 32767
long	4 bytes	− 2,147,483,648 to 2,147,483,647
unsigned char	1 byte	0 to 255
unsigned	2 bytes	0 to 65,535
unsigned short	2 bytes	0 to 65,535
unsigned long	4 bytes	0 to 4,294,967,295
enum	2 bytes	0 to 65,535
float	4 bytes	Approximately 3.4E − 38 to 3.4E + 38 with 7-digit precision
double	8 bytes	Approximately 1.7E − 308 to 1.7E + 308 with 15-digit precision
long double	8 bytes	Approximately 1.7E − 308 to 1.73 + 308 with 15-digit precision

MEMORY MODELS IN MICROSOFT C

The memory-addressing scheme used by the 8086 microprocessor forces the concept of "memory models" onto any C compiler designed to generate code for 8086 machines. The 8086 microprocessor family uses 16-bit registers (the 80386 is a 32-bit processor). Since the processor has to use registers to manipulate memory addresses and 16 bits can only address 64 K of memory, a different scheme is used in the 8086 to address memory. The address of each byte in memory is considered to be composed of two parts: a "segment" address and an "offset" address from the starting byte of the segment. Each "segment" and each "offset" is a 16-bit value that the microprocessor can manipulate using its registers. The segment and the offset addresses are combined to generate the final "physical address," which is only 20 bits long, specifically, using the formula:

Physical Address (20-bit) = Segment Address (16-bit) * 16 + Offset (16-bit)

An advantage of this strategy is that if all of your data fits into a single 64-K segment, the 8086 can set up the segment address in a segment register (specifically, the register named DS) and refer to data items using only the 16-bit offset. This results in faster code because the code does not have to manipulate the segment portion of the address.

A C compiler for 8086 machines has two choices: either it forces you to write programs that use only a single segment of data and code or it provides you with options to mix and match various segment and offset addressing schemes for data and code. The concept of memory models arises from the availability of these choices. A specific memory model refers to one of five ways of addressing code and data, shown in Table 2-2.

Table 2-2. *Microsoft C Compiler Memory Models*

Memory Model	Meaning
Small	All data and code addresses are 16-bit offsets. Program size limited to one segment of code and one segment of data.
	Compiler option: /AS
Medium	All data addresses are 16-bit offsets, but code addresses use explicit segments and offsets. A program can have a single segment of data, but many segments of code.
	Compiler option: /AM
Compact	All code addresses are offset only, but data addresses use segments as well as offsets. Programs can have multiple data segments, but only one code segment.
	Compiler option: /AC
Large	All data and code addresses include explicit segments and offsets. Program size is limited only by available memory (which is limited by the 20-bit physical address), but a single data item cannot exceed a 64-K segment.
	Compiler option: /AL
Huge	Same as the large model, but address arithmetic is performed in such a way that an array can span across multiple segments.
	Compiler option: /AH

In addition to the five standard memory models, with keywords *far*, *near*, and *huge* you can mix data items with an addressing scheme different from the default allowed by the standard model. These keywords can qualify the address of a data item as well as of a function. Table 2-3 summarizes the meaning of these keywords.

Table 2-3. *The* near, far, *and* huge *Keywords in Microsoft C*

Keyword	When Used with Data	When Used with Function
near	Data addresses are 16-bit offsets with respect to the segment address of a default data segment.	Function is assumed to be in the current code segment.
far	Full segment and offset addresses used. Data may be anywhere in memory.	Referenced using full segment and offset address.
huge	Full segment and offset addresses used. An array can be larger than a 64-K segment because 32-bit arithmetic is used on pointers.	Not applicable to functions.

The memory model concept is not a part of the C language, but an artifact necessary to exploit the architecture of the 8086 microprocessor. So programs using the keywords *near*, *far*, and *huge* are not portable.

NEW KEYWORDS CONTROLLING CODE GENERATION

Three new keywords, *_export*, *_loadds*, and *_saveregs*, were introduced in Microsoft C 5.1. Each modifies the code generated for a function.

The *_export* keyword allows you to create functions that will reside in OS/2's dynamic-link libraries (see Richard Letwin's *Inside OS/2*, Microsoft Press, 1988, for a discussion of dynamic-link libraries and other major features of OS/2).

The *_loadds* keyword causes the compiler to generate code to load the data segment register (DS) with a specific value upon entry to the function. The *data_seg* pragma specifies the segment value loaded into DS. If there are no *data_seg* pragmas in the program, the segment value set by the /ND option is used. When none of these sources for the segment value are present, the default group DGROUP is used to derive the segment value. Note that the *_loadds* function modifier has the same effect as the /Au compiler option. For example,

```
#pragma data_seg(MYSEG)

void far _loadds myfunction(int command);
```

declares *myfunction* as a function that loads the segment value MYSEG into the DS register upon entry.

The *_saveregs* keyword instructs the compiler to generate code to save all CPU registers upon entering the function and restore them when exiting it. The AX register is not restored if the function returns a value.

THE INTERRUPT ATTRIBUTE

If you write C applications that require handling interrupts (for example, programming the serial communication ports for interrupt-driven I/O), you will find the *interrupt* keyword useful. Introduced in Microsoft C 5.0, this keyword serves as a qualifier for a function you want to install as the *interrupt handler* for a specific interrupt number. When the compiler translates a function with the *interrupt* attribute, it generates code to push the registers AX, CX, DX, BX, BP, SP, SI, DI, DS, and ES. Then it sets up the DS register to point to the data segment of that function. Next, the code of the function is included. Finally, the compiler uses an IRET instruction (instead of a normal RET) to return from the function. A typical use of the *interrupt* attribute is:

```
void interrupt far int_handler (unsigned es, unsigned ds,
                                unsigned di, unsigned si,
                                unsigned bp, unsigned sp,
                                unsigned bx, unsigned dx,
                                unsigned cx, unsigned ax,
                                unsigned ip, unsigned cs,
                                unsigned flags)
{
/* Place code to handle interrupt referring to registers by
 * name when necessary.
 */
}
```

Within the interrupt handler, you can access the values of registers by referring to them by name. Other precautions that apply to assembly language interrupt handlers also apply to the C function. For example, you should not call a library routine that calls a DOS function, such as stream and low-level I/O routines. On the other hand, such routines as those in the string manipulation category are safe inside the *interrupt* function.

GLOBALS AND PREPROCESSOR CONSTANTS

Microsoft C includes a number of predefined global variables and preprocessor constants. The global variables contain the DOS version number, last error number, and pointer to the process environment block. We refer to these global variables as predefined variables. Table 2-4 summarizes the predefined global variables and their purpose. The four macros introduced in Microsoft 5.1 are indicated.

Table 2-4. *Predefined Global Variables in Microsoft C 5.1*

Variable	Declaration and Purpose
_amblksiz	unsigned _amblksiz; When the Microsoft C memory allocation routines have to allocate memory from the far heap, they first request memory from DOS in a big chunk and then they parcel out memory to satisfy calls made to *malloc* until the chunk is exhausted. The _amblksiz variable contains the size of a single chunk in bytes. The default value is 8,192 bytes (or 8 K). The *halloc* and the _ nmalloc routines do not use this variable. Declared in: malloc.h

Table 2-4. *(cont.)*

Variable	Declaration and Purpose
daylight	int daylight; The *daylight* variable is 1 if a daylight saving time zone is specified in the TZ environment variable. It is used when converting local time to Greenwich Mean Time. (See Time functions for details.) Declared in: time.h
_doserrno	int _doserrno; Contains the MS-DOS error code returned by the last MS-DOS system call. Declared in: stdlib.h
environ	char *environ[]; This is an array of pointers to strings where the strings constitute the environment table of the process. This allows you to access the environment variables for use by a particular program. Declared in: stdlib.h
errno	int errno; Contains an error code corresponding to the last system call. Declared in: stdlib.h
_fmode	int _fmode; Contains the default file translation mode. The default value is 0, which means files are translated in the text mode. (See File Manipulation routines for more details.) Declared in: stdlib.h
_osmajor	unsigned char _osmajor; This is the major version number of MS-DOS. For example, if you have MS-DOS 3.30, _osmajor is 3. Declared in: stdlib.h
_osminor	unsigned char _osminor; This is the minor version number of MS-DOS. For MS-DOS 3.10, _osminor is 10. Declared in: stdlib.h
_osversion	unsigned _osversion; This contains the complete DOS version number. For MS-DOS 3.20, _osversion is 320. Declared in: dos.h
_psp	unsigned int _psp; This variable contains the segment address of the program segment prefix (PSP) of the current process. The PSP contains information about the process, such as the command line arguments, pointer to the environment block, and the return address. The PSP begins at offset 0 of the segment address contained in _psp. Declared in: stdlib.h
sys_errlist	char *sys_errlist[]; This is an array of pointers to a set of strings each corresponding to a system error message. Declared in: stdlib.h
sys_nerr	int sys_nerr; This is the total number of strings in the sys_errlist array.

Table 2-4. *(cont.)*

Variable	Declaration and Purpose
	Declared in: stdlib.h
timestamp	Defined as a string containing the date and time of last modification to the file, expressed in the form *DDD MMM DD HH:MM:SS YYYY*. Here is an example: *Mon Jun 20 19:35:52 1988*.
	The timezone variable contains the difference in seconds between Greenwich Mean Time and the local time. (See Time functions for details.)
	Declared in: time.h
tzname	char *tzname[2];
	The tzname[0] contains the name of the local time zone (for example, EST or PST) and tzname[1] contains the name of the daylight saving time zone. (See Time functions for details.)
	Declared in: time.h

Preprocessor constants are used extensively in the library routines to define values for specific parameters in a more readable fashion. A few of the preprocessor symbols are defined by the compiler itself. These predefined symbols, shown in Table 2-5, can help you write code that can be easily ported to other machines. For example, consider the fragment of code:

```
#ifdef MSDOS
    :
/*   MS-DOS specific code goes here */
    :
#endif
#ifdef vms
    :
/*   DEC VAX/VMS specific code goes here */
    :
#endif
```

When this code is compiled with the Microsoft C compiler, the symbol MSDOS is predefined, so only the first chunk of code appropriate for MS-DOS machines is processed. On the other hand, on a DEC VAX/VMS system, the symbol *vms* is predefined. So on that system we only get the part that applies to DEC VMS systems.

Table 2-5. *Predefined Preprocessor Symbols in Microsoft C 5.1*

Symbol	Purpose
MSDOS	This symbol indicates that the operating system is MS-DOS.
M_I86	This symbol identifies the machine for which the compiler generates code as a member of the Intel 8086 family.
M_I86xM	This symbol, keyed by the substitute for *x*, identifies the memory model. In the small model, the symbol is M_I86SM; in the compact

Table 2-5. *(cont.)*

Symbol	Purpose
	model, M_I86CM; in the medium model, M_I86MM; and in the large model, M_I86LM. In the huge model, two symbols are defined: M_I86LM and M_I86HM.
NO_EXT_KEYS	This symbol is defined when the /Za option is used to disable all extensions specific to Microsoft C.
_CHAR_UNSIGNED	This symbol is defined when the /J option is used. It changes the default type of char variables from signed to unsigned.
DATE	This symbol is defined as the date of compilation, expressed as a string of the form *MMMM DD YYYY*.
STDC	Defined as 1 when the compiler option enforcing strict ANSI conformance is enabled.
TIME	The time when compilation of the file began, expressed as a string of the form *HH:MM:SS*.
TIMEZONE	long timezone;

DISPLAYING DIAGNOSTIC MESSAGES

Version 5.1 also introduces the ANSI-compatible preprocessor directive *#error*. The *#error* directive causes the compiler to display a diagnostic message during compilation. You can use the *#error* directive to remind the user to compile the program with a specific compiler option. The syntax of this directive is

```
#error <message string>
```

in which the rest of the line following *#error* is the message string to be printed by *#error*. For example, suppose you know that your source file contains nonstandard extensions to the C language. If the user wanted to compile with the /Za option enforcing strict ANSI compatibility, you would remind the user to use the /Ze option (which enables the extensions) instead. Here's how:

```
#ifdef NO_EXT_KEYS
   #error Program uses nonstandard extensions. Recompile with /Ze
#endif
```

Since the NO_EXT_KEYS symbol is defined when the /Za option is used, the error message is printed only when you turn off extensions.

Compiler Notes

Writing C code is only one aspect of developing software in Microsoft C. First you compile the code, then link it with libraries to create the executable file, and, finally, you debug the program when it fails to work properly. The Microsoft C 5.1 compiler comes with a set of tools that help with one or more of these steps. Both the compiler and the linker are accessed via a command-line oriented program named CL.EXE, but the linker can also be invoked separately as LINK. Object modules are organized into libraries by the LIB utility. The MAKE utility lets you automate the steps involved in creating an executable file, helping you manage the "compile-link" cycle. Finally, the CodeView full-screen debugger helps you locate the bugs in your program.

CL: COMPILING AND LINKING

CL is your gateway to both the compiler and the linker. A small program with few modules, you can use CL to generate and compile the files and link them as simply as

```
cl test.c rest.c
```

This assumes the main function to be in the file TEST.C and other functions to be in the file REST.C. Using the small memory model as the default, CL will create the object files TEST.OBJ and REST.OBJ and invoke the linker to generate the executable TEST.EXE.

Using CL without any options may be good enough for small test programs, but when you are developing a larger application, you will want to specify the memory model, the type of math library you want to use, and whether you want the compiler to generate information needed by the CodeView debugger among other things. You specify these choices through command-line options to CL. For example, we can use this command to compile the example program using the large model, generate code for the 8087 math coprocessor, and generate supporting information for the debugger:

```
CL /AL /FPi87 /Zi TEST.C REST.C
```

Each option begins with a slash '/'. The next letter tells the compiler the type of the option, and subsequent characters and digits specify your complete choice for that type. In the example, the /AL option specifies the large memory model, the /FPi87 tells the compiler to embed 8087 code in the output, and the /Zi option generates the information needed to debug using the CodeView debugger. The complete list of options for CL is shown in Table 2-6. Table 2-7 shows the options according to the purpose of each category.

Some of the options are straightforward, but a few, such as the optimization options (the /O family), are difficult to use. To use these appropriately, you need to understand the types of optimizations that a compiler can perform and have a general idea of how the compiler will react to your code. The best approach is to begin by using the simple options and then, as you learn more about the capabilities of the Microsoft C compiler, you can add the more exotic ones to your repertoire.

Table 2-6. *List of Options for CL*

Option	Action by CL
/AS	Selects small memory model. (Default.)
/AM	Selects medium memory model.
/AC	Selects compact memory model.

Table 2-6. *(cont.)*

Option	Action by CL
/AL	Selects large memory model.
/AH	Selects huge memory model.
/A⟨string⟩	Sets up a customized memory model. The ⟨string⟩ consists of three characters, one from each group:

Group	Letter	Interpretation
Code size	s	Small
	l	Large
Data Size	n	Near
	f	Far
	h	Huge
Segments	d	SS is equal to DS
	u	SS not same as DS. DS loaded in each module.
	w	SS not same as DS. DS remains fixed.

Option	Action by CL
/C	Retains the comments when preprocessing file (valid with /E, /P, or /EP).
/c	Compiles without linking.
/D⟨name⟩[= text]	Defines the macro with the text. The equal sign and the following text may be omitted.
/E	Preprocesses a file and sends the output to stdout with line numbers.
/EP	Same as option /E, but no line numbers are printed.
/F⟨hex_number⟩	Sets the stack size to the number of bytes specified by the hexadecimal number.
/Fa[filename]	Sends an assembly listing to the file name given. If a file name is omitted, the default is the source file name with the extension .ASM.
/Fc[filename]	Generates a combined source-assembly listing.
/Fe⟨filename⟩	Accepts the file name as the name of the executable file.
/Fl[filename]	Generates an object code listing.
/Fm[filename]	Generates a link map file.
/Fo⟨filename⟩	Accepts the file name as the name of the object file.
/FPa	Generates calls to an alternate math library for floating-point operations.
/FPc	Generates calls to an emulator library for floating-point operations. At run-time, uses the 8087 coprocessor, if one is found.
/FPc87	Generates calls to an 8087 library. Requires 8087 coprocessor at run-time.
/FPi	Generates in-line code that uses the emulator library. Uses 8087 coprocessor at run-time, if one is found. (Default.)
/FPi87	Generates in-line instructions for the 8087 coprocessor. Requires an 8087 at run-time.
/Fs[filename]	Produces a source listing.
/G0	Uses 8086 instructions. (Default.)
/G1	Uses 80186 instructions.
/G2	Uses 80286 instructions.
/Gc	Uses Pascal-style function calls (arguments are pushed on stack in the

Table 2-6. *(cont.)*

Option	Action by CL
	order they appear in the function call and stack is cleaned up by the function before returning). Generates fast, compact code.
/Gm	Force *near const* items to be allocated in the DATA segment. Used for generating ROM code.
/Gs	Stack-checking calls are not generated.
/Gt[number]	Places data items larger than [number] bytes in a new data segment. (Default [number] is 256.)
/H⟨number⟩	Restricts significant characters in external names to specified length.
/HELP	Displays a list of commonly used CL options.
/I⟨pathname⟩	The ⟨pathname⟩ is added to the list of directories that are searched for include files.
/J	Changes the default type of char to unsigned.
/Lc	Compile for DOS 3.x (real mode)
/link⟨options⟩	Passes the ⟨options⟩ to LINK.
/Lp	Compile for OS/2 protected mode
/Lr	Synonym for /Lc
/ND⟨dataseg⟩	Sets the name of the data segment to ⟨dataseg⟩.
/NM⟨module⟩	Sets the name of the module to ⟨module⟩.
/NT⟨textseg⟩	Sets the name of the code segment to ⟨textseg⟩.
/O	Enables optimization. (Same as /Ot.)
/Oa	Ignores aliasing (multiple names for the same memory location).
/Od	Disables optimizations.
/Oi	Enables the use of intrinsic functions.
/Ol	Enables loop optimizations.
/On	Disables "unsafe" optimizations.
/Op	Enables precision optimizations on floating-point calculations.
/Or	Disables in-line return.
/Os	Optimizes for space.
/Ot	Optimizes for speed. (Default.)
/Ox	Enables maximum optimization. (Same as /Oailt /Gs.)
/P	Preprocesses and sends output to the file with same name as source but with the extension .I.
/qc	Invokes the Microsoft QuickC compiler.
/Sl⟨columns⟩	Sets the characters per line in the source listings (should be between 79 and 132).
/Sp⟨lines⟩	Sets the page length in lines for source listings (should be between 15 and 255).
/Ss⟨string⟩	Sets the subtitle string for source listings.
/St⟨string⟩	Sets the title string for source listings.
/Tc⟨file⟩	Specifies a ⟨file⟩ without the .c extension.
/U⟨name⟩	Removes predefined macro ⟨name⟩.
/u	Removes the definition of all predefined macros.
/V⟨string⟩	Puts a version string into the object file.

Table 2-6. *(cont.)*

Option	Action by CL
/W⟨number⟩	Sets the level for compiler warning messages. The ⟨number⟩ is either 0 or 1 or 2 or 3.
/X	Ignores the list of "standard places" when searching for include files.
/Za	Enforces ANSI compatibility by disabling all Microsoft extensions to the language.
/Zd	Generates line number information for the Microsoft SYMDEB symbolic debugger.
/Ze	Enables all features specific to Microsoft C. (Default.)
/Zg	Generates function declarations without compiling program. The result is sent to the standard output.
/Zi	Generates symbolic debugging information required by Microsoft CodeView full-screen debugger.
/Zl	Removes default library information from the object files.
/Zp⟨n⟩	Packs structures on n-byte boundary.
/Zs	Performs a syntax check only.

Note: [. . .] denotes optional items, ⟨ . . . ⟩ indicates required arguments.

CREATING OS/2 EXECUTABLES

Microsoft C 5.1 adds the /L option, which tells the linker whether you are compiling the program for OS/2 protected mode (/Lp) or DOS real mode (/Lr) or (/Lc). Before compiling OS/2 protected mode programs you should use the Microsoft SETUP program to specify the mode-specific libraries you will need. (See section 2 of the Microsoft C 5.1 update—supplied with Microsoft C 5.1—for details.)

Table 2-7. *Option Categories for CL*

Purpose of Option	Options
Selecting a memory model. Default: /AS	/AS /AM /AC /AL /AH
Selecting a floating-point library. Default: /FPi	/FPa /FPc /FPC87 /FPi /FPi87
Controlling optimization. Default: /Ot	/O /Oa /Od /Oi /Ol /On /Op /Or /Os /Ot /Ox
Controlling the preprocessor.	/C /D⟨name⟩[= text] /E /EP /I⟨include path⟩ /P /u /U⟨name⟩ /X
Generating code for specific processor and mixed language calls. Default: /G0	/Gt[number]
Specifying execution mode (real or OS/2 protected)	/Lp /Lr /Lc
Supporting CodeView, error checking, and language extensions. Default: /Ze	/Za /Zd /Ze /Zg /Zi /Zl /Zs /Zp[1 or 2 or 4]

Table 2-7. *(cont.)*

Purpose of Option	Options
Creating listing, object, and executable files.	/Fa[assembly file] /Fc[code file] /Fe⟨executable file⟩ /F1[listing file] /Fm[map file] /Fo⟨object file⟩ / Fs[source listing]
Formatting source listings	/S1⟨column⟩ /Sp[lines] /Ss⟨subtitle⟩ /St⟨title⟩
Linking	/F⟨hex number⟩ /link ⟨linker options⟩
Miscellaneous	/c /H⟨number⟩ /Gm /J /Tc⟨file⟩ /ND⟨dataseg⟩ / NM⟨module⟩ /NT⟨textseg⟩ /V⟨string⟩ /W⟨0 or 1 or 2 or 3⟩

USING BIND TO CREATE DUAL-MODE EXECUTABLES

Use the Microsoft BIND utility to create a single executable file that will run in both real (DOS) and protected (OS/2) mode. Before doing this, you should:

▶ Run the SETUP program to choose the appropriate default protected-mode libraries.

▶ Read Section 4 of the Microsoft C 5.1 update manual and read the Microsoft Codeview and Utilities update for a detailed discussion of the BIND utility.

▶ Note the tables in Section 7.2 of the Microsoft C 5.1 update manual. The first table specifies functions that are only supported in real mode; you cannot create runnable dual-mode programs that contain these functions. The second table lists functions that can be executed simultaneously by more than one thread of execution in OS/2. Programs using multiple execution threads should avoid threads containing functions not on this list.

▶ Read any README files supplied with your version of Microsoft C. They may contain material later than that given in the Microsoft manuals or this book.

The easiest way to invoke BIND is to use the */Fb* option with CL. This specifies that BIND will be invoked to create a bound (dual-mode) executable from the current program. If you want to use a program name other than the current one, give the name following */Fb* (without intervening space). For example, the CL command line:

```
CL /Lp /Fbtest
```

creates the dual-mode executable TEST.EXE. (The extension is supplied automatically.) The */Lp* option specifies that the protected-mode version of the library will be used; alternatively, you can specify protected-mode default libraries in the SETUP program.

It is tedious to type in the options you choose to use with CL to compile and link your program. Additionally, you can enter no more than 128 characters on the command line, so if you select too many options you will not be able to enter them on the command line to CL—even if you were willing to do the keyboarding. Microsoft C provides three ways to solve this problem. You can define an environment variable CL (not the executable CL) with the options you plan to use. For example, defining the CL environment variable by the DOS command

```
SET CL=/AS /Gs /Od /Zi /FPc
```

and invoking the compiler with *CL ⟨filename⟩* is equivalent to typing the command *CL /AS /Gs /Od /Zi /FPc ⟨filename⟩*. The program will be compiled and linked using the small model (/AS), without any stack-checking calls (/Gs), without any optimization (/Od), with support for CodeView (/Zi), and using calls to the floating-point emulator library.

Another approach is to use the batch file to do the job by placing the compile command in a batch file that takes the file name as an argument. An example (using the same options) is

```
echo off
if not "%1" == "" goto run
:usage
echo ! usage:  RUN filename
echo !
echo ! where    filename is the program you are testing
echo !          (do not include extension, .C assumed)
echo !
goto end
:run
if exist %1.c goto filefound
echo ! RUN: File %1.c not found. Exiting...
goto end
:filefound
echo ! Now starting CL...
CL /AS /Gs /Od /Zi /FPc %1.c
:end
```

If this batch file is named RUN.BAT, you can compile and link a file TEST.C by the command *run test*. The batch file first checks whether an argument is present. If it finds an argument, it checks whether the file named by the argument exists. If it does, RUN.BAT invokes CL.

These two approaches are fine when you have the entire program in a single file. If you are working on a larger project, it is best to use the Microsoft MAKE utility. Microsoft MAKE is invoked by the command *MAKE ⟨makefile⟩*, in which ⟨makefile⟩ is a file that contains the commands for MAKE. For a program that consists of several files, you would set up the MAKE commands to generate the object codes and then invoke LINK separately to build the executable. Apart from automating the building of an executable, MAKE also ensures the compilation of only those modules that have changed since the last compilation. It does so by examining the time of last modification stamped on the files. A source file is compiled only if it was modified at a later time than the corresponding object file. The documentation on MAKE included in the manuals distributed by Microsoft with version 5.1 of their C compiler discusses this in depth. Here is a sample ⟨makefile⟩.

```
###############################################################
#    Makefile for Microsoft MAKE
#    Comments start with '#'
#
#    Model set to small

MODEL=S

# Compiler flags -- generate object code only (/c option)
CFLAGS=/A$(MODEL)     /Gs          /Od    /Zi  /FPc   /c

CL=cl $(CFLAGS)

# General inference rules
# Rule to make .OBJ files from .C files

.C.OBJ:
       $(CL) $*.C

# Compile the files

prog.obj: prog.c local.h common.h

file1.obj: file1.c common.h

file2.obj: file2.c local.h

# Make the executable

prog.exe:  prog.obj file1.obj file2.obj
       LINK $**, $@;
```

This MAKE file builds a program named PROG.EXE that has three source files, PROG.C, FILE1.C, and FILE2.C, and two include files, LOCAL.H and COMMON.H. The MAKE commands are dependency rules showing, for each file, the other files that it depends on. The dependency list is followed by a line showing how to prepare the file. If a generic rule is defined (for example, "build an .OBJ file out of a .C by using CL with the following options"), you do not have to state the command to build a file. In our sample MAKE file, PROG.OBJ depends on the source files PROG.C, COMMON.H, and LOCAL.H and PROG.EXE depends on the object files PROG.OBJ, FILE1.OBJ, and FILE2.OBJ. The LINK command to build the executable is stated because we did not provide a rule to arrive at an executable from object modules.

LINK: THE LINKER   Although CL invokes the linker, you might want to invoke the linker alone, especially when no compilation is necessary. The /link option enables you to specify linker options. So you need to know the command line options for the linker as well. Table 2-8 describes the linker options together with their meaning.

Table 2-8. *LINK Options*

Option	Action by LINK
/B[ATCH]	Disables prompting for pathname when library or object file is not found.
/CO[DEVIEW]	Generates executable file with information needed by Microsoft CodeView debugger.
/CP[ARMAXALLOC]:⟨num⟩	Sets the maximum number of 16-byte paragraphs needed by program to ⟨num⟩. Valid range for ⟨num⟩ is from 1 to 65,535.
/DO[SSEG]	Forces segments to be arranged in a particular order in memory. (Default when linking with a Microsoft library.)
/DS[ALLOCATE]	Forces loading of data at the high end of the data segment. *Use this option with assembly language routines only.*
/E[XEPACK]⟨exe⟩ ⟨pack⟩	Packs the executable ⟨exe⟩ during linking and places result in ⟨pack⟩.
/F[ARCALLTRANSLATION]	Converts far calls within the same segment to near calls, so calling far functions is more efficient.
/HE[LP]	Lists the LINK options.
/HI[GH]	Places the executable file as high as possible in memory. *Use this option with assembly language routines only.*
/I[NFORMATION]	Displays informative messages during linking.
/LI[NENUMBERS]	Shows the line numbers of source statements in the map file.
/M[AP]:[number]	Generates a listing of all global symbols in the input modules. The [number] denotes the maximum number of symbols the linker can sort.
/NOD[EFAULTLIBRARYSEARCH]	Ignores default libraries.
/NOE[XTDICTIONARY]	Accepts a user-defined substitute for a standard library function.
/NOF[ARCALLTRANSLATION]	Turns off the /FARCALLTRANSLATION option (Default.)
/NOG[ROUPASSOCIATION]	This is only provided for compatibility with early versions of linker and compiler.
/NOI[GNORECASE]	Begins distingushing between uppercase and lowercase letters.
/NOP[ACKCODE]	Turns off the /PACKCODE option. (Default.)
/O[VERLAYINTERRUPT]:⟨num⟩	Sets up ⟨num⟩ as the interrupt number to be used when an overlay has to be loaded.
/PAC[KCODE]	Packs adjacent code segments into 64-K chunks (use with /FARCALLTRANSLATION).
/PAU[SE]	Pauses before writing executable to disk, allowing you to swap diskettes.

Table 2-8. *(cont.)*

Option	Action by LINK
/Q[UICKLIBRARY]	Produces a library for use with Microsoft QuickC compiler.
/SE[GMENTS]:⟨number⟩	Sets the maximum number of segments to ⟨number⟩. (Default is 128.)
/ST[ACK]:⟨number⟩	Sets the stack size to ⟨number⟩ bytes. (Default is 2,048 bytes [2 K].)

Note: [. . .] denotes optional items, ⟨ . . . ⟩ indicates required arguments.

II Process Control and Memory Management

▶ Process Control

▶ Variable-Length Argument List

▶ Memory Allocation and Management

▶ Buffer Manipulation

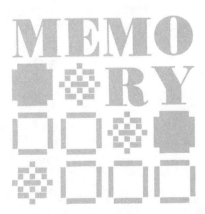

Chapter **3 Process Control**

Introduction

One way to reduce software development time is to reuse existing code. You can use existing C routines by function calls from your C program. Microsoft C even allows you to call routines written in other languages. But what if the existing code that suits your need is an "executable" (an MS-DOS .COM or .EXE) file? Here is an example.

Suppose you are developing an application that provides an electronic mail (e-mail) service. You want the user to enter and edit a message that your application will then send over the network to another computer. An editor is ideal for entering and editing text, and every PC has one. If you can invoke the editor from your application program while you have the text prepared and stored in a temporary file, you won't have to develop and debug an editor from scratch. Luckily, the Microsoft C library provides the facilities that let you run another program from your program. This is called "executing a child" process, or "spawning" or "launching" a child. The Microsoft C library contains a set of "process control" routines that help you launch a child process and control certain aspects of your own process. For our e-mail example, you could use the *spawnlp* function in the process control category to invoke an editor (you can ask the user to enter the name) in which the user can prepare the mail message. Use of the *spawn* functions is demonstrated in the reference pages.

We should note that Microsoft C 5.1 supports OS/2, which has a much more complex (and powerful) notion of processes and the environment. Although our discussion here focuses on MS-DOS, we provide reference material on the two process control functions specific to OS/2 (*cwait* and *wait*). If you are going to be programming in OS/2 protected mode, we recommend that you first read such books as Gordon Letwin's *Inside OS/2* (Microsoft Press, 1988) and the Waite Group's *OS/2 Bible* (Howard W. Sams & Company, due late 1988).

Next we examine what MS-DOS processes are, how they are started and terminated, and how error conditions (exceptions) are handled by processes.

Concepts: Process, Environment, and Signals

A "process" is an executable program in memory and its associated *environment*. Anytime you run a program, you create a process. A program's environment is stored in the PSP and it includes all the information necessary to execute the program. This includes information about the locations of its code and data in memory and which files were opened in the program.

ENVIRONMENT OF A PROCESS

When you run MS-DOS on your PC, and see the familiar *A)* (or *C)*, if you have a hard disk) prompt, you are talking to a "process" that is running the DOS command processor COMMAND.COM. In this case, the environment includes the DOS variables of PATH, COMSPEC, and PROMPT and such variables as INCLUDE, LIB, and TMP that the Microsoft C compiler uses. Specifically, the environment associated with a process in MS-DOS consists of an array of null-terminated strings, with each string defining a symbol in the format *VARIABLE=Value*. For example, the MS-DOS command interpreter, COMMAND.COM, is located by DOS using the definition of an environment variable named COMSPEC. You can see a list of the environment variables by typing SET at the DOS prompt. On my PC-AT, the result of typing SET is

```
C:\> set
COMSPEC=C:\COMMAND.COM
PATH=C:\;C:\DOS31;C:\BIN;C:\KERMIT;C:\TEX
INCLUDE=c:\include
LIB=c:\lib
TMP=c:\tmp
PROMPT=$p$g
```

Each symbol to the left of the equal sign is an environment variable and the string to the right of the equal sign is its value. As shown in Figure 3-1, the environment strings are laid out one after another with a zero byte (a null character) separating one variable's definition from the next. The end of the environment is marked by two consecutive null characters.

You can also define environment variables with the DOS command SET. When defining in batch files, you embed the definition in a line. Typically you define the variables PATH, INCLUDE, LIB, TMP, and PROMPT in the AUTOEXEC.BAT file.

Passing Information Via Environment Variables

The environment variables are used to pass information to processes. For example, when you type the program name, CL, COMMAND.COM will look up the list of directories in the PATH environment variable and search in each directory for an executable file named CL (CL.COM, CL.EXE, or CL.BAT).

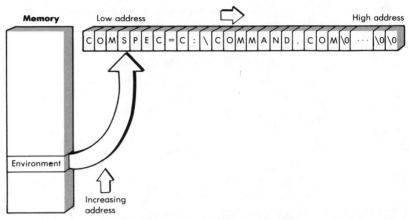

Figure 3-1. *The MS-DOS environment*

Since CL.EXE is the Microsoft C 5.1 compiler's command interface program, COMMAND.COM will find it in the directory C:\BIN (where this program normally resides), load it into memory, and run it. When DOS runs a program, in this case, CL.EXE, it passes a copy of the parent's environment to the child. Thus the environment variables that you saw when you typed SET will be available to the CL.EXE. In fact, the compiler uses the settings of the environment variables INCLUDE, LIB, and TMP, respectively, to locate the include files, and the object libraries and to create temporary files.

Using the Environment in Your Programs

The capability of accessing environment variables can be exploited by your C programs as well. For example, if you are developing an e-mail application, you can decide that you will send a copy of a mail message to all addresses listed in an environment variable DISTLIST. You can get at this environment variable via the library routine *getenv*. There is another routine named *putenv* which lets you add new definitions to your environment table. Keep in mind, however, that these definitions will vanish the moment your program exits because your program's environment table is only a copy of the parent's environment. Changes made to this copy will not affect the parent's table. A little later, we will describe another way of accessing the environment of your process.

CHILD PROCESS Suppose you wrote, compiled, and linked a small C program called TEST.EXE whose source file is

```
#include <stdio.h>
main(int argc, char **argv, char **envp)
{
    int i;
/* Print the command line arguments */
    printf("Number of command line arguments = %d\n", argc);
    for (i = 0; i < argc; i++)
    {
```

```
        printf("Argument %d = %s\n", i, argv[i]);
    }
/* Print the environment */
    printf("\nEnvironment contains:\n");
    for(i = 0; envp[i] != NULL; i++)
    {
        printf("%s\n", envp[i]);
    }
}
```

You run the program by typing *TEST One Two Three* at the DOS prompt. The *One Two Three* following the name of the program are called "command-line arguments." This mechanism is used to pass optional items to the program. As shown in Figure 3-2, COMMAND.COM will execute TEST.EXE as a child process. If the file TEST.EXE is in the directory C:\TEST, COMMAND.COM will find it, no matter what the current default directory is, as long as the environment variable PATH has C:\TEST in it. For example, you may define PATH as PATH=C:\DOS;C:\BIN;C:\TEST. The child process running TEST.EXE also receives a copy of all the DOS environment variables.

To the child process running TEST.EXE, COMMAND.COM is the parent. In this case, the parent waits until the child finishes its job. When TEST.EXE exits, the PC will run the parent process again and you will see the DOS prompt.

ACCESSING COMMAND-LINE ARGUMENTS AND ENVIRONMENT

Let's see how to access the command-line arguments and the environment in a Microsoft C program (this is the second method of accessing the environment, the first is to use the function *getenv*). Note that in the example program, the *main* function has three arguments. The first argument is an integer, *argc*, containing the number of command-line arguments. In MS-DOS versions 3.0 and later, the first argument is always the full pathname of the program. So *argc* will be 4 in our example. The argument *argv* is a pointer to an array of C strings (see Figure 3-2), each containing one command-line argument. In our example, argv[0] will be C:\TEST\TEST.EXE, which is the full pathname of the executable file.

The environment is passed to a process in the same manner as the command-line arguments. Thus, *envp* is also a pointer to an array of null-terminated C strings, each containing one environment setting. A NULL entry signifies the end of the environment table.

OS/2 PROCESSES

OS/2 goes beyond MS-DOS in supporting multiple concurrently executing processes. To accommodate OS/2, two new library routines were introduced in Microsoft C 5.1. These routines, *cwait* and *wait*, work in OS/2's protected mode only and are used to suspend a process until a certain child terminates or any of its child processes terminate. The *cwait* function waits for a specific child process whereas *wait* keeps the calling process suspended until any of its child processes terminate.

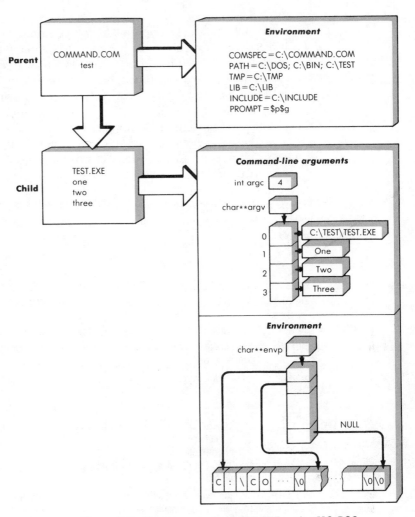

Figure 3-2. *Process running TEST.EXE under MS-DOS*

EXIT CODES FOR PROCESSES   When a child process exits, it returns an integer value, called the "exit code" to its parent just as a function call would return a value. The exit code signifies whether the program executed successfully. An exit code equal to zero normally means that the child process executed successfully. Nonzero exit codes indicate error. If you execute a program from a DOS batch file, the exit code from the program is available in a parameter named ERRORLEVEL. You could check for erroneous return from our example program by using the batch code fragment:

```
TEST One Two Three
if not ERRORLEVEL 0 echo TEST failed
```

SIGNALS   "Signals" are the operating system's way of interrupting a process when certain error conditions, also called "exceptions," occur. The signal mechanism is present in UNIX and is supported by most C libraries, Microsoft C included. Each recognized exception has a routine to handle the exception, and you can use the library routine *signal* to install your own routine to handle a particular signal. When a signal occurs, the appropriate handler is called. The *raise* function can be used to artificially generate a signal.

Constants are defined in the *signal.h* header for each signal that Microsoft C 5.0 can handle. Although there are six signals, as shown in Table 3-1, only three are relevant in MS-DOS systems: SIGABRT, SIGFPE, and SIGINT. Of these, the SIGINT signal is most often used. Generated when you hit a Control-C on the PC's keyboard, it normally terminates the process, but you can install your own handler for SIGINT to do something else. The example in the reference page on *signal* shows how this is done. Microsoft C 5.1 responds to four additional signals. See Table 3-8 in the reference page on *signal* for these.

Table 3-1. *List of Signals in Microsoft C 5.1*

Signal	Exception Condition	Default Action
SIGABRT	Abnormal termination of program.	Terminate program with exit code 3.
SIGFPE	Floating-point error, such as overflow, division by zero, etc.	Terminate program.
SIGILL	Illegal instruction. This exception is not generated by MS-DOS, but is included for ANSI compatibility.	Not applicable in MS-DOS.
SIGINT	Generated when user hits Control-C.	Generate software interrupt number 23h.
SIGSEGV	Illegal memory access. This exception is not generated under MS-DOS, but is included for ANSI compatibility.	Not applicable in MS-DOS.
SIGTERM	Termination request sent to the program. This is not generated in MS-DOS, but is included for ANSI compatibility.	Not applicable in MS-DOS.

NONLOCAL GOTOS IN C: LONGJMP AND SETJMP

Sometimes it is handy to be able to abort what you were doing and get back to where you started. For example, you may want to return to execute some code for error recovery no matter where an error is detected in your application. The *setjmp* and the *longjmp* functions provide the tools to accomplish this. The *setjmp* function saves the "state" or the "context" of the process and the *longjmp* uses the saved context to revert to a previous point in the program. What is the context of the process? In general, the context of a process refers to information that enables you to reconstruct exactly the way the process is at a particular point in its flow of execution. In C programs the relevant information includes quantities such as the address of the current instruction and of the registers SP, BP, SI, DI, DS, ES, and SS.

To understand the mechanics of *setjmp* and *longjmp*, look at the following code fragment:

```
#include <setjmp.h>
jmp_buf saved_context;

main()
{
    if (setjmp(saved_context) == 0)
    {
        do_something();
    }

    else
    {
/* This part executed when longjmp is called */
        handle_error();
    }
}

do_something()
{
    int something_wrong;
    :
    :
    if(something_wrong) longjmp(saved_context, 1);
}
```

Incidentally, the data type *jmp_buf* is defined in the header file *setjmp.h*. This is a system-dependent data type because different systems might require different amounts of information to capture the context of a process. In Microsoft C 5.1, *jmp_buf* is simply an array of nine 2-byte integers, as shown in Figure 3-3. Upon entry to *setjmp*, the stack contains the address of the buffer *saved_context* and the address of the *if* statement in the main function, to which *setjmp* will return. The *setjmp* function copies this return address (2 bytes of segment address and 2 bytes of offset) as well as the current values of the seven registers, SP, BP, SI, DI, DS, ES, and SS, into the buffer *saved_context*. Then *setjmp* returns with a zero. In this case, the *if* statement is satisfied and *do_something( )* is called.

When something goes wrong in *do_something( )* (indicated by the flag *something_wrong*), we call *longjmp* with two arguments: the first is the buffer that contains the context to which we will return. When the stack reverts back to this saved state, and the return statement in *longjmp* is executed, it will be as if we were returning from the call to *setjmp*, which originally saved the buffer *saved_context*. The second argument to *longjmp* specifies the return value to be used during this return. It should be other than zero so that in the *if* statement we can tell whether the return is induced by a *longjmp*.

The *setjmp/longjmp* combination enables you to jump unconditionally from one C function to another without using the conventional return statements. Essentially, *setjmp* marks the destination of the jump and *longjmp* is a nonlocal *goto* that executes the jump.

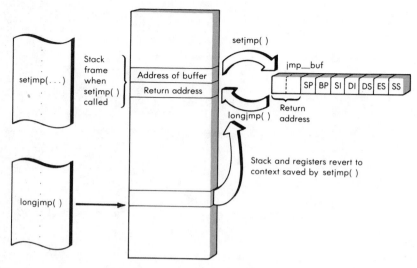

Figure 3-3. setjmp *and* longjmp *in action*

Notes on Process Control

The process control functions (see Table 3-2 for a complete catalog) can perform a variety of functions beyond the task of starting and stopping a process. Table 3-3 shows the process control routines listed by task. As you can see, many of the routines are for spawning or executing a child process.

Table 3-2. *Catalog of Process Control Routines*

Routine	Description
abort	Raises the SIGABRT signal after printing a message to *stderr*. The normal handler for SIGABRT terminates the process without flushing file buffers.
assert	Prints a diagnostic message and aborts program, if a given logical expression is false.
atexit	Installs a routine to a stack of up to 32 routines that will be called in "last-in first-out" order when the process terminates.
cwait	Suspends execution of the calling program until the specified child (or grandchild) process is terminated. (OS/2 protected mode only.)
execl	Executes a child process that overlays the parent in memory. Command-line arguments to the child are passed in a list terminated by a NULL and the child inherits the parent's environment.
execle	Executes a child process that overlays the parent in memory. Command-line arguments and a new environment are passed to the child in the form of a NULL-terminated list.
execlp	Executes a child process that overlays the parent in memory. Command-line arguments to the child are passed in a NULL-terminated list and the PATH environment variable is used to locate the file to be executed as a child.
execlpe	Executes a child process that overlays the parent in memory. Command-line arguments and a new environment are passed to the child in a NULL-terminated list and the PATH environment variable is used to find the file which is executed as a child.

Table 3-2. *(cont.)*

Routine	Description
execv	Executes a child process that overlays the parent in memory. A pointer to a variable-length array of command-line arguments is passed to the child. The child also receives a copy of the parent's environment.
execve	Executes a child process that overlays the parent in memory. Command-line arguments and a new environment are passed in variable length arrays with NULLs indicating the end of each array.
execvp	Executes a child process that overlays the parent in memory. Command-line arguments are passed in a variable-length array that ends with a NULL. The child inherits a copy of the parent's environment and the PATH environment variable is used to locate the program executed as a child.
execvpe	Executes a child process that overlays the parent in memory. Command-line arguments for the child and a specified environment are passed via pointers to NULL-terminated variable-length arrays. The environment variable PATH specifies the directories in which the program to be executed as a child can reside.
exit	Calls the functions installed by *atexit* or *onexit*, flushes all buffers associated with files that are open for I/O, and terminates the process and returns to the parent.
_exit	Terminates the process and immediately returns to the parent without performing the services that *exit* provides.
getenv	Returns the definition of an environment variable from the environment of the process.
getpid	Returns a unique integer process identification number.
longjmp	Restores the context of a process thus affecting an unconditional jump to the place where *setjmp* was called to save that context.
onexit	Installs a routine to a stack of up to 32 routines that are called in "last-in first-out" order when the process terminates.
perror	Prints an error message using your message and the system message corresponding to the value in the global variable *errno*.
putenv	Adds the definition of a new environment variable to the process environment table.
raise	Generates a signal (an exception).
setjmp	Saves the context of a process in a buffer that can be used by *longjmp* to jump back.
signal	Installs a function to handle a specific exception or signal.
spawnl	Executes a child process either by destroying the parent in memory or leaving it intact and returning to it when the child terminates. The command-line arguments to the child are passed in a NULL-terminated list and the child receives a copy of the parent's environment.
spawnle	Functions as *spawnl* does, but a new environment is passed in a list that ends with a NULL.
spawnlp	Functions as *spawnl* does and also searches all the directories named in the PATH environment variable to locate the program that is executed as a child.
spawnlpe	Behaves as *spawnle* does and also uses the setting of the PATH environment variable to locate the executable file to be run as a child.
spawnv	Executes a child process either by destroying the parent in memory or leaving it intact and returning to it when the child terminates. The command-line arguments to the child are passed as a pointer to a variable-length array whose last element is a NULL. The child receives a copy of the parent's environment.

Table 3-2. *(cont.)*

Routine	Description
spawnve	Functions as *spawnv* does, but a new environment is passed via a pointer to a variable-length array that ends with a NULL.
spawnvp	Functions as *spawnv* does and also searches all the directories named in the PATH environment variable to locate the program that is executed as a child.
spawnvpe	Behaves as *spawnve* does and also uses the setting of the PATH environment variable to locate the executable file to be run as a child.
system	Executes an MS-DOS system command.
wait	Suspends execution of the calling program until any of its immediate child processes is terminated. (OS/2 protected mode only.)

Table 3-3. *Process Control Routines by Task*

Task	Name of Routines
Launch a child process that destroys the parent in memory	execl, execle, execlp, execlpe, execv, execve, execvp, execvpe
Launch a child process that optionally overlays the parent in memory or returns to the parent when it exits	spawnl, spawnle, spawnlp, spawnlpe, spawnv, spawnve, spawnvp, spawnvpe
Wait for termination of all or selected OS/2 child processes	cwait, wait
Execute an MS-DOS command	system
Terminate a process	abort, _exit, exit
Handle errors	assert, perror
Get and set environment	getenv, putenv,
Install exception handler and generate an exception	raise, signal
Nonlocal jump from one functiion to another	longjmp, setjmp
Install routines to be called when the process terminates	atexit, onexit
Get identification number of process	getpid

SPAWN *AND EXEC* FUNCTIONS

Just as COMMAND.COM creates a child process and runs your program, the program can, in turn, execute a child of its own and run any other executable. The library routines in the process control category provide you with two choices: the *exec* routines or the *spawn* routines. Both sets of routines rely on the MS-DOS EXEC function to create a process, although they have slightly differing capabilities. The *exec* routines load the child into memory in the space previously used by the parent. Thus, the parent is "overlaid" by the child and destroyed. When the child ends, it returns to DOS. The *spawn* routines are more general. They offer you the choice of either overlaying the parent, in which case they behave exactly like their *exec* counterparts, or loading the child into a different place in memory. While the child executes, the parent waits and when the child terminates, the parent process resumes.

Versions of *spawn* and *exec*

The *exec* and *spawn* routines have eight versions each. This large assortment gives you control over how you pass the command-line arguments and the environment to the child process. It is easy enough to decide which routine to use once you know the naming scheme (see Figure 3-4).

The first part of a routine name is *exec* or *spawn*. The next character must be present. It can be either an "l" or a "v" to indicate how command-line arguments and environment (if a new one is provided) are passed. An "l" indicates that the command-line arguments (each a C string) are listed one after another with a NULL ending the list. This list appears in the call to the *spawn* or the *exec* function. You should use this form when the number of command-line arguments and entries in the environment table are fixed and

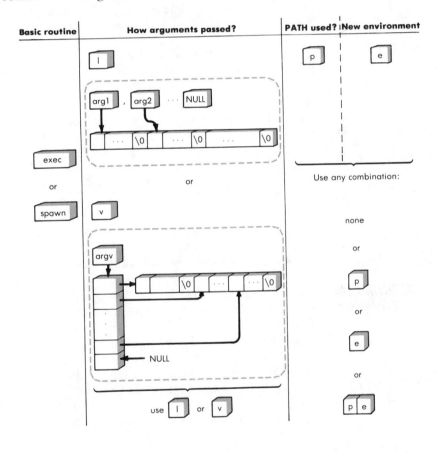

Figure 3-4. *Naming conventions and use of* exec *and* spawn *functions*

known in advance. A "v" indicates that the strings that make up the command-line arguments and environment are placed in an array, and a pointer to this array is passed to the function. The last element in the array is a NULL pointer. Since this array can be constructed at run-time, this form of the routines is suitable when there is a variable number of command-line arguments to be passed to the child process.

The next letters, "p" or "e" or the pair "pe," are optional. Whenever a "p" is included in the name, the PATH environment variable of the parent process is used as the list of directories that will be searched when trying to locate the executable file that will be excuted as a child process. The "e" signifies that instead of inheriting the parent's environment, a new environment is being specified. The format used to specify the environment is the same as that for the command-line arguments and is determined by which of the letters "l" or "v" is present in the function's name.

Spawn or Exec: Which One to Use

The *spawn* and *exec* functions allow you to start a child process and execute another program. The choice of one over the other depends on your application. If you want to use a tool like an editor and return to your program, then one of the *spawn* functions will meet your needs. There are situations in which *exec* is more suitable. Suppose, your application can be broken up into three programs, MODULE1.EXE, MODULE2.EXE, and MODULE3.EXE, each independent of the other. You can run your application by first executing MODULE1.EXE in which you use *exec* to launch a child process, MODULE2.EXE. When MODULE2.EXE ends, you can switch to MODULE3.EXE by another *exec* call. Thus you can chain from one program to another by using the *exec* functions. Despite this, you may decide to use *spawn* exclusively because the functionality of *exec* can be obtained by invoking the *spawn* functions with the execution mode P_OVERLAY.

EXECUTING DOS COMMANDS

What if you want to use an MS-DOS command, like DIR, from your C program? Since DOS commands are only understood by COMMAND.COM, the *exec* or *spawn* functions have to spawn a copy of COMMAND.COM to execute any DOS command. This task is made simple by the Microsoft C library routine *system*, which can accept and execute any MS-DOS command. The *system* function actually looks at the COMSPEC environment variable to locate a copy of COMMAND.COM to run as a child while your program waits. The PATH environment variable is used when executing the command that you provide to *system*.

TERMINATING A PROCESS

Three functions can terminate a process: *abort, _exit,* and *exit.* Of course any process terminates automatically when its body of code ends. When a C process terminates normally via a call to *exit* or when its execution is complete, several things happen. First a set of up to 32 routines (installed earlier by calls to *atexit* or *onexit*) will be called one after another in a last-in first-out (LIFO) manner. Then, all buffers associated with files open for buffered I/O will be "flushed," which involves writing out the contents of a buffer to its associated file. Finally, the process ends and returns to its parent.

The *abort* and *_exit* functions terminate a process without going through the niceties of normal termination. The buffers are not flushed (desirable when you know that the data in the buffers may be corrupted), nor do they call the routines that are supposed to be called upon program termination. The *abort* function even prints a message indicating that the program terminated abnormally.

Cautions

► When you use *exec* or *spawn* to launch a child process, the file translation mode (see the tutorial in Chapter 13) of open files is included in the environment that is passed to the child. Specifically, it is in the entry named ;C_FILE_INFO in the environment. The information on the translation mode is passed in binary form. Normally, when you invoke a C program, the "startup" code (that which is executed before your *main* function is called) reads this entry in the environment and removes it. If you run a non-C program (such as COMMAND.COM), this entry is left behind in the environment and you may see some "junk" when you print the environment in the child although normal functioning of the program should not be affected by this. To see this effect, try the following example program:

```
#include <stdlib.h>
main()
{
/* Execute the DOS command SET to see environment */
    system("set");
}
```

► The child process does not inherit the signal handlers you may have installed in the parent. All signal handlers revert to the default settings.

► The combined length of all the strings that form the command-line arguments to the child cannot exceed 128 bytes.

► You should be aware of some limits on the size of environment table. The total length of the entire environment cannot exceed 32 K and the size of individual definitions is limited to 128 bytes.

Further Reading

The use of the *exec* and the *spawn* functions as well as the handling of signals has been covered in Prata's text[1] and in Hansen's book[2].

1. Stephen Prata, The Waite Group, *Advanced C Primer++*, Howard W. Sams & Company, Indianapolis, IN, 1986, 502 pages.

2. Augie Hansen, *Proficient C*, Microsoft Press, Redmond, WA, 1987, 492 pages.

abort

COMPATIBILITY	MSC 3	MSC 4	MSC 5	QC	TC	ANSI	UNIX V
	▲	▲	▲	▲	▲	▲	▲

PURPOSE Use *abort* to exit your program abnormally.

SYNTAX `void abort(void);`

EXAMPLE CALL `abort();`

INCLUDES `#include <process.h>`   For function declaration

or

`#include <stdlib.h>`

DESCRIPTION The *abort* function first prints the message *Abnormal program termination* to *stderr* and then calls *raise(SIGABRT)*. Subsequent processing depends on your arrangement for the signal SIGABRT. The default action on SIGABRT is to terminate the calling process with exit code 3 and return to the parent process or MS-DOS. Note that *abort,* unlike *exit,* will not flush the file buffers or call the routines set up by *atexit* or *onexit.* You can take care of these chores, however, by correctly setting up the processing for the SIGABRT signal.

RETURNS The default action of SIGABRT raised by *abort* is to terminate the process and return code 3 to the parent process.

COMMENTS In Microsoft C 4.0 *abort* prints the final message and terminates the process without raising the signal SIGABRT.

SEE ALSO `exit, _exit`   To terminate a process

`raise, signal`   To generate and handle exceptions

EXAMPLE Write a program that uses *abort* to exit when it is invoked without any command-line arguments. Otherwise, the program simply prints out the arguments.

```
#include <stdio.h>
#include <stdlib.h>
main(int argc, char **argv)
{
    int i;
    if(argc < 2)
    {
        printf("Not enough arguments!\n");
```

 Process Control

```
        abort();
    }
    for (i=0; i<argc; i++)
    {
        printf("Argument %d = %s\n", i+1, argv[i]);
    }
}
```

assert

COMPATIBILITY	MSC 3	MSC 4	MSC 5	QC	TC	ANSI	UNIX V
	▲	▲	▲	▲	▲	▲	▲

PURPOSE Use *assert* to print an error message and abort the program if a specific assertion is false.

SYNTAX `void assert(<expression>);`

`<expression>`   C statements specifying assertion being tested

EXAMPLE CALL `assert(arg_value >= 0);`

INCLUDES `#include <stdio.h>`   For definition of stderr, used in definition of *assert*

`#include <assert.h>`   For definition of *assert*

DESCRIPTION The *assert* macro is defined in Microsoft C 5.0 and 5.1 in such a way that if the expression is false (i.e., evaluates to zero), it prints a diagnostic message of the form

`Assertion failed: expression, file (filename), line (linenumber)`

and calls *abort*. In the diagnostic message, *filename* is the name of the source file and *linenumber* is the line number where the *assert* macro appears in the source file. In Microsoft C 4.0 the diagnostic message does not include the *expression*.

COMMON USES The *assert* macro identifies program errors during the debugging phase. After the program is debugged, you can disable all occurrences of the *assert* macro either by using the option /DNDEBUG=1 in the compiler's command line or by inserting a *#define NDEBUG 1* in the source file.

SEE ALSO abort: To abort a program

EXAMPLE This program considers it a fatal error if it is invoked without any argument on

assert

the command line. This test is implemented by *assert*. When invoked with one or more arguments, the program simply prints the arguments.

```
#include <stdio.h>
#include <assert.h>
main(int argc, char **argv)
{
    int i;
/* Make sure that there is more than one argument */
    assert(argc > 1);
/* Just print out the arguments */
    printf("Thanks for these \"arguments\"\n");
    for (i=0; i<argc; i++)
    {
        printf("Argument %d = %s\n", i+1, argv[i]);
    }
}
```

atexit

COMPATIBILITY	MSC 3	MSC 4	MSC 5	QC	TC	ANSI	UNIX V
			▲	▲	▲	▲	

PURPOSE   Use *atexit* to set up a stack of up to 32 functions that the system will call in a LIFO manner when your program terminates normally.

SYNTAX   `int atexit(void (*func)(void));`

`void (*func)(void);`   Pointer to function to be called

INCLUDES   `#include <stdlib.h>`   For function declaration

DESCRIPTION   The *atexit* function places the function pointer *func* on a stack of functions to be called when the program terminates. (Note that the name of a function denotes a pointer to it.) Up to 32 functions can be specified with *atexit*. These are invoked in a LIFO manner when the calling program exits. (The function whose address you provide in the first call to *atexit* is called last.) Note that the functions passed to *atexit* cannot take any arguments.

COMMON USES   The *atexit* and *onexit* functions allow you to set up "house cleaning" functions that should be performed when exiting your application program. These might include making sure all files are updated and saving the last setting of internal parameters to a disk file.

Process Control

RETURNS   The *atexit* function returns a zero if successful. If you have already called *atexit* more than 32 times, the return value will be nonzero.

SEE ALSO   exit   To terminate process (after calling functions installed by *atexit*)

onexit   UNIX version of *atexit*

EXAMPLE   Demonstrate the use of *atexit* by calling it with three functions. Let each function print out an identifying message. Notice that the functions are called in the reverse order. Thus the first function "registered" with *atexit* gets called last.

```
#include <stdio.h>
#include <stdlib.h>
main(int argc, char **argv)
{
     void first(void), second(void), third(void);
     atexit(first);
     atexit(second);
     atexit(third);
     printf("Now exiting...\n");
}
/*-------------------------------------------------*/
void first(void)
{
     printf("Function number 1: called last\n");
}
/*-------------------------------------------------*/
void second(void)
{
     printf("Function number 2:\n");
}
/*-------------------------------------------------*/
void third(void)
{
     printf("Function number 3: called first\n");
}
/*-------------------------------------------------*/
```

atexit

cwait

COMPATIBILITY	MSC 3	MSC 4	MSC 5	QC	TC	ANSI	UNIX V
			5.1 only				

PURPOSE
Use *cwait* in OS/2's protected mode to wait until a specified child process terminates.

SYNTAX
```
int cwait(int *p_status, int proc_id, int action);
```

```
int *p_status;
```
Address of integer to hold the termination status code of child

```
int proc_id;
```
Process identification number of the child

```
int action;
```
Action code to indicate whether process waits for child alone or for all grandchildren too

EXAMPLE CALL
```
pid = spawnv(P_NOWAIT, "child.exe", args);
if (cwait(&status, pid, WAIT_GRANDCHILD) == -1)
                                    perror("cwait failed");
```

INCLUDES
```
#include <process.h>
```
For function prototype and action codes

DESCRIPTION
Available in OS/2's protected mode only, the *cwait* function suspends the calling process until the child process specified by the identification number in the argument *proc_id* terminates. Depending on the value of the *action* argument, the parent process either waits only for the child or for all the grandchildren of that child. The *action* can be one of the two values shown in Table 3-4. These constants are defined in the include file *process.h*. When *cwait* returns, the integer at the address *p_status* contains a termination code that can be interpreted by consulting Table 3-5.

Table 3-4. *Action Codes*

Action Code	Meaning
WAIT_CHILD	Parent process waits until the child process ends.
WAIT_GRANDCHILD	Parent waits until the specified child process and all grandchildren of that child terminate.

COMMON USES
The *cwait* function synchronizes processes in OS/2's protected mode environment.

RETURNS
When *cwait* returns after a normal termination of the child process, it returns the process identification of the child. In case of abnormal termination of the child, it returns −1 and sets the global variable *errno* to EINTR. For other

 Process Control

Table 3-5. *Contents of the Status Word*

Byte	Contents
Low order	Zero if child terminated normally. Otherwise, this byte contains the termination code from the service DOSCWAIT, to be interpreted as follows:

Content	Meaning
1	Hard error abort
2	Trap operation
3	SIGTERM signal (asking child to terminate) was not intercepted

Byte	Contents
High order	When child returns normally, this contains the low-order byte of the result code that was passed by the child process to DOSEXIT.

types of errors, *cwait* returns −1 immediately and sets *errno* either to EINVAL to indicate an invalid action code or to ECHILD to signify that the child process specified by *proc_id* does not exist.

COMMENTS   You should be familiar with the protected mode operation of the OS/2 operating system before using the *cwait* function.

SEE ALSO   spawn   To launch a child process

   wait   To wait until any one of the child processes terminates

exec functions

COMPATIBILITY	MSC 3	MSC 4	MSC 5	QC	TC	ANSI	UNIX V
		▲	▲	▲	▲		▲

PURPOSE   Use one of the *exec* functions to load and execute a child process in the memory currently occupied by your program's code.

SYNTAX
```
int execl(char *path, char *arg0, char *arg1,..., NULL);

int execle(char *path, char *arg0, char *arg1,..., NULL,
        char *envp[]);

int execlp(char *path, char *arg0, char *arg1,..., NULL);

int execlpe(char *path, char *arg0, char *arg1,..., NULL,
        char *envp[]);

int execv(char *path, char *argv[]);
```

```
int execve(char *path, char *argv[], char *envp[]);

int execvp(char *path, char *argv[]);

int execvpe(char *path, char *argv[], char *envp[]);
```

char *path;   Pathname of file to be executed as a child process

char *arg0, *arg1, ..., NULL;   Command-line arguments for the child process
                                        (ends with a NULL)

char *argv[];   Array of command-line arguments for the child process

char *envp[];   The environment parameter table

EXAMPLE CALL   execv ("child.exe", argv);

INCLUDES   #include <process.h>   For function declaration

DESCRIPTION   The *exec* functions create a child process to load and execute the program specified by the argument *path*. In doing so, they destroy the calling process. The variations among the different forms of the *exec* functions are due to the way in which arguments and environment variables are passed to the child process. Table 3-6 uses the name of each function as a key to tabulate its action.

As you can see, the fifth letter of the name, "l" or "v," determines how command-line arguments are received by the child process. The next one or two letters indicate how environment variables are passed to the child process.

If the sixth letter of the name is a "p," then the PATH environment variable is used by COMMAND.COM to locate the executable program whose name you specify in the argument *path*. Otherwise, you must specify the full pathname of the file to be executed or specify a path beginning at the current working directory. If the *path* argument does not have an extension, the *exec* function first searches for a file without an extension. If none is found and *path* does not end with a period, it tries the extensions .COM and .EXE, in that order.

Note that the combined length of all the command-line argument strings, including a separating space between each adjoining argument, must not exceed 128 bytes. Although a different string will not produce any error, it is customary to provide the full pathname of the executable file as the first command-line argument to the child process.

The last two points to note are about files and signal handlers. In the child process, all signal handlers are reset to the default ones. Files that were open in the parent remain open in the child, but the translation modes (see *fopen*) in Chapter 13 of the open files are not preserved in the child. You must reset the translation modes by calling the *setmode* function.

COMMON USES   The *exec* functions may be used to chain the execution from one program to another.

 Process Control

Table 3-6. exec *Functions*

Fifth Letter of Name	Meaning
l	Command-line arguments to the child process are listed on the statement that invokes the *exec* function. These forms are useful when the number of arguments is known in advance. The arguments, *arg0, arg1 . . .* , are listed one after another with NULL marking the end.
v	Command-line arguments are passed in the form of a pointer to an array of argument strings. This is useful when the number of arguments is not known in advance. In this case, you prepare an array of null-terminated strings, each representing one command-line argument for the child program, put NULL to mark the end of the list, and pass the pointer to this array, *argv*, to the child process via the *exec* function.

Next Two Letters	How Environment Variables Are Handled
none	Child process inherits parent's environment variables.
p	PATH environment variable is used to locate the executable file. In this case, the *path* argument may specify a program name without any directory information and COMMAND.COM will locate the program if it is present in one of the directories included in your PATH environment variable.
e	Child process receives a pointer *envp* to an array of environment strings. Each environment variable definition is of the form *NAME = value of variable*, and the end of the array is marked by NULL.
pe	This is a combination of letters described above. The PATH environment variable is used and the child process gets a pointer to a table of environment variables that you prepare.

RETURNS If successful, the *exec* functions do not return to the parent. If an error occurs, the return value is −1 and the global variable *errno* is set to one of the constants shown in Table 3-7, indicating the cause of the error.

COMMENTS Since the *exec* functions overwrite the parent in memory, they are good only for chaining one program to another. Use the *spawn* functions if you want to launch a program and return to the original program.

Microsoft warns that because of a bug in DOS versions 2.0 and 2.1, a child process launched by *exec* may cause fatal system errors when it exits. Use DOS versions 3.0 or higher for reliable operation when calling *exec*.

SEE ALSO spawn functions   To launch a program and return when it terminates

EXAMPLE Demonstrate the use of the *exec* functions in a program that allows a child process to run using any one of the eight *exec* functions. Prepare data in a structure allocated in the parent program and pass the data to the child by encoding the address as a character string and using that string as a command-line argument. In the child program, print the command-line arguments and

exec functions

Table 3-7. *Error Codes Returned by* **exec** *Functions*

Error	Cause of Error
E2BIG	Either the total length of the command-line arguments exceeds 128 bytes, or the memory required for the environment variables exceeds 32 K.
EACCES	You are running MS-DOS 3.0 or higher with file-sharing enabled and the file specified in *path* is either locked or not set up for sharing.
EMFILE	COMMAND.COM has to open the specified file first to determine if it is executable. This error means there were already too many files open (20) to prevent COMMAND.COM from doing this.
ENOENT	Either the path or the file specified in the argument *path* was not found.
ENOEXEC	The specified file is not executable because its format does not match the DOS specification for an executable file.
ENOMEM	Either there is not enough memory to load and execute the child process or available memory is corrupted or an invalid block of memory was located, indicating that the parent process was incorrectly loaded.

the environment passed to it. Then access the data structure using the address passed in the command line and display the various fields. *Note:* Remember to compile and link the child program first and save it in a file named *child.exe*.

```
/*===================== PARENT =====================*/
#include <stdio.h>
#include <process.h>
#include <malloc.h>
#include <string.h>
typedef struct TEST_DATA
{
    char name[20];
    int n;
    double x;
} TEST_DATA;
/* PARENT: Test the "exec" functions. Pass address of
 *         data in command line arguments as well as
 *         environment variables when appropriate.
 */
char *envp[] =
{
    "PARENT=EXEC FUNCTIONS",
    NULL
};
main()
{
    char *argv[4], buf[20], rname[40];
    TEST_DATA *pdata;
/* Set up a data structure and initialize it */
    if((pdata=(TEST_DATA *)
```

MEMO⬛⬛RY

Process Control

```
                 malloc(sizeof(TEST_DATA))) == NULL) abort();
        strcpy(pdata->name, "PARENT");
        pdata->n = 100;
        pdata->x = 1000.99;
/* Set up the arguments for the child process */
        argv[0] = "child.exe",
        argv[1] = rname;
        sprintf(buf, "%p", (void far *)pdata);
        argv[2] = buf;
        argv[3] = NULL;
/* Ask user which "exec" routine to call */
        printf("Enter name of \"exec\" function to call:");
        gets(rname);
        strlwr(rname);
/* Call the "exec" function requested by the user */
        if(strcmp(rname, "execl") == 0)
        {
            execl("child.exe",
                    "child.exe", "execl", buf, NULL);
        }
        if(strcmp(rname, "execle") == 0)
        {
            execle("child.exe",
                "child.exe", "execle", buf, NULL, envp);
        }
        if(strcmp(rname, "execlp") == 0)
        {
            execlp("child.exe",
                    "child.exe", "execlp", buf, NULL);
        }
        if(strcmp(rname, "execlpe") == 0)
        {
            execlpe("child.exe",
                "child.exe", "execlpe", buf, NULL, envp);
        }
        if(strcmp(rname, "execv") == 0)
        {
            execv("child.exe", argv);
        }
        if(strcmp(rname, "execve") == 0)
        {
            execve("child.exe", argv, envp);
        }
        if(strcmp(rname, "execvp") == 0)
        {
            execvp("child.exe", argv);
        }
        if(strcmp(rname, "execvpe") == 0)
```

exec functions

```
        {
            execvpe("child.exe", argv, envp);
        }
/* Check if we could call child or not */
        if(strcmp(pdata->name, "CHILD") == 0)
        {
            printf("Back from child: name = %s, n = %d, \
x= %f\n", pdata->name, pdata->n, pdata->x);
        }
        else
        {
            printf("Don't know: %s\n", rname);
        }
}
/*===================== CHILD =====================*/
/*      Must be in a file named:  CHILD.EXE            */
#include <stdio.h>
#include <dos.h>
#include <string.h>
typedef struct TEST_DATA
{
    char name[20];
    int n;
    double x;
} TEST_DATA;
/* Child: First argument is program name,
 *        Second one tells us how child was invoked
 *        Third argument is an address in the form
 *        SSSS:0000 (segment:offset). This is the
 *        address of a data structure allocated in
 *        the parent.
 */
static char far cname[] = "CHILD";
main(int argc, char **argv, char **envp)
{
    char  **p_table;
    TEST_DATA far *pdata;
    void far *p_s1;
    void far *p_s2;
    printf("CHILD: received %d arguments\n", argc);
    if(argc < 3){
        printf("not enough arguments\n");
        exit(1);
    }
    printf("CHILD invoked by a %s call.\n", argv[1]);

/* Now print the environment passed to CHILD     */
    printf("==== CHILD: Environment contains ====\n");
```

```
        for(p_table = envp;
            *p_table != NULL;
            p_table++) printf("%s\n", *p_table);

/* Read in address of parent's data from argv[2] */
        sscanf(argv[2], "%p", (void far *)&pdata);
        printf("In child: name = %Fs, n = %d, x= %f\n",
                pdata->name, pdata->n, pdata->x);
/* Put new values in the data structure. If CHILD was
 * created by a "spawn" function call, this data will
 * be available to the parent when child exits.
 * Notice that we have to use "movedata" to copy
 * "far" data in small or medium model.
 */
        p_s1 = (void far *)cname;
        p_s2 = (void far *)pdata->name;
        movedata(FP_SEG(p_s1), FP_OFF(p_s1),
                FP_SEG(p_s2), FP_OFF(p_s2), 6);
        pdata->n = 101;
        pdata->x = 999.99;
        exit(0);
}
```

exit

COMPATIBILITY	MSC 3	MSC 4	MSC 5	QC	TC	ANSI	UNIX V
	▲	▲	▲	▲	▲	▲	▲

PURPOSE   Use *exit* to terminate your program normally by flushing file buffers, closing files, and invoking functions set up with *atexit* and *onexit*.

SYNTAX   `void exit(int status);`

`intstatus;`   Exit status code

EXAMPLE CALL   `exit(0);`

INCLUDES   `#include <stdlib.h>`   For function declaration

or

`#include <process.h>`

DESCRIPTION   The *exit* function flushes all buffers associated with files opened for buffered I/O, closes all files, and then invokes in LIFO order the functions set up by earlier calls to *atexit* and *onexit*. After the calls are complete, *exit* terminates the program and makes available to the parent process or DOS the low-order byte of the argument *status*. Ordinarily, a *status* of zero means normal exit, whereas nonzero values indicate errors. If the program was invoked from an MS-DOS batch file, the value of *status* can be checked from the batch file with the command IF_ERRORLEVEL. Starting with Microsoft C 5.1, *exit* terminates all threads of a program in OS/2's protected mode operation.

SEE ALSO   _exit   To terminate process without performing the normal "housekeeping" chores

atexit, onexit   To set up functions called when a process terminates normally

EXAMPLE   Illustrate how file buffers are flushed when a program *exit*s by opening a file, writing a line to it, and using *exit* to terminate. The line appears in the file because *exit* flushed the buffer.

```
#include <stdio.h>
main()
{
    FILE *fp;
    char filename[40];
    printf("Enter name of a file to be opened \
for writing:");
    gets(filename);
    if((fp = fopen(filename, "w+")) == NULL)
    {
        perror("File open error");
        abort();
    }
    fprintf(fp, "If you use \"exit\", this line will \
appear in the file\nbecause it flushes buffers\n");
    printf("TYPE %s to see if buffers were flushed\n",
            filename);
    exit(0);
}
```

__exit

COMPATIBILITY	MSC 3	MSC 4	MSC 5	QC	TC	ANSI	UNIX V
	▲	▲	▲	▲	▲		

PURPOSE   Use _exit to terminate your program immediately without flushing file buffers.

SYNTAX   void _exit(int status);

int status;   _exit status code

 Process Control

EXAMPLE CALL   _exit(0);

INCLUDES   #include <stdlib.h>   For function declaration

or

#include <process.h>

DESCRIPTION   The _*exit* function terminates the program immediately, without flushing the buffers associated with files opened for buffered I/O. The files are closed "as-is" and, after terminating the program, _*exit* makes available to the parent process or to DOS the low-order byte of the argument *status*. Ordinarily a *status* of zero means normal exit, whereas nonzero values indicate errors. If the program was invoked from an MS-DOS batch file, the value of *status* can be checked with the command IF_ERRORLEVEL. Starting with Microsoft C 5.1, _*exit* terminates all threads of a program in OS/2's protected mode operation.

SEE ALSO   exit   To terminate process after performing "housekeeping" chores

EXAMPLE   Illustrate that file buffers are not flushed when a program _*exit*s by opening a file, writing a line to it and using _*exit* to terminate the program. Notice that the line does not appear in the file because _*exit* did not flush the buffer when exiting the program.

```
#include <stdio.h>
main()
{
    FILE *fp;
    char filename[40];
    printf("Enter name of a file to be opened \
for writing:");
    gets(filename);
    if((fp = fopen(filename, "w+")) == NULL)
    {
        perror("File open error");
        abort();
    }
    fprintf(fp, "If you use \"_exit\", this line will \
not appear in the file\nbecause buffers are not \
flushed\n");
    printf("TYPE %s to see if buffers were flushed\n",
            filename);
    _exit(0);
}
```

_exit

getenv

COMPATIBILITY	MSC 3	MSC 4	MSC 5	QC	TC	ANSI	UNIX V
	▲	▲	▲	▲	▲	▲	▲

PURPOSE Use *getenv* to get the definition of a variable from the environment table of the process.

SYNTAX `char *getenv(const char *varname);`

`const char *varname;`   Name of environment variable to look for

EXAMPLE CALL `current_path = getenv("PATH");`

INCLUDES `#include <stdlib.h>`   For function declaration

DESCRIPTION The *getenv* function uses the global variable *environ* to locate the list of environment variables and then it searches the list for an entry for the variable named *varname*.

RETURNS If *varname* is found, *getenv* returns a pointer to the string value of *varname*. Thus if the environment variable LIB is defined as LIB=C:\LIB in the environment table, invoking *getenv* with LIB as *varname* returns a pointer to the string C:\LIB. If *varname* is undefined, *getenv* returns a NULL.

COMMENTS Under MS-DOS, the *main* function can get a pointer to the list of environment variables as a third argument, say, *envp*. The library routine *putenv* may alter the location of this list, however, and render *envp* useless. So, it is safer to use the functions *getenv* and *putenv*, respectively, to locate and modify the environment table.

SEE ALSO putenv   To add the definition of a new variable to the environment table of the process

EXAMPLE Prepare a small utility program that lets you see the setting of an environment variable. Assume that the name of the environment variable is given on the command line. Use *getenv* to get the value of that variable and print it.

```
#include <stdio.h>
#include <stdlib.h>
main(int argc, char **argv)
{
    char *value;
    if(argc < 2)
    {
        printf("Usage: %s <env_var_name>\n", argv[0]);
        exit(0);
    }
}
```

 Process Control

```
/* Get the value of the environment variable */
    strupr(argv[1]);
    if ((value = getenv(argv[1])) == NULL)
    {
        printf("%s <-- no such environment variable\n",
                argv[1]);
    }
    else
    {
        printf("%s=%s\n", argv[1], value);
    }
}
```

getpid

COMPATIBILITY	MSC 3	MSC 4	MSC 5	QC	TC	ANSI	UNIX V
	▲	▲	▲	▲			▲

PURPOSE Use *getpid* to obtain the "process ID," an integer value that identifies the calling process to MS-DOS.

SYNTAX `int getpid(void);`

INCLUDES `#include <process.h>`   For function declaration

DESCRIPTION The *getpid* function returns an integer value, the process ID, that identifies the calling process. The process ID is also used by the *mktemp* function to generate temporary file names.

SEE ALSO `mktemp`   To generate temporary file name using process ID

EXAMPLE Use *getpid* to get the identification number of the process and print it. A different number is returned every time you run the program.

```
#include <stdio.h>
#include <process.h>
main()
{
    int process_id;
    process_id = getpid();
    printf("The process ID is: %d\n", process_id);
}
```

getpid

longjmp

COMPATIBILITY	MSC 3	MSC 4	MSC 5	QC	TC	ANSI	UNIX V
	▲	▲	▲	▲	▲	▲	▲

PURPOSE Use *longjmp* to restore a stack environment that was saved by an earlier call to *setjmp*, thus restoring all local variables to their previous states and returning as if from the last call to *setjmp*.

SYNTAX
```
void longjmp(jmp_buf env, int value);
```

`jmp_buf env;`   Data type in which the registers and a return address representing the stack environment are stored

`int value;`   Value that appears to be returned by the earlier call to *setjmp*

EXAMPLE CALL `longjmp(stack_env, 1);`

INCLUDES `#include <setjmp.h>`   For function declaration and definition of the data type *jmp_buf*

DESCRIPTION The *longjmp* function restores the registers saved in *env* as part of the stack environment saved earlier by a call to *setjmp*. Then it jumps to the return address for *setjmp* which is also saved in *env*. This restores all stack-based local variables to their state when the *setjmp* function was called, making it appear as if *setjmp* returned again. The argument *value* is used in this "forced" return from *setjmp*. However, this process might not properly restore all register-based variables to the routine where the call to *setjmp* occurred. Since *longjmp* jumps to the return address of the corresponding call to *setjmp*, you must make sure that the call to *longjmp* occurs before the function in which you called *setjmp* has returned.

COMMON USES The *longjmp* function is used in conjunction with its companion *setjmp* to divert the flow of execution to error-recovery code without using the normal function call and return conventions. First a call to *setjmp* is necessary to set up the place to which *longjmp* can return control when called. After that, when the error condition occurs, you can call *longjmp* and jump to the point where the *setjmp* function would have returned.

COMMENTS It is a little difficult to understand the behavior of *setjmp* and *longjmp* but, essentially, they give you the flexibility of jumping to an arbitrary location from within C. This is akin to a "goto" statement which lets you jump from one function to another.

SEE ALSO `setjmp`   To save a stack environment to be used in a subsequent call to *longjmp*

EXAMPLE The pair of *setjmp* and *longjmp* is ideal for error-handling or handling special

 Process Control

conditions in a program. You call *setjmp* at a place where you have code that you may want to execute later. Then whenever the conditions are met, call *longjmp* with the stack environment variable saved earlier by *setjmp*. This places you where *setjmp* was called originally. It will appear as though the *setjmp* function returned a second time, this time with the value from the second argument to *longjmp*. Here is a small program to illustrate a way to use this versatile duo.

```
#include <stdio.h>
#include <setjmp.h>
static jmp_buf mark_place;
static void call_longjmp(void);
main()
{
    int rvalue;
    rvalue = setjmp(mark_place);
    if(rvalue != 0)
    {
        printf("Second return from \"setjmp\" induced \
by call to \"longjmp\"\n");
        printf("Return value = %d\n", rvalue);
        exit(rvalue);
    }
    printf("Calling \"longjmp\" next...\n");
    call_longjmp();
}
/*-------------------------------------------------*/
static void call_longjmp(void)
{
    longjmp(mark_place, 3);
}
```

onexit

COMPATIBILITY	MSC 3	MSC 4	MSC 5	QC	TC	ANSI	UNIX V
		▲	▲	▲			▲

PURPOSE Use *onexit* to set up a stack of as many as 32 functions that the system will call in a LIFO manner when your program terminates normally.

SYNTAX `onexit_t onexit(onexit_t (*func)(void));`

`onexit_t (*func)(void);`   Pointer to function to be called

INCLUDES `#include <stdlib.h>`   For function declaration and definition of *onexit_t*

DESCRIPTION   The *onexit* function places the function address *func* on a stack of functions to be called when the program terminates. (Note that in C the name of a function denotes a pointer to itself.) Up to 32 functions can be specified using *onexit*. These will be invoked in a LIFO manner when the calling program exits. Thus the function whose address you provide in the first call to *onexit* will actually be called last.

Note that the functions passed to *onexit* cannot take any arguments and it returns a value of type *onexit_t*, a data type defined in *stdlib.h*.

COMMON USES   The *onexit* and *atexit* functions allow your application program to "clean house" before returning to DOS.

RETURNS   The *onexit* function returns a pointer *func* to the function if successful. If there is no more room in its stack for the function, *onexit* returns a NULL.

COMMENTS   The *onexit* function is not a part of the proposed ANSI definition. The *atexit* function performs the same function and *is* a part of the ANSI definition. So if portability is a concern, you may want to use *atexit* instead of *onexit*.

SEE ALSO   exit   To terminate process (after calling functions installed by *onexit*)

   atexit   ANSI version of *onexit*

EXAMPLE   Demonstrate the use of *onexit* by calling it with three different function addresses. Let each function print out an identifying message. Notice that the first function registered with *onexit* gets called last.

```
#include <stdio.h>
#include <stdlib.h>
main(int argc, char **argv)
{
    void first(void), second(void), third(void);
    onexit(first);
    onexit(second);
    onexit(third);
    printf("Now exiting...\n");
}
/*-------------------------------------------------*/
void first(void)
{
    printf("Function number 1: called last\n");
}
/*-------------------------------------------------*/
void second(void)
{
    printf("Function number 2:\n");
}
/*-------------------------------------------------*/
```

 Process Control

```
void third(void)
{
    printf("Function number 3: called first\n");
}
/*---------------------------------------------------*/
```

perror

COMPATIBILITY	MSC 3	MSC 4	MSC 5	QC	TC	ANSI	UNIX V
	▲	▲	▲	▲	▲	▲	▲

PURPOSE   Use *perror* to construct an error message by concatenating your message with that from the system which corresponds to the current value in the global variable *errno*. The message prints to *stderr*.

SYNTAX   `void perror(const char *string);`

`const char *string;`   Your part of the message

EXAMPLE CALL   `perror("Error closing file");`

INCLUDES   `#include <stdio.h>`   For function declaration

DESCRIPTION   The *perror* function takes the message from the argument "string," appends a colon and a space, and concatenates to this the message from the system's error message table corresponding to the value in the global variable *errno*. The value in *errno* is the error number corresponding to the last error that occurred in a C library routine. All error messages are stored in a table of strings called *sys_errlist*. There is no need, however, to declare or to directly access these variables in your program.

COMMON USES   When an error occurs in certain C library routines, the variable *errno* is set to a value that reflects the cause of the error. Typically, *perror* is called immediately after an error return from a library routine to print a message detailing the error. This message then prints to *stderr*.

COMMENTS   Rather than access *errno* and the system error-message list *sys_errlist* directly, you should always use *perror* to print the error message when a library routine returns with an error. This approach is safer because it does not use error numbers, which very well can change during a later release of the compiler.

SEE ALSO   `_strerror, strerror`   Alternate functions to prepare error messages

EXAMPLE   Demonstrate the use of *perror* by creating the error of closing a file with a bad handle and then printing an error message.

```
#include <stdio.h>
#include <io.h>
main()
{
    printf("We'll call \"close\" with an invalid file \
handle\n");
    if (close (100) == -1)
    {
/* Error occurred. Use perror to print error message */
        perror("Error closing file");
    }
}
```

putenv

COMPATIBILITY	MSC 3	MSC 4	MSC 5	QC	TC	ANSI	UNIX V
	▲	▲	▲	▲	▲		▲

PURPOSE   Use *putenv* to enter the definition of a new variable into the environment table of the process.

SYNTAX   `int putenv(char *envstring);`

`char *envstring;`   Definition of environment variable to be added

EXAMPLE CALL   `putenv("TMP=c:\mydir\temp");`

INCLUDES   `#include <stdlib.h>`   For function declaration

DESCRIPTION   The *putenv* function uses the global variable *environ* to locate the copy of the environment table that the process inherits from the parent. To this table it adds the new definition specified in the argument *envstring*, which must be of the form:

`VARNAME=definition`

If the environment variable named VARNAME already exists, its definition is changed to the new definition. Otherwise, an entirely new definition is added to the environment table. Note that the environment table altered by *putenv* is only a copy. Once the process terminates, the environment definitions revert to the original ones under the parent process. Thus, you cannot use *putenv* in a program to alter the environment variable settings seen at DOS command level. Any process launched by your program via *exec* or

Process Control

spawn functions, however, gets a copy of the environment settings with all the alterations you made with *putenv*.

COMMON USES The *putenv* function is useful to add new application-specific definitions to the environment table, which revert to their original meanings once the program exits.

RETURNS The *putenv* function returns a 0 if successful. A return value of −1 indicates failure due to lack of memory in the environment space of the process.

COMMENTS Under MS-DOS, the *main* function can get a pointer to the list of environment variables as a third argument, for instance, *envp*. The library routine *putenv* may alter the location of this list, however, rendering *envp* useless. So it is safer to use the functions *getenv* and *putenv*, respectively, to locate and modify the environment table.

SEE ALSO getenv   To get the definition of a variable from the environment table of the process

EXAMPLE Write a program that enables you to define a new environment variable or redefine an existing one. Accept the definition on the command line and use *putenv* to add the definition to the list of current environment variables. Notice that anything you define is gone when you exit the program.

```
#include <stdio.h>
#include <stdlib.h>
main(int argc, char **argv)
{
    char *value;
    if(argc < 2)
    {
        printf("Usage: %s <env_var_def.>\n", argv[0]);
        exit(0);
    }
/* Add new definition to the environment table */
    strupr(argv[1]);
    if (putenv(argv[1]) == -1)
    {
        printf("Error adding the definition: %s\n",
                argv[1]);
    }
    else
    {
        printf("Added to environment table: %s\n",
                argv[1]);
        printf("This definition will be gone once the \
program exits.\n");
    }
}
```

putenv

raise

COMPATIBILITY	MSC 3	MSC 4	MSC 5	QC	TC	ANSI	UNIX V
			▲	▲	▲	▲	

PURPOSE Use *raise* to "raise a signal" that generates an exception, leading to special handling.

SYNTAX
```
int raise(int signum);
```

```
int signum;     Signal number to be raised
```

INCLUDES
```
#include <signal.h>      For function declaration
```

DESCRIPTION The *raise* function creates an exception condition corresponding to the number *signum*. The exception will be handled by invoking a routine that was set up earlier by calling the function *signal*. If this was not done, certain default actions are performed for that particular exception. Table 3-6 in the reference pages on *signal* shows the default action for each exception condition and the defined constants for signals used as arguments to *raise*. The *abort* function uses *raise* to create the exception SIGABRT to initiate actions to be taken when aborting a program.

RETURNS If successful, *raise* returns a zero. Otherwise, it returns a nonzero value.

SEE ALSO
abort   To terminate a program abnormally and raise the SIGABRT signal

signal   To install exception handlers for signals

EXAMPLE Demonstrate the use of *raise* by generating the signal SIGABRT, signifying "abnormal termination" of a process. This shows how the *abort* function works.

```
#include <stdio.h>
#include <signal.h>
main()
{
    printf("Raising SIGABRT...\n");
    raise(SIGABRT);
}
```

 Process Control

setjmp

COMPATIBILITY	MSC 3	MSC 4	MSC 5	QC	TC	ANSI	UNIX V
	▲	▲	▲	▲	▲	▲	▲

PURPOSE Use *setjmp* to save a stack environment before calling another function. This environment can be restored by a call to *longjmp*, achieving the effect of a nonlocal *goto*.

SYNTAX `int setjmp(jmp_buf env);`

`jmp_buf env;` Data type where the registers and a return address representing the stack environment are stored

EXAMPLE CALL `if (setjmp(env) != 0) printf("Returned from longjmp\n");`

INCLUDES `#include <setjmp.h>` For function declaration and definition of the data type *jmp_buf*

DESCRIPTION The *setjmp* function saves certain registers and its own return address in the argument *env*, which is of type *jmp_buf* as defined in *setjmp.h*. The saved values represent the stack environment at the statement where the call to *setjmp* occurred. When *longjmp* is later called with the saved stack environment, it restores all stack-based local variables in the routine to the values they had when *setjmp* was called and jumps to the return address that *setjmp* had saved. This will feel like a return, one more time, from the last call to *setjmp*. Note that this process does not guarantee the proper restoration of register-based variables.

COMMON USES The *setjmp* function is used in conjunction with *longjmp* to pass control of execution to error-recovery code without using the normal function call and return conventions.

RETURNS After saving the stack environment, *setjmp* returns a zero. When *longjmp* is called with the environment saved by this particular call to *setjmp*, the effect is the same as returning from *setjmp* again, this time with the second argument of *longjmp* as the return value.

COMMENTS It is a little difficult to understand the behavior of *setjmp* and *longjmp*. Essentially, these routines give you the flexibility of jumping to an arbitrary location from within C. This is akin to a "goto" statement that lets you jump from one function to another.

SEE ALSO `longjmp` To jump back to where *setjmp* was called earlier

EXAMPLE Demonstrate the functioning of *setjmp* in a program that sets up the stack environment and then calls a function that in turn calls *longjmp* with the environment saved earlier. Notice how the effect is one of returning twice from the first call to *setjmp*. The second return is with a different return value than the first one, so you can do some extra processing after *longjmp* is called. Note too that you can return from a function without using the normal *return* statement.

```c
#include <stdio.h>
#include <setjmp.h>
static jmp_buf this_place;
static void fake_error(void);
main()
{
    int retval;
    retval = setjmp(this_place);
    if(retval == 0)
    {
        printf("First return from \"setjmp\"\n");
    }
    else
    {
        printf("Second return from \"setjmp\" induced \
by call to \"longjmp\"\n");

/* Do processing that's otherwise skipped. For example,
 * error recovery.
 */
        printf("There may be an error handler here.\n\
We simply exit.\n");
        exit(retval);
    }
/* Somewhere else, in another function call longjmp */
    printf("Everything seemed fine until suddenly...\n");
    fake_error();
}
/*--------------------------------------------------*/
static void fake_error(void)
{
    printf("Illegal instruction\n");
    printf("--- longjmp called ---\n");
    longjmp(this_place, 1);
}
```

 Process Control

signal

COMPATIBILITY	MSC 3	MSC 4	MSC 5	QC	TC	ANSI	UNIX V
	▲	▲	▲	▲	▲	▲	▲

PURPOSE Use *signal* to define a function that handles an exception condition.

SYNTAX
```
void (*signal(int signum,
        void (*func)(int signum[, int subcode])))(int signum);
```

`int signum;`   Signal number for which a handler is being set up

`void (*func)(int , int);`   Pointer to handler that can accept the signal number and an optional subcode as arguments

INCLUDES `#include <signal.h>`   For function declaration

DESCRIPTION The *signal* function sets up the routine *func* as the handler for the exception or signal number (*signum*). The handler is expected to accept the signal number and an optional error code as arguments. The signal number must be one of the constants shown in Table 3-8. These are defined in the include file *signal.h*. The default handling of each exception is also explained in Table 3-8. The argument *func* must be either the address of a C or assembly language routine or one of the constants SIG_DFL or SIG_IGN. Table 3-9 summarizes the action taken by these exception handlers.

RETURNS If successful, *signal* returns the pointer to the previous handler. In case of error, it returns the constant SIG_ERR and sets the global variable *errno* to EINVAL to indicate an invalid signal number.

SEE ALSO `raise`   To generate a signal

EXAMPLE The SIGINT signal is generated when you hit Control-C. The default handler for this signal terminates the program. Use *signal* in a program to install your own handler for SIGINT. This way, instead of abruptly ending the program, the user has a chance to cancel the signal.

```
#include <stdio.h>
#include <signal.h>
int ctrlc_handler(int);
int back_again = 0;
main()
{
/* Take over the Control-C interrupt */
    if(signal(SIGINT, ctrlc_handler) == SIG_ERR)
    {
        perror("signal failed");
```

```
            exit(0);
        }
        printf("Installed SIGINT signal handler\n");
        printf("Hit Control-C to exit:");
        while(1)
        {
            kbhit();
            if(back_again != 0)
            {
                back_again = 0;
                printf("\nHit Control-C to exit:");
            }
        }
    }
/*-----------------------------------------------------*/
int ctrlc_handler(int sig)
{
    int c;
/* First arrange to ignore further SIGINT */
    signal(SIGINT, SIG_IGN);
    printf("\nInterrupted. Quit?");
    c = getche();
    if(c == 'y' || c == 'Y') exit(0);
/* Reenable interrupt handler -- and return */
    back_again = 1;
    signal(SIGINT, ctrlc_handler);
}
```

Table 3-8. *Exception Conditions*

Signal	Exception Condition	Default Action
SIGABRT	Abnormal termination of program	Terminate program with exit code 3.
SIGFPE	Floating-point error, such as overflow, division by zero, etc.	Terminate program.
SIGILL	Illegal instruction. This exception is not generated by MS-DOS, but is included for ANSI compatibility.	Not applicable in MS-DOS.
SIGINT	Generated when user hits Control-C.	Generate software interrupt number 23h.
SIGSEGV	Illegal memory access. This exception is not generated under MS-DOS, but is included for ANSI compatibility.	Not applicable in MS-DOS.
SIGTERM	Termination request sent to the program. This is not generated in MS-DOS, but is included for ANSI compatibility.	Not applicable in MS-DOS.

 Process Control

Table 3-9. *Exception Handlers*

Handler	Action
SIG_DFL	This refers to the default handler. If the program is terminated, files will be closed, but buffers associated with files open for buffered I/O will not be flushed.
SIG_IGN	If you provide this as the handler, the exception condition will be ignored. This should not be used as the handler for the SIGFPE signal because this leaves the floating-point package unusable.
Function Address	The function will be called with the signal and an optional code as the arguments. The SIGINT and SIGFPE exceptions are handled differently. For the SIGINT exception, the handler will be called with SIGINT as the argument. At the same time, SIG_DFL is set up as the handler for subsequent SIGINT signals. Of course, you can reset the handler in the function called as a result of SIGINT.
	For SIGFPE exceptions, the installed handler will be called with the value SIGFPE and an integer code representing the floating-point error. This second argument is a constant of FPE_〈code〉 where the constants are defined in the include file *float.h*. The handler for SIGFPE should call _*fpreset* to reset the floating-point package and clear the error condition.

In addition to the signals defined in Microsoft C 5.0, Table 3-10 lists the four protected-mode only signals introduced in version 5.1.

Table 3-10. *Microsoft C 5.1 Signals*

Constant	Meaning
SIGBREAK	Control-Break signal. Default action is to terminate the program.
SIGUSR1	OS/2 process flag A. Default action is to ignore the signal.
SIGUSR2	OS/2 process flag B. Default action is to ignore the signal.
SIGUSR3	OS/2 process flag C. Default action is to ignore the signal.

A new action code, SIG_ACK, is also available for use in OS/2. If a user-defined handler is installed, OS/2 sends no signals until a SIG_ACK acknowledgment is received for the last signal.

spawn functions

COMPATIBILITY	MSC 3	MSC 4	MSC 5	QC	TC	ANSI	UNIX V
		▲	▲	▲	▲		

PURPOSE Use any one of the *spawn* functions to load and execute a child process and to return to your program when the child process terminates.

SYNTAX
```
int spawnl(int modeflag, char *path, char *arg0, char *arg1,...,
    NULL);
```

```
int spawnle(int modeflag, char *path, char *arg0, char *arg1,...,
        NULL, char *envp[]);

int spawnlp(int modeflag, char *path, char *arg0, char *arg1,...,
        NULL);

int spawnlpe(int modeflag, char *path, char *arg0, char *arg1,...,
        NULL, char *envp[]);

int spawnv(int modeflag, char *path, char *argv[]);

int spawnve(int modeflag, char *path, char *argv[], char *envp[]);

int spawnvp(int modeflag, char *path, char *argv[]);

int spawnvpe(int modeflag, char *path, char *argv[], char *envp[]);
```

`int modeflag;`   Execution mode of calling process

`char *path;`   Pathname of file to be executed as a child process

`char *arg0, *arg1, . . . , NULL;`   Command-line arguments for the child process (ends with a NULL)

`char *argv[];`   Array of command-line arguments for the child process

`char *envp[];`   The environment parameter table

INCLUDES   `#include <process.h>`   For function declaration and definition of the constants P_WAIT, P_OVERLAY, and P_NOWAIT

DESCRIPTION   The *spawn* functions create a child process to load and execute the program specified by the argument *path*. The argument *modeflag* indicates how the parent process should be treated while the child is running. Under MS-DOS, this flag can take either of the values P_WAIT or P_OVERLAY. The P_WAIT flag indicates that the parent process should be suspended until the child finishes, whereas P_OVERLAY means that the child overwrites the parent in memory, destroying the parent. The P_OVERLAY mode has the same effect as the *exec* functions have. A third constant P_NOWAIT, is defined in *process.h* and is meant for concurrent execution of parent and child, but use of this mode under MS_DOS produces an error. This mode might be useful in a multitasking operating system of the future.

The variations among the *spawn* functions are reflections of the way in which arguments and environment variables are passed to the child process. Table 3-11 describes each function's action. The fifth letter of the name, "1" or "v," determines how command-line arguments are received by the child process. The next one or two letters indicate how environment variables are

Process Control

passed to the child process. If the sixth letter of the name is a "p," the PATH environment variable is used by COMMAND.COM to locate the executable program you specify in the argument *path*. Otherwise, you must specify the full pathname of the file to be executed or specify a path beginning at the current working directory. If the *path* argument does not have an extension, the *spawn* function first searches for a file without an extension. If none is found and *path* does not end with a period, it tries the extensions .COM and .EXE, in that order.

Table 3-11. *The spawn Functions*

Fifth Letter of Name	Meaning
l	Command-line arguments to the child process are listed on the statement that invokes the *spawn* function. These forms are useful when the number of arguments is known in advance. The arguments *arg0*, *arg1* . . . are listed one after another with a NULL marking the end.
v	Command-line arguments are passed in the form of a pointer to an array of argument strings. This is useful when the number of arguments is not known in advance. In this case, you prepare an array of null-terminated strings, each representing one command-line argument for the child program, put a NULL to mark the end of the list and pass the pointer to this array (*argv*) to the child process via the *spawn* function.

Two Letters	How Environment Variables Are Handled
none	Child process inherits parent's environment variables.
p	PATH environment variable is used to locate the executable file. In this case, the *path* argument may specify a program name without any directory information and COMMAND.COM will locate the program, if present, in any one of the directories included in your PATH environment variable.
e	Child process receives a pointer *envp* to an array of environment strings. Each environment variable definition is of the form *NAME = value of variable*, and the end of the array is marked by a NULL.
pe	This is a combination of the letters described above. Thus, in this, the PATH environment variable is used and the child process gets a pointer to a table of environment variables that you prepare.

Note that the combined length of all the command-line argument strings, including a separating space between adjoining arguments, must not exceed 128 bytes. It is customary to provide the full pathname of the executable file as the first command-line argument to the child process, although using a different string will not produce an error.

In the child process, all signal handlers are reset to the default ones. Files that were open in the parent remain open in the child, and, unlike the *exec* functions, the translation modes of the open files (see *fopen*) are also preserved in the child process.

spawn functions

Starting with Microsoft C 5.1, under OS/2, the P__NOWAIT mode of execution implies that the child process runs concurrently with the parent. In this case, the return value is the identification number of the child. An additional P__NOWAITO flag allows execution of the parent while ignoring all *cwait* and *wait* calls against the child process.

COMMON USES The *spawn* functions are useful when you want to execute a separately compiled and linked application from your program and return to your main program when that process terminates. The example below illustrates how you can pass pointers to data areas for sharing between the two processes.

RETURNS When used with P__WAIT as *modeflags*, the *spawn* functions return the exit status of the child process to the parent. The return value for P__NOWAIT (when this mode becomes available) will be the process ID of the child process. In this case, if you want the exit code, you will have to call a routine to wait for it. If the child process cannot be started, the return value is −1 and *errno* is set to one of the constants shown in Table 3-12, indicating the cause of the error.

Table 3-12. *Error Codes Returned by* spawn *Functions*

Error	Cause of Error
E2BIG	Either the total length of the command-line arguments exceeds 128 bytes or the memory required for the environment variables exceeds 32 K.
EINVAL	The *modeflag* argument is invalid.
ENOENT	Either the path or the file specified in the argument *path* was not found.
ENOEXEC	The specified file is not executable because its format does not match the DOS specification for an executable file.
ENOMEM	There is not enough memory to load and execute the child process or available memory is corrupted or an invalid block of memory was located, indicating the parent process was incorrectly loaded.

COMMENTS The *spawn* functions provide a powerful mechanism to make your application versatile. Essentially, you can let programs that are "well-behaved" toward your application (in that they do not hinder its performance) run from the application, giving the functionality of terminate-but-stay-resident (TSR) utilities that are so prevalent in the MS-DOS world.

Microsoft warns that because of a bug in DOS versions 2.0 and 2.1, a child process launched by *spawn*, with the P__OVERLAY argument, may cause fatal system errors when it exits. Use DOS versions 3.0 or higher for reliable operation when calling *spawn* with P__OVERLAY.

SEE ALSO `exec functions`   To launch a process that overlays its parent in memory

EXAMPLE Demonstrate their use in a program that allows a child process to run using any one of the eight *spawn* functions. Prepare data in a structure allocated in the

Process Control

parent program and pass this data to the child by encoding the address as a character string and using that string as a command-line argument. In the child program, print the command-line arguments and the environment passed to it. Then, using the address passed in the command line, acces the data structure and display the various fields. Finally, make changes to the data structure and exit. In the parent program, print the values in the data structure to show that the changes made in the child came through. Note: Remember to compile and link the child program first and save it in a file named *child.exe*.

```c
/*====================== PARENT ======================*/
#include <stdio.h>
#include <process.h>
#include <malloc.h>
#include <string.h>
typedef struct TEST_DATA
{
    char name[20];
    int n;
    double x;
} TEST_DATA;
/* PARENT: Test the "spawn" functions. Pass address of
 *         data in command line arguments as well as
 *         environment variables when appropriate.
 */
char *envp[] =
{
    "PARENT=SPAWN FUNCTIONS",
    NULL
};
main()
{
    char *argv[3], buf[20], rname[40];
    TEST_DATA *pdata;
/* Set up a data structure and initialize it */
    if((pdata=(TEST_DATA *)
        malloc(sizeof(TEST_DATA))) == NULL) abort();
    strcpy(pdata->name, "PARENT");
    pdata->n = 100;
    pdata->x = 1000.99;
/* Set up the arguments for the child process */
    argv[0] = "child.exe",
    argv[1] = rname;
    sprintf(buf, "%p", (void far *)pdata);
    argv[2] = buf;
    argv[3] = NULL;
/* Ask user which "spawn" routine to call */
    printf("Enter name of \"spawn\" function to call:");
    gets(rname);
```

spawn functions

```
        strlwr(rname);
/* Call the "spawn" function requested by the user */
    if(strcmp(rname, "spawnl") == 0)
    {
        spawnl(P_WAIT, "child.exe",
            "child.exe", "spawnl", buf, NULL);
    }
    if(strcmp(rname, "spawnle") == 0)
    {
        spawnle(P_WAIT, "child.exe",
        "child.exe", "spawnle", buf, NULL, envp);
    }
    if(strcmp(rname, "spawnlp") == 0)
    {
        spawnlp(P_WAIT, "child.exe",
            "child.exe", "spawnlp", buf, NULL);
    }
    if(strcmp(rname, "spawnlpe") == 0)
    {
        spawnlpe(P_WAIT, "child.exe",
        "child.exe", "spawnlpe", buf, NULL, envp);
    }
    if(strcmp(rname, "spawnv") == 0)
    {
        spawnv(P_WAIT, "child.exe", argv);
    }
    if(strcmp(rname, "spawnve") == 0)
    {
        spawnve(P_WAIT, "child.exe", argv, envp);
    }
    if(strcmp(rname, "spawnvp") == 0)
    {
        spawnvp(P_WAIT, "child.exe", argv);
    }
    if(strcmp(rname, "spawnvpe") == 0)
    {
        spawnvpe(P_WAIT, "child.exe", argv, envp);
    }
/* Check if we could call child or not */
    if(strcmp(pdata->name, "CHILD") == 0)
    {
        printf("Back from child: name = %s, n = %d, \
x= %f\n", pdata->name, pdata->n, pdata->x);
    }
    else
    {
        printf("Don't know: %s\n", rname);
    }
```

Process Control

```
}
/*===================== CHILD =====================*/
/*     Must be in a file named:  CHILD.EXE         */
#include <stdio.h>
#include <dos.h>
#include <string.h>
typedef struct TEST_DATA
{
    char name[20];
    int n;
    double x;
} TEST_DATA;
/* Child: First argument is program name,
 *         Second one tells us how child was invoked
 *         Third argument is an address in the form
 *         SSSS:0000 (segment:offset). This is the
 *         address of a data structure allocated in
 *         the parent.
 */
static char far cname[] = "CHILD";
main(int argc, char **argv, char **envp)
{
    char   **p_table;
    TEST_DATA far *pdata;
    void far *p_s1;
    void far *p_s2;
    printf("CHILD: received %d arguments\n", argc);
    if(argc < 3){
        printf("not enough arguments\n");
        exit(1);
    }
    printf("CHILD invoked by a %s call.\n", argv[1]);

/* Now print the environment passed to CHILD     */
    printf("==== CHILD: Environment contains ====\n");
    for(p_table = envp;
        *p_table != NULL;
        p_table++) printf("%s\n", *p_table);

/* Read in address of parent's data from argv[2] */
    sscanf(argv[2], "%p", (void far *)&pdata);
    printf("In child: name = %Fs, n = %d, x= %f\n",
           pdata->name, pdata->n, pdata->x);
/* Put new values in the data structure. If CHILD was
 * created by a "spawn" function call, this data will
 * be available to the parent when child exits.
 * Notice that we have to use "movedata" to copy
 * "far" data in small or medium model.
```

spawn functions

```
    */
        p_s1 = (void far *)cname;
        p_s2 = (void far *)pdata->name;
        movedata(FP_SEG(p_s1), FP_OFF(p_s1),
                FP_SEG(p_s2), FP_OFF(p_s2), 6);
        pdata->n = 101;
        pdata->x = 999.99;
        exit(0);
    }
```

system

COMPATIBILITY	MSC 3	MSC 4	MSC 5	QC	TC	ANSI	UNIX V
	▲	▲	▲	▲	▲	▲	▲

PURPOSE   Use *system* to execute an MS-DOS command from your program.

SYNTAX   `int system(const char *string);`

`const char *string;`   MS-DOS command to be executed

INCLUDES   `#include <process.h>`   For function declaration

or

`#include <stdlib.h>`

DESCRIPTION   The *system* function uses the environment variable COMSPEC to locate a copy of COMMAND.COM and passes to it the argument *string* as a command to be executed. The environment variable PATH is used to locate any program whose execution may be specified in the command *string*. In Microsoft C 5.0, if *string* is NULL, *system* will only check to see if COMMAND.COM is present. In version 4.0, a NULL argument is not allowed. Starting with Microsoft C 5.1, in OS/2, *system* runs CMD.EXE to execute the command string.

RETURNS   If *string* is not NULL, *system* returns 0 if the command was successfully executed. In case of error, *system* returns −1 and sets *errno* to one of the constants shown in Table 3-13 to indicate the cause of the error. In Microsoft C 5.0, if *string* is NULL and COMMAND.COM is found *system* returns a nonzero value. In case COMMAND.COM cannot be located using the environment variable COMSPEC, *system* will return a zero and set *errno* to ENOENT. Note that syntax errors in the specified command are not considered "errors"; only errors resulting in the inability to execute COMMAND.COM are returned.

 Process Control

Table 3-13. *Error Codes Returned by* System

Error	Cause of Error
E2BIG	Either the argument list for COMMAND.COM exceeds 128 bytes or the memory required for the environment variables exceeds 32 K.
ENOENT	COMMAND.COM not found.
ENOEXEC	The COMMAND.COM file is not executable because it has an invalid format.
ENOMEM	There is not enough memory to load COMMAND.COM and execute the command or available memory is corrupted or an invalid block of memory was located, indicating that the parent process was incorrectly loaded.

SEE ALSO   `exec functions, spawn functions`   To launch a process

EXAMPLE   Write a program that lets you type a command and have it executed by a copy of COMMAND.COM that is launched by calling *system*.

```
#include <stdio.h>
#include <stdlib.h>
main()
{
    char command[80];
    while(1)
    {
        printf("Enter command (\"quit\" to exit):");
        gets(command);
        strlwr(command);
/* Exit if user typed "quit" */
        if(strcmp(command, "quit") == 0) exit(0);
/* Otherwise pass command to a copy of COMMAND.COM */
        if(system(command) == -1)
        {
            perror("error in system");
        }
    }
}
```

wait

COMPATIBILITY	MSC 3	MSC 4	MSC 5	QC	TC	ANSI	UNIX V
				5.1 only			

PURPOSE   Use *wait* in OS/2's protected mode to wait until any one of your immediate child processes terminates.

SYNTAX   `int wait(int *p_status);`

```
int *p_status;
```
Address of integer to hold the termination status code

EXAMPLE CALL
```
if(wait(&status) == -1) perror("wait failed");
```

INCLUDES
```
#include <process.h>
```
For function prototype

DESCRIPTION Available in OS/2's protected mode only, the *wait* function suspends the calling process until any one of the immediate child process of the calling process terminates. When *wait* returns, the integer at the address *p_status* will contain a termination code that can be interpreted by consulting Table 3-5.

COMMON USES The *wait* function synchronizes processes in OS/2's protected mode environment.

RETURNS When *wait* returns after a normal termination of the child process, it returns the process identification of the child. In case of abnormal termination of the child, it returns −1 and sets the global variable *errno* to EINTR. For other types of errors, *wait* returns −1 immediately and sets *errno* to ECHILD to indicate that no child processes exist for the calling process.

COMMENTS You should be familiar with the protected mode operation of the OS/2 operating system before using the *wait* function.

SEE ALSO spawn   To launch a child process

cwait   To wait for a specific child of the calling process

 **Process Control**

Variable-Length Argument List

Introduction

In writing C programs you encounter functions, such as *printf*, that can take a variable number of arguments. Take, for instance, a routine (*findmax*) that picks the largest integer from an array (*a,b,c,d*). If the routine can accept a variable number of arguments, you can use such calls as *findmax(1,2,3)* and *findmax(a,b,c,d)* to find the maximum of any number of arguments. Fortunately this can be done quite easily in C because of its convention of passing arguments on the stack. A set of macros in the Microsoft C library makes a straightforward task of handling a variable number of arguments. This section explains how this is done.

Concepts

The secret to handling a variable number of arguments in C lies in the way arguments are passed to a function. Figure 4-1 shows the contents of the state at the moment a C and a FORTRAN or a Pascal function are entered. When a function is called, the arguments followed by the return address (the place in the calling program to which the microprocessor will ultimately return) are placed on the stack.

THE STACK: C AND FORTRAN OR PASCAL As you can see in Figure 4-1, in FORTRAN and Pascal the arguments of the function are placed on the stack in the order they appear in the function call, exactly the opposite of a C function call. The result is that the first argument in C is always at a fixed positive offset (the number of bytes needed to store the return address) from the stack pointer SP, so no matter how many arguments are passed to a C function, the first argument is always easily reachable. This is not true in FORTRAN and Pascal. In fact, in these, if you do not pass the required number of arguments, the addresses computed for each argument will be erroneous.

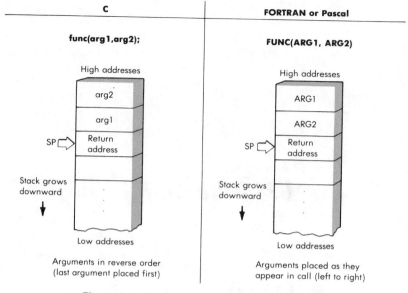

Figure 4-1. *The stack upon entry to a function*

GETTING TO
THE ARGUMENTS
IN C The parameter-passing conventions in C help us access a variable number of arguments. As shown in Figure 4-2, upon entry to the C function the first argument appears on the stack just above the return address (meaning it has the next higher address). Additional arguments have successively higher addresses. If you could get to the first argument on the stack and you knew the size of all other arguments you could retrieve the arguments one by one. This, respectively, is what the *va_start* and the *va_arg* macros do.

While the macros help us access the arguments on the stack, they can-

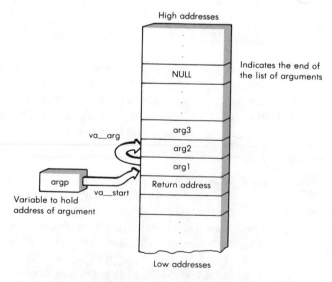

Figure 4-2. *Accessing a variable number of arguments in C*

not tell us when the argument list ends. In fact, the only way to find this is by adopting a convention. If each argument were a pointer, for example, you could mark the end of the argument list with a NULL value. To illustrate how the arguments are accessed using these macros, suppose we are writing the *findmax* function to accept a variable number of integers and return the largest of the arguments. Since we want positive numbers only, we assume that a value of −9999 indicates the end of the argument list. Here is one way to implement the *findmax* function, using the ANSI version of the macros:

```
int findmax(int firstint, ...)
{
    int maxval = -9999, x = 0;
    va_list argp;
/* Get the first optional parameter using "va_start" */
    va_start(argp, firstint);
    x = firstint;
    while(x != -9999)   /* -9999 marks end of arguments */
    {
            if(maxval < x) maxval = x;
            x = va_arg(argp, int);
    }
    return (maxval);
}
```

The variable *argp* of type *va_list* is used to point to arguments. (In Microsoft C, *va_list* is defined to be a pointer to a character.) The first step in accessing the arguments is to use *va_start* to initialize *argp*. The ANSI standard requires that a function accepting a variable number of arguments must have at least one argument. The *va_start* macro uses the address of this compulsory first argument to set up *argp*. Once this is done, you can get subsequent arguments by repeatedly using the *va_arg* macro. (See the reference pages that follow for the UNIX version of these macros.) The UNIX System V and the proposed ANSI approaches to accessing the arguments are based on the stack layout shown in Figure 4-2. The function accepting variable-length arguments must declare a pointer to hold the address of the current argument. The macro *va_start* must be used first to initialize this pointer. Each successive use of the macro *va_arg* sets the pointer to the next argument. The type of variables on the stack must be given as an argument to these macros. The macro *va_end* is not needed because it sets the local argument pointer to NULL, which you can do yourself if you want to repeat the process. See Table 4-1 for a description of these macros.

Notes

Two sets of macros handle variable-length argument lists. One set conforms to the proposed ANSI standard for C and is defined in the header file *stdarg.h*.

The other set is for UNIX System V compatibility and is defined in the *varargs.h* header file. The method of using each set is described in the reference pages.

Table 4-1. *Variable-Length Argument List Macros*

Macro	Description
va_arg	Gets the next argument from the stack.
va_end	Sets the argument pointer to NULL.
va_start	Initializes the argument pointer to the address of the first argument on the stack.

Cautions

► The UNIX version of the macros requires that you use a specific format in declaring the function that will accept variable-length arguments. Two macros appear in the declaration as shown in this sample:

```
int func(va_alist)
va_dcl
{
/* ... body of function ... */
}
```

Note the use of macros *va_alist* in the argument list and *va_dcl* where you would normally declare the arguments. The second macro, *va_dcl*, must appear *without* a terminating semicolon.

va__start, va__arg, va__end

COMPATIBILITY	MSC 3	MSC 4	MSC 5	QC	TC	ANSI	UNIX V
		▲	▲	▲	▲	▲	

PURPOSE   Use the *va_start*, *va_arg*, and *va_end* macros to access arguments in a function that accepts a variable number of arguments. This entry describes the ANSI-compatible version of the macros.

SYNTAX   `void va_start(va_list arg_ptr, prev_param);`

`<type> va_arg(va_list arg_ptr, <type>);`

`void va_end(va_list arg_ptr);`

`va_list arg_ptr;`   Pointer to list of arguments

`prev_param`   Name of parameter preceding first optional argument

`<type>`   Type of argument to be retrieved

INCLUDES   `#include <stdarg.h>`   For macro declarations and definition of data type *va_list*

DESCRIPTION   The *va_start, va_arg*, and *va_end* macros provide an ANSI-compatible method for accessing the arguments of a function when the function takes a fixed number of required arguments followed by a variable number of optional arguments. The required arguments are in standard style and are accessed by parameter names. The optional arguments are accessed using the macros *va_start, va_arg*, and *va_end*. These, respectively, are used to initialize a pointer to the beginning of the list of optional arguments, to advance the pointer to the next argument of a particular type, and to reset the pointer to NULL when all the arguments are used. The procedure for accessing the optional arguments is outlined below:

1. Access the required arguments by name. These arguments are declared as parameters in the usual manner. Declare a variable *arg_ptr* of type *va_list*.

2. Use the *va_start* macro with *arg_ptr* and the name of the last required argument. This sets *arg_ptr* to the beginning of the list of optional arguments to the function. *Caution:* If the last required argument is declared with the *register* storage class, *va_start* will not work properly.

3. Use the *va_arg* macro to retrieve the next argument. This macro updates *arg_ptr* and returns a pointer to the argument being sought. Repeat this step until you have accessed all the arguments. You have to decide on a value that will mark the end of the list. For example, if you

are accessing integer arguments, you might use a value of −1 to mark the end of the argument list.

4. Use the *va_end* macro to set *arg_ptr* to NULL.

Note that an identical set of macros with slightly different usage exists to access variable-length arguments as specified by the UNIX System V standard. These macros are defined in the header file *varargs.h* and are described under a separate heading.

COMMON USES   These macros can be used in conjunction with the routines *vfprintf*, *vprintf*, and *vsprintf* to design error-handling routines that accept variable-length arguments.

RETURNS   The *va_arg* macro returns a pointer to the next argument of a given type. The *va_start* macro sets a pointer to the beginning of the list of arguments; *va_end* resets this pointer to NULL.

SEE ALSO   Unix V version of va_start, va_arg, va_end

EXAMPLE   Demonstrate the use of ANSI-style variable-length argument processing by writing a function that accepts a variable number of integer arguments and returns the largest value. Assume that a value of −999 marks the end of the argument list. Write a main program that shows how the function is used.

```
#include <stdio.h>
#include <stdarg.h>
int findmax(int, ...);
main()
{
    int maxvalue;
/* The end of the list of integers is marked by -9999 */
    maxvalue = findmax(-1, 20, 30, 50, -9999);

    printf("findmax(-1, 20, 30, 50, -9999) returns: \
    %d\n", maxvalue);
    maxvalue = findmax(1, 2, 3, 4, 5, 6, 7, 8, -9999);
    printf("findmax(1, 2, 3, 4, 5, 6, 7, 8, -9999)\
returns: %d\n", maxvalue);
}
/*-----------------------------------------------------*/
/* The "findmax" finds the largest value in a list
 * of integers. It uses the "va_..." macros to get
 * the arguments. This is the ANSI version.
 */
int findmax(int firstint, ...)
{
    int maxval = -9999, x = 0;
    va_list argp;
```

 Variable-Length Argument List

```
/* Get the first optional parameter using "va_start" */
    va_start(argp, firstint);
    x = firstint;
    while(x != -9999)
    {
            if(maxval < x) maxval = x;
            x = va_arg(argp, int);
    }
    return (maxval);
}
```

UNIX V version

va__start, va__arg, va__end

COMPATIBILITY	MSC 3	MSC 4	MSC 5	QC	TC	ANSI	UNIX V
		▲	▲	▲			▲

PURPOSE   Use the *va__start*, *va__arg*, and *va__end* macros to access arguments in a function that accepts a variable number of arguments. This entry describes the UNIX V version of the macros.

SYNTAX   `void va_start(va_list arg_ptr);`

`<type> va_arg(arg_ptr, <type>);`

`void va_end(va_list arg_ptr);`

`va_alist`   Name that must appear at the end of all required arguments to the function

`va_dcl`   Declaration of *va__alist*

`va_list arg_ptr;`   Pointer to list of arguments

`<type>`   Type of argument to be retrieved

INCLUDES   `#include <varargs.h>`   For macro declarations and definition of data types *va__list*, *va__alist*, and *va__dcl*

DESCRIPTION   The *va__start*, *va__arg*, and *va__end* macros provide a UNIX System V-compatible method for accessing the arguments of a function when the function takes a fixed number of required arguments followed by a variable number of optional arguments. The required arguments are in standard style and are accessed by parameter names. The optional arguments are accessed using the macros *va__start*, *va__arg*, and *va__end*. These, respectively, are used to initialize a pointer to the beginning of the list of optional arguments, to advance the pointer to the next argument of a particular type, and to reset the pointer

va__start, va__arg, va__end

to NULL when all the arguments are used. The procedure for accessing the optional arguments is outlined below:

1. Declare the required arguments as parameters in the usual manner. End the list of parameters with the name *va_alist* which denotes all optional arguments to the function. Place the macro *va_dcl* (no semicolon at the end) between the function declaration and its definition. This declares the variable *va_alist*. In the function, declare a variable *arg_ptr* of type *va_list*.

2. Use the *va_start* macro with *arg_ptr* as the parameter. This sets *arg_ptr* to the beginning of the list of optional arguments to the function.

3. Use the *va_arg* macro to retrieve the next argument. This macro updates *arg_ptr* and returns a pointer to the argument being sought. Repeat this step until you have accessed all the arguments. You have to decide on a value that will mark the end of the list. For example, if you are accessing string arguments, you might use a value of NULL to mark the end of the argument list.

4. Use the *va_end* macro to set *arg_ptr* to NULL.

Note that an identical set of macros with slightly different usage exists to accesss variable-length arguments as specified by the proposed ANSI C standard. These macros are defined in the header file *stdarg.h* and are described under a separate heading.

COMMON USES   These macros can be used in conjunction with the routines *vfprintf*, *vprintf*, and *vsprintf* to implement error-handling routines that accept variable-length arguments.

RETURNS   The *va_arg* macro returns a pointer to the next argument of a given type. The *va_start* macro sets a pointer to the beginning of the list of arguments; *va_end* resets this pointer to NULL.

SEE ALSO   ANSI version of va_start, va_arg, va_end

EXAMPLE   Demonstrate the use of UNIX-style variable-length argument processing by writing a function that accepts a variable number of character strings and returns the longest string. Assume that a NULL marks the end of the argument list. Write a main program that shows how the function is used.

```
#include <stdio.h>
#include <string.h>
#include <varargs.h>
char *findlong();
main()
{
    char *longest;
/* The end of the list of strings is marked by NULL */
    longest = findlong("Microsoft C", "Turbo C",
```

 Variable-Length Argument List

```
                        "QuickC",  NULL);
        printf("Longest of: Microsoft C Turbo C QuickC =\
        %s\n", longest);
        longest = findlong("a", "ab", "abc", "x",
                            "xy", NULL);
        printf("Longest of: a  ab  abc  x xy  = %s\n",
                longest);
}
/*---------------------------------------------------*/
/* The "findlong" finds the longest string in a list
 * of strings. It uses the "va_..." macros to get
 * the arguments. This is the UNIX version.
 */
char *findlong(va_alist)    /* Note declaration      */
va_dcl        /* Macro must appear without semicolon */
{
    size_t length, maxlen = 0;
    char *longest = NULL, *str;
    va_list argp;
/* Get the first optional parameter using "va_start" */
    va_start(argp);

    while((str = va_arg(argp, char*)) != NULL)
    {
        length = strlen(str);
        if(maxlen < length)
        {
            maxlen = length;
            longest = str;
        }
    }
    return (longest);
}
```

va__start, va__arg, va__end

Chapter *5* *Memory Allocation and Management*

Introduction

Most computer systems, including the PC, operate on a single basic concept. They store instructions and data in memory and use a central processing unit (CPU) such as the 8086 microprocessor to repeatedly retrieve instructions from memory and execute them. The operating system, itself a program residing in memory, takes care of loading other programs and executing them. It has its own scheme of managing the available memory for its data and the memory for other programs as well.

In older programming languages, such as FORTRAN, there is no provision for requesting memory at run-time. All data items and arrays have to be declared before the program is compiled. You have to guess the maximum size of an array beforehand and you cannot exceed the maximum other than by recompiling the program. This is inefficient because you are locking in your program's maximum amount of memory. With the prevalence of terminate-and-stay-resident (TSR) programs, memory is often a scarce resource.

In most modern languages, including C, you can request blocks of memory at run-time and release the blocks when your program no longer needs them. A major advantage of this capability is that you can design your application to exploit all available memory in the system. For example, if your application is a text editor, and your system has a limited amount of memory, using this dynamic memory allocation you can design your application so only a small portion of a file is loaded into memory. The rest is swapped in and out of the disk as needed. On the other hand, when running on a system with more memory, the editor can load more of the file into memory at once, providing increased speed. Such a thoughtful design can also win you the support of your users. For nothing is more annoying than to discover that your investment in additional kilobytes for your system is useless because your favorite application ignores the extra memory.

Like most other capabilities in C, this capability comes in the form of a set of library routines, known as the "memory allocation" routines. The set that comes with Microsoft C 5.1 has many more routines than UNIX has. We will go through the salient features of this set of routines next.

Concepts: Memory Layout and Addressing

First, we present some concepts and terminology necessary for understanding memory allocation in Microsoft C 5.1 under MS-DOS. The questions we answer here include how is memory addressed in an 8086 microprocessor? What is the layout of memory during the execution of a C program? How does DOS manage the PC's memory, and how does Microsoft C add another level of management?

MEMORY ADDRESSING IN THE IBM PC Physically, the 8086 microprocessor uses a 20-bit address to access memory. This usually means that systems based on the 8086 can accommodate a maximum memory size of 1,024 K—one megabyte (note that 1 K = 1,024 bytes). We said "usually" because it is possible to circumvent this limit with the so-called "expanded memory" mechanisms. Also, the newer members of the 8086 family, from the 80286 on, have larger memory address spaces, which can be accessed as extended memory under what is called "protected" mode. When these newer microprocessors run DOS in the "real" mode, however, the limit on memory size still applies.

Segments and Offsets

The 8086 microprocessors have 16-bit internal registers (except the 80386, which has 32-bit registers) and a single register cannot hold the entire 20-bit physical address. Thus a different approach is taken in the implementation of memory addressing in the 8086 microprocessor. Each memory address is constructed of two parts: a segment address and an offset, each a 16-bit value. In this model, as shown in Figure 5-1, we view the physical memory as a collection of segments. The segment address is the address of the first byte of a segment. The offset tells us the location of an arbitrary byte with respect to the beginning of the segment. In hexadecimal (hex) notation, it is customary to denote the segment and offset addresses in the form *SSSS:OOOO* in which the two sets of hexadecimal digits are separated by a colon. With this scheme, two registers, one containing the segment address and the other the offset, can specify the address of any byte in memory.

Since both the segment address and the offset use a 16-bit representation, we can have at most 65,536 segments with each segment at most 64 K in size. Although this implementation of the addressing scheme implies a much larger amount of memory size than we previously claimed, the mapping of segment and offset addresses to a physical address explains the apparent discrepancy: the physical address is 20 bits, so the maximum number of bytes that can be addressed is 2^{20}, which is equal to 1,024 K or 1 megabyte (Mb). The physical address of a memory location is computed by shifting the segment address to the left by four bits and adding the offset to the result.

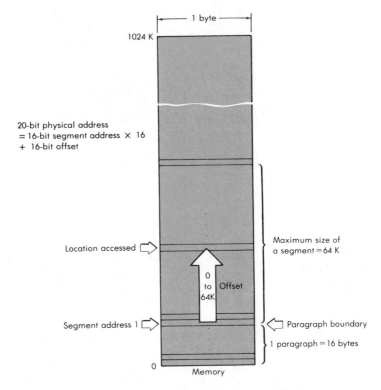

Figure 5-1. *Memory addressing in IBM PC*

Paragraphs

Shifting the segment address to the left by four bits corresponds to multiplying it by 16 (which is the same as 10 hex). In fact, a group of 16 contiguous bytes has a special name in the PC: a "paragraph". This means that in the PC we can have, at most, 65,536 paragraphs. The address of a paragraph is that of the first byte in the paragraph. Since paragraphs are located at 16-byte boundaries, in terms of segment and offset notation each paragraph address has a zero offset. Thus when DOS allocates a certain number of paragraphs, it only returns the segment address.

MEMORY LAYOUT OF A TYPICAL C PROGRAM

Suppose you have written, compiled, and linked a C program into an executable file. Now you begin running the program. How are the different components of the program laid out in memory?

Code Segment

Let's take a snapshot of low memory just as the program begins executing. Starting at a paragraph boundary, you find all the instructions of your program. This is the so-called "code" segment (see Figure 5-2). The segment register CS holds the segment address of the code segment, and the instruction pointer (IP) in the 8086 microprocessor by holding its offset keeps track of the current instruction to execute.

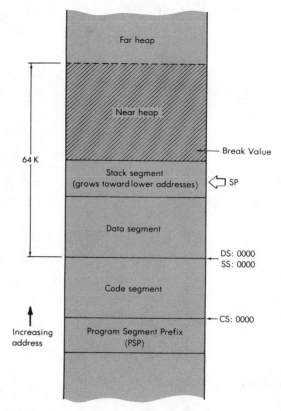

Figure 5-2. *Memory layout of a Microsoft C program in IBM PC*

Data Segment and the Stack

At the next highest paragraph address after the program's code, you find the data for your program. This is called the "data segment," and its address is stored in the DS register. After the data, a fixed size block (2 K by default) of memory is used for passing arguments during function calls and for storing local variables. This block is known as the "stack segment," and it is used as a LIFO buffer. The 8086 microprocessor uses a stack pointer (SP) register to keep track of the current place in the stack. The segment address of the stack is kept in the segment register SS.

In 8086-based computers, the stack always grows downward. This means that when placing an element on the stack, the stack pointer is first decremented and then the element is saved at the address SS:SP. By default, in Microsoft C programs the stack segment begins at the same place as the data segment. The compiler options /Au or /Aw can be used to instruct the compiler to use separate stack and data segments.

The Break Value

The first address beyond the data segment of a program is called the "break value" of the process, and it denotes the boundary of the memory allocated to the process (see Figure 5-2). To alter the break value and enlarge the memory currently in use by your process, you can use the *sbrk* function in the library.

Because of the segment:offset addressing scheme in the PC several "memory models" are available in the Microsoft C compiler. For each item of code or data, the compiler can either generate explicit segment and offset addresses or can use the offset alone with a default segment address. Each combination of code and data address generation defines a specific memory model.

Near and Far Data

When the compiler uses offsets alone for data addresses, the data items are said to have "near" addresses. Often the items are referred to as "near data." All near data items have the same segment address which is stored in the segment register DS. Analogously, when explicit segment and offset addresses are generated for data items, they are called "far data." Far data items can be located anywhere in memory, and the compiler generates code that explicitly loads an 8086 segment register, such as ES, to access them.

Segment:Offset or Offset Alone: Pros and Cons

The selection of a memory model also has other implications. For example, when offsets alone are used in addressing data or accessing instructions in the code segment, the code executes faster because it does not have to explicitly load a segment register. But the drawback is that at most 64 K of data is available. Instead of forcing a decision like this upon users, the Microsoft C compiler provides users the option of selecting one out of five different memory models, each trading off execution speed against program size.

Small and Medium Models

The small and medium memory models allow only a single segment of data. The small model also limits code to a single segment, but the medium model allows multiple segments of code. As shown in Figure 5-3, all data addresses for these models use offsets with respect to the segment address in the register DS. These models are most useful when the amount of data is expected to be limited. When program size is also small, select the small model; for lengthy programs, use the medium model.

Compact and Large Models

In these two models, the compiler generates explicit segment and offset addresses for all data items. Thus these models allow an unlimited amount of data with only one constraint: *no single data item can exceed 64 K.* The compact model allows only a single code segment, whereas the large model allows unlimited code and data, subject only to the condition that each data item fit into a single 64-K segment. Actually, when we say "unlimited" we mean "limited only by available physical memory." Some operating systems support "virtual memory," which allows code or data to be swapped out to disk when physical memory is exceeded.

Although these two models allow multiple data segments, all initialized global and static data is still placed in a segment whose address is in DS. Normally, the stack is also located in this segment, which is called the "default data segment" because it is present in each memory model.

Huge Memory Model

The huge memory model removes the single data item's 64-K barrier. A single array can exceed 64 K, but the size of each element in any array larger than 128 K must be a power of two. The huge model is identical to the large model except that all address calculations are performed by considering each address as a full 32-bit value stored in an unsigned long integer (with the segment address in the high-order bytes).

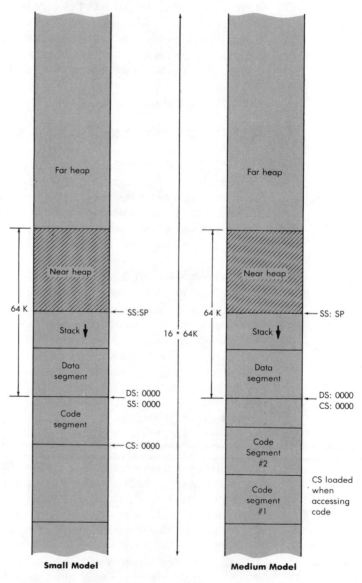

Figure 5-3. *Memory layout for Microsoft C memory models*

Custom Memory Models: *near*, *far*, and *huge* Keywords

The five predefined memory models suffice for most applications, but occasionally you want to address a far data item (for instance, to access video memory directly) in a small model, which lacks such capability. Fortunately, the Microsoft C compiler allows you to mix and match an occasional data item of a type not available in the selected model. In the compact, large, and huge models, you can use the keyword *near* to signify that certain pieces of data reside in the default data segment (one whose segment address is in the DS register). Similarly, in the small and the medium memory models you can use the *far* keyword to tell the compiler to use explicit segment and offset

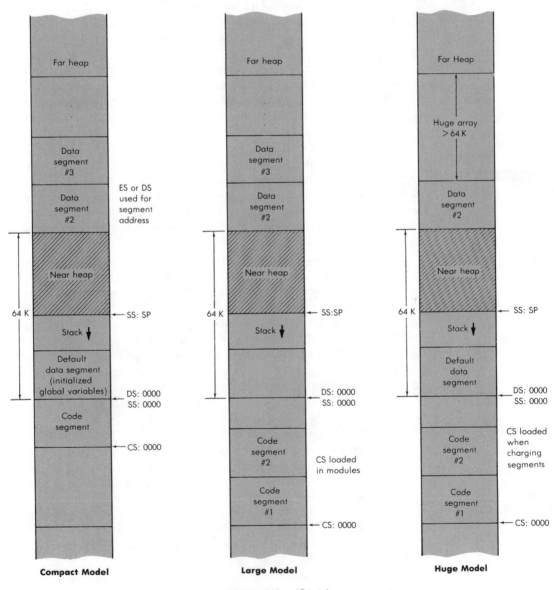

Figure 5-3. *(Cont.)*

addresses when generating code that accesses a specific data item (the ES segment register is used to hold the segment addresses of such data items). A third keyword, *huge*, allows you to use a huge data item (size exceeding 64 K) in any memory model.

THE HEAP: NEAR AND FAR

Now we are ready to identify the region of memory from which allocation normally takes place. Of the 64-K "default data segment," 2 K is used as a stack and an indeterminate amount is used by the data and static variables of the program. The rest of the memory in the segment, in the region above the stack (see Figures 5-2 and 5-3), is known as the "heap"—or more accurately, the "near heap"—because all locations in this block are reached by an offset from the segment address in DS. When allocation of far data items is requested, an area beyond the default data segment is used and this pool is called the "far heap."

The heap is a bit more than simply a block of memory—it is partitioned into smaller blocks, some of which are in use and some, free. Also, there are links allowing the memory allocation routines to search for a free block and assign the block to a requesting function. These tasks fall under the category of memory management.

MEMORY MANAGEMENT: A TWO-STEP PROCESS

Memory management is done in two steps in programs compiled and linked with the Microsoft C memory allocation routines. As an operating system, MS-DOS has to keep track of the memory so that it can load and execute programs. Essentially, it keeps track of the first free paragraph address and provides a service that can dole out a specified number of paragraphs to a requesting process.

The steps involved in accessing the heap depend on the memory model. In the small and medium models, the memory remaining in the default data segment (near heap) after allocating the stack is used as a free pool.

In the compact and large models, which use far data, the Microsoft C allocation routine first gets a segment of a size equal to the value in the global variable _amblksiz (initially set to 8,192 bytes or 8 K) from MS-DOS. This segment becomes the far heap from which smaller blocks are handed out to satisfy calls made to *malloc* or _fmalloc. When the 8-K block is exhausted, the allocation routine gets another 8-K chunk from DOS. You can alter this block size of the far heap by setting _amblksiz (which is already declared in the header file *malloc.h*) to a value of your choice.

The allocation of huge data is handled differently. The Microsoft C routine *halloc* gets the requested memory directly from MS-DOS and when *hfree* is called to free this memory, it is returned to DOS.

Other than *halloc*, the allocation routines keep track of the memory pool in a linked list in which each entry contains the starting address of the block, the size of the block in bytes, and whether it is currently in use or not. Initially, the entire block, excluding the bytes needed to store a single list entry, is maintained as a contiguous free block. As blocks of memory get allocated and freed, the list grows.

The heap is the pool of memory together with the linked list data structure, which keeps track of which component blocks are free and which are in use. (See Figure 5-4.) When we refer to heap elements, we mean the entries in the linked list data structure. The "consistency of a heap" refers to the requirement that all entries in the heap's linked list data structure have reasonable values. For example, the address of a block, as it appears in an entry, must lie within the bounds of the heap. The Microsoft C library includes a set of routines that lets you verify the consistency of the heap as well as find out further information about each entry in the heap.

Notes

The memory allocation routines, cataloged in Table 5-1, give you all the memory management and debugging tools necessary for building complex applications that use the available memory intelligently. Note that many of these routines perform similar functions but for different heaps. See Table 5-2 for a breakdown of generic and heap-specific routines.

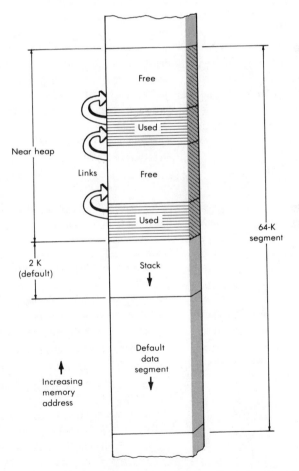

Figure 5-4. *The heap in memory (the near heap is shown here)*

Table 5-1. *Memory Allocation Routines*

Routine	Description
alloca	Allocates a number of bytes from the stack.
calloc	Allocates a number of bytes from the heap (near heap in small and medium models, far heap in large, compact, and huge models) and initializes them to zero.
_expand	Enlarges or shrinks a previously allocated block of memory without moving the block in the heap.
_ffree	Frees previously allocated memory to the far heap.
_fheapchk	Tests the far heap for consistency.
_fheapwalk	Traverses the far heap and returns information on each block of memory.
_fmalloc	Allocates a number of bytes from the far heap.
free	Frees previously allocated memory (near heap in small and medium models, far heap in large and compact models).
_freect	Returns the approximate number of elements of a given size that can be allocated on the heap (near heap in small and medium models, far heap in large and compact models).
_fmsize	Returns the size of a block allocated on the far heap.
halloc	Allocates a huge array (size can exceed 64 K, but size of each element must be a power of 2 when it exceeds 128 K).
_heapchk	Checks heap for consistency (near heap in small and medium models, far heap in large and compact models).
_heapset	Sets heap elements to specified value (near heap in small and medium models, far heap in large and compact models).
_heapwalk	Traverses heap entries and returns information on each entry (near heap in small and medium models, far heap in compact, large, and huge models).
hfree	Frees block of memory allocated by *halloc*.
malloc	Allocates a number of bytes from the heap (near heap in small and medium models, far heap in large, compact, and huge models).
_memavl	Returns approximate number of bytes available for allocation on the heap.
_memmax	Returns the largest number of contiguous bytes available for allocation on the near heap.
_msize	Returns the size of a memory block allocated earlier by *calloc, malloc,* or *realloc* (near heap in small and medium models, far heap in large, compact, and huge models).
_nfree	Frees previously allocated memory to near heap.
_nheapchk	Checks the near-heap for consistency.
_nheapset	Sets all free near-heap elements to a specified value.
_nheapwalk	Traverses the near heap and returns information on the each block of memory.
_nmalloc	Allocates a number of bytes from the near heap.
realloc	Enlarges or shrinks a previously allocated block of memory, moving the block in the heap, if necessary.
sbrk	Sets to a new value the address of the first byte of memory beyond that used by all the data in the program (this is the break value).
stackavail	Gets the amount of memory available in the stack.

THE MEMORY
ALLOCATION
ROUTINES BY TASK

Table 5-2 lists the memory allocation routines grouped according to the tasks they perform. The most important purpose of these routines is the allocation and the deallocation of memory from the heap, but they can also allocate memory from the stack. Another crucial task is obtaining size information about memory blocks: both allocated and available. Lastly, an entire subcategory of routines provides the capability of "snooping" around in the heap and helping debug problems related to the heap. Note that the routines marked GENERIC call the routine for the appropriate heap dependent on the selected memory model of the program.

Table 5-2. *Memory Allocation Routines by Task*

Task	Routines
Allocate memory.	calloc, malloc (generic), _nmalloc (near heap), _fmalloc (far heap), halloc (huge data)
Free memory.	free (generic), _nfree (near heap), _ffree (far heap), hfree (huge data)
Alter size of allocated block.	realloc, _expand
Determine size of allocated block.	msize (generic), _nmsize (near heap), _fmsize (far heap)
Determine amount available in the near heap for allocation.	_freect, _memavl, _memmax
Allocate from the stack.	alloca
Determine amount available in the stack.	stackavail
Check consistency of heap.	heapchk (generic), _nheapchk (near heap), _fheapchk (far heap)
Fill heap with specified value.	heapset (generic), _nheapset (near heap), _fheapset (far heap)
Step through elements in heap.	heapwalk (generic), _nheapwalk (near heap), _fheapwalk (far heap)
Set the break value (address of first byte beyond all data in the program).	sbrk

TYPICAL USE OF
MEMORY
ALLOCATION

You need memory allocation capabilities when you cannot determine in advance the exact amount of space you will need to store the data used or generated in your program. If the data is generated during the course of the program, you may simply want to get space as and when needed. (You may also want to free memory when it is no longer needed.) Typically, the data elements are in the form of a C structure with a field containing pointers to the next element. This enables you to link one element to the next and keep them accessible via a single pointer to the beginning of the linked list. It is also common to want to allocate, at run-time, a number of data elements contiguously. Such a structure, called an "array," provides faster access to arbitrary data elements than linked lists because you do not have to start at the beginning and trace through the links. In either case, the allocation of memory proceeds as described below. (Huge arrays are handled differently and are described later.)

Requesting Memory

You can use either *malloc* or *calloc* to get the needed memory. While *malloc* simply returns a block of memory of specified size, *calloc* allocates room for an array of a specified number of elements, each of a given size, and it also initializes all the allocated bytes to zero. Use the *sizeof* statement to get the size of a data element.

Whether you use *calloc* or *malloc*, the actual allocation is done by calling *malloc*. Depending on the memory model being used, the call to *malloc* is mapped either to a call to _nmalloc or to _fmalloc. The _nmalloc function allocates memory from the near heap while _fmalloc gets its memory from the far heap. These routines can also be explictly called when you allocate room for data items of either *near* or *far* type.

Using the Allocated Block

The allocation routines return the address of the allocated block as a pointer to a *void* data item. You should always cast this pointer into a pointer of the type of data for which you requested space in order to handle data items correctly. This pointer is the only way to access the newly allocated block. By assigning it to a pointer variable, you ensure that it cannot be destroyed. If the request for memory fails, the return value will be NULL. So you must always check for a NULL return value when you call an allocation routine. Otherwise, you will see the error message "Null pointer assignment" when you exit your program.

Releasing Memory

If the data you have stored in a block of memory is no longer needed and you do not plan to store anything in that memory, you should call *free* to release that block to the heap for use by other routines. Just like *malloc*, *free* maps to _nfree in the small and the medium models, and to _ffree in the compact, large, and huge models.

Altering the Size of a Block

What if you allocated room for an array and later discovered that you need room for more elements? The C library includes routines that can either enlarge or shrink the size of an allocated block. Both the *realloc* and the _expand routines do the job. When enlarging a block, _expand tries to expand the block in its current position in the heap; it fails if it cannot. The *realloc* function, however, relocates the block in the heap to satisfy the request for enlargement. Both routines guarantee that the data taking up to the old size of the block will remain intact.

Getting the Size Information

The Microsoft C library includes several routines that let you determine the size of an allocated block as well as the amount available for allocation. The _msize routine returns the size of an allocated block in bytes. You have to provide it with the pointer that was returned by the allocation routine. Similar to *malloc* and *free*, *msize* maps to *_nmsize* for the small and the medium models and to *_fmsize* for the compact, the large, and the huge memory models. You can also call the *_nmsize* and *_fmsize* routines explicitly. For example, if you allocate a far data item using *_fmalloc* in a small model, you can use *_fmsize* to determine the size of the block.

The other routines that return size information are *_freect*, *_memavl*, and *_memmax*. All deal exclusively with the near heap in the default data segment. Thus they work in small and medium models or with any near data in other models. The *_freect* routine tells you how many elements of a given size will fit into the memory available for allocation in the near heap. The *_memavl* routine is similar, but it returns the total number of bytes available for allocation in the near heap. Typically, the pool of memory in the near heap is a number of blocks, some in use and some free. The *_memmax* routine returns the size, in bytes, of the largest contiguous block of memory you can allocate from the near heap. Thus, if you wanted to get as large a block as possible in the near heap, you could do it by the call *_nmalloc(_memmax( ))*.

HUGE ARRAYS   The allocation and deallocation of huge arrays (whose size exceeds the 64-K limit on segment size) is handled by the routines *halloc* and *hfree*, respectively. You have to observe a few restrictions when requesting room for a huge array. When the size of the array exceeds 128 K (131,072 bytes), the size of each element must be a power of two. Unlike the other memory allocation routines, *halloc* gets its memory directly from MS-DOS and *hfree* returns the block by using a DOS function call. There is no concept of a heap in this case. These routines can be used in the huge memory model or to allocate any data item of type *huge*. The pointer returned by *halloc* is of type *huge*, which is similar to *far* except that any pointer arithmetic is performed using a full 32-bit representation of the pointer.

ALLOCATING FROM THE STACK   The stack is used for passing arguments during function calls and also for storage for any local variables. If you have too many local variables you run the risk of running out of stack space, a condition known as "stack overflow." A solution to this problem is to allocate local variables dynamically, meaning that you do not declare them in the function, but allocate them on the stack using *alloca*. Of course, you should check that there is enough room on the stack before taking up space on it. This can be done by calling the library routine *stackavail* which lets you determine the number of bytes available on the stack. You can manage storage, even on the stack, using these two routines from the Microsoft C library.

SNOOPING AROUND THE HEAP   Dynamic memory allocation often can be a source of strange errors. For example, you may allocate an array of 100 integers and by mistake write into array indices above 99 (the last element position). This may overwrite critical information in the heap's data structures and cause the program to fail when a memory allocation routine is called later in your program. Microsoft C 5.1 includes several routines that can help you track down such errors.

The *_heapchk* routine checks the consistency of the heap. It ensures all the entries have valid addresses for the blocks of memory used and it reports any bad node entry it finds. By calling _heapset, you can set each byte in all free blocks of memory in the heap to a specified *fill character*. Lastly, the _heapwalk routine lets you examine each entry in the linked list data structure of the heap. Using a combination of these routines, you can isolate problems that are caused by damage to the heap. In the small and the medium memory models, the _heapchk, _heapset, and _heapwalk routines map to _nheapchk, _nheapset, and _nheapwalk, respectively. These routines are meant for use with the near heap. In the compact, the large, and the huge models, they map respectively to _fheapchk, _fheapset, and _fheapwalk, which are for use with the far heap.

Cautions

▶ Do not mix the *halloc* and *hfree* functions with the other routines for memory allocation and deallocation because each set manages the memory in a different manner.

▶ Always pass a valid pointer to the deallocation routine *free* (*hfree* for huge data). If you pass a pointer that was not returned by the corresponding allocation routine, later calls to the memory allocation functions will produce errors.

▶ The *sbrk* routine that adjusts the "break value" should not be used together with other allocation routines. Decreasing the break value using *sbrk* may cause other memory allocation routines to misbehave.

Further Reading

Memory management is covered in most textbooks on operating systems. The book on XINU by Comer[1] and the book on MINIX by Tanenbaum[2] describe memory management from the point of view of an operating system. Each includes samples of C code that implement the memory management algorithms. Knuth's classic text[3] describes the basic algorithms used in deciding how to assign a particular block of memory to satisfy a request. For a more practical and relevant description of the C memory allocation routines and their usage, consult Prata's book[4].

1. Douglas Comer, *Operating System Design The XINU Approach*, Prentice-Hall, Inc. Englewood Cliffs, NJ, 1984, 486 pages.

2. Andrew S. Tanenbaum, *Operating Systems Design and Implementation*, Prentice-Hall, Inc. Englewood Cliffs, NJ, 1987, 719 pages.

3. Donald E. Knuth, *The Art of Computer Programming, Volume 1: Fundamental Algorithms*, Addison-Wesley, Reading, MA, 1968.

4. Stephen Prata, The Waite Group, *Advanced C Primer++*, Howard W. Sams & Company, Indianapolis, IN, 1986, 502 pages.

alloca

COMPATIBILITY	MSC 3	MSC 4	MSC 5	QC	TC	ANSI	UNIX V
		▲	▲	▲			▲

PURPOSE Use *alloca* to obtain a specified amount of space in the program's stack for temporary use.

SYNTAX `void *alloca(size_t num_bytes);`

`size_t num_bytes;` Number of bytes to be allocated from the stack

EXAMPLE CALL `ptr = alloca(80);`

INCLUDES `#include <malloc.h>` For function declaration and definition of data type *size_t*

DESCRIPTION The *alloca* function allocates the number of bytes specified in the argument *num_bytes* to the program's stack. Before calling *alloca* you should call *stackavail* to determine the amount of space available on the stack for allocation. The *alloca* function only creates room for local variables; it does not increase the size of a program's stack. The allocated bytes begin at an address that satisfies all requirements for storage of any C data type. There is no need to deallocate this memory from the stack because the space is freed as soon as the calling function returns.

COMMON USES The *alloca* function allocates temporary storage on the stack. In fact, all local variables in a function are allocated on the stack, but *alloca* enables us to get only as much space on the stack as we need, when we need it. For temporary needs, this is more efficient than allocating memory in the default segment with *malloc*.

RETURNS The return value from *alloca* is a pointer to a type *void*, representing the address of the first byte of the space allocated on the stack. If the function fails because of insufficient space on the stack, a NULL is returned.

COMMENTS Since the stack is used for passing parameters and storing return addresses during function calls, you cannot use *alloca* inside an argument to another function. Attempting to free the space by calling other memory deallocation functions such as *free* will most likely crash your program.

SEE ALSO `stackavail` To determine the space available on the stack

`malloc` To allocate memory from the heap

`free` To release memory allocated earlier

EXAMPLE Use *alloca* to allocate room for a buffer to hold 80 characters on the program's stack. Prompt the user for a string and store it in the buffer you allocate.

alloca

```
#include <stdio.h>
#include <malloc.h>
main()
{
    char *buffer;
/* Get 80 bytes from stack */
    buffer = (char *) alloca(80);
    if (buffer == NULL)
    {
        printf("alloca failed.\n");
        exit(0);
    }
    printf("Buffer allocated. Enter string to store: ");
    gets(buffer);
    printf("\nYou entered: %s\n",buffer);
}
```

calloc

COMPATIBILITY	MSC 3	MSC 4	MSC 5	QC	TC	ANSI	UNIX V
	▲	▲	▲	▲	▲	▲	▲

PURPOSE Use *calloc* to allocate memory for an array of a given number of elements, each having a specified size. All bytes of the allocated array are initialized to zero. Note that *calloc* can only allocate memory for an array whose size is smaller than 64 K. For larger arrays, use *halloc*.

SYNTAX `void *calloc(size_t num_elems, size_t elem_size);`

`size_t    num_elems;`   Number of elements

`size_t    elem_size;`   Size of each element in bytes

EXAMPLE CALL `p_int = (int *) calloc(100, sizeof(int));`

INCLUDES `#include <malloc.h>`   For function declaration and definition of data type *size_t*

`#include <stdlib.h>`   For ANSI compatibility

DESCRIPTION The *calloc* function computes the number of bytes it must allocate by multiplying the number of elements *num_elems* by the size of each *elem_size*. Then it calls *malloc* to allocate the memory. Finally, it calls the *memset* function to set each byte of the allocated memory to zero. Since the compiler maps the call to *malloc* to a routine appropriate for the memory model in use, *calloc* works for all memory models except *huge*. To allocate huge (that is, longer than 64 K) arrays, use the *halloc* function.

 Memory Allocation and Management

COMMON USES The *calloc* function creates and initializes to zero arrays of data objects at run-time. This allows your application to get memory as needed instead of setting aside a fixed amount and running the risk of filling up the space with no way of getting additional room. You can use *calloc*, for example, to set aside memory for 100 elements, each 80 bytes long.

RETURNS The return value from *calloc* is a pointer to a type *void*, representing the address of the allocated memory. The storage locations are guaranteed to be able to hold data objects of any kind. If the memory allocation is unsuccessful because of insufficient space or bad values of the arguments, a NULL is returned.

COMMENTS In Microsoft C 4.0 you could get a valid pointer even if the element size was given as zero. This pointer could be used with the function *realloc* to enlarge the memory to a desired size. This is no longer true in Microsoft C 5.0 and 5.1.

The *calloc* function merely computes the total memory requested in bytes and calls *malloc*, which is the most general-purpose memory allocation routine in the Microsoft C run-time library.

SEE ALSO

malloc   General-purpose memory allocation routine

halloc   To allocate huge (greater than 64 K) arrays

free   To release memory allocated earlier

EXAMPLES Use *calloc* to allocate room for a buffer to hold 100 lines of text, each 80 characters long. Prompt the user for a string and store it in the buffer.

```
#include <stdio.h>
#include <stdlib.h>
#include <malloc.h>
char *buffer;
main()
{
    buffer = (char *) calloc(100, 80);
    if (buffer == NULL)
    {
        printf("Allocation Failed.\n");
        exit(0);
    }
    printf("Buffer allocated. Enter string to store: ");
    gets(buffer);
    printf("\nYou entered: %s\n",buffer);
}
```

Suppose you are developing a small data base of your client's vital statistics. You have grouped all information about a single client in a C data structure of type CLIENT_T. Define this data type and use *calloc* to allocate enough memory for 100 clients.

calloc

```
#include <stdio.h>
#include <malloc.h>
#include <stdlib.h>
#define MAX_CHR       80
#define MAX_CLIENTS 100
typedef struct CLIENT_T        /* Define a data structure */
{
        char      name[MAX_CHR];
        unsigned  age;
        double    networth;
} CLIENT_T;

main()
{
    CLIENT_T *client_list;  /* Define pointer to data */
    if( (client_list =       /* Cast returned pointer  */
        (CLIENT_T *) calloc(MAX_CLIENTS,
                            sizeof(CLIENT_T))) == NULL)
    {
        fprintf(stderr,"No room for clients!\n");
    }
    else
    {
        printf("Client list allocated successfully.\n");
    }
/* The array of structures can now be accessed by using
 * the pointer "client_list". For example the net worth
 * of client number 10 is --   client_list[10].networth
 */
}
```

__expand

COMPATIBILITY	MSC 3	MSC 4	MSC 5	QC	TC	ANSI	UNIX V
		▲	▲	▲			

PURPOSE Use the *__expand* function to enlarge or shrink an allocated block of memory without changing the location of the block.

SYNTAX `void *_expand(void *mem_address, size_t newsize);`

`void *mem_address;`   Pointer to allocated block of memory

`size_t newsize;`   Requested size of block in number of bytes

  Memory Allocation and Management

EXAMPLE CALL   `_expand(p_old_block, 2000*sizeof(int));`

INCLUDES   `#include <malloc.h>`   For function declaration and definition of data type *size_t*

DESCRIPTION   The *_expand* function alters the size of an allocated block of memory to the number of bytes specified in the argument *newsize*. The address of the block is provided, as a pointer to a *void* data type, in the argument *mem_address*, which itself is a pointer returned by an earlier call to one of the memory allocation routines such as *malloc, calloc,* or *realloc.* It can also be the address of a block of memory that was just freed, as long as there have been no calls to any memory allocation routine since the block had been freed.

Unlike *realloc,* which also provides the same services, *_expand* will not move the block of memory to another location in the heap in an attempt to satisfy the requested change in size.

RETURNS   The return value from *_expand* is a pointer to the block of memory whose size was altered. Since *_expand* does not move the block around, the value returned, if successful, is the same as the argument *mem_address.* When the size cannot be enlarged to the amount requested in the call, *_expand* makes the block as large as possible and returns a NULL to indicate the error.

COMMENTS   For normal allocation and reallocation needs, it is best to stick to the portable routines: *malloc, calloc,* and *realloc.* Using *realloc* to enlarge the size of a block gives the added advantage of providing a greater possibility of success because *realloc* moves the block around in the heap in an attempt to find enough space. In fact, it is hard to find a situation where *realloc* won't do and *_expand* must be used.

SEE ALSO   `realloc`   More portable way to alter the size of an allocated block of memory

EXAMPLE   Allocate an 80-byte buffer using *malloc.* Prompt the user for a string and store it in the buffer. Now call the *_expand* function to enlarge the size to 8,000 bytes. Verify that the contents remain unaltered.

```
#include <stdio.h>
#include <malloc.h>
main()
{
    char *buffer;

    if( (buffer = (char *) malloc(80) ) == NULL)
    {
        printf("Error allocating buffer\n");
        exit(0);
    }
    printf("Buffer allocated. Enter string to store:");
    gets(buffer);
    printf("Before _expand, string is: %s\n", buffer);
```

_expand

```
    if( _expand(buffer, 8000) == NULL)
    {
        printf("_expand failed. Buffer still usable\n");
    }
    printf("After _expand, string is still: %s\n",
            buffer);
}
```

__ffree

COMPATIBILITY	MSC 3	MSC 4	MSC 5	QC	TC	ANSI	UNIX V
		▲	▲	▲			

PURPOSE Use _ffree to deallocate a block of memory previously allocated by _fmalloc.

SYNTAX `void _ffree(void far *mem_address);`

`void far *mem_address;`   Far pointer to block of memory being deallocated

EXAMPLE CALL `_ffree((void far *)buffer);`

INCLUDES `#include <free.h>`   For function declaration

DESCRIPTION The _ffree function deallocates memory blocks outside the default data segment. The address of the block to be deallocated is given as a far pointer to a *void* type in the argument *mem_address*. This pointer should be the one that was returned when this block of memory was allocated by the function _fmalloc.

COMMON USES The _ffree function is useful for deallocating memory originally allocated by _fmalloc.

COMMENTS The _ffree function should be used only when the original allocation was done by _fmalloc. An instance of this would be when you use a mixed-memory model when you require storage outside the default data segment while working in the small model.

SEE ALSO free   More portable way of allocating memory

_fmalloc   To allocate storage outside the default data segment

EXAMPLE Use _fmalloc to allocate room for an 80-character string. Prompt the user for a string and store it in the buffer you allocate. Display the string and then deallocate the storage by calling _ffree.

 Memory Allocation and Management

```
#include <stdio.h>
#include <stdlib.h>
#include <malloc.h>
#define MAX_CHR 80
main()
{
    unsigned char far *buffer;
/* Allocate room for string and check for NULL pointer*/
    if( (buffer = (char far *)_fmalloc(MAX_CHR)) == NULL)
    {
        printf("Allocation Failed.\n");
        exit(0);
    }
    printf("Buffer allocated. Enter string to store: ");
    gets(buffer);
    printf("\nYou entered: %s\n",buffer);
    _ffree((void far*)buffer); /* Deallocate the space*/
    printf("Buffer deallocated.\n");
}
```

__fheapchk

COMPATIBILITY	MSC 3	MSC 4	MSC 5	QC	TC	ANSI	UNIX V
			▲	▲			

PURPOSE Use _fheapchk to check the consistency of the far heap, the linked list outside the default data segment of memory blocks from which functions such as _fmalloc allocate memory.

SYNTAX `int _fheapchk(void);`

INCLUDES `#include <malloc.h>`   For function declaration

DESCRIPTION The _fheapchk function is similar to _heapchk, except the former checks the linked list of memory blocks, the heap, located *outside* the default data segment. The heap is the pool of memory from which data blocks referenced by far pointers (see the tutorial) are allocated by the _fmalloc function. The check ensures that entries in the heap data structure make sense; if an entry is the address of a block of memory in use, for example, it must be within the limits of the pool of memory currently assigned to the far heap.

RETURNS The return value from _fheapchk is interpreted in the same manner as the value returned by _heapchk. See Table 5-3 for a list of defined constants for the meaning of the return value. The example below illustrates the use of the value returned by the _fheapchk function.

COMMENTS The *_fheapchk* function is intended to check the consistency of the far heap, the free memory pool from which memory is allocated for data objects that are to be accessed by far pointers. (See the tutorial.) It is not necessary to call *_fheapchk* directly unless you are mixing memory models, for example, allocating a data array with far addresses in a small or a medium model.

SEE ALSO

_heapset   To fill all unallocated memory in the heap with a specified character

_heapwalk   To navigate through the heap's linked list data structure and check the size and status (free or used) of blocks

_heapchk   To check the heap in any memory model

_nheapchk   To check the near heap (in the default data segment)

EXAMPLE Use *_fmalloc* and *_ffree* to allocate and deallocate a few blocks of memory in the far heap. Then call *_fheapchk* to check the heap and display the returned information. Note that you can compile and link this program in any memory model because we are explicitly using far data pointers and calls to the far allocation routine *_fmalloc*.

```
#include <stdio.h>
#include <malloc.h>
main()
{
    char far *buffer;
    int heapstatus;
/* Perform some allocations and deallocations */
    buffer = (char far *) _fmalloc(500);
    _fmalloc(800);
    _ffree((void far *)buffer);
/* Now get the status of the far heap by calling _fheapchk */
    heapstatus = _fheapchk();
    switch (heapstatus)
    {
        case _HEAPOK:       printf("Heap OK\n");
                            break;
        case _HEAPEMPTY:    printf("Heap not initialized\n");
                            break;
        case _HEAPBADBEGIN: printf("Heap header bad\n");
                            break;
        case _HEAPBADNODE:  printf("Heap has bad node/s\n");
                            break;
    }
}
```

 Memory Allocation and Management

__fheapset

COMPATIBILITY	MSC 3	MSC 4	MSC 5	QC	TC	ANSI	UNIX V
			▲	▲			

PURPOSE Use _fheapset to set to a specific character each byte in every unused block in the far heap, the linked list of memory blocks from which functions such as _fmalloc allocate memory. (See the tutorial.)

SYNTAX `hint _fheapset(unsigned fill_char);`

`unsigned int fill_char;`   Character used to fill all unused memory location in the heap

EXAMPLE CALL `heapstatus = _fheapset('X');`

INCLUDES `#include <malloc.h>`   For function declaration

DESCRIPTION The _fheapset routine performs a function similar to that of _heapset except that it works with the far heap. The _fheapset function first checks the consistency of the far heap and then fills all unused blocks with the character specified in the argument *fill_char*.

RETURNS The return value from _fheapset is the result of the consistency check performed on the far heap. The return value must be interpreted by comparing it with the constants shown in Table 5-3, just as it is done for the function _heapchk. The example below shows how to use the value returned by the _fheapset function.

Table 5-3. *Possible Results of a Heap Check*

Constant	Interpretation
_HEAPOK	All entries in the linked list that make up the heap appear to be consistent (all addresses are within the limits of the memory block assigned to the heap).
_HEAPEMPTY	The heap is probably not initialized. This means the heap-checking utility routine could not find any linked list data structure that would indicate an existing heap. This is the condition before any of the allocation routines are called.
_HEAPBADBEGIN	The initial header information of the heap data structure could not be found.
_HEAPBADNODE	A node in the linked list data structure of the heap was found to be bad. This may indicate overwriting beyond the array limits in a dynamically allocated array.

COMMENTS The *_fheapset* function should be called directly only when you are mixing memory models, for example, allocating a data array with far address in a small or a medium model.

SEE ALSO _heapset To fill all unallocated memory in the heap with a specified character (for all memory models)

_heapwalk To navigate through the heap's linked list data structure and check the size and status (free or used) of blocks

_nheapset To fill unused locations in the near heap (in the default data segment)

EXAMPLE Use *_fheapset* to set each byte in the unused parts of the far heap to the character 'F'. Now call *_fmalloc* to allocate an 80-byte buffer and show, by printing the buffer, that the fill operation worked.

```
#include <stdio.h>
#include <malloc.h>
main()
{
    char far *buffer;
    int heapstatus;
/* Call _fmalloc once to initialize the far heap  */
    _fmalloc(1);
/* Fill all free memory with F */
    heapstatus = _fheapset('F');
/* Allocate a buffer in the far heap */
    buffer = (char far *) _fmalloc(80);
/* Display the buffer and also show status returned by
 * _fheapset
 */
    buffer[79] = '\0'; /* Mark the end of the string */
    printf("The buffer contains:\n%Fs\n", buffer);
    switch (heapstatus)
    {
        case _HEAPOK:        printf("Heap OK\n");
                             break;
        case _HEAPEMPTY:     printf("Heap not initialized\n");
                             break;
        case _HEAPBADBEGIN:  printf("Heap header bad\n");
                             break;
        case _HEAPBADNODE:   printf("Heap has bad node/s\n");
                             break;
    }
}
```

Memory Allocation and Management

__fheapwalk

COMPATIBILITY	MSC 3	MSC 4	MSC 5	QC	TC	ANSI	UNIX V
			▲	▲			

PURPOSE Use the _fheapwalk function to obtain information about the entries in the far heap, from which memory allocation routines such as _fmalloc allocate data objects to be referenced by far pointers. (See the tutorial.)

SYNTAX `int _fheapwalk(struct _heapinfo *heap_entry);`

`struct _heapinfo *heap_entry;`   Pointer to data structure in which information about next heap entry is returned

INCLUDES `#include <malloc.h>`   For function declaration and definition of structure _heapinfo

DESCRIPTION The _fheapwalk function returns information about the next entry in the far heap in a data structure of type _heapinfo, which is defined in the header file malloc.h and whose structure is shown in the description of the function _heapwalk. You must allocate a structure of type _heapinfo and provide its address in the argument heap_entry. The _fheapwalk function is used in the same manner as _heapwalk. The reference section on _heapwalk has a detailed description of its use.

RETURNS The return value from _fheapwalk should be interpreted by comparing it with the constants shown in Table 5-4.

Table 5-4. *Return Values from __heapwalk*

Constant	Interpretation
__HEAPOK	The entries of the heap are all right up to the current one. In this case, the __heapinfo structure contains information about the next entry in the heap's linked list data.
__HEAPEMPTY	The heap is probably not initialized. This means no calls have been made to a memory allocation routine.
__HEAPBADPTR	The __pentry field in the __heapinfo data structure does not contain a valid pointer to an entry in the heap.
__HEAPBADBEGIN	The initial header information of the heap data structure could not be found.
__HEAPBADNODE	A node in the linked list data structure of the heap was found to be bad. This may indicate overwriting beyond the array limits in a dynamically allocated array.
__HEAPEND	The end of the heap was reached successfully.

COMMENTS The _*fheapwalk* function should be called only when you are mixing memory model in your programs. For example, you may be allocating some data objects to be addressed by far pointers in a small or medium model program. In programs where a single memory model is used throughout, the _*heapwalk* function is a better choice because the compiler automatically uses the version appropriate for the memory model being used. This makes it easier to change memory models at a later date.

SEE ALSO

_heapchk   To check the heap's linked list data structure for consistency

_heapwalk   To step through the heap's linked list data structure and check the size and status (free or used) of blocks—for any memory model

_nheapwalk   To inspect entries in the near heap (in the default data segment)

EXAMPLE Use _*fmalloc* to allocate one or two data arrays in the far heap. Then call _*fheapwalk* to traverse through the entries of the heap and print a short report about the entries.

```
#include <stdio.h>
#include <malloc.h>
main()
{
    struct _heapinfo heapentry;
    char far *buffer;
/* Allocate a buffer in the far heap */
    buffer = (char far *) _fmalloc(80);
    _fmalloc(500);      /* Another one ...   */
    _ffree(buffer);     /* Free the first one */
/* Now check the heap entries. Set the _pentry field to
 * NULL to begin at first entry
 */
    heapentry._pentry = NULL;
/* Keep calling _fheapwalk as long as return value
 * is _HEAPOK. Print information about entry from the
 * structure 'heapentry'
 */
    printf("-------- BEGIN HEAP TRAVERSAL ---------\n");
    while ( _fheapwalk(&heapentry) == _HEAPOK)
    {
        printf("Address: %p  Status: %6s  Size: %5u\n",
                heapentry._pentry, (heapentry._useflag ==
                _FREEENTRY ? "FREE" : "USED"),
                heapentry._size);
    }
    printf("---------- END HEAP TRAVERSAL --------\n");
}
```

**MEMO
RY**

Memory Allocation and Management

__fmalloc

COMPATIBILITY	MSC 3	MSC 4	MSC 5	QC	TC	ANSI	UNIX V
		▲	▲	▲			

PURPOSE Use _fmalloc to allocate memory in the compact or large memory model when all data addresses are far pointers. The _fmalloc function allocates memory of the requested size outside the default data segment.

SYNTAX `void far *_fmalloc(size_t num_bytes);`

`size_t    num_bytes;`   Number of bytes needed

EXAMPLE CALL `far_int_buffer = (int far *)_fmalloc(10000);`

INCLUDES `#include <malloc.h>`   For function declaration and definition of data type *size_t*

DESCRIPTION The _fmalloc function allocates the number of bytes requested in the argument *num_bytes* outside the default data segment and returns a *far* pointer to the memory allocated.

COMMON USES The _fmalloc function allocates memory in compact and large memory model C programs. The *malloc* function calls _fmalloc in these memory models.

RETURNS The _nmalloc function returns a *far* pointer to the allocated memory. A NULL is returned if it is not possible to allocate the requested amount of memory because of insufficient space or bad values of the arguments.

COMMENTS The *malloc* function should normally be used instead of _fmalloc because calls to *malloc* are mapped to _fmalloc in models with far data addresses and *malloc* is guaranteed to be portable. Microsoft C allows you to call the _fmalloc function explicitly so that you can mix memory models—for example, to allocate a *far* data array in a small memory model.

SEE ALSO

`malloc`	More portable way of allocating memory
`calloc`	To allocate and initialize an array
`halloc`	To allocate huge (greater than 64 K) arrays
`_nmalloc`	To allocate memory in small and medium models
`_ffree`	To free memory allocated by _fmalloc

EXAMPLE Use _fmalloc to allocate room for an 80-character string. Prompt the user for a string and store it in the buffer you allocate.

__fmalloc

```
#include <stdio.h>
#include <stdlib.h>
#include <malloc.h>
#define MAX_CHR 80
main()
{
     unsigned char far *buffer;
/* Allocate room for string and check for NULL pointer*/
     if( (buffer = (char far *)_fmalloc(MAX_CHR))
          == NULL)
     {
             printf("Allocation Failed.\n");
             exit(0);
     }
     printf("Buffer allocated. Enter string to store: ");
     gets(buffer);
     printf("\nYou entered: %s\n",buffer);
}
```

__fmsize

COMPATIBILITY	MSC 3	MSC 4	MSC 5	QC	TC	ANSI	UNIX V
		▲	▲	▲			

PURPOSE Use the _fmsize function to obtain the total number of bytes in a block of memory allocated earlier by the function _fmalloc.

SYNTAX size_t _fmsize(void far *mem_address);

void far *mem_address; Pointer to allocated block of memory whose size is to be determined

EXAMPLE CALL blocksize = _fmsize((void far *)buffer);

INCLUDES #include <malloc.h> For function declaration and definition of data type *size_t*

DESCRIPTION The _fmsize function accepts in the argument *mem_address* a *far* pointer to a *void* data type obtained by a successful call to the allocation routine _fmalloc. It returns the size of the block in number of bytes.

RETURNS The _fmsize function returns the number of bytes allocated in the specified block of memory in a data type *size_t*, an unsigned integer in the include file *malloc.h*.

Memory Allocation and Management

SEE ALSO   _msize   Similar function, but not specific to any memory model

                 _nmsize   To determine size of a block of memory located in the default data segment

EXAMPLE   Allocate an 8,000-byte buffer outside the default data segment by using _fmalloc. Call the _fmsize to check the size of the allocated buffer.

```
#include <stdio.h>
#include <malloc.h>
main()
{
    size_t max_bytes;
    char far *buffer;

    if( (buffer = (char far *) _fmalloc(80) ) == NULL)
    {
        printf("Error allocating buffer\n");
        exit(0);
    }
/* Find size of block now */
    max_bytes = _fmsize(buffer);
    printf("Buffer size is: %u bytes\n", max_bytes);
}
```

free

COMPATIBILITY	MSC 3	MSC 4	MSC 5	QC	TC	ANSI	UNIX V
	▲	▲	▲	▲	▲	▲	▲

PURPOSE   Use the *free* function to release an allocated storage block to the pool of free memory. Only blocks allocated by *malloc, calloc,* and *realloc* can be safely deallocated by *free*; memory allocated by *halloc* must be released by calling *hfree*.

SYNTAX   void free(void *mem_address);

                 void *mem_address;   Pointer to block of memory to be released

EXAMPLE CALL free(buffer);

INCLUDES   #include <malloc.h>   For function declaration

                 #include <stdlib.h>   For ANSI compatibility

DESCRIPTION   The *free* function returns to the pool of free memory a block of memory that was allocated earlier by *malloc, calloc*, or *realloc*. The address of the block is specified by the argument *mem_address*, which is a pointer to the starting byte of the block. A NULL pointer argument is ignored by *free*.

　　The Microsoft C compiler maps *free* to specific deallocation routines depending on the memory model in use. In the small and medium models, in which data addresses are all *near* pointers, the function maps to *_nfree*. It maps to *_ffree* in the large and compact models, in which the compiler uses *far* data pointers.

COMMON USES   The *free* function is used with *malloc, calloc*, and *realloc* to free memory used by data objects that are no longer needed.

COMMENTS   Use *free* with *malloc, calloc*, and *realloc* only. If you use *free* with the model-specific allocation routines *_nmalloc* and *_fmalloc* the Microsoft C heap management algorithm may not work properly for future allocation and deallocation requests.

　　Memory allocated by *halloc* must be released by calling *hfree* because *halloc* fulfils memory requests by directly calling MS-DOS, rather than using the memory management facilities of Microsoft C.

SEE ALSO

malloc　　　To allocate a block of storage

calloc　　　To allocate and initialize an array

realloc　　　To alter size of allocated block of memory

free　　　To release memory allocated earlier

_nfree　　　Actual routine invoked in small and medium models

_ffree　　　Actual routine invoked in compact and large models

EXAMPLE   Use *malloc* to allocate room for an 80-character string. Prompt the user for a string and store it in the buffer you allocate. Print the string and then deallocate the buffer by calling *free*.

```
#include <stdio.h>
#include <stdlib.h>
#include <malloc.h>
#define MAX_CHR 80
main()
{
    unsigned char *buffer;
/* Allocate room for string and check for NULL */
    if( (buffer = (char *)malloc(MAX_CHR)) == NULL)
    {
```

Memory Allocation and Management

```
            printf("Allocation Failed.\n");
            exit(0);
    }
    printf("Buffer allocated. Enter string to store: ");
    gets(buffer);
    printf("\nYou entered: %s\n",buffer);
    free((void *)buffer);    /* Deallocate the memory */
    printf("Buffer deallocated.\n");
}
```

__freect

COMPATIBILITY	MSC 3	MSC 4	MSC 5	QC	TC	ANSI	UNIX V
		▲	▲	▲			

PURPOSE Use the _freect function to determine the approximate number of elements of a given size that can be allocated in the default data segment.

SYNTAX `unsigned int _freect(size_t elem_size);`

`size_t elem_size;`   Size of each data element in bytes

EXAMPLE CALL `room_for_integers = _freect(sizeof(int));`

INCLUDES `#include <malloc.h>`   For function declaration and definition of data type *size_t*

DESCRIPTION The _freect function computes the total number of data elements, each of size *elem_size* bytes, that can fit into the free space in the default data segment. So it is usually called with the argument sizeof(type). In contrast to this, the _memavl function simply returns the total number of bytes available for allocation in the default data segment.

RETURNS The _freect function returns an unsigned integer with the number of elements of the specified size that can fit into the available memory in the default data segment.

SEE ALSO _memavl   To determine the total bytes in the available memory in the default data segment

EXAMPLE Call _freect in a small program to determine how many integers can fit into the free memory in the default data segment. Then call *malloc* to allocate 1,000 integers and repeat the call to _freect to see how many more integers will fit into the leftover space.

```
#include <stdio.h>
#include <malloc.h>
main()
{
    int *iarray;
    printf("There is room for %u integers in the free \
space\n", _freect(sizeof(int)) );    /* call _freect */
    printf("in default data segment\n");
/* Now allocate memory for 1000 integers */
    if( (iarray = (int *) malloc(1000) ) == NULL)
    {
        printf("Error allocating memory\n");
        exit(0);
    }
    printf("Room for %u integers left after allocating \
1000 integers\n",
    _freect(sizeof(int)) );    /* Call _freect again */
}
```

halloc

COMPATIBILITY	MSC 3	MSC 4	MSC 5	QC	TC	ANSI	UNIX V
		▲	▲	▲			

PURPOSE Use *halloc* to allocate memory for an array of data elements when the total size of requested memory exceeds the size of a 64-K segment. You can use *halloc*, for example, to set aside memory for an array of 100,000 short integers (2 bytes each).

SYNTAX `void huge *halloc(long num_elems, size_t elem_size);`

`long num_elems;`   Number of elements

`size_t elem_size;`   Size of each element in bytes

EXAMPLE CALL `p_huge = (short huge *)halloc(100000, sizeof(short));`

INCLUDES `#include <malloc.h>`   For function declaration and definition of data type *size_t*

DESCRIPTION The *halloc* function allocates the memory necessary to hold the number of data elements specified in the argument *num_elems*, each of size *elem_size*, by calling the MS-DOS memory allocation function (function number 48H). Each byte in the allocated memory is set to 0. Similar to *calloc*, except that the size of *halloc*'s block of memory can be huge—it can exceed 64 K. When allocating memory blocks larger than 128 K (131,072 bytes), the size of each data element must be a power of 2. You release the allocated memory by calling *hfree* before exiting the program.

Memory Allocation and Management

COMMON USES The *halloc* function creates room for very large arrays of data objects at run-time. This may be necessary, for example, when you want to load a large bit-mapped image into memory for manipulation or a large text file for editing.

RETURNS The *halloc* function returns a *huge* pointer (see the tutorial section) to the first byte of the allocated memory. The allocated memory is properly aligned for storing any type of data. If the memory allocation fails because of insufficient space or bad values of the arguments, a NULL is returned.

SEE ALSO

calloc Same function as *halloc* but for smaller arrays (<64 K)

hfree To free huge (greater than 64 K) arrays allocated by *halloc*

EXAMPLE Use *halloc* to allocate room for a huge array of 100,000 short integers and initialize each element to zero. Deallocate the array by calling *hfree* before exiting the program.

```
#include <stdio.h>
#include <stdlib.h>
#include <malloc.h>
#define MAX_SIZE 100000L
main()
{
    short huge *larray;
/* Allocate room for string and check for NULL pointer*/
    if( (larray = (short huge *)halloc(MAX_SIZE,
                         sizeof(short)))  == NULL)
    {
        printf("Allocation by halloc Failed.\n");
        exit(0);
    }
    printf("Array of 100,000 short ints allocated.\n");
/* Free the array and exit */
    hfree((void huge *)larray);
    printf("Huge array deallocated\n");
}
```

__heapchk

COMPATIBILITY	MSC 3	MSC 4	MSC 5	QC	TC	ANSI	UNIX V
			▲	▲			

PURPOSE Use *__heapchk* to check the consistency of the heap, the linked list of memory blocks from which functions such as *malloc* allocate memory. This is a debugging tool to pinpoint problems related to memory allocation from the heap.

__heapchk

SYNTAX   `int _heapchk(void);`

EXAMPLE CALL   `heapstatus = _heapchk();`

INCLUDES   `#include <malloc.h>`   For function declaration

DESCRIPTION   The *_heapchk* function checks the heap. The entries in the heap are addresses of free and used blocks of memory. The *_heapchk* function checks to see that the entries are within the first and the last addresses of the heap and it returns code signifying the results of the check.

Just as the function *malloc* gets linked to different versions depending on the memory model in use, the *_heapchk* function is mapped to *_nheapchk* for small and medium memory models and to *_fheapchk* in compact, large, or huge models. In mixed memory models, you can explicitly call *_nheapchk* or *_fheapchk*, respectively, to check the near heap or the far heap.

COMMON USES   The *_heapchk* function is used with its companions, *_heapset* and *_heapwalk*, to pinpoint problems related to the heap, for example, over-writing allocated memory.

RETURNS   The return value from *_heapchk* should be defined in the include file *malloc.h* and interpreted by comparing it with the constants shown in Table 5-3.

COMMENTS   The *_heapchk* function is used in conjunction with *_heapset* and *_heapwalk* to locate causes of program failure that are related to the heap. A typical problem is allocating room, for example, for an 80-character string and then storing 100 characters in the string. Such mistakes can overwrite information in the heap's own linked list data structure and cause the program to fail.

SEE ALSO   `_heapset`   To fill all unallocated memory in the heap with a specified character

`_heapwalk`   To navigate through the heap's linked list data structure and check the size and status (free or used) of blocks

`_nheapchk`   To check the near heap (inside the default data segment)

`_fheapchk`   To check the far heap (outside the default data segment)

EXAMPLE   Use *malloc* and *free* to allocate and deallocate a few blocks of memory. Then call *_heapchk* to check the condition of the heap. Display the information returned by *_heapchk*.

```
#include <stdio.h>
#include <malloc.h>
main()
{
    char *buffer;
    int heapstatus;
```

 Memory Allocation and Management

```
/* Perform some allocations and deallocations */
   buffer = (char *) malloc(500);
   malloc(800);
   free((void *)buffer);
/* Now get the status of the heap by calling _heapchk */
   heapstatus = _heapchk();
   switch (heapstatus)
   {
       case _HEAPOK:        printf("Heap OK\n");
                            break;
       case _HEAPEMPTY:     printf("Heap not initialized\n");
                            break;
       case _HEAPBADBEGIN:  printf("Heap header bad\n");
                            break;
       case _HEAPBADNODE:   printf("Heap has bad node/s\n");
                            break;
   }
}
```

__heapset

COMPATIBILITY	MSC 3	MSC 4	MSC 5	QC	TC	ANSI	UNIX V
			▲	▲			

PURPOSE Use the _heapset function to fill each byte in unused blocks of memory in the heap with a specified character value. For example, you can use _heapset to fill all unallocated memory with a specific character so that later on you can tell by examining the contents of arrays if anything was overwritten.

SYNTAX `int _heapset(unsigned fill_char);`

`unsigned int fill_char;`   Character used to fill all unused memory location in the heap

EXAMPLE CALL `heapstatus = _heapset('Z');`

INCLUDES `#include <malloc.h>`   For function declaration

DESCRIPTION The _heapset function first checks the consistency of the heap, from which memory is allocated by Microsoft C's heap management routines. This check is similar to the one performed by _heapchk. After the check, _heapset fills every byte of each unused block of memory with the character specified in the argument *fill_char*.

The _heapset function is mapped to _nheapset for small and medium memory models, and to _fheapset in the compact, large, and huge models.

__heapset

In mixed memory models, you can explicitly call *_nheapset* or *_fheapset* to fill the near heap or the far heap, respectively.

COMMON USES   The *_heapset* function is used to locate errors in the program that may be overwriting dynamically allocated data in the heap. By first filling the unused memory with a known character, you can determine overwritten locations by examining them. If necessary, you can call the *_heapwalk* function in order to access and examine each individual block of memory in the heap.

RETURNS   The return value from *_heapset* is the result of the consistency check performed before the unused memory locations are filled. This value must be interpreted in the same manner as the value returned by *_heapchk*. See Table 5-3 for a list of defined constants that may be returned by the heap check. The example below illustrates use of the return value.

COMMENTS   The *_heapset* function is used with *_heapwalk* to locate causes of program failure due to overwriting dynamically created data objects in the heap. You use *_heapset* to fill the unused memory with a known character, and *_heapwalk* to access each block individually. Introduced in Microsoft C 5.0, these functions are helpful in debugging mishaps caused by inadvertent damage to the heap. You need to call a memory allocation function before using *_heapset* so that the heap is initialized, otherwise there will not be any blocks, free or used, to work with.

SEE ALSO   _heapchk   To check the heap's linked list data structure for consistency

_heapwalk   To traverse the heap's linked list data structure and check the size and status (free or used) of blocks

_nheapset   To fill the free memory blocks in the near heap (inside the default data segment)

_fheapset   To check the unused memory blocks in the far heap (outside the default data segment)

EXAMPLE   Use *_heapset* to fill all free memory blocks in the heap with the character 'X'. Now allocate an 80 byte buffer by calling *malloc*. Display the contents of the allocated buffer to verify that it contains the character 'X'. Remember to call *malloc* once before using *_heapset* so that the heap gets initialized.

```
#include <stdio.h>
#include <malloc.h>
main()
{
    char *buffer;
    int heapstatus;
/* Call malloc once to initialize the heap    */
    malloc(1);
```

 Memory Allocation and Management

```
/* Fill all free memory with X */
   heapstatus = _heapset('X');
/* Allocate a buffer */
   buffer = (char *) malloc(80);
/* Display the buffer and also show status returned by
 * _heapset
 */
   buffer[79] = '\0';  /* Mark the end of the string */
   printf("The buffer contains:\n%s\n", buffer);
   switch (heapstatus)
   {
       case _HEAPOK:       printf("Heap OK\n");
                           break;
       case _HEAPEMPTY:    printf("Heap not initialized\n");
                           break;
       case _HEAPBADBEGIN: printf("Heap header bad\n");
                           break;
       case _HEAPBADNODE:  printf("Heap has bad node/s\n");
                           break;
   }
}
```

__heapwalk

COMPATIBILITY	MSC 3	MSC 4	MSC 5	QC	TC	ANSI	UNIX V
			▲	▲			

PURPOSE Use the _heapwalk function to traverse the entries in the heap, the pool of free memory blocks from which functions such as *malloc* allocate memory. Each call to _heapwalk returns the address of the next block of memory in the heap, its size, and whether it is free or in use.

SYNTAX `int _heapwalk(struct _heapinfo *heap_entry);`

`struct _heapinfo *heap_entry;` Pointer to data structure in which information about the next heap entry is returned

EXAMPLE CALL `heapstatus = _heapwalk(&heapinfo);`

INCLUDES `#include <malloc.h>` For function declaration and definition of structure _heapinfo

DESCRIPTION The _heapwalk function returns information about the next entry in the heap. This information is returned in a data structure of type _heapinfo, which is defined in the header file *malloc.h* and whose structure is shown in the C declaration below:

__heapwalk

```
struct _heapinfo
{
    int far *_pentry;    /* Pointer to next heap entry        */
    size_t _size;        /* Size of this block of memory      */
    int     _useflag;    /* Flag to indicate if block is "in use" */
};
```

You must allocate a structure of type *_heapinfo* and provide its address to *_heapwalk* in the argument *heap_entry*. Set the *_pentry* field in the *_heapinfo* structure to NULL to begin traversing the heap from the first node onwards. For each call that returns the constant _HEAPOK, the *_pentry* field will have the address of the next heap entry, the *_size* field will have its size in bytes, and the *_useflag* will contain either of the constants _FREEEN-TRY or _USEDENTRY to indicate, respectively, whether the entry is unused or already allocated.

Just as *malloc*, *_heapset*, and *_heapchk* map to an appropriate version, depending on the memory model in use, *_heapwalk* is defined by the compiler as *_nheapwalk* in the small and medium memory models and as *_fheapwalk* in the compact, large, and huge models.

COMMON USES The *_heapwalk* function locates errors in the program that may be inadvertently overwriting dynamically allocated data in the heap. You first call *_heapset* to fill all the free memory in the heap with a known character and then determine overwritten locations by examining them. Use the *_heapwalk* function to step through the blocks in the heap to examine each one, if necessary.

RETURNS The return value from *_heapwalk* should be interpreted according to the constants shown in Table 5-4.

Table 5-4. *Return Values from* _heapwalk

Constants	Interpretation
_HEAPOK	The entries of the heap are all right up to the current one. In this case, the _heapinfo structure contains information about the next entry in the heap's linked list data.
_HEAPEMPTY	The heap is probably not initialized. This means no calls have been made to a memory allocation routine.
_HEAPBADPTR	The _pentry field in the _heapinfo data structure does not contain a valid pointer to an entry in the heap.
_HEAPBADBEGIN	The initial header information of the heap data structure could not be found.
_HEAPBADNODE	A node in the linked list data structure of the heap was found to be bad. This may indicate overwriting beyond the array limits in a dynamically allocated array.
_HEAPEND	The end of the heap was reached successfully.

Memory Allocation and Management

COMMENTS The *_heapwalk* function together with *_heapset* gives you the tools needed to pinpoint if a program failure is due to overwriting dynamically created data objects in the heap.

SEE ALSO _heapchk   To check the heap's linked list data structure for consistency

_heapwalk   To navigate through the heap's linked list data structure and check the size and status (free or used) of blocks

_nheapwalk   To inspect entries in the near heap (inside the default data segment)

_fheapwalk   To inspect entries in the far heap (outside the default data segment)

EXAMPLE Write a C routine that uses *_heapwalk* to traverse the entries of the heap and then prints a short report about the entries. Test the routine by calling it from a main program where a number of allocation and deallocation operations are performed. Notice that the heap is not initialized until the first call to a memory allocation function.

```
#include <stdio.h>
#include <malloc.h>
main()
{
    char *buffer;

    traverse_heap();              /* Uninitialized heap */
    buffer = (char *) malloc(80); /* Allocate a buffer*/
    traverse_heap();     /* Check heap entries now   */
    free(buffer);        /* Release the buffer       */
    traverse_heap();     /* Check heap entries again */
}

static traverse_heap()
{
    struct _heapinfo heapentry;
    int heapstatus;
/* Set _pentry field to NULL to begin at first entry */
    heapentry._pentry = NULL;
/* Now keep calling _heapwalk as long as return value
 * is _HEAPOK. Print information about entry from the
 * structure 'heapentry'
 */
    printf("-------- BEGIN HEAP TRAVERSAL ---------\n");
    while ( (heapstatus = _heapwalk(&heapentry)) ==
                _HEAPOK)
    {
        printf("Address: %p  Status: %6s  Size: %5u\n",
                heapentry._pentry, (heapentry._useflag ==
```

_heapwalk

```
                        _FREEENTRY ? "FREE" : "USED"),
                    heapentry._size);
        }
        switch (heapstatus)  /* Print last status */
        {
            case _HEAPOK:      printf("Heap OK\n");
                               break;
            case _HEAPEMPTY:   printf("Heap not initialized\n");
                               break;
            case _HEAPBADBEGIN: printf("Heap header bad\n");
                                break;
            case _HEAPBADNODE: printf("Heap has bad node/s\n");
                               break;
        }
        printf("----------- END HEAP TRAVERSAL --------\n");
}
```

hfree

COMPATIBILITY	MSC 3	MSC 4	MSC 5	QC	TC	ANSI	UNIX V
		▲	▲	▲			

PURPOSE Use the *hfree* function to release a block of memory previously allocated by *halloc*.

SYNTAX `void hfree(void huge *mem_address);`

`void huge *mem_address;`   Pointer to block of memory to be released

EXAMPLE CALL `hfree((void huge *)bigbuf);`

INCLUDES `#include <malloc.h>`   For function declaration

DESCRIPTION The *hfree* function deallocates a block of memory whose address is specified by the *huge* pointer *mem_address*. The memory is released by calling the MS-DOS memory deallocation function (number 49H). The pointer *mem_address* was earlier returned by a call to *halloc*.

COMMON USES The *hfree* function is used to free memory allocated by *halloc*, allowing your program to use memory for data objects that are no longer needed.

COMMENTS Use *hfree* only to free memory that was earlier allocated by *halloc*.

SEE ALSO `halloc`   To allocate and initialize huge arrays (>64 K)

EXAMPLE Use *halloc* to allocate room for a huge array of 65,000 characters. Then deallocate the array by calling *hfree* before exiting the program.

Memory Allocation and Management

```
#include <stdio.h>
#include <stdlib.h>
#include <malloc.h>
#define MAX_SIZE 65000L
main()
{
    char huge *bigbuf;
/* Allocate room for string and check for NULL */
    if( (bigbuf = (char huge *)halloc(MAX_SIZE,
                        sizeof(char))) == NULL)
    {
        printf("Allocation by halloc Failed.\n");
        exit(0);
    }
    printf("Array of 65,000 characters allocated.\n");
/* Free the array and exit */
    hfree((void huge *)bigbuf);
    printf("Huge array deallocated\n");
}
```

malloc

COMPATIBILITY	MSC 3	MSC 4	MSC 5	QC	TC	ANSI	UNIX V
	▲	▲	▲	▲	▲	▲	▲

PURPOSE   Use *malloc* to allocate memory for an array of a given number of bytes. Note that *malloc* can only allocate memory for an array whose size is less than 64 K. Use *halloc* for arrays larger than 64 K.

SYNTAX   `void *malloc(size_t num_bytes);`

`size_t num_bytes;`   Number of bytes needed

EXAMPLE CALL   `buffer = (char *)malloc(100*sizeof(char));`

INCLUDES   `#include <malloc.h>`   For function declaration and definition of data type *size_t*

`#include <stdlib.h>`   For ANSI compatibility

DESCRIPTION   The *malloc* function allocates the number of bytes requested in the argument *num_bytes* by calling internal Microsoft C heap management routines. The *malloc* function will work properly for all memory models except *huge*. Specifically, the compiler maps *malloc* to *_nmalloc* for small and medium (near data) models, and to *_fmalloc* for compact and large (far data) models. For the huge model, use *halloc*.

COMMON USES The *malloc* function creates room for arrays of data objects at run-time, allowing you to write programs without having to guess beforehand the amount of storage you will need at run-time.

RETURNS The *malloc* function returns a pointer that is the starting address of the memory allocated. The allocated memory is properly aligned (the address of the first byte meets the requirements for storing any type of C variable). If the memory allocation is unsuccessful because of insufficient space or bad values of the arguments, a NULL is returned.

COMMENTS The *malloc* function is the basic memory allocation function in the Microsoft C run-time library. Use the *calloc* function to call *malloc*.

Note that when using *malloc* to allocate storage for a specific data type, you should cast the returned *void* pointer to that type.

SEE ALSO calloc   To allocate and initialize an array

halloc   To allocate huge (greater than 64 K) arrays

realloc   To alter size of previously allocated block of memory

_nmalloc   Actual routine invoked in small and medium models

_fmalloc   Actual routine invoked in compact and large models

free   To release memory allocated earlier

EXAMPLE Use *malloc* to allocate room for an 80-character string. Prompt the user for a string and store it in the buffer you allocate.

```
#include <stdio.h>
#include <stdlib.h>
#include <malloc.h>
#define MAX_CHR 80
main()
{
    char *buffer;
/* Allocate room for string and check for NULL pointer*/
    if( (buffer = (char *)malloc(MAX_CHR)) == NULL)
    {
        printf("Allocation Failed.\n");
        exit(0);
    }
    printf("Buffer allocated. Enter string to store: ");
    gets(buffer);
    printf("\nYou entered: %s\n",buffer);
}
```

 Memory Allocation and Management

__memavl

COMPATIBILITY	MSC 3	MSC 4	MSC 5	QC	TC	ANSI	UNIX V
		▲	▲	▲			

PURPOSE Use the _memavl function to determine the number of bytes available in the default data segment beyond the space already being used by the program's data. For example, you can use _memavl in small and medium models to determine memory available for allocation before calling *calloc* or *malloc*.

SYNTAX `size_t _memavl(void);`

EXAMPLE CALL `available_memory = _memavl();`

INCLUDES `#include <malloc.h>`　　For function declaration and definition of data type *size_t*

DESCRIPTION The _memavl function returns the number of bytes available in the default data segment from which *malloc*, *calloc*, and *realloc* allocate memory in the small and medium models. In *all* memory models the function _nmalloc can be used to allocate memory in the default data segment. You can use _memavl in all memory models to make sure enough memory is available before calling the allocation routine. Note, however, that the size returned by _memavl is not necesarily contiguous bytes. There is no guarantee, therefore, that a call to _nmalloc to allocate the entire amount will succeed. To find the largest block of contiguous bytes, you can use _memmax.

RETURNS The return value from _memavl is an unsigned integer of type *size_t* containing the number of bytes available for allocation in the default data segment.

SEE ALSO `malloc, calloc, realloc`　　To allocate memory from the heap

`_nmalloc`　　Always allocates memory from the default data segment

`free`　　To release memory allocated earlier

EXAMPLE Call the _memavl function to determine the number of bytes available in the default data segment. Use *malloc* to allocate room for a buffer to hold 8,000 characters. Now call _memavl again to see how many bytes are available after allocating these 8,000 bytes. Compile and run the program in the small model, then in the large model, and note the difference. In the large model the amount of available memory remains unchanged because *malloc* allocates outside the default data segment.

```
#include <stdio.h>
#include <malloc.h>
main()
```

```
{
    size_t max_bytes;
    char *large_buffer;
/* Check how much room is available in the default data
 * segment
 */
    max_bytes = _memavl();
    printf("%u bytes available in the data segment\n",
            max_bytes);
/* Allocate 8000 bytes */
    large_buffer = (char *) malloc(8000);
/* Check available memory again */
    max_bytes = _memavl();
    printf("%u bytes available after allocating 8000 \
bytes\n", max_bytes);
}
```

__memmax

COMPATIBILITY	MSC 3	MSC 4	MSC 5	QC	TC	ANSI	UNIX V
		▲	▲	▲			

PURPOSE   Use the *__memmax* function to determine the maximum number of *contiguous* bytes that can be allocated from the default data segment. Use *__memmax* in the small or the medium models, for example, to find the largest chunk of memory that you can allocate by using *malloc*.

SYNTAX   `size_t _memmax(void);`

EXAMPLE CALL   `max_single_block_size = _memmax();`

INCLUDES   `#include <malloc.h>`   For function declaration and definition of data type *size_t*

DESCRIPTION   The *__memmax* function returns the size of the largest block of memory available in the default data segment. Use *__memavl* to determine the *total* amount of memory available, which together with *__memmax* suggests how many smaller sized blocks may be allocated.

COMMON USES   In the small and medium memory models *malloc* allocates memory from the default data segment while *__nmalloc* allocates space from this segment in all memory models. Before calling the allocation routine, it is useful to call *__memmax* to determine the largest chunk of memory that can be allocated. A call of the form *malloc(__memsize( ))* can also be used to allocate the largest available block.

   Memory Allocation and Management

RETURNS The return value from _memmax_ is the size of the largest block of contiguous memory available for allocation in the default data segment.

SEE ALSO _memavl   To determine the total number of bytes available for allocation in the default data segment

EXAMPLE Use _memmax_ with _nmalloc_ to allocate the largest chunk of contiguous memory from the default data segment.

```
#include <stdio.h>
#include <malloc.h>
main()
{
    char near *buffer;
    size_t max_bytes;
/* Find size of largest block */
    max_bytes = _memmax();
    printf("%u bytes in largest contiguous block\n",
        max_bytes);
    if( (buffer = (char near *) _nmalloc(max_bytes) )
        == NULL)
    {
        printf("Error allocating buffer\n");
        exit(0);
    }
    printf("%u contiguous bytes allocated \
successfully\n", max_bytes);
}
```

__msize

COMPATIBILITY	MSC 3	MSC 4	MSC 5	QC	TC	ANSI	UNIX V
		▲	▲	▲			

PURPOSE Use the _msize_ function to determine the size, in number of bytes, of a block of memory that has been allocated or manipulated by _malloc, calloc,_ or _realloc._

SYNTAX `size_t _msize(void *mem_address);`

`void *mem_address;`   Pointer to allocated block of memory whose size is to be determined

EXAMPLE CALL `blocksize = _msize(p_block);`

INCLUDES   `#include <malloc.h>`   For function declaration and definition of data type *size_t*

DESCRIPTION   The *_msize* function returns the size of an allocated block of memory in number of bytes. The address of the the block is provided, as a pointer to a *void* data type, in the argument *mem_address*. This pointer was returned by an earlier call to one of the memory allocation routines such as *malloc, calloc,* or *realloc.* In the small and medium memory models, *_msize* is mapped to *_nmsize* and in the compact and large models it maps to *_fmsize.*

COMMON USES   After a failed call to a routine such as *_expand, _msize* can be used to determine the actual size of the block.

RETURNS   The return value from *_msize* is the size of the block of memory in number of bytes. The return value is of type *size_t,* which is defined to be an unsigned integer in the include file *malloc.h.*

SEE ALSO   _nmsize   To determine size of a block of memory inside the default data segment

   _fmsize   To determine size of a block of memory located outside the default data segment

EXAMPLE   Allocate an 80-byte buffer using *malloc* and call the *_expand* function to enlarge the size to 65,000 bytes, so that the function fails and enlarges the block to the maximum possible value. Use *_msize* to check how much the buffer was enlarged.

```
#include <stdio.h>
#include <malloc.h>
main()
{
    size_t max_bytes = 65000;
    char *buffer;

    if( (buffer = (char *) malloc(80) ) == NULL)
    {
        printf("Error allocating buffer\n");
        exit(0);
    }
/* Now enlarge the buffer to maximum possible size */
    if( _expand((void *)buffer, max_bytes) == NULL)
    {
        printf("_expand failed. Buffer still usable\n");
    }
    max_bytes = _msize(buffer); /* Find size of block */
    printf("Buffer size was increased to: %u bytes\n",
        max_bytes);
}
```

Memory Allocation and Management

__nfree

COMPATIBILITY	MSC 3	MSC 4	MSC 5	QC	TC	ANSI	UNIX V
		▲	▲	▲			

PURPOSE Use _nfree to deallocate an allocated block of memory by calling _nmalloc.

SYNTAX `void _nfree(void near *mem_address);`

`void near *mem_address;`   Near pointer to block of memory being deallocated

EXAMPLE CALL `_nfree((void near *)near_buffer);`

INCLUDES `#include <malloc.h>`   For function declaration

DESCRIPTION The _nfree function deallocates a block of memory whose address, in the form of a *near* pointer to a *void* data type, is given in the argument *mem_address*. This is the pointer that was returned during the allocation of this block by _nmalloc.

COMMON USES The _nfree function deallocates memory allocated by _nmalloc.

COMMENTS Do not call _nfree unless the memory was allocated by an explicit call to _nmalloc because you were mixing memory models. An example of this is calling a data block with a *near* address while working in a large memory model.

SEE ALSO free   More portable way of allocating memory

         _nmalloc   To allocate memory in the default data segment

EXAMPLE Use _nmalloc to allocate room for an 80-character string. Prompt the user for a string and store it in the buffer you allocated. After displaying the string, deallocate the buffer by calling _nfree.

```
#include <stdio.h>
#include <stdlib.h>
#include <malloc.h>
#define MAX_CHR 80
main()
{
    unsigned char near *buffer;
/* Allocate room for string and check for NULL pointer*/
    if( (buffer = (char near *)_nmalloc(MAX_CHR))
        == NULL)
        {
            printf("Allocation Failed.\n");
```

```
            exit(0);
        }
        printf("Buffer allocated. Enter string to store: ");
        gets(buffer);
        printf("\nYou entered: %s\n",buffer);
/* Deallocate the buffer */
        _nfree((void near *)buffer);
        printf("Buffer deallocated.\n");
    }
```

__nheapchk

COMPATIBILITY	MSC 3	MSC 4	MSC 5	QC	TC	ANSI	UNIX V
			▲	▲			

PURPOSE Use _nheapchk to check the consistency of the heap in the default data segment.

SYNTAX `int _nheapchk(void);`

EXAMPLE CALL `heapstatus = _nheapchk();`

INCLUDES `#include <malloc.h>`   For function declaration

DESCRIPTION The _nheapchk function checks the heap, the linked list of memory blocks. (See the tutorial.) The check ensures that all entries in the heap data structure make sense. As an example, if an entry is the address of a free block of memory, the check determines whether it is within the limits of the pool of memory assigned to the heap.

RETURNS The return value from _nheapchk should be interpreted in the same manner as the value returned by _heapchk. See Table 5-3 for a list of defined constants for the meaning of the return value.

COMMENTS The _nheapchk function should be called to check the consistency of the near heap only when you are mixing memory models in your program. For example, you may be allocating some data objects to be addressed by near pointers in a large model program. In programs in which a single memory model is used throughout, the _heapchk function is a better choice because the compiler automatically uses the version appropriate for the memory model being used, making it easier to change memory models at a later date.

SEE ALSO _heapset   To fill all unallocated memory in the heap with a specified character

_heapwalk   To go through the heap's linked list data structure and check the size and status (free or used) of each block

Memory Allocation and Management

_heapchk	To check the heap in any memory model
_fheapchk	To check the far heap (outside the default data segment)

EXAMPLE Use _nmalloc and _nfree to allocate and deallocate a few blocks of memory. Then call _nheapchk to check the heap and display the information returned.

```
#include <stdio.h>
#include <malloc.h>
main()
{
    char near *buffer;
    int heapstatus;
/* Perform some allocations and deallocations */
    buffer = (char near *) _nmalloc(500);
    _nmalloc(800);
    _nfree((void near *)buffer);
/* Now get the status of the near heap by calling
 * _nheapchk
 */
    heapstatus = _nheapchk();
    switch (heapstatus)
    {
        case _HEAPOK:       printf("Heap OK\n");
                            break;
        case _HEAPEMPTY:    printf("Heap not initialized\n");
                            break;
        case _HEAPBADBEGIN: printf("Heap header bad\n");
                            break;
        case _HEAPBADNODE: printf("Heap has bad node/s\n");
                            break;
    }
}
```

__nheapset

COMPATIBILITY	MSC 3	MSC 4	MSC 5	QC	TC	ANSI	UNIX V
			▲	▲			

PURPOSE When mixing memory models, use _nheapset to fill the free memory locations in the near heap with a specified character value.

SYNTAX `int _nheapset(unsigned fill_char);`

`unsigned int fill_char;`   Character used to fill all unused memory location in the heap

EXAMPLE CALL   `heapstatus = _nheapset('N');`

INCLUDES   `#include <malloc.h>`   For function declaration

DESCRIPTION   The *_nheapset* function first checks the consistency of the near heap, the linked list of memory blocks located in the default data segment. (See the tutorial.) If the near heap is all right, *_nheapset* fills every unused memory location with the character specified in the argument *fill_char*.

RETURNS   The return value from *_nheapset* should be interpreted in the same manner as the value returned by *_heapchk*. See Table 5-3 for a list of defined constants to interpret this return value.

COMMENTS   Call *_nheapset* to fill unallocated memory blocks in the near heap only when you are mixing memory models in your program. For example, you may be allocating and manipulating data arrays with near addresses in a compact, large, or huge model. If your program uses a single memory model, the *_heapset* function is a better choice because the compiler automatically uses the version appropriate for the memory model being used, making it easier to change memory models at a later date.

SEE ALSO   `_heapset`   To fill all unallocated memory in the heap with a specified character

   `_heapwalk`   To navigate through the heap's linked list data structure and check the size and status (free or used) of blocks

   `_fheapset`   To fill unused locations in the far heap (outside the default data segment)

EXAMPLE   Use *_nheapset* to fill the free locations in the near heap with the letter N. Then allocate a small buffer by calling *_nmalloc* and print the buffer to show that the fill worked.

```
#include <stdio.h>
#include <malloc.h>
main()
{
    char near *buffer;
    int heapstatus;
/* Call _nmalloc once to initialize the heap */
    _nmalloc(1);
/* Fill all free memory with N */
    heapstatus = _nheapset('N');
/* Allocate a buffer   */
    buffer = (char near *) _nmalloc(80);
/* Display the buffer and also show status returned by
 * _nheapset
 */
    buffer[79] = '\0';  /* Mark the end of the string */
```

Memory Allocation and Management

```
        printf("The buffer contains:\n%s\n", buffer);
        switch (heapstatus)
        {
            case _HEAPOK:        printf("Heap OK\n");
                                 break;
            case _HEAPEMPTY:     printf("Heap not initialized\n");
                                 break;
            case _HEAPBADBEGIN:  printf("Heap header bad\n");
                                    break;
            case _HEAPBADNODE:   printf("Heap has bad node/s\n");
                                 break;
        }
    }
```

__nheapwalk

COMPATIBILITY	MSC 3	MSC 4	MSC 5	QC	TC	ANSI	UNIX V
			▲	▲			

PURPOSE Use the _nheapwalk function to obtain information about the entries in the near heap.

SYNTAX `int _nheapwalk(struct _heapinfo *heap_entry);`

`struct _heapinfo *heap_entry;`   Pointer to data structure in which information about the next heap entry is returned

EXAMPLE CALL `heapstatus = _nheapwalk(&heapinfo);`

INCLUDES `#include <malloc.h>`   For function declaration and definition of structure _heapinfo

DESCRIPTION The _nheapwalk function returns information about the next entry in the near heap in a data structure of type _heapinfo, which is defined in the header file *malloc.h* and whose structure is shown in the description of the function _heapwalk. You must allocate a structure of type _heapinfo and provide its address to _nheapwalk in the argument *heap_entry*. The _nheapwalk and *heapwalk* functions are used similarly. See the reference pages on _heapwalk for a detailed description of appropriate usage.

RETURNS The return value from _nheapwalk should be interpreted according to the constants shown in Table 5-4.

COMMENTS The _nheapwalk function should be called to examine blocks of memory in the near heap only when you are mixing memory models in your program.

For example, you may be allocating some data objects to be addressed by near pointers in a large model program. In programs in which a single memory model is used throughout, the *_heapwalk* function is a better choice because the compiler automatically uses the version appropriate for the memory model being used, making it easier to change memory models at a later date.

SEE ALSO

_heapchk   To check the heap's linked list data structure for consistency

_heapwalk   To navigate through the heap's linked list data structure and check the size and status (free or used) of memory blocks

_fnheapwalk   To inspect entries in the far heap (outside the default data segment)

EXAMPLE   Write a C program that uses *_nmalloc* to allocate one or two data arrays in the near heap then calls *_nheapwalk* to traverse the entries of the heap and prints a short report about the entries.

```c
#include <stdio.h>
#include <malloc.h>
main()
{
    struct _heapinfo heapentry;
    char near *buffer;
/* Allocate a buffer */
    buffer = (char near *) _nmalloc(80);
    _nmalloc(200);               /* Another one ...    */
    _nfree(buffer);              /* Free the first one */
/* Now check the heap entries */
/* Set _pentry field to NULL to begin at first entry */
    heapentry._pentry = NULL;
/* Now keep calling _nheapwalk as long as return value
 * is _HEAPOK. Print information about entry from the
 * structure 'heapentry'
 */
    printf("-------- BEGIN HEAP TRAVERSAL ---------\n");
    while ( _nheapwalk(&heapentry) == _HEAPOK)
    {
        printf("Address: %p  Status: %6s Size: %5u\n",
            heapentry._pentry, (heapentry._useflag ==
            _FREEENTRY ? "FREE" : "USED"),
            heapentry._size);
    }
    printf("----------- END HEAP TRAVERSAL --------\n");
}
```

Memory Allocation and Management

__nmalloc

COMPATIBILITY	MSC 3	MSC 4	MSC 5	QC	TC	ANSI	UNIX V
		▲	▲	▲			

PURPOSE   Use _nmalloc to allocate memory in programs of small and medium memory models where all data addresses are *near* pointers. The _nmalloc function allocates memory in the single default data segment allowed in these models.

SYNTAX   `void near *_nmalloc(size_t num_bytes);`

`size_t   num_bytes;`   Number of bytes needed

EXAMPLE CALL   `near_int_buffer = (int near *)_nmalloc(100*sizeof(int));`

INCLUDES   `#include <malloc.h>`   For function declaration

`#include <stdlib.h>`   For definition of data type *size_t*

DESCRIPTION   The _nmalloc function allocates the number of bytes requested in the argument *num_bytes* from the default data segment and returns a *near* pointer to a *void* data type.

COMMON USES   The _nmalloc function allocates memory in small and medium memory model C programs. The *malloc* function actually maps to _nmalloc in these memory models.

RETURNS   The return value from _nmalloc is a *near* pointer of a *void* data type. If the memory allocation fails because of insufficient space or bad values of the arguments, a NULL is returned.

COMMENTS   Normally you should not call _nmalloc directly because calls to *malloc* are mapped to _nmalloc in models with near data addresses. Because *malloc* is portable it is the more useful. The explicit use of _nmalloc is necessary only when mixing memory models.

SEE ALSO   `malloc`   More portable way of allocating memory

`calloc`   To allocate and initialize an array

`halloc`   To allocate huge (greater than 64 K) arrays

`_fmalloc`   To allocate memory in compact and large models

`_nfree`   To free memory allocated by _nmalloc

__nmalloc

EXAMPLE Use _nmalloc to allocate room for an 80-character string. Prompt the user for a string and store it in the buffer you allocate.

```
#include <stdio.h>
#include <stdlib.h>
#include <malloc.h>
#define MAX_CHR 80
main()
{
    unsigned char near *buffer;
/* Allocate room for string and check for NULL */
    if( (buffer = (char near *)_nmalloc(MAX_CHR))
        == NULL)
    {
        printf("Allocation Failed.\n");
        exit(0);
    }
    printf("Buffer allocated. Enter string to store: ");
    gets(buffer);
    printf("\nYou entered: %s\n",buffer);
}
```

__nmsize

COMPATIBILITY	MSC 3	MSC 4	MSC 5	QC	TC	ANSI	UNIX V
		▲	▲	▲			

PURPOSE Use the _nmsize function to determine the size, in number of bytes, of a block of memory allocated in the default data segment by the routine _nmalloc.

SYNTAX `size_t _nmsize(void near *mem_address);`

`void near *mem_address;`   Pointer to allocated block of memory whose size is to be determined

EXAMPLE CALL `bufsize = _nmsize(near_buffer);`

INCLUDES `#include <malloc.h>`   For function declaration and definition of data type *size_t*

DESCRIPTION The _nmsize function returns the size of a block of memory allocated by the function _nmalloc. The pointer returned during the earlier call to _nmalloc, a *near* pointer to a *void* data type, is given as the input argument *mem_address*.

RETURNS The return value from _nmsize is the size of the block of memory in number of bytes in a data type *size_t*, which is defined to be an unsigned integer in the include file *malloc.b*.

Memory Allocation and Management

SEE ALSO   _msize   Similar function, but not specific to any memory model

_fmsize   To determine size of a block of memory located outside the default data segment

EXAMPLE   Allocate an 80-byte buffer using _*nmalloc* and call the _*nmsize* to check the size of the allocated buffer.

```
#include <stdio.h>
#include <malloc.h>
main()
{
    size_t max_bytes;
    char near *buffer;
    if( (buffer = (char near *) _nmalloc(80) ) == NULL)
    {
        printf("Error allocating buffer\n");
        exit(0);
    }
/* Find size of block now */
    max_bytes = _nmsize(buffer);
    printf("Buffer size is: %u bytes\n", max_bytes);
}
```

realloc

COMPATIBILITY	MSC 3	MSC 4	MSC 5	QC	TC	ANSI	UNIX V
	▲	▲	▲	▲	▲	▲	▲

PURPOSE   Use *realloc* to adjust the size of a block of memory allocated by *malloc* or *calloc*.

SYNTAX   `void *realloc(void *mem_address, size_t newsize);`

`void *mem_address;`   Pointer to the block of memory whose size is to be altered

`size_t newsize;`   New size of the block in bytes

EXAMPLE CALL   `new_buffer = realloc(old_buffer, old_size+100);`

INCLUDES   `#include <malloc.h>`   For function declaration

`#include <stdlib.h>`   For ANSI compatibility and definition of data type *size_t*

realloc

DESCRIPTION The *realloc* function alters the size of an allocated block of memory to a size given in the argument *newsize*. The address of the block is specified by the pointer to a *void* type, *mem_address*. This pointer must be either NULL or a value returned by an earlier call to *malloc, calloc,* or *realloc*. If the argument *mem_address* is a NULL, then *realloc* behaves like *malloc* and allocates a new block of memory of size *newsize*. The memory block of altered size may not be located at the same address, but the contents of the new block (up to its old size) is guaranteed to be unchanged.

COMMON USES Normally the *realloc* function is used to enlarge a block of memory as the need arises to store more data elements, enabling you to write programs that work with arrays that enlarge or shrink as data is added or removed.

RETURNS The *realloc* function returns the address of the block of memory cast as a pointer to a *void* data type. The resized block of memory is guaranteed to meet the alignment requirements for any type of data storage. The alignment refers to a requirement often imposed by hardware that the address of the first byte have certain properties, for example, that it be even or a multiple of 16. If the new size is zero or if there is no more room to enlarge the block of memory, *realloc* frees the block and returns a NULL.

SEE ALSO calloc   To allocate and initialize an array

  malloc   To allocate a block of memory

  free   To release memory allocated earlier

EXAMPLE Use *malloc* to allocate room for a string of 10 characters. Read in a short string and store it in the allocated buffer. Then enlarge the buffer to hold an 80-character string. Show the user the contents again to verify that the original string is still there.

```
#include <stdio.h>
#include <stdlib.h>
#include <malloc.h>

main()
{
    unsigned char *buffer;
/* Allocate room for string and check for NULL */
    if( (buffer = (char *)malloc(10)) == NULL )
    {
            printf("Allocation Failed.\n");
            exit(0);
    }
    printf("Buffer allocated. Enter string to store: ");
    gets(buffer);
    printf("\nYou entered: %s\n",buffer);
```

 Memory Allocation and Management

```
/* Now enlarge size of buffer and redisplay string */
    if( (buffer = (char *)realloc((void *)buffer, 80))
        == NULL )
    {
        printf("Reallocation Failed.\n");
        exit(0);
    }
    printf("Buffer still contains: %s\n",buffer);
}
```

sbrk

COMPATIBILITY	MSC 3	MSC 4	MSC 5	QC	TC	ANSI	UNIX V
	▲	▲	▲	▲	▲		▲

PURPOSE Use *sbrk* in small and medium memory models to alter the break value of a process. The break value is the address of the first available byte in the default data segment beyond the memory already being used by the data in the process.

SYNTAX `void *sbrk(int change);`

`int change;` Number of bytes by which the break value is to be changed

EXAMPLE CALL `buffer = (char *) sbrk(80);`

INCLUDES `#include <malloc.h>` For function declaration

DESCRIPTION The *sbrk* function adds the number of bytes specified in the argument *change* to the break value of the process from which *sbrk* is called. The break value indicates the number of bytes that the process is currently using in the default data segment. In fact, it is the offset at which the heap (the chunk of memory from which new blocks may be allocated) begins. Since *sbrk* adds the argument *change* to the current break value, specifying a negative value in *change* reduces the memory being used by the process.

Since all address specifications in this function work with the default data segment, only models using near data addresses—small and medium—can use the *sbrk* function.

COMMON USES The *sbrk* function is used in small and medium models as an alternate memory allocation routine.

RETURNS The return value from *sbrk* is a pointer to a type *void*, representing the address of the previous break value. If the break value could not be altered because of insufficient space or if the memory model is compact, large, or huge, a character pointer to a value of −1 is returned. See the example below for a sample error check.

COMMENTS The *sbrk* function provides compatibility with UNIX System V library. It is better to use *malloc* for memory allocation because it is portable, it conforms to the proposed ANSI standard, and it works in all memory models except the huge model. Use *halloc* in the huge model.

SEE ALSO `malloc`   Most general-purpose memory allocation routine

          `halloc`   To allocate huge (greater than 64 K) arrays

          `free`   To release memory allocated earlier

EXAMPLE Use *sbrk* to allocate room for a buffer to hold 80 characters at the end of the default data segment in a small model program. Prompt the user for a string and store it in the buffer you allocated. Call *sbrk* with a negative argument to deallocate this memory.

```
#include <stdio.h>
#include <malloc.h>
unsigned char *buffer;
main()
{
/* Allocate a buffer by adding 80 to the break value */
    buffer = (char *) sbrk(80);
    if (buffer == -1)
    {
            printf("sbrk failed.\n");
            exit(0);
    }
    printf("Buffer allocated. Enter string to store: ");
    gets(buffer);
    printf("\nYou entered: %s\n",buffer);
    sbrk(-80);   /* Deallocate the buffer */
    printf("Buffer deallocated\n");
}
```

MEMO RY

Memory Allocation and Management

stackavail

COMPATIBILITY	MSC 3	MSC 4	MSC 5	QC	TC	ANSI	UNIX V
		▲	▲	▲			

PURPOSE Use *stackavail* before calling *alloca* to determine the approximate size in bytes of the space available on the stack for allocation.

SYNTAX `size_t stackavail(void);`

EXAMPLE CALL `room_in_stack = stackavail();`

INCLUDES `#include <malloc.h>`   For function declaration and definition of data type *size_t*

DESCRIPTION The *stackavail* function returns the number of bytes available on the program's stack for allocation by the function *alloca*. This space can be used for storing temporary arrays or other data.

RETURNS The return value from *stackavail* is the approximate number of bytes available on the stack. The return value is of type *size_t*, which is defined in *malloc.h* as the type *unsigned int*.

COMMENTS Since function calls use the stack to hold arguments, it is important to leave some space on the stack rather than using all the space indicated by *stackavail*.

SEE ALSO
`alloca`   To allocate space on the stack

`malloc`   To allocate memory from the heap

`free`   To release memory allocated earlier

EXAMPLE Call the *stackavail* function to determine the number of bytes available on the stack. Use *alloca* to allocate room for a buffer to hold 80 characters on the program's stack. Call *stackavail* again to see how many bytes are available after allocating these 80 bytes. Don't be surprised if the numbers do not quite add up; each allocated chunk may be required to start at a specific address to meet the requirement that the space be suitable for storing any type of data.

```
#include <stdio.h>
#include <malloc.h>
main()
{
    size_t max_bytes;
    char *buffer;
/* Check how much room is available on the stack */
    max_bytes = stackavail();
```

```
    printf("%u bytes available on the stack\n",
           max_bytes);
/* Get 80 bytes from stack */
    buffer = (char *) alloca(80);
    max_bytes = stackavail();
    printf("%u bytes available after allocating 80 \
bytes\n", max_bytes);
}
```

Memory Allocation and Management

Chapter **6 Buffer Manipulation**

Introduction

The buffer manipulation routines manipulate bytes in memory. They allow you to copy data from one area of memory to another, initialize a block of memory, search for the occurrence of a specific character (actually, this can be any value that fits into a byte), and compare the contents of two buffers. These routines are helpful, for example, when you are directly copying a screenful of text (or, image) from a buffer to the video memory. Another interesting example of using the buffer manipulation routines is in a file comparison utility. Provided you have enough memory, you could copy two files into memory and use a routine *memcmp* to see if the files match.

Concepts: Buffers, Pointers, and Byte Ordering

To use the buffer manipulation routines effectively, you need to be familiar with the concept of a buffer and its address. The routines are similar to the string manipulation routines we discuss in Chapter 10.

BUFFERS A buffer is a contiguous set of bytes in the computer's memory. The contents of the buffer can be ASCII characters, which most of the routines expect to operate on, or numerical (binary) values. As shown in Figure 6-1, the buffer is accessed by a pointer to the first byte. The figure shows Buffer 2 with the string *Hello*. Strings in C are similar to buffers except they always end with a null character (\0—a byte containing zero) while buffer manipulation routines require an argument to specify the number of bytes to be manipulated. Many buffer routines have corresponding string versions. Although the buffer manipulation routines can handle strings as well, there are many functions that deal specifically with strings and these are usually easier to use.

167

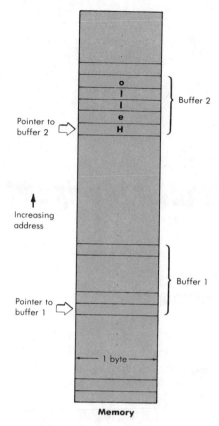

Figure 6-1. *Buffers in memory*

**BUFFER
POINTERS:
SEGMENTS AND
OFFSETS**

The pointer to the buffer is an address that consists of two parts, segment and offset, each 16 bits long, as we explained in the tutorial in Chapter 5. The 20-bit physical address used by the 8086 microprocessor is constructed by shifting the segment address 4 bits to the left and adding the offset to the result. The buffer address is specified as the name of an array or as a pointer variable. The segment and offset addresses are implicit in the memory model of the program. For example, in the small and medium memory models all data is assumed to reside within a single 64-K segment of memory whose address is specified in the DS segment register (see Chapter 2). In this case, the pointer to a buffer is the 16-bit offset of the first byte of the buffer within that segment (which can be 64 K at most). Thus in the small and the medium models the buffers being manipulated, like all other data items, are confined to a single segment.

In the compact, large, and huge memory models, all pointers have full segment and offset addresses. In these models, the buffers can be anywhere in memory. The size of a single buffer in the compact and large models is still limited to 64 K; in huge models, the size of a buffer is limited only by available memory. The buffer manipulation routines *memccpy, memchr, memcmp, memcpy, memicmp, memmove,* and *memset* accept huge pointers as arguments in the compact, large, and huge memory models.

BYTE ORDERING One special buffer manipulation routine, *swab,* provides a special service: it swaps adjacent pairs of bytes in a buffer. This routine takes care of the mismatch among different computer systems in "byte ordering," which refers to how the bytes of a 2- or 4-byte integer are arranged in memory. Consider, as an example, a short integer variable *shortvar* that occupies 2 bytes in memory. Suppose, we store the hexadecimal value 0x0201 into this variable. What will the byte at the address of *shortvar* contain? What about the byte at the next higher address? In the 8086 family, as illustrated in Figure 6-2, the least significant byte (in this case, 01) is at the address of *shortvar* while the most significant byte is at the next higher address. And if we load the value 0x04030201 into a long integer variable *longvar,* the ordering in the 8086 family would again start with the least significant byte at the lowest address with the bytes of ever higher significance placed at successive higher addresses (Figure 6-2). So the order of bytes in short and long integers is the same in the 8086 family of computers. This ordering scheme is sometimes called "little-endian" because the least significant byte is at the lowest ad-

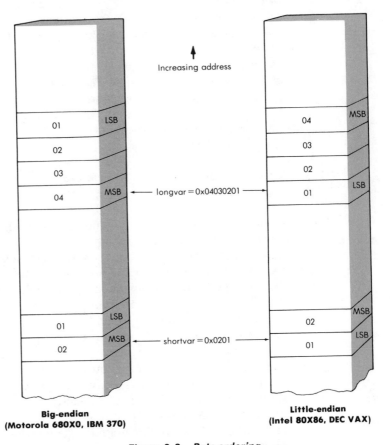

Figure 6-2. *Byte ordering*

dress. Exactly the reverse order of placing the bytes is used in many other microprocessors—most notably the 680×0 family and the IBM 370. These machines are called "big-endian" systems because the most significant byte is at the lowest address.

Normally you need not worry about the exact ordering of bytes. But today many different computer systems are often connected together in networks. In such an environment, you do have to worry about the byte ordering if you transfer binary data between a little-endian system (IBM PC, for instance) and a big-endian one (Macintosh, for instance). And, back where we started, the Microsoft C library includes the *swab* routine which can swap adjacent bytes and you can use it to convert short integers from one form of ordering to another.

Notes on Using the Buffer Routines

The buffer manipulation routines (see Table 6-1) are a more general form of the string manipulation routines which operate on C strings. The operation of a buffer routine is clarified by comparing it with its string counterpart. The difference between them is that the buffer manipulation routines always need a byte count whereas the string routines determine the end of a string by looking for the null character. For example, *memchr* works like *strchr*, *memcmp* like *strcmp*, *memcpy* and *memmove* like *strcpy*, *memicmp* like *stricmp*, and *memset* like *strset*. The *memccpy* function works like *memcpy* except that it takes an additional argument: a character that it uses as a marker. It copies the source buffer to the destination until either a specified number of bytes has been used or until *memccpy* encounters that character in the source buffer. So the call

```
char title[81], this_book[] = "Microsoft C Bible";
memccpy(title, this_book, '\0', 81);
```

copies 81 characters or up to (and including) the null character, from *this _book* into *title*. In this case, since the string *this_book* has a null character before the eighty first position, the entire string is copied to *title*.

The *movedata* is a special-purpose routine to move data from two buffers anywhere in memory. In the small and medium memory models, the buffers are constrained to be in the same segment because all addresses are offsets from the segment address specified in the DS register. In this case, you cannot use the buffer copy routines, such as *memcpy*, to copy data from a buffer in your program to the video memory (treated as a buffer at a specified address) because the video memory is outside your program's data segment. The *movedata* routine lets you specify the segment and offset addresses of the source and destination buffers explicitly. Use the function *segread* or the macros *FP_SEG* and *FP_OFF* to get the necessary values for your buffers. For example, in the color graphics adapter and the Enhanced Graphics Adapter in text mode, the video memory begins at the address B800:0000.

Table 6-1. *Buffer Manipulation Routines*

Routine	Description
memccpy	Copies bytes from one buffer to another until a specific character is encountered or until a specified number of bytes have been copied.
memchr	Searches for a specific character in a given number of bytes of the buffer.
memcmp	Compares a specified number of bytes of two buffers.
memcpy	Copies a specified number of bytes from one buffer to another (*not for overlapping source and destination*).
memicmp	Compares a specified number of bytes of two buffers without regard to the case of the letters.
memmove	Copies a specified number of bytes from one buffer to another (*handles overlapping source and destination*).
memset	Sets specified number of bytes of a buffer to a given value.
movedata	Copies a specified number of bytes from one buffer to another in possibly different segment.
swab	Takes an array of bytes and swaps contents of each pair of adjacent bytes.

You can view this as 25 rows by 80 columns of 2-byte values, laid out by row starting at the address B800:0000. Each 2-byte value corresponding to a screen position has 1 byte (the high-order byte) with the attribute (such as normal, reverse video, blinking) and the other byte with the actual character. If we have another buffer in memory with the same organization, we can prepare a screenful of text in this buffer and display it by copying the buffer to the video memory. Here is an example:

```
    void far *address;
    short dispbuf[25][80]; /* Display buffer */
/* Set all locations to zero */
    memset(dispbuf, '\0', sizeof(dispbuf));
/* Get segment, offset of dispbuf */
    address = (void far *)dispbuf;
    bufseg = FP_SEG(address);
    bufoff = FP_OFF(address);
/* Copy buffer into video memory -- clears screen */
    movedata( bufseg, bufoff, 0xb800, 0x0000,
              sizeof(dispbuf));
```

We set up a buffer, *dispbuf*, which is set to all zeroes by calling *memset*. The segment and offset of the buffer are obtained using FP_SEG and FP_OFF, respectively. We had to copy the address of *dispbuf* into a far pointer variable *address* because the FP_SEG and FP_OFF macros work properly with far addresses only. In the last statement, we call *movedata* to copy *dispbuf* to the video memory. The result is a cleared screen.

Table 6-2 summarizes the buffer manipulation routines by task. As you can see, the routines are primarily intended for copying, comparing, and initializing regions of memory.

Table 6-2. *Buffer Manipulation Routines by Task*

Task	Routines
Copies one buffer into another.	memccpy, memcpy, memmove, movedata
Compares two buffers.	memcmp, memicmp
Initializes all bytes of a buffer.	memset
Locates a specific character in buffer.	memchr
Swaps the contents of the high-order byte with that of the low-order one in a 2-byte word.	swab

Cautions

There are a few pitfalls you must be wary of when using the buffer manipulation routines.

▶ In Microsoft C 4.0, *memcpy* properly handled copying between overlapping source and destination buffers. This is not true under Microsoft C 5.0 or 5.1 in which only *memmove* is guaranteed to handle overlapping buffers. If you have programs that were developed under version 4.0, you should check the usage of *memcpy* carefully, and, if necessary, replace instances of *memcpy* with *memmove*.

▶ In the small and the medium memory models, the source and destination buffers are both in the same segment (because addresses are offsets from the segment address in the DS register). If you have to copy bytes between buffers in different segments, use *movedata* because it accepts explicit segment:offset addresses of the buffers being manipulated.

memccpy

COMPATIBILITY	MSC 3	MSC 4	MSC 5	QC	TC	ANSI	UNIX V
	▲	▲	▲	▲	▲		▲

PURPOSE   Use *memccpy* to copy bytes from one memory buffer to another. Copying continues until *memccpy* encounters a specified character or until a specified number of bytes have been copied, whichever happens first.

SYNTAX   `void *memccpy(void *dest, void *source, int c, unsigned count);`

`void *dest;`   Pointer to buffer to which data will be copied

`void *source;`   Pointer to buffer from which data will be copied

`int c`   Last character to be copied

`unsigned count;`   Maximum number of bytes to be copied

EXAMPLE CALL   `memccpy(dest_buf, inbuf, '\0', 81);`

INCLUDES   `#include <memory.h>`   For function declaration

or

`#include <string.h>`

DESCRIPTION   The *memccpy* function copies bytes from the buffer at the *source* address to another buffer at *dest*. The copying starts at the first byte of the source and continues until one of two events occur: *memccpy* encounters a byte containing the character *c* in the source buffer or the total number of bytes copied from the source to *dest* equal the count specified in the argument *count*. When *memccpy* stops because of the first event, it copies the character *c* before returning.

Note that you are responsible for allocating enough space for the destination buffer. If you copy more bytes than the size allocated, *memccpy* may destroy other data and cause the program to fail in mysterious ways.

COMMON USES   The *memccpy* function and its counterparts *memcpy*, *memmove*, and *movedata*, are efficient tools for copying large blocks of data from one array to another.

RETURNS   If *memccpy* stops after encountering the character *c* in *source*, it returns a pointer to the character following *c* in the *source* buffer. Otherwise, *memccpy* returns a NULL.

COMMENTS   Be sure that there is enough room in the destination buffer before calling any string or memory copy functions. This is a major source of error in C programs.

SEE ALSO `memcpy, memmove`   To copy one buffer to another

`movedata`   To copy buffers even if the source and destination are in different segments

EXAMPLE Use *memccpy* to copy a string typed in by the user from an input buffer to an internal buffer. Copy until the null character (\0) is encountered or until 81 bytes are copied.

```
#include <stdio.h>
#include <memory.h>
static char dest[81];   /* Destination buffer */
main()
{
    char inbuf[81];
    printf("Enter a string: ");
    gets(inbuf);
    memccpy(dest, inbuf, '\0', 81);
    printf("Destination buffer has: %s\n", dest);
}
```

memchr

COMPATIBILITY	MSC 3	MSC 4	MSC 5	QC	TC	ANSI	UNIX V
	▲	▲	▲	▲	▲	▲	▲

PURPOSE Use the *memchr* function to search a memory buffer for a specific character.

SYNTAX `void *memchr(const void *buffer, int c, size_t count);`

`const void *buffer;`   Pointer to buffer in which search takes place

`int c;`   Character to look for

`size_t count;`   Maximum number of bytes to be examined

EXAMPLE CALL
```
/* Look for the first occurrence of 'I' in a 100 byte buffer */
    first_i = memchr(start_address, 'I', 100);
```

INCLUDES `#include <memory.h>`   For function declaration and definition of *size_t*

or

`#include <string.h>`

DESCRIPTION The *memchr* function looks through the first *count* bytes in the buffer at the address buffer and stops when it finds the character *c*. The search terminates if *memchr* does not find *c* after examining all the *count* bytes.

 Buffer Manipulation

RETURNS   If *memchr* finds the character *c*, it returns a pointer to it. Otherwise, *memchr* returns a NULL.

SEE ALSO   `memcmp, memicmp`   To compare characters in two buffers

EXAMPLE   The listing of the ROM BIOS in the IBM PC Technical Reference manual shows that IBM's copyright notice appears at offset E000h in the BIOS segment F000h. Use *memchr* in a large memory model program to look for the I in IBM's copyright notice. If you do not have an IBM, substitute an appropriate character and address. On successful return, copy the next eight characters into a local buffer and print them out.

```
/* Use the the large memory model (-AL flag)       */
#include <stdio.h>
#include <memory.h>
/* Copyright notice begins at segment F000 and offset
 * E000
 */
#define  COPYRIGHT_NOTICE  0xf000e000L
static char dest[81];             /* Destination buffer */
main()
{
    void *copr_address, *first_i;
    copr_address = COPYRIGHT_NOTICE;
/* Look for the 'I' of IBM in the copyright notice   */
    if((first_i = memchr(copr_address, 'I', 24))
        == NULL)
    {
        printf("Search failed!\n");
    }
    else
    {
        printf("Found an 'I'at %p\n", first_i);
/* Copy next 8 characters into buffer 'dest' for
 * printing
 */
        memcpy(dest, first_i, 8);
        dest[8] = '\0';
        printf("The next 8 characters are: %s\n", dest);
    }
}
```

memchr

memcmp

COMPATIBILITY	MSC 3	MSC 4	MSC 5	QC	TC	ANSI	UNIX V
	▲	▲	▲	▲	▲	▲	▲

PURPOSE Use *memcmp* to compare a number of bytes from one buffer with those in another.

SYNTAX
```
int memcmp(const void *buffer1, const void *buffer2,
           size_t count);
```

const void *buffer1;   Pointer to first buffer

const void *buffer2;   Pointer to second buffer

size_t count;   Number of bytes to be compared

EXAMPLE CALL
```
if (memcmp(buffer1, buffer2, sizeof(buffer1)) == 0)
              printf("The buffers are identical\n");
```

INCLUDES
```
#include <memory.h>
```
For function declaration and definition of *size_t*

```
#include <string.h>
```

DESCRIPTION The *memcmp* function compares the first *count* bytes of *buffer1* and *buffer2* and returns an integer value indicating the order in which these two sets of characters would have appeared in a dictionary.

COMMON USES Because the other string-comparison routine, *strcmp*, can be used only with null-terminated strings, the *memcmp* function is preferable for comparing portions of two strings.

RETURNS The integer values returned by *memcmp* have the following meanings:

Value	Interpretation
Less than 0	The first *count* characters in *buffer1* are less than those of *buffer2*, meaning *buffer1* would have appeared before *buffer2* if they were in a dictionary.
Equal to 0	The two buffers are equal up to the first *count* characters.
Greater than 0	*buffer1* is greater than *buffer2*.

COMMENTS The "intrinsic" form of the *memcmp* function does not support huge arrays in compact or large model programs. You have to use the huge memory model (with compiler option /AH) to get this support with the intrinsic version of *memcmp*.

 Buffer Manipulation

SEE ALSO memicmp   To compare one buffer to another without regard to case of the characters

EXAMPLE Use *memcmp* to compare two buffers. Let one be in uppercase and the other in lowercase. Notice that unlike *memicmp*, *memcmp* considers *buffer1* greater than *buffer2*.

```
#include <stdio.h>
#include <memory.h>
static char buffer1[81] = "Buffer 1",
            buffer2[81] = "BUFFER 1";
main()
{
    int result;
    printf("First buffer = %s\nSecond buffer = %s\n",
            buffer1, buffer2);
    result = memcmp(buffer1, buffer2, sizeof(buffer1));
    if(result == 0) printf("The buffers are equal.\n");
    if(result < 0) printf("%s less than %s\n", buffer1,
                            buffer2);
    if(result > 0) printf("%s greater than %s\n",
                            buffer1, buffer2);
}
```

memcpy

COMPATIBILITY	MSC 3	MSC 4	MSC 5	QC	TC	ANSI	UNIX V
	▲	▲	▲	▲	▲	▲	▲

PURPOSE Use *memcpy* to copy bytes from one memory buffer to another.

SYNTAX `void *memcpy(void *dest, const void *source, size_t count);`

`void *dest;`   Pointer to buffer to which data will be copied

`const void *source;`   Pointer to buffer from which data will be copied

`size_t count;`   Maximum number of bytes to be copied

EXAMPLE CALL `memcpy(dest, src, 80); /* Copy 80 bytes from dest to src */`

INCLUDES `#include <memory.h>`   For function declaration and definition of *size_t*

or

`#include <string.h>`

memcpy

DESCRIPTION The *memcpy* function copies *count* bytes from the buffer at address *source* to another buffer at *dest*. This function can be used to copy a screen image from an offscreen buffer to the video memory. (This is true only in large data models; use *movedata* in small and medium models.)

RETURNS The *memcpy* function returns a pointer to the destination buffer *dest*.

COMMENTS In Microsoft C 5.0 and 5.1, if some parts of the source and destination buffers overlap, *memcpy* does not ensure that the bytes in *source* are copied before being overwritten. This used to work correctly in version 4.0. In versions 5.0 and 5.1, the *memmove* function still handles copying between overlapping buffers properly so you should use *memmove* when you copy to and from overlapping buffers.

The intrinsic version of *memcpy* cannot handle huge arrays in compact or large memory model programs.

SEE ALSO memccpy, memmove   To copy one buffer to another

movedata   To copy buffers even if the source and destination are in different segments

EXAMPLE Use *memcpy* to copy 80 bytes from one buffer to another. Print both buffers before and after the move to verify the results.

```
#include <stdio.h>
#include <memory.h>
static char src[80]="This is the SOURCE buffer\n";
static char dest[80]="Destination\n";
main()
{
    printf("Before memcpy: Source = %s Destination \
= %s", src, dest);
/* Copy from source to destination */
    memcpy(dest, src, 80);
    printf("After  memcpy: Source = %s Destination \
= %s", src, dest);
}
```

memicmp

COMPATIBILITY	MSC 3	MSC 4	MSC 5	QC	TC	ANSI	UNIX V
	▲	▲	▲	▲	▲		▲

PURPOSE Use *memicmp* to compare a number of bytes from one buffer with those in another without regard to the case of the letters in the two buffers.

SYNTAX int memicmp(void *buffer1, void *buffer2, unsigned count);

 Buffer Manipulation

```
void *buffer1;        Pointer to first buffer

void *buffer2;        Pointer to second buffer

unsigned count;       Number of bytes to be compared
```

EXAMPLE CALL
```
if(memicmp(buffer1, buffer2, 10) == 0)
     puts("The buffers are equal up to the first 10 bytes\n");
```

INCLUDES
```
#include <memory.h>       For function declaration
```

or

```
#include <string.h>
```

DESCRIPTION The *memicmp* function converts the first *count* characters in *buffer1* and *buffer2* into lowercase letters. Then it compares the first *count* bytes of the two buffers and returns an integer value indicating the order in which these two sets of characters would have appeared in a dictionary.

RETURNS The integer values returned by *memicmp* have the following meanings:

Value	Interpretation
Less than 0	The first *count* characters in *buffer* are less than those of *buffer2*, meaning *buffer* would have appeared before *buffer2* if they were in a dictionary.
Equal to 0	The two buffers are equal up to the first *count* characters.
Greater than 0	*buffer1* is greater than *buffer2*.

SEE ALSO memcmp   To compare one buffer to another (the case of letters matters)

EXAMPLE Use *memicmp* to compare two buffers. Let one be in uppercase and the other in lowercase. Note that unlike *memcmp*, *memicmp* considers the buffers equal regardless of the case of the letters.

```
#include <stdio.h>
#include <memory.h>
static char buffer1[81] = "Buffer 1",
            buffer2[81] = "BUFFER 1";
main()
{
    int result;
    printf("First buffer = %s\nSecond buffer = %s\n",
            buffer1, buffer2);
    result = memicmp(buffer1, buffer2, sizeof(buffer1));
```

memicmp

```
        if(result == 0) printf("The buffers are equal.\n");
        if(result < 0) printf("%s less than %s\n", buffer1,
                                buffer2);
        if(result > 0) printf("%s greater than %s\n",
                                buffer1, buffer2);
    }
```

memmove

COMPATIBILITY	MSC 3	MSC 4	MSC 5	QC	TC	ANSI	UNIX V
	▲	▲	▲	▲	▲	▲	

PURPOSE Use *memmove* to copy bytes from one memory buffer to another. The *memmove* function can correctly copy to and from overlapping buffers.

SYNTAX `void *memmove(void *dest, const void *source, size_t count);`

`void *dest;`   Pointer to buffer to which data will be copied

`const void *source;`   Pointer to buffer from which data will be copied

`size_t count;`   Maximum number of bytes to be copied

EXAMPLE CALL `memmove(dest, src, sizeof(src));`

INCLUDES `#include <string.h>`   For function declaration and definition of *size_t*

DESCRIPTION The *memmove* function copies *count* bytes from the buffer at address *source* to another buffer at *dest*. The source and destination buffers may overlap. The *memmove* function handles *huge* pointers properly.

RETURNS The *memmove* function returns a pointer to *dest*.

SEE ALSO `memccpy, memcpy`   To copy one buffer to another

`movedata`   To copy buffers even if the source and destination are in different segments

EXAMPLE Use *memmove* to copy 80 bytes from one part of a buffer to another. Print the buffer before and after the move to verify that *memmove* can handle overlapping source and destination buffers properly.

```
#include <stdio.h>
#include <string.h>
static char src[80]="FirstSecond";
main()
{
```

 Buffer Manipulation

```
    printf("Before memmove:Source = %s\n", src);
/* Copy from source to itself */
    memmove(&src[5], src, sizeof(src));
    printf("After  memmove:Source = %s\n", src);
}
```

memset

COMPATIBILITY	MSC 3	MSC 4	MSC 5	QC	TC	ANSI	UNIX V
	▲	▲	▲	▲	▲	▲	▲

PURPOSE Use *memset* to set a specified number of bytes in memory to a specific character.

SYNTAX `void *memset(void *buffer, int c, size_t count);`

`void *buffer;`   Pointer to memory where bytes are to be set

`int c;`   Each byte in buffer is set to this character

`size_t count;`   Maximum number of bytes to be set

EXAMPLE CALL `memset(big_buffer, '\0', 2048);`

INCLUDES `#include <memory.h>`   For function declaration and definition of *size_t*

or

`#include <string.h>`

DESCRIPTION The *memset* function sets the first *count* bytes in the buffer to the character *c*.

COMMON USES The *memset* function is useful for initializing large chunks of memory. For example, *calloc* calls *memset* to set each byte of the allocated block of memory to zero.

RETURNS The *memset* function returns a pointer *buffer* to the buffer.

COMMENTS There is an intrinsic version of *memset* also, but that version cannot handle huge arrays in compact or large model programs.

SEE ALSO `memccpy, memcpy, memmove`   To copy one buffer to another

EXAMPLE Set all bytes in a buffer to the letter Z, append a null character, and print the resulting C string.

memset

```
#include <stdio.h>
#include <memory.h>
static char buffer[41];     /* Destination buffer */
main()
{
    char *result;
    result = memset(buffer, 'Z', 40);
    buffer[40] = '\0';
    printf("The buffer now contains: %s\n", buffer);
}
```

movedata

COMPATIBILITY	MSC 3	MSC 4	MSC 5	QC	TC	ANSI	UNIX V
	▲	▲	▲	▲	▲		

PURPOSE   Use the *movedata* function to copy a specified number of bytes from a source address to a destination address that can be in a different segment.

SYNTAX
```
void movedata(unsigned source_seg, unsigned source_off,
              unsigned dest_seg, unsigned dest_off, unsigned count);
```

unsigned source_seg;   Segment address of source buffer

unsigned source_off;   Offset address of source buffer

unsigned dest_seg;   Segment address of destination

unsigned dest_off;   Offset address of destination

unsigned count;   Number of bytes to be copied

EXAMPLE CALL   `movedata(src_seg, src_off, dest_seg, dest_off, 4096);`

INCLUDES   `#include <memory.h>`   For function declaration

or

`#include <string.h>`

DESCRIPTION   The *movedata* function copies *count* bytes from the source address given by *source_seg:source_off* to the destination address *dest_seg:dest_off*. Since the addresses are in segment and offset format, *movedata* can copy from one segment to another.

 Buffer Manipulation

COMMON USES The *movedata* function is useful for moving data from one *far* array to another in small and medium memory models. It can also be used to copy data directly into the video memory.

COMMENTS In large and compact models, the *memcpy* and *memmove* functions perform the same as *movedata* because all data objects in these models are addressed using explicit segment and offset values.

SEE ALSO
memcpy, memmove   To copy one buffer to another

segread   To get current values of the segment registers

FP_OFF, FP_SEG   Macros to determine segment and offset addresses of a *far* data item

EXAMPLES Write a C program that calls *movedata* to copy the first 22 bytes from the address F000:E000 (in ROM BIOS) to a buffer in your program. Append a null character (\0) and print the resulting C string. On an IBM PC-AT this will print the IBM copyright notice.

```
#include <stdio.h>
#include <dos.h>            /* For FP_OFF and FP_SEG    */
#include <memory.h>
static char far buffer[41];   /* Destination buffer */
main()
{
    void far *address;
    unsigned bufseg, bufoff;
/* Get segment and offset address of buffer */
    address = (void far *)buffer;
    bufseg = FP_SEG(address);
    bufoff = FP_OFF(address);
    movedata(0xf000, 0xe000, bufseg, bufoff, 22);
    buffer[22] = '\0';
/* Use the 'F' address modifier when printing buffer */
    printf("The buffer now contains: %Fs\n", buffer);
}
```

In a Color Graphics Adapter (and EGA in text mode), the video memory starts at the address B800:0000. Prepare a buffer with 2,000 (25 rows by 80 columns) short integers. Initialize the entire buffer to zero (use *memset*). Now use *movedata* to copy the contents of the buffer into video memory. The effect of setting the video memory to zeroes is to clear the display screen. This approach is used for preparing text output offscreen and for updating the display very rapidly.

movedata

```
#include <stdio.h>
#include <dos.h>
#include <memory.h>
static short dispbuf[25][80]; /* Display buffer */
main()
{
    void far *address;
    unsigned bufseg, bufoff;
/* Initialize display buffer to zero */
    memset(dispbuf, '\0', sizeof(dispbuf));
/* Get segment and offset address of buffer */
    address = (void far *)dispbuf;
    bufseg = FP_SEG(address);
    bufoff = FP_OFF(address);
/* Copy buffer into video memory -- clears screen */
    movedata( bufseg, bufoff, 0xb800, 0x0000,
             sizeof(dispbuf));
}
```

swab

COMPATIBILITY	MSC 3	MSC 4	MSC 5	QC	TC	ANSI	UNIX V
	▲	▲	▲	▲	▲		▲

PURPOSE Use *swab* to copy an even number of bytes from one location to another, at the same time swapping each pair of adjacent bytes.

SYNTAX `void swab(char *source, char *destination, int n);`

`char *source;`   Data to be copied after byte swapping

`char *destination;`   Buffer for byte-swapped data

`int n;`   Number of bytes to copy (must be even)

EXAMPLE CALL `swab("badc", result, 4); /* result will be "abcd" */`

INCLUDES `#include <stdlib.h>`   For function definition

DESCRIPTION The *swab* function copies *n* bytes of data from the buffer *source* to another buffer at *dest*, taking two adjacent bytes at a time and swapping their positions in *dest*. The number *n* should be even to allow *swab* to perform the byte swapping.

 Buffer Manipulation

COMMON USES The byte-swapping capability afforded by *swab* is useful when preparing binary data to be read by a system in which the ordering of least significant and most significant bytes in a short integer is just the opposite of the order in the current system.

COMMENTS Although most computer systems today use the 8-bit byte as the smallest unit for data storage, there is no such standard for which byte is least significant and which most significant in multibyte data objects. Even in the simplest case of a short integer with 2 bytes in it you have two possibilities: the least significant byte is either the one at the lower address or the one at the higher memory address. The situation is more complicated in a network environment where machines with differing conventions may be connected together. In these situations you have to use such functions as *swab* to convert the byte ordering of one machine to the liking of another.

EXAMPLE Illustrate the use of *swab* in a program that takes a string on the command line (with no blanks embedded) and copies it into another buffer. Print the copy made by *swab*.

```c
#include <stdio.h>
#include <stdlib.h>
#include <string.h>
main(int argc, char **argv)
{
    size_t len;
    char src[80], dst[80];
/* Make sure that there are at least 2 arguments */
    if(argc < 2)
    {
        printf("Usage: %s <string for \"swab\">\n",
                argv[0]);
        abort();
    }
/* Take an even no. of characters and feed it to swab */
    len = 2*(strlen(argv[1])/2);
    strncpy(src, argv[1], len);
/* Mark the end of string in both source and dest.    */
    src[len] = '\0';
    dst[len] = '\0';
/* Now copy after swapping adjacent bytes */
    swab(src, dst, len);
    printf("Input string to \"swab\" : %s\n\
Output string to \"swab\": %s\n", src, dst);
}
```

swab

III Data Processing

- ► Data Conversion Routines
- ► Math Routines
- ► Character Classification and Conversion
- ► String Comparison and Manipulation
- ► Searching and Sorting
- ► Time Routines

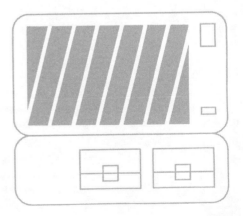

Chapter *7* *Data Conversion Routines*

Introduction

Information management with microcomputers frequently requires crunching numbers. These numbers are represented internally in several forms depending on the type of C variable in which the value is held. The Microsoft C data conversion routines allow us to convert back and forth between the internal form of a C variable and the character string representations that we can read.

Concepts: Internal Representations of Data

The data conversion routines rely on several internal representations of a number—as a series of bytes in memory containing a binary representation as well as in a character string (with the values expressed in decimal and hexadecimal, among other numbering systems).

NUMBERS IN MANY FORMS

All computers store numbers in binary representation in their memory locations. This is true of all types of numbers, floating point or integer. As illustrated in Figure 7-1, the character string representation of a value depends on the radix, or the base of the number system in which the value is being expressed. For example, decimal 100 is written as 64 in hexadecimal, 144 in octal, and 1100100 in binary. Figure 7-1 also shows the internal binary representations of the value 100 stored as a short integer and as an Institute of Electrical and Electronics Engineers (IEEE) format double-precision floating-point number. The character string, though, is the form we deal with to obtain numbers from the user or to format and print numbers calculated by the program.

NUMBERS FOR THE MICRO- PROCESSORS

The pattern of bits that represents a value (such as decimal 100) in memory is determined by the type of C variable used to hold that value. If the variable type is *int*, which has a size of two bytes on the IBM PC, the value will be stored

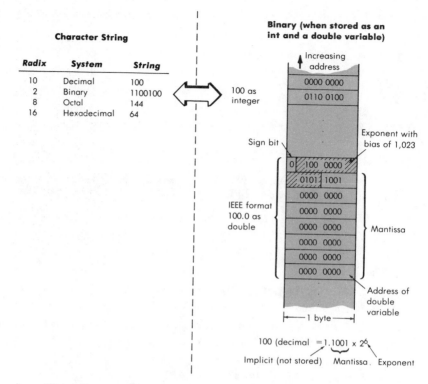

Figure 7-1. *Decimal 100 as a character string and in internal forms*

in binary in these two bytes (Figure 7-1). On the other hand, if we were to store 100 in a variable of type *double*, eight bytes will be used to hold the value and the bit pattern will depend on a format known as the IEEE format for double-precision numbers. Both the 8086 microprocessor and its "math whiz" companion 8087 store floating-point numbers in the IEEE format. See Chapter 6 of the book by Angermeyer and Jaeger[1] for a detailed presentation of binary representation of floating-point numbers in the 8087 math coprocessor.

Notes on Using the Data Conversion Routines

The Microsoft C data conversion routines help us create a bridge between the two styles of representing numbers: the human readable text string and the machine readable binary form. Table 7-1 lists the routines at our disposal.

The conversion routines are ideal for converting command-line arguments from their string representation into the internal format. For example, we may want the user to invoke a small calculator utility in the form

```
eval 4.5 + 2.3
```

where *eval* is the name of the program that accepts command-line arguments

Table 7-1. *Data Conversion Routines*

Routine	Description
atof	Converts a string to a double-precision floating-point value.
atoi	Converts a string to an integer.
atol	Converts a string to a long integer.
ecvt	Converts a double-precision floating-point value into a string without an embedded decimal point (the sign of the value and the position of the decimal point are returned separately).
fcvt	Almost identical to ecvt, but it rounds the value to a specified number of digits.
gcvt	Converts a double-precision floating-point value into a string using a specified number of significant digits and having an embedded decimal point.
itoa	Converts an integer value to a string.
ltoa	Converts a long integer value to a string.
strtod	Converts a string to a double-precision floating-point value.
strtol	Converts a string to a long integer.
strtoul	Converts a string to an unsigned long integer.
ultoa	Converts an unsigned long integer value to a string.

of the form ⟨*value1*⟩ ⟨*operator*⟩ ⟨*value2*⟩ and prints out the answer to the operation. In the sample invocation above, we get back 6.8 as the answer. When implementing the program *eval*, we can make use of the function *atof* to convert the second and the fourth command-line argument (the first argument is always the name of the program) to *double* variables. The code implementing the addition operator might be:

```
    :
value1 = atof(argv[1]);
value2 = atof(argv[3]);
switch(argv[2][0])
{
    :
    case '+': result = value1 + value2;
            break;
    :
}
printf("%f", result);
```

In this example, we asssumed a decimal calculator. If we want a hexadecimal calculator (so that all input and output is in hexadecimal), we can use *strtoul* to convert the input arguments to unsigned long integers. Use *ultoa* and specify a hexadecimal base to convert the result to a string.

Since the conversion routines are mostly used to read numerical values typed in by the user and to convert them to internal formats, you must consider the maximum values that each type of C variable can hold. Table 7-2 summarizes this information. Note that the range of values and the sizes shown in Table 7-2 apply only to Microsoft C on the IBM PC, XT, AT, and compatibles.

Table 7-2. *Limits of Values that Can Fit into C Variables*

Type	Bytes	Limits
double	8	15 significant digits, exponent ranging from −306 to 306
int	2	−32,767 to 32,767
long	4	−2,147,483,647 to 2,147,483,647
unsigned int	2	0 to 65,535
unsigned long	4	0 to 4,294,967,295

DATA CONVERSION ROUTINES BY TASK

The twelve data conversion routines perform two basic tasks: converting a C numerical value to a string or converting a string to a specific type of C variable. Table 7-3 shows the routines grouped by task.

Table 7-3. *Data Conversion Routines by Task*

Task	Routines
Convert character string to floating-point value.	atof, strtod
Convert character string to integer.	atoi
Convert character string to long integer.	atol, strtol
Convert character string to unsigned long integer.	strtoul
Convert floating-point values to character string.	ecvt, fcvt, gcvt
Convert integer values to string.	itoa
Convert long integer to string.	ltoa
Convert unsigned long integer to string.	ultoa

OTHER DATA CONVERSION RESOURCES

A few other routines in the C library provide data conversion facilities. The *sprintf* and the *sscanf* functions in the I/O category convert internal values to strings and strings back to internal representations, respectively. The *sprintf* routine, however, lacks the ability to convert an integer to a string using an arbitrary radix—only decimal and hexadecimal formats are supported. To print a value in binary or octal you have to use such routines as *itoa, ltoa,* or *ultoa*.

Further Reading

Angermeyer and Jaeger[1] devote their Chapter 6 to the subject of writing programs for the 8087 math coprocessor. In that chapter they also describe the binary representation of floating-point numbers.

1. John Angermeyer and Kevin Jaeger, The Waite Group, *MS-DOS Developer's Guide*, Howard W. Sams & Company, Indianapolis, IN, 1987, 440 pages.

atof

COMPATIBILITY	MSC 3	MSC 4	MSC 5	QC	TC	ANSI	UNIX V
	▲	▲	▲	▲	▲	▲	▲

PURPOSE Use *atof* to convert a character string to a double-precision floating-point value.

SYNTAX ```double atof(const char *string);```

```const char *string;```   String to be converted

EXAMPLE CALL ```dbl_value = atof(input_string);```

INCLUDES ```#include <math.h>```   For function declaration

or

```#include <stdlib.h>```

DESCRIPTION The *atof* function converts the argument "string" into a double value. The string is expected to be of the form:

[whitespace][sign][digits.digits]

[exponent_letter][sign][digits]

The "whitespace" characters are optional blanks and tab characters, the "sign" is optional, and "digits" refer to decimal digits. The "exponent_letter" is either d, D, e, or E, marking the beginning of the exponent field (no matter which letter appears in the exponent field, the exponent always denotes a power of 10). If a decimal point appears without any digits preceding it, at least one digit must appear after the decimal point. The conversion of characters from the string continues until *atof* encounters a character it cannot handle (the null character will suffice).

In the compact and large memory models *atof* can only handle strings with a maximum length of 100 characters.

RETURNS The *atof* function returns the double-precision value after conversion. The return value is undefined if an overflow occurred during conversion.

SEE ALSO ```atoi, atol```   To convert strings to integers and long integer values

```ecvt, fcvt, gcvt```   To convert floating-point values to strings

EXAMPLE Write a program that accepts a floating-point number, uses *atof* to convert it to internal representation, and then prints that value.

atof
```

```
#include <stdio.h>
#include <math.h>
main(int argc, char **argv)
{
    double value;
    if(argc < 2)
    {
        printf("Usage: %s <value>\n", argv[0]);
    }
    else
    {
        value = atof(argv[1]);
        printf("Value entered = %g\n", value);
    }
}
```

atoi

COMPATIBILITY	MSC 3	MSC 4	MSC 5	QC	TC	ANSI	UNIX V
	▲	▲	▲	▲	▲	▲	▲

PURPOSE Use *atoi* to convert a character string to an *int* value.

SYNTAX `int atoi(const char *string);`

`const char *string;`   String to be converted

EXAMPLE CALL `int_value = atoi(input_string);`

INCLUDES `#include <stdlib.h>`   For function declaration

DESCRIPTION The *atoi* function converts the argument *string* into an *int* value. The string is expected to be of the form:

[whitespace][sign][digits]

The "whitespace" characters are optional blanks and tab characters, the "sign" is optional, and "digits" refer to decimal digits. The conversion of characters from the string continues until *atoi* encounters a character it cannot handle (for example, a terminating null character, a decimal point, or a letter).

RETURNS The *atoi* function returns the integer value as an *int* variable. The return value is undefined if it is too large to fit an *int* variable.

 Data Conversion Routines

SEE ALSO atof   To convert strings to floating-point values

atol   To convert strings to long integers

itoa, ltoa, ultoa   To convert integers to strings

EXAMPLE Write a program that accepts a sequence of decimal integers, uses *atoi* to convert it to an integer, and then prints that integer.

```
#include <stdio.h>
#include <stdlib.h>
main(int argc, char **argv)
{
    int value;
    if(argc < 2)
    {
        printf("Usage: %s <value>\n", argv[0]);
    }
    else
    {
        value = atoi(argv[1]);
        printf("Value entered = %d\n", value);
    }
}
```

atol

COMPATIBILITY	MSC 3	MSC 4	MSC 5	QC	TC	ANSI	UNIX V
	▲	▲	▲	▲	▲	▲	▲

PURPOSE Use *atol* to convert a character string to a *long* integer value.

SYNTAX `int atol(const char *string);`

`const char *string;`   String to be converted

EXAMPLE CALL `long_value = atol(input_string);`

INCLUDES `#include <stdlib.h>`   For function declaration

DESCRIPTION The *atol* function converts the argument *string* into a *long* integer value. The string is expected to be of the form:

[whitespace][sign][digits]

atol

The "whitespace" characters are optional blanks and tab characters, the "sign" is optional, and "digits" refer to decimal digits. The conversion of characters from the string continues until *atol* encounters a character it cannot handle (for example, a terminating null character, a decimal point, or a letter).

RETURNS The *atol* function returns the integer value as a *long* variable. The return value is undefined if it is too large to fit a *long* integer.

SEE ALSO

atof To convert strings to floating-point values

atoi To convert strings to integers

itoa, ltoa, ultoa To convert integers to strings

EXAMPLE Write a program that accepts a sequence of decimal integers, uses *atol* to convert it to a long integer and then prints that long integer.

```
#include <stdio.h>
#include <stdlib.h>
main(int argc, char **argv)
{
    long value;
    if(argc < 2)
    {
        printf("Usage: %s <value>\n", argv[0]);
    }
    else
    {
        value = atol(argv[1]);
        printf("Value entered = %ld\n", value);
    }
}
```

ecvt

COMPATIBILITY	MSC 3	MSC 4	MSC 5	QC	TC	ANSI	UNIX V
	▲	▲	▲	▲	▲		▲

PURPOSE Use *ecvt* to convert a floating-point value to a character string.

SYNTAX char *ecvt(double value, int count, int *dec, int *sign);

double value; Floating-point value to be converted to string

int count; Number of digits to be stored

 Data Conversion Routines

int *dec;   Pointer to integer where position of decimal point is returned

int *sign;   Pointer to integer where sign of the number is returned

EXAMPLE CALL   string = ecvt(value, precision, &d_position, &sign);

INCLUDES   #include <stdlib.h>   For function declaration

DESCRIPTION   The *ecvt* function converts the *double* argument *value* into a null-terminated character string with *count* digits. If the number of digits in *value* exceeds *count*, the last digit is rounded. On the other hand, if there are fewer than *count* digits, the string is padded with zeroes.

You must specify the addresses of integer variables *dec* and *sign*, which are used by *ecvt* to return the location of the decimal point from the beginning of the string and the sign of the number, respectively. If *ecvt* returns a zero or a negative number in *dec*, the decimal point lies at the beginning of the string or to the left of the first digit. If the value in *sign* is zero, the number is positive. Otherwise, it is negative.

RETURNS   The *ecvt* function returns a pointer to an internal string where the string of digits is stored. The next call to either *ecvt* or *fcvt* destroys the result.

SEE ALSO   atof   To convert strings to floating-point values

fcvt, gcvt   To convert floating-point numbers to strings

itoa, ltoa, ultoa   To convert integers to strings

EXAMPLE   Write a program that accepts a floating-point number, uses *atof* to convert it to internal form, and prepares a character string representing the value of that number by calling *ecvt* with a precision of 10 digits. Print the buffer prepared by *ecvt*, the location of the decimal point, and the value of the sign indicator.

```
#include <stdio.h>
#include <math.h>
#include <stdlib.h>
main(int argc, char **argv)
{
    int dec, sign, precision = 10;
    double value;
    char  *p_buffer;
    if(argc < 2)
    {
        printf("Usage: %s <value>\n", argv[0]);
    }
    else
    {
/* Convert the number to internal form. Then call ecvt */
```

ecvt

```
            value = atof(argv[1]);
            p_buffer = ecvt(value, precision, &dec, &sign);
            printf("Buffer from ecvt contains: %s\n\
Location of decimal point: %d\n\
Sign (0 = pos, 1 = neg)  : %d\n", p_buffer, dec, sign);
         }
    }
```

fcvt

COMPATIBILITY	MSC 3	MSC 4	MSC 5	QC	TC	ANSI	UNIX V
	▲	▲	▲	▲	▲		▲

PURPOSE Use *fcvt* to convert a floating-point value to a character string. The function of *fcvt* is similar to that of *ecvt* but *fcvt* rounds the number to a specified number of digits.

SYNTAX `char *fcvt(double value, int count, int *dec, int *sign);`

`double value;`   Floating-point value to be converted to string

`int count;`   Number of digits to be stored

`int *dec;`   Pointer to integer where position of decimal point is returned

`int *sign;`   Pointer to integer where sign of the number is returned

EXAMPLE CALL `string = fcvt(value, precision, &d_position, &sign);`

INCLUDES `#include <stdlib.h>`   For function declaration

DESCRIPTION Like *ecvt*, the *fcvt* function converts the *double* argument *value* into a character string with *count* digits. If the number of digits in *value* exceeds *count*, the excess digits are rounded off to *count* places. On the other hand, if there are fewer than *count* digits, the string is padded with zeroes. You must specify the addresses of integer variables *dec* and *sign*, which are used by *fcvt* to return the location of the decimal point from the beginning of the string and the sign of the number, respectively. If *fcvt* returns a zero or a negative number in *dec*, the decimal point lies at the beginning of the string or to the left of the first digit. If the value in *sign* is zero, the number is positive. Otherwise, it is negative.

RETURNS The *fcvt* function returns a pointer to an internal string where the string of digits is stored. The next call to either *fcvt* or *ecvt* destroys the result.

 Data Conversion Routines

SEE ALSO atof   To convert strings to floating-point values

ecvt, gcvt   To convert floating-point numbers to strings

itoa, ltoa, ultoa   To convert integers to strings

EXAMPLE Write a program that accepts a floating-point number, uses *atof* to convert it to internal form, and prepares a character string representing the value of that number by calling *ecvt* with a precision of 10 digits. Print the buffer prepared by *fcvt*, the location of the decimal point, and the value of the sign indicator.

```
#include <stdio.h>
#include <math.h>
#include <stdlib.h>
main(int argc, char **argv)
{
    int dec, sign, precision = 10;
    double value;
    char  *p_buffer;

    if(argc < 2)
    {
        printf("Usage: %s <value>\n", argv[0]);
    }
    else
    {
/* Convert the number to internal form. Then call fcvt */
        value = atof(argv[1]);
        p_buffer = fcvt(value, precision, &dec, &sign);
        printf("Buffer from fcvt contains: %s\n\
Location of decimal point: %d\n\
Sign (0 = pos, 1 = neg)  : %d\n", p_buffer, dec, sign);
    }
}
```

gcvt

COMPATIBILITY	MSC 3	MSC 4	MSC 5	QC	TC	ANSI	UNIX V
	▲	▲	▲	▲	▲		▲

PURPOSE Use *gcvt* to convert a floating-point value to a character string. Unlike *ecvt* and *fcvt*, *gcvt* returns the results in a character buffer supplied by you.

SYNTAX char *gcvt(double value, int digits, char *buffer);

double value;   Floating-point value to be converted to string

gcvt

```
int digits;        Number of significant digits to be stored

char *buffer;      Pointer to character array where result is returned
```

EXAMPLE CALL `gcvt(value, significant_digits, resulting_string);`

INCLUDES `#include <stdlib.h>`   For function declaration

DESCRIPTION The *gcvt* function converts the *double* argument *value* into a character string that it saves in the buffer whose address is given in the argument *buffer*. You must allocate enough room in the buffer to hold all digits of the converted string and the terminating null character (\0).

The argument *digits* specifies the number of significant digits that *gcvt* should produce in the character string. If *gcvt* cannot meet this requirement in normal decimal format, it generates a string in scientific notation using mantissa and exponent (e.g., 1.234e−7 as opposed to 0.0000001234).

RETURNS The *gcvt* function returns a pointer to the string of digits, i.e., it returns the argument *buffer*.

COMMENTS Unlike *ecvt* and *fcvt*, *gcvt* uses a string supplied by you and it includes the decimal point and the sign in the result.

SEE ALSO `atof`   To convert strings to floating-point values

`ecvt, fcvt`   To convert floating-point numbers to strings

`itoa, ltoa, ultoa`   To convert integers to strings

EXAMPLE Write a program that accepts a floating-point number, uses *atof* to convert it to internal form, and prepares a formatted representation of that number (with six significant digits) by calling *gcvt*. Print the resulting string.

```
#include <stdio.h>
#include <math.h>
#include <stdlib.h>
main(int argc, char **argv)
{
    int significant_digits = 6;
    double value;
    char  buffer[80];                /* Buffer for gcvt */
    if(argc < 2)
    {
        printf("Usage: %s <value>\n", argv[0]);
    }
    else
    {
/* Convert the number to internal form. Then call gcvt */
```

 Data Conversion Routines

```
value = atof(argv[1]);
gcvt(value, significant_digits, buffer);
printf("Buffer from gcvt contains: %s\n",
        buffer);
    }
}
```

itoa

COMPATIBILITY	MSC 3	MSC 4	MSC 5	QC	TC	ANSI	UNIX V
	▲	▲	▲	▲	▲		

PURPOSE Use *itoa* to convert an integer value to a null-terminated character string.

SYNTAX `char *itoa(int value, char *string, int radix);`

`int value;`   Integer value to be converted to string

`char *string;`   Pointer to character array where result is returned

`int radix;`   Radix in which the result is expressed (in the range 2–36)

EXAMPLE CALL `itoa(32, buffer, 16); /* buffer will contain "20" */`

INCLUDES `#include <stdlib.h>`   For function declaration

DESCRIPTION The *itoa* function converts the *int* argument *value* into a null-terminated character string using the argument *radix* as the base of the number system. The resulting string with a length of up to 17 bytes is saved in the buffer whose address is given in the argument *string*. You must allocate enough room in the buffer to hold all digits of the converted string plus the terminating null character (\0). For radixes other than 10, the sign bit is not interpreted; instead, the bit pattern of *value* is simply expressed in the requested *radix*.

The argument *radix* specifies the base (between 2 and 36) of the number system in which the string representation of *value* is expressed. For example, using either 2, 8, 10, or 16 as *radix*, you can convert *value* into its binary, octal, decimal, or hexadecimal representation, respectively. When *radix* is 10 and the *value* is negative the converted string will start with a minus sign.

RETURNS The *itoa* function returns the pointer to the string of digits (i.e., it returns the argument *string*).

SEE ALSO `ecvt, fcvt, gcvt`   To convert floating-point numbers to strings

    `ltoa, ultoa`   To convert long and unsigned long integers to strings

itoa

EXAMPLE　Write a program to print an integer value using a specified radix. Assume the program will be invoked with the decimal value and the radix on the command line. Use *itoa* to generate the formatted string.

```c
#include <stdio.h>
#include <stdlib.h>
main(int argc, char **argv)
{
    char buffer[17];                /* Buffer for itoa  */
    int value, radix;
    if(argc < 3)
    {
        printf("Usage: %s <value> <radix>\n", argv[0]);
    }
    else
    {
        value = atoi(argv[1]);
        radix = atoi(argv[2]);
        itoa(value, buffer, radix);
        printf("%s in radix %s = %s\n", argv[1], argv[2],
                buffer);
    }
}
```

ltoa

COMPATIBILITY	MSC 3	MSC 4	MSC 5	QC	TC	ANSI	UNIX V
	▲	▲	▲	▲	▲		

PURPOSE　Use *ltoa* to convert a *long* integer value to a null-terminated character string.

SYNTAX　`char *ltoa(long value, char *string, int radix);`

`long value;`　　Long integer value to be converted to string

`char *string;`　　Pointer to character array where result is returned

`int radix;`　　Radix in which the result is expressed (in the range 2–36)

EXAMPLE CALL　`ltoa(0x10000, string, 10); /* string = "65536" */`

INCLUDES　`#include <stdlib.h>`　　For function declaration

DESCRIPTION　The *ltoa* function converts the *long* argument *value* into a character string using the argument *radix* as the base of the number system. A *long* integer

Data Conversion Routines

has 32 bits when expressed in radix 2, so the string can occupy a maximum of 33 bytes with the terminating null character. The resulting string is returned in the buffer whose address is given in the argument *string*.

The argument *radix* specifies the base (between 2 and 36) of the number system in which the string representation of *value* is expressed. For example, using either 2, 8, 10, or 16 as *radix*, you can convert *value* into its binary, octal, decimal, or hexadecimal representation, respectively. When *radix* is 10 and the *value* is negative the converted string will start with a minus sign.

RETURNS   The *ltoa* function returns the pointer to the converted string (i.e., it returns the argument *string*).

SEE ALSO   `ecvt, fcvt, gcvt`   To convert floating-point numbers to strings

   `itoa, ultoa`   To convert *int* and *unsigned long* integers to strings

EXAMPLE   Write a program that accepts a long integer value and a radix on the command line and then calls *ltoa* to prepare a character representation of that number in the specified radix and prints the string.

```
#include <stdio.h>
#include <stdlib.h>
main(int argc, char **argv)
{
    char buffer[17];              /* Buffer for ltoa  */
    int  radix;
    long value;
    if(argc < 3)
    {
        printf("Usage: %s <value> <radix>\n", argv[0]);
    }
    else
    {
        value = atol(argv[1]);
        radix = atoi(argv[2]);
        ltoa(value, buffer, radix);
        printf("%s in radix %s = %s\n", argv[1], argv[2],
                buffer);
    }
}
```

ltoa

strtod

PURPOSE Use *strtod* to convert a character string to a double-precision value.

SYNTAX `double strtod(const char *string, char **endptr);`

`const char *string;`   Pointer to character array from which double-precision value is extracted

`char **endptr;`   On return, points to character in *string* where conversion stopped

EXAMPLE CALL `dbl_value = strtod(input_string, &endptr);`

INCLUDES `#include <stdlib.h>`   For function declaration

`#include <float.h>`   For the definition of the constant HUGE_VAL

`#include <math.h>`   For the definition of ERANGE

DESCRIPTION The *strtod* function converts the *string* to a double-precision value. The string is expected to be of the form

[whitespace][sign][digits.digits][exponent_letter][sign][digits]

where "whitespace" refers to (optional) blanks and tab characters, "sign" is a + or a −, and the "digits" are decimal digits. The "exponent_letter" can be either d, D, e, or E (no matter which exponent letter is used, the exponent always denotes a power of 10). If there is a decimal point without a preceding digit, there must be at least one digit following it.

The *strtod* function begins the conversion process with the first character of *string* and continues until it finds a character that does not fit the above form. Then it sets *endptr* to point to the leftover string. In compact and large model programs *strtod* can only handle strings with a maximum length of 100 characters.

RETURNS The *strtod* function returns the double-precision value as long as it is not too large. If it is too large, an overflow occurs and the return value is the constant HUGE_VAL with the same sign as the number represented in *string*. Additionally, the global variable *errno* is set to the constant ERANGE.

COMMENTS The advantage of using *strtod* over *atof* is that *strtod* returns a pointer to the character where the conversion stopped, enabling you to handle the rest of the string any way you wish.

 Data Conversion Routines

SEE ALSO   atof   To convert strings to double-precision values

          strtol, strtoul   To convert strings to long and unsigned long integers

EXAMPLE   Prompt the user for a floating-point number followed by arbitrary characters. Then call *strtod* to convert the floating-point number to internal form. Print the number and the rest of the string, which in a more realistic program would be processed further.

```
#include <stdio.h>
#include <stdlib.h>
main()
{
    char input[80], *stop_at;
    double value;
    printf(
    "Enter a number followed by other characters:\n");
    gets(input);
/* Now convert the number to internal value */
    value = strtod(input, &stop_at);
    printf("Value = %g\n\
Stopped at: %s\n", value, stop_at);
}
```

strtol

COMPATIBILITY	MSC 3	MSC 4	MSC 5	QC	TC	ANSI	UNIX V
		▲	▲	▲	▲	▲	▲

PURPOSE   Use *strtol* to convert a character string to a long integer value.

SYNTAX   long strtol(const char *string, char **endptr, int radix);

          const char *string;   Pointer to character array from which the long integer value is extracted

          char **endptr;   On return, points to character in *string* where conversion stopped

          int radix;   Radix in which the value is expressed in the string (radix must be in the range 2–36)

EXAMPLE CALL   value = strtol(input, &endptr, radix);

INCLUDES   #include <stdlib.h>   For function declaration

strtol

`#include <limits.h>`   For the definition of the constants LONG＿MIN and LONG＿MAX

`#include <math.h>`   For the definition of ERANGE

DESCRIPTION   The *strtol* function converts the *string* to a long integer value. The string is expected to be of the form

[whitespace][sign][0][x or X][digits]

where "whitespace" refers to optional blanks and tab characters, "sign" is a + or a −, and the "digits" are decimal digits. The string is expected to contain a representation of the long integer using the argument *radix* as the base of the number system. If *radix* is given as zero, though, *strtol* will use the first character in *string* to determine the radix of the value. The rules are given in the table.

First Character	Next Character	Radix Selected
0	0–7	Radix 8 is used (octal digits expected)
0	x or X	Radix 16 (hexadecimal digits expected)
1–9	—	Radix 10 (decimal digits expected)

Of course, other radixes may be specified via the argument *radix*. The letters a through z (or A through Z) are assigned values of 10 through 35. For a specified radix, *strtol* expects only those letters whose assigned values are less than the *radix*.

The *strtol* function begins the conversion process with the first character of *string* and continues until it finds a character that meets the above requirements. Then, before returning, *strtol* sets *endptr* to point to that character.

RETURNS   The *strtol* function returns the long integer value except when it would cause an overflow. In which case, *strtol* sets *errno* to ERANGE and returns either LONG＿MIN or LONG＿MAX depending on whether the value was negative or positive.

COMMENTS   The advantage of using *strtol* over *atol* is that *strtol* allows radix values other than 10 and it can determines the radix automatically based on the first two characters of the string. Unlike *atol*, *strtol* returns a pointer to the character where the conversion stopped, enabling you to handle the rest of the string any way you wish.

SEE ALSO   `atol`   To convert strings to long integer values

`ltoa`   To convert long integers to strings

`strtoul`   To convert strings to unsigned long integers

 Data Conversion Routines

EXAMPLE Write a program that accepts on the command line a long integer value followed by the radix in which the value is represented. Use *strtol* with the radix to convert the representation of that number to an internal value. Print this value.

```
#include <stdio.h>
#include <stdlib.h>
main(int argc, char **argv)
{
    char *stop_at;    /* Marks where strtol stopped  */
    int  radix;
    long value;
    if(argc < 3)
    {
        printf("Usage: %s <value> <radix>\n", argv[0]);
    }
    else
    {
        radix = atoi(argv[2]);
        value = strtol(argv[1], &stop_at, radix);
        printf("Value read in radix %d = %ld\n\
Stopped at: %s\n", radix, value, stop_at);

    }
}
```

strtoul

COMPATIBILITY	MSC 3	MSC 4	MSC 5	QC	TC	ANSI	UNIX V
			▲	▲	▲	▲	

PURPOSE Use *strtoul* to convert a character string to an unsigned long integer.

SYNTAX
```
unsigned long strtoul(const char *string, char **endptr,
                      int radix);
```

`const char *string;` Pointer to character array from which the unsigned long value is extracted

`char **endptr;` On return, points to character in *string* where conversion stopped

`int radix;` Radix in which the value is expressed in the string (radix must be in the range 2–36)

EXAMPLE CALL `value = strtoul(input_string, &stop_at, radix);`

strtoul

INCLUDES   `#include <stdlib.h>`   For function declaration

`#include <limits.h>`   For the definition of the constants LONG_MIN and LONG_MAX

`#include <math.h>`   For the definition of ERANGE

DESCRIPTION   The *strtoul* function converts the *string* to an unsigned long integer value. The string is expected to be of the form

[whitespace][0]x or X][digits]

where "whitespace" refers to optional blanks and tab characters, "sign" is a + or a −, and the "digits" are decimal digits. The string is expected to contain a representation of the unsigned long integer with the argument *radix* as the base of the number system. If *radix* is given as zero, however, *strtoul* uses the first character in *string* to determine the radix of the value. The rules are shown in the table.

First Character	Next Character	Radix Selected
0	0–7	Radix 8 is used (octal digits expected)
0	x or X	Radix 16 (hexadecimal digits expected)
1–9	—	Radix 10 (decimal digits expected)

Of course, other radix may be specified via the argument *radix*. The letters a through z (or A through Z) are assigned values 10 through 35. For a specified radix, *strtoul* expects only those letters whose assigned values are less than the *radix*.

The *strtoul* function begins the conversion process with the first character of *string* and continues until it finds a character that meets the above requirements. Then before returning, *strtoul* sets *endptr* to point to that character.

RETURNS   The *strtoul* function returns the unsigned long integer value except when it will cause an overflow. In which case, *strtoul* sets *errno* to ERANGE and returns the value ULONG_MAX.

SEE ALSO   `atol`   To convert strings to long integer values

`ultoa`   To convert unsigned long integers to strings

`strtol`   To convert strings to long integers

EXAMPLE   Write a program that accepts on the command line an unsigned long integer value followed by the radix in which the value is represented. Use *strtoul* with

Data Conversion Routines

the radix to convert the representation of that number to an internal value. Print this value.

```
#include <stdio.h>
#include <stdlib.h>
main(int argc, char **argv)
{
    char *stop_at;    /* Marks where strtoul stopped */
    int  radix;
    unsigned long value;
    if(argc < 3)
    {
        printf("Usage: %s <value> <radix>\n", argv[0]);
    }
    else
    {
        radix = atoi(argv[2]);
        value = strtoul(argv[1], &stop_at, radix);
        printf("Value read in radix %d = %lu\n\
Stopped at: %s\n", radix, value, stop_at);

    }
}
```

ultoa

COMPATIBILITY	MSC 3	MSC 4	MSC 5	QC	TC	ANSI	UNIX V
	▲	▲	▲	▲	▲		

PURPOSE Use *ultoa* to convert an *unsigned long* integer value to a character string.

SYNTAX char *ultoa(unsigned long value, char *string, int radix);

unsigned long value;   Unsigned long integer value to be converted to string

char *string;   Pointer to character array where result is returned

int radix;   Radix in which the result is expressed (in the range 2–36)

EXAMPLE CALL ultoa(0x100000, string, 10); /* string = "131072" */

INCLUDES #include <stdlib.h>   For function declaration

DESCRIPTION The *ultoa* function converts the *unsigned long* argument *value* into a null-terminated character string using the argument *radix* as the base of the number system. A *long* integer has 32 bits when expressed in radix 2, so the string can occupy a maximum of 33 bytes with the terminating null character. The resulting string is returned by *ultoa* in the buffer whose address is given in the argument *string*.

The argument *radix* specifies the base (between 2 and 36) of the number system in which the string representation of *value* is expressed. For example, using either 2, 8, 10, or 16 as *radix*, you can convert *value* into its binary, octal, decimal, or hexadecimal representation, respectively.

RETURNS The *ultoa* function returns the pointer to the converted string (i.e., it returns the argument *string*).

SEE ALSO ecvt, fcvt, gcvt   To convert floating-point numbers to strings

itoa, ltoa   To convert *int* and *long integers to strings*

EXAMPLE Write a program to print an unsigned long integer value in a specific radix. Assume that the program accepts the value followed by the radix on the command line. Use *ultoa* to prepare the character representation of the number in the radix.

```
#include <stdio.h>
#include <stdlib.h>

main(int argc, char **argv)
{
    char buffer[17];            /* Buffer for ultoa */
    int   radix;
    unsigned long value;
    if(argc < 3)
    {
        printf("Usage: %s <value> <radix>\n", argv[0]);
    }
    else
    {
        value = atol(argv[1]);
        radix = atoi(argv[2]);
        ultoa(value, buffer, radix);
        printf("%s in radix %s = %s\n", argv[1], argv[2],
                buffer);
    }
}
```

Data Conversion Routines

Chapter **8 Math Routines**

Introduction

You often need computational capabilities beyond basic arithmetic operations. The 8086 microprocessor does not have machine instructions to perform such arithmetic operations as addition or multiplication of real or floating-point numbers directly. It needs support from an 8087 math coprocessor (or a software library) to do these computations. In Microsoft C, the support for all floating-point operations is provided by a floating-point package. Using compiler options, you can ask the compiler to generate code for an 8087 coprocessor or to use its software library that implements similar capabilities using 8086 instructions. In addition to the support for basic floating-point operations, the Microsoft C library also includes a set of functions, the *math functions*, to control the operational characteristics of the underlying floating-point package and to compute common mathematical functions such as the sine and the cosine. This tutorial provides a summary of the capabilities of the math library in Microsoft C 5.1.

Concepts: Floating-Point Operations

Most of the math functions operate on floating-point variables, so we begin by explaining how floating-point numbers are stored and manipulated in the PC.

FLOATING-POINT FORMATS *Floating-point variables* hold floating-point numbers— numbers with fractional parts. When writing such numbers, we usually use a decimal point, for example, 1.2345×10^5. This way of writing floating-point numbers is known as scientific or engineering notation. In fact, any floating-point number can be represented in this form: a "mantissa" (the number's significant digits) multiplied by 10 raised to the power of an integer "exponent." The mantissa and exponent form is how floating-point numbers are represented in the PC, except that instead of the exponent representing a power of 10, it represents a power of 2, since base 2 is a computer's natural format.

Precision: Single and Double

The number of bytes used to represent a floating-point number depends on the precision of the variable. The C variable type *float* is used to declare *single-precision* floating-point variables. The type *double* denotes *double-precision* values. As shown in Figure 8-1, the single-precision *float* variables require 4 bytes of storage while *double* variables use 8 bytes. The representation of the mantissa and the exponent in the variables is in accordance with the IEEE floating-point standards and is used in Microsoft C and understood by the 8087 math coprocessor.

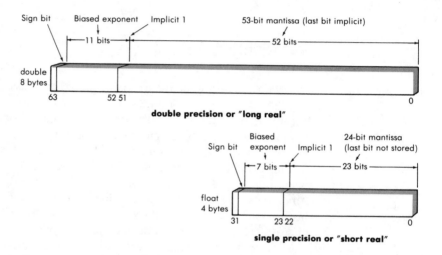

Figure 8-1. *IEEE format for binary representation of floating-point numbers*

IEEE Format for Floating-Point Numbers

The IEEE format expresses a floating-point number in binary form known as "normalized." Normalization involves adjusting the exponent so that the "binary point" (the binary analog of the decimal point) in the mantissa always lies to the right of the most significant nonzero digit. In binary representation, this means that the most significant digit of the mantissa is always a 1. This property of the normalized representation is exploited by the IEEE format when storing the mantissa.

Consider an example of generating the normalized form of a floating-point number. Suppose, we want to represent the decimal number 5.375. Since this can be written as

$$4 + 1 + \frac{1}{4} + \frac{1}{8}$$

the binary form will be

101.011

The normalized form is obtained by adjusting the exponent until the decimal point is to the right of the 1 in the most significant position. In this case, the result is

1.01011×2^2

The IEEE format for floating-point storage uses a sign bit, a mantissa, and an exponent representing the power of 2. The "sign bit" denotes the sign of the number: a 0 represents a positive value and a 1 denotes a negative value. The mantissa is represented in binary. Constraining the floating-point number to be in normalized form results in a mantissa whose most significant binary digit is always 1. The IEEE format takes advantage of this by not storing this bit at all. The exponent is an integer stored in unsigned binary format after adding a positive integer "bias" to ensure that the stored exponent is always positive. The value of the bias depends upon the precision of the floating-point representation.

The single-precision *float* variable uses 4 bytes (32 bits) comprising 1 sign bit and 7 bits for the exponent and allows a 24-bit mantissa that can be stored in the rest of the 23 bits because the most significant bit is always 1 (Figure 8-1). The exponent is stored with a bias of 127. Thus, the smallest positive value you can store in a *float* variable is 2^{-126}, which is approximately 1.175×10^{-38}. The largest positive value is 2^{128}, which is about 3.4×10^{38}. About seven significant decimal digits can be handled in a *float* variable.

The double-precision *double* variable uses 8 bytes providing 64 bits of storage. As shown in Figure 8-1, the first bit is used for the sign bit, the next 11 bits hold the exponent, which has a bias of 1,023 added to it. The rest of the 52 bits contain the 53-bit mantissa. This representation allows about 15 significant decimal digits and the smallest positive value is 2^{-1022}, which is approximately 2.23×10^{-308}. The largest positive value that can be held in a *double* variable is 2^{1024}, which is approximately 1.8×10^{308}.

The IEEE format also specifies certain bit-patterns that represent such special conditions as infinite values or NANs (for "not a number"), but we will not go into the details here.

Other Formats: Microsoft Binary Format

The IEEE standard format for binary representation of floating-point numbers is a recent one. Prior to its development, Microsoft used its own binary representation of floating-point numbers in Microsoft BASIC. The single- and double-precision versions of the Microsoft formats use the same number of bytes for storage as the corresponding IEEE representation, but the meaning of the internal bits differ. If you need to pass floating-point data between Microsoft BASIC and Microsoft C, you can use the following library routines: *dieeetomsbin* for converting double-precision IEEE format to the corresponding Microsoft Binary format and *dmsbintoieee* for the reverse. For single-precision numbers, use the routines *fieeetomsbin* and *fmsbintoieee*, respectively.

**COMPILER
OPTIONS FOR THE
FLOATING-POINT
LIBRARY**
If an 8087 math coprocessor is not present in your system, the Microsoft C library is equipped with alternatives to handle all floating-point calculations. Table 8-1 lists the compiler options providing an array of choices, from generating in-line 8087 instructions to using an alternate math library which is also supplied with Microsoft C. The options */FPc87* and */FPi87* require a math coprocessor at run-time and should not be used for applications that will be distributed widely. For such applications, the options */FPc* or */FPi* generate code that uses the 8087 if the PC has one, but also uses a software emulator.

Table 8-1. *Compiler Options for Floating-Point Libraries*

Option	8087 or 80287 Required?	Description
/FPa	No	Generates function call to an alternate math library. Will not use an 8087 even if system has it. This alternate math library is provided with Microsoft C.
/FPc	No	Generates function calls and uses the math coprocessor if one is present (otherwise uses an emulator library).
/FPc87	Yes	Generates function calls to routines that use 8087 instructions.
/FPi	No	Generates in-line 8087 instructions that will use the 8087 if found. Otherwise, these instructions will be fielded by the emulator library. This is the default.
/FPi87	Yes	Generates in-line 8087 instructions that require the coprocessor at run-time.

**THE FLOATING-
POINT PACKAGE**
The IEEE standard for binary floating-point arithmetic is used in the 8087 family of math coprocessors. The software implementation that emulates the 8087 when no coprocessor is present in the system also uses the IEEE standard. The routines that handle floating-point calculations are collectively called the "floating-point package."

You can control certain parameters of the floating-point package, such as precision of the calculations and method of rounding the numbers, with the library routines *_clear87*, *_control87*, and *_status87*. The floating-point package maintains two 16-bit registers, the control word and the status word, for this purpose. There are similarly named registers in the 8087 processors. As their names imply, the "status word" maintains the current status of the floating-point package and the "control word" lets you control the precision of the computations and decide how a floating-point result should be truncated to fit in the number of bits available for that precision. The alternate math library does not have these provisions, when you see the compiler option */FPa* these routines are not available. The entire floating-point package can be reset by the library routine *_fpreset*.

**FLOATING-POINT
EXCEPTIONS**
When certain errors occur in the floating-point package, it raises the signal SIGFPE (see the tutorial in Chapter 3 for details on signals). The exceptional conditions, "exceptions" for short, that raise the signal can be controlled by setting bits in the control word with the function *_control87*. The floating-

point package has six exceptions (as does the 8087): invalid operation, un-normalized operand, divide by zero, overflow, underflow, and loss of precision (inexact result).

Error Handling in the Floating-Point Package

When an error occurs in a math function, function *matherr* is called. A default, *matherr* is supplied in the Microsoft C library, but you can write your own version of *matherr* to handle errors differently. You have to use the linker option /NOE (see Chapter 2 for details) when adding your own version of *matherr*. Otherwise, the linker will complain when it finds another *matherr* in the library.

Notes

Table 8-2 catalogs the math functions available in the Microsoft C 5.1 library. While most routines are for computing specific functions, a few are meant for other chores, such as error handling, format conversion, and controlling the floating-point package.

Table 8-2. *Library Math Functions*

Routine	Description
abs	Returns the absolute value of an integer argument.
acos	Computes the arc cosine of a value between -1 and 1 and returns an angle between 0 and π radian.
asin	Computes the arc sine of a value between -1 and 1 and returns an angle between $-\pi/2$ and $\pi/2$ radians.
atan	Computes the arc tangent of a value and returns an angle between $-\pi/2$ and $\pi/2$ radians.
atan2	Computes the arc tangent of one argument divided by the other and returns an angle between $-\pi$ and π radians.
bessel functions	Evaluates the Bessel functions of first and second kind for integer orders.
cabs	Computes the magnitude of a complex number.
ceil	Finds the smallest integer larger than or equal to the function's floating-point argument.
_clear87	Clears the status word of the floating-point package (not available in the alternate math library which is used when compiler option /FPa is specified).
_control87	Gets and sets the control word of the floating-point package (not available in the alternate math library which is used when compiler option /FPa is specified).
cos	Evaluates the cosine of an angle in radians.
cosh	Evaluates the hyperbolic cosine of its argument.
dieeetomsbin	Converts a double-precision number from IEEE format to Microsoft Binary format (used in Microsoft BASIC).
div	Divides one integer by another and returns an integer quotient and an integer remainder.

Table 8-2. *(cont.)*

Routine	Description
dmsbintoieee	Converts a double-precision number from Microsoft Binary format (used in Microsoft BASIC) to IEEE format.
exp	Computes the exponential of a floating-point argument.
fabs	Returns the absolute value of a floating-point argument.
fieeetomsbin	Converts a single-precision number from IEEE format to Microsoft Binary format (used in Microsoft BASIC).
floor	Finds the largest integer smaller than or equal to the function's floating-point argument.
fmod	Computes the floating-point remainder after dividing one floating-point value by another so that the quotient is the largest possible integer for that division.
fmsbintoieee	Converts a single-precision number from Microsoft Binary format (used in Microsoft BASIC) to IEEE format.
_fpreset	Reinitializes the floating-point math package.
frexp	Breaks down a floating-point value into a mantissa between 0.5 and 1 and an integer exponent so that the value is equal to the mantissa × 2 raised to the power of the exponent.
hypot	Computes the length of the hypotenuse of a right-angled triangle.
labs	Returns the absolute value of a long integer argument.
ldexp	Computes a floating-point value equal to a mantissa × 2 raised to power of an integer exponent.
ldiv	Divides one long integer by another and returns a long integer quotient and a long integer remainder.
log	Evaluates the natural logarithm of its floating-point argument.
log10	Evaluates the logarithm to the base 10 of its floating-point argument.
_lrotl	Rotates an unsigned long integer left by a given number of bits.
_lrotr	Rotates an unsigned long integer right by a given number of bits.
matherr	Handles error conditions occurring in the functions of the math library package.
modf	Breaks down a floating-point value into its integer part and its fractional part.
pow	Computes the value of one argument raised to the power of a second one.
rand	Returns a random integer between 0 and 32,767.
_rotl	Rotates an unsigned integer left by a given number of bits.
_rotr	Rotates an unsigned integer right by a given number of bits.
sin	Evaluates the sine of an angle in radians.
sinh	Evaluates the hyperbolic sine of its argument.
sqrt	Computes the square root of a positive floating-point number.
srand	Sets the starting point for the sequence of random numbers generated by *rand*.
_status87	Gets the status word of the floating-point package (not available in the alternate math library which is used when compiler option /FPa is specified).
tan	Evaluates the tangent of an angle in radians.
tanh	Evaluates the hyperbolic tangent of its argument.

THE MATH FUNCTIONS BY TASK

When we categorize the math functions in terms of the tasks (Table 8-3), we find that several important types of computation are supported in the library.

Table 8-3. *Math Functions by Task*

Task	Routines
Evaluate trigonometric functions.	acos, asin, atan, atan2, cos, sin, tan
Evaluate powers and logarithms.	exp, frexp, ldexp, log, log10, pow
Compute square root.	sqrt
Compute magnitudes and absolute values.	abs, cabs, fabs, hypot
Find integer limits (lower and upper) for floating-point numbers.	ceil, floor
Evaluate hyperbolic functions.	cosh, sinh, tanh
Evaluate Bessel functions of first and second kind of integral orders.	j0, j1, jn, y0, y1, yn
Break down floating-point number into integer and fraction.	modf
Find floating-point remainder.	fmod
Integer arithmetic.	abs, div, labs, ldiv
Rotate bits.	_lrotl, _lrotr, _rotl, _rotr
Generate random numbers.	rand, srand
Handle errors.	matherr
Manipulate floating-point package (status and control information)	_clear87, _control87, _fpreset, _status87
Convert from one format to another.	dieeetomsbin, dmsbintoieee, fieeetomsbin, fmsbintoieee

Basic Math Functions

The trigonometric functions *cos, sin, tan, acos, asin, atan*, and *atan2* respectively evaluate the cosines, sines, and tangents of any angle in radian and compute their respective inverses. You will find these routines useful for tasks such as changing from rectangular to polar coordinates, which often occurs in graphics programs.

The Bessel functions *j0, j1, jn, y0, y1*, and *yn* are generally not encountered in everyday programming, unless you happen to be in a research group studying such phenomena as sound and radio wave reflection. The hyperbolic functions *cosh, sinh*, and *tanh* are also uncommon, but they are available if you need them.

Unlike FORTRAN, which has built-in support for complex variables and has an exponentiation operator, you have to use library routines in C for these tasks. The *pow* routine lets you raise one number to the power of another. The *cabs* and the *hypot* functions can compute the magnitude of a complex number. Other commonly needed functions include *sqrt* to compute square roots. The *log, log10* return the logarithm, natural and to the base 10, respectively, of an argument. Exponentials (for example, $e^{1.5}$) can be computed by *exp*. The *abs* and *fabs* functions return the absolute value of an argument. The *ceil* and *floor* routines find the nearest integer larger or smaller than a given floating-point number.

INTEGER ARITHMETIC

There are four routines that use integer arguments to handle arithmetic. The routines *abs* and *labs* return the absolute value of an integer and a long integer, respectively. The *div* function divides one integer by another and returns the integer quotient and an integer remainder. The *ldiv* function operates similarly, but with long integer arguments.

ROTATING BITS

The bit shift operators are ideal for extracting a specified number of bits from an integer variable. Sometimes, however, you may want to *rotate* the bits rather than shift. For example, you can implement the byte-swapping capability of *swab* by rotating the bits of each 2-byte integer to the right by 8 bits.

At each step in the shift operation, one bit is discarded at one end while a zero bit is inserted at the other end, as shown in Figure 8-2. Rotation is similar to shift *except* that the bit being shifted out is brought into the other end. The routines *_rotl* and *_lrotl* rotate an unsigned integer and an unsigned long integer, respectively, to the left by a specified number of bits. The corresponding routines for rotating right are *_rotr* and *_lrotr*.

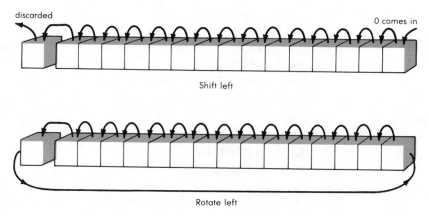

Shift left

Rotate left

Figure 8-2. *Shift vs rotate*

GENERATING RANDOM NUMBERS

If you need to generate random numbers for a random screen pattern, a game, or a statistical analysis problem, for instance, the Microsoft C library includes a routine *rand* that can generate a random positive integer in the range 0– 32,767. Using it is like throwing a die with 32,768 faces. The numbers are generated by an algorithm that, given a starting number, always generates the same sequence of numbers. So instead of being truly random, the sequence generated by *rand* is a pseudo-random sequence. If the algorithm used to generate the numbers is good, the sequence will have such good properties as not repeating itself too soon and any of the numbers between 0 and 32,767 will appear with equal probability. (A poor algorithm is analogous to a loaded die.) The function *srand* sets the starting point of the random sequence. Although Microsoft C does not provide a routine to generate a random sequence of random numbers, you can use the system time as the argument to *srand* to set a new random seed for *rand*.

Cautions

▶ When the compiler option */FPa* is used to select an alternate math library, the functions *_clear87, _control87,* and *_status87* should not be called in the program.

▶ If you install your own handler for the floating-point exception SIGFPE, your handler should call *_fpreset* to reset the floating-point package before returning.

▶ If you provide an alternate *matherr* to handle errors, use the linker option /NOE during linking.

▶ The basic math function capabilities exist in all C libraries, but the functions that deal with the floating-point package are specific to MS-DOS.

Further Reading

Consult the book by Morgan and Waite[1] for further details on the floating-point data types supported by the 8087 math coprocessor (or, Numeric Data Processor). If you need to use the trigonometric and the Bessel functions often, the handbook by Abramowitz and Stegun[2] is a good reference. If you are interested in programming the 8087 math coprocessor in assembly language, the developer's guide by Angermeyer and Jaeger[3] devotes a chapter to this topic.

1. Christopher L. Morgan and Mitchell Waite, *8086/8088 16-bit Microprocessor Primer*, BYTE/McGraw-Hill, Peterborough, NH, 1982, 355 pages.

2. Milton Abramowitz and Irene A. Stegun, Eds., *Handbook of Mathematical Functions with Formulas, Graphs and Mathematical Tables*, Dover Publications, New York, NY, 1972, 1046 pages.

3. John Angermeyer and Kevin Jaeger, The Waite Group, *MS-DOS Developer's Guide*, Howard W. Sams & Company, Indianapolis, IN, 1987, 440 pages.

abs

COMPATIBILITY	MSC 3	MSC 4	MSC 5	QC	TC	ANSI	UNIX V
	▲	▲	▲	▲	▲	▲	▲

PURPOSE Use *abs* to get the absolute value of an integer.

SYNTAX `int abs(int n);`

`int n;`   Integer whose absolute value is returned

EXAMPLE CALL `x = abs(-5); /* x will be 5 now */`

INCLUDES `#include <stdlib.h>`   For function declaration

DESCRIPTION The *abs* function returns the absolute value of the integer argument *n*. Thus *abs (−10)* returns +10.

RETURNS The integer returned by *abs* is the absolute value of *n*.

SEE ALSO
`cabs`   To obtain the magnitude (or absolute value) of a complex number

`fabs`   To get the absolute values of a floating-point number

`labs`   To get the absolute values of a long integer

EXAMPLE Write a program that reads an integer value as a command-line argument and prints its absolute value.

```
#include <stdio.h>
#include <stdlib.h>
main(int argc, char **argv)
{
    int value, result;
    if(argc < 2)
    {
        printf("Usage: %s <integer_value>\n", argv[0]);
    }
    else
    {
        value = atoi(argv[1]);
        result = abs(value);
        printf("Absolute value of %d = %d\n",
                value, result);
    }
}
```

 Math Routines

acos

COMPATIBILITY	MSC 3	MSC 4	MSC 5	QC	TC	ANSI	UNIX V
	▲	▲	▲	▲	▲	▲	▲

PURPOSE Use *acos* to compute the arc cosine of a *double* variable whose value lies between −1 and 1.

SYNTAX `double acos(double x);`

`double x;` Argument whose arc cosine is to be computed

EXAMPLE CALL `angle = acos(0.5); /* angle is "pi"/3 */`

INCLUDES `#include <math.h>` For function declaration and definition of constants EDOM and DOMAIN

DESCRIPTION The *acos* function accepts an argument *x* whose value lies in the range −1 to 1 and computes its arc cosine. The result is an angle with value between 0 and π radians.

RETURNS When the value of the argument *x* is in the valid range of −1 to 1, *acos* returns the result. If the argument's value is outside the acceptable range, *acos* sets the global variable *errno* to the constant EDOM which is defined in *math.h*, prints a DOMAIN error message to *stderr*, and returns a value of zero. You can write your own error-handling routine with the name *matherr* to perform differently when an error occurs.

SEE ALSO `matherr` To handle math errors (you can add your own)

`cos` To compute a cosine of an angle

EXAMPLE Write a program that accepts a floating-point number on the command line and computes the arc cosine of that number if it lies between −1 and 1.

```
#include <stdio.h>
#include <math.h>
#include <stdlib.h>        /* errno is defined here */
#define  R_TO_D   57.29578 /* radians to degrees  */
main(int argc, char **argv)
{
    double result;
    if(argc < 2)
    {
        printf("Usage: %s <value>\n", argv[0]);
    }
    else
```

```
            {
                result = acos(atof(argv[1])) * R_TO_D;
                if(errno != EDOM)
                {
                    printf("Arc cosine (%s) = %f deg.\n",
                            argv[1], result);
                }
            }
        }
```

asin

COMPATIBILITY	MSC 3	MSC 4	MSC 5	QC	TC	ANSI	UNIX V
	▲	▲	▲	▲	▲	▲	▲

PURPOSE Use *asin* to compute the arc sine of a *double* variable whose value lies between −1 and 1.

SYNTAX `double asin(double x);`

`double x;` Argument whose arc sine is to be computed

EXAMPLE CALL `angle = asin(0.707)  /* angle is roughly "pi"/4  */`

INCLUDES `#include <math.h>` For function declaration and definition of constants EDOM and DOMAIN

DESCRIPTION The *asin* function computes the arc sine of the argument *x* provided its value lies in the range −1 to 1. The result is an angle with value between $-\pi/2$ and $\pi/2$ radians.

RETURNS For a valid argument *x* with values between −1 and 1, *asin* returns an angle whose sine is equal to *x*. If the argument's value lies outside the acceptable range, however, *asin* sets the global variable *errno* to the constant EDOM which is defined in *math.h*, prints a DOMAIN error message to *stderr*, and returns a value of zero. You can write your own error-handling routine with the name *matherr* to perform differently when an error occurs.

SEE ALSO `matherr` To handle math errors (you can add your own)

`sin` To compute a sine of an angle

EXAMPLE Write a program that computes and prints the arc sine of 10 numbers between −1 and 1, starting with −1 and advancing to 1 with a stepsize of 0.2.

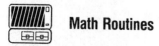 **Math Routines**

```
#include <stdio.h>
#include <math.h>
#include <stdlib.h>          /* errno is defined here */
#define R_TO_D   57.29578 /* radians to degrees  */
main()
{
    double value, result;
    for (value = -1.0; value <= 1.0; value += 0.2)
    {
        result = asin(value) * R_TO_D;
        if(errno != EDOM)
        {
            printf("Arc sine (%f) = %f deg.\n",
                    value, result);
        }
    }
}
```

atan

COMPATIBILITY	MSC 3	MSC 4	MSC 5	QC	TC	ANSI	UNIX V
	▲	▲	▲	▲	▲	▲	▲

PURPOSE Use *atan* to compute the arc tangent of a variable.

SYNTAX `double atan(double x);`

`double x;`   Argument whose arc tangent is to be computed

EXAMPLE CALL `angle = atan(1.0)  /* angle is "pi"/4  */`

INCLUDES `#include <math.h>`   For function declaration

DESCRIPTION The *atan* function computes the arc tangent of the argument x. The result is an angle with value between $-\pi/2$ and $\pi/2$ radians.

RETURNS The *atan* function returns the angle in the range $-\pi/2$ and $\pi/2$ whose tangent is equal to x.

SEE ALSO atan2   To compute arc tangent of the ratio of two arguments

EXAMPLE Write a program that prompts for a floating-point number and then computes the arc tangent of that number.

atan

```c
#include <stdio.h>
#include <math.h>
#include <stdlib.h>        /* errno is defined here */
#define  R_TO_D   57.29578 /* radians to degrees  */
main()
{
    double tanvalue, result;
    printf("Enter value whose arctangent you want \
to evaluate: ");
    scanf(" %le", &tanvalue);
    result = atan(tanvalue) * R_TO_D;
    if(errno != EDOM)
    {
        printf("Arc tangent (%f) = %f deg.\n",
                tanvalue, result);
    }
}
```

atan2

COMPATIBILITY	MSC 3	MSC 4	MSC 5	QC	TC	ANSI	UNIX V
	▲	▲	▲	▲	▲	▲	▲

PURPOSE Use *atan2* to compute the arc tangent of the ratio of two nonzero variables.

SYNTAX `double atan2(double y, double x);`

`double x, y;`   Arc tangent of y/x will be computed

EXAMPLE CALL `angle = atan2(y, x);`

INCLUDES `#include <math.h>`   For function declaration and definition of constants EDOM and DOMAIN

DESCRIPTION The *atan2* function computes the arc tangent of the ratio of the arguments y/x. The result is an angle with value between $-\pi$ and π radians. In contrast to *atan*, which takes a single argument, *atan2* can use the sign of its two arguments to determine the quadrant (a 90° sector in cartesian coordinates) in which the angle should lie.

RETURNS Provided both arguments x and y are nonzero, *atan2* returns an angle whose tangent is equal to x. If both arguments are zero, however, *atan2* sets the global variable *errno* to the constant EDOM, prints a DOMAIN error message to *stderr*, and returns a value of zero. You can write your own error-handling routine to perform differently when an error occurs with the name *matherr*.

 Math Routines

SEE ALSO atan   To compute arc tangent of an argument

matherr   To handle math errors (you can add your own)

tan   To compute a tangent of an angle

EXAMPLE Write a program that accepts two floating-point numbers y and x on the command line and computes the arc tangent of y/x.

```
#include <stdio.h>
#include <math.h>
#include <stdlib.h>          /* errno is defined here */
#define  R_TO_D   57.29578 /* radians to degrees  */
main(int argc, char **argv)
{
    double result;
    if(argc < 3)
    {
        printf("Usage: %s <y> <x>\n", argv[0]);
    }
    else
    {

        result = atan2(atof(argv[1]),
                       atof(argv[2])) * R_TO_D;
        if(errno != EDOM)
        {
            printf("Arc tangent (%s/%s) = %f deg.\n",
                argv[1], argv[2], result);
        }
    }
}
```

Bessel functions

COMPATIBILITY	MSC 3	MSC 4	MSC 5	QC	TC	ANSI	UNIX V
	▲	▲	▲	▲			▲

PURPOSE Use the functions in this group to evaluate Bessel functions of first and second kind of any integer order for an argument. (For further details, see a reference book such as *Handbook of Mathematical Functions* by M. Abramowitz and I.A. Stegun, Dover, 1970.)

SYNTAX double j0(double x);

Bessel functions

```
double j1(double x);

double jn(int n, double x);

double y0(double x);

double y1(double x);

double yn(int n, double x);

double x;        Positive argument for the Bessel function

int n;        Integer order of the Bessel function for jn and yn
```

INCLUDES `#include <math.h>`   For function declaration and definition of constants EDOM, DOMAIN, and HUGE_VAL

DESCRIPTION This group of functions evaluates the Bessel function of first and second kind of integer order at an argument *x*. The functions *jn* and *yn* also accept an integer *n* that denotes the order of the Bessel function being evaluated. The argument *x* must be positive when calling the functions *y0, y1* and *yn*, which compute Bessel functions of the second kind.

COMMON USES Bessel functions appear in mathematical theories of electromagnetic wave propagation. You may not need them for everyday programming, but they are available in the Microsoft C library if your application requires them.

RETURNS Normally, the functions return the value of the appropriate Bessel function at the specified argument *x*, and for the order *n* in the case of *jn* and *yn*. But if the Bessel functions of the second kind are called with a negative *x*, the routines return the value HUGE_VAL, set *errno* to the constant EDOM, and print a DOMAIN error message on *stderr*. Additional error handling can be provided by linking your version of the routine named *matherr*.

SEE ALSO `matherr`   To handle math errors (you can add your own)

EXAMPLE Write a program that accepts a command line of the form *bessel ⟨j or y⟩ ⟨n⟩ ⟨x⟩* and computes the value of the appropriate Bessel function by calling *jn* or *yn* with argument *x*. Remember to handle the cases *n = 0* and *n = 1* separately.

```
#include <stdio.h>
#include <math.h>
#include <stdlib.h>   /* errno is declared here */
main(int argc, char **argv)
{
    int    n;
    double x, result;
```

 Math Routines

```
        if(argc < 4)
        {
            printf("Usage: %s <j or y> <n> <x>\n",
                    argv[0]);
        }
        else
        {
            n = atoi(argv[2]);
            x = atof(argv[3]);
            switch(argv[1][0])
            {
                case 'j':
                case 'J':
                    if(n == 0) result = j0(x);
                    if(n == 1) result = j1(x);
                    if (n != 0 && n != 1) result = jn(n, x);
                    break;
                case 'y':
                case 'Y':
                    if(n == 0) result = y0(x);

                    if(n == 1) result = y1(x);
                    if (n != 0 && n != 1) result = yn(n, x);
                    break;
                default:
                    printf("Unknown function: %s\n", argv[1]);
                    exit(0);
            }
            if (errno != EDOM)
                printf("%s %d (%f) = %f\n",
                        argv[1], n, x, result);
        }
    }
```

cabs

COMPATIBILITY	MSC 3	MSC 4	MSC 5	QC	TC	ANSI	UNIX V
	▲	▲	▲	▲	▲		▲

PURPOSE Use *cabs* to compute the magnitude of a complex number stored in a structure of type *complex*.

SYNTAX `double cabs(struct complex z);`

`struct complex z;`   Structure containing the complex number whose magnitude is computed

cabs

EXAMPLE CALL   `magnitude = cabs(z);`

INCLUDES   `#include <math.h>`   For function declaration and definition of the structure complex

DESCRIPTION   The *cabs* function computes the magnitude of a complex number z stored in a structure of type *complex* which is defined in *math.h* as follows:

```
struct complex
{
    double x;    /* Real part of the complex number      */
    double y;    /* Imaginary part of the complex number */
};
```

The magnitude of z is computed with the expression

```
magnitude = sqrt(z.x*z.x + z.y*z.y);
```

RETURNS   If the magnitude of z is too large, *cabs* calls the routine *matherr* to handle the error. In this case, it returns a value HUGE_VAL defined in *math.h* and sets the variable *errno* to the constant ERANGE. If all goes well, *cabs* returns the magnitude of the complex number.

SEE ALSO   `matherr`   To handle math errors (you can add your own)

`hypot`   To compute the length of the hypotenuse of a right triangle

`fabs`   To compute the absolute value of a *double* variable

EXAMPLE   Write a program that accepts the real and the imaginary part of a complex number on the command line and computes the magnitude of the complex number by using *cabs*.

```
#include <stdio.h>
#include <math.h>
#include <stdlib.h>        /* errno is defined here */
main()
{
    struct complex z;
    double result;
    printf("Enter complex number in the form \
\"(real, imaginary)\":");
    scanf(" ( %le , %le )", &z.x, &z.y);
    result = cabs(z);
    if(errno != ERANGE)
    {
        printf("Magnitude of (%f, %f) = %f\n",
                z.x, z.y, result);
    }
}
```

 Math Routines

ceil

COMPATIBILITY	MSC 3	MSC 4	MSC 5	QC	TC	ANSI	UNIX V
	▲	▲	▲	▲	▲	▲	▲

PURPOSE Use *ceil* to compute the *ceiling*, the smallest integer value that is greater than or equal to a *double* variable.

SYNTAX `double ceil(double x);`

`double x;` Variable whose "ceiling" is to be returned

EXAMPLE CALL `x_ceiling = ceil(4.1);  /* x_ceiling is 5.0 */`

INCLUDES `#include <math.h>` For function declaration

DESCRIPTION The *ceil* function finds the ceiling of a *double* argument x. The ceiling is the smallest integral value that is equal to or that just exceeds x. This can be used in rounding a *double* value *up*to the next integer.

RETURNS The return value is the ceiling of $x$expressed as a *double*.

SEE ALSO `floor` To determine the largest integer that is just less than a variable

EXAMPLE Write a program that accepts a floating-point number on the command line and prints the ceiling of that number.

```
#include <stdio.h>
#include <math.h>
main(int argc, char **argv)
{
    double result;
    if(argc < 2)
    {
        printf("Usage: %s <value>\n", argv[0]);
    }
    else
    {
        result = ceil(atof(argv[1]));
        printf("ceil of %s = %f\n", argv[1], result);
    }
}
```

__clear87

COMPATIBILITY	MSC 3	MSC 4	MSC 5	QC	TC	ANSI	UNIX V
		▲	▲	▲	▲		

PURPOSE Use *_clear87* to retrieve the current contents of the floating-point status word and reset all bits to zero.

SYNTAX `unsigned int _clear87(void);`

EXAMPLE CALL `status = _clear87();`

INCLUDES `#include <float.h>`   For function declaration and definition of constants denoting status-word bit settings

DESCRIPTION The *_clear87* function retrieves the status word of the floating-point package of the C library and clears all its bits before returning. This status word is a composite of the status word of the 8087 math coprocessor and other conditions detected by the 8087 exception handler. (See the reference page on *_status87* for details on the bit settings of the status word.)

RETURNS The *_clear87* function returns the prior contents of the floating-point status word.

SEE ALSO _status87   To get the floating-point status word

 _control87   To alter bits in the floating-point control word

EXAMPLE Copy a small *double* variable into a *float* variable and generate an underflow and an inexact result. Now call *_clear87* to clear the status word. The return value reflects the error that occurred, but if you read the status again with *_status87*, it will show a cleared status word.

```
#include <stdio.h>
#include <float.h>
main()
{
    float a;
    double b = 1.e-40;
    unsigned fpstatus;
/* Perform operation that produces underflow and
 * an inexact result
 */
    a = b;   /* This will produce inexact result */
    printf("After undeflow/inexact ");
/* Clear status word. It'll return prior status */
    fpstatus = _clear87();
```

 Math Routines

```
printf("status word was: %X\n", fpstatus);
fpstatus = _status87();
printf("After _clear87, status word is: %X\n",
                                      fpstatus);
}
```

__control87

COMPATIBILITY	MSC 3	MSC 4	MSC 5	QC	TC	ANSI	UNIX V
		▲	▲	▲	▲		

PURPOSE Use _control87 to get and set the floating-point control word. When an 8087 math coprocessor is being used, _control87 sets its control word.

SYNTAX `unsigned int _control87(unsigned new, unsigned mask);`

`unsigned int new;`   New control word bit values

`unsigned int mask;`   Mask to indicate which bits of control word to set

EXAMPLE CALL `status = _control87(PC_24, MCW_PC); /* 24-bit precision */`

INCLUDES `#include <float.h>`   For function declaration and definition of constants denoting control-word bit settings

DESCRIPTION The _control87 function gets and sets the floating-point control word. The settings control the precision, the rounding, the infinity mode, and the exceptions that will be generated. The value of the argument *mask* determines which of these four categories is being changed. The possible values are shown in Table 8-4 in terms of constants defined in *float.h*. If the *mask* is zero, _control87 simply returns the value of the status word. For any other mask setting from Table 8-4, you must specify the new value, given in the argument *new*, for that option from the list under that mask value. Thus, to set the precision to 24 bits, you need the call _control87(PC_24, MCW_PC);.

RETURNS The _control87 function returns the floating-point control word.

SEE ALSO _status87   To get the floating-point status word

_clear87   To get and clear the floating-point status word

EXAMPLE Get and display the current contents of the floating-point control word. Now set the precision to 24 bits and compute the product of 0.1 with itself. Display the result and note the difference from 0.01. Use the constant CW_DEFAULT to set the control word back to its default. The precision will now be 64 bits.

Table 8-4. *Floating-Point Control Word*

Mask Constant	Mask Meaning	Values	Meaning of Value
MCW_EM	Controls the conditions under which interrupts will be generated by the floating-point package. Choose from these values:	EM_INVALID	Exception on invalid operation
		EM_DENORMAL	Exception if denormalized argument
		EM_ZERODIVIDE	Exception on divide by zero
		EM_OVERFLOW	Exception on overflow
		EM_UNDERFLOW	Exception on underflow
		EM_INEXACT	Exception on loss of precision
MCW_IC	Controls the interpretation of "infinity" by the package.	IC_AFFine	Use "affine" infinity (affine infinity distinguishes between positive and negative infinity, projective infinity does not)
		IC_PROJECTIVE	Use "projective" infinity
MCW_RC	Controls the rounding options.	RC_CHOP	Round off results by chopping
		RC_UP	Round to next higher number
		RC_DOWN	Round to next lower number
		RC_NEAR	Round to nearest number
MCW_PC	Controls the level of precision of the results.	PC_24	24-bits precision
		PC_53	53-bits precision
		PC_64	64-bits precision

Repeat the previous computation and note the improvement in the accuracy of the results.

```
#include <stdio.h>
#include <float.h>
main()
{
    double a = 0.1;
/* Read current floating point control word     */
    printf("Current control word = %.4X\n",
            _control87(0,0));
/* Now lower the precision to 24 bits           */
    _control87(PC_24, MCW_PC);
/* Perform a math operation and see the result  */
    printf("0.1 x 0.1 = 0.01 in 24 bit precision\
 = %.15e\n", a*a);
/* Restore precision to default 64 bits and redo */
    _control87(CW_DEFAULT, 0xffff);
```

Math Routines

```
        printf("0.1 x 0.1 = 0.01 in 64 bit precision\
    = %.15e\n", a*a);
    }
```

COS

COMPATIBILITY	MSC 3	MSC 4	MSC 5	QC	TC	ANSI	UNIX V
	▲	▲	▲	▲	▲	▲	▲

PURPOSE · Use *cos* to compute the cosine of an angle whose value is given in radians.

SYNTAX `double cos(double x);`

`double x;`   Angle in radians whose cosine is to be computed

EXAMPLE CALL `cos_angle = cos(ang_radian);`

INCLUDES `#include <math.h>`   For function declaration and definition of error constants

DESCRIPTION The *cos* function computes the cosine of *double* argument *x*.

RETURNS As long as the angle *x* is less than approximately 1.34×10^8 radians (this was found by experimentation), *cos* accurately computes and returns the cosine of *x*. If the value of *x* is large enough to cause a loss of significance (i.e., the result is correct up to a few digits only), *cos* will generate a PLOSS error to indicate "partial loss of precision." If the value is so large that the result is totally useless, a TLOSS error will be sent to *stderr* and the return value is zero and *errno* is set to the constant ERANGE.

SEE ALSO `acos`   To compute the arc cosine of a variable

`sin`   To compute the sine of an angle

EXAMPLE Write a program that prints a table showing the cosine of the angles between 0 and 180° in steps of 10°.

```
#include <stdio.h>
#include <math.h>
#include <stdlib.h>        /* errno is defined here */
#define  R_TO_D   57.29578 /* radians to degrees   */
main()
{
    double angle, result;
    printf("------- Table of Cosines --------\n");
    printf("Angle\t\tCosine\n");
    for(angle = 0.0; angle <= 180.0; angle += 10.0)
```

```
        {
            result = cos(angle / R_TO_D);
            if(errno != ERANGE)
            {
                printf("%f deg.\t%f\n", angle, result);
            }
        }
    }
```

cosh

COMPATIBILITY	MSC 3	MSC 4	MSC 5	QC	TC	ANSI	UNIX V
	▲	▲	▲	▲	▲	▲	▲

PURPOSE   Use *cosh* to compute the hyperbolic cosine of a *double* variable.

SYNTAX   `double cosh(double x);`

`double x;`   Variable whose hyperbolic cosine is to be computed

EXAMPLE CALL   `result = cosh(x);`

INCLUDES   `#include <math.h>`   For function declaration and definition of error constants

DESCRIPTION   The *cosh* function computes the hyperbolic cosine of the *double* variable *x*.

RETURNS   Normally, *cosh* returns the hyperbolic cosine of *x*. If the value of the result is too large (a *double* variable can be as large as 10^{308}), *cosh* returns the value HUGE_VAL and, at the same time, sets *errno* to the constant ERANGE.

SEE ALSO   `sinh`   To compute the hyperbolic sine of a variable

EXAMPLE   Write a program that accepts a floating-point number on the command line and computes its hyperbolic cosine.

```
#include <stdio.h>
#include <math.h>
#include <stdlib.h>        /* errno is defined here */
main(int argc, char **argv)
{
    double result;
    if(argc < 2)
    {
        printf("Usage: %s <value>\n", argv[0]);
    }
    else
```

 Math Routines

```
{
    result = cosh(atof(argv[1]));
    if(errno != ERANGE)
    {
        printf("Hyperbolic cosine of %s = %f\n",
                argv[1], result);
    }
}
}
```

dieeetomsbin

COMPATIBILITY	MSC 3	MSC 4	MSC 5	QC	TC	ANSI	UNIX V
		▲	▲	▲			

PURPOSE Use the *dieeetomsbin* function to convert a double-precision number from IEEE format to Microsoft Binary format.

SYNTAX `int dieeetomsbin(double *src8, double *dst8);`

`double *src8;`   Pointer to double variable with value in IEEE format

`double *dst8;`   Pointer to double variable where Microsoft Binary representation is returned

EXAMPLE CALL `dieeetomsbin(&d_ieee, &d_msbin);`

INCLUDES `#include <math.h>`   For function declaration

DESCRIPTION The *dieeetomsbin* function converts the double precision-value in IEEE format stored at the address *src8* to Microsoft Binary format and returns this value at the address *dst8*. This routine can not handle IEEE NAN (not-a-number) and infinities. Also, IEEE "denormals" are treated as zeroes.

RETURNS The *dieeetomsbin* function returns a 0 if conversion is successful and a 1 if conversion caused an overflow.

COMMENTS In Microsoft C programs double-precision values are kept in the IEEE format, but Microsoft BASIC stores such values in the Microsoft Binary format. The *dieeetomsbin* function allows C programs to create data files that may be read by Microsoft BASIC.

SEE ALSO `dmsbintoieee`   To convert from Microsoft Binary format to IEEE format

`fieeetomsbin, fmsbintoieee`   Conversion routines for single-precision *float* variables

EXAMPLE Write a program that uses *dieeetomsbin* to convert some *double* values (by default in IEEE double precision-format) to Microsoft Binary format and saves the result in a binary file. In the example for *dmsbintoieee* we will use this data file as input.

```c
#include <math.h>
#include <stdio.h>
double data[10] = {1.0, 2.0, 3.0, 4.0, 5.0, 6.0, 7.0,
                   8.0, 9.0, 10.0};
double conv[10];
main()
{
    int i;
    char filename[80];
    FILE *outfile;
/* Convert data to MS binary format */
    for(i=0; i<10; i++)
        dieeetomsbin(data+i, conv+i);
/* Save in a file */
    printf("Enter file name for MS binary data:");
    gets(filename);
    if ((outfile = fopen(filename, "wb")) == NULL)
    {
        printf("Error opening file: %s\n", filename);

        exit(0);
    }
    i = fwrite(conv, sizeof(double), 10, outfile);
    printf("Saved %d bytes in file: %s\n", i, filename);
}
```

div

COMPATIBILITY	MSC 3	MSC 4	MSC 5	QC	TC	ANSI	UNIX V
			▲	▲	▲	▲	

PURPOSE Use *div* to divide one integer value by another and get the quotient and remainder in a structure of type *div_t*.

SYNTAX `div_t div(int numer, int denom);`

`int numer;`   Numerator

`int denom;`   Denominator

 Math Routines

EXAMPLE CALL
```
result = div(32, 5);
/* result.quot = 6 and result.rem = 2 */
```

INCLUDES
```
#include <stdlib.h>
```
For function declaration and definition of structure *div_t*

DESCRIPTION
The *div* function divides the first integer *numer* by the second one *denom* and returns the resulting quotient and remainder packed in a structure of type *div_t*. The structure of type *div_t* is defined in *stdlib.h* as

```
typedef struct
{
    int quot;   /* The quotient  */
    int rem;    /* The remainder */
} div_t;
```

RETURNS
The *div* function returns a structure of type *div_t* containing the quotient and remainder of the division.

SEE ALSO
```
ldiv
```
To divide one long integer by another

EXAMPLE
Write a program that accepts a numerator and a denominator on the command line and uses *div* to compute the quotient and the remainder of the division.

```
#include <stdio.h>
#include <stdlib.h>
main(int argc, char **argv)
{
    int x, y;
    div_t result;
/* Make sure that there is at least 3 arguments */
    if(argc < 3)
    {
        printf("Usage: %s <int numerator> <int denom>\n",
                argv[0]);
        exit(0);
    }
/* Divide first integer by second and display
 * quotient and remainder
 */
    x = atoi(argv[1]);
    y = atoi(argv[2]);
    result = div(x,y);
    printf("Dividing %d by %d. Quotient = %d and \
remainder = %d\n", x, y, result.quot, result.rem);
}
```

div

dmsbintoieee

COMPATIBILITY	MSC 3	MSC 4	MSC 5	QC	TC	ANSI	UNIX V
		▲	▲	▲			

PURPOSE Use the *dmsbintoieee* function to convert a double-precision number from Microsoft Binary format to the IEEE format.

SYNTAX `int dmsbintoieee(double *src8, double *dst8);`

`double *src8;`   Pointer to double variable with value in Microsoft Binary format

`double *dst8;`   Pointer to double variable where IEEE representation will be returned

EXAMPLE CALL `dmsbintoieee(&d_msbin, &d_ieee);`

INCLUDES `#include <math.h>`   For function declaration

DESCRIPTION The *dmsbintoieee* function converts the double-precision value in Microsoft Binary format stored at the address *src8* to IEEE format and returns this value at the address *dst8*.

RETURNS The *dmsbintoieee* function returns a 0 if conversion is successful and a 1 if conversion caused an overflow.

COMMENTS In Microsoft C programs double-precision values are kept in the IEEE format, but Microsoft BASIC stores such values in the Microsoft Binary format. The *dmsbintoieee* function allows C programs to read binary data files with double-precision values stored by Microsoft BASIC.

SEE ALSO `dieeetomsbin`   To convert from IEEE format to Microsoft Binary format

`fieeetomsbin, fmsbintoieee`   Conversion routines for single-precision *float* variables

EXAMPLE In the example for *dieeetomsbin* we wrote a binary file with 10 floating-point values in Microsoft Binary format. Now write a program that reads this data and converts it back to IEEE format using *dmsbintoieee*. Print the converted values.

```
#include <math.h>
#include <stdio.h>
double data[10], conv[10];
main()
{
    int i;
    char filename[80];
```

 Math Routines

```
        FILE *infile;
/* Read data from binary file */
    printf("Enter file name for MS binary data:");
    gets(filename);
    if ((infile = fopen(filename, "rb")) == NULL)
    {
        printf("Error opening file: %s\n", filename);
        exit(0);
    }
    i = fread(data, sizeof(double), 10, infile);
    printf("Read %d bytes from file: %s\n", i, filename);
/* Convert from MS binary to IEEE format */
    printf("Values are: ");
    for(i=0; i<10; i++)
    {
        dmsbintoieee(data+i, conv+i);

        printf("%g ", *(conv+i));
    }
    printf("\n");
}
```

exp

COMPATIBILITY	MSC 3	MSC 4	MSC 5	QC	TC	ANSI	UNIX V
	▲	▲	▲	▲	▲	▲	▲

PURPOSE Use *exp* to compute the exponential of a *double* variable.

SYNTAX `double exp(double x);`

`double x;`   Variable whose exponential is to be computed

EXAMPLE CALL `y = exp(x);`

INCLUDES `#include <math.h>`   For function declaration and definition of error constants

DESCRIPTION The *exp* function computes the exponential of the *double* variable x. The exponential of a variable x is e^x where e is the base of natural logarithm ($e = 2.7182818$).

RETURNS Normally, *exp* returns the exponential of x. In case of overflow (the value of the result is too large), *exp* returns the value HUGE_VAL and sets *errno* to the constant ERANGE. On underflow, the return value will be zero, but *errno* is not set.

SEE ALSO

log   To compute the natural logarithm (the inverse of the exponential) of a variable

pow   To raise *x* to the power *y*

EXAMPLE   Write a program that accepts a floating-point number on the command line and computes its exponential.

```c
#include <stdio.h>
#include <math.h>
#include <stdlib.h>  /* errno is declared here */
main(int argc, char **argv)
{
    double result;
    if(argc < 2)
    {
        printf("Usage: %s <value>\n", argv[0]);
    }
    else
    {
        result = exp(atof(argv[1]));
        if (errno != EDOM)
            printf("exp (%s) = %f\n", argv[1], result);
    }
}
```

fabs

COMPATIBILITY	MSC 3	MSC 4	MSC 5	QC	TC	ANSI	UNIX V
	▲	▲	▲	▲	▲	▲	▲

PURPOSE   Use *fabs* to compute the absolute value of a *double* variable.

SYNTAX   `double fabs(double x);`

`double x;`   Variable whose absolute value is to be returned

EXAMPLE CALL   `y = fabs(-5.15); /* y will be 5.15 */`

INCLUDES   `#include <math.h>`   For function declaration

DESCRIPTION   The *fabs* function returns the absolute value of its argument *x*.

RETURNS   The return value is of type *double* with a positive value that is the absolute value of *x*.

 Math Routines

SEE ALSO   cabs   To compute the magnitude of a complex variable

EXAMPLE   Write a program that accepts a floating-point number on the command line and computes the absolute value of the number by using *fabs*.

```
#include <stdio.h>
#include <math.h>
main(int argc, char **argv)

{
    double result;
    if(argc < 2)
    {
        printf("Usage: %s <value>\n", argv[0]);
    }
    else
    {
        result = fabs(atof(argv[1]));
        printf("Absolute value of %s = %f\n",
                argv[1], result);
    }
}
```

fieeetomsbin

COMPATIBILITY	MSC 3	MSC 4	MSC 5	QC	TC	ANSI	UNIX V
		▲	▲	▲			

PURPOSE   Use the *fieeetomsbin* function to convert a single-precision number from IEEE format to Microsoft Binary format.

SYNTAX   `int fieeetomsbin(float *src4, float *dst4);`

`float *src4;`   Pointer to float variable with value in IEEE format

`float *dst4;`   Pointer to float variable where Microsoft Binary representation is returned

EXAMPLE CALL   `fieeetomsbin(&f_ieee, &f_msbin);`

INCLUDES   `#include <math.h>`   For function declaration

DESCRIPTION   The *fieeetomsbin* function converts the single-precision value in IEEE format stored at the address *src4* to Microsoft Binary format and returns this value at the address *dst4*. This routine cannot handle IEEE NANs (not-a-number) and infinities. Also, IEEE "denormals" are treated as zeroes.

COMMON USES The *fieeetomsbin* function is useful in writing from C programs binary data files with single-precision values that can be read by Microsoft BASIC, which uses the Microsoft Binary format.

RETURNS The *fieeetomsbin* function returns a zero if conversion is successful and a one if conversion caused an overflow.

SEE ALSO fmsbintoieee   To convert from Microsoft Binary format to IEEE format

dieeetomsbin, dmsbintoieee   Conversion routines for double-precision *double* variables

EXAMPLE Write a program that uses *fieeetomsbin* to convert some *float* values (by default in IEEE double-precision format) to Microsoft Binary format and saves the result in a binary file. In the example for *fmsbintoieee* we will use this data file as input.

```c
#include <math.h>
#include <stdio.h>
float data[10] = {0.1, 0.2, 0.3, 0.4, 0.5, 0.6, 0.7,
                  0.8, 0.9, 1.0};
float conv[10];
main()
{
    int i;
    char filename[80];
    FILE *outfile;
/* Convert data to MS binary format */
    for(i=0; i<10; i++)
        fieeetomsbin(data+i, conv+i);
/* Save in a file */
    printf("Enter file name for MS binary data:");
    gets(filename);
    if ((outfile = fopen(filename, "wb")) == NULL)
    {
        printf("Error opening file: %s\n", filename);
        exit(0);
    }
    i = fwrite(conv, sizeof(float), 10, outfile);
    printf("Saved %d bytes in file: %s\n", i, filename);
}
```

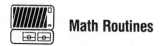 **Math Routines**

floor

COMPATIBILITY	MSC 3	MSC 4	MSC 5	QC	TC	ANSI	UNIX V
	▲	▲	▲	▲	▲	▲	▲

PURPOSE Use *floor* to compute the "floor," the largest integer value that is less than or equal to a *double* variable.

SYNTAX `double floor(double x);`

`double x;` Variable whose floor is to be returned

EXAMPLE CALL `x = floor(4.15); /* x will be 4.0 */`

INCLUDES `#include <math.h>` For function declaration

DESCRIPTION The *floor* function finds the floor of a *double* argument *x*. The floor is the largest integral value that is less than or equal to *x*. This can be used in rounding a *double* value *down* to the preceding integer.

RETURNS The return value is the floor of *x* expressed as a *double*.

SEE ALSO `ceil` To determine the smallest integer that just exceeds a variable

EXAMPLE Write a program that accepts a floating-point number on the command line and prints the floor of that number.

```c
#include <stdio.h>
#include <math.h>
main(int argc, char **argv)
{
    double result;
    if(argc < 2)
    {
        printf("Usage: %s <value>\n", argv[0]);
    }
    else
    {
        result = floor(atof(argv[1]));
        printf("floor of %s = %f\n", argv[1], result);
    }
}
```

fmod

COMPATIBILITY	MSC 3	MSC 4	MSC 5	QC	TC	ANSI	UNIX V
	▲	▲	▲	▲	▲	▲	▲

PURPOSE Use *fmod* to compute the floating-point remainder after dividing one floating-point number by another and ensuring that the quotient is the largest possible integer.

SYNTAX `double fmod(double x, double y);`

`double x, y;`　　　The remainder after the division x/y is returned

EXAMPLE CALL `rem = fmod(24.95, 5.5); /* rem will be 2.95 */`

INCLUDES `#include <math.h>`　　　For function declaration

DESCRIPTION The *fmod* function divides x by y and finds the integral floor of the quotient, the largest integer that is less than or equal to the quotient. If this result is n, *fmod* returns the value r computed from the expression $r = x - n*y$. The entire operation is equivalent to

```
double n, r;
    :
    :
n = floor(x/y);
r = x - n*y;
```

RETURNS When y is zero, *fmod* returns a zero. Otherwise, it returns the remainder computed as described above.

SEE ALSO `floor`　　　To find the largest integer that is less than or equal to a floating-point value

EXAMPLE Write a program that takes two real numbers and computes the floating-point remainder after dividing the first number by the second and ensuring that the quotient is the largest integer possible.

```
#include <stdio.h>
#include <math.h>
#include <stdlib.h>        /* errno is defined here */
main(int argc, char **argv)
{
    double x, y, result;
    if(argc < 3)
    {
        printf("Usage: %s <x> <y>\n", argv[0]);
    }
```

 Math Routines

```
            else
            {
                x = atof(argv[1]);

                y = atof(argv[2]);
                result = fmod(x,y);
                if(errno != ERANGE)
                {
                    printf("fmod(%s, %s) = %f\n",
                            argv[1], argv[2], result);
                }
            }
        }
```

fmsbintoieee

COMPATIBILITY	MSC 3	MSC 4	MSC 5	QC	TC	ANSI	UNIX V
		▲	▲	▲			

PURPOSE Use the *fmsbintoieee* function to convert a single-precision number from Microsoft Binary format to the IEEE format.

SYNTAX `int fmsbintoieee(float *src4, float *dst4);`

`float *src4;`   Pointer to float variable with value in Microsoft Binary format

`float *dst4;`   Pointer to float variable where IEEE representation is returned

EXAMPLE CALL `fmsbintoieee(&f_msbin, &f_ieee);`

INCLUDES `#include <math.h>`   For function declaration

DESCRIPTION The *fmsbintoieee* function converts the single-precision value in Microsoft Binary format stored at the address *src4* to IEEE format and returns this result at the address *dst4*.

COMMON USES Since Microsoft C uses the IEEE format, the *fmsbintoieee* function is useful in reading binary data files with single-precision values in Microsoft Binary format that might have been created by Microsoft BASIC.

RETURNS The *fmsbintoieee* function returns a 0 if conversion is successful and a 1 if the conversion caused an overflow.

SEE ALSO `fieeetomsbin`   To convert from IEEE format to Microsoft Binary format

`dieeetomsbin, dmsbintoieee`   Conversion routines for double-precision variables

fmsbintoieee

EXAMPLE   In the example for *fieeetomsbin* we wrote a binary file with 10 single-precision floating-point values in Microsoft Binary format. Write a program here that reads that data and uses *fmsbintoieee* to convert it back to IEEE format. Print the result. Compare these results with those in the example for *fieeetomsbin*.

```
#include <math.h>
#include <stdio.h>
float data[10], conv[10];
main()
{
    int i;
    char filename[80];
    FILE *infile;
/* Read data from binary file */
    printf("Enter file name for MS binary data:");
    gets(filename);
    if ((infile = fopen(filename, "rb")) == NULL)
    {
        printf("Error opening file: %s\n", filename);
        exit(0);
    }
    i = fread(data, sizeof(float), 10, infile);
    printf("Read %d bytes from file: %s\n", i, filename);
/* Convert from MS binary to IEEE format */
    printf("Values are: ");
    for(i=0; i<10; i++)
    {
        fmsbintoieee(data+i, conv+i);
        printf("%g ", *(conv+i));
    }
    printf("\n");
}
```

_fpreset

COMPATIBILITY	MSC 3	MSC 4	MSC 5	QC	TC	ANSI	UNIX V
		▲	▲	▲	▲		

PURPOSE   Use *_fpreset* to reinitialize the floating-point math package.

SYNTAX   void _fpreset(void);

EXAMPLE CALL   _fpreset();

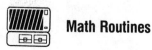 **Math Routines**

INCLUDES   `#include <float.h>`   For function declaration

DESCRIPTION   The *_fpreset* function reinitializes the floating-point math package. This function is provided so that you can begin with a clean floating-point system after using functions from the *system, signal* and *spawn, exec* families, which Microsoft suggests not be used within floating-point calculations. As an example, if you trap floating-point errors using *signal* with the constant SIGFPE, the exception handler can safely recover from floating-point errors by calling *_fpreset* followed by a *longjmp*.

SEE ALSO   `signal`   This can be used to trap floating-point exceptions

EXAMPLE   The *signal* function of the C library allows you to set up SIGFPE signals to handle floating-point errors. When a floating-point error occurs, the handler is invoked. As suggested above, inside the handler you should initialize the floating-point package before returning. Test the program by using *setjmp* and *longjmp* and a deliberate divide-by-zero error.

```
#include <stdio.h>
#include <float.h>
#include <setjmp.h>
#include <signal.h>
int myfphandler(int, int);
jmp_buf this_point;
main()
{
    double a = 1.0, b = 0.0, c;
/* Set up floating point error handler            */
    if(signal(SIGFPE, myfphandler) == SIG_ERR)
    {
        abort();
    }
/* Mark the place where we jump back after error */
    if(setjmp(this_point) == 0)
    {
/* Create a math error, divide by zero            */
        c = a/b;
    }
/* "longjmp" will get up here from "myfphandler" */
    printf("Recovered from floating point error\n");
}
/*----------------------------------------------------*/
int myfphandler(int sig, int num)
{
    printf("In handler: signal = %d, subcode = %d\n",
            sig, num);
/* As recommended, initialize floating point package */
    _fpreset();
```

```
/* Use "longjmp" to return                              */
    longjmp(this_point, -1);
}
```

frexp

COMPATIBILITY	MSC 3	MSC 4	MSC 5	QC	TC	ANSI	UNIX V
	▲	▲	▲	▲	▲	▲	▲

PURPOSE   Use *frexp* to compute a mantissa with an absolute value between 0.5 and 1.0 and an integer exponent such that the floating-point argument to *frexp* is equal to the mantissa × 2^n.

SYNTAX   `double frexp(double x, int *expptr);`

`double x;`   Floating-point argument to be decomposed

`int *expptr;`   Pointer to an integer where the exponent is returned

EXAMPLE CALL   `mantissa = frexp(5.1, &exponent);`

INCLUDES   `#include <math.h>`   For function declaration

DESCRIPTION   The *frexp* function breaks down the floating-point number *x* into a mantissa *m*, whose absolute value lies between 0.5 and 1.0, and an integer exponent *n*, so that $x = m \times 2^n$.

The exponent *n* is stored by *frexp* in the location whose address is given in the argument *expptr*. If *x* is zero, the exponent will also be zero.

COMMON USES   You can use *frexp* to generate the binary representation of a floating-point number. (The tutorial section explains how floating-point numbers are represented in binary form in computers.)

RETURNS   Normally *frexp* returns the mantissa *m* computed as described above. When *x* is zero, *frexp* returns a zero as the mantissa.

SEE ALSO   dexp   To reconstruct a floating-point number from mantissa and exponent, as computed by *frexp*

           modf   To decompose a floating-point number into its fractional and integral parts

EXAMPLE   Use *frexp* in a program to decompose a real value into a mantissa (between 0.5 and 1) and an exponent of 2.

```
#include <stdio.h>
#include <math.h>
```

 Math Routines

```
#include <stdlib.h>        /* errno is defined here */
main(int argc, char **argv)
{
    int exponent;
    double x, mantissa;
    if(argc < 2)
    {
        printf("Usage: %s <x>\n", argv[0]);
    }
    else
    {
        x = atof(argv[1]);
        mantissa = frexp(x, &exponent);
        printf("%s = %f times 2 raised to %d\n",
                    argv[1], mantissa, exponent);
    }
}
```

hypot

COMPATIBILITY	MSC 3	MSC 4	MSC 5	QC	TC	ANSI	UNIX V
	▲	▲	▲	▲	▲		▲

PURPOSE Use *hypot* to compute the length of the hypotenuse of a right triangle, given the length of the other two sides.

SYNTAX `double hypot(double x, double y);`

`double x, y;`   sqrt(x*x + y*y) will be returned

EXAMPLE CALL `length = hypot(3.0, 4.0); /* length = 5.0 */`

INCLUDES `#include <math.h>`   For function declaration and definition of constants ERANGE and HUGE_VAL

DESCRIPTION The *hypot* function computes the square root of the sum of the squares of the arguments x and y, giving the return value:

`return_value = sqrt(x*x + y*y);`

If x and y are the sides of a right triangle (i.e., these two sides met at a right angle), by the Pythagorean theorem the value returned by *hypot* corresponds to the length of the hypotenuse of the right triangle. If x and y represented the real and the imaginary parts of a complex number, respectively, the value returned by *hypot* is the magnitude (i.e., the absolute value) of the complex number represented by x and y. Thus *hypot* can be used to achieve the functionality of *cabs* as well.

RETURNS The normal return value is the length of the hypotenuse as described above. If the result is too large, however, *hypot* returns the value HUGE_VAL and sets *errno* to the constant ERANGE.

SEE ALSO cabs   To compute magnitude of a complex number

EXAMPLE Write a program that computes the length of the hypotenuse of a right triangle whose sides are entered on the command line.

```
#include <stdio.h>
#include <math.h>
#include <stdlib.h>        /* errno is defined here */
main(int argc, char **argv)
{
    double x, y, result;
    if(argc < 3)
    {
        printf("Usage: %s <x> <y>\n", argv[0]);
    }
    else
    {
        x = atof(argv[1]);
        y = atof(argv[2]);
        result = hypot(x,y);
        if(errno != ERANGE)
        {
            printf("hypot(%s, %s) = %f\n",
                    argv[1], argv[2], result);
        }
    }
}
```

labs

COMPATIBILITY	MSC 3	MSC 4	MSC 5	QC	TC	ANSI	UNIX V
	▲	▲	▲	▲	▲	▲	

PURPOSE Use *labs* to get the absolute value of a long integer value.

SYNTAX long labs(long n);

long n;   Long integer whose absolute value is returned

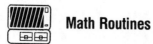 **Math Routines**

EXAMPLE CALL `lresult = labs(-65540L); /* result will be 65540 */`

INCLUDES `#include <stdlib.h>`   For function declaration

DESCRIPTION The *labs* function returns the absolute value of the long integer argument *n*. For example, *labs(-999999L)* returns 999999.

RETURNS The long integer returned by *labs* is the absolute value of *n*.

SEE ALSO `abs`   To get the absolute value of an integer

`cabs`   To obtain the magnitude (or absolute value) of a complex number

`fabs`   To get the absolute value of a floating-point number

EXAMPLE Use *labs* to obtain the absolute value of a long integer entered as a command-line argument to a program.

```
#include <stdio.h>
#include <stdlib.h>
main(int argc, char **argv)
{
    long value, result;
    if(argc < 2)
    {
        printf("Usage: %s <long_integer_value>\n",
                argv[0]);
    }
    else
    {
        value = atol(argv[1]);
        result = labs(value);
        printf("Absolute value of %ld = %ld\n",
                value, result);
    }
}
```

ldexp

COMPATIBILITY	MSC 3	MSC 4	MSC 5	QC	TC	ANSI	UNIX V
	▲	▲	▲	▲	▲	▲	▲

PURPOSE Use *ldexp* to compute a floating-point number from a mantissa and an integer exponent such that the floating-point number is equal to the mantissa × 2^{exp}.

SYNTAX `double ldexp(double x, int exp);`

```
double x;        Floating-point value of the mantissa

int exp;         Integer exponent
```

EXAMPLE CALL
```
value = ldexp(mantissa, binary_exponent);
```

INCLUDES
```
#include <math.h>        For function declaration
```

DESCRIPTION The *ldexp* function computes and returns the floating-point number equal to $x \times 2^{exp}$.

COMMON USES The *ldexp* complements *frexp* by enabling you to determine the floating-point value corresponding to a binary representation in the mantissa-exponent form. (See the tutorial section for an explanation.)

RETURNS Normally *ldexp* returns the value computed as described above. When the result is too large, *ldexp* returns the value HUGE_VAL (with the sign of *x*) and sets *errno* to ERANGE.

SEE ALSO frexp   To decompose a floating-point number into a mantissa and an exponent as required by *ldexp*

modf   To decompose a floating-point number into its fractional and integral parts

EXAMPLE Write a program to accept a mantissa and an exponent of 2 and compute the number they represent.

```
#include <stdio.h>
#include <math.h>
#include <stdlib.h>        /* errno is defined here */
main(int argc, char **argv)
{
    double mantissa, result;
    int    exponent;
    if(argc < 3)
    {
        printf("Usage: %s <mantissa> <exponent>\n",
                argv[0]);
    }
    else
    {
        mantissa = atof(argv[1]);
        exponent = atoi(argv[2]);
        result = ldexp(mantissa, exponent);
        if(errno != ERANGE)
        {
            printf("%s times 2 raised to %s = %f\n",
```

 Math Routines

```
                    argv[1], argv[2], result);
            }
        }
    }
```

ldiv

COMPATIBILITY	MSC 3	MSC 4	MSC 5	QC	TC	ANSI	UNIX V
			▲	▲	▲	▲	

PURPOSE Use *ldiv* to divide one long integer value by another and get the quotient and remainder in a structure of type *ldiv_t*.

SYNTAX `ldiv_t ldiv(long numer, long denom);`

`long numer;`   Numerator

`long denom;`   Denominator

EXAMPLE CALL
```
lresult = ldiv(65540L, 65536L);
/* lresult.quot = 1, lresult.rem = 4 */
```

INCLUDES `#include <stdlib.h>`   For function declaration and definition of structure *ldiv_t*

DESCRIPTION The *ldiv* function divides the long integer *numer* by another long integer, *denom*, and returns the resulting quotient and remainder packed in a structure of type *ldiv_t*. The structure type *ldiv_t* is defined in *stdlib.h* as

```
typedef struct
{
    long quot;    /* The quotient  */
    long rem;     /* The remainder */
} ldiv_t;
```

RETURNS The *ldiv* function returns a structure of type *ldiv_t* containing the quotient and remainder of the division.

SEE ALSO `div`   To divide one integer by another

EXAMPLE Write a program that accepts two long integers, a numerator and a denominator, on the command line and uses *ldiv* to compute the quotient and remainder of the division.

```
#include <stdio.h>
#include <stdlib.h>
```

ldiv

```
main(int argc, char **argv)
{
    long int x, y;
    ldiv_t result;
/* Make sure that there is at least 3 arguments */
    if(argc < 3)
    {
        printf("Usage: %s <long numerator> <long denom>\n",
                argv[0]);
        exit(0);

    }
/* Divide first long integer by second and display
 * quotient and remainder
 */
    x = atol(argv[1]);
    y = atol(argv[2]);
    result = ldiv(x,y);
    printf("Dividing %ld by %ld. Quotient = %ld and \
remainder = %ld\n", x, y, result.quot, result.rem);
}
```

log, log10

COMPATIBILITY	MSC 3	MSC 4	MSC 5	QC	TC	ANSI	UNIX V
	▲	▲	▲	▲	▲	▲	▲

PURPOSE Use *log* and *log10* respectively to compute the natural logarithm and logarithm to the base 10 of a positive *double* variable.

SYNTAX `double log(double x);`

`double log10(double x);`

`double x;`   Variable whose logarithm is to be computed

EXAMPLE CALL
```
y = log(x);
a = log10(b);
```

INCLUDES `#include <math.h>`   For function declaration and definition of error constants

DESCRIPTION The *log* function computes the natural logarithm (base *e*) of the *double* variable *x* (i.e., the exponential of the result should be equal to *x*).

The *log10* function computes the logarithm of *x* with respect to base 10. Thus 10 raised to the power of the result should be *x*.

 Math Routines

RETURNS   Normally, *log* and *log10* return the logarithm of *x*. If *x* is negative, both functions return the value HUGE_VAL, print a DOMAIN error on *stderr*, and set *errno* to the constant EDOM. If *x* is zero, both functions will print a SING error message to indicate a singularity (a point where the function's value is infinity), return the value HUGE_VAL, and set *errno* to ERANGE.

    Note that under Microsoft C 4.0 both *log* and *log10* set *errno* to EDOM when *x* was either zero or negative.

SEE ALSO   exp   To compute the exponential (the inverse of the natural logarithm) of a variable

               pow   To compute the value of one variable raised to the power of another

EXAMPLE   Write a small program that accepts a number and computes its natural logarithm as well as its logarithm to the base 10.

```
#include <stdio.h>
#include <math.h>
#include <stdlib.h>   /* errno is declared here */
main(int argc, char **argv)
{
    double result;
    if(argc < 2)
    {
        printf("Usage: %s <value>\n", argv[0]);
    }
    else
    {
/* Compute the natural logarithm                         */
        result = log(atof(argv[1]));
        if (errno != EDOM && errno != ERANGE)
            printf("log (%s) = %f\n", argv[1], result);

/* Now compute the logarithm to the base 10              */
        result = log10(atof(argv[1]));
        if (errno != EDOM && errno != ERANGE)
            printf("log10 (%s) = %f\n", argv[1], result);
    }
}
```

log, log10

__lrotl

COMPATIBILITY	MSC 3	MSC 4	MSC 5	QC	TC	ANSI	UNIX V
			▲	▲	▲		

PURPOSE Use *__lrotl* to rotate to the left the bits in an unsigned long integer variable.

SYNTAX `unsigned long int _lrotl(unsigned long value, int shift);`

`unsigned long value;`   Value to be rotated left

`int shift;`   Number of bits to shift

EXAMPLE CALL `result = _lrotl(0x0123454567L, 4) /* result is 0x12345670 */`

INCLUDES `#include <stdlib.h>`   For function declaration

DESCRIPTION The *__lrotl* function rotates to the left the bits in the unsigned long variable *value* by shifting bit positions. Bit rotation to the left by one position means that the leftmost bit is shifted out and inserted into the rightmost bit and all the other bits shift one step to the left.

RETURNS The unsigned long integer returned by *__lrotl* is the *value* rotated left.

SEE ALSO `_lrotr`   To rotate an unsigned long integer to the right

`_rotl, _rotr`   To rotate unsigned integers

EXAMPLE Write a program to illustrate the effect of rotating a long integer to the left. Ask the user for a value (up to eight digits) in hexadecimal. Use *__lrotl* to rotate the number to the left 32 times, printing the result in hexadecimal after each rotation.

```
#include <stdio.h>
#include <stdlib.h>
main()
{
    char input[80];
    int bits;
    unsigned long value;
    char **eptr;
    printf("Enter long integer to rotate (in hex): ");
    gets(input);
/* Convert string to unsigned long integer */
    value = strtoul(input, eptr, 16);
    for (bits = 1; bits < 33; bits++)
        printf(
```

 Math Routines

```
"%#8.8lx rotated left by %d bits = %#8.8lx\n",
value, bits, _lrotl(value,bits));
}
```

__lrotr

COMPATIBILITY	MSC 3	MSC 4	MSC 5	QC	TC	ANSI	UNIX V
			▲	▲	▲		

PURPOSE Use _lrotr_ to rotate to the right the bits in an unsigned long integer variable.

SYNTAX `unsigned long int _lrotr(unsigned long value, int shift);`

`unsigned long value;`   Value to be rotated right

`int shift;`   Number of bits to shift

EXAMPLE CALL `result = _lrotr(0x0123454567L, 16) /* result is 0x45670123 */`

INCLUDES `#include <stdlib.h>`   For function declaration

DESCRIPTION The _lrotr_ function rotates to the right the bits in the unsigned long variable _value_ by shifting bit positions. Bit rotation to the right by one position means that the rightmost bit is shifted out and inserted into the leftmost bit and all the other bits shift one step to the right.

RETURNS The unsigned long integer returned by _lrotr_ is the _value_ rotated right.

SEE ALSO `_lrotl`   To rotate an unsigned long integer to the left

`_rotl, _rotr`   To rotate unsigned integers

EXAMPLE Write a program to illustrate the effect of rotating a long integer to the right. Assume that the value (up to eight digits) in hexadecimal and the number of bits to rotate are entered on the command line. Use _lrotr_ to perform the rotation and then print the result. You can see the effect of rotation best if the number of bits to rotate is a multiple of 4.

```
#include <stdio.h>
#include <stdlib.h>
main(int argc, char **argv)
{
    int bits;
    unsigned long value;
    char **eptr;
```

__lrotr

```
        if(argc < 3)

        {
            printf("Usage: %s <hex value (max 8 digits)>\
<no. bits to rotate right>\n",
                     argv[0]);
            exit(0);
        }
/* Convert argument to unsigned long integer */
        value = strtoul(argv[1], eptr, 16);
        bits = atoi(argv[2]);
        printf("%#8.8lx rotated right by %d bits = %#8.8lx\n",
                value, bits, _lrotr(value,bits));
}
```

matherr

PURPOSE
The default *matherr* function is called by a math function when an error occurs. You can develop your own version of *matherr* to customize error handling.

SYNTAX
```
int matherr(struct exception *error_info);
```

struct exception *error_info;   Pointer to a structure that contains information about the error that just occurred

INCLUDES
`#include <math.h>`   For function declaration

DESCRIPTION
The *matherr* function is called with a pointer to a structure of type *exception*, which is defined in *math.h* as follows:

```
struct exception
{
    int type;          /* exception type - see below          */
    char *name;        /* name of function where error occurred */
    double arg1;       /* first argument to function          */
    double arg2;       /* second argument (if any) to function */
    double retval;     /* value to be returned by function    */
};
```

The value put into *retval* by *matherr* is returned by the math function to its calling process.

Math Routines

A *matherr* is present in the library, but you can supply your own version as long as it conforms to the description provided here.

RETURNS   The *matherr* function returns a zero to indicate an error and a nonzero to indicate successful corrective action. If *matherr* returns a zero the math function that called *matherr* displays an error message and sets *errno* to an appropriate value. Keep this in mind when writing your own *matherr* function.

SEE ALSO   acos, asin, atan, atan2, bessel, cabs cos, cosh, exp, hypot, log, log10, pow, sin, sinh, sqrt, tan   How the math functions behave with the default *matherr*

EXAMPLE   As described above, you can write your own version of *matherr* to handle mathematical errors your way. As an example, write a *matherr* function that handles the DOMAIN error by returning the square root of the absolute value of a number when *sqrt* is called with a negative argument. You will have to use the linker option /NOE to stop LINK from complaining when it finds a duplicate *matherr* in the default library.

```
/*  Use /NOE option with linker to use our copy of
 *  matherr error handler without complaining.
 */
#include <stdio.h>
#include <math.h>
#include <string.h>
main(int argc, char **argv)
{
    double result;
    if(argc < 2)
    {
        printf("Usage: %s <value>\n", argv[0]);
    }
    else
    {
        result = sqrt(atof(argv[1]));
        printf("sqrt (%s) = %f\n", argv[1], result);
    }
}
/*-------------------------------------------------*/
/*  Our own custom error handler. We will check if
 *  the function is "sqrt". If yes, and the error type
 *  is DOMAIN, we will return square root of the
 *  absolute value. Otherwise, our matherr will return
 *  zero to force the default actions.
 */
int matherr(struct exception *errorinfo)
{
    if(errorinfo->type == DOMAIN)
```

matherr

```
{
    if(strcmp(errorinfo->name, "sqrt") == 0)

    {
      errorinfo->retval = sqrt(-(errorinfo->arg1));
      return(1);   /* return 1 == no more error  */
    }
}
return(0); /* return 0 to indicate error       */
}
```

max

COMPATIBILITY	MSC 3	MSC 4	MSC 5	QC	TC	ANSI	UNIX V
			▲	▲	▲		

PURPOSE Use the *max* macro to obtain the larger of two values of any numerical data type, signed or unsigned.

SYNTAX `<type> max(<type> a, <type> b);`

`<type> a, b;`   Values to be compared, ⟨type⟩ denotes any numerical data type

EXAMPLE CALL
```
double dbl1, dbl2, dblmax;
int i1, i2, intmax;
dblmax = max(dbl1, dbl2);
intmax = max(i1, i2);
```

INCLUDES `#include <stdlib.h>`   For definition of the macro

DESCRIPTION The *max* macro is defined in *stdlib.h*:

```
#define max(a,b)    (((a) > (b)) ? (a) : (b))
```

It accepts two values (constants or variables) of any numerical data type and returns the value of the larger of the two. For example, if a = 9 and b = 11, max(a,b) returns b.

RETURNS The *max* macro evaluates to the larger value of the two arguments *a* and *b*.

SEE ALSO `min`   Macro to get the smaller of two values

EXAMPLE Write a utility program that accepts a single character to indicate the variable type (*i* for integer, *l* for long, and *d* for floating-point), followed by two values, and prints the maximum of the two values. Use *max* to obtain the larger of the two values.

 Math Routines

```
#include <stdio.h>
#include <stdlib.h>
main(int argc, char **argv)
{
    int    i1, i2, ir;
    long   l1, l2, lr;
    double d1, d2, dr;
    if(argc < 4)
    {
        printf("Usage: %s <type> <value1> <value2>\n",
                argv[0]);
    }
    else
    {
        switch(argv[1][0])
        {
            case 'i':
            case 'I':
                i1 = atoi(argv[2]);
                i2 = atoi(argv[3]);
                ir = max(i1, i2);
                printf("Larger of %d and %d = %d\n",
                        i1, i2, ir);
                break;
            case 'l':
            case 'L':
                l1 = atol(argv[2]);
                l2 = atol(argv[3]);
                lr = max(l1, l2);
                printf("Larger of %ld and %ld = %ld\n",
                        l1, l2, lr);
                break;
            case 'd':
            case 'D':
                d1 = atof(argv[2]);
                d2 = atof(argv[3]);
                dr = max(d1, d2);
                printf("Larger of %g and %g = %g\n",
                        d1, d2, dr);
                break;

            default:  printf("Don't know type: %c\n",
                            argv[1][0]);
        }
    }
}
```

max

min

PURPOSE Use the *min* macro to obtain the smaller of two values of any numerical data type, signed or unsigned.

SYNTAX `<type> min(<type> a, <type> b);`

`<type> a, b;`   Values to be compared, ⟨type⟩ denotes any numerical data type

EXAMPLE CALL
```
double dbl1, dbl2, dblmin;
int i1, i2, intmin;
dblmin = min(dbl1, dbl2);
intmin = min(i1, i2);
```

INCLUDES `#include <stdlib.h>`   For definition of the macro

DESCRIPTION The *min* macro is defined in *stdlib.h*:

```
#define min(a,b)    (((a) < (b)) ? (a) : (b))
```

It accepts two values (constants or variables) of any numerical data type and returns the smaller of the two. For example, if a = 9 and b = 11, min(a,b) returns a.

RETURNS The *min* macro evaluates to the smaller of the two arguments *a* and *b*.

SEE ALSO max   Macro to get the larger of two values

EXAMPLE Write a program that accepts a single character to indicate the variable type (*i* for integer, *l* for long and *d* for floating-point), followed by two values, and prints the smaller of the two values. Use *min* to obtain the minimum of the two values.

```
#include <stdio.h>
#include <stdlib.h>
main(int argc, char **argv)
{
    int    i1, i2, ir;
    long   l1, l2, lr;
    double d1, d2, dr;
    if(argc < 4)
    {
        printf("Usage: %s <type> <value1> <value2>\n",
               argv[0]);
```

 Math Routines

```
    }
    else
    {
        switch(argv[1][0])
        {
            case 'i':
            case 'I':
                i1 = atoi(argv[2]);
                i2 = atoi(argv[3]);
                ir = min(i1, i2);
                printf("Smaller of %d and %d = %d\n",
                        i1, i2, ir);
                break;
            case 'l':
            case 'L':
                l1 = atol(argv[2]);
                l2 = atol(argv[3]);
                lr = min(l1, l2);
                printf("Smaller of %ld and %ld = %ld\n",
                        l1, l2, lr);
                break;
            case 'd':
            case 'D':
                d1 = atof(argv[2]);
                d2 = atof(argv[3]);
                dr = min(d1, d2);
                printf("Smaller of %g and %g = %g\n",
                        d1, d2, dr);
                break;

            default:  printf("Don't know type: %c\n",
                            argv[1][0]);
        }
    }
}
```

modf

COMPATIBILITY	MSC 3	MSC 4	MSC 5	QC	TC	ANSI	UNIX V
	▲	▲	▲	▲	▲	▲	▲

PURPOSE   Use *modf* to decompose a floating-point number into its fractional and integral parts.

modf

SYNTAX
```
double modf(double x, double *intptr);
```

```
double x;        Floating-point value to be decomposed
```

```
double *intptr;        Integral part of x is returned here
```

EXAMPLE CALL
```
fraction = modf(24.95, &int_part); /* fraction is .95 */
```

INCLUDES
```
#include <math.h>        For function declaration
```

DESCRIPTION The *modf* function separates the floating-point number *x* into its fractional part and its integral part. The integer part is returned as a floating-point value in the location whose address is given in the argument *intptr*.

RETURNS The *modf* function returns the signed fractional part of *x*.

SEE ALSO
frexp   To decompose a floating-point number into a mantissa and an exponent

ldexp   To construct a floating-point number from its mantissa and exponent

EXAMPLE Write a program that accepts a real number and decomposes it into its integral part and its fractional part.

```
#include <stdio.h>
#include <math.h>
#include <stdlib.h>        /* errno is defined here */
main(int argc, char **argv)
{
    double x, intpart, fract;
    if(argc < 2)
    {
        printf("Usage: %s <x>\n", argv[0]);
    }
    else
    {
        x = atof(argv[1]);
        fract = modf(x, &intpart);
        printf("Integer part of %s   = %f\n\
Fractional part of %s = %f\n", argv[1], intpart,
        argv[1], fract);
    }
}
```

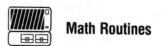 **Math Routines**

pow

COMPATIBILITY	MSC 3	MSC 4	MSC 5	QC	TC	ANSI	UNIX V
	▲	▲	▲	▲	▲	▲	▲

PURPOSE Use *pow* to compute the value of one argument raised to the power of another.

SYNTAX `double pow(double x, double y);`

`double x, y;` x raised to the power y is computed

EXAMPLE CALL `x = pow(2.0, 3.0); /* x will be 8.0 */`

INCLUDES `#include <math.h>` For function declaration and definition of constants EDOM, ERANGE, DOMAIN, and HUGE_VAL

DESCRIPTION The *pow* function computes the value of x raised to the power y. Neither argument can be zero and when x is negative, y can only take integral values less than 2^{64}.

RETURNS When both x and y are nonzero positive numbers, *pow* returns the value x raised to the power y. If x is nonzero and y is zero, the return value is unity (one). When x is zero and y is negative, *pow* returns the value HUGE_VAL and sets *errno* to EDOM. If both x and y are zero or if x is negative and y is not an integral value, *pow* returns a zero, sets *errno* to EDOM, and prints a DOMAIN error message to *stderr*. If the result is too large, *pow* prints no message but returns the value HUGE_VAL.

SEE ALSO exp To compute exponential

matherr To handle math errors (you can add your own)

log, log10 To compute logarithms

sqrt To compute square root

EXAMPLE Write a program to accept floating-point numbers x and y on the command line and compute the value of x raised to the power y.

```
#include <stdio.h>
#include <math.h>
#include <stdlib.h>        /* errno is defined here */
main(int argc, char **argv)
{
    double x, y, result;
    if(argc < 3)
```

```
{
    printf("Usage: %s <x> <y>\n", argv[0]);
}
else
{
    x = atof(argv[1]);
    y = atof(argv[2]);
    result = pow(x,y);
    if(errno != ERANGE)
    {
        printf("%s raised to the power %s = %f\n",
                argv[1], argv[2], result);
    }
}
}
```

rand

COMPATIBILITY	MSC 3	MSC 4	MSC 5	QC	TC	ANSI	UNIX V
	▲	▲	▲	▲	▲	▲	▲

PURPOSE Use *rand* to generate a pseudorandom integer with a value in the range 0–32,767.

SYNTAX `int rand(void);`

EXAMPLE CALL `random_value = rand();`

INCLUDES `#include <stdlib.h>`   For function definition

DESCRIPTION The *rand* function generates a pseudorandom integer with a value between 0 and 32,767. The starting point of the pseudorandom integers (the "seed") is set by calling *srand*.

RETURNS The *rand* function returns the pseudorandom integer it generates.

COMMENTS We say the integer returned by *rand* is pseudorandom, instead of random, because, given the seed, the sequence of numbers to be generated is predictable. After all, they are generated by a fixed algorithm. If the algorithm is well designed, though, the numbers within the sequence appear to be random.

Select a random seed each time you call *srand* to get a new sequence of numbers each time.

SEE ALSO `srand`   To set a new seed for the random number generator

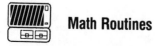 **Math Routines**

EXAMPLE   Call *rand* and generate 20 pseudorandom integers. Print the integers and note that the same sequence is generated every time the program is run. A different sequence can be obtained by changing the starting seed.

```
#include <stdio.h>
#include <stdlib.h>
main()
{
    int i;
/* Generate and display 20 pseudorandom integers */
    printf("20 pseudorandom integers from \"rand\"\n");
    for(i=0; i<20; i++)
    {
        printf("%d\n", rand());
    }
}
```

__rotl

COMPATIBILITY	MSC 3	MSC 4	MSC 5	QC	TC	ANSI	UNIX V
			▲	▲	▲		

PURPOSE   Use *_rotl* to rotate to the left the bits in an unsigned integer variable.

SYNTAX   `unsigned _rotl(unsigned value, int shift);`

`unsigned int value;`   Value to be rotated left

`int shift;`   Number of bits to shift

EXAMPLE CALL   `new_pattern = _rotl(0x1234, 8); /* result is 3412h */`

INCLUDES   `#include <stdlib.h>`   For function declaration

DESCRIPTION   The *_rotl* function rotates to the left the bits in the *value* by shifting bit positions. Bit rotation to the left by one position means that the leftmost bit is shifted out and inserted into the rightmost bit and all the other bits shift one step to the left.

RETURNS   The unsigned integer returned by *_rotl* is the *value* rotated left. For example, *_rotl(0x0123, 4* returns *0x1230*.

SEE ALSO   `_lrotl, _lrotr`   To rotate unsigned long integers

`_rotr`   To rotate an unsigned integer to the right

EXAMPLE Write a program that accepts an integer value in hexadecimal form and the number of bits to rotate, uses *_rotl* to rotate that number to the left, and displays the result in hexadecimal. The effect of left rotation is most apparent if you run the program with shifts of 4 and 8.

```
#include <stdio.h>
#include <stdlib.h>
main(int argc, char **argv)
{
    int bits;
    unsigned value;
    if(argc < 3)
    {
        printf("Usage: %s <hex value (max 4 digits)>\
<no. bits to rotate left>\n",
                argv[0]);
        exit(0);
    }
/* Convert argument to unsigned long integer */
    sscanf(argv[1], "%4x", &value);
    bits = atoi(argv[2]);
    printf("%#4.4x rotated left by %d bits = %#4.4x\n",
            value, bits, _rotl(value,bits));
}
```

__rotr

COMPATIBILITY	MSC 3	MSC 4	MSC 5	QC	TC	ANSI	UNIX V
			▲	▲	▲		

PURPOSE Use *_rotr* to rotate to the right the bits in an unsigned integer variable.

SYNTAX unsigned _rotr(unsigned value, int shift);

unsigned int value;   Value to be rotated right

int shift;   Number of bits to shift

EXAMPLE CALL rotated_value = _rotr(0x1234, 4); /* result is 4123h */

INCLUDES #include <stdlib.h>   For function declaration

DESCRIPTION The *_rotr* function rotates the bits in the *value* to the right by shifting bit positions. Bit rotation to the right by one position means that the rightmost

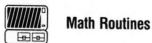 **Math Routines**

bit is shifted out and inserted into the leftmost bit and all the other bits shift one step to the right.

RETURNS The unsigned integer returned by *_rotr* is the *value* rotated right. For example, *_rotr(0x0123, 4)* will return *0x2301*.

SEE ALSO `_lrotl, _lrotr`   To rotate unsigned long integers

`_rotl`   To rotate an unsigned integer to the left

EXAMPLE Write a program that accepts an integer value in hexadecimal form, uses *_rotl* to rotate that number 16 times to the right, and displays the result in hexadecimal at each step.

```
#include <stdio.h>
#include <stdlib.h>
main()
{
    int bits;
    unsigned value;
    printf("Enter a hexadecimal value to be rotated :");
    scanf("%4x", &value);
    for (bits = 1; bits < 17; bits++)
        printf(
        "%#4.4x rotated right by %d bits = %#4.4x\n",
        value, bits, _rotr(value,bits));
}
```

sin

COMPATIBILITY	MSC 3	MSC 4	MSC 5	QC	TC	ANSI	UNIX V
	▲	▲	▲	▲	▲	▲	▲

PURPOSE Use *sin* to compute the sine of an angle whose value is expressed in radians.

SYNTAX `double sin(double x);`

`double x;`   Angle in radians whose sine is to be computed

EXAMPLE CALL `y = sin(x)`

INCLUDES `#include <math.h>`   For function declaration and definition of error constants

DESCRIPTION The *sin* function computes the sine of *double* argument *x*, which represents an angle in radians.

sin

RETURNS   As long as the angle *x* is less than approximately $1.34e^8$ radians (found by experimentation), *sin* computes and returns the sine of *x*. If the value of *x* is larger, a loss of significance (the result is correct up to a few digits only) occurs and *sin* generates a PLOSS error to indicate "partial loss of precision." If the value is so large that the result is totally useless, a TLOSS error is sent to *stderr*, the return value is zero, and *errno* is set to the constant ERANGE.

SEE ALSO   asin   To compute the arc sine of a variable

                cos   To compute cosine of an angle

EXAMPLE   Write a program that accepts an angle in degrees and prints its sine.

```
#include <stdio.h>
#include <math.h>
#include <stdlib.h>        /* errno is defined here */
#define  R_TO_D   57.29578 /* radians to degrees   */
main(int argc, char **argv)
{
    double result;
    if(argc < 2)
    {
        printf("Usage: %s <degrees>\n", argv[0]);
    }
    else
    {
        result = sin(atof(argv[1]) / R_TO_D);
        if(errno != ERANGE)
        {
            printf("Sine (%s deg.) = %f\n",
                    argv[1], result);
        }
    }
}
```

sinh

COMPATIBILITY	MSC 3	MSC 4	MSC 5	QC	TC	ANSI	UNIX V
	▲	▲	▲	▲	▲	▲	▲

PURPOSE   Use *sinh* to compute the hyperbolic sine of a *double* variable.

SYNTAX   double sinh(double x);

                double x;   Variable whose hyperbolic sine is to be computed

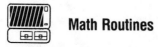 **Math Routines**

EXAMPLE CALL `a = cosh(b);`

INCLUDES `#include <math.h>`   For function declaration and definition of error constants

DESCRIPTION The *sinh* function computes the hyperbolic sine of the *double* variable *x*.

RETURNS Normally, *sinh* returns the hyperbolic sine of *x*. If the result is too large (a *double* variable can be as large as approximately 10^{308}), *sinh* returns the value HUGE_VAL and sets *errno* to the constant ERANGE.

SEE ALSO `cosh`   To compute the hyperbolic cosine of a variable

EXAMPLE Write a program that accepts a floating-point number on the command line and computes its hyperbolic sine.

```
#include <stdio.h>
#include <math.h>
#include <stdlib.h>        /* errno is defined here */
main(int argc, char **argv)
{
    double result;
    if(argc < 2)
    {
        printf("Usage: %s <value>\n", argv[0]);
    }
    else
    {
        result = sinh(atof(argv[1]));
        if(errno != ERANGE)
        {
            printf("Hyperbolic sine of %s = %f\n",
                    argv[1], result);
        }
    }
}
```

sqrt

COMPATIBILITY	MSC 3	MSC 4	MSC 5	QC	TC	ANSI	UNIX V
	▲	▲	▲	▲	▲	▲	▲

PURPOSE Use *sqrt* to compute the square root of a non-negative *double* variable.

SYNTAX `double sqrt(double x);`

`double x;`   Variable whose square root is to be computed

EXAMPLE CALL   `sqrt_2 = sqrt(2.0); /* sqrt_2 = 1.414 */`

INCLUDES   `#include <math.h>`   For function declaration

DESCRIPTION   The *sqrt* function computes the square root of the *double* variable *x*, provided *x* is not negative.

RETURNS   The *sqrt* function returns the square root of *x*. If *x* is negative, though, *sqrt* prints a DOMAIN error message to *stderr*, sets the global variable *errno* to EDOM, and returns a zero.

SEE ALSO   pow   To compute the value of one argument raised to the power of another

EXAMPLE   Write a program that accepts a number and computes its square root.

```
#include <stdio.h>
#include <math.h>
#include <stdlib.h>  /* errno is declared here */
main(int argc, char **argv)
{
    double result;
    if(argc < 2)
    {
        printf("Usage: %s <value>\n", argv[0]);
    }
    else
    {
        result = sqrt(atof(argv[1]));
        if (errno != EDOM)
            printf("sqrt (%s) = %f\n", argv[1], result);
    }
}
```

srand

COMPATIBILITY	MSC 3	MSC 4	MSC 5	QC	TC	ANSI	UNIX V
	▲	▲	▲	▲	▲	▲	▲

PURPOSE   Use *srand* to set the starting value (seed) for generating a sequence of pseudo-random integer values.

SYNTAX   `void srand(unsigned seed);`

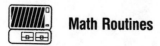

Math Routines

unsigned seed;   Starting point for random number generator

EXAMPLE CALL   srand(new_seed);

INCLUDES   #include <stdlib.h>   For function definition

DESCRIPTION   The *srand* function sets the seed of the random number generation algorithm used by the function *rand*.

   If the seed is 1, the random number generator is initialized to its default starting point, generating the sequence that is produced when *rand* is called without prior calls to *srand*. Any other value for the seed sets a random starting point for the pseudorandom sequence to be generated by *rand*.

SEE ALSO   rand   To obtain a random integer value

EXAMPLE   Write a program that uses *srand* to set the seed for a sequence of pseudorandom integers generated by *rand*. Notice that the same seed always generates the same sequence of numbers (instead of its being purely random). That is why we call the sequence of numbers "pseudorandom" (instead of being purely random).

```
#include <stdio.h>
#include <stdlib.h>
main()
{
    int i;
    unsigned seed;
/* Ask user to enter a new seed */
    printf("Enter a seed: ");
    scanf(" %u", &seed);
/* Set new seed by calling "srand" */
    srand(seed);
/* Generate and display 20 pseudorandom integers */
    printf("20 pseudorandom integers from \"rand\"\n");
    for(i=0; i<20; i++)
    {
        printf("%d\n", rand());
    }
    printf("Try again with the same seed.\n\
You'll get the same sequence.\n");
}
```

srand

__status87

COMPATIBILITY	MSC 3	MSC 4	MSC 5	QC	TC	ANSI	UNIX V
		▲	▲	▲	▲		

PURPOSE Use *__status87* to get the contents of the floating-point status word, which is a combination of the 8087 math coprocessor status word and other conditions detected by the 8087 exception handler.

SYNTAX `unsigned int _status87(void);`

EXAMPLE CALL `if(_status87() & SW_ZERODIVIDE) puts("Zero divide error");`

INCLUDES `#include <float.h>`   For function declaration and definition of constants denoting status-word bit settings

DESCRIPTION The *__status87* function returns the status word of the floating-point package. This status word is a composite of the status word of the 8087 math coprocessor and other conditions detected by the 8087 exception handler. You can use the status word to detect error conditions in your own floating-point exception handler.

You should check the return value by performing a bitwise AND with the constant from Table 8-5 that matches the condition you are verifying and then comparing that result for equality with the constant itself. In other words, if the return value is *status*, checking for a loss of precision is done by the code fragment

```
status = _status87();
if ((status & SW_INEXACT) == SW_INEXACT)
{
/* A loss of precision has occurred */
    :
    :
}
```

RETURNS The bits in the value returned by *__status87* indicate the status of the floating-point package. Table 8-5 shows the constants defined in *float.h* to indicate specific conditions.

Table 8-5. *The Floating-Point Status Word*

Status Constant	Meaning
SW_INVALID	Invalid operation.
SW_DENORMAL	Operands are stored in a "normalized" form in in the 8087 math coprocessor. This bit indicates a denormalized operand.

 Math Routines

Table 8-5. *(cont.)*

Status Constant	Meaning
SW_ZERODIVIDE	Divide-by-zero attempted.
SW_OVERFLOW	Floating-point overflow.
SW_UNDERFLOW	Floating-point underflow.
SW_INEXACT	Loss of precision in result.
SW_UNEMULATED	The floating-point package can use a library that emulates 8087 instructions. This bit indicates that an unemulated instruction was encountered. (SW_INVALID also set.)
SW_SQRTNEG	Computation of the square root of a negative number attempted. (SW_INVALID also set.)
SW_STACKOVERFLOW	Floating-point stack overflow. (SW_INVALID also set.)
SW_STACKUNDERFLOW	Floating-point stack underflow. (SW_INVALID also set.)

SEE ALSO   _clear87   To reset the floating-point status word

             _control87   To alter bits in the floating-point control word

EXAMPLE Read and display the current floating-point status word. Now copy a small double variable into a *float* one and create an underflow and an inexact result. Read and display the status word again; the new value reflects the error.

```
#include <stdio.h>
#include <float.h>
main()
{
    float a;
    double b = 1.e-40;
    unsigned fpstatus;
    printf("Before any computations ");
    fpstatus = _status87();
    printf("status word is: %X\n", fpstatus);
/* Perform operation that produces underflow and
 * an inexact result
 */
    a = b;   /* This will produce inexact result */
    printf("After undeflow/inexact ");
    fpstatus = _status87();
    printf("status word is: %X\n", fpstatus);
}
```

__status87

tan

COMPATIBILITY	MSC 3	MSC 4	MSC 5	QC	TC	ANSI	UNIX V
	▲	▲	▲	▲	▲	▲	▲

PURPOSE Use *tan* to compute the tangent of an angle whose value is expressed in radians.

SYNTAX `double tan(double x);`

`double x;` Angle in radians whose tangent is to be computed

EXAMPLE CALL `y = tan(x);`

INCLUDES `#include <math.h>` For function declaration and definition of error constants

DESCRIPTION The *tan* function computes the tangent of *double* argument *x*, which represents an angle in radians.

RETURNS As long as the angle *x* is less than approximately $1.34e^8$ radians (found by experimentation), *tan* correctly computes and returns the tangent of *x*. If the value of *x* is larger, a loss of precision results (the result is correct up to a few digits only) and *tan* generates a PLOSS error to indicate "partial loss of precision." If the value is so large that the result is totally void of precision, a TLOSS error is sent to *stderr* and the return value is zero. At the same time, *errno* is set to the constant ERANGE.

SEE ALSO atan To compute the arc tangent of a variable

EXAMPLE Write a program that accepts an angle in degrees and prints its tangent.

```
#include <stdio.h>
#include <math.h>
#include <stdlib.h>       /* errno is defined here */
#define  R_TO_D   57.29578 /* radians to degrees   */
main(int argc, char **argv)
{
    double result;
    if(argc < 2)
    {
        printf("Usage: %s <degrees>\n", argv[0]);
    }
    else
    {
        result = tan(atof(argv[1]) / R_TO_D);
        if(errno != ERANGE)
        {
```

 Math Routines

```
        printf("Tangent (%s deg.) = %f\n",
                argv[1], result);
    }
  }
}
```

tanh

COMPATIBILITY	MSC 3	MSC 4	MSC 5	QC	TC	ANSI	UNIX V
	▲	▲	▲	▲	▲	▲	▲

PURPOSE Use *tanh* to compute the hyperbolic tangent of a *double* variable.

SYNTAX `double tanh(double x);`

`double x;`   Variable whose hyperbolic tangent is to be computed

EXAMPLE CALL `a = tanh(b);`

INCLUDES `#include <math.h>`   For function declaration

DESCRIPTION The *tanh* function computes the hyperbolic tangent of the *double* variable *x*.

RETURNS The *tanh* function returns the hyperbolic tangent of *x*.

SEE ALSO `cosh, sinh`   To compute the hyperbolic cosine and hyperbolic sine of a variable

EXAMPLE Write a program that accepts a floating-point number on the command line and computes its hyperbolic tangent.

```
#include <stdio.h>
#include <math.h>
#include <stdlib.h>        /* errno is defined here */
main(int argc, char **argv)
{
    double result;
    if(argc < 2)
    {
        printf("Usage: %s <value>\n", argv[0]);
    }
    else
    {
        result = tanh(atof(argv[1]));
        if(errno != ERANGE)
        {
```

```
        printf("Hyperbolic tangent of %s = %f\n",
               argv[1], result);
    }
  }
}
```

 Math Routines

Chapter **9** *Character Classification and Conversion*

Introduction

C uses the American Standard Code for Information Interchange (ASCII) character set, which contains characters that can be printed as well as some that have special meanings and are not printable. Often you need to determine the category of a character or to convert a character from one case to another. The C library includes character classification macros for this purpose. (See Table 9-1.)

THE ASCII CHARACTER SET The ASCII character set relies on a 7-bit code to represent all letters, numbers, punctuation symbols, and some special (unprintable) control characters. The 128 ASCII characters are shown in Figure 9-1. The single-character entries are printable. The two- and three-letter codes are unprintable (except SP which denotes a blank space).

Beyond the basic 128, the IBM PC also supports character codes from 128 through 255 that a single unsigned C character variable can represent.

		Second digit														
	0	**1**	**2**	**3**	**4**	**5**	**6**	**7**	**8**	**9**	**A**	**B**	**C**	**D**	**E**	**F**
0	NUL	SOH	STX	ETX	EOT	ENQ	ACK	BEL	BS	HT	LF	VT	FF	CR	SO	SI
1	DLE	DC1	DC2	DC3	DC4	NAK	SYN	ETB	CAN	EM	SUB	ESC	FS	GS	RS	US
2	SP	!	"	#	$	%	&	'	(	)	*	+	,	–	.	/
3	0	1	2	3	4	5	6	7	8	9	:	;	<	=	>	?
4	@	A	B	C	D	E	F	G	H	I	J	K	L	M	N	O
5	P	Q	R	S	T	U	V	W	X	Y	Z	[	\	]	^	_
6	`	a	b	c	d	e	f	g	h	i	j	k	l	m	n	o
7	p	q	r	s	t	u	v	w	x	y	z	{	|	}	~	DEL
	0	**1**	**2**	**3**	**4**	**5**	**6**	**7**	**8**	**9**	**A**	**B**	**C**	**D**	**E**	**F**

First hexadecimal digit

Figure 9-1. *The ASCII character set*

Often called the "IBM PC extended ASCII character set," these are a collection of Greek, accented, and graphical characters. In fact, even the nonprinting ASCII characters can be displayed on the IBM PC and some are useful for drawing borders of pop-up menus and windows in PC applications. Most printers meant for the IBM PC also support the extended character set. The Microsoft C character classification macros, however, work with the ASCII (128) character set only.

Notes on Character Classification and Conversion

Table 9-1 shows catalogs of the available character classification macros. The macros are defined in the header file *ctype.h* where you can examine them. Table 9-2 groups the macros by task.

Table 9-1. *Character Classification Macros*

Macro	Description
isalnum	Tests if a character is alphanumeric.
isalpha	Tests if a character is alphabetic.
isascii	Tests if an integer value is a valid ASCII character.
iscntrl	Tests if a character belongs to the set of control characters.
isdigit	Tests if a character is a numerical digit.
isgraph	Tests if a character is printable (excluding the space character).
islower	Tests if a character is lowercase.
isprint	Tests if a character is printable (including the space character).
ispunct	Tests if a character belongs to the set of punctuation characters.
isspace	Tests if a character belongs to the set of whitespace characters.
isupper	Tests if a character is uppercase.
isxdigit	Tests if a character is a hexadecimal digit.
toascii	Converts an integer value to a valid ASCII character.
tolower	Converts a character to lowercase if that character is an uppercase letter.
_tolower	Converts a character to lowercase without checking if it is a uppercase letter.
toupper	Converts a character to uppercase if that character is a lowercase letter.
_toupper	Converts a character to uppercase without checking if it is a lowercase letter.

Table 9-2. *Character Classification Macros by Task*

Task	Macros
Classify a character.	isalnum, isalpha, isascii, iscntrl, isdigit, isgraph, islower, isprint, ispunct, isspace, isupper, isxdigit
Convert from uppercase to lowercase.	tolower, _tolower
Convert from lowercase to uppercase.	toupper, _toupper

CHARACTER CLASSIFICATION: BEHIND THE SCENES

The Microsoft C library maintains an array named _ctype_ containing unsigned characters and information that is used in the macro definitions to classify the characters. If 'c' is an ASCII character, the unsigned character _ctype [c+1] contains the classification information about that character. By testing the contents of _ctype[c+1], the macros determine whether 'c' belongs to a category (for example, uppercase letters). That information is encoded in the bits of the single byte in the array _ctype that corresponds to the character 'c'. For example, the uppercase 'c' has bit 0 of _ctype[c+1] set to 1. Thus 'c' is uppercase if

```
(_ctype[c+1] & 1)
```

is true (or 1). We could rewrite the test for uppercase letters to compare the ASCII code of the test character with the ASCII codes 'A' and 'Z' and to conclude that the character is uppercase if it satisfies

```
if(c >= 'A' && c <= 'Z') /* character is uppercase */
```

Both approaches work fine, but the library macros are faster because they use a single test while our method needs two logical tests.

The bit patterns in _ctype that determine the classification of characters comprise eight basic categories. These and the range of ASCII characters that belong to each are shown in Table 9-3.

Table 9-3. *Basic Categories of Character Classification*

Category	ASCII Characters
Uppercase letter	'A' through 'Z'
Lowercase letter	'a' through 'z'
Digit (0 through 9)	'0' through '9'
Whitespace	tab, line feed (newline), vertical feed, form feed and carriage return
Punctuation character	! " # $ % & ' ( ) * + , – . / : ; < = > ? @ [\ ] ^ _ ['] { ¦ } ~
Control character	All characters with codes 0 through 1F and the final character 7F
Blank space	The blank space character
Hexadecimal digit	'0' through '9', 'A' through 'F' and 'a' through 'f'

All the macros are based on these basic classification categories. Table 9-4 summarizes the categories of characters that satisfy the classification macros.

Table 9-4. *Tests Performed by Classification Macros*

Macro	Test for Basic Categories
isalpha	Uppercase or lowercase letter
isupper	Uppercase letter

Table 9-4. *(cont.)*

Macro	Test for Basic Categories
islower	Lowercase letter
isdigit	Digit
isxdigit	Hexadecimal digit
isspace	Whitespace
ispunct	Punctuation character
isalnum	Uppercase or lowercase letter or digit
isprint	Blank space or punctuation character or uppercase letter or lowercase letter or digit
isgraph	Punctuation character or uppercase letter or lowercase letter or digit
iscntrl	Control character
isascii	Value less than 80 hex

Cautions

► The possibility of "side effects" constitutes a common pitfall of using macros. This is best illustrated by an example. Consider the *tolower* macro, defined in *ctype.h* as

```
#define _tolower(c)      ( (c)-'A'+'a' )
#define tolower(c)       ( (isupper(c)) ? _tolower(c) : (c) )
```

which says you subtract the ASCII code of 'A' and add the ASCII equivalent of 'a' to get lowercase letters from uppercase ones. You can confirm the derivation of this formula with the ASCII codes shown in Figure 9-1. Now suppose you used the macro in your program as follows

```
int c;
c = tolower(getch());
```

hoping to get a single keystroke converted to lowercase when you press a key. Will this happen?

In the first step of the compilation process, the C preprocessor replaces *tolower* with its definition and produces

```
int c;
c = ( (isupper(getch())) ? ( (getch())-'A'+'a' ) : (getch()) );
```

Since the macro's argument is *getch( )*, that function call is inserted wherever *c* appears in the macro definition. Notice that *getch* is called three times in the expanded macro. Instead of processing a single keystroke, the statement consumes two characters from the keyboard; if the first is an uppercase character, the second is converted to a value by subtracting the value of 'A' and adding 'a'. For any other type of first keystroke, the second key hit at the keyboard will be copied to the variable *c* without any change.

All the extra function calls that occurred in this example are the side effects of using a macro. Because of this, you should avoid using as an argument to a macro any expression or function that when evaluated changes your program's behavior. If you use the conversion macros (with possible side effects), you might consider linking to the function versions of the *toupper* and *tolower* macros. You can do this by "undefining" the macros (use *#undef*) after the statement *#include ⟨ctype.h⟩* in your program. Insert an *#include ⟨stdlib.h⟩* after this to include the definition of the function versions.

► Although the macros *_tolower* and *_toupper* run faster because they do no checking of the characters, do not use them unless the character is known to be of the appropriate case. Otherwise, the character will be mapped to another, possibly invalid, value.

► Note that the *toascii* macro converts an integer value to ASCII by chopping off all high-order bits above the seventh one.

isalnum

COMPATIBILITY	MSC 3	MSC 4	MSC 5	QC	TC	ANSI	UNIX V
	▲	▲	▲	▲	▲	▲	▲

PURPOSE Use the *isalnum* macro to check whether an ASCII character is alphanumeric.

SYNTAX `int isalnum(int c);`

`int c;` Integer with ASCII character

EXAMPLE CALL `if(isalnum(c) != 0) printf("%c is alphanumeric\n", c);`

INCLUDES `#include <ctype.h>` For macro definition

DESCRIPTION The *isalnum* macro determines if the value in the integer argument *c* is one of the digits 0 to 9, a lowercase letter from a to z, or an uppercase letter from A to Z. The *isalnum* macro can only handle valid ASCII values (from 0 to 127) and the constant EOF, defined in *stdio.h*.

RETURNS The *isalnum* macro returns a nonzero value if the *c* is an alphanumeric character. Otherwise it returns a zero.

SEE ALSO `isascii` To test if an arbitrary integer value is a valid ASCII character

EXAMPLE Write a program that prints out the ASCII table with a special mark next to each character that satisfies *isalnum*.

```
#include <stdio.h>
#include <ctype.h>
main()
{
    int ch, count,
        mark = 0xdb; /* to mark characters */
/* Go over entire ASCII table and display the
 * alphanumeric ones.
 */
    printf(
    "Alphanumeric ones are marked with a %c\n",
            mark);
    for(count = 0, ch = 0; ch <= 0x7f; ch++)
    {
        printf("%#02x ", ch);
/* Print character -- if printable          */
        if(isprint(ch))
        {
            printf(" %c", ch);
```

Character Classification and Conversion

```
        }
        else
        {
            printf("  ");
        }
/* Perform test and put a mark if test succeeds */
        if(isalnum(ch) != 0)
        {
            printf(" %c", mark);
        }
        else
        {
            printf("  ", ch);
        }
        count++;
        if(count == 8)
        {
            printf(" \n");
            count = 0;
        }
    }
}
```

isalpha

COMPATIBILITY	MSC 3	MSC 4	MSC 5	QC	TC	ANSI	UNIX V
	▲	▲	▲	▲	▲	▲	▲

PURPOSE   Use the *isalpha* macro to check whether an ASCII character is alphabetic.

SYNTAX   `int isalpha(int c);`

       `int c;`   Integer with ASCII character

EXAMPLE CALL   `if(isalpha(c) != 0) printf("%c is letter\n", c);`

INCLUDES   `#include <ctype.h>`   For macro definition

DESCRIPTION   The *isalpha* macro determines if the value in the integer argument *c* is a lowercase letter from a to z or an uppercase letter from A to Z. The *isalpha* macro can only handle valid ASCII values (from 0 to 127) and the constant EOF, defined in *stdio.h*.

RETURNS   The *isalpha* macro returns a nonzero value if the *c* is indeed a letter. Otherwise it returns a zero.

isalpha

SEE ALSO   isascii   To test whether an arbitrary integer value is a valid ASCII character

EXAMPLE   Write a program that prints out the ASCII table with a special mark next to each character that satisfies *isalpha*.

```c
#include <stdio.h>
#include <ctype.h>
main()
{
    int ch, count,
        mark = 0xdb; /* to mark characters */
/* Go over entire ASCII table and display the
 * alphabetic ones.
 */
    printf(
    "Letters are marked with a %c\n", mark);
    for(count = 0, ch = 0; ch <= 0x7f; ch++)
    {
        printf("%#02x ", ch);
/* Print character -- if printable             */
        if(isprint(ch))
        {
            printf(" %c", ch);
        }
        else
        {
            printf("  ");
        }
/* Perform test and put a mark if test succeeds */
        if(isalpha(ch) != 0)
        {
            printf(" %c", mark);
        }
        else
        {
            printf("  ", ch);
        }
        count++;
        if(count == 8)
        {
            printf(" \n");
            count = 0;
        }
    }
}
```

Character Classification and Conversion

isascii

COMPATIBILITY	MSC 3	MSC 4	MSC 5	QC	TC	ANSI	UNIX V
	▲	▲	▲	▲	▲		▲

PURPOSE Use the *isascii* macro to check whether an arbitrary integer value is a valid ASCII character.

SYNTAX `int isascii(int c);`

`int c;`   Integer value being checked

EXAMPLE CALL `if(isascii(c) != 0) printf("%d <- not ASCII value\n", c);`

INCLUDES `#include <ctype.h>`   For macro definition

DESCRIPTION The *isascii* macro determines if the value of the integer argument *c* is in the range 0–127 (the range of values that the ASCII character set occupies).

RETURNS The *isascii* macro returns a nonzero value if the *c* is a valid ASCII character. Otherwise it returns a zero.

COMMENTS The IBM PC supports extended ASCII characters (those with codes from 128 to 255). The *isascii* macro treats these as non-ASCII.

SEE ALSO `toascii`   To convert an arbitrary integer value to a valid ASCII character

EXAMPLE Write a program that accepts an integer value on the command line and prints out a message indicating whether that value is an ASCII character. (This is true if the value is between 0 and 127.)

```
#include <stdio.h>
#include <ctype.h>
main(int argc, char **argv)
{
    int ch;
    if(argc < 2)
    {
        printf("Usage: %s <integer_value>\n",
                argv[0]);
    }
    else
    {
        if (isascii(ch = atoi(argv[1])) != 0)
        {
            printf("%s is an ASCII character\n\
It prints as %c on the IBM PC\n", argv[1],  ch);
```

```
            }
            else
            {
                printf("%s is not an ASCII char.\n",
                       argv[1]);
            }
        }
    }
```

iscntrl, isdigit, isgraph, islower, isprint, ispunct, isspace, isupper, isxdigit

COMPATIBILITY	MSC 3	MSC 4	MSC 5	QC	TC	ANSI	UNIX V
	▲	▲	▲	▲	▲	▲	▲

PURPOSE Use this group of macros to determine specific properties of an ASCII character: whether it is a control character, a digit, a lowercase letter, printable, and so on.

SYNTAX
```
int iscntrl(int c);

int isdigit(int c);

int isgraph(int c);

int islower(int c);

int isprint(int c);

int ispunct(int c);

int isspace(int c);

int isupper(int c);

int isxdigit(int c);

int c;        Integer with ASCII character
```

EXAMPLE CALL
```
if(isprint(c) != 0) printf("%c is printable\n", c);
if(isdigit(c) != 0) printf("%c is a digit\n", c);
if(iscntrl(c) != 0) printf("%d is a control char\n", c);
```

INCLUDES
```
#include <ctype.h>        For macro definitions
```

Character Classification and Conversion

DESCRIPTION This group of macros determines if the value in the integer argument *c* satisfies a specific condition. The macros can only handle valid ASCII values (from 0 to 127) and the constant EOF, defined in *stdio.h*. Table 9-5 shows the test performed by each of the macros.

Table 9-5. *Character Classification Tests*

Macro	Tests for	Acceptable Values
iscntrl	Control character	7Fh or in the range 0 to 1Fh
isdigit	Decimal digit	'0' to '9'
isgraph	Printable character excluding the space	21h to 7Eh
islower	Lowercase character	'a' to 'z'
isprint	Printable character	'a' to 'z'
ispunct	Punctuation character	21h to 2Fh or 3Ah to 40h or 5Bh to 60h or 7Bh to 7Ch
isspace	Whitespace character	9h to Dh or 20h (space)
isupper	Uppercase character	'A' to 'Z'
isxdigit	Hexadecimal digit	'0' to '9' or 'A' to 'F' or 'a' to 'f'

RETURNS Each macro returns a nonzero value if the *c* satisfies the criteria for that macro. Otherwise it returns a zero.

COMMENTS You should use *isascii* first to verify that the integer value is indeed a valid ASCII character. Only then should you use any one of these macros to test for specific properties of that ASCII value.

 The Microsoft C library maintains a list of characters classified according to these tests, allowing the macros to perform the tests swiftly. You can determine how these tests work by studying the file *ctype.h*. In particular, try printing out the external array *(_ctype+1)* for index 0 through 127. For example, each character code for which a 10 (which is equal to the defined constant _PUNCT in *ctype.h*) appears in the array is a punctuation character.

SEE ALSO isascii   To test whether an arbitrary integer value is a valid ASCII character

EXAMPLE Write a program that accepts the name of one of the macros *iscntrl, isdigit, isgraph, islower, isprint, ispunct, isspace, isupper,* or *isxdigit* and prints the ASCII table with a mark next to each character that satisfies the test. This is a convenient tool. Figure 9-2 shows the output for the macro *ispunct.* See if your understanding of punctuation characters matches those of the C library.

```
#include <stdio.h>
#include <string.h>
#include <ctype.h>
/* Define a table of function names and numbers */
typedef struct FUNC_TABLE
{
    char name[16];
```

iscntrl, isdigit, isgraph, islower, isprint, ispunct, isspace, isupper, isxdigit

```
        int   funcnum;
    } FUNC_TABLE;
    #define CNTRL  0
    #define DIGIT  1
    #define GRAPH  2
    #define LOWER  3
    #define PRINT  4
    #define PUNCT  5
    #define SPACE  6
    #define UPPER  7
    #define XDIGIT 8
    /* Now declare the table and initialize it        */
    static FUNC_TABLE isfuncs[9] =
    {
        "iscntrl", CNTRL, "isdigit", DIGIT,
        "isgraph", GRAPH, "islower", LOWER,
        "isprint", PRINT, "ispunct", PUNCT,
        "isspace", SPACE, "isupper", UPPER,
        "isxdigit", XDIGIT
    };
    static int numfunc = sizeof(isfuncs)/sizeof(FUNC_TABLE);
    main(int argc, char **argv)
    {
        int ch, count, i, test_result,
            mark = 0xdb; /* to mark characters */
        if (argc < 2)
        {
            printf("Usage: %s <function_name>\n", argv[0]);
            exit(0);
        }
    /* Search table for function name and pointer */
        for(i=0; i<numfunc; i++)
        {
            if (strcmp(argv[1], isfuncs[i].name) == 0)
                break;
        }
        if (i >= numfunc)
        {
            printf("Unknown function: %s\n", argv[1]);
            exit(0);
        }
    /* Now go over entire ASCII table and mark the
     * characters that satisfy requested test.
     */
        printf(
        "Those marked with a %c satisfy %s\n",
            mark, argv[1]);
        for(count = 0, ch = 0; ch <= 0x7f; ch++)
```

 Character Classification and Conversion

```
        {
            printf("%#02x ", ch);
/* Print character -- if printable              */
            if(isprint(ch))
            {
                printf(" %c", ch);
            }
            else
            {
                printf("  ");
            }
/* Perform the test and put a mark if test succeeds */
            switch(isfuncs[i].funcnum)
            {
                case CNTRL: test_result = iscntrl(ch);
                        break;
                case DIGIT: test_result = isdigit(ch);
                        break;
                case GRAPH: test_result = isgraph(ch);
                        break;
                case LOWER: test_result = islower(ch);
                        break;
                case PRINT: test_result = isprint(ch);
                        break;
                case PUNCT: test_result = ispunct(ch);
                        break;
                case SPACE: test_result = isspace(ch);
                        break;
                case UPPER: test_result = isupper(ch);
                        break;
                case XDIGIT: test_result = isxdigit(ch);
                        break;
            }
            if(test_result != 0)
            {
                printf("%c ", mark);
            }
            else
            {
                printf("  ", ch);
            }
            count++;
            if(count == 8)
            {
                printf(" \n");
                count = 0;
            }
        }
    }
```

iscntrl, isdigit, isgraph, islower, isprint, ispunct, isspace, isupper, isxdigit

Those marked with a ■ satisfy ispunct

00	0×01	0×02	0×03	0×04	0×05	0×06	0×07
0×08	0×09	0×0a	0×0b	0×0c	0×0d	0×0e	0×0f
0×10	0×11	0×12	0×13	0×14	0×15	0×16	0×17
0×18	0×19	0×1a	0×1b	0×1c	0×1d	0×1e	0×1f
0×20	0×21 ! ■	0×22 " ■	0×23 # ■	0×24 $ ■	0×25 % ■	0×26 & ■	0×27 ' ■
0×28 (■	0×29) ■	0×2a * ■	0×2b + ■	0×2c , ■	0×2d - ■	0×2e . ■	0×2f / ■
0×30 0	0×31 1	0×32 2	0×33 3	0×34 4	0×35 5	0×36 6	0×37 7
0×38 8	0×39 9	0×3a : ■	0×3b ; ■	0×3c < ■	0×3d = ■	0×3e > ■	0×3f ? ■
0×40 @ ■	0×41 A	0×42 B	0×43 C	0×44 D	0×45 E	0×46 F	0×47 G
0×48 H	0×49 I	0×4a J	0×4b K	0×4c L	0×4d M	0×4e N	0×4f O
0×50 P	0×51 Q	0×52 R	0×53 S	0×54 T	0×55 U	0×56 V	0×57 W
0×58 X	0×59 Y	0×5a Z	0×5b [■	0×5c \ ■	0×5d] ■	0×5e ^ ■	0×5f _ ■
0×60 ` ■	0×61 a	0×62 b	0×63 c	0×64 d	0×65 e	0×66 f	0×67 g
0×68 h	0×69 i	0×6a j	0×6b k	0×6c l	0×6d m	0×6e n	0×6f o
0×70 p	0×71 q	0×72 r	0×73 s	0×74 t	0×75 u	0×76 v	0×77 w
0×78 x	0×79 y	0×7a z	0×7b { ■	0×7c | ■	0×7d } ■	0×7e ~ ■	0×7f

Figure 9-2. *ASCII characters that satisfy the macro* **ispunct**

toascii

COMPATIBILITY	MSC 3	MSC 4	MSC 5	QC	TC	ANSI	UNIX V
	▲	▲	▲	▲	▲		▲

PURPOSE Use the *toascii* macro to convert an arbitrary integer value to a valid ASCII character.

SYNTAX `int toascii(int c);`

`int c;`   Integer to be converted

EXAMPLE CALL `c = toascii(int_value);`

INCLUDES `#include <ctype.h>`   For macro definition

DESCRIPTION The *toascii* macro sets all but the low-order seven bits of the integer *c* to zero so that the converted value represents a valid ASCII character. If *c* is already an ASCII character, it remains unchanged. As an example, this macro could be used to remove the high bit (the most significant bit) from characters in a WordStar document file. (WordStar uses the high bit to store formatting information.)

RETURNS The *toascii* macro returns the converted character.

SEE ALSO `isascii`   To test whether an arbitrary integer value is a valid ASCII character

EXAMPLE Write a program to convert an integer value to an ASCII character.

Character Classification and Conversion

```
#include <stdio.h>
#include <stdlib.h>
#include <ctype.h>
main(int argc, char **argv)
{
    int ch;
    if(argc < 2)
    {
        printf("Usage: %s <integer_value>\n",
                argv[0]);
    }
    else
    {
        ch = toascii(atoi(argv[1]));
        printf("%s converted to ASCII character = %#x\n\
It prints as %c on the IBM PC\n", argv[1], ch, ch);
    }
}
```

__tolower, tolower

COMPATIBILITY	MSC 3	MSC 4	MSC 5	QC	TC	ANSI	UNIX V
	▲	▲	▲	▲	▲	only tolower	▲

PURPOSE Use the _tolower and tolower macros to convert an uppercase ASCII character to lowercase. Use _tolower only when you are sure that the character being converted is an uppercase letter.

SYNTAX int _tolower(int c);

int tolower(int c);

int c;   ASCII character to be converted

EXAMPLE CALL c = tolower('Q'); /* c will become 'q' */

INCLUDES #include <ctype.h>   For macro definition

DESCRIPTION Both _tolower and tolower macros apply a formula to the ASCII character c that will convert it to lowercase if c is indeed an uppercase letter. Since tolower checks to see if c is actually an uppercase letter before making the conversion it is safer to use it than to take the risk with _tolower.

RETURNS The _tolower and tolower macros return a lowercase character.

COMMENTS Since *tolower* is implemented as a macro, if you give it an integer expression with side effects, things may go awry. In such cases you may choose to use a version of *tolower* implemented as a function. The prototype for this version appears in *stdlib.h*, and you can use it either by "undefining" the macro with the *#undef* preprocessor directive or by simply not including *ctype.h*.

SEE ALSO isascii To test whether an arbitrary integer value is a valid ASCII character

_toupper, toupper To convert lowercase letters to uppercase

EXAMPLE Write a program that accepts a string from the user and calls *tolower* to convert the characters to lowercase until a blank is encountered or the string ends. Print the results of the conversion.

```
#include <stdio.h>
#include <ctype.h>
main()
{
    int i, ch;
    char input[81];
    printf("Enter a string: ");
    gets(input);
    for(i=0; (input[i] != ' ') && (input[i] != '\0');
        i++)
    {
        input[i] = tolower(input[i]);
    }
    printf("Result: %s\n", input);
}
```

_toupper, toupper

COMPATIBILITY	MSC 3	MSC 4	MSC 5	QC	TC	ANSI	UNIX V
	▲	▲	▲	▲	▲	only toupper	▲

PURPOSE Use the *_toupper* and *toupper* macros to convert a lowercase ASCII character to uppercase. Use the *_toupper* macro only when you are sure that the character being converted is a lowercase letter.

SYNTAX int _toupper(int c);

int toupper(int c);

int c; ASCII character to be converted

 Character Classification and Conversion

EXAMPLE CALL `c = toupper('q'); /* c will become 'Q' */`

INCLUDES `#include <ctype.h>`   For macro definition

DESCRIPTION The _*toupper* applies a formula to the ASCII character *c* that will convert it to uppercase if *c* is indeed a lowercase letter. Since *toupper* first checks to see if *c* is actually a lowercase letter before making the conversion it is safer to use it than _*toupper*.

RETURNS Both _*toupper* and *toupper* macros return an uppercase character.

COMMENTS A version of *toupper* in the Microsoft C library is implemented as a function. The prototype for this version appears in *stdlib.h*, and you can use it either by "undefining" the macro with the *#undef* preprocessor directive or by simply not including *ctype.h*. This is sometimes necessary because when you feed a macro an integer expression with side effects, things may go awry.

SEE ALSO `isascii`   To test whether an arbitrary integer value is a valid ASCII character

`_tolower, tolower`   To convert uppercase letters to lowercase

EXAMPLE Write a program that accepts a string from the user and calls *toupper* to convert the characters to uppercase until a blank is encountered or the string ends. Print the results of the conversion.

```
#include <stdio.h>
#include <ctype.h>
main()
{
    int i, ch;
    char input[81];
    printf("Enter a string: ");
    gets(input);
    for(i=0; (input[i] != ' ') && (input[i] != '\0');
        i++)
    {
        input[i] = toupper(input[i]);
    }
    printf("Result: %s\n", input);
}
```

_toupper, toupper

Chapter **10 String Comparison and Manipulation**

Introduction

Manipulating text is a major part of many computer applications. The manipulation might involve text editing, word processing, or that part of your application that reads commands typed by the user and interprets them. Typically you read a single line of command into a C string and interpret it. Depending on the syntax of your application's command set, the interpretation might involve such chores as extracting the command and parameters from the string, comparing the command against entries in a stored table, or copying the parameters to separate strings for later use. Although C has no built-in operators for handling strings, the Microsoft C compiler has a set of string manipulation routines that provides all the capabilities needed to process strings.

Concepts: Strings in C

C has no basic data type for strings. Instead, strings are treated as arrays of characters, each of which occupies a byte. By convention, the end of a string in C is marked by a byte containing a null character (\0). Because of this, C strings are known as null-terminated strings or ASCIIZ (ASCII characters with a zero marking the end) strings.

DECLARING STRINGS IN C Since strings are treated as an array of characters, they can be declared in your programs by such a statement as

```
char str1[81], str2[]="A string";
```

Here, *str1* will be a string with room for 81 characters, but because one position is always used by the terminating null (\0), *str1* can hold 80 characters at most. The second string, *str2*, does not show a size, but the compiler can guess its size since it is being initialized. In this case, *str2* takes 9 bytes including the terminating null (see Figure 10-1). By the way, remember that you can declare a local string but cannot initialize it. To initialize a string, you have to declare it outside the function definitions.

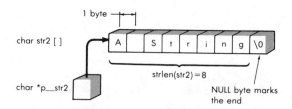

Figure 10-1. *Strings in C*

Another way of accessing a string is through a "pointer," which can hold the address of a variable (see Chapter 1). If you wanted to access the string *str2* using a pointer named *p_str2*, you could use the C code fragment:

```
char  str2[] = "A string";
char *p_str2;
p_str2 = str2;
```

Once *p_str2* is initialized, it can be used to access the string in the same manner *str2* is used (see Figure 10-1). Of course, the pointer requires some additional storage space.

You can also declare and initialize a string at the same time with

```
char *p_str = "A string";
```

in which the character pointer *p_str* is initialized to the address of a string constant "A string".

LEXICOGRAPHIC ORDERING

The string comparison routines compare and order strings as they would appear in a dictionary. The comparison is based on the ASCII value of the characters in corresponding bytes of the two strings, but the order of the ASCII codes is such that the collating sequence of the letters correspond to their place in the lexicon. Thus the ordering is known as "lexicographic" ordering.

Notes on String Manipulation

The string manipulation routines provide a host of capabilities (see Table 10-1 for a catalog). If you group the capabilities into categories, you will find that most routines are for comparing two strings, copying one string into another, and searching for the occurrence of a character in a string. (See Table 10-2 for a list by task.)

Table 10-1. *String Manipulation Routines*

Routine	Description
strcat	Appends one string to another.
strchr	Locates the first occurrence of a character in a string.
strcmp	Compares one string to another and differentiates between lowercase and uppercase letters.
strcmpi	Compares one string to another without regard to case of the letters.
strcpy	Copies one string to another.
strcspn	Returns the position in the string of the first character that belongs to a given set of characters.
strdup	Allocates memory and makes a duplicate copy of a string.
strerror	Returns a string containing the system error message corresponding to an error number.
_strerror	Returns a string constructed out of a user-supplied message concatenated to the system error message for the last error that occurred in a library routine.
stricmp	Identical to strcmpi.
strlen	Returns the length of a string as the number of bytes in the string, excluding the terminating null (\0).
strlwr	Converts all characters in a string to lowercase.
strncat	Appends a specified number of characters of one string to another.
strncmp	Compares a specified number of characters of two strings while maintaining the distinction between lowercase and uppercase letters.
strncpy	Copies a specified number of characters from one string to another (Note that the resulting string will not automatically have a null character appended.)
strnicmp	Compares a specified number of characters of two strings without regard to the case of the letters.
strnset	Copies the same character into a specified number of positions in a string.
strpbrk	Locates the first occurrence of any character from one string in another.
strrchr	Locates the last occurrence of a character in a string.
strrev	Reverses a string.
strset	Copies the same character to every position in a string.
strspn	Returns the position in the string of the first character that does not belong to a given set of characters.
strstr	Locates the first occurrence of one string in another.
strtok	Returns the next token in a string with the token delimiters specified in a string.
strupr	Converts all characters in a string to uppercase.

LENGTH OF A STRING

The length of a C string is determined by the number of bytes in the string, not counting the terminating null byte. For example, the string *str2* in Figure 10-1 is 8 bytes long, although 9 bytes are needed to store the entire string.

Table 10-2. *String Manipulation Routines by Task*

Task	Routines
Find length of a string.	strlen
Compare two strings lexicographically.	strcmp, strcmpi, stricmp, strncmp, strnicmp
Copy, append, and duplicate.	strcat, strcpy, strdup, strncat, strncpy
Convert a string from uppercase to lowercase and back.	strlwr, strupr
Search for a character or a substring.	strchr, strcspn, strpbrk, strrchr, strspn, strstr
Extract tokens from a string.	strtok
Load the same character into every position in a string.	strnset, strset
Reverse a string.	strrev
Prepare error message in a string.	strerror, _strerror

COMPARING C STRINGS

Five functions, *strcmp, strcmpi, stricmp, strncmp,* and *strnicmp,* in the library can compare two strings. Each function returns a zero when the strings match. A value less than zero indicates that the first string argument is lexicographically less than the second, which means that it appears before the second one in a dictionary. Similarly, a positive return value indicates that the first string is lexicographically greater than the second.

The routine *strcmp* compares the entire length of two strings, and it differentiates between lowercase and uppercase letters. The *strncmp* function is like *strcmp,* but it only compares a specified number of characters from the beginning of each string.

Identical in function, *strcmpi* and *stricmp* perform like *strcmp* except that they ignore the case of letters when comparing the strings. The *strncmpi* function is a case-insensitive version of *strnicmp.* Thus, if we compare the two strings *Microsoft* and *MICROSOFT* with *strcmp* it would conclude that *MICROSOFT* is less than *Microsoft* (because capital letters come before lowercase in the ASCII code sequence), but *strcmpi* or *stricmp* would find the strings identical and return a zero.

COPYING, APPENDING, AND DUPLICATING

The *strcat, strcpy, strdup, strncat,* and *strncpy* are for copying, concatenating, and duplicating strings.

The *strcat* function appends the second string argument to the first one, producing a null-terminated string as the result. The *strncat* function is a version of *strcat* that copies only a specified number of characters from the second string to the first.

The *strcpy* function copies the whole second string argument to the first one while *strncpy* only copies a specified number of bytes. When *strncpy* does not copy the entire string, it does not automatically append a null to the result. You must ensure that there is enough room in the first string to hold the second one by declaring an array of characters or by allocating memory at run-time. Because it will perform both steps for you, the *strdup* function is handy. It allocates memory to hold a string and then copies the string into the newly allocated memory.

PARSING A COMMAND LINE: EXTRACTING TOKENS

Earlier we alluded to the need for interpretation of application commands. To enable interpretation, you need to separate the command string into its component parts. For example, if you chose a command syntax of the form:

```
<COMMAND> <PARAMETER_1> <PARAMETER_2>
```

your command strings will consist of a command word followed by two parameters with blank spaces or tabs as the characters that separate the parts of the command. Now you read a command line of the form

```
copy x y
```

which to your application means copy the value of x into y. In this case, the parts are

```
<COMMAND> = copy
<PARAMETER_1> = x
<PARAMETER_2> = y
```

The process of separating the command line into parts is known as "parsing." Each part is a token.

Extracting Tokens

The C library has routines that help parse a string. The *strtok* function can get the tokens one by one. If you prefer, you can use the routines *strcspn* and *strspn* to construct your own parser, especially if your command language is much more complicated than the one in our example. The *strcspn* function returns the index of the first character (its location in the array) that matches one of the characters in a second string, and *strspn* does just the opposite, returning the first character that does not belong to the second string.

The *strpbrk* routine functions the same as *strcspn*, but it returns a pointer to the matched character rather than the index. The *strstr* function searches for the occurrence of one string in another, and *strchr* and *strrchr* locate a single character in a string. The *strchr* function searches for a character from the beginning, and *strrchr* searches from the end of the string.

Converting Case

Once you parse the command line in our example and get the token ⟨COMMAND⟩, you can compare that with entries in an internal array of strings to identify the task to be performed. If you decide to store commands in either lowercase or uppercase, you can use either *strlwr* or *strupr* to get the entire command string into lowercase or uppercase, respectively. Following this, you can use *strcmp* to see if the command matches any in your stored table. To avoid the case-conversion step, you would use one of the routines *strcmpi* or *stricmp* that ignore case when performing the string comparison.

MISCELLANEOUS UTILITIES

A few functions in the string manipulation group are hard to categorize. The *strnset* and *strset* functions let you set all positions in a string to the same character; *strnset* sets only a specified number of characters while *strset* works on the whole string. The *strrev* function reverses the characters in a string and *strerror* and *_strerror* returns a string containing an error message corresponding to an error number.

THE BUFFER MANIPULATION CATEGORY

Since a string is a special kind of buffer, the buffer manipulation routines (see Chapter 6) can also be used to manipulate strings. The reverse is not possible, however, because the string manipulation category always looks for a null byte as the marker indicating the end of a buffer (except for the functions with the *strn* prefix, which take a character count as argument).

Cautions

▶ When allocating memory for a string, remember to count the null character. If you are allocating memory to hold another copy of a specific string named, say, *str*, you compute the number of bytes you need by adding 1 to the value returned from the call *strlen(str)*.

▶ When copying a string to another, you must ensure that the destination string has enough room to hold the incoming characters. You will see no error messages if the copy operation continues beyond the last character of the destination string, but the program is likely to fail in a strange way.

▶ If you use *strncpy* to copy a specific number of bytes—less than the length of the source string—to another one, the resulting string will not have a null character automatically appended to it. So, you have to append a \0 yourself to convert the result to a valid C string.

strcat

COMPATIBILITY	MSC 3	MSC 4	MSC 5	QC	TC	ANSI	UNIX V
	▲	▲	▲	▲	▲	▲	▲

PURPOSE Use *strcat* to concatenate (append) one string to another.

SYNTAX `char *strcat(char *string1, const char *string2);`

`char *string1;`   Destination string

`const char *string2;`   String to be appended to the first one

EXAMPLE CALL
```
char metoo[7] = "Me ";
strcat(metoo, "too"); /* Result is "Me too" */
```

INCLUDES `#include <string.h>`   For function declaration

DESCRIPTION The *strcat* function accepts the C strings *string1* and *string2* as arguments. It appends the second string to the first one, terminating the resulting string with a null character (\0). The terminating NULL of the first string is removed and *string1* becomes the concatenation of the old *string1* and *string2*. Note that you are responsible for allocating enough space for the destination string *string1*. If, after appending *string2* to *string1*, the length of the resulting string exceeds the allocated size of *string1*, *strcat* may destroy other data and cause the program to fail.

RETURNS The *strcat* function returns a pointer to the concatenated string (i.e., it returns *string1*).

SEE ALSO `strncat`   To concatenate a specified number of characters of one string to another

`strcpy, strncpy`   To copy one string into another

`strdup`   To allocate storage and create a duplicate of a string

EXAMPLE Write a program that prompts the user for first name, last name, and middle initial. Then use *strcat* to construct the full name.

```
#include <stdio.h>
#include <string.h>
main()
{
    char fullname[80], last[40], middle[10];
    printf("Enter your first name: ");
    gets(fullname);
    printf("Last name: ");
    gets(last);
```

```
    printf("Middle initial: ");
    gets(middle);
/* Append the parts together to get full name */
    strcat(fullname," ");
    strcat(fullname, middle);
    strcat(fullname," ");
    strcat(fullname, last);
    printf("Greetings! %s\n", fullname);
}
```

strchr

COMPATIBILITY	MSC 3	MSC 4	MSC 5	QC	TC	ANSI	UNIX V
	▲	▲	▲	▲	▲	▲	▲

PURPOSE Use *strchr* to find the first occurrence of a particular character in a given string.

SYNTAX `char *strchr(const char *string, int c);`

`const char *string;`   String to be searched

`int c;`   Character to be located

EXAMPLE CALL
```
cost_is = strchr("Estimated cost = $120", '$');
/* Now cost_is will be the C string "$120"  */
```

INCLUDES `#include <string.h>`   For function declaration

DESCRIPTION The *strchr* function searches for the first occurrence of the character *c* in the C string *string*. The terminating null character is included in the search; it can also be the character to be located.

RETURNS If the character *c* is found, *strchr* returns a pointer to the first occurrence of *c* in *string1*. For example,

```
printf("%s", strchr("Annual salary = $35,750", '$'));
```

will print *$35,750*. If the search fails, *strchr* returns a NULL.

SEE ALSO `strrchr`   To locate the last occurrence of a character in a string

`strcspn, strpbrk`   To locate the first character in a string that matches one of the characters in another

`strstr`   To locate the occurrence of one string in another

String Comparison and Manipulation

EXAMPLE   Prompt the user for a string and a character whose first occurrence in the string will be found by using *strchr*. Display the result of the search.

```
#include <stdio.h>
#include <conio.h>
#include <string.h>
main()
{
    int c;
    char buf[80], *result;
    printf("Enter a string: ");
    gets(buf);
    printf(
"Enter character to be located (first occurrence):");
    c = getche();
    if ((result = strchr(buf, c)) == NULL)
    {
        printf("\n'%c' <-- not in \"%s\"\n", c, buf);
    }
    else
    {
        printf("\n'%c' first occurs at: %s\n",
                                   c, result);
    }
}
```

strcmp

COMPATIBILITY	MSC 3	MSC 4	MSC 5	QC	TC	ANSI	UNIX V
	▲	▲	▲	▲	▲	▲	▲

PURPOSE   Use *strcmp* to compare one string to another. The comparison is case sensitive.

SYNTAX   `int strcmp(const char *string1, const char *string2);`

`const char *string1;`   First string

`const char *string2;`   Second string

EXAMPLE CALL   `if( strcmp(username, "sysmgr") != 0 ) exit(0);`

INCLUDES   `#include <string.h>`   For function declaration

DESCRIPTION   The *strcmp* function accepts the C strings *string1* and *string2* as arguments.

strcmp

It compares the two strings lexicographically and returns an integer value indicating the lexicographic order of *string1* with respect to *string2*. Note that unlike *strcmpi* and *stricmp*, *strcmp* is case sensitive.

RETURNS The *strcmp* function returns an integer indicating the lexicographic ordering of *string1* with respect to *string2*. The return value is zero if the two strings are identical. If *string1* is less than *string2*, the return value is less than zero. When *string1* is greater than *string2*, *strcmp* returns an integer greater than zero. For example,

```
result = strcmp("ABC", "abc"); /* result less than 0    */
result = strcmp("abc", "abc"); /* result equal to  0    */
result = strcmp("xy",  "abc"); /* result greater than 0 */
```

SEE ALSO strncmp   To compare a specified number of characters of two strings

strcmpi, stricmp, strnicmp   To compare two strings regardless of the case of the characters

EXAMPLE Write a program that uses *strcmp* to compare two strings typed by the user and display the result.

```c
#include <stdio.h>
#include <string.h>
main()
{
    int result;
    char str1[80], str2[80];
    printf("Enter a string: ");
    gets(str1);
    printf("Enter string to compare with first: ");
    gets(str2);
    printf("Case sensitive comparison shows that\n");
    result = strcmp(str1, str2);
    if(result == 0)
    {
        printf("\"%s\" == \"%s\"\n", str1, str2);
    }
    if(result < 0)
    {
        printf("\"%s\" < \"%s\"\n", str1, str2);
    }
    if(result > 0)
    {
        printf("\"%s\" > \"%s\"\n", str1, str2);
    }
}
```

 String Comparison and Manipulation

strcmpi

COMPATIBILITY	MSC 3	MSC 4	MSC 5	QC	TC	ANSI	UNIX V
	▲	▲	▲	▲			

PURPOSE Use *strcmpi* to compare one string to another without regard to case.

SYNTAX `int strcmpi(const char *string1, const char *string2);`

`const char *string1;`   First string

`const char *string2;`   Second string

EXAMPLE CALL `if( strcmpi(command, "delete") == 0 ) do_delete();`

INCLUDES `#include <string.h>`   For function declaration

DESCRIPTION The *strcmpi* function first converts all alphabetic characters in strings *string1* and *string2* to lowercase. Then it compares the two strings and returns an integer value indicating the lexicographic order of *string1* with respect to *string2*.

RETURNS The *strcmpi* function returns a zero if the two strings are identical. If *string1* is less than *string2*, the return value is less than zero. When *string1* is greater than *string2*, *strcmpi* returns an integer greater than zero. Thus *strcmpi* (*"XYZ"*, *"xyz"*); returns zero.

SEE ALSO `strnicmp`   Same as *strcmpi*, but only compares a specified number of characters of the two strings

`strcmp, strncmp`   To compare two strings (case sensitive)

`stricmp`   Identical to *strcmpi*

EXAMPLE Demonstrate the use of *strcmpi* by comparing two strings entered by user.

```
#include <stdio.h>
#include <string.h>
main()
{
    int result;
    char str1[80], str2[80];
    printf("Enter a string: ");
    gets(str1);
    printf("Enter string to compare with first: ");
    gets(str2);
    printf("Case insensitive comparison shows that\n");
```

```
    result = strcmpi(str1, str2);
    if(result == 0)
    {
        printf("\"%s\" == \"%s\"\n", str1, str2);
    }
    if(result < 0)
    {
        printf("\"%s\" < \"%s\"\n", str1, str2);
    }
    if(result > 0)
    {
        printf("\"%s\" > \"%s\"\n", str1, str2);
    }
}
```

strcpy

COMPATIBILITY	MSC 3	MSC 4	MSC 5	QC	TC	ANSI	UNIX V
	▲	▲	▲	▲	▲	▲	▲

PURPOSE Use *strcpy* to copy one string to another.

SYNTAX `char *strcpy(char *string1, const char *string2);`

`char *string1;`   Destination string

`const char *string2;`   String to be copied to the first one

EXAMPLE CALL `strcpy(dos_command, "DIR");`

INCLUDES `#include <string.h>`   For function declaration

DESCRIPTION The *strcpy* function copies the string *string2* to the buffer whose address is given by *string1*. The terminating null character of the second string is also copied so *string1* becomes an exact copy of *string2*.

RETURNS The *strcpy* function returns a pointer to the copied string (i.e., it returns *string1*).

COMMENTS The string manipulation routines *strcpy* and *strncpy* can be harmful to your program if you forget to allocate enough room in the buffer *string1* for the entire destination string, including the terminating null character. If, after appending *string2* to *string1*, the length of the resulting string exceeds the allocated size of *string1*, *strcpy* may destroy other data and cause the program to fail.

 String Comparison and Manipulation

SEE ALSO   `strcat, strncat`   To concatenate one string to another

            `strncpy`   To copy a specified number of characters of one string into another

            `strdup`   To allocate storage and create a duplicate copy of a string

EXAMPLE   Write a program to accept a string and use *strcpy* to copy it into another internal buffer.

```
#include <stdio.h>
#include <string.h>
main()
{
    char str1[80], str2[80];
    printf("Enter a string: ");
    gets(str2);
    strcpy(str1, str2);
    printf("String copied. Result is: %s\n", str1);
}
```

strcspn

COMPATIBILITY	MSC 3	MSC 4	MSC 5	QC	TC	ANSI	UNIX V
	▲	▲	▲	▲	▲	▲	▲

PURPOSE   Use *strcspn* to locate the position of the first occurrence in a string of any character from another.

SYNTAX   `size_t strcspn(const char *string1, const char *string2);`

        `const char *string1;`   String to be searched

        `const char *string2;`   String describing set of characters to be located

EXAMPLE CALL   `first_q = strcspn("soliloquy", "q"); /* first_q = 6 */`

INCLUDES   `#include <string.h>`   For function declaration

DESCRIPTION   The *strcspn* function locates the first occurrence in *string1* of any character other than the terminating null in *string2*.

RETURNS   If successful, the *strcspn* function returns the index of the first character in *string1* that belongs to the set of characters *string2*. Thus this value is the length of the initial substring of *string1* that consists of characters *not* in *string2* (i.e., the substring that does not "span" the character set *string2*).

strcspn

If *string1* begins with a character from *string2*, the return value is zero. If *string1* is devoid of characters from *string2*, *strcspn* returns the length of *string1*.

SEE ALSO   strpbrk   To search for the first occurrence of any character from one string in another

strspn   To find the length of the initial substring made up entirely of characters in another string

EXAMPLE   Prompt the user for a string with some numeric values followed by other characters. Then use *strcspn* to locate the first occurrence of a non-numeric character in the string. This can be used to catch input errors when only numeric values are expected.

```
#include <stdio.h>
#include <string.h>
char *digits = "0123456789";
main()
{
    int loc;
    char str1[80];
    printf("Enter a number followed by other \
characters: ");
    gets(str1);
    loc = strcspn(str1, digits);
    printf("First non-numeric character in \
\n%s\nis at location %d\n", str1, loc);
}
```

strdup

COMPATIBILITY	MSC 3	MSC 4	MSC 5	QC	TC	ANSI	UNIX V
	▲	▲	▲	▲	▲		

PURPOSE   Use *strdup* to allocate memory and copy a given string into that space.

SYNTAX   `char *strdup(const char *string);`

`const char *string;`   String to be duplicated

EXAMPLE CALL   `saved_command = strdup(command);`

INCLUDES   `#include <string.h>`   For function declaration

 String Comparison and Manipulation

DESCRIPTION The *strdup* function first calls *malloc* to allocate enough memory to hold *string*. It then copies the string into the newly allocated buffer.

RETURNS If the *strdup* function succeeds, it returns a pointer to the new copy of the string. If memory allocation fails, *strdup* returns a NULL.

SEE ALSO `strcat, strncat`   To concatenate one string to another

`strcpy, strncpy`   To copy one string into another

EXAMPLE Read in a string and make a duplicate by calling the function *strdup*.

```
#include <stdio.h>
#include <string.h>
main()
{
    char str1[80], *str1_copy;
    printf("Enter a string: ");
    gets(str1);
    str1_copy = strdup(str1);
    printf("String duplicated. Result is: %s\n",
            str1_copy);
}
```

strerror

COMPATIBILITY	MSC 3	MSC 4	MSC 5	QC	TC	ANSI	UNIX V
		▲	▲	▲	▲	▲	

PURPOSE Use *strerror* to retrieve an error message corresponding to an error number.

SYNTAX `char *strerror(int errnum);`

`int errnum;`   Error number

EXAMPLE CALL `error_message = strerror(errno);`

INCLUDES `#include <string.h>`   For function declaration

DESCRIPTION The *strerror* function finds the system error message corresponding to the error number given in the argument *errnum*. The *strerror* function gets the system error message by using the value in the global variable *errno* as the index of a table of error messages called *sys_errlist*, which is declared in the header file *stdlib.h*. In a typical use, you should call *strerror* immediately after an error return from a library routine and provide the value of *errno* as the argument. Note that *strerror* only returns the error message; printing the message is up to you.

RETURNS   The *strerror* function returns a pointer to the error message from the table *sys _errlist*.

COMMENTS   The *strerror* function of Microsoft C 4.0 is called *_strerror* in versions 5.0 and 5.1. The new *strerror* is a version conforming to ANSI standards.

SEE ALSO   `_strerror`   To construct an error message by appending the system message to one supplied by you

            `perror`   To print an error message

EXAMPLE   Write a program in which you create an error by attempting to close a nonexistent file handle (say, 100). Once the error occurs, call *strerror* with *errno* as argument and print the error message returned by *strerror*. Note that *stdlib.h* is included to provide the appropriate declaration of *errno*.

```
#include <stdio.h>
#include <stdlib.h>
#include <io.h>
#include <string.h>
main()
{
    int handle=100;
    char *errmsg;
/* Generate an error condition by closing a
 * file with non-existent handle 100
 */
    if(close(handle) == -1)
    {
        errmsg = strerror(errno);
        printf("Error closing file: %s", errmsg);
    }
}
```

__strerror

COMPATIBILITY	MSC 3	MSC 4	MSC 5	QC	TC	ANSI	UNIX V
			▲	▲	▲		

PURPOSE   Use *_strerror* to construct an error message consisting of your message concatenated with a system message corresponding to the last error that occurred in a library routine.

 String Comparison and Manipulation

SYNTAX   `char *_strerror(char *string);`

          `char *string;`   String containing user-supplied error message

EXAMPLE CALL   `error_message = _strerror("Error opening file");`

INCLUDES   `#include <string.h>`   For function declaration

DESCRIPTION   The *_strerror* function constructs an error message by appending a colon to the contents of *string* and appending a system message that corresponds to the last error occurring in a library routine. The length of *string* can be at most 94 bytes. If *string* is NULL, the message constructed by *_strerror* only contains the system message. The message always has a newline character (\n) at the end.

The *_strerror* function gets the system error message by using the value in the global variable *errno* as the index of a table of error messages called *sys_errlist*. You should call *_strerror* immediately after a library routine returns with an error. Otherwise, subsequent calls to other routines may overwrite the value of *errno*. Note that *_strerror* only prepares the error message; printing the message is up to you.

RETURNS   The *_strerror* function returns a pointer to the error message it constructed.

COMMENTS   The *_strerror* function of Microsoft C 5.0 and 5.1 is identical to the *strerror* function of version 4.0. The name was changed in version 5.0 so that Microsoft could include an ANSI version of the *strerror* function.

SEE ALSO   `strerror`   To get system message corresponding to error number (ANSI version)

          `perror`   To print an error message

EXAMPLE   Write a program that illustrates the use of *_strerror* to construct error messages. Generate an error by attempting to duplicate the file handle 100 (a file not yet open). Display the error message returned by *_strerror*.

```
#include <stdio.h>
#include <io.h>
#include <string.h>
main()
{
    int handle=100;
    char *errmsg;
/* Generate an error condition by attempting to
 * duplicate a unused file handle (100)
 */
    if(dup(handle) == -1)
    {
        errmsg = _strerror("Error duplicating handle");
```

_strerror

```
        printf(errmsg);
    }
}
```

stricmp

COMPATIBILITY	MSC 3	MSC 4	MSC 5	QC	TC	ANSI	UNIX V
		▲	▲	▲	▲		

PURPOSE Use *stricmp* to compare one string to another without regard to the case of the letters.

SYNTAX int stricmp(const char *string1, const char *string2);

const char *string1;   First string

const char *string2;   Second string

EXAMPLE CALL if(stricmp(answer, "yes") == 0) delete_file(fname);

INCLUDES #include <string.h>   For function declaration

DESCRIPTION The *stricmp* function converts all alphabetic characters in *string1* and *string2* to lowercase. Then it compares the two strings and returns an integer value indicating the lexicographic order of *string1* with respect to *string2*.

RETURNS The *stricmp* function returns an integer indicating the lexicographic ordering of *string1* with respect to *string2* after all alphabetic characters have been converted to lowercase. The return value is zero if the two strings are identical. If *string1* is less than *string2*, the return value is less than zero. When *string1* is greater than *string2*, *stricmp* returns an integer greater than zero.

SEE ALSO strnicmp   Same as *stricmp*, but only compares a specified number of characters of the two strings

strcmp, strncmp   To compare two strings (case sensitive)

strcmpi   Identical to *stricmp*

EXAMPLE Write a program that uses *stricmp* to perform a comparison of two strings, regardless of cases.

```
#include <stdio.h>
#include <string.h>
main()
```

 String Comparison and Manipulation

```
{
    int result;
    char str1[80], str2[80];
    printf("Enter a string: ");
    gets(str1);
    printf("Enter string to compare with first: ");
    gets(str2);
    printf("Case insensitive comparison shows that\n");
    result = stricmp(str1, str2);
    if(result == 0)
    {
        printf("\"%s\" == \"%s\"\n", str1, str2);
    }
    if(result < 0)
    {
        printf("\"%s\" < \"%s\"\n", str1, str2);
    }
    if(result > 0)
    {
        printf("\"%s\" > \"%s\"\n", str1, str2);
    }
}
```

strlen

COMPATIBILITY	MSC 3	MSC 4	MSC 5	QC	TC	ANSI	UNIX V
	▲	▲	▲	▲	▲	▲	▲

PURPOSE Use *strlen* to find the length of a string in bytes, not counting the terminating null character.

SYNTAX `size_t strlen(const char *string);`

`const char *string;`   String whose length is to be returned

EXAMPLE CALL `length = strlen(name);`

INCLUDES `#include <string.h>`   For function declaration

DESCRIPTION The *strlen* function counts the number of bytes in *string*, not including the terminating null character.

RETURNS The *strlen* function returns the length in bytes of *string*.

EXAMPLE Use *strlen* to determine and print the length of a string.

```
#include <stdio.h>
#include <string.h>
main()
{
    size_t len;
    char buf[80];
    printf("Enter a string: ");
    gets(buf);
    len = strlen(buf);
    printf("The length of the string is: %u\n", len);
}
```

strlwr

COMPATIBILITY	MSC 3	MSC 4	MSC 5	QC	TC	ANSI	UNIX V
	▲	▲	▲	▲	▲		

PURPOSE Use *strlwr* to convert any uppercase letters in a string to lowercase.

SYNTAX `char *strlwr(char *string);`

`char *string;`   String to be converted to lowercase

EXAMPLE CALL
```
char command[] = "QUIT";
strlwr(command); /* Now command = "quit" */
```

INCLUDES `#include <string.h>`   For function declaration

DESCRIPTION The *strlwr* function converts any uppercase letters in the *string* to lowercase. Other characters in the string are unaffected.

RETURNS The *strlwr* function returns a pointer to the converted string, (i.e., it returns *string*).

COMMENTS The *strlwr* routine and its companion *strupr* are not part of the proposed ANSI definition. You can implement your own versions of these using the macros *tolower* and *toupper*, respectively.

SEE ALSO `strupr`   To convert a string to uppercase

`tolower`   To convert a single uppercase letter to lowercase

EXAMPLE Use *strlwr* to convert a string to lowercase.

String Comparison and Manipulation

```
#include <stdio.h>
#include <string.h>
main()
{
    char buf[80];
    printf("Enter a string with uppercase letters: ");
    gets(buf);
    strlwr(buf);
    printf("The string in lowercase is:\n%s\n", buf);
}
```

strncat

COMPATIBILITY	MSC 3	MSC 4	MSC 5	QC	TC	ANSI	UNIX V
	▲	▲	▲	▲	▲	▲	▲

PURPOSE Use *strncat* to concatenate a specified number of characters of one string to another.

SYNTAX `char *strncat(char *string1, const char *string2, size_t n);`

`char *string1;`   Destination string

`const char *string2;`   String whose first *n* characters are to be appended to the destination string

`size_t n;`   Number of characters of *string2* to be appended to *string1*

EXAMPLE CALL
```
char id[16] = "ID = ";
strncat(id, name, 10); /* id is first 10 char of name */
```

INCLUDES `#include <string.h>`   For function declaration

DESCRIPTION The *strncat* function appends the first *n* characters of *string2* to *string1* and terminates the resulting string with a null character. The terminating null of the first string is removed and *string1* becomes the resulting concatenation. If *n* is larger than the length of *string2*, the entire second string is appended to *string1*.

RETURNS The *strncat* function returns a pointer to the concatenated string (i.e., it returns *string1*).

SEE ALSO `strcat`   To concatenate one string to another

`strcpy, strncpy`   To copy one string into another

`strdup`   To allocate storage and create a duplicate a string

EXAMPLE Use *strncat* to generate and print the sequence of strings:

```
a
ab
abc
abcd
...
...
abcdefghijklmnopqrstuvwxyz
```

```c
#include <stdio.h>
#include <string.h>
char result[40] = "a";
char rest[] = "bcdefghijklmnopqrstuvwxyz";
unsigned length = sizeof(rest)/sizeof(char);
main()
{
    unsigned i;
    for(i = 0; i<length; i++, result[1]='\0')
    {
        strncat(result, rest, i);
/* Show the current result */
        printf("%s\n", result);
    }
}
```

strncmp

COMPATIBILITY	MSC 3	MSC 4	MSC 5	QC	TC	ANSI	UNIX V
	▲	▲	▲	▲	▲	▲	▲

PURPOSE Use *strncmp* to compare a specified number of characters of two strings to one another. The comparison is case sensitive.

SYNTAX `int strncmp(const char *string1, const char *string2, size_t n);`

`const char *string1;`   First string

`const char *string2;`   Second string

`size_t n;`   Number of characters of strings to be compared

EXAMPLE CALL `if(strncmp(command, "quit", 2) == 0) quit_program();`

INCLUDES `#include <string.h>`   For function declaration

 String Comparison and Manipulation

DESCRIPTION The *strncmp* function compares the first *n* characters of *string1* and *string2*. The result of the case-sensitive comparison is returned as an integer value indicating the lexicographic order of the first *n* characters of *string1* with respect to the same part of *string2*.

RETURNS The *strncmp* function returns an integer indicating the lexicographic ordering of the first *n* characters of *string1* with respect to the same part of *string2*. The return value will be zero if the two substrings are identical. If *substring1* is less than *substring2*, the return value is less than zero. When *substring1* is greater than *substring2*, *strncmp* returns an integer greater than zero.

SEE ALSO   strcmp   To compare two strings

strncmpi, stricmp, strnicmp   To compare two strings disregarding the case of
the characters

EXAMPLE Write a program that accepts two strings and specifies the number of characters that are to be compared. Use *strncmp* to perform the comparison and then display the result.

```c
#include <stdio.h>
#include <string.h>
main()
{
    int len, result;
    char str1[80], str2[80];
    printf("Enter a string: ");
    gets(str1);
    printf("Enter string to compare with first: ");
    gets(str2);
    printf("How many characters to compare:");
    scanf(" %d", &len);
    printf("Based on case sensitive comparison of \
the first %d characters\n", len);
    result = strncmp(str1, str2, len);
    if(result == 0)
    {
        printf("\"%s\" == \"%s\"\n", str1, str2);
    }
    if(result < 0)
    {
        printf("\"%s\" < \"%s\"\n", str1, str2);
    }
    if(result > 0)
    {
        printf("\"%s\" > \"%s\"\n", str1, str2);
    }
}
```

strncmp

strncpy

COMPATIBILITY	MSC 3	MSC 4	MSC 5	QC	TC	ANSI	UNIX V
	▲	▲	▲	▲	▲	▲	▲

PURPOSE Use *strncpy* to copy a specified number of characters of one string to another.

SYNTAX `char *strncpy(char *string1, const char *string2, size_t n);`

`char *string1;`   Destination string

`const char *string2;`   String whose first *n* characters are to be copied to the destination string

`size_t n;`   Number of characters to be copied

EXAMPLE CALL `strncpy(fname, "tmp12345678", 8); /* fname = "tmp12345" */`

INCLUDES `#include <string.h>`   For function declaration

DESCRIPTION The *strncpy* function copies the first *n* characters of *string2* to the buffer whose address is given by *string1*. The copy is placed starting at the first character position of *string1*. If *n* is less than the length of *string2*, no terminating null character is appended to *string1*. If *n* exceeds the length of *string2*, however, *string1* is padded with null characters until it is *n* bytes long.

You should avoid situations where the *n* bytes following *string1* overlap *string2* because the behavior of *strcpy* with such arguments is not guaranteed to be correct.

RETURNS The *strncpy* function returns a pointer to the copied string (i.e., it returns *string1*).

SEE ALSO `strcat, strncat`   To concatenate one string to another

`strcpy`   To copy one string into another

`strdup`   To allocate storage and create a duplicate of a string

EXAMPLE Read in a string and copy the first half into another buffer using *strncat*. Note that no null character is appended to the copied string so you have to add one if you want to use it as a C string (for example, when you print it using *printf*).

```
#include <stdio.h>
#include <string.h>
main()
{
    size_t len;
```

 String Comparison and Manipulation

```
        char str1[80], str2[80];
        printf("Enter a string: ");
        gets(str2);
        len = strlen(str2)/2;
        strncpy(str1, str2, len);
/* Since '\0' is not appended automatically, we have
 * to do so before printing string
 */
        str1[len] = '\0';
        printf("Half the length of string copied. Result:\
%s\n", str1);
}
```

strnicmp

COMPATIBILITY	MSC 3	MSC 4	MSC 5	QC	TC	ANSI	UNIX V
		▲	▲	▲	▲		

PURPOSE Use *strnicmp* to compare a specified number of characters of two string without regard to case.

SYNTAX `int strnicmp(const char *string1, const char *string2, size_t n);`

`const char *string1;`   First string

`const char *string2;`   Second string

`size_t n;`   Number of characters of strings to be compared

EXAMPLE CALL `if (strnicmp(command, "exit", 2) == 0) exit_program();`

INCLUDES `#include <string.h>`   For function declaration

DESCRIPTION The *strnicmp* function compares the first *n* characters of *string1* with the corresponding ones in *string2*, but during the comparison it converts each uppercase letter to lowercase. The result of this comparison is returned as an integer value indicating the lexicographic ordering of the first *n* characters of *string1* with respect to *string2*.

RETURNS The *strnicmp* function returns zero if the two substrings are identical. If *substring1* is less than *substring2*, the return value is less than zero. When *substring1* is greater than *substring2*, *strnicmp* returns an integer greater than zero.

SEE ALSO `strcmpi, stricmp`   To compare two strings (case sensitive)

```
strcmp, strncmp        To compare two strings (case sensitive)
```

EXAMPLE Use *strnicmp* in a program that compares two strings without regard to case. Let the program accept two strings and the number of characters to compare and then display the result of the comparison.

```
#include <stdio.h>
#include <string.h>
main()
{
    int len, result;
    char str1[80], str2[80];
    printf("Enter a string: ");
    gets(str1);
    printf("Enter string to compare with first: ");
    gets(str2);
    printf("How many characters to compare:");
    scanf(" %d", &len);
    printf("Based on case insensitive comparison of \
the first %d characters\n", len);
    result = strnicmp(str1, str2, len);
    if(result == 0)
    {
        printf("\"%s\" == \"%s\"\n", str1, str2);
    }
    if(result < 0)
    {
        printf("\"%s\" < \"%s\"\n", str1, str2);
    }
    if(result > 0)
    {
        printf("\"%s\" > \"%s\"\n", str1, str2);
    }
}
```

strnset

COMPATIBILITY	MSC 3	MSC 4	MSC 5	QC	TC	ANSI	UNIX V
	▲	▲	▲	▲	▲		

PURPOSE Use *strnset* to set a specified number of characters in a string, excluding the terminating null, to a specific character value.

SYNTAX `char *strnset(char *string, int c, size_t n);`

`char *string;`   String whose first *n* characters are to be set to *c*

 String Comparison and Manipulation

int c;   Value to be copied into first *n* character positions of *string*

size_t n;   Number of characters to be set

EXAMPLE CALL   `strnset(all_zzz, 'z', 40);`

INCLUDES   `#include <string.h>`   For function declaration

DESCRIPTION   The *strnset* function copies the character in the integer *c* to the first *n* character positions in *string*. If *n* exceeds the length of the string, all character positions, except the last one (the terminating null character), are set.

RETURNS   The *strnset* function returns a pointer to the altered string (i.e., it returns *string*).

SEE ALSO   `strset`   To set all characters of a string to a specific character value

EXAMPLE   Use *strnset* to fill the first half of a string entered by the user with a character also entered by the user.

```
#include <stdio.h>
#include <conio.h>
#include <string.h>
main()
{
    int c;
    size_t len;
    char buf[80];

    printf("Enter a string: ");
    gets(buf);
    printf(
"Enter character you want half the string set to:");
    c = getche();
    len = strlen(buf)/2;
/* Set first half of string to character in c */
    strnset(buf, c, len);
    printf("\nString is now: %s\n", buf);
}
```

strnset

strpbrk

COMPATIBILITY	MSC 3	MSC 4	MSC 5	QC	TC	ANSI	UNIX V
	▲	▲	▲	▲	▲	▲	▲

PURPOSE Use *strpbrk* to locate the first occurrence of any of the characters from one string in another string.

SYNTAX `char *strpbrk(const char *string1, const char *string2);`

`const char *string1;`   String to be searched

`const char *string2;`   String describing set of characters to be located

EXAMPLE CALL `first_vowel = strpbrk(word, "aeiou");`

INCLUDES `#include <string.h>`   For function declaration

DESCRIPTION The *strpbrk* function searches for the first occurrence in *string1* of any of the characters from *string2*. The terminating null is not included in the search.

RETURNS If successful, the *strpbrk* function returns a pointer to the first occurrence of any character from *string2* in *string1*. If the search fails, *strpbrk* returns a NULL. Failure implies that *string1* and *string2* have no characters in common.

SEE ALSO strchr   To search for the first occurrence of a character in a string

strcspn   To locate the first character in a string that matches one of the characters in another

EXAMPLE Use *strpbrk* to locate the first occurrence of a vowel in a word and print the word up to and including the vowel (this will tend to extract the first syllable from the word).

```
#include <stdio.h>
#include <string.h>
char *vowels = "aeiou";
main()
{
    char str1[80], *result;
    printf("Enter a word: ");
    gets(str1);
    if ((result = strpbrk(str1, vowels)) == NULL)
    {
        printf("No vowels in word\n");
    }
```

 String Comparison and Manipulation

```
        else
        {
            printf("First syllable in %s ", str1);
/* Put a null character just after the first vowel */
            result++;
            *result = '\0';
            printf("is: %s\n", str1);
        }
    }
```

strrchr

COMPATIBILITY	MSC 3	MSC 4	MSC 5	QC	TC	ANSI	UNIX V
	▲	▲	▲	▲	▲	▲	▲

PURPOSE Use *strrchr* to find the last occurrence of a particular character in a given string.

SYNTAX `char *strrchr(const char *string, int c);`

`const char *string;`   String to be searched

`int c;`   Character to be located

EXAMPLE CALL
```
char line_cost[] = "10 units at $1.20 ea. = $12.00";
total_cost = strrchr(line_cost, '$');
/* Now total_cost will be the string "$12.00" */
```

INCLUDES `#include <string.h>`   For function declaration

DESCRIPTION The *strrchr* function searches for the last occurrence of the character *c* in *string*. The terminating null character is included in the search and can be the character to be located.

RETURNS If the character *c* is found, *strrchr* returns a pointer to the last occurrence of *c* in *string*. If the search fails, *strrchr* returns a NULL.

SEE ALSO strchr   To locate the first occurrence of a character in a string

EXAMPLE Write a program that accepts a date in the form "MM/DD/YY" and uses *strrchr* to locate the last occurrence of the / character and print the returned string as a year.

strrchr

```
#include <stdio.h>
#include <string.h>
main()
{
    char buf[80], *result;
    printf("Enter date: ");
    gets(buf);
    if ((result = strrchr(buf, '/')) == NULL)
    {
        printf("%s <-- not a date!\n", buf);
    }
    else
    {
        result++;     /* Skip the '/' */
        printf("The year is: 19%s\n", result);
    }
}
```

strrev

COMPATIBILITY	MSC 3	MSC 4	MSC 5	QC	TC	ANSI	UNIX V
	▲	▲	▲	▲	▲		

PURPOSE Use *strrev* to reverse the order of characters in a string.

SYNTAX `char *strrev(char *string);`

`char *string;`   String to be reversed

EXAMPLE CALL `strrev(input_string);`

INCLUDES `#include <string.h>`   For function declaration

DESCRIPTION The *strrev* function reverses the order of the characters in *string*. The terminating null character remains at the same place.

RETURNS The *strrev* function returns a pointer to the reversed string (it returns the argument *string*).

SEE ALSO `strcpy, strncpy`   To copy one string to another

EXAMPLE Use *strrev* to reverse a string typed at the keyboard and print the result. One use of this program is to check whether a string is a "palindrome," that is, whether it reads the same backward and forward.

 String Comparison and Manipulation

```
#include <stdio.h>
#include <string.h>
main()
{
    char buf[80];
    printf("Enter a string: ");
    gets(buf);
    strrev(buf);
    printf("Reversed string is:\n%s\n", buf);
}
```

strset

COMPATIBILITY	MSC 3	MSC 4	MSC 5	QC	TC	ANSI	UNIX V
	▲	▲	▲	▲	▲	▲	▲

PURPOSE Use *strset* to set all characters in a string, excluding the terminating null, to a specific character value.

SYNTAX `char *strset(char *string, int c);`

`char *string;` String to be set to *c*

`int c;` Value to be copied into each character position of *string*

EXAMPLE CALL `char password[16];`
`strset(password, 'x'); /* Set password to all 'x' */`

INCLUDES `#include <string.h>` For function declaration

DESCRIPTION The *strset* function copies the character in the integer *c* to every character position in *string*, except the terminating null character. This is useful for setting a string to blanks or other default values.

RETURNS The *strset* function returns a pointer to the altered string (i.e, it returns *string*).

SEE ALSO `strnset` To set a specified number of characters of a string to a specific character value

EXAMPLE Write a C program that reads in a string from the keyboard, prompts for a fill character, and uses *strset* to set the entire string to that character. Then the program displays the result.

```
#include <stdio.h>
#include <conio.h>
#include <string.h>
main()
```

```
{
    int c;
    char buf[80];
    printf("Enter a string: ");
    gets(buf);
    printf(
"Enter character you want entire string set to:");
    c = getche();
    strset(buf, c);
    printf("\nString is now: %s\n", buf);
}
```

strspn

COMPATIBILITY	MSC 3	MSC 4	MSC 5	QC	TC	ANSI	UNIX V
	▲	▲	▲	▲	▲	▲	▲

PURPOSE Use *strspn* to locate the position of the first character in a string that does not belong to the set of characters in another.

SYNTAX `size_t strspn(const char *string1, const char *string2);`

`const char *string1;`   String to be searched

`const char *string2;`   String describing set of characters

EXAMPLE CALL
```
char *input = "280ZX";
first_nondigit_at = strspn(input, "1234567890");
/* first_nondigit_at will be  3 */
```

INCLUDES `#include <string.h>`   For function declaration

DESCRIPTION The *strspn* function locates the first character in *string1* that is not present in *string2*. The terminating null is not included in the search.

RETURNS If successful, the *strspn* function returns the index of the first character in *string1* that does not belong to the set of characters *string2*. Thus, this value is the length of the initial substring of *string1* that consists entirely of characters in *string2*, i.e., the substring that spans the character set in *string2*.

If *string1* begins with a character that does not appear in *string2*, the return value is zero. On the other hand, if *string1* only contains characters from *string2*, *strspn* returns the length of *string1*.

SEE ALSO strpbrk   To search for the first occurrence of any of the characters from one string in another string

String Comparison and Manipulation

strcspn   To find the length of the initial substring that is made up entirely of characters
               not in another string

EXAMPLE   Read in a string and use *strspn* to locate the first nonwhitespace character in
               the string.

```
#include <stdio.h>
#include <string.h>
/*space, tab and newline are the whitespace characters */
char *whitespace = " \t\n";
main()
{
    int loc;
    char str1[80];
    printf("Enter a string with preceding blanks: ");
    gets(str1);
    loc = strspn(str1, whitespace);
    printf("First non-whitespace character in\
\n%s\nis at location %d\n", str1, loc);
}
```

strstr

COMPATIBILITY	MSC 3	MSC 4	MSC 5	QC	TC	ANSI	UNIX V
	▲	▲	▲	▲	▲	▲	

PURPOSE   Use *strstr* to locate the first occurrence of one string in another.

SYNTAX   char *strstr(const char *string1, const char *string2);

               const char *string1;   String to be searched

               const char *string2;   String to be located

EXAMPLE CALL   char input[]="The account number is MSCB-87-08-01";
                    acc_no = strstr(input, "MSCB");
               /* Now the string acc_no will be "MSCB-87-08-01" */

INCLUDES   #include <string.h>   For function declaration

DESCRIPTION The *strstr* function searches for the first occurrence of *string2* in *string1*.

RETURNS   If successful, the *strstr* function returns a pointer to the first occurrence of
               string2 as a substring in *string1*. If the search fails, *strstr* returns a NULL.

SEE ALSO   `strchr`   To search for the first occurrence of a character in a string

`strcspn`, `strpbrk`   To locate the first character in a string that matches one of the characters in another string

EXAMPLE   Read in a string and then a substring that you want to find in the first string. Use *strstr* to perform the search. Display the results of the search.

```
#include <stdio.h>
#include <string.h>
main()
{
    char str1[80], str2[80], *result;
    printf("Enter a string: ");
    gets(str1);
    printf("Enter string to locate in the first: ");
    gets(str2);
    if((result = strstr(str1, str2)) == NULL)
    {
        printf("\"%s\" NOT IN \"%s\"\n", str2, str1);
    }
    else
    {
        printf("\"%s\" FOUND.\n\Rest of string: %s\n",
            str2, result);
    }
}
```

strtok

PURPOSE   Use *strtok* to get the next token, or substring, in a string delimited by any character from a second string.

SYNTAX   `char *strtok(char *string1, const char *string2);`

`char *string1;`   String from which tokens are returned

`const char *string2;`   String describing set of characters that delimit tokens

EXAMPLE CALL   `next_token = strtok(input, "\t, ");`

INCLUDES   `#include <string.h>`   For function declaration

 String Comparison and Manipulation

DESCRIPTION   The *strtok* function isolates a token, or substring, from *string1*. The token is marked by delimiting characters given in the second string argument *string2*. All tokens in a particular string *string1* can be extracted through successive calls to *strtok* in the following way. Make the first call to *strtok* with the string to be "tokenized" as the first argument. Provide as the second argument a C string composed from the delimiting characters. After that, call *strtok* with a NULL as the first argument and the delimiting characters appropriate for that token in the second string. This tells *strtok* to continue returning tokens from the old *string1*. The example below illustrates how this is done.

Note that the set of delimiters can change in each call to *strtok*. In the process of separating tokens, *strtok* modifies the string *string1*. It inserts null characters in place of delimiters to convert tokens to C strings.

COMMON USES   The *strtok* function is handy when you are developing an application in which the user enters commands using a specified syntax. The routine that parses the command lines can use *strtok* to isolate the tokens. Quite complex syntax can be accommodated by using a different set of delimiters for each token.

RETURNS   The first call to *strtok* with the argument *string1* returns a pointer to the first token. Subsequent calls with a NULL as the first argument will return the next tokens. When there are no tokens left, *strtok* returns a NULL.

SEE ALSO   strpbrk, strcspn   To search for the first occurrence of any character from one string in another

strspn   To find the first occurrence of a character in a string that does not belong to another string

EXAMPLE   Write a C program that reads a string and separates it into tokens. The tokens are separated by blank spaces, tabs, or commas. This process of converting input strings to tokens is known as "parsing" and is one of the first things any command interpreter or compiler has to do.

```
#include <stdio.h>
#include <string.h>
char tokensep[] = " \t,";
main()
{
    int i = 0;
    char buf[80], *token;
    printf("Enter a string of tokens separated by comma\
 or blank:");
    gets(buf);
/* Call strtok once to get first token and initialize it */
    token = strtok(buf, tokensep);
/* Keep calling strtok to get all tokens                 */
    while(token != NULL)
```

strtok

```
    {
        i++;
        printf("Token %d = %s\n", i, token);
        token = strtok(NULL, tokensep);
    }
}
```

strupr

COMPATIBILITY	MSC 3	MSC 4	MSC 5	QC	TC	ANSI	UNIX V
	▲	▲	▲	▲	▲		

PURPOSE Use *strupr* to convert any lowercase letters in a string to uppercase.

SYNTAX `char *strupr(char *string);`

`char *string;` String to be converted to uppercase

EXAMPLE CALL `strupr("help"); /* converts it to "HELP" */`

INCLUDES `#include <string.h>` For function declaration

DESCRIPTION The *strupr* function converts any lowercase letters in the *string* to uppercase. Other characters in the string are unaffected.

RETURNS The *strupr* function returns a pointer to the converted string (i.e., it returns "string").

COMMENTS The *strupr* routine and its companion *strlwr* are not part of the proposed ANSI definition. Using the macros *toupper* and *tolower*, respectively, you can implement your own versions.

SEE ALSO `strlwr` To convert a string to lowercase

`toupper` To convert a single lowercase letter to uppercase

EXAMPLE Write a program that reads a string from the keyboard and converts the entire screen to uppercase by calling the function *strupr*.

```
#include <stdio.h>
#include <string.h>
main()
{
    char buf[80];
```

 String Comparison and Manipulation

```
        printf("Enter a string with lowercase letters: ");
        gets(buf);
        strupr(buf);
        printf("The string in uppercase is:\n%s\n", buf);
}
```

Chapter *11* *Searching and Sorting*

Introduction

Searching and *sorting* are commonplace in business applications of the PC. All commercial data base programs have these capabilities. If you implement your own data base program tailored to your specific requirements, you invariably need search and sort capabilities. For example, if your data base contains the names and addresses of the customers of your company, you may want to search the list for information about a certain customer. And for mailings, you might want to print labels for all entries in your data base, sorted by zip code.

If you are developing your data base in C, Microsoft C makes your job easier by providing four library routines for sorting and searching lists in memory. We describe these routines in this section.

Concepts

Many algorithms are used for searching and sorting, some meant for arrays that fit into memory and others that can handle files much too large to fit into the memory of the PC. The sort and search functions in the Microsoft C library are for in-memory operations only.

SORTING The typical sort operation involves a data layout like that shown in Figure 11-1. You have an array of pointers each of which contains the address of a data structure (for example, a structure with fields that contain the name, address, and zip code for a customer). Sorting is done not by rearranging the data records themselves, which would be inefficient, but by rearranging the pointers to cause a particular field in the data structure (the "key" for the sort) to appear in ascendant or descendant position. In Figure 11-1 we show the

335

original list and the list after it was sorted with the ZIP code (the key field) ascendant. Notice that only the pointers were rearranged; the data structures stayed put. This improves sorting speed because the pointers are much smaller than the structures themselves, but the pointers require extra storage space.

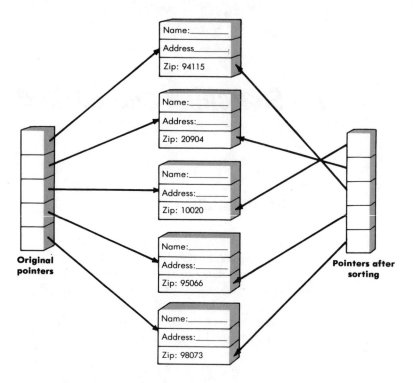

Figure 11-1. *Sorting*

In its sort and search routines the Microsoft C library supplies the basic algorithms but you supply the starting address of the array, the number of elements in it, the size (in bytes) of each element, and a pointer to a function that performs the comparison of two elements.

You write the function that compares two elements from the array. The function receives the pointers to the two elements and returns an integer value. A positive return value signifies that the first element is "greater than" the second one. A zero signifies equality, and a negative number means that the first element is "less than" the second one. You define what less than and greater than mean. In the name and address data base example, you could compare the zip code field of the two structures and return a value based on which zip is higher. If you wanted to sort by the name field, you could compare the names alphabetically. With your definition, the Microsoft *qsort* function sorts the array in ascending order. You can change the order by reversing the less than and greater than definitions in the function performing the comparison.

The Quicksort Algorithm

The only sort routine in the library, *qsort*, is based on the well-known "quicksort" algorithm. This popular, general-purpose sort algorithm was invented by C. A. R. Hoare in 1962. The quicksort algorithm is based on the principle of divide and conquer. The array being sorted is partitioned into two parts and the algorithm is applied to each part. The algorithm can be implemented with the following recursive program:

```
quicksort(lower_bound, upper_bound)
int lower_bound, upper_bound;
{
    int i;
    if (upper_bound > lower_bound)
    {
        i = partition_array(upper_bound, lower_bound);
        quicksort(lower_bound, i);
        quicksort(i+1, upper_bound);
    }
}
```

The *upper_bound* and *lower_bound* are the array indices describing a particular partition. As you can see from the code, the *partitioning of the array* is at the heart of the quicksort algorithm. The partitioning algorithm must satisfy three conditions. First, after the partitioning is complete, one element we'll call X must move to its final position in the sorted array. Second, all elements in the lower half of the new partition must be less than X. Third, all elements in the upper half must be greater than X.

One way to implement the partitioning is to arbitrarily select the element X, at the *upper_bound*, as the one to move into its final place in the sorted array. Then we scan the array from bottom to top until we find an element greater than X, and we also scan it from top to bottom until we find an element less than X. Next we exchange these two elements with one another. This step is repeated until the partitioning is complete, which is indicated by the condition that the scan from top down crosses the one from bottom up. The C code fragment below illustrates this partitioning algorithm (for simplicity, we assume that the array is named *array* and that it contains integer values only):

```
int partition_array(lower_bound, upper_bound)
int lower_bound, upper_bound;
{
    int i, j, X, temp;

    X = array[upper_bound];
    i = lower_bound - 1;
    j = upper_bound;
    while(j <= i)          /* Till partitioning is done */
    {
```

```
        while(a[i] >= X) i++;        /* Scan array */
        while(a[j] <= X) j--;        /* Scan array */
/* Exchange elements */
        temp = a[i];
        a[i] = a[j];
        a[j] = temp;
    }
    return(i); /* Return index to indicate partition */
}
```

SEARCHING The Microsoft C library includes two searching algorithms: the linear search and the binary search.

The Linear Search Algorithm

The linear search is the simpler method of searching: we look through the array sequentially until the specific element is found or, if the array ends before the element is found, the search fails. The *lfind* routine implements this search.

The Binary Search Algorithm

The binary search algorithm is implemented by the function *bsearch*. Like quicksort, binary search uses a divide and conquer approach to find an element in an array. This approach is analogous to searching for a word in the dictionary. You flip to a page around the middle of the dictionary and if the words on that page occur later in alphabetic order than the word you are looking for, you repeat the search in the first half of the dictionary. This method works because the dictionary is already sorted in a particular order.

The array also must be sorted in ascending order. On such a sorted array, the binary search proceeds as follows. The value of the key field in the middle entry of the array is compared with the value being sought. If the entry has a value either too high or too low, this search step is repeated on the upper half or lower half of the array, respectively. Thus at every step of the search you reduce the length of the array to be searched by half, allowing even a large array to be searched very quickly.

General Usage

Microsoft provides four sort and search routines (see Table 11-1). One, *qsort*, is meant for sorting an array of elements. The others, *bsearch, 1find*, and *1search* are for searching an array of elements for a given value. These routines are designed to be used in a standard way. Figure 11-2 shows the arguments that you pass to the routines. These include the starting address of the array; the number of elements in it; the size (in bytes) of each element, and a pointer to a function, *compare( )*, that performs the comparison of two elements. Figure 11-2 shows sorting or searching the command-line arguments that are passed to the *main* function in your program. For a declaration of the form *main(int argc, char **argv)*, the number of arguments is in *argc* (the standard way a program accesses its command-line arguments) and the starting address of the array is *argv*. Each element is a pointer to a C string, so the size of each element is given by *sizeof(char *)*. The comparison function is called as *compare(char **elem1, char **elem2)* with two arguments, each a pointer to a variable that points to a string. We can use a string comparison routine such as *strcmp* to perform the comparison inside *compare( )*.

Table 11-1. *Search and Sort Routines*

Routine	Description
bsearch	Performs binary search for an element in a sorted array.
lfind	Performs linear search for an element in an array. The array need not be sorted.
lsearch	Performs linear search like *lfind*, but appends the value being searched to the array if the value is not found.
qsort	Sorts an array of elements using the "quicksort" algorithm.

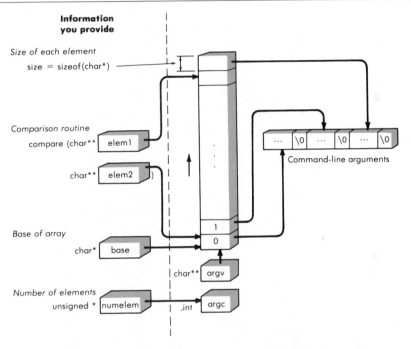

Figure 11-2. *Sorting and searching command-line arguments*

The Routines

The sorting routine is named *qsort* and it uses the quicksort algorithm. The other three routines, *bsearch, lfind*, and *lsearch*, are for searching. The *bsearch* function performs binary search on a sorted array. You can use *qsort* to perform the sorting before calling *bsearch*. The *lfind* and *lsearch* routines implement a linear search technique, but *lsearch* also provides the additional service of inserting the element into the array if it is not found during the search.

Further Reading

Search and sort algorithms are covered in every computer science text on data structures and algorithms. An entire volume by Knuth[1] deals with sort and search algorithms alone. For a shorter introduction to these algorithms, you can consult the books by Sedgewick[2] and Tremblay and Sorenson[3].

1. Donald E. Knuth, *The Art of Computer Programming, Volume 3: Sorting and Searching*, Addison-Wesley Publishing Co., Reading, MA, 1973.

2. Robert Sedgewick, *Algorithms*, Addison-Wesley Publishing Co., Reading, MA, 1983, 551 pages.

3. Jean-Paul Tremblay and Paul G. Sorenson, *An Introduction to Data Structures with Applications*, Second Edition, McGraw-Hill, Inc., New York, NY, 1984, 861 pages.

bsearch

COMPATIBILITY	MSC 3	MSC 4	MSC 5	QC	TC	ANSI	UNIX V
	▲	▲	▲	▲	▲	▲	▲

PURPOSE Use *bsearch* to perform a binary search of a sorted array with a specific number of elements, each a fixed number of bytes long.

SYNTAX
```
void *bsearch(const void *key, const void *base, size_t num,
              size_t width,
              int (*compare)(const void *elem1, const void *elem2));
```

`const void *key;` Pointer to element value being searched for

`const void *base;` Pointer to beginning of array being searched

`size_t num;` Number of elements in array

`size_t width;` Size of each element in bytes

`int (*compare)(const void *elem1, const void *elem2);`
Pointer to a function that compares two elements, *elem1* and *elem2*, each of type *const void* *

EXAMPLE CALL
```
int mycompare(const void *, const void *);
result = (char **) bsearch((const void *)keyword,
                           (const void *)envp,
                           (size_t)count,
                           (size_t)sizeof(char *),
                           mycompare);
```

INCLUDES
`#include <search.h>` For function declaration and definition of *size_t*

or

`#include <stdlib.h>` For function declaration, definition of *size_t* and for ANSI compatibility

DESCRIPTION The *bsearch* function performs a binary search (see the tutorial section) of a sorted array, beginning at the address *base* and comprising *num* elements, each of size *width* bytes. The argument *key* points to the value being sought.
    In the argument *compare*, you supply the address of a routine which should accept two arguments *elem1* and *elem2*, each a pointer to an element in the array. The *bsearch* function calls your routine when it has to compare two elements of the array, passing the address of the array elements as arguments. Your routine should compare the two elements and return one of the

values shown in the table (for strings, "greater than" and "less than" usually refer to alphabetic order).

Return Value	To Indicate
Negative	First element is less than the second one
Zero	The two elements are identical to each other
Positive	First element is greater than the second one

Note that you can use the *qsort* routine to sort the array before calling *bsearch*.

RETURNS   The *bsearch* function returns a pointer to the first occurrence of the value *key* in the array. If the value is not found, *bsearch* returns a NULL.

SEE ALSO   lfind, lsearch   To perform a linear search

qsort   To sort an array using the "quick sort" algorithm

EXAMPLE   In Microsoft C under MS-DOS, the *main* function is invoked with three arguments: the number of strings in the command line, the command line itself, and the MS-DOS environment table, which is also an array of strings. Write a program that accepts a keyword on the command line and uses *bsearch* to search the environment table for the string beginning with this keyword. First it sorts the environment table using *qsort*, prints it, and then calls *bsearch* to perform the search. Count the number of entries in the table, noting that the end of the environment table is marked by a NULL.

```
#include <stdio.h>
#include <string.h>
#include <search.h>
int mycompare(const void *, const void *);
main(int argc, char **argv, char **envp)
{
    unsigned int i, count;
    char **p_table, **result;
    if(argc < 2)
    {
        printf("Usage: %s <KEYWORD>\n", argv[0]);
        exit(0);
    }
/* Find length of environment table                    */
    for(count = 0, p_table = envp;
        *p_table != NULL;
        p_table++, count++);          /* a null loop    */
```

  Searching and Sorting

```
    /* Sort the environment table using "qsort"        */
        qsort((void *) envp, (size_t)count,
            (size_t)sizeof(char *), mycompare);
/* Print sorted environment table                      */
        printf("===== Sorted environment table =====\n");
        for(i = 0, p_table = envp; i < count; i++)
        {
            printf("%s\n", *p_table);
            p_table++;
        }
/* Search for the KEY variable in the environment    */
        result = (char **) bsearch((const void *)&argv[1],
                                    (const void *)envp,
                                    (size_t)count,
                                    (size_t)sizeof(char *),
                                    mycompare);
        if(result != NULL)
        {
            printf("\nFound %s in\n%s\n", argv[1], *result);
        }
        else
        {
            printf("\n%s not found.\
Try with uppercase keyword\n", argv[1]);
        }
}
/*-------------------------------------------------*/
int mycompare(char **arg1, char **arg2)
{
/* Compare two strings up to the length of the key    */
    return(strncmp(*arg1, *arg2, strlen(*arg1)));
}
```

lfind

COMPATIBILITY	MSC 3	MSC 4	MSC 5	QC	TC	ANSI	UNIX V
		▲	▲	▲	▲		▲

PURPOSE Use *lfind* to make a linear search through an array with a specific number of elements, each a fixed number of bytes long.

SYNTAX
```
char *lfind(char *key, char *base, unsigned *num, unsigned width,
            int (*compare)(const void *elem1, const void *elem2));
```

char *key;   Pointer to element value being searched for

```
char *base;         Pointer to beginning of array being searched

unsigned *num;         Pointer to number of elements in array

unsigned width;         Size of each element in bytes

int (*compare)(const void *elem1, const void *elem2);
```
Pointer to a function that compares two elements, *elem1* and *elem2*, each of type *const void* *

EXAMPLE CALL
```
int mycompare(void *, void *);
result = (char **)lfind((char *)keyword,
                        (char *)envp,
                        &count,
                        sizeof(char *),
                        mycompare);
```

INCLUDES
```
#include <search.h>      For function declaration
```

or

```
#include <stdlib.h>      For function declaration and ANSI compatibility
```

DESCRIPTION The *lfind* function makes a linear search through an array that begins at the address *base* and consists of *num* elements, each of size *width* bytes. The argument *key* points to the value being sought.

In the argument *compare*, *lfind* expects the address of a routine to compare a pair of elements from the array. This routine should accept arguments *elem1* and *elem2*, each a pointer to an element in the array. The *lfind* function calls this routine with the address of two array elements as arguments. The routine compares the two elements and returns a zero if the elements are identical. Otherwise, it returns a nonzero value.

RETURNS If the value *key* is found, *lfind* returns a pointer to its first occurrence in the array. If it is not found, *lfind* returns a NULL.

SEE ALSO
lsearch   To perform a linear search of an array

bsearch   To perform a binary search of a sorted array

EXAMPLE Write a program that accepts a keyword on the command line and uses *lfind* to find the first occurrence in the process environment table of a string that begins with the keyword. Note that the environment table is automatically the third parameter in the *main* function with Microsoft C on an MS-DOS system.

 Searching and Sorting

```
#include <stdio.h>
#include <stdlib.h>
#include <string.h>
#include <search.h>
int mycompare(void *, void *);
main(int argc, char **argv, char **envp)
{
    unsigned int count;
    char **p_table, **result;
    if(argc < 2)
    {
        printf("Usage: %s <KEYWORD>\n", argv[0]);
        exit(0);
    }
/* Find length of environment table and print it    */
    printf("==== Environment table contains ====\n");
    for(count = 0, p_table = envp;
        *p_table != NULL;
        p_table++, count++) printf("%s\n", *p_table);
/* Search for the KEY variable in the environment    */
    result = (char **)lfind((char *)&argv[1],
                            (char *)envp,
                            &count,
                            sizeof(char *),
                            mycompare);

    if(result != NULL)
    {
        printf("\nFound %s in\n%s\n", argv[1], *result);
    }
    else
    {
        printf("\n%s not found.\
Try with uppercase keyword\n", argv[1]);
    }
}
/*---------------------------------------------------*/
int mycompare(char **arg1, char **arg2)
{
    return(strncmp(*arg1, *arg2, strlen(*arg1)));
}
```

lsearch

PURPOSE Use *lsearch* to perform a linear search of an array with a specified number of elements, each a fixed number of bytes long. The value being sought is added to the array if it is not found.

SYNTAX
```
char *lsearch(char *key, char *base, unsigned *num, unsigned width,
              int (*compare)(const void *elem1, const void *elem2));
```

`char *key;`   Pointer to element value being searched for

`char *base;`   Pointer to beginning of array being searched

`unsigned *num;`   Pointer to number of elements in array

`unsigned width;`   Size of each element in bytes

`int (*compare)(const void *elem1, const void *elem2);`
     Pointer to a function that compares two elements, *elem1* and *elem2*, each of type *const void **

EXAMPLE CALL
```
int client_compare(void *, void *);
result = (char **) lsearch((char *)client_name,
                           (char *)client_table,
                           &count,
                           sizeof(char *),
                           client_compare);
```

INCLUDES `#include <search.h>`   For function declaration

or

`#include <stdlib.h>`   For function declaration and ANSI compatibility

DESCRIPTION The *lsearch* function performs a linear search (see the tutorial section) of an array beginning at the address *base* and comprising *num* elements, each of size *width* bytes. The argument *key* points to the value being sought.

The *lsearch* function needs a routine that it can call or compare a pair of elements from the array. It should find the address of such a routine in the argument *compare*. You should write this routine to accept arguments *elem1* and *elem2*, each a pointer to an element in the array. The *lsearch* function calls this routine with the address of two array elements as arguments. The routine compares the elements and returns a zero if the elements are identical. Otherwise, the routine returns a nonzero value.

 Searching and Sorting

RETURNS The *lsearch* function returns a pointer to the first occurrence of the value *key* in the array. If the value is not found, *lsearch* adds the element at the end of the array, updates the value in *num*, and returns a pointer to the newly added item. If you don't want to add missing items to the array, use *lfind* instead.

SEE ALSO lfind   To perform a linear search without adding element to array

bsearch   To perform a binary search of a sorted array

EXAMPLE Write a program using *lsearch* to search in a small table of C strings for an entry beginning with a keyword entered on the command line. When the entry is not found, *lsearch* inserts the entry into the array and updates the element count. You can verify this by providing a keyword you know is not in the table.

```c
#include <stdio.h>
#include <string.h>
#include <search.h>
int mycompare(void *, void *);
char *our_table[20] =
{
        "Microsoft C 5.1",
        "Quick C 1.0",
        "Turbo C 1.0",
        NULL
};
main(int argc, char **argv)
{
    unsigned int i, count, oldcount;
    char **p_table, **result;
    if(argc < 2)
    {
        printf("Usage: %s <KEYWORD>\n", argv[0]);
        exit(0);
    }
/* Find length of our table  and print it   */
    printf("==== Our table contains ====\n");
    for(count = 0, p_table = our_table;
        *p_table != NULL;
        p_table++, count++) printf("%s\n", *p_table);
    oldcount = count;
/* Search for the PATH variable in the environment   */
    result = (char **) lsearch((char *)&argv[1],
                            (char *)our_table,
                            &count,
                            sizeof(char *),
                            mycompare);

    if(count == oldcount)
```

lsearch

```
        {
            printf("\nFound %s in\n%s\n", argv[1], *result);
        }
        else
        {
            printf("\n%s was added to table\n", argv[1]);
/* Print table again */

            printf("==== Now table contains ====\n");
            for(i=0; i<count; i++)
                printf("%s\n", our_table[i]);
        }
}
/*-------------------------------------------------*/
int mycompare(char **arg1, char **arg2)
{
/* Compare two strings up to the length of the key    */
    return(strncmp(*arg1, *arg2, strlen(*arg1)));
}
```

qsort

COMPATIBILITY	MSC 3	MSC 4	MSC 5	QC	TC	ANSI	UNIX V
	▲	▲	▲	▲	▲	▲	▲

PURPOSE Use *qsort* to sort an array having a given number of elements, each a fixed number of bytes long.

SYNTAX
```
void qsort(void *base, size_t num, size_t width,
            int (*compare)(const void *elem1, const void *elem2));
```

`const void *base;`   Pointer to beginning of array being sorted

`size_t num;`   Number of elements in array

`size_t width;`   Size of each element in bytes

`int (*compare)(const void *elem1, const void *elem2);`
Pointer to a function that compares two elements, *elem1* and *elem2*, each of type *const void ***

EXAMPLE CALL
```
int compare(const void *, const void *);
qsort((void *) envp, (size_t)count,
        (size_t)sizeof(char *), compare);
```

Searching and Sorting

INCLUDES   #include <search.h>   For function declaration and definition of *size_t*

or

#include <stdlib.h>   For function declaration and definition of *size_t* and for ANSI compatibility

DESCRIPTION   The *qsort* function uses the quick sort algorithm (see the tutorial section) to sort an array beginning at the address *base* and comprising of *num* elements, each of size *width* bytes.

During the sort, *qsort* compares pairs of elements from the array by calling a routine whose address you provide in the argument *compare*. This function should accept arguments *elem1* and *elem2*, each a pointer to an element in the array. The *qsort* function calls this routine using the address of two array elements as arguments. Your routine should compare the two elements and return one of the values shown in the table (for strings, "greater than" and "less than" usually refer to alphabetic order):

Return Value	To Indicate
Negative	First element is less than the second one.
Zero	The two elements are identical to each other.
Positive	First element is greater than the second one.

On the basis of these values, the array is sorted in ascending order of element values, but you can reverse the order by changing the return value of the greater than and less than tests in the function that compares elements from the array.

SEE ALSO   find, lsearch   To perform a linear search

bsearch   To perform a binary search on a sorted array

EXAMPLE   Illustrate the use of *qsort* by sorting the environment table (an array of strings with a NULL string at the end) that is the third argument in the *main* function with Microsoft C under MS-DOS.

```
#include <stdio.h>
#include <string.h>
#include <search.h>
int mycompare(const void *, const void *);
main(int argc, char **argv, char **envp)
{
    unsigned int i, count;
```

```
        char **p_table, **result;
/* Find length of environment table and print it      */
        printf("==== Unsorted environment table ====\n");
        for(count = 0, p_table = envp;
            *p_table != NULL;
            p_table++, count++) printf("%s\n", *p_table);
/* Sort the environment table using "qsort"            */
        qsort((void *) envp, (size_t)count,
            (size_t)sizeof(char *), mycompare);
/* Print sorted environment table                      */
        printf("===== Sorted environment table =====\n");
        for(i = 0, p_table = envp; i < count; i++)
        {
            printf("%s\n", *p_table);
            p_table++;
        }
}
/*----------------------------------------------------*/
int mycompare(char **arg1, char **arg2)
{
/* Compare two strings up to the length of the key     */
    return(strncmp(*arg1, *arg2, strlen(*arg1)));
}
```

Chapter **12 Time Routines**

Introduction

Time is of the essence in a computer. The computer executes instructions at a steady rate, once every clock tick—and the clock ticks very fast indeed. You may have noticed advertisements proclaiming 8-, 10- or 12-MHz machines. Each MHz translates to one million clock ticks per second. This is the fast-moving time kept by the system's clock. Time, in hours, minutes, and seconds is also important and is used by the operating system, MS-DOS, for a variety of tasks. An example is the date and time *stamp* on each file in the system, used to record when a file was created and when it was last modified. You see this information when you list the directory with a DIR command at the DOS prompt.

Your C programs may use the date and time information as well. If, for example, you develop a graphical user interface and you wish to display current date and time in a corner of the screen, the Microsoft C library includes routines for just this kind of task. In fact, it contains many different routines, giving you a choice of getting the date and time information in a variety of formats, each suitable for a specific job.

Concepts: Time in MS-DOS Systems

The 8086 microprocessor uses a *system clock* which ticks several million times a second to execute its instructions. The hardware requires this fast clock, but humans prefer a slower pace. So the PC provides circuitry to generate an interrupt at the rate of 18.2 times a second and includes code in the ROM BIOS (see the tutorial in Chapter 16) to handle these interrupts. The interrupt handler updates a count of such interrupts since the PC was last turned on. In the early days of the IBM PC, if you knew the time when the PC was turned on, these tick counts could be used to compute the current time. This is why MS-DOS always asks for the date and time when you power up your PC. Now, however, most PCs have a "clock/calendar" card or, in the case of the PC-AT and PS/2, a built-in "real-time clock." These are similar to digital clocks and they can keep running even when your PC is off because they use a battery as a backup power supply. The PC-AT and PS/2 get the system date and time at power-up from the real-time clock, so the user is not asked for it by MS-DOS.

THE CLOCK DRIVER

MS-DOS uses device drivers to communicate with peripheral devices and it uses a special driver, identified by a particular bit in the attribute word in the driver's header, to get or set the date and the time. As shown in Figure 12-1, this CLOCK driver, maintains the current time and date as a 6-byte sequence. The time is expressed in hours, minutes, seconds, and hundredths of seconds and the date is expressed as the number of days elapsed since January 1, 1980. In fact, none of the time routines understands any date prior to January 1, 1980, since that's when time began for MS-DOS. The CLOCK driver marks directory entries with date and time stamps and provides date and time services to application programs (via DOS functions numbered 2Ah through 2Dh). The fact that MS-DOS uses a driver for those functions made it easy to add a clock/calendar board to the original PC. You just popped the board into your system and loaded the CLOCK driver by placing a statement like *DE-VICE=⟨path name of driver⟩* in your CONFIG.SYS file.

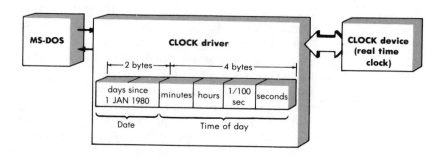

Figure 12-1. *Time in MS-DOS*

TIME IN UNIX AND IN MICROSOFT C

You need not worry about the CLOCK driver when using the time functions in the Microsoft C library, but you do need to know how time is maintained in UNIX systems. This is because Microsoft C has maintained a high degree of compatibility with UNIX, helping to ensure portability.

In UNIX, and in Microsoft C, the date and the time is expressed jointly by the number of seconds elapsed since 00:00:00 hours Greenwich Mean Time (GMT) on January 1, 1970. This is a more universal representation than in MS-DOS because it uses the same reference (GMT) at any location in the world. How is this universal time derived from the local time kept by MS-DOS? Here is the scheme used by Microsoft C.

The TZ Environment Variable

An environment variable (see Chapter 3) named TZ defines the time zone (for example, PST, MST, EST), the difference between the local time and GMT in hours, and whether daylight saving time is honored. You can use the DOS command SET to define the environment variable TZ. For a PC in the Eastern Standard Time with daylight saving honored, for example, the definition of TZ will be *TZ=EST5EDT* because there is a difference of 5 hours between EST and GMT. If TZ is not defined, a default of *TZ=PST8PDT* is assumed.

Global Variables: *daylight, timezone,* and *tzname*

Three global variables store time zone information that is used by several time functions for their operation. The library function *tzset* sets these variables from the setting of the environment variable TZ.

The variable *daylight* is an integer that contains either a 1 or a 0 depending on whether the daylight saving is honored in this time zone. The long integer variable *timezone* contains the number of seconds to be added to the local time to get GMT when both are expressed as seconds elapsed since 00:00:00 hour, January 1, 1970. The *tzname* variable is an array of two strings, the first containing the name of the time zone and the second, the corresponding daylight-saving time zone (for example, EST and EDT).

Conversion from Local Time to GMT

Figure 12-2 illustrates the conversion of local time from MS-DOS to the format used in Microsoft C. The date and time from MS-DOS are converted to seconds elapsed since the 00:00:00 hour, January 1, 1970, and the value of *timezone* is added to this number. If daylight savings is honored and on at that time, the value is further modified. The result is what the function *time* returns: the current date and time expressed as seconds elapsed since 00:00:00 hours GMT, 1970.

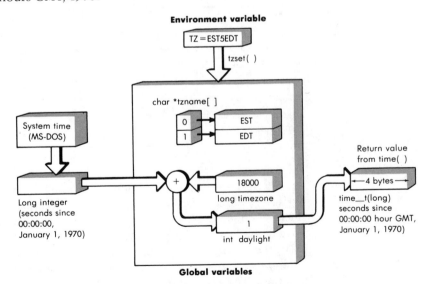

Figure 12-2. *Time in Microsoft C*

The main function of the time routines is to get the current date and time in various formats and to convert from one format to another. A list of the functions is given in Table 12-1 and the functions are classified by task in Table 12-2.

Table 12-1. *Time Routines*

Routine	Description
asctime	Converts time from a structure of type *tm* to a string.
clock	Returns the elapsed processor time in number of ticks.
ctime	Converts time from a value of type *time_t* to a string.
difftime	Computes the difference of two values of type *time_t*.
ftime	Returns the current time in a structure of type *timeb*.
gmtime	Converts time from a value of type *time_t* to a structure of type *tm* that corresponds to GMT.
localtime	Converts time from a value of type *time_t* to a structure of type *tm* that corresponds to the local time.
mktime	Converts the local time from a structure of type *tm* to a value of type *time_t*.
_strdate	Returns the current date as an eight-character string of the form *11/26/87*.
_strtime	Returns the current time as an eight-character string of the form *17:09:35*.
time	Returns the seconds elapsed since 00:00:00 hour, GMT, January 1, 1970, as a value of type *time_t*.
tzset	Assigns values to the global variables *timezone*, *daylight*, and *tzname* based on the time zone specified in the environment variable TZ.
utime	Sets the "last modified" time stamp of a file to which you have write access.

Table 12-2. *Time Routines by Task*

Task	Routines
Get current date and time.	ftime, _strdate, _strtime, time
Convert time from one form to another.	asctime, ctime, gmtime, localtime, mktime
Compute elapsed time.	clock, difftime
Set file modification time.	utime
Load environment variable setting into internal variables.	tzset

Figure 12-3 depicts the different formats of date and time and conversion among them. The basic function *time* returns a value of type *time_t*, which is defined to be a long integer in the *time.h* header file. This long integer value is converted to a structure named *tm* (defined in the *time.h* header file) by the *gmtime* and *localtime* routines. The *gmtime* function sets all fields in the *tm* structure to correspond to GMT while *localtime* sets them to the local time. The *mktime* function converts time back from structure *tm* to a value of type *time_t*.

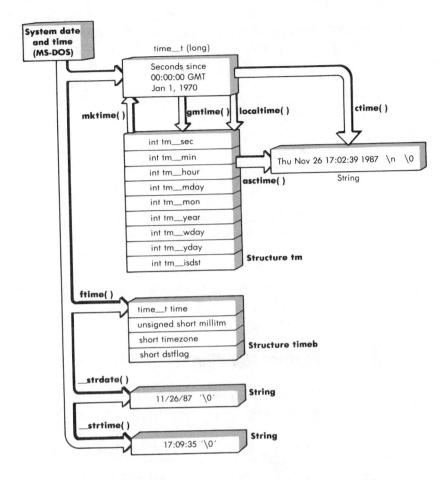

Figure 12-3. *Conversion among different forms of date and time*

A different structure, *timeb*, defined in the file *sys\timeb.h*, is used by the *ftime* function to return the current date and time. The field *time* in the *timeb* structure is identical to the value returned by the *time* function.

Printing Date and Time

The *asctime* function converts the value in a structure of type *tm* to a C string that you can print. The *ctime* function converts the output of *time* directly to a string. The functions *_strdate* and *_strtime* return in printable strings the date and the time, respectively.

ELAPSED TIME   Sometimes you have to compute the time elapsed between two events. The *difftime* function returns the difference of two values of type *time_t* in seconds. The *clock* function returns the number of *clock ticks* used by the process so far. The number of ticks per second is defined in the constant CLK _TCK (in file *time.h*) to be 1,000 (see the example program in the *clock* reference page). Although this implies an accuracy of a millisecond, it is misleading for the PC because the actual updating of the clock happens only 18.2 times a second or approximately once every 55 milliseconds.

Cautions

▶ If the TZ environment variable is not set on your system, the GMT will be computed wrongly. Since everything in MS-DOS is done in local time, this is important only if you need an accurate universal time. The default settings of TZ imply that local time is Pacific Standard Time.

▶ The functions *gmtime* and *localtime* use a single structure of type *tm* to store the time. Each call to either function overwrites the result of the previous call.

▶ The *ctime* and *asctime* functions also use a single character string to store results. Thus any call to one overwrites the result of the previous call.

Further Reading

The time functions have not received much attention in books about C programming on the PC. One exception is Hansen's book[1], which includes a detailed discussion of the time routines in the Microsoft C 4.0 library. Consult Duncan's book[2] on MS-DOS for further information on the CLOCK driver, and on drivers in general, in MS-DOS.

1. Augie Hansen, *Proficient C*, Microsoft Press, Redmond, WA, 1987, 492 pages.

2. Ray Duncan, *Advanced MS-DOS*, Microsoft Press, Redmond, WA, 1986, 468 pages.

asctime

COMPATIBILITY	MSC 3	MSC 4	MSC 5	QC	TC	ANSI	UNIX V
	▲	▲	▲	▲	▲	▲	▲

PURPOSE Use *asctime* to convert a time stored in a structure of type *tm* to a character string.

SYNTAX `char *asctime(const struct tm *time);`

`cons struct tm *time;`   Pointer to a structure containing time to be converted to a string

EXAMPLE CALL `printf("The time is %s\n", asctime(&timedata));`

INCLUDES `#include <time.h>`   For function declaration and definition of structure *tm*

DESCRIPTION The *asctime* function converts to a character string the value of a time stored in the structure of type *tm* at the address *time*. The value is set up by an earlier call to *gmtime* or *localtime*, both of which accept a long integer value for the time, prepare the fields of a structure of type *tm*, and return a pointer to that structure. The structure *tm* is defined in *time.h* as follows:

```
struct tm
{
    int tm_sec;      /* seconds after the minute - [0,59] */
    int tm_min;      /* minutes after the hour - [0,59]   */
    int tm_hour;     /* hours since midnight - [0,23]     */
    int tm_mday;     /* day of the month - [1,31]         */
    int tm_mon;      /* months since January - [0,11]     */
    int tm_year;     /* years since 1900                  */
    int tm_wday;     /* days since Sunday - [0,6]         */
    int tm_yday;     /* days since January 1 - [0,365]    */
    int tm_isdst;    /* daylight savings time flag        */
};
```

The string prepared by *asctime* is 26 characters long, counting the null character at the end, and has the form:

`Thu Nov 26 17:02:39 1987\n\0`

As the definition shows, a 24-hour clock is used for the time.

RETURNS The *asctime* function returns a pointer to the data area where the string is stored.

COMMENTS To prepare the time for printing, the *asctime* and *ctime* functions use a single static string so it will be destroyed by subsequent calls to these routines.

asctime

SEE ALSO   ctime, gmtime, localtime, time

EXAMPLE   Use *asctime* to get and display the local time.

```
#include <stdio.h>
#include <time.h>
main()
{
    struct tm *curtime;
    time_t bintime;
/* Get time in seconds since 00:00:00 GMT, 1/1/70 */
    time(&bintime);
/* Convert time to local time (default is PST)    */
    curtime = localtime(&bintime);
/* Use asctime to print the date and time         */
    printf("Current time: %s\n", asctime(curtime));
}
```

clock

COMPATIBILITY	MSC 3	MSC 4	MSC 5	QC	TC	ANSI	UNIX V
			▲	▲	▲	▲	

PURPOSE   Use *clock* to obtain in number of ticks the amount of processor time used by the current process.

SYNTAX   clock_t clock(void);

EXAMPLE CALL   ticks_now = clock();

INCLUDES   #include <time.h>   For function declaration and definition of type *clock_t*

DESCRIPTION   The *clock* function tells how much processor time has been used by the calling process. The value is expressed as the number of ticks. The constant CLK_TCK, defined in *time.h*, is the number of ticks per second, so the value returned by *clock* should be divided by CLK_TCK to get the elapsed processor time in seconds.

RETURNS   If processor time is available to *clock*, it returns the current time in ticks, cast as a value of type *clock_t* which is defined in *time.h*. Otherwise, it returns the value −1, cast as *clock_t*.

SEE ALSO   difftime   To get the difference of two time values

   time   To get the current time as a long integer

 **Time Routines**

EXAMPLE   Use *clock* to determine and display the processor time used in a program that performs a computational loop 10,000 times.

```c
#include <stdio.h>
#include <time.h>
main()
{
    unsigned i, tused, count=10000;
    double a, b, c, d;
    clock_t ticksnow;
    for(i=0; i<count; i++)
    {
        a = (double)(i-1);
        b = (double)(i+1);
        c = (double)(i*i);
        d = a*b - c;
    }
/* Get current clock ticks by calling "clock"     */
    if((ticksnow = clock()) == (clock_t)-1)
    {
        printf("Processor time not available!\n");
        abort();
    }
/* Convert processor time to seconds. Use CLK_TCK  */
    tused = (unsigned)ticksnow/CLK_TCK;
    printf("10,000 loops ran for %u seconds\n", tused);
}
```

ctime

COMPATIBILITY	MSC 3	MSC 4	MSC 5	QC	TC	ANSI	UNIX V
	▲	▲	▲	▲	▲	▲	▲

PURPOSE   Use *ctime* to convert to a character string a time stored as a value of type *time_t*.

SYNTAX   `char *ctime(const time_t *time);`

   `const time_t *time;`   Pointer to variable containing time to be converted to a string

EXAMPLE CALL   `printf("Current time = %s\n", ctime(&bintime));`

INCLUDES   `#include <time.h>`   For function declaration and definition of *time_t*

DESCRIPTION   The *ctime* function converts to a character string the value of time stored in the variable of type *time_t* at the address *time*. This value is obtained by an earlier

ctime

call to the function *time*, which returns the number of seconds elapsed since 00:00:00 hours GMT, January 1, 1970. The string prepared by *ctime* is 26 characters long, counting the null character at the end, and has the form:

```
Thu Nov 26 17:02:39 1987\n\0
```

As the preceding example shows, a 24-hour clock is used for the time.

RETURNS   As long as the value in *time* represents a date on or after the year 1980, *ctime* returns a pointer to the data area where the character string is stored. If the value in *time* represents a date prior to 1980, *ctime* returns a NULL in Microsoft C 5.0 and 5.1. Under similar circumstances in version 4.0, *ctime* returns the date and time of January 1, 1980, and 00:00:00 hours.

COMMENTS   To prepare the time for printing, the *ctime* and *asctime* functions use a single static string so it will be destroyed by subsequent calls to these routines.

SEE ALSO   asctime   To convert time from a *tm* structure into a character string

                time   To get the current time as a long integer value

EXAMPLE   Use *ctime* to prepare a string version of the value returned by a call to *time* and print this string.

```
#include <stdio.h>
#include <time.h>
main()
{
    time_t bintime;
/* Get time in seconds since 00:00:00 GMT, 1/1/70 */
    time(&bintime);
/* Use ctime to print the date and time          */
    printf("Current time: %s\n", ctime(&bintime));
}
```

difftime

COMPATIBILITY	MSC 3	MSC 4	MSC 5	QC	TC	ANSI	UNIX V
	▲	▲	▲	▲	▲	▲	▲

PURPOSE   Use *difftime* to obtain the difference of two time values, each of type *time_t*.

SYNTAX   double difftime(time_t time2, time_t time1);

            time_t time2;   Value of time from which *time1* will be subtracted

            time_t time1;   Value of time to be subtracted from *time2*

 Time Routines

EXAMPLE CALL   `seconds_used = difftime(oldtime, newtime);`

INCLUDES   `#include <time.h>`   For function declaration definition of *time_t*

DESCRIPTION   The *difftime* function computes the difference between time values *time2* and *time1*. These times are obtained by calling *time*, which returns the current time in seconds since 00:00:00 hours GMT, January 1, 1970. This function is useful for computing elapsed time between arbitrary events. Use *clock* for determining how long the current program has been running.

RETURNS   The *difftime* function returns the elapsed time, *time2 − time1*, in seconds as a double-precision number.

SEE ALSO   `time`   To get current time in seconds since 00:00:00 hours GMT, January 1, 1970

EXAMPLE   Use *difftime* to determine the time it takes to perform a computational loop a specified number of times.

```
#include <stdio.h>
#include <time.h>
main()
{
    unsigned long i, count;
    double a, b, c, d, tused, tperstep;
    time_t tstart, tstop;
/* Ask user number of times "multiply" to be done */
    printf("Enter number of times loop is run:");
    scanf(" %lu", &count);
/* Get current time by calling "time"              */
    time(&tstart);
    for(i=0; i<count; i++)
    {
        a = (double)(i-1);
        b = (double)(i+1);
        c = (double)(i*i);
        d = a*b - c;
    }
/* Get time again and print time used.            */
    time(&tstop);
    tused = difftime(tstop, tstart);  /* in sec   */
    tperstep = tused/(double)count;
    printf("Total time = %f seconds\n\
Time per iteration: %f milliseconds\n", tused,
            tperstep*1000.0);
}
```

difftime

ftime

PURPOSE Use *ftime* to get the current time and store it in a structure of type *timeb*.

SYNTAX `void ftime(struct timeb *timeptr);`

`struct timeb *timeptr;`   Pointer to structure of type *timeb* to which time is returned

EXAMPLE CALL `ftime(&time_buffer);`

INCLUDES `#include <sys\timeb.h>`   For function declaration and definition of structure *timeb*

DESCRIPTION The *ftime* function gets the current time and stores it in a structure of type *timeb* that you allocate and whose address you provide in the argument *timeptr*. The fields in the structure at *timeptr* are set to appropriate values by *ftime*. The *timeb* structure is defined in the include file *sys\timeb.h* as:

```
struct timeb
{
    time_t          time;      /* Time in seconds since 00:00:00
                                  GMT, January 1, 1970           */
    unsigned short  millitm;   /* Fraction of a second in milli-
                                  seconds                        */
    short           timezone;  /* Difference in minutes moving
                                  westward, between GMT and local
                                  time                           */
    short           dstflag;   /* Nonzero if daylight saving is
                                  in effect in the local time zone*/
};
```

The *ftime* function uses the settings of the global variables *timezone* and *daylight* in setting the values of the fields *timezone* and *dstflag* in the *timeb* structure. These variables are set by calling *tzset* and using the environment variable TZ. (See the reference page on *tzset* for more details.)

SEE ALSO `time`   To get current time as a long integer value

`tzset`   To set environment variables that indicate time zones and enable daylight saving hours

EXAMPLE Use *ftime* to get the current time. Use *ctime* to display the *time* field of the *timeb* structure.

 Time Routines

```
#include <stdio.h>
#include <sys\types.h>
#include <sys\timeb.h>
#include <time.h>
main()
{
    struct timeb time_buffer;
    char *date_time;
/* Use "ftime" to get current time into time_buffer */
    ftime(&time_buffer);
/* Convert "time" field to a string and print it    */
    printf("Time = %s", ctime(&time_buffer.time));
}
```

gmtime

COMPATIBILITY	MSC 3	MSC 4	MSC 5	QC	TC	ANSI	UNIX V
	▲	▲	▲	▲	▲	▲	▲

PURPOSE Use *gmtime* to separate a time value of type *time_t* into fields of a structure of type *tm*. This results in values that represent the GMT relative to the time zone specified in the environment variable TZ.

SYNTAX `struct tm *gmtime(const time_t *time);`

`const time_t *time;` Pointer to stored time in seconds elapsed since 00:00:00 GMT, January 1, 1970

EXAMPLE CALL `t_gmt = gmtime(&bintime);`

INCLUDES `#include <time.h>` For function declaration and definition of structure *tm* and data type *time_t*

DESCRIPTION The *gmtime* function breaks down a time value, stored at the location *time*, to year, month, day, hour, minutes, seconds, and several other fields that it saves in a structure of type *tm*. The value at *time* is the number of seconds elapsed from 00:00:00 hours GMT, January 1, 1970, to a time obtained by calling the function *time*. The structure *tm* is defined in *time.h* as follows:

```
struct tm
{
    int tm_sec;      /* seconds after the minute - [0,59] */
    int tm_min;      /* minutes after the hour - [0,59]   */
    int tm_hour;     /* hours since midnight - [0,23]     */
    int tm_mday;     /* day of the month - [1,31]         */
```

```
    int tm_mon;        /* months since January - [0,11]    */
    int tm_year;       /* years since 1900                 */
    int tm_wday;       /* days since Sunday - [0,6]        */
    int tm_yday;       /* days since January 1 - [0,365]   */
    int tm_isdst;      /* daylight savings time flag, nonzero
                          if enabled                       */
};
```

The fields set up by *gmtime* correspond to GMT as dictated by the environment variable TZ, which indicates the time zone and the daylight saving zone for use in converting from local time to GMT. TZ must be set to a three-letter time zone name (such as PST, EST, etc.), followed by a signed number giving the difference between GMT and the local time zone (a positive sign can be omitted). An optional three-letter daylight saving zone name can be added to the setting. The *gmtime* function uses this information to convert the local time to GMT based on the time zone and the daylight saving season. If TZ is not defined, a default setting of PST8PDT is used. Note that TZ is not a part of the proposed ANSI definition; it is a Microsoft extension.

RETURNS   Provided the value in *time* does not represent a date prior to 1980, *gmtime* returns a pointer to the structure where the converted time is stored. Otherwise, in Microsoft C 5.0 and 5.1, it returns a NULL and in version 4.0, it returns the date and time: January 1, 1980, 00:00:00 hours.

COMMENTS   MS-DOS does not understand dates prior to 1980, so time values provided to the library routines *gmtime* and *localtime* must be later than 1980. Note that *gmtime* uses the static structure of type *tm* to return the result so each call to this routine destroys the result of the preceding call.

SEE ALSO   asctime   To convert time from a structure of type *tm* into a character string

localtime   To convert from GMT to local time

time   To get current time in seconds elapsed since 00:00:00 hours GMT, January 1, 1970

EXAMPLE   Get the current time using *time*, convert it to GMT using *gmtime*, and display this latter time.

```
#include <stdio.h>
#include <time.h>
main()
{
    time_t tnow;
    struct tm *tmnow;
/* Get the time in seconds since 0 hrs GMT, 1/1/70  */
    time(&tnow);
/* Convert it to string showing Greenwich Mean Time */
    tmnow = gmtime(&tnow);
```

 Time Routines

```
printf("Greenwich Mean Time = %s\n",
    asctime(tmnow));
}
```

localtime

COMPATIBILITY	MSC 3	MSC 4	MSC 5	QC	TC	ANSI	UNIX V
	▲	▲	▲	▲	▲	▲	▲

PURPOSE Use *localtime* to separate a time value of type *time_t* into various fields of a structure of type *tm*.

SYNTAX `struct tm *localtime(const time_t *time);`

`const time_t *time;`   Pointer to stored time in seconds elapsed since 00:00:00 hours GMT, January 1, 1970

EXAMPLE CALL `t_local = localtime(&bintime);`

INCLUDES `#include <time.h>`   For function declaration and definition of structure *tm* and data type *time_t*

DESCRIPTION The *localtime* function breaks down the time value, stored at the location *time*, to year, month, day, hour, minutes, seconds, and several other fields that it saves in a structure of type *tm*. The fields set up by *localtime* correspond to local time. The value at *time* is the number of seconds elapsed from 00:00:00 hours GMT, January 1, 1970, to a time obtained by calling the function *time*. The structure *tm* is defined in *time.h* as shown in the reference pages on *gmtime*.

RETURNS Provided the value in *time* does not represent a date prior to 1980, *localtime* returns a pointer to the structure where the converted time is stored. Otherwise, in Microsoft C 5.0, it returns a NULL and in version 4.0, it returns the date and time: January 1, 1980, 00:00:00 hours.

COMMENTS MS-DOS does not understand dates prior to 1980, so time values provided to the library routines *localtime* and *gmtime* must be later than 1980. Note that *localtime* uses the static structure of type *tm* to return the result so each call to this routine destroys the result of the preceding call.

SEE ALSO `asctime`   To convert time from a structure of type *tm* into a character string

`gmtime`   To convert from local time to GMT

`time`   To get current time in seconds elapsed since 00:00:00 hours GMT, January 1, 1970

localtime

EXAMPLE Use *time* to get the current time. Convert it to a detailed representation of the local date and time by using *localtime*. Use *asctime* to print the date and time.

```
#include <stdio.h>
#include <time.h>
main()
{
    time_t tnow;
    struct tm *tmnow;
/* Get the time in seconds since 0 hrs GMT, 1/1/70 */
    time(&tnow);
/* Convert it to string showing local time. Use the
 * environment variable TZ and the function "tzset"
 * to set the timezone appropriately.
 * Default time is PST.
 */
    tmnow = localtime(&tnow);
    printf("Local Time = %s\n", asctime(tmnow));
}
```

mktime

COMPATIBILITY	MSC 3	MSC 4	MSC 5	QC	TC	ANSI	UNIX V
			▲	▲		▲	

PURPOSE Use *mktime* to convert the local time from a structure of type *tm* into a value of type *time_t*.

SYNTAX `time_t mktime(struct tm *timeptr);`

`struct tm *timeptr;`   Pointer to structure of type *tm* where local time is stored

EXAMPLE CALL `bintime = mktime(&timebuf);`

INCLUDES `#include <time.h>`   For function declaration and definition of structure *tm*

DESCRIPTION The *mktime* function converts the local time currently at the address *timeptr* from the form of year, month, day, and so on, to the number of seconds elapsed since 00:00:00 hours GMT, January 1, 1970. This is the same format in which *time* returns the current time and is the format used in the argument to the functions *ctime*, *difftime*, and *localtime*.

Two fields in the structure of type *tm* are ignored by *mktime*: *tm_wday* and *tm_yday*, denoting the day of the week and day of the year, respectively. The *mktime* function sets the fields in the *tm* structure to appropriate values before returning.

 Time Routines

RETURNS   If successful, *mktime* returns the contents of *timeptr* as a value of type *time _t*. If the local time in *timeptr* cannot be handled by *mktime* (e.g., the date is prior to 1980), the return value will be a −1 cast to the type *time_t*.

SEE ALSO   asctime   To convert time from a structure of type *tm* into a character string

time   To get current time in seconds elapsed since 00:00:00 hours GMT, January 1, 1970

EXAMPLE   Note that *mktime* adjusts if the fields in the *tm* data structure are not within a valid range. For instance, you could set the number of days since first of the month to 45 and *mktime* would alter other fields (such as making it the next month) to bring all entries to valid ranges. This feature is useful for setting up a utility program that prints the date a specified number of days from today. Write a program that accepts as a command-line argument the number of days to look ahead.

```c
#include <stdio.h>
#include <time.h>
main(int argc, char **argv)
{
    time_t    tresult, tnow;
    struct tm *tmnow;
    if(argc<2)
    {
        printf("Usage: %s <number of days>\n", argv[0]);
        exit(0);
    }
/* Get todays's date and convert it to a "tm" structure */
    time(&tnow);
    tmnow = localtime(&tnow);
/* Adjust the number of days */
    tmnow->tm_mday += atoi(argv[1]);
/* Now call "mktime" to set everything in tmnow */
    if((tresult = mktime(tmnow)) == (time_t)-1)
    {
        printf("mktime failed\n");
    }
    else
    {
        printf("%d days from now it'll be %s\n",
                atoi(argv[1]), ctime(&tresult));
/*              atoi(argv[1]), asctime(tmnow)); */
    }
}
```

mktime

__strdate

COMPATIBILITY	MSC 3	MSC 4	MSC 5	QC	TC	ANSI	UNIX V
			▲	▲			

PURPOSE Use *_strdate* to obtain the current date as an eight-character string of the form *11/26/87*.

SYNTAX `char *_strdate(char *date);`

`char *date;` Current date in the form MM/DD/YY returned by *_strdate*

EXAMPLE CALL `_strdate(date_buffer);`

INCLUDES `#include <time.h>` For function declaration

DESCRIPTION The *_strdate* function gets the current date, formats it into an eight-character string of the form MM/DD/YY, and copies it into a nine-character buffer that you allocate and whose address you provide in the argument *date*. For example, November 26, 1987 is returned by *_strdate* as 11/26/87 with a null at the end.

RETURNS The *_strdate* function returns the argument *date*.

SEE ALSO `ctime, time` To get and convert date and time into a string

`_strtime` To get current time in a string

EXAMPLE Use *_strdate* to convert today's date to a string and then print the string.

```
#include <stdio.h>
#include <time.h>
main()
{
    char date_buffer[9];
    _strdate(date_buffer);
    printf("Today is: %s\n", date_buffer);
}
```

 **Time Routines**

__strtime

COMPATIBILITY	MSC 3	MSC 4	MSC 5	QC	TC	ANSI	UNIX V
			▲	▲			

PURPOSE Use _strtime to obtain the current time as an eight-character string of the form *17:09:35*.

SYNTAX `char *_strtime(char *time);`

`char *time;`   Current time in the form HH:MM:SS returned by _strtime

EXAMPLE CALL `_strtime(time_buffer);`

INCLUDES `#include <time.h>`   For function declaration

DESCRIPTION The _strtime function gets the current time, formats it into an eight-character string of the form HH:MM:SS, and copies it into a nine-character buffer that you allocate and whose address you provide in the argument *time*. For example, the current time of 9 minutes and 35 seconds past 5 pm, returns as 17:09:35 with a null at the end.

RETURNS The _strtime function returns the argument *time*.

SEE ALSO `ctime, time`   To get and convert date and time into a string

`_strdate`   To get current date in a string

EXAMPLE Use _strtime to convert the current time to a C string and then print the string.

```
#include <stdio.h>
#include <time.h>
main()
{
    char time_buffer[9];
    _strtime(time_buffer);
    printf("Time now: %s\n", time_buffer);
}
```

__strtime

time

PURPOSE Use *time* to obtain the number of seconds elapsed since 00:00:00 hours, GMT, January 1, 1970.

SYNTAX `time_t time(time_t *timeptr);`

`time_t *timeptr;`   Pointer to variable where result is returned

EXAMPLE CALL `time(&bintime);`

INCLUDES `#include <time.h>`   For function declaration and definition of *time_t*

DESCRIPTION The *time* function gets the current time and adjusts it according to the value in the global variable *_timezone* which is set by the function *tzset*). Then it computes the number of seconds elapsed since 00:00:00 hour GMT, January 1, 1970, till the adjusted current time. The result is stored as a variable of type *time_t* at the location *timeptr*. If *timeptr* is NULL, the result is not stored.

RETURNS The *time* function returns the number of elapsed seconds.

COMMENTS The value obtained from *time* can be converted to a string by calling *ctime* and the fields of the date and time can be separated by calling *gmtime* or *localtime*.

SEE ALSO `ctime`   To convert time into a string

`gmtime, localtime`   To convert time into a *tm* structure

`tzset`   To set environment variables that indicate the local time zone

EXAMPLE Get and display the current time.

```
#include <stdio.h>
#include <time.h>
main()
{
    time_t tnow;
/* Get the time in seconds since 0 hrs GMT, 1/1/70 */
    time(&tnow);
/* Convert the time to a string and print it. This
 * will be your local time provided you have set the
 * environment variable TZ to your time zone. The
 * default is PST with daylight saving enabled.
```

 Time Routines

```
 * See "tzset" for details.
 */
    printf("Current time = %s\n", ctime(&tnow));
}
```

tzset

COMPATIBILITY	MSC 3	MSC 4	MSC 5	QC	TC	ANSI	UNIX V
	▲	▲	▲	▲	▲		▲

PURPOSE   Use *tzset* to assign values to the global variables *timezone, daylight* and *tzname* based on the time zone specified in the environment variable TZ.

SYNTAX   `void tzset(void);`

INCLUDES   `#include <time.h>`   For function declaration and declaration of the global variables

DESCRIPTION   The *tzset* function uses the current setting of the environment variable TZ to assign appropriate values to the global variables shown in Table 12-3. TZ indicates the time zone and the daylight saving zone for use in converting from GMT to local time. TZ must be set to a three-letter time zone name (PST, EST, etc.), followed by a signed number giving the difference between GMT and the local time zone (a positive sign can be omitted). An optional three-letter daylight saving zone name can be added to the setting. The *tzset* function uses this information to compute and save the values of the global variables shown in Table 12-3. If TZ is not defined, a default setting of PST8PDT is used. TZ and *tzset* are not part of the proposed ANSI definition; they are Microsoft extensions.

Table 12-3. *Global Variables for Time Zone and Daylight Saving*

Variable	Type and Value
timezone	Long integer. The difference in seconds between GMT and local time. Default value is 28800 (this means that the local time is Pacific Standard Time which is 28,800 seconds or 8 hours later than GMT).
daylight	Integer. Nonzero if a daylight saving time zone is specified TZ. Otherwise it is zero. Default value is 1.
tzname[0]	Character string. Three-letter time zone name from TZ. Default is PST.
tzname[1]	Character string. Three-letter daylight saving time zone name from TZ, or an empty string if omitted from TZ. Default is PDT.

COMMENTS   The functions *ftime* and *localtime* use the global variables as set by *tzset*.

SEE ALSO `ftime, localtime, time`   Functions that use the environment variables set up by *tzset*

EXAMPLE Use *putenv* to set the environment variable TZ to the value EST5EDT. Then call *tzset* and print the values of the global variables *timezone* and *daylight* and the strings in the array *tz*.

```
#include <stdio.h>
#include <stdlib.h>
#include <time.h>
main()
{
    time_t tnow;
/* Set the environment variable TZ to Eastern Standard
 * Time with daylight saving enabled. See text for
 * information on defining TZ.
 */
    if(putenv("TZ=EST5EDT") == -1)
    {
        printf("Error defining TZ\n");
        exit(1);
    }
/* Now call "tzset" to set up internal global variables */
    tzset();
/* Print the current values of the global variables     */
    printf("timezone = %ld, daylight = %d,\n\
tzname[0] = %s\ntzname[1] = %s\n", timezone, daylight,
            tzname[0], tzname[1]);
/* Get and display current local time -- should be EDT   */
    time(&tnow);
    printf("Local time = %s", ctime(&tnow));
}
```

utime

COMPATIBILITY	MSC 3	MSC 4	MSC 5	QC	TC	ANSI	UNIX V
	▲	▲	▲	▲			▲

PURPOSE Use *utime* to change the "last modified" time stamp of a file to which you have write access.

SYNTAX `int utime(char *path, struct utimbuf *timeptr);`

`char *path;`   Pathname of file whose last modified time is set

 Time Routines

```
        struct utimbuf *timeptr;         Pointer to a structure through which the modification
                                         time is specified
```

EXAMPLE CALL
```
/* Set modification time of file to current time */
        utime(file_name, NULL);
```

INCLUDES `#include <sys\utime.h>`   For function declaration and definition of structure
utimbuf

DESCRIPTION The *utime* function sets the last modified time of the file specified by the pathname *path* to the value provided in the *modtime* field of a structure of type *utimbuf* whose address is given in the argument *timeptr*. The structure *utimbuf* is defined in the include file *sys\utime.h*, as shown below. Under MS-DOS, only the modification time is significant. If the second argument to *utime* is NULL, the modification time of the file is set to the current time.

```
struct utimbuf
{
    time_t actime;      /* access time       */
    time_t modtime;     /* modification time */
};
```

For *utime* to succeed, you must have write access to *path*.

RETURNS If *utime* is successful, it returns a zero. In case of an error, it returns a −1 and sets *errno* to one of the constants shown in the table.

Error	Cause of Error
EACCES	File cannot be accessed. This means the file specified by *path* is either a directory or a read-only file.
EINVAL	The structure *timesptr* has invalid values.
EMFILE	The file has to be opened by *utime* before it can change the modification time. This means there are too many files open to allow *utime* to perform this step.
ENOENT	File specified by *path* not found or the pathname includes nonexistent directory names.

SEE ALSO `time`   To get current time in seconds elapsed since 00:00:00 hours GMT, January 1, 1970

EXAMPLE Utilities such as MAKE use the modification times of files to decide whether, for example, a recompilation or relinking is necessary. Often a utility called TOUCH is available to update the modification time of a file. Use *utime* to write such a program. The program should accept a file name as an argument and set the file's modification time to the current time. Try the program on a file and see if it works.

utime

```
/* Utility to update the modification time of a file */
#include <stdio.h>
#include <sys\types.h>
#include <sys\utime.h>
main(int argc, char **argv)
{
    if(argc < 2)
    {
        printf("Usage: %s <file_name>\n", argv[0]);
        exit(0);
    }
/* Use "utime" to set modification time of file to
 * current time.
 */
    if(utime(argv[1], NULL) == -1)
    {
        perror("\"utime\" failed");
    }
    else
    {
        printf("%s: mod time changed\n", argv[1]);
    }
}
```

Time Routines

IV
Files and I/O

- ► File Manipulation
- ► Directory Manipulation
- ► Input and Output Routines
- ► System Calls

13 **File Manipulation**

Introduction

The file system is a key system component of the PC. All applications and data reside in files. If you develop an application, it is likely to use files for temporary storage of its data and results so that they can be reused at a later date. We cover reading from and writing to files in the I/O discussion in Chapter 15. File manipulation covers routines that enable us to determine status of a file and to perform certain housekeeping chores to keep the files in order.

Concepts

The concepts of file system and of mechanisms used to access files are central to file manipulation.

HIERARCHICAL FILE SYSTEM IN MS-DOS

The file system describes the way files are organized under an operating system. MS-DOS uses a hierarchical file system, which refers to its tree-like structure. As illustrated in Figure 13-1, that file system has a root directory under which there are directories and files. Each directory can have more files and directories under it.

PATHNAMES TO ACCESS FILES

Files under MS-DOS can be specified by their pathnames. This is a string (see Figure 13-2) with four major components: the drive letter, the directory names, the file name, and the extension. The drive letter is a single letter followed by a colon specifying the disk drive in which the file resides. Each directory name starts with the root directory (indicated by a \) followed by all its subdirectories, each separated from the previous one by a \. The last directory name is followed by a \ and then a file name with up to eight characters and, optionally, a three-letter extension. A period separates the extension from the file name. Files can be renamed with the Microsoft C routine *re-name*. The *_makepath* and *_splitpath* routines, respectively, let you combine and take apart a pathname by its component parts.

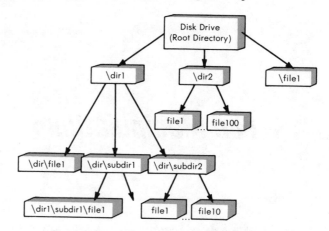

Figure 13-1. *MS-DOS hierarchical file system*

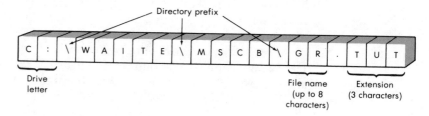

Figure 13-2. *Pathname of a file in MS-DOS*

FILE HANDLES The pathname of a file is one way of identifying it, but there is another way to reach a file. When you create or open a file using the functions *open, sopen* or *creat*, an integer identifier, called the "handle" of the file, is returned. The handle is used by the system to access a structure where certain pertinent information about the open file is stored. When you query the system about an open file, its handle suffices as an identifier.

PERTINENT FILE INFORMATION To manipulate files, certain pieces of information are crucial to your application, among them permission and permission mask settings, file size and status, and translation mode.

Permission Settings

Normally, you can read from and write to a file. You may not want to allow others to read from a file, however, if the data is confidential. You may also want certain files to be "read only" because you don't want others to overwrite the data in these files inadvertently. Each operating system provides a means to control access to a file. In MS-DOS certain "permission settings" are associated with a file. If you think of the read and write access to a file as one-way doors, the permission settings indicate which of these doors are open. As shown in Figure 13-3, for example, in a read-only file, only the read door is open and the write door is locked.

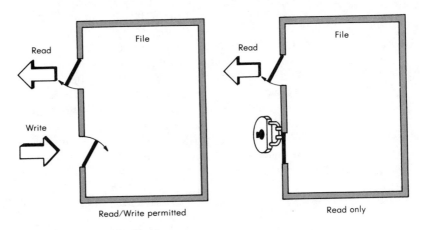

Figure 13-3. *Permission settings of a file*

There are three types of permission settings. In Microsoft C the include file *sys\stat.h* contains the constants S_IREAD and S_IWRITE which denote read and write permissions, respectively. When both reading and writing are permitted, permission is set to the bitwise-OR of the two, S_IREAD¦S _IWRITE. Under MS-DOS reading and writing are allowed on all directories. Also, all files are always readable under MS-DOS. Thus a file's permission setting to S_IWRITE is equivalent to the Microsoft setting S_IREAD¦S _IWRITE.

The *access* function lets you check the permission settings of a file while *chmod* lets you alter the permission setting of an open file.

Permission Mask

The "permission mask" is not associated with individual files, but is a bit pattern used by the file creation routines to determine the permission settings of a newly created file. You specify the permission mask with the same permission constants, S_IREAD and S_IWRITE, but their interpretation is different. If the permission mask is S_IREAD, reading from the file is not allowed, so the file will be write only. (This is ignored in MS-DOS, but included for compatibility with UNIX System V). On the other hand, a permission mask of S_IWRITE implies the file will be read only. You use the routine *umask* to specify the default permission mask.

The permission mask is applied in the following manner. When you create a file by a call to *creat, open* or *sopen*, you specify the desired permission setting for the new file. If necessary, the file creation routines use the current value of the permission mask to override the requested permission setting. For example, if the mask says that all files should be read only (remember, you

cannot have a write-only file in MS-DOS), a request for a permission setting of
S_IREAD¦S_IWRITE is changed to S_IREAD.

File Size and Status

The size or length of a file refers to the number of bytes in the file. For example, the length of the file shown in Figure 13-4 is 8 bytes. You can use the routine *filelength* to determine the length of a file that is already open. The size of an open file can be altered by the routine *chsize*. If the file is not open, you can find its length from its status. The status includes when the file was last modified, its size, and the disk drive where it is located. The information is provided in a structure of type *stat* defined in the header file *sys\stat.h*. Several other fields are included for compatibility with System V UNIX, but they are not used in MS-DOS. For an open file, use *fstat* to get the status. The *stat* provides the same information for a file specified by its pathname.

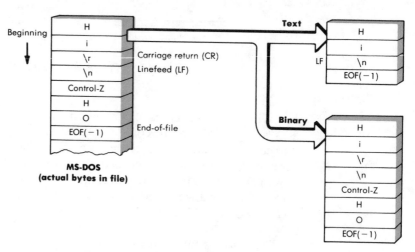

Figure 13-4. *Text and binary translation modes*

Translation Mode

In Chapter 15 we discuss the way the contents of a file can be interpreted when reading from or writing to the file under MS-DOS. The interpretation depends on which of the two "translation modes" is associated with the open file: text or binary. "Text mode" is useful for reading to and writing from ASCII text files. "Binary mode" is used to read data files.

In binary mode each byte in the file is treated as a value with no special significance, as shown in Figure 13-4. Since the number of bytes in the file is known, the end-of-file is encountered when all the bytes have been read; there is no specific end-of-file value in the binary mode.

In text mode, a carriage return (\r) followed by a linefeed, or newline \n, is translated to a single newline. Also, as soon as a Control-Z is encountered, the file is considered to have ended. Thus anything after a Control-Z cannot be read in this mode.

Figure 13-4 illustrates how the contents of a file are treated when opened in both modes. In text mode, the contents of the file are checked to see if a Control-Z or a carriage return is encountered, but in binary mode, the file's contents are taken literally, without any translation. Use the function *setmode* if you want to change the translation mode of a file that is already open.

Table 13-1 details the routines for file manipulation. Next we explain some of the capabilities described.

Table 13-1. *File Manipulation Routines*

Routine	Description
access	Checks for existence as well as read/write permission settings of a file.
chmod	Changes the read/write permission settings of a file.
chsize	Extends or truncates a file.
filelength	Returns length of a file in bytes.
fstat	Returns information about an open file specified by handle.
isatty	Checks if a file handle refers to a character device.
locking	When file-sharing is enabled (MS-DOS 3.0 and higher), locks or unlocks a specified number of bytes in an open file.
_makepath	Constructs a DOS pathname out of component parts.
mktemp	Generates a unique file name by use of a template.
remove	Deletes a file specified by its pathname.
rename	Changes the pathname of a file to a new value (can be used to move file to new directory).
setmode	Changes the translation mode of an open file specified by its handle.
_splitpath	Separates a DOS pathname into its component parts.
stat	Returns information about a file specified by its pathname.
umask	Sets the default read/write permission mask for the current process.
unlink	Deletes a file specified by its pathname.

FILE MANIPULATION BY TASK

The file manipulation routines let you modify and obtain certain information about MS-DOS files. They also allow you to delete files (using *remove*, and *unlink*) and perform certain utility functions such as generating temporary file names (with *mktemp*) and locking certain parts of a file that has been opened for sharing. Table 13-2 shows the routines grouped by task.

File or Device

In MS-DOS, devices are opened like files and I/O with devices can be done using a common set of routines. For each open file, the system maintains information to tell devices apart from disk files. The *isatty* function lets you determine if a file handle refers to a device or to a disk file. For example, the preopened files *stdin* and *stdout* are initially connected to the keyboard and the monitor, which are *devices*. If either of these are redirected to a disk file, MS-DOS will mark the handles as such. You can use the *isatty* function to determine whether a handle refers to a disk file or a device.

Table 13-2. *File Manipulation Routines by Task*

task	Routines
Delete a file.	remove, unlink
Alter and set permission setting.	access, chmod, umask
Get status information of a file.	fstat, stat
Name file.	mktemp, rename
Change or check file size.	chsize, filelength
Check if file is a character device.	isatty
Set translation mode (text or binary).	setmode
Lock/unlock portions of file.	locking
Assemble and disassemble MS-DOS pathnames.	_makepath, _splitpath

File-Sharing

Under MS-DOS 3.0 and higher, the command SHARE installs the file-sharing option that allows multiple processes to open and access a file. After opening a file for sharing (with *sopen*), the actual sharing is achieved by a mechanism (the *locking* function) that enables you to lock and unlock specific portions of the file.

Cautions

▶ File-sharing is not available in MS-DOS versions below 3.0 because the *locking* function does not work in those versions.

▶ Note that several functions require the file handle as an input parameter. If you open the file using a higher-level stream I/O routine (see Chapter 15), use *fileno* to get the handle.

▶ Remember that MS-DOS imposes a limit of 20 open files per process. You can change this under DOS 3.3 by following instructions included in the README.DOC file of the Microsoft C 5.1 distribution disk.

Further Reading

Consult Prata's book[1] for a detailed exposition of the file manipulation routines. Permission settings and translation modes are also explained.

1. Stephen Prata, The Waite Group, *Advanced C Primer++*, Howard W. Sams & Company, Indianapolis, IN, 1986, 502 pages.

access

COMPATIBILITY	MSC 3	MSC 4	MSC 5	QC	TC	ANSI	UNIX V
	▲	▲	▲	▲	▲		▲

PURPOSE Use *access* to check whether a file exists and if so, whether read and/or write operations are permitted.

SYNTAX `int access(char *path, int mode);`

`char *path;` Pathname of file being checked

`int mode;` Integer denoting permission setting being checked

EXAMPLE CALL `if(access("temp.dat", 4) == 0) puts("Data file exists");`

INCLUDES `#include <io.h>` For function declaration

DESCRIPTION The *access* function determines whether the file specified by the pathname *path* exists and whether the permission setting of the file allows the operation indicated by the argument *mode*. Use one of the values shown in the table for the argument *mode*. If the pathname *path* specifies a directory, *access* only verifies whether the directory exists. Under MS-DOS all directories have both read and write permissions, and all files have read permission.

Value of *mode*	Interpretation
00	Only existence of file will be checked.
02	Check if file has write permission.
04	Check if file has read permission.
06	Check if file has read and write permission.

RETURNS If *access* finds that the file or directory specified by *path* exists and allows the access specified by *mode*, it returns a 0. If the pathname does not exist or is not accessible in the specified *mode*, the return value is −1 and the global variable *errno* is set to ENOENT to indicate that the specified pathname is invalid or to EACCES to denote that the requested type of access is not allowed.

SEE ALSO `chmod` To alter the permission setting of a file

`fstat, stat` To find information about an open file, including permission settings

EXAMPLE Using *access*, write a program that checks the existence of the file CONFIG.SYS in the root directory of drive C. If the file exists and has read permission, open it with *fopen* and display its contents.

```
#include <stdio.h>
#include <io.h>
char filename[] = "c:\\config.sys";
main()
{
        FILE *infile;
        char buffer[80];
/* Check if the file exists. Note that we need two '\'*/
        if(access(filename, 4) == -1)
        {
            perror("access failed");
            exit(1);
        }
        if ( (infile = fopen(filename, "r")) == NULL)
        {
            perror("fopen failed");
            exit(1);
        }
        printf("Contents of %s\n", filename);
        while ( fgets(buffer, 80, infile) != NULL)
        {
            printf(buffer);
        }
}
```

chmod

COMPATIBILITY	MSC 3	MSC 4	MSC 5	QC	TC	ANSI	UNIX V
	▲	▲	▲	▲	▲		▲

PURPOSE   Use *chmod* to alter the read/write permission settings of a file.

SYNTAX   `int chmod(char *path, int pmode);`

`char *path;`   Pathname of file whose permission is being changed

`int pmode;`   Integer denoting new permission setting for the file

EXAMPLE CALL   `chmod("inventory.lis", S_IWRITE);`

INCLUDES   `#include <io.h>`   For function declaration

`#include <sys\types.h>`   Required by <sys\stat.h>

`#include <sys\stat.h>`   For definition of constants denoting permission settings

File Manipulation

DESCRIPTION The *chmod* function sets the read/write permission setting of the file whose pathname is given in the argument *path* to the new setting specified in the integer *pmode*. The permission settings are specified in terms of constants defined in the include file *sys\stat.h*. The table below shows the possible combinations of the permission settings and their meanings. Under MS-DOS all files are readable, so it is not possible to give write-only permission to a file.

Constant	Interpretation
S_IWRITE	Both reading and writing permitted.
S_IREAD	Only reading permitted.
S_IREAD ¦ S_IWRITE	Both reading and writing permitted.

RETURNS If *chmod* successfully changes the permission setting to *pmode*, it returns a 0. In case of error, the return value is −1 and the global variable *errno* is set to ENOENT to indicate that the specified pathname is invalid.

SEE ALSO access   To check if read/write operations are permitted on a file

fstat, stat   To find information about an open file, including permission settings

EXAMPLE Write a small utility program using *chmod* to enable the user to change the read/write permission of a file. Assume that the command-line syntax is: "CHMOD ⟨pathname⟩ ⟨permission⟩" in which "permission" is a single character R (for read-only) or W (both read and write).

```
#include <stdio.h>
#include <sys\types.h>

#include <sys\stat.h>
#include <io.h>
main(int argc, char **argv)
{
    int pmode=-999;
    if(argc < 3)
    {
        printf(
          "Usage: %s <pathname> <R¦W>\n", argv[0]);
    }
    else
    {
/* Convert last argument to permission code          */
        if(argv[2][0]=='R') pmode = S_IREAD;
        if(argv[2][0]=='W') pmode = S_IREAD¦S_IWRITE;
        if(pmode==-999)
        {
```

chmod

```
                              printf("Unknown permission: %s\n",
                                    argv[2]);
                              exit(1);
                      }
                      if(chmod(argv[1], pmode) == -1)
                      {
                              perror("Error in \"chmod\"");
                      }
              }
      }
```

chsize

COMPATIBILITY	MSC 3	MSC 4	MSC 5	QC	TC	ANSI	UNIX V
	▲	▲	▲	▲	▲		▲

PURPOSE Use *chsize* to extend or truncate a file open for unbuffered, unformatted write operations.

SYNTAX `int chsize(int handle, int size);`

`int handle;`   Handle of file whose size is being changed

`long size;`   New length of file in bytes

EXAMPLE CALL `chsize(filehandle, 0L);  /* Truncate file to zero length */`

INCLUDES `#include <io.h>`   For function declaration

DESCRIPTION The *chsize* function truncates or extends the file specified by the argument *handle* to match the new length in bytes given in the argument *size*. When the file is extended, null characters are appended to the file. When the file is truncated, all data beyond the new *size* is lost.

RETURNS The *chsize* returns a 0 to indicate success. In case of error, the return value is −1 and the global variable *errno* is set to one of the constants shown in Table 13-3.

Table 13-3. *Values of* errno *on Return from* chsize

Error Constant	Interpretation of Error Code
EACCES	Access to file was denied. For DOS 3.0 and above this means the file is locked against writing.
EBADF	File is read only or the handle does not refer to an open file.
ENOSPC	No more space left on the device where the file is stored. This can occur when trying to extend a file on a nearly full disk.

 **File Manipulation**

SEE ALSO   access   To check if read/write operations are permitted on a file

　　　　　　　chmod   To change read/write permissions of a file

　　　　　　　fstat, stat   To find information about an open file, including permission settings

EXAMPLE   Prompt the user for the name of an existing file to open and truncate to size zero.

```c
#include <stdio.h>
#include <fcntl.h>
#include <io.h>
main()
{
    int  filehandle, answer = 0;
    char filename[80];
    printf("Enter name of file to truncate: ");
    gets(filename);
    if((filehandle = open(filename, O_RDWR)) == -1)
    {
        perror("open failed");
        exit(1);
    }
/* Now give user a warning and a chance to abort      */
    while(answer != 'N' && answer != 'Y')

    {
        printf("Truncate %s to size zero? (Y or N)",
                filename);
        scanf(" %1s", &answer);
        answer = toupper(answer);
    }
    if(answer == 'Y')
    {
        if(chsize(filehandle, 0L) == -1)
        {
            perror("chsize failed");
        }
        else
        {
            printf("%s successfully truncated.\n",
                    filename);
        }
    }
}
```

chsize

filelength

COMPATIBILITY	MSC 3	MSC 4	MSC 5	QC	TC	ANSI	UNIX V
		▲	▲	▲	▲		

PURPOSE Use the *filelength* function to determine the length of a file in bytes. To use this function, you have to specify the file handle (see the tutorial).

SYNTAX
```
long filelength(int file_handle);
int file_handle;        Handle of file whose length is to be returned
```

EXAMPLE CALL
```
filesize = filelength(filehandle);
```

INCLUDES
```
#include <stdio.h>        For function declaration
```

DESCRIPTION The *filelength* function returns the size in number of bytes of the file whose handle is specified in the argument *file_handle*. To get the handle of a file opened by *fopen*, you use *fileno* and then use *filelength* to get its length.

RETURNS The long integer value returned by *filelength* is the size of the file in number of bytes. If an error occurs, the return value is −1L. If the error is due to an invalid handle, the global variable *errno* is set to constant EBADF.

SEE ALSO fileno   To obtain the handle of a file whose pointer to the associated FILE data structure is known

EXAMPLE Ask the user for a file name. Open the file with *fopen* for read only. Now call *filelength* to determine the size of the file. Use *fileno* to get the handle for the file.

```
#include <stdio.h>
main()
{
        char filename[80];
        FILE *infile;
        long filesize;
        printf("Enter the name of an existing file: ");
        gets(filename);
/* Open the file */
        if ( (infile = fopen(filename, "r")) == NULL)
        {
            printf("fopen failed to open: %s\n", filename);
            exit(0);
        }
    /* Get file size and display it. Use fileno to get the handle. */
        if( (filesize = filelength(fileno(infile))) != -1L)
            {
```

 **File Manipulation**

```
            printf("Size of %s = %ld bytes\n", filename, filesize);
        }
        else
        {
            printf("Error getting file size\n");
        }
}
```

fstat

COMPATIBILITY	MSC 3	MSC 4	MSC 5	QC	TC	ANSI	UNIX V
	▲	▲	▲	▲	▲		▲

PURPOSE Use the *fstat* function to retrieve information about a file that has been opened for unbuffered, unformatted I/O.

SYNTAX `int fstat(int handle, struct stat *buffer);`

`int handle;`   Handle of file whose "vital statistics" will be returned

`struct stat *buffer;`   Pointer to structure where result will be returned

EXAMPLE CALL `fstat(filehandle, &stat_buffer);`

INCLUDES `#include <sys\types.h>`   Required by ⟨sys\stat.h⟩

`#include <sys\stat.h>`   For function declaration and definition of structure *stat*

DESCRIPTION The *fstat* function returns information about the file specified by the argument *handle*. You must allocate a structure of type *stat* and provide a pointer to this structure in the argument *buffer*. After *fstat* returns successfully, this structure contains the information about the file. The structure *stat* is defined in ⟨sys\stat.h⟩ and a commented version of its declaration is shown below. Several fields in the *stat* structure are used in UNIX but not in MS-DOS and are included here for compatibility.

```
struct stat
{
    dev_t          st_dev;   /* Drive number of disk or handle of
                                device containing the file      */
    ino_t          st_ino;   /* Unused in MS-DOS. The "i-node"
                                number of file in UNIX           */
    unsigned short st_mode;  /* Bit mask of file's mode          */
    short          st_nlink; /* Always set to 1 under MS-DOS     */
    short          st_uid;   /* Unused in MS-DOS. For "user-id"
                                under UNIX                       */
```

```
        short          st_gid;   /* Unused in MS-DOS. For "group-id"
                                     under UNIX                       */
        dev_t          st_rdev;  /* Same as the field st_dev         */
        off_t          st_size;  /* Size of file in bytes            */
        time_t         st_atime; /* Time of last modification        */
        time_t         st_mtime; /* Same as st_atime                 */
        time_t         st_ctime; /* Same as st_atime                 */
};
```

RETURNS   If *fstat* is successful in obtaining the information about the file, it returns a 0.
In case of error, the return value is −1 and the global variable *errno* is set to
the constant EBADF to indicate that the specified handle is invalid.

SEE ALSO   access   To check if read/write operations are permitted on a file

               chmod   To change read/write permissions for a file

               stat   To find information about a file specified by a pathname

EXAMPLE   Use *fstat* to display information about the standard output file *stdout* (you
can get its handle by using *fileno*).

```
#include <stdio.h>
#include <sys\types.h>
#include <sys\stat.h>
#include <io.h>
main()
{
    struct stat info;
    if (fstat(fileno(stdout), &info) != 0)
    {
        perror("fstat failed");
        exit(1);
    }
    if ((info.st_mode & S_IFCHR) == S_IFCHR)
    {
        printf("stdout is a device\n");
    }
    if ((info.st_mode & S_IFREG) == S_IFREG)
    {
/* This means stdout has been redirected to a file */
        printf("stdout is a regular file on drive %c\n",
            info.st_dev+65);
    }
}
{
    struct stat info;
    if (fstat(fileno(stdout), &info) != 0)
```

File Manipulation

```
      {
          perror("fstat failed");
          exit(1);
      }
      if ((info.st_mode & S_IFCHR) == S_IFCHR)
      {
          printf("stdout is a device\n");
      }
      if ((info.st_mode & S_IFREG) == S_IFREG)
      {
/* This means stdout has been redirected to a file */
          printf("stdout is a regular file on drive %c\n",
                 info.st_dev+65);
      }
  }
```

isatty

COMPATIBILITY	MSC 3	MSC 4	MSC 5	QC	TC	ANSI	UNIX V
	▲	▲	▲	▲	▲		

PURPOSE Use the *isatty* function to determine whether a particular file handle refers to a "character device" which, under MS-DOS, means the console, printer, or a serial port.

SYNTAX `int isatty(int handle);`

`int handle;`   Handle about which this query is being made

EXAMPLE CALL `if(isatty(fileno(stdout)) != 0) puts("stdout is console");`

INCLUDES `#include <io.h>`   For function declaration

DESCRIPTION The *isatty* function determines whether a specified handle refers to a character device.

COMMON USES The *isatty* function provides a way to determine if I/O redirection is in effect (the return value is zero when the I/O stream is redirected to a file). Knowing that it is might cause you to do things differently in your program. For example, when your application, XYZ, is executed with a command like XYZ>OUTFILE (meaning output from the program XYZ goes to the file OUTFILE), you might not want to make any calls to graphics functions because the user would not be expecting any output on the screen.

RETURNS The *isatty* function returns a nonzero value if the handle refers to a character device. If not, it returns a zero.

isatty

EXAMPLE Write a program using *isatty* that determines whether *stdout* is a character device or not. If it is a device, the program must run in interactive mode, in which characters are sent to the display rather than a file.

```c
#include <stdio.h>
#include <io.h>
main()
{
    if(!isatty(fileno(stdout)))
    {
        printf("stdout redirected to a file\n");
    }
    else
    {
        printf("Executing in interactive mode\n");
    }
}
```

locking

COMPATIBILITY	MSC 3	MSC 4	MSC 5	QC	TC	ANSI	UNIX V
	▲	▲	▲	▲			

PURPOSE Use the *locking* function, under MS-DOS version 3.0 and higher, to lock or unlock a number of bytes in a file. This feature is of use when file-sharing.

SYNTAX `int locking(int handle, int mode, long nbytes);`

`int handle;` Handle of file where data is being locked

`int mode;` Integer denoting file-locking mode

`long nbytes;` Number of bytes to be locked or unlocked

EXAMPLE CALL `locking(handle, LK_NBLCK, 256); /* Lock 256 bytes */`

INCLUDES `#include <io.h>` For function declaration

`#include <sys\locking.h>` For definition of constants denoting lock-unlock modes

DESCRIPTION The *locking* function is for use when file-sharing is enabled by executing the MS-DOS command SHARE. Because earlier versions of DOS do not have the SHARE command the *locking* function should be used only under MS-DOS versions 3.0 and later. Starting with Microsoft C 5.1, under OS/2, *locking* can

 **File Manipulation**

be used to coordinate file-sharing even when SHARE.COM or SHARE.EXE is not installed.

When called, *locking* performs the lock or unlock action requested by the argument *mode* on the file specified by the handle. The action affects the file's next *n* bytes (or to the end-of-file) from its current position. The argument *mode* must be specified by one of the constants shown in Table 13-4. These constants are defined in the include file *sys\locking.h*.

Table 13-4. *Constants Denoting File-Locking Modes*

Locking-Mode Constant	Interpretation
LK_LOCK	Locks the specified bytes. If they cannot be locked, *locking* retries every second, up to a maximum of 10 attempts. It returns error if it fails even after these attempts.
LK_RLCK	Performs same function as LK_LOCK.
LK_NBLCK	Locks the specified bytes and returns an error immediately if it fails.
LK_NBRLCK	Performs same function as LK_NBLCK.
LK_UNLCK	Unlocks previously locked bytes.

Locking a number of bytes (a region) prevents further reading and writing of those bytes by any process. Unlocking removes this restriction, but each region that is locked must be unlocked individually, even if two locked regions are adjacent to each other. Many separate regions in a file can be locked simultaneously, but no two regions can overlap. Finally, all locked regions must be unlocked before closing the file or exiting the program. Microsoft warns that under MS-DOS 3.0 and 3.1 locked files may become unlocked when a child process exits.

RETURNS   If *locking* succeeds, it returns a 0. Otherwise, it returns a −1 and sets the global variable *errno* to one of the constants shown in Table 13-5.

Table 13-5. *Values of errno on Return from* locking

Error Constant	Interpretation
EACCES	Access to file was denied. File is already locked or unlocked.
EBADF	The handle does not refer to an open file.
EDEADLOCK	This code is set if the mode is set to LK_LOCK or LK_RLCK and the file could not be locked even after 10 retries at 1-second intervals.
EINVAL	Either *mode* or *nbytes* is invalid. This error means the argument values are erroneous.

COMMENTS   Under MS-DOS versions earlier than 3.0, the *locking* function does not operate.

locking

SEE ALSO   sopen   To open with various file-sharing options

EXAMPLE   Assuming that you are writing an application to be used in a networked environment with file-sharing under DOS, write a sample program that locks a part of the file using *locking* (presumably it updates that portion of the file) and then unlocks it for use by other processes. Remember to run SHARE before executing the program.

```
#include <stdio.h>
#include <io.h>
#include <fcntl.h>
#include <sys\locking.h>
main()
{
    long curpos;
    int filehandle;

    char filename[80], buffer[80];
    printf("Enter name of file to test with:");
    gets(filename);
    if ((filehandle = open(filename, O_RDONLY)) == -1)
    {
        perror("open failed");
        exit(1);
    }
/* Read 80 characters from the file                    */
    if (read(filehandle, buffer, 80) == -1)
    {
        perror("read error");
        exit(1);
    }
/* Get and save current position                       */
    curpos = tell(filehandle);
/* Now go to beginning of file and lock 80 bytes       */
    lseek(filehandle, 0L, SEEK_SET);
    if (locking(filehandle, LK_NBLCK, curpos) == -1)
    {
        perror("locking failed");
    }
    else
    {
        printf("First %ld bytes of file %s locked\n",
                curpos, filename);
/* In an actual program, you would make changes and
 * write these bytes back to the file before unlocking
 */
        lseek(filehandle, 0L, SEEK_SET);
        if (locking(filehandle, LK_UNLCK, curpos)
```

 **File Manipulation**

```
                                == -1)
                        {
                            perror("unlocking failed");
                        }
                        else
                        {
                            printf("File unlocked\n");
                        }
                }
        }
```

__makepath

COMPATIBILITY	MSC 3	MSC 4	MSC 5	QC	TC	ANSI	UNIX V
			▲	▲	fnmerge		

PURPOSE Use _makepath_ to create a full pathname composed of a drive letter, directory path, file name, and file extension.

SYNTAX
```
void _makepath(char *path, char *drive, char *dir,
               char *fname, char *ext);
```

char *path;   Pointer to buffer where full pathname will be returned

char *drive;   Drive letter

char *dir;   Directory path

char *fname;   File name

char *ext;   File extension

EXAMPLE CALL
```
_makepath(pathname, "c", "temp", "result", "dat");
/* pathname will be "c:\temp\result.dat"  */
```

INCLUDES `#include <stdlib.h>`   For function declaration and definition of the constant _MAX
_PATH

DESCRIPTION The _makepath_ function combines the strings *drive, dir, fname*, and *ext* to construct a full pathname and store it in the buffer *path*. You must allocate enough room in the buffer to hold the complete pathname, but the individual strings may be of any length. The constant _MAX_PATH, defined in *stdlib.h*, describes the maximum-length pathname that MS-DOS can handle so a size of _MAX_PATH for *path* is a safe choice, assuming that the combined of the strings does not exceed _MAX_PATH. The arguments *drive, dir, fname,* and *ext* are described in Table 13-6.

Table 13-6. *Components of Pathname*

Argument	Description
drive	Contains the drive letter (A, B, C, etc.) followed by an optional colon. If the colon is missing, _makepath inserts it automatically in the pathname. If this string is empty, no drive letter and colon appear in the pathname.
dir	Contains the path of directories, excluding the drive letter and the actual file name. Either forward (/) or backward (\) slashes may be used as separators in directory names and the trailing slash is optional. A trailing slash is automatically added after *dir.* If *dir* is an empty string, nothing is inserted in this position in the complete pathname. Remember that to get a single backslash character, you must have two backslashes in the string.
fname	Contains the file name without the extension.
ext	This is the file's extension with or without a leading period (.); _makepath automatically inserts a period. If this string is empty, no extension appears in the pathname.

SEE ALSO   _splitpath   To separate a pathname into its components

EXAMPLE   Illustrate the use of *_makepath* by constructing a complete pathname out of component strings entered by the user.

```
#include <stdio.h>
#include <stdlib.h>
main()
{
    char pathname[_MAX_PATH], drive[_MAX_DRIVE],
        dir[_MAX_DIR], filename[_MAX_FNAME],
        ext[_MAX_EXT];
/* Prompt user for various components               */
    printf("Enter drive letter:");
    gets(drive);
    printf("       directory path (%d characters max):",
            _MAX_DIR-1);
    gets(dir);
    printf("       filename (%d characters max):",
            _MAX_FNAME-1);
    gets(filename);
    printf("       extension (up to 3 letters):");
    gets(ext);
/* Construct the complete path name and display it  */
    _makepath(pathname, drive, dir, filename, ext);
    printf("Path name is: %s\n", pathname);
}
```

 **File Manipulation**

mktemp

COMPATIBILITY	MSC 3	MSC 4	MSC 5	QC	TC	ANSI	UNIX V
	▲	▲	▲	▲	▲		▲

PURPOSE   Use the *mktemp* function to generate unique file names by modifying a given template for the names.

SYNTAX   `char *mktemp(char *template);`

   `char *template;`   Pattern string to be used in constructing file names

EXAMPLE CALL
```
char tfilename = "mscbXXXXXX";
mktemp(tfilename);
```

INCLUDES   `#include <io.h>`   For function declaration

DESCRIPTION   The *mktemp* function uses the string *template* and modifies a portion of it to generate unique file names. The *template* string must be of the form: baseXXXXXX. The "base" of the template consists of one or more characters that appear in every file name. The Xs are treated as place holders to be replaced by a single alphanumeric character followed by five digits, which is a unique number identifying the calling process (no attention is paid to the eight-character limit on DOS file names). For the alphanumeric digit, *mktemp* starts with 0 and goes on to the lowercase alphabet, a through z. Before returning a file name, *mktemp* checks that no file with that name exists in the working directory. Note that *mktemp* is not creating or opening a file, only creating a file name.

COMMON USES   If your program creates many temporary files, *mktemp* relieves you of the responsibility of coming up with unique file names.

RETURNS   The *mktemp* function returns a pointer to the modified template. In case of an error, for example, when no more unique file names can be created out of a given template, the return value will be NULL.

SEE ALSO   `tempnam, tmpnam`   Other routines to create temporary file names

   `tmpfile`   To open an unnamed temporary file that is deleted when closed

EXAMPLE   Use *mktemp* to get a unique file name with the prefix "naba" and open the file. The file name returned by *mktemp* will be 10 characters long, if you check the directory (using the DIR command), you will find that the newly created file uses only the first eight characters of the name.

```
#include <stdio.h>
#include <io.h>
```

mktemp

```
static char *our_template = "nabaXXXXXX";
main()
{

    char unique_name[9];
/* First copy template into placeholder for name      */
    strcpy(unique_name, our_template);
    if(mktemp(unique_name) == NULL)
    {
        printf("Could not create unique file name!\n");
    }
    else
    {
        fopen(unique_name, "w");
        printf("File %s opened\n", unique_name);
    }
}
```

remove

COMPATIBILITY	MSC 3	MSC 4	MSC 5	QC	TC	ANSI	UNIX V
	▲	▲	▲	▲	▲	▲	

PURPOSE Use *remove* to delete a file specified by its pathname.

SYNTAX `int remove(const char *path);`

`const char *path;`   Pathname of file to be deleted

EXAMPLE CALL `remove("c:\\tmp\\tmp01234"); /* Delete temporary file */`

INCLUDES `#include <io.h>`   For function declaration

or

`#include <stdio.h>`

DESCRIPTION The *remove* function deletes the file specified by *path*.

RETURNS If *remove* successfully deletes the specified file, it returns a 0. Otherwise, the return value is −1 and the global variable *errno* is set to either ENOENT if the pathname is not found or to EACCES if the pathname is that of a directory or a read-only file.

SEE ALSO `unlink`   Also deletes a file

 **File Manipulation**

EXAMPLE Write a utility program that uses *remove* to delete a file. Assume that the program will be invoked with a command of the form "rm ⟨filename⟩" where "rm.exe" is the program name.

```
#include <stdio.h>
#include <io.h>
main(int argc, char **argv)
{
    if(argc < 2)
    {
        printf("Usage: %s <pathname>\n", argv[0]);
    }
    else
    {
        printf("File %s ", argv[1]);
        if(remove(argv[1]) != 0)
        {
            perror("remove failed");
        }
        else
        {
            printf("deleted\n");
        }
    }
}
```

rename

COMPATIBILITY	MSC 3	MSC 4	MSC 5	QC	TC	ANSI	UNIX V
	▲	▲	▲	▲	▲	▲	

PURPOSE Use *rename* to change the name of a file or directory specified by its pathname. For example, you can use *rename* to write a program that provides the function of the UNIX command *mv* (to move a file from one directory to another).

SYNTAX `int rename(const char *oldname, const char *newname);`

`const char *oldname;` Current pathname of file or directory

`const char *newname;` New pathname

EXAMPLE CALL
```
/* Copy "text.exe" from c:\tmp to c:\bin and give it a new name */
rename("c:\\tmp\\test.exe", "c:\\bing\\rview.exe");
```

rename

INCLUDES   `#include <io.h>`   For function declaration

or

`#include <stdio.h>`

DESCRIPTION   The *rename* function changes the name of a file or directory from *oldname* to *newname*. Use *rename* to move a file from one directory to another, but only in the same device. Directories cannot be moved.

RETURNS   If *rename* is successful, it returns a zero. In case of an error, it returns a non-zero value and the global variable *errno* contains further information. This variable equals the constant EACCES if a file or directory called *newname* exists, if a file with *newname* could not be created, or if *oldname* is a directory and *newname* specifies a different directory path. Attempting to specify a different drive letter results in *errno* set to EXDEV or to ENOENT if the pathname *oldname* does not refer to an existing file or directory.

SEE ALSO   `creat, fopen, open`   To create and open a file

EXAMPLE   Write a program using *rename* that mimics the UNIX command *mv*.

```c
#include <stdio.h>
#include <io.h>
main(int argc, char **argv)
{
    if(argc < 3)
    {
        printf("Usage: %s <oldname> <newname>\n",
                argv[0]);
    }
    else
    {
        printf("File %s ", argv[1]);
        if(rename(argv[1], argv[2]) != 0)
        {
            perror("rename failed");
        }
        else
        {
            printf("renamed to %s\n", argv[2]);
        }
    }
}
```

 **File Manipulation**

setmode

COMPATIBILITY	MSC 3	MSC 4	MSC 5	QC	TC	ANSI	UNIX V
	▲	▲	▲	▲	▲		

PURPOSE Use the *setmode* function to set the translation mode (see the tutorial section) of a file opened for unbuffered, unformatted I/O.

SYNTAX
```
int setmode(int handle, int mode);
```

```
int handle;        Handle of open file
```

```
int mode;          Integer denoting new translation mode
```

EXAMPLE CALL
```
setmode(filehandle, O_BINARY); /* Set file mode to binary */
```

INCLUDES
```
#include <io.h>      For function declaration
```

```
#include <fcntl.h>        For definition of constants that are used to specify translation
                          modes
```

DESCRIPTION The *setmode* function changes to *mode* the translation mode of the file specified by *handle*. The translation mode specifies how carriage return-linefeed pairs are treated during file I/O. The value of the argument *mode* is either the constant 0_TEXT to open in text, or translated, mode or 0_BINARY to open in binary, or untranslated, mode. These are both defined in *fcntl.h*.

COMMON USES Typically, the *setmode* is used to change the default translation modes associated with the files *stdin, stdout, stderr, stdaux,* and *stdprn.* For other files, you can specify the translation mode when opening the file with *open* or *fopen.*

RETURNS When there are no errors, *setmode* returns the previous value of the translation mode. Otherwise, it returns a −1 and sets the global variable *errno* to EBADF if the file handle is invalid or to EINVAL if the value given for the argument *mode* is not equal to one of the constants O_TEXT or O_BINARY.

SEE ALSO
```
fopen, open        To open a file and specify a translation mode
```

EXAMPLE Use *setmode* to write a program that changes the translation mode of *stdout* from its default "text" to "binary." Now print a string with a newline (\n). You will see that only a single linefeed appears (instead of the normal carriage return-linefeed pair).

```
#include <stdio.h>
#include <io.h>
#include <fcntl.h>
```

```
main()
{
/* Set mode of stdout to O_BINARY (binary mode) */
    if(setmode(fileno(stdout), O_BINARY) == -1)
    {
        perror("setmode failed");
    }
    else
    {
        printf("stdout is in binary mode now.\n");
        printf("Notice how this output looks\n");
    }
}
```

__splitpath

COMPATIBILITY	MSC 3	MSC 4	MSC 5	QC	TC	ANSI	UNIX V
			▲	▲			

PURPOSE Use *_splitpath* to separate a full pathname into its components: drive letter, directory path, file name, and file extension.

SYNTAX
```
void _splitpath(char *path, char *drive, char *dir,
                char *fname, char *ext);
```

char *path;   Pointer to buffer where full pathname is stored

char *drive;   Drive letter

char *dir;   Directory path

char *fname;   File name

char *ext;   File extension

EXAMPLE CALL _splitpath(pathname, drive, dir, filename, extension);

INCLUDES #include <stdlib.h>   For function declaration and definition of the constants _MAX_DRIVE, _MAX_DIR, _MAX_NAME, and _MAX_EXT

DESCRIPTION The *_splitpath* function splits the full pathname given in the argument *path* into its component substrings, which are returned in the strings *drive, dir, fname,* and *ext.* You must allocate enough room for each of these strings. The constants _MAX_DRIVE, _MAX_DIR, _MAX_NAME, and _MAX_EXT,

 **File Manipulation**

defined in *stdlib.h*, denote the maximum lengths of the strings *drive, dir, fname,* and *ext,* respectively, and should be used to declare the strings.

When *_splitpath* returns, *drive* contains the drive letter followed by a colon; *dir* has the directory path with either forward or backward slashes as separators; *fname* is the file name; and *ext,* is the extension with a leading period. If a component is absent in the argument *path,* the corresponding string will be empty (it contains a single null character (\0).

SEE ALSO   _makepath   To construct a pathname from its components

EXAMPLE   Write a program that uses *_splitpath* to parse a complete pathname entered by the user.

```
#include <stdio.h>
#include <stdlib.h>
main()
{
    char pathname[_MAX_PATH], drive[_MAX_DRIVE],
        dir[_MAX_DIR], filename[_MAX_FNAME],
        ext[_MAX_EXT];
/* Prompt user for a complete path name              */
    printf("Enter complete path name to parse:\n");
    gets(pathname);
/* Decompose complete path name and display result   */
    _splitpath(pathname, drive, dir, filename, ext);
    printf("Drive        : %s\n", drive);
    printf("Directory path: %s\n", dir);
    printf("Filename     : %s\n", filename);
    printf("Extension    : %s\n", ext);
}
```

stat

COMPATIBILITY	MSC 3	MSC 4	MSC 5	QC	TC	ANSI	UNIX V
	▲	▲	▲	▲	▲		▲

PURPOSE   Use the *stat* function to obtain information about an existing file specified by its pathname.

SYNTAX   `int stat(char *path, struct stat *buffer);`

   `char *path;`   Pathname of file whose "vital statistics" will be returned

   `struct stat *buffer;`   Pointer to structure where result will be returned

stat

EXAMPLE CALL stat("result.dat", &stat_buffer);

INCLUDES #include <sys\types.h>   Required by ⟨sys\stat.h⟩

#include <sys\stat.h>   For function declaration and definition of structure *stat*

DESCRIPTION The *stat* function returns certain information about the file or directory specified by the pathname in the argument *path*. The information is stored by *stat* in a structure of type *stat*. A pointer to an allocated structure of this type must be provided in the argument *buffer*. The structure *stat* is defined in ⟨sys\stat.h⟩ and its declaration is of the form:

```
struct stat
{
    dev_t          st_dev;   /* Drive number of disk or handle of
                                device containing the file       */
    ino_t          st_ino;   /* Unused in MS-DOS. The "i-node"
                                number of file in UNIX            */
    unsigned short st_mode;  /* Bit mask of file's mode           */
    short          st_nlink; /* Always set to 1 under MS-DOS       */
    short          st_uid;   /* Unused in MS-DOS. For "user-id"
                                under UNIX                        */
    short          st_gid;   /* Unused in MS-DOS. For "group-id"
                                under UNIX                        */
    dev_t          st_rdev;  /* Same as the field st_dev          */
    off_t          st_size;  /* Size of file in bytes             */
    time_t         st_atime; /* Time of last modification         */
    time_t         st_mtime; /* Same as st_atime                  */
    time_t         st_ctime; /* Same as st_atime                  */
};
```

If the pathname refers to a directory, the field *st_mode* has the bit corresponding to the constant S_IFDIR set. For a file, on the other hand, the bit corresponding to the value S_IFREG is set. Other bits in this field indicate read/write permissions and whether the *path* refers to a device. When it refers to a device, the values in the time and size fields are meaningless.

RETURNS The *stat* function returns 0 to indicate its success in obtaining the information about the file. Otherwise, the return value is −1 and the global variable *errno* is set to the constant ENOENT, indicating that no file, directory, or device exists by the specified pathname.

SEE ALSO access   To check if read/write operations are permitted on a file

chmod   To change read/write permissions of a file

fstat   To find information about a file specified by a valid handle

 **File Manipulation**

EXAMPLE   Use *stat* to write a utility program that prints useful information about a file.

```
#include <stdio.h>
#include <sys\types.h>
#include <sys\stat.h>
#include <time.h>
main(int argc, char **argv)
{
    struct stat info;
    if(argc < 2)
    {
        printf("Usage: %s <pathname>\n", argv[0]);
    }
    else
    {
        if(stat(argv[1], &info) != 0)
        {
            perror("Error in \"stat\"");
            exit(1);
        }
/* Print out information about the file            */
        printf("File: %s\n\
Drive        :  %c\n\
Size         :  %ld bytes,\n\
Last modified: %s\n",  argv[1], info.st_dev+65,
                info.st_size, ctime(&info.st_atime));
    }
}
```

umask

COMPATIBILITY	MSC 3	MSC 4	MSC 5	QC	TC	ANSI	UNIX V
	▲	▲	▲	▲	▲		▲

PURPOSE   Use the *umask* function to set the read/write permission mask that modifies the read/write permission settings of subsequent files created by this process.

SYNTAX   `int umask(int pmode);`

`int pmode;`   Permission mask to be used in all subsequent new files

EXAMPLE CALL
```
/* Make all future files read-only */
    oldmask = umask(S_IWRITE);
```

INCLUDES   `#include <io.h>`   For function declaration

```
#include <sys\types.h>        For definition of data types used in ⟨sys\stat.h⟩

#include <sys\stat.h>         For definition of constants to specify permission settings of
                              a file
```

DESCRIPTION The *umask* function accepts a read/write permission setting mask (see the tutorial) in the integer argument *pmode*. The mask modifies the permission settings for new files created by calls to *creat*, *open*, or *sopen*.

The mask *pmode* is interpreted as follows. If a particular bit is set to 1, the corresponding bit in the file's permission setting is 0 (which means that operation will not be allowed). On the other hand, a 0 in a particular bit of *pmode* implies that the corresponding bit in the permission setting is left unchanged.

The *pmode* argument can take one of the values shown in Table 13-7 expressed in terms of constants that are defined in the include file *sys\stat.h*.

Because MS-DOS always allows reading from a file, only the S_IWRITE setting has use in an MS-DOS system.

Table 13-7. *Possible Values of Permission Mask in* umask

Constant	Interpretation
S_IWRITE	Writing is not allowed.
S_IREAD	Reading is not allowed (that is ignored in MS-DOS).
S_IREAD ¦ S_IWRITE	Both reading and writing disallowed (reading is always allowed in MS-DOS).

RETURNS The *umask* function returns the previous value of the permission mask.

SEE ALSO creat, open, sopen   To create and open new files for unformatted I/O

EXAMPLE Write a program to set the permission mask so that future files are read only. Display the previous value of the mask.

```
#include <stdio.h>
#include <sys\types.h>
#include <sys\stat.h>
#include <io.h>

main()
{
    int oldmask;
/* Make all future files read-only */
    oldmask = umask(S_IWRITE);
    printf("Previous value of permission mask was %X\n",
            oldmask);
}
```

 **File Manipulation**

unlink

COMPATIBILITY	MSC 3	MSC 4	MSC 5	QC	TC	ANSI	UNIX V
	▲	▲	▲	▲	▲		▲

PURPOSE Use *unlink* to delete a file specified by its pathname.

SYNTAX `int unlink(const char *path);`

`const char *path;`   Pathname of file to be deleted

EXAMPLE CALL `unlink("old.dat");`

INCLUDES `#include <io.h>`   For function declaration

or

`#include <stdio.h>`

DESCRIPTION The *unlink* function deletes the file specified by the pathname *path*. (This function is more useful under UNIX, in which a file can be linked to multiple directories.)

RETURNS If *unlink* successfully deletes the specified file, it returns a 0. A return value of −1 indicates error. If *unlink* cannot find the file specified by the pathname, the global variable *errno* is set to ENOENT. If the file is read only or if it is a directory, *errno* is set to EACCES.

SEE ALSO `remove`   Also deletes a file

EXAMPLE Use *unlink* in a program that deletes a file chosen by the user.

```
#include <stdio.h>
#include <io.h>
main(int argc, char **argv)
{
    if(argc < 2)
    {
        printf("Usage: %s <pathname>\n", argv[0]);
    }
    else
    {
        printf("File %s ", argv[1]);
        if(unlink(argv[1]) != 0)
        {
            perror("unlink failed");
        }
```

```
        else
        {
            printf("deleted\n");
        }
    }
}
```

File Manipulation

14 Directory Manipulation

Introduction

The MS-DOS operating system comes with a file system that takes care of the physical storage of data and presents a clean model of the filing system.

MS-DOS, like UNIX, uses a hierarchical file system enabling you to organize your files in directories and subdirectories. The "directory manipulation" routines in Microsoft C provide the basic tools necessary to create, modify, and remove directories from your C program. There is also a host of routines that manipulate the files, which we describe in Chapter 13.

Concepts

Proper use of the directory manipulation routines in Microsoft C requires an understanding of the MS-DOS file system and where directories fit in that model.

DOS FILE SYSTEM As we saw in Figure 13-1, the hierarchical file system used by DOS (and many other operating systems) consists of a root directory (on a certain disk drive) under which there are more directories and files. Each directory, in turn, can have additional directories and files under it. In this model of the hierarchical file system, a directory is just a file capable of storing other files inside it. Although the conceptual model is the same for all such file systems, the naming conventions and the way data is stored on the physical medium (the hard disk or the floppy) varies from one operating system to another.

DOS Pathnames

"Pathname" refers to the complete specification necessary to locate a file—the drive (a letter followed by a colon), then the hierarchy of directories leading to the file being located. The pathname of a file is constructed by concatenating the drive name to a list of directory names ending with the name of the file, as we illustrated in Figure 13-2. The topmost directory, known as the "root directory," is represented by a single backslash (\). The individual directory names are separated by backslashes.

Another backslash follows the last directory name. The file name, which can be eight characters followed by an optional three-character extension separated by a period, concludes the pathname. Since a directory is also a file, this naming convention also applies to directories.

Notes

MS-DOS includes such commands as MD, RD, and CD that enable you to create or delete a directory and change the current working directory, respectively. With the directory manipulation routines you can perform these tasks from a C program. The four C routines in this category are summarized in Table 14-1. The fifth routine, named _searchenv, is useful when you want to find a particular file in a list of directories, including the current working directory, defined in a specific environment variable. For example, you can use _searchenv to locate the file AUTOEXEC.BAT in the directories defined in the PATH environment variable by the call

```
_searchenv("autoexec.bat", "PATH", buffer);
```

where *buffer* is a character array in which _searchenv places the full pathname of the file being sought. In this example, if *autoexec.bat* is found in the root directory of drive C, after returning from _searchenv, *buffer* will contain "C:\AUTOEXEC.BAT".

Table 14-1. *Directory Manipulation Routines*

Routine	Description
chdir	Changes the current working directory.
getcwd	Returns the current working directory.
mkdir	Creates a new directory.
rmdir	Deletes a directory, provided it is empty.
_searchenv	Searches for a file in directories listed in a specified environment variable.

Cautions

► The directory manipulation routines do not allow you to switch to a different drive. To do so, use a call to *_dos_setdrive* or a call such as *system("c:")*.

► Watch out for a small detail when initializing C strings with DOS pathnames. The problem stems from the embedded backslashes in DOS pathnames and the special meaning C attaches to backslashes in strings. For example, a newline character is represented by \n and a backspace character is denoted by \b. To avoid misinterpretation, use *two* backslashes to embed a single backslash in a string being initialized to contain a pathname.

► The root directory in the MS-DOS file system is assigned limited space on the storage medium. This limits the number of files you can have at the root level. On double-sided double-density disk with 9 tracks, the number of files is 112; the PC-AT high-density disk has room for 224 files; and the hard disk can hold 512 files at the root level. Since a directory is just a file, the number of files you can have in other directories is limited only by the storage space on that drive.

Further Reading

One aspect of the DOS file system we did not discuss is the physical storage of files. The developer's guide by Angermeyer and Jaeger[1] devotes a chapter to the physical layout files on disks in MS-DOS. Duncan's book[2] is another source for such information.

1. John Angermeyer and Kevin Jaeger, The Waite Group, *MS-DOS Developer's Guide*, Howard W. Sams & Company, Indianapolis, IN, 1987, 440 pages.

2. Ray Duncan, *Advanced MS-DOS*, Microsoft Press, Redmond, WA, 1986, 468 pages.

chdir

COMPATIBILITY	MSC 3	MSC 4	MSC 5	QC	TC	ANSI	UNIX V
	▲	▲	▲	▲	▲		▲

PURPOSE Use *chdir* to change the current working directory. The *chdir* function works exactly like the MS-DOS command CD.

SYNTAX `int chdir(char *path);`

`char *path;` Pathname of new working directory

EXAMPLE CALL `chdir("c:\\bin\\sample");`

INCLUDES `#include <direct.h>` For function declaration

DESCRIPTION The *chdir* function changes the current working directory to the one specified by the argument *path*. As with the MS-DOS command, CD, you cannot change the default drive. Use the *_dos_setdrive* function to change the drive.

COMMON USES The *chdir* function allows you to change working directories while in your application program.

RETURNS When *chdir* succeeds in changing the current directory, it returns a 0. In case of error, it returns a −1 and sets the global variable *errno* to ENOENT to indicate that the specified pathname is invalid.

COMMENTS A call to *chdir* with a pathname that includes a drive specification sets the current working directory to the one on that drive, but the drive name remains unchanged. To use that directory, set the default drive with a call to the DOS function *_dos_setdrive* or with the use of *system*.

SEE ALSO `mkdir, rmdir` Other functions to manipulate directories

`_dos_setdrive` To change the default drive

`system` To execute an MS-DOS command from a program

EXAMPLE Write a program using *chdir* that provides the functionality of the MS-DOS command CD.

```
#include <stdio.h>
#include <direct.h>
main(int argc, char **argv)
{
    if(argc < 2)
```

Directory Manipulation

```
    {
        printf("Usage: %s <pathname>\n", argv[0]);
    }
    else
    {
        if(chdir(argv[1]) != 0)
        {
            perror("Error in \"chdir\"");
        }
    }
}
```

getcwd

COMPATIBILITY	MSC 3	MSC 4	MSC 5	QC	TC	ANSI	UNIX V
	▲	▲	▲	▲	▲		▲

PURPOSE Use *getcwd* to get the full pathname of the current working directory, including the drive name.

SYNTAX `char *getcwd(char *path, int numchars);`

`char *path;`   Buffer where pathname of current working directory is returned

`int numchars;`   Number of bytes available in the buffer for pathname

EXAMPLE CALL `getcwd(path_buffer, 80);`

INCLUDES `#include <direct.h>`   For function declaration

DESCRIPTION The *getcwd* function gets the pathname of the current working directory, including the drive specification, and stores it in the buffer specified by the argument *path*. The integer argument *numchars* tells *getcwd* the maximum number of characters the buffer *path* can hold. If the *path* argument is NULL, *getcwd* allocates *numchars* bytes using *malloc* and stores the pathname in this space. When you no longer need the space, you can free it by calling *free* with the pointer returned by *getcwd* as argument.

COMMON USES The *getcwd* function is useful for getting the current directory name and saving it. If your program changes working directories during its execution, it can use the saved name to restore the original working directory before exiting.

RETURNS The *getcwd* function returns a pointer to the buffer in which the pathname is stored. If *path* is not NULL, the return value is equal to *path* or a pointer to the buffer allocated to hold the pathname. A return value of NULL indicates an error. The global variable *errno* is set to ENOMEM if the *path* argument is

NULL and *getcwd* fails when allocating a buffer. If the pathname has more characters than *numchars*, *errno* is set to ERANGE.

SEE ALSO   chdir   To change current working directory

EXAMPLE   Use *getcwd* to get the pathname of the current working directory and display it.

```
#include <stdio.h>
#include <direct.h>
main()
{
    char pathname[81];
    if (getcwd(pathname, 80) == NULL)
    {
        perror("Error in getcwd");
    }
    else
    {
        printf("Current directory: %s\n", pathname);
    }
}
```

mkdir

COMPATIBILITY	MSC 3	MSC 4	MSC 5	QC	TC	ANSI	UNIX V
	▲	▲	▲	▲	▲		

PURPOSE   Use *mkdir* to create a new directory with a specified pathname.

SYNTAX   int mkdir(char *path);

           char *path;   Pathname of new directory

EXAMPLE CALL   mkdir("c:\\waite\\mscb"); /* c:\waite must already exist */

INCLUDES   #include <direct.h>   For function declaration

DESCRIPTION   The *mkdir* function creates a new directory with the pathname *path*. The pathname can include drive specification and directory/subdirectory names, but because *mkdir* can only create one directory at a time all but the last subdirectory must already exist. For example, if you have an existing directory named TEMP in the root directory of drive C, you can create a new directory with the pathname *C:\TEMP\NEW_1*, but *C:\TEMP\NEW_1\NEW_2* is illegal because it requires the creation of two directories.

 **Directory Manipulation**

COMMON USES The *mkdir* function is convenient in "setup" programs that you might distribute with your application. It can be used to implement, for example, the setup program provided with Microsoft C 5.1 for installing the compiler. Essentially, *mkdir* lets you create new directories from your program.

RETURNS When *mkdir* succeeds in creating the directory, it returns a 0. In case of error, it returns a −1 and sets the global variable *errno* to ENOENT, indicating that the specified pathname is invalid, or to EACCES, indicating that that pathname is that of a drive or an existing file or directory.

SEE ALSO

rmdir   To delete a directory

chdir   To change the current working directory

EXAMPLE Write a program using *mkdir* that provides the functionality of the MS-DOS command *md*.

```
#include <stdio.h>
#include <direct.h>
main(int argc, char **argv)
{
    if(argc < 2)
    {
        printf("Usage: %s <pathname>\n", argv[0]);
    }

    else
    {
        if(mkdir(argv[1]) != 0)
        {
            perror("Error in \"mkdir\"");
        }
    }
}
```

rmdir

COMPATIBILITY	MSC 3	MSC 4	MSC 5	QC	TC	ANSI	UNIX V
	▲	▲	▲	▲	▲		

PURPOSE Use *rmdir* to delete an existing directory with a specified pathname.

SYNTAX int rmdir(char *path);

char *path;   Pathname of directory to delete

EXAMPLE CALL `rmdir("c:\\temp\\last"); /* c:\temp\last must be empty */`

INCLUDES `#include <direct.h>`   For function declaration

DESCRIPTION The *rmdir* function deletes an existing directory with the pathname *path*. The pathname can include drive specification, directory, and subdirectory names. As with the MS-DOS command RD, the directory must be empty before it can be deleted. For example, if you have an existing directory named TEMP in the root directory of drive C, you can use *rmdir("c:\\temp")* to delete it, provided it is empty.

RETURNS If *rmdir* successfully deletes the directory, it returns a 0. In case of error, it returns a −1 and sets the global variable *errno* to ENOENT if the specified pathname is invalid or to EACCES if the pathname is that of a drive or an existing file, if the directory is not empty, or if the specified directory is the root directory or the current working directory.

SEE ALSO mkdir   To create a new directory

chdir   To change the current working directory

EXAMPLE Write a program using *rmdir* that provides the functionality of the MS-DOS command *rd*.

```
#include <stdio.h>
#include <direct.h>
main(int argc, char **argv)
{
    if(argc < 2)
    {
        printf("Usage: %s <pathname>\n", argv[0]);
    }
    else
    {
        if(rmdir(argv[1]) != 0)
        {
            perror("Error in \"rmdir\"");
        }
    }
}
```

Directory Manipulation

__searchenv

COMPATIBILITY	MSC 3	MSC 4	MSC 5	QC	TC	ANSI	UNIX V
			▲	▲	searchpath		

PURPOSE Use _searchenv to search for a particular file in a list of directories, including the current working directory and those defined in a specific environment variable.

SYNTAX `void _searchenv(char *name, char *env_var, char *path);`

`char *name;` Name of file to find

`char *env_var;` Environment variable that defines directories to search through

`char *path;` Buffer you supply to hold the full pathname of the file if it is found

EXAMPLE CALL `_searchenv(fname, "PATH", buffer);`

INCLUDES `#include <stdlib.h>` For function declaration

DESCRIPTION The _searchenv function first searches in the current working directory for the file whose name is given in the argument *name*. If the file is not found in the current directory, _searchenv continues the search in each directory path specified in the definition of the environment variable *env_var*. The definition of this variable is of the same form as that of the DOS environment variable PATH in that the directory names are separated by semicolons. If the file is found, _searchenv copies the file's pathname into the buffer at address *path* which must be large enough to hold the full pathname. If _searchenv fails to locate the file, *path* will contain a single null character.

SEE ALSO `getenv, putenv` To access and alter the environment table

EXAMPLE Write a utility that accepts a file name and searches for that file in all directories listed in the PATH environment variable. If found, print the full pathname of the file. Use _searchenv to locate the file.

```
#include <stdio.h>
#include <stdlib.h>
main(int argc, char **argv)
{
    char path_buffer[80];
    printf("This program searches for a file in all\n\
the directories specified in the PATH \n\
environment variable\n");
    if(argc < 2)
    {
```

```
            printf("Usage: %s <filename>\n", argv[0]);
            exit(0);
    }
/* Use "_searchenv" to locate the file */
    _searchenv(argv[1], "PATH", path_buffer);
    if(path_buffer[0] == '\0')
    {
        printf("File: %s not found\n", argv[1]);
    }
    else
    {
        printf("Found as: %s\n", path_buffer);
    }
}
```

Directory Manipulation

Introduction

Input and output (I/O) make computers useful as information processing tools. I/O can involve reading from and writing to files in the disk or reading input from the keyboard and sending output to the display screen or sending commands to peripherals. The Microsoft C library provides a large assortment of I/O routines for each of these tasks. We will discuss the salient features of the Microsoft C I/O routines here.

The C programming language has no built-in capability to perform any I/O. This is the responsibility of the library accompanying your C compiler. Fortunately, the C library under UNIX has a core of routines that constitutes the de facto standard I/O library (until, at least, the ANSI standard for C is finalized). The Microsoft C library includes this UNIX core together with a group of I/O routines that provide access to hardware in the PC. Microsoft C also adheres to the I/O library specifications of the proposed ANSI standard for C which is likely to be formally adopted in the near future.

We will describe the available file types in MS-DOS and the types of I/O necessary to access all IBM PC hardware features. The I/O categories include file I/O and I/O operations with registers in peripheral devices. Then we will describe all Microsoft C I/O routines, grouping them by common function, and finally we provide some cautions that should help you use these routines properly.

Concepts of File and Other I/O

The concept of a "file" is universal to almost all I/O in MS-DOS and Microsoft C, with the exception of reading or writing to *port* addresses in the peripheral devices attached to the 8086 microprocessor. You can think of a file as a sequence of bytes of data stored on a diskette, a RAM disk, CD ROM, or some external media. A file must be able to receive or impart a stream of bytes; physical storage need not underlie a file, as is shown in Figure 15-1A. Thought of in this manner, the keyboard, the serial communications port, and the display screen are all files—precisely the model used by the file I/O routines in Microsoft C.

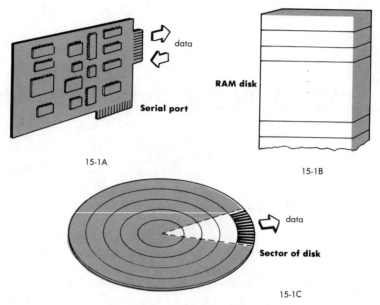

15-1A

15-1B

15-1C

Figure 15-1. *Files in Microsoft C*

TEXT AND BINARY FILES

In addition to this abstract view of a file as a stream of bytes, C programmers have to remember another distinction among files: how the constituent bytes are interpreted. Under MS-DOS, a file can be either text or binary.

In "text" files, each byte is interpreted as an ASCII character with a Control-Z representing the end of the file. In C (and in UNIX), a newline character (\n) signifies the end of a line (newline is an ASCII 10). In an MS-DOS text file, however, the end of a line of text is marked by a pair of characters: a carriage return (CR) followed by a linefeed (LF). We call this pair the CR-LF. By the way, CR and LF are represented in C by \r and \n respectively. This end-of-line difference between C and MS-DOS can be a problem during file I/O.

Microsoft C solves this problem by allowing the file I/O routines to perform some translation when interacting with a text file. A Control-Z character in an MS-DOS file opened in text mode signifies the end of that file (even if there is more data after the character). When reading from the file, a CR-LF pair is translated by the C I/O routines to LF (which is the newline character \n in C). When writing to the file using the C I/O routines, a single LF causes a CR-LF pair to be written, allowing proper formatting under MS-DOS. This approach keeps the model of text files fixed in your C program whether it is running under UNIX or MS-DOS. There is little impact on your programming because the translation takes place automatically whenever you open an MS-DOS file in the text mode.

In reading and writing "binary" files using C I/O routines, the bytes are not interpreted in any manner. To understand and use the contents of a binary file you must know what was stored there in the first place. After all, a 4-byte value in the file could be a long integer, a *float* variable, or even two short integers. When you know how the binary file was written, reading from it is straightforward. For example, if you write 1,000 short integer values to a binary file from a 2,000-byte buffer in memory, each two-byte value you later read from the file represents a short integer—a perfect match.

Binary files are ideal for storing numeric data because of the efficient manner of storage. To represent an integer value, say 32,767, in a text file, you would need 5 bytes to store the ASCII representation of the five digits. In binary form, 2 bytes are enough to hold this number. So if you had two files full of such data, the binary one would be 2.5 times smaller than the ASCII counterpart. Note, however, that the binary file would not be readable by a word processor or a text editor.

TYPES OF I/O ROUTINES IN MICROSOFT C

The Microsoft C library has three types of I/O routine: the stream routines, followed by the low-level file I/O routines, and finally the console and port I/O routines.

The "stream" routines refer to I/O performed using the model of files as a stream of bytes together with a buffer associated with a file. The "buffer" is a temporary storage area for the stream of bytes being read from or written to the file. The "low-level" routines are similar except that they do not use a buffer. "Console and port I/O" is meant for direct input and output from the keyboard, the monitor, and any peripheral devices (such as the serial adapter) attached to the PC.

Buffered Stream I/O

The stream I/O routines use a buffer to hold data in transit to and from a file. In a buffered read operation from a disk file, as Figure 15-2 illustrates, a fixed chunk of bytes is read from the disk into a buffer of the same size. The routines requesting data from the file actually read from the buffer. When the buffer has no characters left, it is automatically refilled by a disk read operation. A similar sequence occurs when writing to a file.

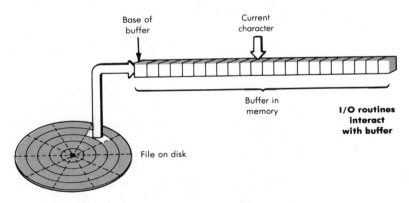

Figure 15-2. *Buffered file I/O*

The use of a buffer leads to efficient I/O on disk files because there are fewer disk accesses which are much slower than reading from a buffer in memory. There is only one drawback of the buffered approach to I/O; data written to a buffer do not actually appear in the disk file until the buffer is written out. This is "flushing" the buffer, a housekeeping chore normally handled automatically in C programs. In certain cases, however, the buffers are not flushed. These include ending the program abnormally because of a fatal error, exiting a C program with a call to the _exit function, or a hardware error occurring.

The Microsoft C stream I/O functions use an internal data structure to maintain information about the file being accessed. The data structure, named FILE, is defined in the include file *stdio.h*. As shown in Figure 15-3, the FILE structure has room for information about the current buffer, including an identifying number for the file (known as the file's "handle") and a single byte flag to indicate such status and control information as whether an end-of-file occurred during a read operation or an error occurred during I/O. When a file is opened by a stream I/O routine such as *fopen*, a pointer to a FILE structure is returned to the calling program. Subsequent stream I/O operations identify the file by the pointer to the associated FILE data structure. In fact, this pointer to the FILE data structure is commonly referred to as the *stream*. Thus, when we say read from the stream *stdin*, we mean read from the file whose associated FILE structure's address is in *stdin*. Incidentally, *stdin* is a stream that refers to the keyboard and it is already open when a C program begins running.

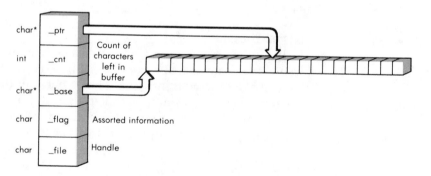

Figure 15-3. *FILE data structure*

Another important feature of the stream I/O routines is *formatting I/O*, the process of converting internal binary values of variables to character strings that can be written out to a file. For example, suppose a single byte contains the bit pattern: 01100100 (which is a binary representation of the decimal value 100). Converting this binary pattern into three ASCII characters in the string *100* involves formatting. Thus formatting is the step that makes the binary representations printable. Not all stream I/O routines are meant for formatted I/O; the *fread* and *fwrite* routines are for reading and writing unformatted binary data.

Unbuffered Low-Level I/O

Low-level I/O refers to unbuffered I/O, thus no buffer holds data read from the disk. Instead, each read request results in accessing the disk (or the device the file refers to) to fetch a requested number of bytes. Since disk accesses are time-consuming, the low-level routines are meant for reading or writing a significant number of bytes at a time.

The low-level I/O routines include no formatting capability. Since formatting is necessary when reading and writing text files (because we have to convert from character strings to internal representations), the low-level I/O routines are not suitable for performing I/O with text files. Binary files, on the other hand, do not require formatting during read/write operations so the low-level routines are ideal for I/O with binary files.

Like the buffered stream I/O routines, the low-level routines maintain data structures that contain such information as the current read/write position in the file and the permission settings for the file. Instead of the FILE pointer used by the stream routines, the low-level routines use the handle, a unique number, to identify each file. A stream file, with its associated FILE data structure, can also be accessed by a handle, which you can get by using the Microsoft C library function *fileno*. Similarly, a buffer may be associated with a file opened by a low-level call so that high-level stream I/O routines can be used on that file. This is accomplished by the library routine *fdopen*.

Console and Port I/O

This last category of I/O is not related to file I/O. Instead, these routines are meant for direct access to the keyboard, the screen, and any I/O port in the PC. Note that the keyboard and the monitor together are called the "console." Access to the keyboard and screen using the console I/O routines is similar to using BIOS calls (described in Chapter 16). There is no buffering of any sort and you do not have to formally open the device to perform these I/O operations.

Various hardware subsystems in the IBM PC can be controlled by sending commands to specific registers known as "ports." These registers are similar to memory locations, but they are accessed by an addressing mechanism in the 8086 microprocessor that is separate from the one used to reach conventional memory and video memory. Thus these ports have their own address space—the I/O address space. The port I/O routines allow you to read from and write to the hardware registers using the assembly language instructions IN and OUT, respectively.

Communications and the Serial Port

The *serial port* on the PC is an example of peripheral hardware that can be programmed by reading from and writing to I/O ports. The serial port on the PC is used for communicating with other computers and on-line services such as CompuServe, BIX, Genie, or your local bulletin board system. A plug-in card that fits into a slot in your PC, the serial port has an RS 232C serial adapter for sending data out. In the typical arrangement, shown in Figure 15-4, individual bytes from the computer are converted into an on-off, or digital, signal by a Universal Asynchronous Receiver Transmitter (UART) on the

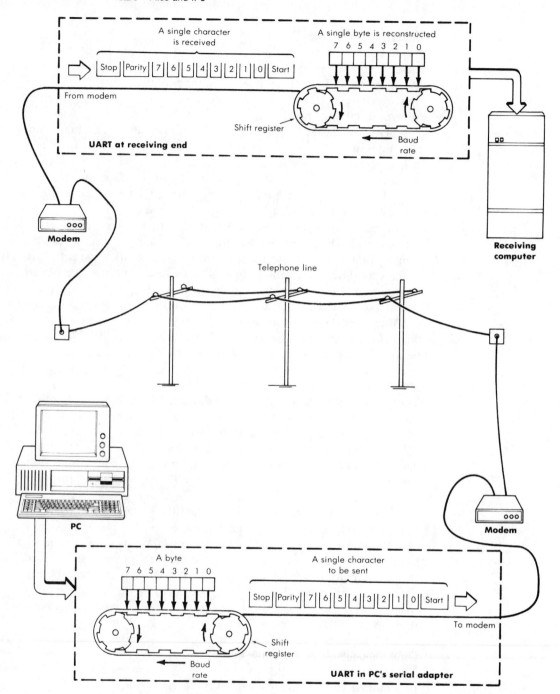

Figure 15-4. *Communicating via the serial port in the IBM PC*

serial adapter. This signal goes out through the serial port into a "modem," which converts the signals into a continuously variable form ("analog" signal) suitable for transmission over telephone lines. At the receiving end, another modem converts the signal back into digital form and finally another UART at the receiving end packs the individual bits from the digital signal into bytes. The UART is controlled by writing to or reading from a set of internal registers which can be accessed via port addresses. Because the port addresses are assigned sequentially, it is enough to know the address of the first port, commonly known as the "base address," of the serial adapter. In the IBM PC, the two serial ports COM1 and COM2 are assigned base port addresses 3F8h and 2F8h, respectively. Thus for the serial adapter COM1, the first register is at 3F8h, the next at 3F9h, and so on.

We will not discuss the function of each register in the UART, except to say that they allow you to control all parameters necessary for communicating data (such as baud rate and word length) and to enable hardware "interrupts" to be generated when certain events occur (such as an incoming byte being ready at the UART or the UART being free to send a byte out). The programming of the registers in the UART can be done by using the Microsoft C I/O functions *inp* and *outp*.

We discuss the concept of interrupts in the section on *System Calls* (Chapter 16). To handle the physical interrupts, you must also program another device—the Intel 8259A Programmable Interrupt Controller in your PC. This device acts as a gatekeeper deciding which device can interrupt the 8086 microprocessor and which ones cannot. The 8259A is also programmed by sending commands to its registers accessible via I/O port addresses (20h and 21h). If your interest is piqued by this summary description of *communications programming* on the PC, you can get more information in Chapter 13 of the *MS-DOS Papers* (Howard W. Sams & Company, 1988), a compendium on MS-DOS programming by The Waite Group.

FILE-SHARING The concept of sharing files is important because computers are being increasingly connected in networks so users can reach across and create, open, or modify files in another PC. MS-DOS version 3.0 introduced certain mechanisms to allow multiple processes on different computers in the network to access files at a common node. If you are using MS-DOS version 3.0 or higher, you can enable this file-sharing capability by issuing the DOS command SHARE.

At the programmer's level, file-sharing is achieved by opening the file with a call to the *sopen* library function with the exact mode of sharing specified with flags. Then you use the Microsoft C function *locking* to lock those parts of the file that you want to work on. When you are finished, *unlocking* them makes these portions of the file again available to others. There are several other MS-DOS services that manage shared access to files in MS-NET, Microsoft's network for PCs. Since a detailed discussion of these services is beyond the scope of this tutorial, we refer you to the *Microsoft MS-DOS Programmer's Reference Manual* (available from Microsoft Corporation and sold at many bookstores) for further details.

In general, the file I/O routines, both stream and low-level, are meant to be used as follows: open the file (where a file can be a device as well), perform the read and write operations, and close the file. In addition to these tasks other routines allow I/O from a specific position in the file, or format a value for printing, or read a single line or a single character, and so on. The console and port I/O routines do not open or close a device; you simply read from or write to the console or the I/O port.

I/O Routines in Microsoft C 5.1 Library

In this section we describe the I/O routines included in Microsoft C 5.1 library to enable you to use these routines effectively.

DEFAULT MODE: TEXT OR BINARY

In Microsoft C, the default mode of a file is determined by the value of the global integer variable _fmode. This is normally set to the constant O _TEXT (a preprocessor constant defined in *fcntl.h*), so all files, by default, are opened as text files. You can change the mode to binary by setting _fmode to O_BINARY. You can also select the mode of a file when opening it or you can use the *setmode* library function to change the translation mode of a file that is already open.

FILES ALREADY OPENED FOR YOUR CONVENIENCE

When your C program starts up, the five files shown in Table 15-1 are opened for you by Microsoft C. These may be called as streams or by handles. The first three files, *stdin, stdout*, and *stderr*, get input from the user, display the output, and display error messages, respectively. From DOS, you can redirect *stdin* and *stdout* to other files.

Table 15-1. *Preopened Files in Microsoft C*

File	Stream Name	Handle Number	Connected to/Mode
Standard input	stdin	0	Console (keyboard)/Text mode
Standard output	stdout	1	Console (display screen)/Text mode
Standard error	stderr	2	Console (display screen)/Text mode
Standard auxliary	stdaux	3	Cannot be connected/Binary mode
Standard print	stdprn	4	Printer port on PC/Binary mode

OPEN FILE LIMIT IN MS-DOS

MS-DOS imposes a limit of 20 open files per process (processes are defined in Chapter 11). Since 5 files are already opened, your program can open 15 files. Files opened for buffered as well as unbuffered I/O count towards this limit.

The number of open streams that use pointers to FILE data structures remains fixed at 20 at all times. But in MS-DOS 3.3, the number of open file handles for the low-level I/O routines such as *open, read, write*, and *lseek* can be made larger. Increasing the number of open file handles involves changing an assembly language file named CRTODAT.ASM, which is distributed with Microsoft C 5.0 and 5.1. This file contains code that runs at the beginning and end of every C program. At the beginning of the file you will find the line

```
_NFILE_ = 20 ; Maximum number of file handles
```

which initializes the symbol _NFILE_ to 20. By editing this line and changing 20 to a higher value you alter the upper limit on the number of file handles. Assemble this file using Microsoft Macro Assembler MASM version 4.0 or later. If you link the new object file CRT0DAT.OBJ explicitly with your program, the new maximum takes effect. You can make the change permanent by replacing the CRT0DAT.OBJ module in the C run-time library for the memory model you plan to use.

GLOBAL VARIABLES AND CONSTANTS THAT MATTER

The I/O routines are affected by certain global variables and preprocessor constants defined by the Microsoft C library. (We have already mentioned one of the variables, _fmode_, which determines the default translation mode of a file.) Table 15-2 lists the most important of these as they relate to the I/O routines. Many more predefined constants are significant to individual I/O routines, but these are described in the reference pages for the relevant I/O routines.

Table 15-2. *Certain Constants and Global Variables Relevant to I/O Routines*

Name	Meaning and Default Value
BUFSIZ	Defines the size of each buffer associated with a stream. Constant is defined in *stdio.h* to be equal to 512.
EOF	Denotes end-of-file. Constant is defined in *stdio.h* as −1.
_fmode	Controls the translation modes (text or binary) of files opened in the program. Global integer's default setting is O_TEXT.
NFILE	Denotes the maximum number of files that can be opened by a process. Constant is defined in *stdio.h* to 20 and can be redefined under MS-DOS 3.3.
NULL	Signifies error returns defined in *stdio.h* to 0 (or 0L for compact, large, and huge memory models).

THE I/O ROUTINES

Table 15-3 catalogs the I/O routines. Since the number of routines in the entire I/O category is quite large, in addition to listing the routines alphabetically, in Table 15-4 we group them according to the specific tasks they perform. In listing the I/O routines by function, we start with the ones that perform file I/O. This group also includes routines that perform I/O with the preopened streams: *stdin* and *stdout*.

Table 15-3. *I/O Library Routines*

Routine	Description
	Stream Routines
clearerr	Clears the error indicator of a stream.
fclose	Closes a stream.

Table 15-3. *(cont.)*

Routine	Description
fcloseall	Closes all streams that are currently open.
fdopen	Associates a stream with a file already opened by a low-level call.
feof	Returns a nonzero value if current position in a stream is at the end of file.
ferror	Returns a nonzero value if an error had occurred during read/write operations on a stream.
fflush	Writes to the file the contents of the buffer associated with a stream.
fgetc	Reads a character from a stream.
fgetchar	Reads a character from the stream *stdin*.
fgetpos	Returns current position of a stream in an internal format suitable for use by *fsetpos*.
fgets	Reads a line (up to and including the first newline character) from a stream.
fileno	Returns the file handle associated with a stream.
flushall	Flushes all buffers of all open streams to the respective files.
fopen	Opens a named file as a buffered stream (includes options for selecting translation modes and access types).
fprintf	Performs formatted output to a stream.
fputc	Writes a character to a stream.
fputchar	Writes a character to the stream *stdout*.
fputs	Writes a string of characters to a stream.
fread	Reads a specified amount of binary data from a stream.
freopen	Closes a stream and reassigns it to a new file.
fscanf	Performs formatted input from a stream.
fseek	Sets current position to a specific location in the file.
fsetpos	Sets current position of a stream using value returned by an earlier call to *fgetpos*.
ftell	Returns the current position in the file associated with a stream.
fwrite	Writes a specified number of bytes of binary data to a stream.
getc	Reads a character from a stream.
getchar	Reads a character from the stream *stdin*.
gets	Reads a string up to a newline character from the stream *stdin*.
getw	Reads two bytes of binary data from a stream.
printf	Performs formatted output to the stream *stdout*.
putc	Writes a character to a stream.
putchar	Writes a character to the stream *stdout*.
puts	Writes a C string to the stream *stdout*.
putw	Writes two bytes of binary data to a stream.
rewind	Sets the current position to the beginning of the file associated with a stream.
rmtmp	Deletes all files created by *tmpfile*.
scanf	Performs formatted input from the stream *stdin*.
setbuf	Assigns a fixed-length user-defined buffer to an open stream.
setvbuf	Assigns a variable-length user-defined buffer to an open stream.
sprintf	Performs formatted output to a buffer.

Table 15-3. *(cont.)*

Routine	Description
sscanf	Performs formatted input from a buffer.
tempnam	Generates a temporary file name with arbitrary directory name.
tmpfile	Creates a temporary file open for buffered stream I/O.
tmpnam	Generates a temporary file name with the directory name specified by the constant *P_tmpdir*.
ungetc	Pushes a character back into the buffer associated with a stream.
vfprintf	Version of *fprintf* that accepts a pointer to a list of arguments and performs formatted output to a stream.
vprintf	Version of *printf* that accepts a pointer to a list of arguments and performs formatted output to the stream *stdout*.
vsprintf	Version of *sprintf* that accepts a pointer to a list of arguments and performs formatted output to a buffer.

Low-Level Routines

Routine	Description
close	Closes a file using its handle.
creat	Creates a new file, opens it, and returns its handle.
dup	Creates a second handle given an existing handle associated with an open file.
dup2	Assigns a specified second handle to an existing handle so that both handles refer to the same file.
eof	Checks for end-of-file condition of a file specified by a handle.
lseek	Sets the current position in a file referenced by a handle.
open	Opens a file for low-level I/O and returns a handle.
read	Reads a specified number of bytes of binary data from a file open for low-level I/O.
sopen	Opens a file for shared low-level I/O and returns a handle.
tell	Returns the current position in a file referenced by a handle.
write	Writes a specified number of bytes of binary data to a file open for low-level I/O.

Console and Port Routines

Routine	Description
cgets	Reads a string of characters from the console.
cprintf	Performs formatted output to the console.
cputs	Writes a string to the console.
cscanf	Performs formatted input from the console.
getch	Reads (without echoing) a single unbuffered character from the console.
getche	Reads and echoes a single unbuffered character from the console.
inp	Reads a single byte from a specified I/O port address.
inpw	Reads two contiguous bytes from a specified I/O port address.
kbhit	Tests whether there are any keystrokes waiting to be read.
outp	Writes a single byte to a specified I/O port address.
outpw	Writes two bytes to a specified I/O port address.
putch	Writes a single unbuffered character to the console.
ungetch	Pushes a character back to the console.

Table 15-4. *Library Routines by Task*

I/O Task	Stream I/O	Low-level I/O
Create a file	fopen	creat, open, sopen
Open a file	fopen, freopen	open, sopen
Close a File	fclose, fcloseall	close
Formatted read	fscanf, scanf	—
Formatted write	fprintf, printf, vfprintf, vprintf	—
Read a character	fgetc, fgetchar, getc, getchar	—
Write a character	fputc, fputchar, putc, putchar	—
Read a line	fgets, gets	—
Write a line	fputs, puts	—
Set read/write position	fseek, fsetpos, rewind	lseek
Get read/write position	fgetpos, ftell	tell
Binary read	fread, getw	read
Binary write	fwrite, putw	write
Flush buffer	fflush, flushall	—
Get handle of a stream	fileno	—
Assign buffer to a handle	fdopen	—
Duplicate a handle	—	dup, dup2
Check error/eof	clearerr, feof, ferror	eof
Manage temporary files	rmtmp, tempnam, tmpfile, tmpnam	—
Control buffering	setbuf, setvbuf	—
Push character to buffer	ungetc	—

String I/O

If you think of files as a stream of bytes, the data sources or destinations do not have to be disk files or devices; they can also be buffers in memory. A group of Microsoft C I/O routines provide the capability to read from and write to arrays of characters ("strings"). These routines allow you to format data and place the result in a string or get characters from a string and convert the characters to internal values. This is often convenient because you can prepare a string that can be output by routines that do not have any formatting capability (for example, the *_outtext* routine in the Graphics category). Table 15-5 lists the three string I/O routines according to the task they perform.

Table 15-5. *String I/O Routines by Task*

I/O Task	Routines
Format input from a string	sscanf
Format output to a string	sprintf, vsprintf

Console and Port I/O Routines by Task

Table 15-6 shows the console and port I/O routines that interact with the keyboard and the screen, grouped by task. As you can see, the console I/O routines also support formatting. The formatting capabilities are identical to those supported by *printf* and *scanf* which we describe next.

Table 15-6. *Console and Port I/O Routines Grouped by Task*

I/O Task	Routines
Read from an I/O port address	inp, inpw
Write to an I/O port address	outp, outpw
Read character from console	getch, getche
Write character to console	putch
Check for waiting keystrokes	kbhit
Push a character back to console	ungetch
Read a string from console	cgets
Write a string to console	cputs
Format input from the console	cscanf
Format output to the console	cprintf

FORMATTED I/O: PRINT AND SCANF

The formatting I/O capabilities of *printf* and *scanf* deserve special attention because they are widely used in C programs and a large number of formatting options are available under each function. Many other functions, such as *cprintf, cscanf, fprintf, fscanf, sprintf*, and *sscanf*, provide identical formatting options. Thus understanding *printf* and *scanf* should help you use all the formatted I/O routines in the Microsoft C library.

Formatting involves converting internal representation of a variable into a character string that humans can understand. To interpret the contents of a set of memory locations you must know the type of C variable being stored there. For example, a set of four bytes can hold a long integer and it can also hold a single-precision floating-point number. The *printf* and *scanf* functions, responsible for formatting the data, have to be told how the contents of these bytes are to be interpreted. This is done by embedding formatting commands in the arguments passed to *printf* and *scanf*.

Formatted Output with printf

In the simplest case, when printing out values of variables, you can use *printf* with a minimal amount of formatting code:

```
float    floatvar = 24.95;
double   dblvar = 99.95;
int      intvar = 100;
char     string[] = "Microsoft C 5.1";
      :
      :
```

```
printf("Float = %f, Double = %f, Integer = %d,\nString = %s\n",
       floatvar, dblvar, intvar, string);
```

In this case, each formatting command consists of a percent sign (%) followed by a single letter that indicates the type of the variable. The format codes are embedded in a string and each command appears exactly where you want the variable to be printed. The string with the formatting codes is followed by the variables that you want printed. Here's what you get if you embed the code fragment above in a C program and execute it.

```
Float = 24.950001, Double = 99.950000, Integer = 100, String =
Microsoft C 5.1
```

You may have noticed the discrepancy between the assigned value of the *float* variable and the value shown by *printf*. The single-precision *float* variables are accurate to 7 significant digits. When we used the %f format to print the value, *printf* used more than 7 significant digits (by default it used 6 digits following the decimal point). Since the stored value is only accurate to 7 significant digits, the value prints as *24.950001* instead of the expected *24.950000*. This illustrates an important point about formatted output: you can only print results that can have at best the accuracy present in the stored value. Since a *float* variable is accurate to 7 digits, you cannot expect to get a more accurate value just by asking *printf* to use a formatting option that requires the use of, say, 15 significant digits.

Notice too that both *float* and *double* floating-point values are printed with six digits after the decimal place. The integer value is printed without any leading blanks and the string is printed in its entirety. These are the default settings of the respective formats: %f, %d, and %s. Additional qualifiers can be placed between the percent sign and the type letter to indicate options, such as the number of digits after the decimal point or a fixed size of field within which to print a value.

Other data types can also be printed out, including the *long* and *unsigned* forms of integers as well as single characters and addresses of variables in hexadecimal format. See the reference pages on *printf* for complete coverage of the formatting options and commands. We will not repeat the information here except to note that while *printf* is meant for writing to the stream *stdout*, *fprintf* performs the same operation to a file and *sprintf* writes formatted output to a string. There is even a formatted console output routine named *cprintf*. Each of these accepts the same formatting commands as *printf*.

Formatted Input with scanf

The *scanf* function is meant for formatting input which involves reading characters and converting groups of them into internal representation of C variables. Like *printf*, a string with embedded format codes specifies how the input characters are to be treated during the conversion process. In fact, a call to *scanf* looks like a call to *printf*, except that the argument list has addresses of the variables into which *scanf* loads the values converted from the input string. If we were reading a *float*, a *double*, and an integer, the call might look like:

```
float    floatvar;
double   dblvar;
int      intvar;
:
:
scanf(" %f %lf %d", &floatvar, &dblvar, &intvar);
```

This formatted read statement reads the three values with any number of blank spaces between them. Note that the format code meant for the *float* variable is different from that for the *double*. The %f code tells *scanf* to convert the string into the internal representation of a *float* variable. The qualifier l between the % and the f tells *scanf* to use the internal representation of a *double* instead of a *float*.

Like *printf*, *scanf* is used with formatted input from the stream *stdin*. The Microsoft C I/O library also includes *fscanf* for formatted reading from a file and *sscanf* for formatted input from a string. Lastly, there is a formatted input routine for the console called *cscanf*. All of these routines use the same formatting commands as *scanf*. The reference page on *scanf* gives a detailed discussion of the formatting options available to you as a programmer.

Cautions

► Do not mix low-level I/O read and write routines with the buffered stream routines because the two sets are not compatible.

► Remember that the translation mode O_TEXT causes interpretation of the bytes in a file and the number of bytes read or written does not correspond to the number in the file. This means that you cannot rely on absolute byte positions when accessing a file in the text mode.

► Single keystrokes from the console cannot be read by *getchar* (it waits until a carriage return is hit). Use the console routines *getch* or *getche* for this purpose. For example, if you wanted to end a program when the user presses any key, you could use

```
{
    :
    :
    printf("Press any key to exit:");
    getch()  /* Read a keystroke and exit */
}
```

If you use *getchar*, the function does not return immediately after a key is pressed. It waits until a carriage return to end the read operation.

► When using the buffered I/O routines, the buffers sometimes have to be explicitly written out (flushed) with the library routines *fflush* or *flushall* before output data actually appears in a file. Normally, buffers are flushed during program termination, but not when a program ends with a call to *_exit*.

▶ The formatting options available in the *printf* and the *scanf* family are quite extensive and several format codes are specific to Microsoft C 5.0 and 5.1. When portability is a concern, check the appropriate reference pages carefully before using a particular format code.

▶ Note that file-sharing is supported only under MS-DOS 3.0 and higher.

Further Reading

The standard I/O routines are covered in almost every book on C. Prata's book[1] provides a gentle introduction to these functions, yet includes a detailed exposition of the concepts behind the C I/O library. The basic file I/O routines are also carefully explained in Lafore's text on C[2].

Chapter 13 of the *MS-DOS Papers*[3] covers in detail how you can program the serial port of a PC in Microsoft C, and it includes an example program illustrating the use of the port I/O routines *inp* and *outp*.

1. Stephen Prata, The Waite Group, *Advanced C Primer++*, Howard W. Sams & Company, Indianapolis, IN, 1986, 502 pages.

2. Robert Lafore, The Waite Group, *Microsoft C Programming for the IBM*, Howard W. Sams & Company, Indianapolis, IN, 1987, 681 pages.

3. The Waite Group, *MS-DOS Papers*, Howard W. Sams & Company, Indianapolis, IN, 1988, 608 pages.

clearerr

COMPATIBILITY	MSC 3	MSC 4	MSC 5	QC	TC	ANSI	UNIX V
	▲	▲	▲	▲	▲	▲	▲

PURPOSE Use the *clearerr* function to reset the error and end-of-file indicators of a file specified by a file pointer (i.e., a pointer to the associated FILE data structure).

SYNTAX `void clearerr(FILE *file_pointer);`

`FILE *file_pointer;`   Pointer to FILE data structure associated with the file whose error flag is being cleared

EXAMPLE CALL `clearerr(outfile);`

INCLUDES `#include <stdio.h>`   For function declaration and definition of the FILE data type

DESCRIPTION The *clearerr* function sets to zero a flag in the FILE data structure associated with the file specified by the argument *file_pointer*. This flag has a nonzero value after an error or an end-of-file condition occurs. The error indicator for the file remains set until cleared by calling *clearerr*. These conditions may be verified by calling *ferror* and *feof*, respectively.

SEE ALSO `ferror`   To detect an error condition of a file

`feof`   To determine an end-of-file condition

EXAMPLE Write a C program that prompts the user for a file name. Open the file with *fopen* for read operations only. Then create an error condition by trying to write to the file. Call *ferror* to detect the error and call *clearerr* to reset the error flag.

```
#include <stdio.h>
main()
{
    char filename[81];
    FILE *infile;
    long filesize;
    printf("Enter the name of an existing file: ");
    gets(filename);
/* Open the file */
    if ( (infile = fopen(filename, "r")) == NULL)
    {
        printf("fopen failed to open: %s\n", filename);
        exit(0);
    }
```

```
        fprintf(infile, "Test..."); /* Try to read a line*/
        if (ferror(infile) != 0)   /* Check for the error*/
        {
            printf("Error detected\n");
            clearerr(infile);       /* Now clear the error */
            printf("Error cleared\n");
        }
    }
```

Stream I/O
fclose

COMPATIBILITY	MSC 3	MSC 4	MSC 5	QC	TC	ANSI	UNIX V
	▲	▲	▲	▲	▲	▲	▲

PURPOSE Use *fclose* to close a file opened earlier for buffered input and output using *fopen*.

SYNTAX `int fclose(FILE *file_pointer);`

`FILE *file_pointer;` Pointer to file to be closed

EXAMPLE CALL `fclose(infile);`

INCLUDES `#include <stdio.h>` For function declaration and efinition of FILE data type

DESCRIPTION The *fclose* function closes the file specified by the argument *file_pointer*. This pointer must have been one returned earlier when the file was opened by *fopen*. If the file is open for writing, the contents of the buffer associated with the file are flushed before the file is closed. The buffer is then released.

COMMON USES To ensure that all buffers get flushed and freed for reuse and that the file is properly closed, use *fclose* for files that you no longer intend to use in your program.

RETURNS If the file is successfully closed, *fclose* returns a zero. In case of an error, the return value is equal to the constant EOF defined in *stdio.h*.

COMMENTS You can use the *fcloseall* function to close all open files at the same time. Since only 20 files opened by *fopen* can be present at the same time, however, for file-intensive applications you may find it necessary to close files with *fclose* when you are done with a file.

SEE ALSO fopen To open a file for buffered I/O

fcloseall To close all open files at the same time

 **Input and Output Routines**

EXAMPLE   Use *fopen* to open a file specified by the user. Read and display the file's contents. Close the file by calling *fclose* and then exit.

```
#include <stdio.h>
char filename[80],      /* Name of file to open      */
     line[81];          /* For lines from the file   */
FILE *inputfile;        /* File pointer to opened file */
main()
{
    printf("Enter name of file to open: ");
    gets(filename);
/* Open the file */
    if ((inputfile = fopen(filename,"r")) == NULL)
    {
        printf("Error opening file: %s\n", filename);
        exit(0);
    }
    printf("==== Contents of input file ====\n");
    while(fgets(line, 80, inputfile) != NULL)
    {
        printf(line);
    }
/* Now close the file and exit */
    fclose(inputfile);
}
```

Stream I/O
fcloseall

COMPATIBILITY	MSC 3	MSC 4	MSC 5	QC	TC	ANSI	UNIX V
	▲	▲	▲	▲	▲		

PURPOSE   Use *fcloseall* to close all files opened for buffered input and output with *fopen* or *tmpfile*, respectively.

SYNTAX   int fcloseall(void);

EXAMPLE CALL   number_closed = fcloseall();

INCLUDES   #include <stdio.h>   For function declaration

DESCRIPTION   The *fcloseall* function closes all files that have been opened by *fopen* or *tmpfile* for buffered I/O. Buffers associated with files opened for writing are written out to the corresponding file before closing.

    Note that *fcloseall* does not close the five I/O *streams* (*stdin, stdout, stderr, stdaux,* and *stdprn)* that are preopened by the system (see the tutorial section).

COMMON USES   You can use *fcloseall* to close, in a single stroke, all files opened by your program.

RETURNS   If files are successfully closed, *fcloseall* returns the number closed. In case of an error, the return value is equal to the constant EOF defined in *stdio.h.*

SEE ALSO   fopen   To open a file for buffered I/O

fclose   To close a single file

EXAMPLE   We'll illustrate two features of the file I/O routines with this example. The function *tmpfile* enables you to create a temporary file. Write a sample C program in which you attempt to open 20 temporary files. Since MS-DOS allows only 20 files (for buffered I/O) and 5 are already open, the *tmpfile* call will fail after 15 files are open. Now call *fcloseall* to close them all at once. Print the number returned by *fcloseall* to verify that it's 15.

```
#include <stdio.h>
main()
{
    int i;
/* Try opening 20 temporary files -- we'll just throw
 * away the returned pointers because we are not going

 * to use these files. The file open will fail after 15
 * files are opened. So the number of closed files
 * should be 15.
 */
    for (i=0; i<20; i++)
    {
        if (tmpfile() == NULL)
            printf("Error opening file # %d\n", i);
        else
            printf("Temporary file #%d opened\n", i);
    }
/* Now close all the files and inform user how many were
 * closed
 */
    i = fcloseall();
    printf("%d files were closed -- should be 15\n", i);
}
```

Input and Output Routines

fdopen

COMPATIBILITY	MSC 3	MSC 4	MSC 5	QC	TC	ANSI	UNIX V
	▲	▲	▲	▲	▲		▲

PURPOSE   Use *fdopen* to associate a buffer with a file that has been opened for unbuffered, unformatted I/O. This allows subsequent buffered, formatted read/write operations with the file.

SYNTAX   `FILE *fdopen(int handle, char *access_mode);`

         `int handle;`   Handle of open file being upgraded for buffered I/O

         `char *access_mode;`   A character string denoting whether file is being opened for read/write.

EXAMPLE CALL   `p_datafile = fdopen(handle, "rb");`

INCLUDES   `#include <stdio.h>`   For function declaration and definition of FILE data type

DESCRIPTION   The *fdopen* function associates a FILE data structure with the file specified by the argument *handle*. The *handle* is an integer returned by low-level I/O routines such as *open, creat,* and *sopen* that originally opened the file. Once buffered I/O becomes permissible, the type of operations you intend to perform on the file must be indicated by the argument *access_mode*. Table 15-7 lists the possible values of *access_mode* and their meanings.

Table 15-7. *Access Modes When Opening Files for Buffered I/O*

Access Mode String	Interpretation
r	Opens file for read operations only. The *fopen* function fails if the file does not exist.
w	Opens a new file for writing. If the file exists, its contents are destroyed.
a	Opens file for appending. A new file is created if the file does not exist.
r+	Opens an existing file for both read and write operations. Error is returned if file does not exist.
w+	Creates a file and opens it for both reading and writing. If file exists, current contents are destroyed.
a+	Opens file for reading and appending. Creates a new file if one does not exist.

In addition to the basic access modes shown in Table 15-7, one of the characters shown in Table 15-8 can be appended to each of the strings in Table 15-7 to specify how the contents of the file are to be translated. Note that the character denoting the translation mode (see the tutorial section) can come before or after the + in the strings above. For example, *w+b* is considered the same as *wb+* and means "open the file for reading and writing in the binary mode." If no translation mode is specified, the default mode is determined by the global variable *_fmode*, which is declared in the header file *stdio.b*. When a file is opened for appending with the *a* or *a+* access mode, existing data can never be destroyed because the *file pointer* is moved to the end of the file before writing occurs. This pointer keeps track of the current position where writing occurs. When a file is opened for updating, using the *r+*, *w+* or *a+* access modes, you must call one of the functions *fsetpos, fseek*, or *rewind* when switching between read and write operations. These calls serve to set the file pointer properly before the operation. You can also call *fsetpos* or *fseek* and set the file pointer to the current position.

Table 15-8. *File Translation Modes for Buffered I/O*

Translation Mode	Interpretation
b	Opens file in untranslated or binary mode. Every character in the file is read as is without the changes described below.
t	Opens file in translated mode. This is a Microsoft C extension and not an ANSI standard mode. Its purpose is to accommodate MS-DOS file conventions. In this mode, the following interpretations will be in effect: (1) Carriage Return-Line Feed (CR-LF) combinations on input are translated to single linefeeds. During output, single linefeed characters are translated to CR-LF pairs. (2) During input, the Control-Z character is interpreted as the end-of-file character.

COMMON USES The *fdopen* function is used to enable buffered, formatted I/O on a file that was originally opened for unbuffered, unformatted I/O.

RETURNS If successful, *fdopen* returns a pointer to the FILE structure that is associated with the file. In case of an error, *fdopen* returns a NULL. See below for an example of checking for error return from *fdopen*.

COMMENTS The *access-mode* specified in the call to *fdopen* must be compatible with the access and sharing modes used when the file was first opened by *open, creat*, or *sopen*. Microsoft warns against using *fdopen* with a file that was opened with *sopen* and file-sharing enabled. The buffered operations are inherently incompatible with the concept of file-sharing because the file is not up to date and ready for sharing as long as some of the data resides in the buffer.

SEE ALSO fclose   To close a file opened by *fdopen*

open   To open a file using a handle, a lower-level routine

EXAMPLE Use *open* to open a file, say, *autoexec.bat* (this is one file every PC has) in the

Input and Output Routines

root directory of your current drive, say, drive C. Now call *fdopen* to allow buffered I/O on the file. Read and display all lines in the file.

```
#include <stdio.h>
#include <io.h>
#include <fcntl.h>

main()
{
        int handle;
        FILE *infile;
        char buffer[80];
/* Open the file. Note that we need two '\'  */
        if ( (handle = open("c:\\autoexec.bat",
            O_RDONLY)) == -1)
        {
            perror("open failed");
            exit(1);
        }
/* Use fdopen to assign a FILE data structure to file */
        if ((infile = fdopen(handle, "r")) == NULL)
        {
                perror("fdopen failed");
                exit(1);
        }
/* All's well. Read and print the contents of the file*/
        printf("Contents of c:autoexec.bat:\n");
        while ( fgets(buffer, 80, infile) != NULL)
        {
            printf(buffer);
        }
}
```

Stream I/O

feof

COMPATIBILITY	MSC 3	MSC 4	MSC 5	QC	TC	ANSI	UNIX V
	▲	▲	▲	▲	▲	▲	▲

PURPOSE Use the *feof* macro, defined in *stdio.h*, to determine whether the end of a file has been reached.

SYNTAX `int feof(FILE *file_pointer);`

`FILE *file_pointer;`   Pointer to FILE data structure associated with the file whose status is being checked

feof

EXAMPLE CALL `if (feof(infile) != 0) printf("File ended\n");`

INCLUDES `#include <stdio.h>`   For function declaration and definition of the FILE data type

DESCRIPTION The *feof* macro returns a value indicating whether the file specified by the argument *file_pointer* has reached its end.

COMMON USES When you get an error return from a read operation, you can call *feof* to determine if the error occurred because you tried to read past the end-of-file.

RETURNS If the end of the file is reached, *feof* returns a nonzero value after the first read operation beyond the end-of-file. Otherwise, it returns a zero.

COMMENTS Since *feof* is implemented as a macro, checking for end-of-file with *feof* does not involve the overhead of calling a function.

SEE ALSO `clearerr`   To reset the end-of-file and error indicator of a file

`rewind`   To move the file pointer to the beginning of a file

`fclose`   To close a single file

EXAMPLE Use *fopen* to open the file *autoexec.bat* for buffered read operations. Read and display each line until an error is returned by the read routine *fgets*. Then call *feof* to check whether end-of-file is reached. If not, there is another error in reading from the file.

```
#include <stdio.h>
main()
{
        FILE *infile;
        unsigned char buffer[81];
/* Open the file "c:\autoexec.bat". We need two '\'  */
        if ( (infile = fopen("c:\\autoexec.bat", "r"))
             == NULL)
        {
            printf("fopen failed.\n");
            exit(0);
        }
        printf("Contents of c:autoexec.bat:\n");
        while ( fgets(buffer, 80, infile) != NULL)
        {
            printf(buffer);
        }
        if (feof(infile) != 0) /* Check end-of-file */
        {
            printf("*** End-of-file reached ***");
        }
```

 Input and Output Routines

```
        else
        {
            printf("ERROR: reading from file!\n");
        }
    }
}
```

ferror

COMPATIBILITY	MSC 3	MSC 4	MSC 5	QC	TC	ANSI	UNIX V
	▲	▲	▲	▲	▲	▲	▲

PURPOSE Use the *ferror* macro, defined in *stdio.h*, to determine if an error has occurred during a previous read or write operation on a file that had been opened for buffered I/O.

SYNTAX `int ferror(FILE *file_pointer);`

`FILE *file_pointer;` Pointer to FILE data structure associated with the file whose status is being checked

EXAMPLE CALL `if (ferror(infile) != 0) printf("Error detected\n");`

INCLUDES `#include <stdio.h>` For function declaration and definition of the FILE data type

DESCRIPTION The *ferror* macro returns a value indicating whether there has been an error during a prior read/write operation on the file specified by the argument *file _pointer*. The FILE data structure associated with the file has a flag field that holds the information about the end-of-file and error conditions during read or write operations. The *ferror* macro checks whether the flag equals a predefined constant that indicates an error condition.

COMMON USES If you have not checked for error returns from read/write operations, you can check after the fact by calling *ferror*. If there was an error, you can call *clearerr* to clear the error flag. Rewinding the file also clears the error flag.

RETURNS If an error has occurred during a read or a write operation on the file, *ferror* returns a nonzero value. Otherwise, it returns a zero.

COMMENTS Since *ferror* is implemented as a macro, checking for errors with it does not involve calling a function. On the other hand, it may be best to check for error returns during calls to read and write routines *fprintf, fgets,* and *fscanf.*

SEE ALSO `clearerr` To clear the error condition of a file

EXAMPLE Use *fopen* to open the file *autoexec.bat* for buffered read operations only.

Now create an error condition by attempting to write a line to it. Call *ferror* to confirm that there was an error and then call *clearerr* to clear the error condition.

```
#include <stdio.h>
char buffer[81] = "This will not be written";
main()
{
        FILE *infile;
/* Open the file "c:\autoexec.bat". Note the two '\' */
        if ( (infile = fopen("c:\\autoexec.bat", "r"))
                == NULL)
        {
           printf("fopen failed.\n");
           exit(0);
        }
        fprintf(infile, "%s\n", buffer);
        if (ferror(infile) != 0)    /* Check for error */
        {
           printf("Error detected\n");
           clearerr(infile);        /* Now clear the error */
           printf("Error cleared\n");
        }
}
```

Stream I/O

fflush

COMPATIBILITY	MSC 3	MSC 4	MSC 5	QC	TC	ANSI	UNIX V
	▲	▲	▲	▲	▲	▲	▲

PURPOSE Use the *fflush* function to process the current contents of the buffer associated with a file opened for buffered I/O (see the tutorial section).

SYNTAX `int fflush(FILE *file_pointer);`

`FILE *file_pointer;` Pointer to FILE data structure associated with the file whose buffer is being flushed

EXAMPLE CALL `fflush(stdin);`

INCLUDES `#include <stdio.h>` For function declaration and definition of the FILE data type

DESCRIPTION The *fflush* function flushes the buffer associated with the file specified by the argument *file_pointer*. This pointer to the FILE data structure is the value returned by an earlier call to *fopen*. If the file is open for write operations, the

Input and Output Routines

flushing involves writing the contents of the buffer to the file. Otherwise, the buffer is cleared.

COMMON USES You can use *fflush* to ignore and discard data read from a file opened for buffered read operations. For a file opened for write or update operations, you can call *fflush* to ensure that the contents of the buffer are written without waiting for the buffer to get full. This may be necessary when launching a child process (see Chapter 11) to ensure that a file is up to date before the child process uses it.

RETURNS If the buffer is successfully flushed, *fflush* returns a zero. In case of an error, the return value is the constant EOF defined in *stdio.h*.

COMMENTS During buffered I/O from files, the actual read or write operation is performed only when the buffer associated with the file becomes full, the file is closed, or the program exits normally. In most cases, you never have to explicitly call *fflush*. But if you must ensure that when you say "write" you mean write to the file and not hold in a buffer, you can insert a call to *fflush* to accomplish this. This helps ensure data integrity at the cost of some loss in efficiency.

SEE ALSO fopen   To open a file for buffered I/O

 fclose   To close a single file

EXAMPLE Use *fopen* to open the file *autoexec.bat* for buffered read operations. Read the first 5 characters with calls to *fgetc* and save them in an array called *line*. Flush the buffer by using *fflush*. Continue reading with *fgetc* until you reach the end of the line or until you have read 80 characters. Now display the array—it should have the first 5 characters of the first line in your *autoexec.bat*, but the rest will be missing because we flushed the buffer after reading those characters.

```
#include <stdio.h>
main()
{

        int i;
        char line[81];
        FILE *infile;
/* Open the file. Note that we need two '\' */
        if ( (infile = fopen("c:\\autoexec.bat", "r"))
              == NULL)
         {
            printf("fopen failed.\n");
            exit(0);
         }
/* Now read characters using fgetc */
```

fflush

```
        for (i=0; i<80; i++)
        {
            line[i] = fgetc(infile);
            if (i==4) fflush(infile); /* Flush buffer */
            if(line[i] == '\n') break;
        }
        line[i+1] = '\0';        /* Mark end of string */
/* Now print the line and see how it looks */
        printf("The line is: %s", line);
    }
```

Stream I/O

fgetc

COMPATIBILITY	MSC 3	MSC 4	MSC 5	QC	TC	ANSI	UNIX V
	▲	▲	▲	▲	▲	▲	▲

PURPOSE Use *fgetc* to read a single character from a file opened for buffered input.

SYNTAX `int fgetc(FILE *file_pointer);`

`FILE *file_pointer;`   Pointer to FILE data structure associated with the file from which a character is to be read

EXAMPLE CALL `char_read = fgetc(infile);`

INCLUDES `#include <stdio.h>`   For function declaration and definition of FILE data type

DESCRIPTION The *fgetc* function reads a character from the current position of the file specified by the argument *file_pointer* and then increments this position. The character is returned as an integer. Note that *getc*, defined in *stdio.h* as a macro, also reads a character from a file.

RETURNS If there are no errors, *fgetc* returns the character read. Otherwise, it returns the constant EOF. Call *ferror* and *feof* to determine if there was an error or the file simply reached its end.

SEE ALSO getc   Macro to read a character from a file

fgetchar   Function to read a character from *stdin*

fputc, fputchar,
    putc, putchar   To write a character to a file

EXAMPLE Use *fgetc* to read a line (maximum length of 80 characters or to the newline

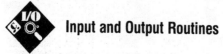

Input and Output Routines

character \n) from the file *autoexec.bat* and display the line on the screen using *printf*.

```
#include <stdio.h>
main()
{
        FILE *infile;
        char buffer[81];
        int i, c;
/* Open the file. */
        if ( (infile = fopen("c:\\autoexec.bat", "r"))
             == NULL)
        {
           printf("fopen failed.\n");
           exit(0);
        }
        c = fgetc(infile);
        for(i=0; (i<80) && (feof(infile) == 0) &&
                    (c != '\n'); i++)
        {
           buffer[i] = c;
           c = fgetc(infile);
        }
        buffer[i] = '\0';  /* make a C-style string */
        printf("First line of c:autoexec.bat: %s\n",
                buffer);
}
```

Stream I/O

fgetchar

COMPATIBILITY	MSC 3	MSC 4	MSC 5	QC	TC	ANSI	UNIX V
	▲	▲	▲	▲	▲		

PURPOSE Use *fgetchar* to read a single character from the file *stdin*, normally the keyboard.

SYNTAX `int fgetchar(void);`

EXAMPLE CALL `c = fgetchar();`

INCLUDES `#include <stdio.h>`   For function declaration

DESCRIPTION The *fgetchar* function reads a character from the file *stdin*. This function is equivalent to *fgetc(stdin)*.

fgetchar

RETURNS If there are no errors, *fgetchar* returns the character read. Otherwise, it returns the constant EOF.

SEE ALSO fgetc   General function to read a character from a file

fputc, fputchar,
   putc, putchar   To write a character to a file

EXAMPLE Use *fgetchar* to read a line (maximum length of 80 characters or up to the newline character \n) from the keyboard and display the line on the screen using *printf*. Even if you wanted to read only one character, because of the buffered input mechanism, the input does not end until you hit the carriage return key.

```
#include <stdio.h>
main()
{
        char buffer[81];
        int i, c;
        printf("Enter a line (end with a return):\n");
        c = fgetchar();
        for(i=0; (i<80) && (c != '\n'); i++)
        {
            buffer[i] = c;
            c = fgetchar();
        }
        buffer[i] = '\0';  /* make a C-style string */
        printf("You entered: %s\n", buffer);
}
```

Stream I/O
fgetpos

COMPATIBILITY	MSC 3	MSC 4	MSC 5	QC	TC	ANSI	UNIX V
			▲	▲	▲	▲	

PURPOSE Use *fgetpos* to get and save the current position where reading or writing occurs in a file opened for buffered I/O.

SYNTAX int fgetpos(FILE *file_pointer, fpos_t *current_pos);

FILE *file_pointer;   Pointer to FILE data structure associated with file whose current position is requested

fpos_t *current_pos;   Pointer to location where file's current position is returned

 **Input and Output Routines**

EXAMPLE CALL   `fgetpos(infile, &curpos);`

INCLUDES   `#include <stdio.h>`   For function declaration and definition of FILE and *fpos_t*
data types

DESCRIPTION   The *fgetpos* function gets the current read or write position of the file specified by the argument *file_pointer*, which is a pointer to the FILE data structure associated with a file that is already open. Next *fgetpos* saves this position
in a location specified by the pointer *current_pos*. This location is of type
fpos_t, which is defined in *stdio.h* to be a *long* integer.

COMMON USES   The *fgetpos* function is used with its counterpart *fsetpos* to remember a location in the file and return to it at a later time.

RETURNS   The *fgetpos* returns a zero when successful. In case of error, the return value
is nonzero and the global variable *errno* is set to the constant EINVAL if the
file_pointer is invalid or to EBADF if *file_pointer* does not point to a file or if
it points to an inaccessible file.

COMMENTS   The value of the current read/write position in the file is meaningful only to
the buffered input and output routines. Although you can access this value,
you should not interpret it in any way. Thus the retrieved file position should
be used only as an input argument to *fsetpos*. Use *ftell* if you want the position
expressed in terms of byte offsets from the beginning of the file.

SEE ALSO   `fsetpos`   To change the current position indicator of a file

EXAMPLE   Open a file using *fopen* for reading. Read 10 characters into a buffer and save
the current position by calling *fgetpos*. Now read in 10 more characters and
call *fsetpos* to return to the position saved earlier. Read in another 10 characters. Print the buffer out and note that the last 10 characters are the same as
the 10 read earlier.

```
#include <stdio.h>
void read10char(FILE *, char *);
main()
{
        fpos_t curpos;
        FILE *infile;
        char filename[81], buffer[40];
        printf("Enter name of a text file: ");
        gets(filename);
/* Open the file for reading */
        if ( (infile = fopen(filename, "r")) == NULL)
        {
            printf("fopen failed.\n");
            exit(0);
        }
```

fgetpos

```
                read10char(infile, buffer);
/* Save current position */
        if (fgetpos(infile, &curpos) != 0)
            perror("fgetpos failed!");
/* Read another 10 characters */
        read10char(infile, &buffer[11]);
/* Reset to previous position in file */
        if (fsetpos(infile, &curpos) != 0)
            perror("fsetpos failed!");
/* Read another 10 characters -- these should be same
 * as last 10.
 */
        read10char(infile, &buffer[21]);
        buffer[32] = '\0';   /* Convert to C string */
        printf("Buffer now has:\n%s", buffer);
}
/*-----------------------------------------------------*/
void read10char(FILE *infile, char *buffer)
{
        int i;
        for(i=0; i<10; i++)

        {
            if((*buffer = fgetc(infile)) == EOF)
            {
                printf("file ended. buffer so far has: \
%s\n", buffer);
                exit(0);
            }
            buffer++;
        }
        *buffer = '\n';
}
```

fgets

COMPATIBILITY	MSC 3	MSC 4	MSC 5	QC	TC	ANSI	UNIX V
	▲	▲	▲	▲	▲	▲	▲

PURPOSE Use the *fgets* function to read a line from a file opened for buffered input. The line is read until a newline (\n) character is encountered or until the number of characters reaches a specified maximum.

SYNTAX `char *fgets(char *string, int maxchar, FILE *file_pointer);`

 **Input and Output Routines**

`char *string;`	Pointer to buffer where characters are stored

`int maxchar;`	Maximum number of characters that can be stored

`FILE *file_pointer;`	Pointer to FILE data structure associated with file from which a line is read

EXAMPLE CALL   `fgets(buffer, 80, infile);`

INCLUDES   `#include <stdio.h>`   For function declaration and definition of FILE data type

DESCRIPTION   The *fgets* function reads a line from the file specified by the argument *file _pointer* and stores the characters in the buffer whose address is given in the argument *string*. Characters are read until a newline (\n) character is encountered or until the total number of characters read is one less than the number specified in *maxchar*. The buffer is converted to a C string by storing a null character (\0) after the last character stored in the buffer. Any newline characters are also included in the string.

Note that *gets* performs similarly but, unlike *fgets*, it reads up to the newline character and then replaces the newline character with a null character (thus the resulting string does not include a newline).

RETURNS   If there are no errors, *fgets* returns the argument *string*. Otherwise, it returns a NULL. You can call *ferror* and *feof* to determine whether the error is genuine or if it occurred because the file reached its end.

SEE ALSO   `gets`   To read a line from *stdin*

                `fputs`   To write a string to a file

                `puts`   To write a string to *stdout*

EXAMPLE   Use *fgets* to read lines (maximum length, 80 characters) from the file *autoexec.bat* and display the lines on the screen using *fputs* with the file *stdout*.

```
#include <stdio.h>
main()
{
        FILE *infile;
        char string[81];
/* Open the file. Because of the special significance
 * of '\' in C, we need two of them in the path name for
 * autoexec.bat
 */
        if ( (infile = fopen("c:\\autoexec.bat", "r"))
             == NULL)
        {
```

fgets

```
                    printf("fopen failed.\n");
                    exit(0);
            }
            printf("Contents of c:autoexec.bat:\n");
            while ( fgets(string, 80, infile) != NULL)
            {
                    fputs(string,stdout);
            }
    }
```

Stream I/O
fileno

COMPATIBILITY	MSC 3	MSC 4	MSC 5	QC	TC	ANSI	UNIX V
	▲	▲	▲	▲	▲		▲

PURPOSE Use the *fileno* macro, defined in *stdio.h*, to obtain the handle of the file currently associated with a specified file pointer. You must have the file handle in order to use some file I/O routines in the run-time library.

SYNTAX `int fileno(FILE *file_pointer);`

`FILE *file_pointer;`   Pointer to FILE data structure associated with the file whose handle is to be returned

EXAMPLE CALL `handle = fileno(file_pointer);`

INCLUDES `#include <stdio.h>`   For function declaration and definition of the FILE data type

DESCRIPTION The *fileno* macro returns an integer which constitutes the handle for the file specified by the argument *file_pointer*.

The FILE data structure associated with the file has a field that includes the handle for the file. A call to *fileno* returns this handle. Handles are necessary when performing lower-level, unbuffered I/O using calls to such routines as *read* or *write*.

RETURNS The integer value returned by *fileno* is the handle of the specified file. The return value is undefined if the argument *file_pointer* does not correspond to an open file.

SEE ALSO fopen   To open a file for buffered I/O

EXAMPLE Use *fileno* to get and display the handles for the five files, *stdin, stdout, stderr, stdaux,* and *stdprn,* which are already open in your program.

 **Input and Output Routines**

```
#include <stdio.h>
main()
{
    printf("Handle for stdin: %d\n", fileno(stdin));
    printf("Handle for stdout: %d\n", fileno(stdout));
    printf("Handle for stderr: %d\n", fileno(stderr));
    printf("Handle for stdaux: %d\n", fileno(stdaux));
    printf("Handle for stdprn: %d\n", fileno(stdprn));
}
```

Stream I/O
flushall

COMPATIBILITY	MSC 3	MSC 4	MSC 5	QC	TC	ANSI	UNIX V
	▲	▲	▲	▲	▲		

PURPOSE   Use the *flushall* function to flush all buffers associated with files opened for buffered I/O, including those that are opened as soon as your program begins executing: *stdin, stdout, stderr, stdaux,* and *stdprn.*

SYNTAX   `int flushall(void);`

EXAMPLE CALL   `flushall();`

INCLUDES   `#include <stdio.h>`   For function declaration

DESCRIPTION   The *flushall* function flushes all buffers associated with files opened for buffered I/O. This includes the five files already open when you start up your program: *stdin, stdout, stderr, stdaux,* and *stdprn.* If the file is open for write operations, the flushing involves writing the contents of the buffer to the file. Otherwise, the buffer is cleared.

Note that buffers are automatically flushed when they are full, when a file is closed, or when the program terminates normally.

RETURNS   The *flushall* function returns the number of buffers it has flushed, which should match the total number of files currently open for input and output.

SEE ALSO   `fflush`   To flush the buffer of a single file

`fclose`   To close a single file

EXAMPLE   Call *flushall* in a program and print the number of buffers that were flushed. The number should be 5, corresponding to the preopened files.

```
#include <stdio.h>
main()
```

```
{
        int files_open;
/* Flush all buffers */
        files_open = flushall();
/* Now print the total number of buffers flushed */
        printf("%d buffers flushed. So this many files \
are open now.\n", files_open);
}
```

Stream I/O

fopen

COMPATIBILITY	MSC 3	MSC 4	MSC 5	QC	TC	ANSI	UNIX V
	▲	▲	▲	▲	▲	▲	▲

PURPOSE Use *fopen* to open a file for buffered input and output operations.

SYNTAX `FILE *fopen(const char *filename, const char *access_mode);`

`const char *filename;`   Name of file to be opened including drive and directory specification

`const char *access_mode;`   Character string denoting whether file is being opened for reading or writing, or both

EXAMPLE CALL `input_file = fopen("data.in", "rb");`

INCLUDES `#include <stdio.h>`   For function declaration and definition of FILE data type

DESCRIPTION The *fopen* function opens the file specified in the argument *filename*. The type of operations you intend to perform on the file must be given in the argument *access_mode*. Table 15-7 explains the values that the *access_mode* string can take.

In addition to the basic access modes shown in Table 15-7, one of the characters from Table 15-8 can be appended to each of the strings in Table 15-7 to specify how the contents of the file are to be translated. Note that the character denoting the translation mode can come before or after the + in the strings above. For example, *w+b* is considered the same as *wb+* and means "create the file and open it for reading and writing in binary mode." If no translation mode is specified, the default mode is determined by the global variable *_fmode*, which is declared in the header file *stdio.h*. When a file is opened for appending with the *a* or *a+* access mode, existing data can never be destroyed because the *file pointer* is moved to the end of the file before writing occurs. This pointer keeps track of the current position where writing occurs.

When a file is opened for updating, using the *r+*, *w+*, or *a+* access

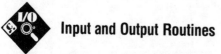 **Input and Output Routines**

modes, you must call one of the functions *fsetpos, fseek*, or *rewind* when switching between read and write operations. These calls serve to set the file pointer properly before the operation. You can also call *fsetpos* or *fseek* and set the file pointer to the current position.

COMMON USES The *fopen* function is used to open a file before performing buffered I/O operations on it. You must open a file with *fopen* before performing any read or write operations. You can, for example, use *fopen* to open the file *c:\autoexec.bat* and read its contents by calling *fgets*.

RETURNS If the file is opened successfully, *fopen* returns a pointer to the file. Actually, this is a pointer to a structure of type FILE, which is defined in the header file *stdio.h*. The actual structure is allocated elsewhere and you do not have to allocate it. In case of an error, *fopen* returns a NULL. See below for an example of checking for an error return from *fopen*.

COMMENTS A maximum of 20 files may be opened by a single process for buffered I/O in MS-DOS. Of these, 5 are already open when the program begins running: *stdin, stdout, stderr, stdprn*, and *stdaux*. This leaves 15 files that your program can simultaneously open with the function *fopen*.

SEE ALSO fclose   To close a file opened by *fopen*

open   To open a file using a handle (a lower-level routine)

setmode, fdopen,
freopen, fileno,
ferror, fcloseall   Other functions related to opening files

EXAMPLES Use *fopen* to open the file *autoexec.bat* for read operations only in the root directory of your current drive, say, drive C. Now read each line and display it on the screen. Use *fclose* to close the file before exiting.

```c
#include <stdio.h>
main()
{
        FILE *infile;
        unsigned char buffer[81];
/* Open the file. Note that we need two '\'  because
 * backslash denotes the beginning of a C escape
 * sequence.
 */
        if ( (infile = fopen("c:\\autoexec.bat", "r"))
            == NULL)
        {
            printf("fopen failed.\n");
            exit(0);
        }
```

fopen

```
        printf("Contents of c:autoexec.bat:\n");
        while ( fgets(buffer, 80, infile) != NULL)
        {
            printf(buffer);
        }
        fclose(infile); /* Close file before exiting */
}
```

Write a C program to save lines typed by the user. Prompt the user for a file name, then open the file for reading and appending in the translation mode (access mode is a+). Next, ask the user to enter lines that you will save in this file. Finally, rewind the file, read it, and display its contents.

```
#include <stdio.h>
char filename[81],      /* Name of file to open       */
     input[80] = "xx"; /* To hold user's input lines */
FILE *scriptfile;      /* File pointer to opened file */
main()
{
    printf("Enter name of file to save your input: ");
    gets(filename);
/* Open the file where we will save the user's input */
    if ((scriptfile = fopen(filename,"a+")) == NULL)
    {
        printf("Error opening file: %s\n", filename);
        exit(0);
    }
/* Accept input lines and save them in the file */
    printf("Enter lines. Hit 'q' to stop.\n");
    while(input[0] != 'q' || input[1] !='\0')
    {
        gets(input);                    /* Read a line  */
        fprintf(scriptfile, "%s\n",  /* Write to file */
                input);
    }
/* Now rewind file, read each line and display it */
    rewind(scriptfile);
    printf("==== Contents of script file ====\n");
    while(fgets(input, 80, scriptfile) != NULL)
    {
        printf(input);
    }
/* Now close the file and exit */
    fclose(scriptfile);
}
```

 Input and Output Routines

COMPATIBILITY	MSC 3	MSC 4	MSC 5	QC	TC	ANSI	UNIX V
	▲	▲	▲	▲	▲	▲	▲

PURPOSE Use the *fprintf* function to format and write character strings and values of C variables to a specified file opened for buffered output.

SYNTAX `int fprintf(FILE *file_pointer, const char *format_string,...);`

`FILE *file_pointer;`   Pointer to FILE data structure of the file to which the output goes

`const char *format_string;`   Character string that describes the format to be used

`...`   Variable number of arguments depending on the number of items being printed

EXAMPLE CALL `fprintf(resultfile, "The result is %f\n", result);`

INCLUDES `#include <stdio.h>`   For function declaration

DESCRIPTION Like *printf*, *fprintf* accepts a variable number of arguments and prints them out to the file specified in the argument *file_pointer* which must be open for buffered output operations. Although *printf* is more widely used and better known, *fprintf* is more general because it can write formatted output to any file, whereas *printf* can send output to *stdout* only. The values of the arguments are printed in the format specified by *format_string*, an array of characters with embedded formatting commands. The formatting commands begin with a percentage sign (%) and *fprintf* accepts the same formatting commands as *printf* does. By the way, use two percentage signs together to actually print a % to the file. The description of the formats is too long to display here; see Tables 15-9, 15-10, 15-11, and 15-12 in the reference pages on *printf* for more detail.

COMMON USES Although *fprint* can be used in every situation where *printf* is used, one of its common uses is to print error messages to the file *stderr*.

RETURNS The *fprintf* function returns the number of characters it has printed.

SEE ALSO `printf`   For printing to *stdout* and for detailed information on formats

`vfprintf, vprintf`   For formatted printing to a file using a pointer to a list of arguments

`sprintf, vsprintf`   For formatted printing to a string

EXAMPLE Ask the user for a file to open for writing. After opening the file with *fopen*, use *fprintf* to send output to the file. Later, use the DOS TYPE command to see how *fprintf* worked.

```
#include <stdio.h>
char    str[] = "Testing fprintf...";
char    c     = '\n';
int     i     = 100;
double  x     = 1.23456;
main()
{
    FILE *outfile;
    char filename[81];
    printf("Enter name of a file to open for WRITING:");
    gets(filename);
/* Open the file for reading */
    if ( (outfile = fopen(filename, "w")) == NULL)
    {
        printf("fopen failed.\n");
        exit(0);
    }
/* Write to this file ... */
    fprintf(outfile, "%s writing to file %s%c", str,
            filename, c);
    fprintf(outfile, "Integer: decimal = %d, \
octal = %o, hex = %X\n", i, i, i);
    fprintf(outfile, "Double: %f(in default f format)\n",
            x);
    fprintf(outfile, "        %.2f(in .2f format)\n",
            x);
    fprintf(outfile, "        %g(in default g format)\n",
            x);
/* Tell user to type file to see results */
    fprintf(stdout,
            "Use the command 'TYPE %s' to see results\n",
            filename);
}
```

Here is how the contents of the file should look:

```
Testing fprintf... writing to file junk1
Integer: decimal = 100, octal = 144, hex = 64
Double: 1.234560(in default f format)
        1.23(in .2f format)
        1.23456(in default g format)
```

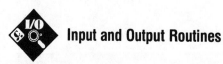

Input and Output Routines

fputc

COMPATIBILITY	MSC 3	MSC 4	MSC 5	QC	TC	ANSI	UNIX V
	▲	▲	▲	▲	▲	▲	▲

PURPOSE Use *fputc* to write a single character to a file opened for buffered output.

SYNTAX `int fputc(int c, FILE *file_pointer);`

`int c;` character to be written

`FILE *file_pointer;` Pointer to FILE data structure associated with file to which the character is to be written

EXAMPLE CALL `fputc('X', p_datafile);`

INCLUDES `#include <stdio.h>` For function declaration and definition of FILE data type

DESCRIPTION The *fputc* function writes a character given in the integer argument *c* to the file specified by the argument *file_pointer*. It writes to the current position of the file and increments this position after writing the character. Note that the *putc* macro, defined in *stdio.h*, also writes a character to a file.

RETURNS If there are no errors, *fputc* returns the character written. Otherwise, it returns the constant EOF. You should call *ferror* to determine whether there was an error or the integer argument *c* just happened to be equal to EOF.

SEE ALSO putc Macro to write a character to a file

fputchar Function to write a character to *stdout*

fgetc, fgetchar,
getc, getchar To read a character from a file

EXAMPLE Use *fputc* to write a line (maximum length of 80 characters or up to the null character \0) to *stdout*.

```
#include <stdio.h>
char buffer[81] = "Testing fputc on stdout...\n";
main()
{
    int i;
/* A for loop that uses fputc to print to stdout */
    for(i=0; (i<81) &&
        (fputc(buffer[i], stdout) != EOF);
        i++);
}
```

fputchar

COMPATIBILITY	MSC 3	MSC 4	MSC 5	QC	TC	ANSI	UNIX V
	▲	▲	▲	▲	▲		

PURPOSE Use *fputchar* to write a single character to the file *stdout*, which is connected to the display on program startup. The *fputchar* function is equivalent to using *fputc* with *stdout* as the argument.

SYNTAX `int fputchar(int c);`

`int c;` Character to be written to *stdout*

EXAMPLE CALL `fputchar('q');`

INCLUDES `#include <stdio.h>` For function declaration

DESCRIPTION The *fputchar* function writes a character to the file *stdout*. This function is equivalent to *fputc(stdout)*.

RETURNS If there are no errors, *fputchar* returns the character written. Otherwise, it returns the constant EOF.

SEE ALSO `fputc` General function to write a character to a file

`fgetc, fgetchar,`
`getc, getchar` To read a character from a file

EXAMPLE Use *fputchar* to write a line (maximum length of 80 characters or up to the null character \0) to *stdout*.

```
#include <stdio.h>
char buffer[81] = "Testing fputchar...\n";
main()
{
    int i;
/* A for loop that uses fputchar to print to stdout */
    for(i=0; (i<81) && (fputchar(buffer[i]) != EOF);
        i++);
}
```

 **Input and Output Routines**

fputs

COMPATIBILITY	MSC 3	MSC 4	MSC 5	QC	TC	ANSI	UNIX V
	▲	▲	▲	▲	▲	▲	▲

PURPOSE Use the *fputs* function to write a C string (an array of characters ending with a null character, \0) to a file opened for buffered output.

SYNTAX `int fputs(char *string, FILE *file_pointer);`

`char *string;`   Null-terminated character string to be output

`FILE *file_pointer;`   Pointer to FILE data structure associated with file to which string is output

EXAMPLE CALL `fputs("Sample Input Data", p_datafile);`

INCLUDES `#include <stdio.h>`   For function declaration and definition of FILE data type

DESCRIPTION The *fputs* function writes the C string given in the argument "string" to the file specified by the argument *file_pointer*, which is a pointer to the FILE data structure associated with a file that has been opened for write operations.

RETURNS In versions 5.0 and 5.1, the *fputs* function returns a zero if it completes its task successfully. Otherwise it returns a nonzero value. In earlier versions, *fputs* returns the last character printed when all goes well. In case of error, it returns the constant EOF.

SEE ALSO

fgets   To read in a line from a file

puts   To write a string to the display

gets   To read a line from the console

EXAMPLE Write a program using *fputs* to print a string to the display (which corresponds to the preopened file *stdout*).

```
#include <stdio.h>
char string[81] =
    "Using fputs with stdout is equivalent to puts\n";
main()
{
        fputs(string, stdout);
}
```

Stream I/O
fread

COMPATIBILITY	MSC 3	MSC 4	MSC 5	QC	TC	ANSI	UNIX V
	▲	▲	▲	▲	▲	▲	▲

PURPOSE Use the *fread* function to read a specified number of data items, each of a given size, from the current position in a file opened for buffered input. The current position is updated after the read.

SYNTAX
```
size_t fread(void *buffer, size_t size, size_t count,
                              FILE *file_pointer);
```

`void *buffer;` Pointer to memory where *fread* stores the bytes it reads

`size_t size;` Size in bytes of each data item

`size_t count;` Maximum number of items to be read

`FILE *file_pointer;` Pointer to FILE data structure associated with file from which data items are read

EXAMPLE CALL `numread = fread(buffer, sizeof(char), 80, infile);`

INCLUDES `#include <stdio.h>` For function declaration and definition of FILE and *size_t*

DESCRIPTION The *fread* function reads *count* data items, each of *size* bytes, starting at the current read position of the file specified by the argument *file_pointer*. After the read is complete, the current position is updated.

You must allocate storage for a buffer to hold the number of bytes that you expect to read. The address of this buffer, in the form of a pointer to a *void* data type, is given in the argument *buffer*. The data items read are saved in this buffer.

COMMON USES The common use of *fread* is to read binary data files. As an example, if you devise a scheme for storing images to a file, you would probably use *fwrite* to write the file and *fread* to read the images back.

RETURNS The *fread* function returns the number of items it successfully read. If the return value is less than you expected, you can call *ferror* and *feof* to determine if a read error has occurred or if end-of-file has been reached.

COMMENTS When *fread* is used on a file opened in the text mode, the CR-LF pairs are translated to single-line feeds.

SEE ALSO `fwrite` To write data items from a buffer to a file

`read` Same function as *fread*, but uses file number or handle

 **Input and Output Routines**

EXAMPLE Open a file using *fopen* for binary read operations (mode *rb*). Read 80 characters, and then display the buffer and the number of data items that *fread* says it read.

```
#include <stdio.h>
main()
{
    int numread;
    FILE *infile;
    char filename[80], buffer[80];
    printf("Enter name of a text file: ");
    gets(filename);
/* Open the file for reading */
    if ( (infile = fopen(filename, "rb")) == NULL)
    {
        printf("fopen failed.\n");
        exit(0);
    }
/* Read 80 characters and display the buffer */
    numread = fread((void *)buffer, sizeof(char), 80,
                    infile);
    printf("Read these %d characters:\n %s\n",
           numread, buffer);
}
```

Stream I/O
freopen

COMPATIBILITY	MSC 3	MSC 4	MSC 5	QC	TC	ANSI	UNIX V
	▲	▲	▲	▲	▲	▲	▲

PURPOSE Use *freopen* to close a file and open another file with the same file pointer. For example, you can use *freopen* to redirect I/O from the preopened file *stdout* to a file of your choice.

SYNTAX
```
FILE *freopen(const char *filename, const char *access_mode,
                                    FILE *file_pointer);
```

`const char *filename;` Name of file to be reopened, including drive and directory specification

`const char *access_mode;` Character string denoting whether file is being reopened for read/write

`FILE *file_pointer;` Pointer to FILE data structure associated with file being closed

freopen

EXAMPLE CALL ` freopen("output.txt", "w", stdout);`

INCLUDES `#include <stdio.h>`   For function declaration and definition of FILE data type

DESCRIPTION The *freopen* function closes the file specified by the argument *file_pointer*, a pointer to the FILE data structure associated with an open file. Next *freopen* opens a new file with the name specified in the argument *filename* and associates the old file pointer with this new file. Use the argument *access_mode* to indicate the type of operations you intend to perform on the file. Tables 15-6 and 15-7 explain the various values that the *access_mode* string can take.

COMMON USES The *freopen* function is often used to redirect input and output for the pre-opened files *stdin* and *stdout*.

RETURNS If all goes well, *freopen* returns a pointer to the newly opened file. This pointer is the same as the argument *file_pointer*. In case of error, a NULL is returned. See below for an example of checking for an error return from *freopen*.

SEE ALSO `fopen`   To open a file

`fclose`   To close a file opened by *fopen* or *freopen*

EXAMPLE Use *freopen* to redirect *stdout* to a file instead of the monitor. Prompt the user for the file name. Use *printf* to print a few lines that go to the file and do not appear on your screen. Exit and observe the contents of the file with the DOS TYPE ⟨filename⟩ command.

```
#include <stdio.h>
main()
{
    char filename[81];
    printf("Enter file name where output should go: ");
    gets(filename);
    printf("If all goes well, use TYPE %s to see \
result.\n", filename);
/* Redirect stdout to this file */
    if ( freopen(filename, "w", stdout) == NULL)
    {
        printf("freopen failed.\n");
        exit(0);
    }
/* Print some lines ... */
    printf("Redirecting stdout to the file %s\n",
            filename);
    printf("All output will be in this file.\n");
}
```

 Input and Output Routines

fscanf

COMPATIBILITY	MSC 3	MSC 4	MSC 5	QC	TC	ANSI	UNIX V
	▲	▲	▲	▲	▲	▲	▲

PURPOSE Use the *fscanf* function to read characters from a file that has been opened for buffered I/O and to convert the strings to values of C variables according to specified formats.

SYNTAX `int fscanf(FILE *file_pointer, const char *format_string,...);`

`FILE *file_pointer;` Pointer to the FILE data structure of file from which reading occurs

`const char *format_string;` Character string that describes the format to be used

`...` Variable number of arguments representing addresses of variables whose values are being read

EXAMPLE CALL `fscanf(infile, "Date: %d/%d/%d", &month, &day, &year);`

INCLUDES `#include <stdio.h>` For function declaration and definition of the FILE data structure

DESCRIPTION The *fscanf* function reads a stream of characters from the file specified by the argument *file_pointer*, converts the characters to values according to format specifications embedded in the argument *format_string*, and stores the values into C variables whose addresses are provided in the variable length argument list.

Each optional argument indicating a value to be read has a corresponding format specification in the argument *format_string*. The format specification begins with a percentage sign and the formatting commands are identical to the ones used with the function *scanf*. A list of the formats is provided in the reference pages on *scanf*.

RETURNS The *fscanf* function returns the number of input items that were successfully read, converted, and saved in variables. If an end-of-file is encountered during the read, the return value will be equal to the constant EOF (defined in *stdio.h*).

COMMENTS The *fscanf* function is used more generally than *scanf*. You can read from any file using *fscanf* and the functions of *scanf* can be duplicated by using the file *stdin* as an argument to *fscanf*. It is customary in C reference books, including ours, however, to describe the format specifications in detail under *scanf*.

fscanf

SEE ALSO   scanf   Formatted reading from *stdin*

sscanf   For formatted reading from a string

cscanf   Formatted, unbuffered input from console

EXAMPLE   The %s format reads strings separated by blanks, tabs, or newline characters. Open the file *autoexec.bat* for buffered I/O and then use *fscanf* to read and display the first 10 tokens, character sequences separated by blanks and newlines.

```c
#include <stdio.h>
main()
{
    int i;
    FILE *infile;
    char token[80];
/* Open the file. Note that we need two '\' */
    if ( (infile = fopen("c:\\autoexec.bat", "r"))
            == NULL)
    {
        perror("fopen failed");
        exit(1);
    }
    printf("First 10 blank separated strings in \
c:\\autoexec.bat:\n");
    for(i=0; i<10; i++)
    {
        if( fscanf(infile, " %s", token) == EOF)
        {
            printf("File ended!\n");
            break;
        }
        else
        {
            printf("Token %d = \"%s\"\n", i, token);
        }
    }
}
```

Input and Output Routines

fseek

COMPATIBILITY	MSC 3	MSC 4	MSC 5	QC	TC	ANSI	UNIX V
	▲	▲	▲	▲	▲	▲	▲

PURPOSE Use the *fseek* function to move to a new position in a file opened for buffered I/O.

SYNTAX
```
int fseek(FILE *file_pointer, long offset, int origin);
```

`FILE *file_pointer;`   Pointer to FILE data structure associated with file whose current position is to be set

`long offset;`   Offset of new position (in bytes) from origin

`int origin;`   Constant indicating the position from which to offset

EXAMPLE CALL
```
fseek(infile, 0L, SEEK_SET); /* Go to the beginning */
```

INCLUDES
```
#include <stdio.h>
```
    For function declaration and definition of FILE

DESCRIPTION The *fseek* function sets the current read or write position of the file specified by the argument *file_pointer* to a new value indicated by the arguments "offset" and "origin." The "offset" is a long integer indicating how far away the new position is from a specific location given in "origin." One of the constants, defined in *stdio.h* and shown in the table below, *must* be the "origin."

Origin	Interpretation
SEEK_SET	Beginning of file
SEEK_CUR	Current position in the file
SEEK_END	End of file

COMMON USES The *fseek* function is commonly used when reading data from a file in the binary read mode. For example, an application may create a data file with a specific format, say, a header of 512 bytes followed by actual data. When reading from such a file you can use *fseek* to skip over the header and move around in the file to retrieve specific pieces of information with *fread*.

RETURNS When successful, *fseek* returns a zero. In case of error, for example when attempting to set a position before the beginning of the file, *fseek* returns a nonzero value. If the file is associated with a device where setting the current position does not make sense (such as a printer), the return value is meaningless.

fseek

COMMENTS   You should be aware of a few nuances of *fseek*.

▶ In text mode (see the tutorial section), you may not be able to give a proper value for offset because of the translation of CR-LF combinations. So only these arguments are guaranteed to work when using *fseek* in the text mode: (1) an offset of OL from any of the origins, and (2) an offset returned by *ftell* with an origin of SEEK_SET.

▶ In append mode, the current position is determined solely by the last I/O operation. Even if you move around in the file, the writing always takes place at the end of the file opened for appending.

SEE ALSO   ftell   To get the offset of the current position in number of bytes from the beginning

lseek   Same function as *fseek*, but works with file handles

EXAMPLE   Open a file using *fopen* for reading. Read and display a line. Now call *fseek* to go back to the beginning and read a line again. The two lines should be identical.

```
#include <stdio.h>
main()
{
    FILE *infile;
    char filename[80], buffer[81];
    printf("Enter name of a text file: ");
    gets(filename);
/* Open the file for reading */
    if ( (infile = fopen(filename, "r")) == NULL)
    {
        printf("fopen failed.\n");
        exit(0);
    }
/* Read and display a line */
    fgets(buffer, 80, infile);
    printf("Line read (before fseek): %s", buffer);
/* Move to beginning using fseek and read a line again */
    if (fseek(infile, OL, SEEK_SET) != 0)
    {
        perror("fseek failed!");
    }
    else
    {
        fgets(buffer, 80, infile);
        printf("Line read (after fseek) : %s", buffer);
    }
}
```

 Input and Output Routines

Stream I/O
fsetpos

COMPATIBILITY	MSC 3	MSC 4	MSC 5	QC	TC	ANSI	UNIX V
			▲	▲	▲	▲	

PURPOSE Use *fsetpos* to set the position where reading or writing can take place in a file opened for buffered I/O.

SYNTAX `int fsetpos(FILE *file_pointer, const fpos_t *current_pos);`

`FILE *file_pointer;` Pointer to FILE data structure associated with file whose current position is to be set

`const fpos_t *current_pos;` Pointer to location containing new value of file position

EXAMPLE CALL `fgetpos(infile, &curpos);`

INCLUDES `#include <stdio.h>` For function declaration and definition of FILE and *fpos_t* data types

DESCRIPTION The *fsetpos* function sets to a new value the current read or write position of the file specified by the argument *file_pointer*. The new value is given in a location whose address is in the argument *current_pos*. The data type of this variable is *fpos_t*, which is defined in the include file *stdio.h* to be a *long*.

COMMON USES The *fsetpos* function resets the file position to a value obtained by an earlier call to its counterpart *fgetpos*.

RETURNS If successful, *fsetpos* returns a zero. Otherwise, the return value will be non-zero, and the global variable *errno* is set to the constant EINVAL if the value of the argument *file_pointer* is invalid or to EBADF if the file is not accessible or if the object to which *file_pointer* points is not a file.

COMMENTS Since the value of the current read/write position in the file is meaningful only to the buffered input and output routines, you should always use *fsetpos* with a position obtained by an earlier call to *fgetpos*. You can use *fseek* if you want to set the position to a value expressed in terms of byte offsets from specific locations in the file.

SEE ALSO `fgetpos` To retrieve the current position indicator of a file

EXAMPLE Open a file using *fopen* for reading. Call *fgetpos* and remember the current position. Read 10 characters into a buffer and return to the saved position by calling *fsetpos*. Now read in 10 more characters. Display the buffer and note that the first 10 characters are the same as the last 10.

```
          #include <stdio.h>
          main()
          {
              fpos_t curpos;
              FILE *infile;
              char filename[81], buffer1[20], buffer2[20];
              printf("Enter name of a text file: ");
              gets(filename);
     /* Open the file for reading */
              if ( (infile = fopen(filename, "r")) == NULL)
              {
                  printf("fopen failed.\n");
                  exit(0);
              }
     /* Save current position */
              if (fgetpos(infile, &curpos) != 0)
                                   perror("fgetpos failed!");
     /* Read 10 characters */
              if (fgets(buffer1, 10, infile) == NULL)
                                   perror("fgets failed");
     /* Reset to previous position in file */
              if (fsetpos(infile, &curpos) != 0)
                                   perror("fsetpos failed!");
     /* Read another 10 characters --
      * these should be same as last 10.
      */
              if (fgets(buffer2, 10, infile) == NULL)
                                     perror("fgets failed");
              printf("We read:\n");
              puts(buffer1);
              puts(buffer2);
          }
```

Stream I/O
ftell

	MSC 3	MSC 4	MSC 5	QC	TC	ANSI	UNIX V
COMPATIBILITY	▲	▲	▲	▲	▲	▲	▲

PURPOSE Use *ftell* to obtain the current position in a file opened for buffered I/O. The position is expressed as a byte offset from the beginning of the file.

SYNTAX `long ftell(FILE *file_pointer);`

`FILE *file_pointer;`   Pointer to FILE data structure associated with file whose current position is to be returned

Input and Output Routines

EXAMPLE CALL   `curpos = ftell(infile));`

INCLUDES   `#include <stdio.h>`   For function declaration and definition of FILE

DESCRIPTION   The *ftell* function returns the current read or write position of the file specified by the argument *file_pointer*.

RETURNS   When successful, *ftell* returns a long integer containing the number of bytes the current position is offset from the beginning of the file. In case of error, *ftell* returns −1L. Also, the global variable *errno* is set to EINVAL if the *file_pointer* argument is invalid or to EBADF if the *file_pointer* does not point to a valid open file. The return value is undefined if the *file_pointer* is associated with a device (such as the keyboard) it would not make any sense to move to a new position in the file.

COMMENTS   When *ftell* is used on a file opened in the text mode, the physical byte offset in the file may not be the same as the value reported by *ftell*. This is due to the translation of the CR-LF pairs in this mode. Everything works correctly, however, if you use *fseek* in combination with *ftell* to return to a specific position in a file opened in text mode.

SEE ALSO   fseek   To set the the current position in a file

   tell   Same function as *ftell*, but uses file handles

EXAMPLE   Use *fopen* to open a file for binary read operations (mode *rb*). Read 80 characters and display the buffer. Now call *ftell* and print the value it returns.

```
#include <stdio.h>
main()
{
    long curpos;
    FILE *infile;
    char filename[80], buffer[80];
    printf("Enter name of a text file: ");
    gets(filename);
/* Open the file for reading */
    if ( (infile = fopen(filename, "rb")) == NULL)
    {
        printf("fopen failed.");
        exit(0);
    }
/* Read 80 characters and display the buffer */
    fread(buffer, sizeof(char), 80, infile);
    printf("Read these 80 characters:\n %s\n", buffer);
/* Get and display current position */
    if ((curpos = ftell(infile)) == -1L)
    {
```

ftell

```
        perror("ftell failed!");
    }
    else
    {
        printf("Currently at %ld bytes from beginning \
of file\n", curpos);
    }
}
```

Stream I/O

fwrite

COMPATIBILITY	MSC 3	MSC 4	MSC 5	QC	TC	ANSI	UNIX V
	▲	▲	▲	▲	▲	▲	▲

PURPOSE Use the *fwrite* function to write a specified number of data items, each of a given size, from a buffer to the current position in a file opened for buffered output. The current position is updated after the write.

SYNTAX
```
size_t fwrite(const void *buffer, size_t size, size_t count,
                              FILE *file_pointer);
```

const void *buffer;   Pointer to buffer in memory from which *fwrite* will get the bytes it writes

size_t size;   Size in bytes of each data item

size_t count;   Maximum number of items to be written

FILE *file_pointer;   Pointer to FILE data structure associated with file to which the data items are to be written

EXAMPLE CALL `numwrite = fwrite(buffer, sizeof(char), 80, outfile);`

INCLUDES `#include <stdio.h>`   For function declaration and definition of FILE and *size_t*

DESCRIPTION The *fwrite* function writes *count* data items, each of *size* bytes, to the file specified by the argument *file_pointer*, starting at the current position. After the write operation is complete, the current position is updated. The data to be written is in the buffer whose address is passed to *fwrite* in the argument *buffer*.

COMMON USES The most common use of *fwrite* is to write binary data files. For example, if you want to save the current status of your application, you can save the values of all the key variables into a file using *fwrite*. Later, you can read these back with the function *fread*.

 Input and Output Routines

RETURNS The *fwrite* function returns the number of items it actually wrote. If that value is less than you expected, an error may have occurred.

COMMENTS If *fwrite* is used on a file opened in the text mode, each carriage return is replaced by a CR-LF pair.

SEE ALSO

fread To read data items from a file to a buffer

write Same function as *fwrite*, but uses file number, or handle

EXAMPLE Open a file using *fopen* for binary write operations (mode *wb*). Write 80 characters and display the number of data items that *fwrite* says it wrote. Type out the file to verify that the write worked.

```
#include <stdio.h>
char buffer[80] = "Testing fwrite\n\
This is the second line.\n";
main()
{
    int numwrite;
    FILE *infile;
    char filename[80];
    printf("Enter name of a file to write to: ");
    gets(filename);
/* Open the file for writing */
    if ( (infile = fopen(filename, "wb")) == NULL)
    {
        printf("fopen failed.\n");
        exit(0);
    }
/* write 80 characters and display the buffer */
    numwrite = fwrite((void *)buffer, sizeof(char), 80,
                        infile);
    printf("%d characters written to file %s\n",
        numwrite, filename);
    printf("Use 'TYPE %s' to see if it worked\n",
            filename);
}
```

fwrite

Stream I/O

getc

COMPATIBILITY

COMPATIBILITY	MSC 3	MSC 4	MSC 5	QC	TC	ANSI	UNIX V
	▲	▲	▲	▲	▲	▲	▲

PURPOSE Use the *getc* macro to read a single character from a file opened for buffered input.

SYNTAX `int getc(FILE *file_pointer);`

`FILE *file_pointer;`   Pointer to file from which a character is to read

EXAMPLE CALL `in_char = getc(p_txtfile);`

INCLUDES `#include <stdio.h>`   For function declaration definition of FILE data structure

DESCRIPTION The *getc* macro reads a character from the file specified by the argument *file _pointer*. The character is read from the current position in the file, and the current position then is advanced to the next character. The *file_pointer* must be a pointer returned earlier by an *fopen* or a *freopen* function call. Note that *fgetc* performs the same as *getc*, but *fgetc* is implemented as a function.

RETURNS The *getc* macro returns the character read as an integer value. A return value of EOF indicates an error. In that case, call the *ferror* and *feof* functions to determine if there was an error or if the file ended.

SEE ALSO `getchar`   Macro to read a character from *stdin*

`fgetc`   Function to read a character from a file

`fputc, fputchar,`
`putc, putchar`   To write a character to a file

EXAMPLE Use *getc* to read a line (maximum length of 80 characters or up to the newline character) from the file *config.sys* and display the line on the screen using *printf*.

```
#include <stdio.h>
main()
{
    FILE *infile;
    char buffer[81];
    int i, c;
/* Open the file -- assuming its at the root directory
 * of drive C:
 */
```

 Input and Output Routines

```
if ( (infile = fopen("c:\\config.sys", "r"))
     == NULL)
{
    printf("fopen failed.\n");
    exit(0);
}
c = getc(infile);
for(i=0; (i<80) && (feof(infile) == 0) &&
            (c != '\n'); i++)
{
    buffer[i] = c;
    c = getc(infile);
}
buffer[i] = '\0';  /* to make a C-style string */
printf("First line of c:config.sys: %s\n",
        buffer);
}
```

Stream I/O

getchar

COMPATIBILITY	MSC 3	MSC 4	MSC 5	QC	TC	ANSI	UNIX V
	▲	▲	▲	▲	▲	▲	▲

PURPOSE Use the *getchar* macro to read a single character from the preopened file *stdin*, which is normally connected to your keyboard input.

SYNTAX `int getchar(void);`

EXAMPLE CALL `c = getchar();`

INCLUDES `#include <stdio.h>`   For function declaration

DESCRIPTION The *getchar* macro reads a character from *stdin* and is equivalent to the use *getc(stdin)*. Note that *getchar* is the macro equivalent of the *fgetchar* function.

RETURNS The *getchar* macro returns the character read from *stdin* as an integer value. In case of an error, the return value is equal to the constant EOF (defined in *stdio.h*).

COMMENTS You cannot use *getchar* to read a single character from the console because a carriage return must be entered to complete a single buffered read from the keyboard. Use *getch* or *getche* for unbuffered input from the keyboard.

SEE ALSO `getc`   Macro to read a character from a file

getchar

fgetc, fgetchar   To read a character from a file

fputc, fputchar,
putc, putchar   To write a character to a file

EXAMPLE   Use *getchar* to read a line (maximum 80 characters) from the standard input. Call *printf* to display the line.

```
#include <stdio.h>
main()
{
    int i, c;
    char buffer[81];
    printf("Enter a line (end with a return):\n");
    c = getchar();
    for(i=0; (i<80) && (c != '\n'); i++)
    {
        buffer[i] = c;
        c = getchar();
    }
    buffer[i] = '\0';  /* to make a C-style string */
    printf("You entered: %s\n", buffer);
}
```

Stream I/O

gets

COMPATIBILITY	MSC 3	MSC 4	MSC 5	QC	TC	ANSI	UNIX V
	▲	▲	▲	▲	▲	▲	▲

PURPOSE   Use *gets* to read a line from the standard input file *stdin*, by default, the keyboard.

SYNTAX   char *gets(char *buffer);

char *buffer;   Buffer where string will be stored

EXAMPLE CALL   gets(command_line);

INCLUDES   #include <stdio.h>   For function declaration

DESCRIPTION   Until it encounters a newline character, the *gets* function reads and stores characters in the *buffer* from the standard input file *stdin*. When it does, it replaces the newline character with a null character and creates a C string. You must allocate room for the buffer in which the characters will be stored.

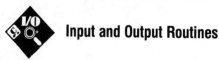 **Input and Output Routines**

Note that while *fgets* performs like *gets*, unlike *gets*, it retains the newline character in the final string.

RETURNS If there is no error, *gets* returns its argument. Otherwise, it returns a NULL. Call *ferror* and *feof* to determine whether the error is a read error or if it occurred because the file reached its end.

SEE ALSO

fgets	To read a line from a file
fputs	To write a string to a file
puts	To write a string to the display

EXAMPLE Use *gets* to read a line to the standard input. Call *printf* to display the line.

```c
#include <stdio.h>
main()
{
    char string[81];
    printf("Enter a line: ");
    gets(string);
    printf("You entered: %s\n", string);
}
```

Stream I/O
getw

COMPATIBILITY	MSC 3	MSC 4	MSC 5	QC	TC	ANSI	UNIX V
	▲	▲	▲	▲	▲		▲

PURPOSE Use *getw* to read a word (two bytes) from a file that has been opened for buffered binary read operations.

SYNTAX `int getw(FILE *file_pointer);`

`FILE *file_pointer;` Pointer to FILE data structure associated with file from which a word is read

EXAMPLE CALL `word = getw(infile);`

INCLUDES `#include <stdio.h>` For function declaration and definition of FILE

DESCRIPTION The *getw* function reads a word from the current position of the file specified by the argument *file_pointer*. The current position is incremented by the size of an *int* (2 bytes).

getw

RETURNS   If successful, *getw* returns the integer value it read. Otherwise, the return value is the constant EOF (defined in *stdio.h*). Since EOF is also a legitimate integer value, you should call *feof* and *ferror* to determine if the end-of-file was reached or if an error occurred.

COMMENTS   The *getw* function is provided only for compatibility with previous Microsoft C libraries. Do not use this function in new programs because the differences in size of words and arrangement of bytes (which one is most significant and which one is least significant) among microprocessors may cause problems when you move your program from one computer to another.

SEE ALSO   putw   To write a word into a file

EXAMPLE   Use *fopen* to open a file for reading in the binary mode. Use *getw* to read the first word and print its value in hexadecimal. To get a feeling for byte ordering, give the name of a text file when running the program. Consult the ASCII code table to see which characters the hexadecimal value printed by the program represents. Use DOS TYPE to print the file out and compare the first two characters with the printed value.

```
#include <stdio.h>
main()
{
    int word1;
    FILE *infile;
    char filename[81];
    printf("Enter name of a file to read from: ");
    gets(filename);
/* Open the file for reading */
    if ( (infile = fopen(filename, "rb")) == NULL)
    {
        printf("fopen failed.\n");
            exit(0);
    }
/* Get first word from file */
    if( (word1 = getw(infile)) == EOF)
    {
/* Check if there was a real error */
        if(feof(infile) != 0)
        {
            printf("File: %s at EOF\n", filename);
            exit(0);
        }
        if(ferror(infile) != 0)
        {
            printf("File: %s Read error\n", filename);
            exit(0);
        }
```

Input and Output Routines

```
            }
/* Print out the first word in hexadecimal */
        printf("The first word in file %s is: %X\n",
                filename, word1);

        printf("Use 'TYPE %s' to confirm this.\n", filename);
        }
```

printf

COMPATIBILITY	MSC 3	MSC 4	MSC 5	QC	TC	ANSI	UNIX V
	▲	▲	▲	▲	▲	▲	▲

PURPOSE Use *printf* to write character strings and values of C variables, formatted in a specified manner, to the standard output file *stdout* (normally the screen).

SYNTAX `int printf(const char *format_string,...);`

`const char *format_string;`   Character string that describes the format to be used

`...`   Variable number of arguments depending on the number of items being printed

EXAMPLE CALL `printf("The product of %d and %d is %d\n", x, y, x*y);`

INCLUDES `#include <stdio.h>`   For function declaration

DESCRIPTION The *printf* function accepts a variable number of arguments and prints them out to the standard output file *stdout*. The value of each argument is formatted according to the codes embedded in the format specification *format _string*. The first argument must be present in a call to *printf*. Calling *printf* is equivalent to using *fprintf* with the file *stdin*.

If the *format_string* does not contain a % character (except for the pair % %, which appears as a single % in the output), no argument is expected and the *format_string* is written out to *stdout*. For example,

`printf("Hello there!\n");`

prints "Hello there!" on the screen and skips to the next line because of the newline (\n) in the string. In fact, the *format_string* may contain commonly accepted special characters with a "backslash" as prefix, such as \n (newline), \t (tab), \a (alert or bell), or an ASCII character in octal notation (such as \004, which prints as a diamond in the IBM PC). You can use these characters to align the printed values properly. For example, *printf("Name\t\tPhone Number\n");* will print "Name" and "Phone Number" separated by two tabs.

To print the values of C variables, a format specification must be embedded in the *format_string* for each variable listed in the argument list to *printf*. For most routine printing chores, you can use the formatting commands in their simplest form:

```
int    ivalue = 100;
double dvalue = 95.5;
char   name = "Microsoft C";
:
printf("Integer = %d, Double = %f, String = %s\n", ivalue,
           dvalue, name);
```

Here we are printing out the values of an *int*, a *double*, and a character string. The formatting command for each variable consists of a percent sign, followed by a single letter denoting the type of variable being printed.

When you need fine control over the appearance of the printed values, *printf* provides it in the form of optional characters between the % and the character denoting the type of C variable being printed. The complete format specification accepted by the *printf* function in Microsoft C 5.1 has the following form:

Print Format Specification in Microsoft C

%[Flags][Width].[Precision][Addressing_mode][Size][Type]

Table 15-9 summarizes the purpose of each field in the format specification. Additional details for each field are given in Tables 15-10, 15-11, and 15-12.

Table 15-9. *Fields in a Format Specification for* printf

Field	Explanation
Flags (Optional)	One or more of the −, +, # characters or a blank space specifies justification, and the appearance of plus/minus signs and the decimal point in the values printed (see Table 15-11).
Width (Optional)	A number that indicates how many characters, at a minimum, must be used to print the value (see Table 15-12).
Precision (Optional)	A number that specifies how many characters, at maximum, can be used to print the value. When printing integer variables, this is the minimum number of digits used (see Table 15-12).
Addressing_mode (Optional)	This field is specific to Microsoft C 5.0 and 5.1. F (for "far") or N (for "near") can be used to override the default addressing mode of the memory model. Use this field only when the variable being passed to *printf* is a pointer (for example, when printing a string or the value of a pointer). As an example, use F in this field when printing a far string in the small memory model.

 Input and Output Routines

Table 15-9. *(cont.)*

Field	Explanation
Size (Optional)	A character that modifies the *Type* field which comes next. One of the characters h, l, or L appears in this field to differentiate between short and long integers and between float and double. Shown below is a summary of this field:

Prefix	When to Use
h	Use when printing integers using *Type* d, i, o, x, or X to indicate that the argument is a short integer. Also, use with *Type* u to indicate that the variable being printed is an unsigned short integer.
l	Use when printing integers or unsigned integers with a *Type* field of d, i, o, x, X, or u to specify that the variable to be printed is a long integer. Also use with floating-point variables (when the *Type* field is e, E, g, or G) to specify a double, rather than a float.
L	Use when the floating-point variable being printed is a long double and the *Type* specifier is one of e, E, f, g, or G.

Field	Explanation
Type (Required)	A letter that indicates the type of variable being printed. Table 15-10 lists the characters and their meanings.

The most important among these fields is the *Type* field which tells *printf* the type of C variable it has to convert to characters and print. Table 15-10 lists the characters that can appear in this field and the kind of C variable each signifies.

Table 15-10. Type *Field in Format Specification for* printf

Type	Type in C	Resulting Output Format
c	char	Single character. *printf("%c", 'Z');* prints a *Z*.
d	int	Signed decimal integer as a sequence of digits with or without a sign depending on the flags used. *printf("%d", 95);"* prints *95*.
e	double or float	Signed value in the scientific format. *double x =* -123.4567 printf("%e", x); prints $-1.234567e+002$.
E	double or float	Signed value in the scientific format, the above example prints $-1.234567E+002$ if the %E format is used.
f	double or float	Signed value in the format, (sign)(digits).(digits), the example for *Type* e will print -123.456700 if the %f format is used. The number of digits before the decimal point depends on the magnitude of the variable, and the number of digits that comes after the decimal point depends on the *Precision* field in the format specification. The default precision is 6. Thus a %f format alone always produces 6 digits after the decimal point, but a %.3f prints the value -123.457 which is -123.4567 rounded off to three decimal places.
g	double or float	Signed value printed using either the e or f format. The format that

printf

Table 15-10. *(cont.)*

Type	Type in C	Resulting Output Format
		generates the most compact output, for the given *Precision* and value, is selected. The e format is used only when the exponent is less than −4 or when it is greater than the value of the *Precision* field. Printing the value −123.4567 using a %g format results in −123.457 because the g format rounds off the number.
G	double or float	Signed value printed using the g format, with the letter G in place of e when exponents are printed.
i	int	Signed decimal integer as a sequence of digits with or without a sign depending on the *Flags* field. For example, *printf("%d %+d", x, x);* prints as *123 +123* when the *int* variable *x* has the value 123.
n	Pointer to int	This is not really a printing format. The argument corresponding to this format is a pointer to an integer. Before returning, the *printf* function stores in this integer the total number of characters it has printed to the output file or to the file's buffer. The EXAMPLES section illustrates the use of the n format.
o	unsigned	Octal digits without any sign.
p	far pointer to void	The address is printed in the form *SSSS:0000* where *SSSS* denotes the segment address and *0000* is the offset. In small and medium memory models, the argument should be cast as (void far *). If the *Flag* character N is used, as in %Np, only the offset of the address is printed. This format is only available in Microsoft C versions 4.0 and above under MS-DOS.
u	unsigned	Unsigned decimal integer as a sequence of digits.
x	unsigned	Hexadecimal digits using lowercase letters, abcdef.
X	unsigned	Hexadecimal digits using uppercase letters, ABCDEF.

Now we'll examine the rest of the components of the format specification and tabulate the choices. First comes the *Flags* field. One or more of the characters shown in Table 15-11 can appear in the *Flags* field. The Default column in Table 15-11 shows what happens when you do not include this optional field in the format specification.

The *Width* field, if present, should be a non-negative decimal number indicating the minimum number of characters output when printing the value to which the format specification applies. If the value being printed does not occupy the entire *Width*, blanks are added to the left or to the right depending on the justification indicated by the *Flags* field. When the *Width* is prefixed with a zero, all numbers being output are padded with zeroes instead of blanks. Note that specifying a *Width* does not imply that the value being printed will be truncated; this is determined by the *Precision* field.

An asterisk in the *Width* field indicates that an integer variable appearing in the argument list contains the value of width to be used for this format. This integer variable has to precede the actual variable to be printed. This is useful because you can compute the width at run-time and generate appropriately tabulated results.

The *Precision* field is separated from the *Width* field by a decimal point

Input and Output Routines

that is present only when *Precision* is explicitly specified. This field must be a non-negative decimal number that, as shown in Table 15-12, is interpreted by *printf* differently for each type of variable. The Default column in Table 15-12 indicates what *printf* does when *Precision* is not specified.

Table 15-11. Flags *Field in Format Specification for* print

Flag	Meaning	Default
–	Left justify output value within a field wide enough to hold the specified maximum number of characters that can be used for this value.	Right justification.
+	If the output value is a numerical one, print a + or a – according to the sign of the value.	A negative sign is printed for negative numerical values.
blank	Positive numerical values are prefixed with blank spaces. This flag is ignored if the + flag also appears.	No blanks are printed.
#	When used in printing variables of type o, x, or X (i.e., octal or hexadecimal), nonzero output values are prefixed with 0, 0x, or 0X, respectively.	No special prefix appears.
	When the *Type* field in the format specification is e, E, or f, this flag forces the printing of a decimal point.	Decimal point appears only when digits follow it.
	For a g or a G in the *Type* field, the # flag prints a decimal point and all trailing zeroes.	Trailing zeroes are truncated and decimal point appears only when digits follow.

Table 15-12. *Interpretation of* Precision *for* Type *Fields*

Type	Meaning	Default
c	*Precision* is ignored.	A single character is printed.
d u i o x X	The *Precision* specifies the minimum number of digits to be printed. When the value occupies fewer characters than the *Precision*, the output is padded on the left with zeroes. The value is always expressed fully, even if it requires more characters than the *Precision*, *printf* will not truncate it.	If *Precision* is not specified, or if it is zero or just a decimal point without a number after it, a value of 1 is used for the *Precision*.
e E	The *Precision* tells *printf* the number of digits it should print after the decimal point.	*Precision* is 6. If the decimal point appears with 0 or no number after it, the decimal point is not printed.

printf

Table 15-12. *(cont.)*

Type	Meaning	Default
f	*Precision* specifies the number of digits to be printed after the decimal point. If a decimal point is printed, at least one digit appears before it.	Default is 6. When *Precision* is explicitly given as 0, no decimal point is printed.
g G	The *Precision* specifies the maximum number of significant digits to be printed.	Default is to print all significant digits.
s	The *Precision* indicates the maximum number of characters to be printed. In this case, *printf* truncates the string and prints only up to *Precision* characters.	The character string is printed until a null character is encountered.

COMMON USES The *printf* function is one of the most commonly used functions in any C run-time library. It is rare that anyone uses all the possible fields in the format specifications, but when your application needs them the choices are available.

RETURNS The *printf* function returns the number of characters it has printed.

COMMENTS Use two percentage signs when you need to print a percentage sign. In fact, if *printf* finds a character after the % character, it simply prints the character.

Note that several features of *printf* in Microsoft C library are nonstandard extensions. In particular, should you want your application program to be portable across multiple systems, avoid the N and F addressing mode modifiers and the p and n formats for printing pointers.

SEE ALSO

vprintf   Another routine for printing to *stdout*

fprintf, vfprintf   For formatted printing to a file

sprintf, vsprintf   For formatted printing to a string

cprintf   Formatted, unbuffered output to console

EXAMPLES Use *printf* to prompt the user for a string. Print it out, together with a count of characters printed during the first prompt.

```
#include <stdio.h>
main()
{
    int numprint;
    char inbuf[81];
    numprint = printf("Enter a string: ");
    gets(inbuf);
```

 Input and Output Routines

```
    printf("I printed %d characters and \
You entered:\n%s\n", numprint, inbuf);
}
```

Using the formatting capabilities of *printf*, print a table showing the numbers from 1 to 10 with their squares.

```
#include <stdio.h>
main()
{
    int i;
    printf("Table of squares\n");
    for (i=1; i<=10; i++)
    {
        printf("%4d\t%6d\n", i, i*i);
    }
}
```

Write a small C program to illustrate some of the special features of *printf*: Show the addressing mode modifiers, printing values of pointers, and width and precision fields of a format at run-time.

```
#include <stdio.h>
char far  strf[] = "Far string...";
char near strn[] = "Near string...";
char *var_name[] = {"long_name_variable",
                    "shorter_var", "short"};
double values[] = { 1.23,  3.4567, 9.87654321};
unsigned int num_vars = sizeof(values)/sizeof(double);
main()
{
    int i, j, numprint, chcount, width, precision=0;
    numprint = printf("Some special features of \
printf\n%n", &chcount);
    printf("printf returned %d and character count in \
variable is %d\n", numprint, chcount);
/* Use of addressing mode modifiers */
    printf("\nYou can print 'near' and 'far' data \
items properly:\n");
    printf("Example: %Fs (far),\n%Ns (near) will print \
in any model\n", strf, strn);
/* Printing addresses of variables */
    printf("\nYou can even print the addresses:\n");
    printf("Item           Segment:Offset\n");
    printf("'far'  string:    %4p\n", (void far *)strf);
```

printf

```
    printf("'near' string:    %4p\n", (void far *)strn);

/* Width and precision can be decided at run-time */
    printf("\nThe format can even be decided \
at run-time\n");
    for(i = 0; i < num_vars; i++)


    {
/* Find maximum length of variable names */
        if( (j = strlen(var_name[i])) > precision)
            precision = j;
    }
/* Make the width 4 characters longer and print names
 * left justified
 */
    width = precision + 4;
    printf("--- Table of Variables ---\n");
    for(i = 0; i < num_vars; i++)
    {
        printf("%-*.*s  %12.8f\n", width, precision,
                            var_name[i], values[i]);
    }
}
```

This example program produces the following listing (the addresses printed using the p format differ according to machine).

```
Some special features of printf
printf returned 32 and character count in variable is 32

You can print 'near' and 'far' data items properly:
Example: Far string... (far),
Near string... (near) will print in any model

You can even print the addresses:
Item            Segment:Offset
'far'  string:    2A4D:0000
'near' string:    2A64:0042

The format can even be decided at run-time
--- Table of Variables ---
long_name_variable      1.23000000
shorter_var             3.45670000
short                   9.87654321
```

 Input and Output Routines

Stream I/O
putc

COMPATIBILITY	MSC 3	MSC 4	MSC 5	QC	TC	ANSI	UNIX V
	▲	▲	▲	▲	▲	▲	▲

PURPOSE Use the *putc* macro to write a single character to a file opened for buffered output.

SYNTAX
```
int putc(int c, FILE *file_pointer);
int c;       Character to be written

FILE *file_pointer;      Pointer to file to which the character is written
```

EXAMPLE CALL
```
putc('*', outfile);
```

INCLUDES
```
#include <stdio.h>
```
For function declaration definition of FILE data structure

DESCRIPTION The *putc* macro writes the character *c* to the current position of the file specified by the argument *file_pointer*. After writing the character, the current position is advanced to the next character. The *file_pointer* must be a pointer returned earlier by an *fopen* or a *freopen* function call or it can be one of the preopened files such as *stdout* or *stderr* for which writing a character makes sense.

Note that *fputc* performs in the same manner as *putc*, except that *fputc* is implemented as a function.

RETURNS The *putc* macro returns the character it wrote as an integer value. A return value of EOF indicates either an error or end-of-file condition. The *ferror* function should be called to determine if there was an error.

SEE ALSO
putchar   Macro to write a character to *stdout*

fputc   Function to write a character to a file

fgetc, fgetchar,
getc, getchar   To read a character from a file

EXAMPLE Use *putc* to write a line (maximum length of 80 characters or up to the null character) to *stdout*.

```
#include <stdio.h>
char buffer[81] = "Testing putc on stdout...\n";
main()
{
    int i;
/* An empty for loop that uses putc to print to stdout */
```

```
    for(i=0; (i<81) && (putc(buffer[i],stdout) != EOF);
        i++);
}
```

Stream I/O

putchar

COMPATIBILITY	MSC 3	MSC 4	MSC 5	QC	TC	ANSI	UNIX V
	▲	▲	▲	▲	▲	▲	▲

PURPOSE   Use the *putchar* macro to write a single character to the preopened file *stdout*, which is initially connected to your display.

SYNTAX   `int putchar(int c);`

`int c;`   Character to be written

EXAMPLE CALL   `putchar('?');`

INCLUDES   `#include <stdio.h>`   For function declaration

DESCRIPTION   The *putchar* macro writes the character *c* to *stdout* and is equivalent to the use *putc(stdout)*. Note that *putchar* is the macro equivalent of the *fputchar* function.

RETURNS   The *putchar* macro returns the character written to *stdout*. In case of any error, the return value is equal to the constant EOF (defined in *stdio.h*).

COMMENTS   Note that you cannot use *putchar* to write a single character to the console because a carriage return must be entered to complete a single buffered write to the keyboard. Use *putch* or *putche* for unbuffered output to the keyboard.

SEE ALSO   putc   Macro to write a character to a file

fputc, fputchar   To write a character to a file

fputc, fputchar,
putc, putchar   To write a character to a file

EXAMPLE   Use *putchar* to write a line (maximum length of 80 characters) to *stdout*.

```
#include <stdio.h>
char buffer[81] = "Testing putchar...\n";
main()
{
    int i;
```

 Input and Output Routines

```
/* A for loop that uses putchar to print to stdout */
    for(i=0; (i<81) && (putchar(buffer[i]) != EOF);
        i++);
}
```

puts

COMPATIBILITY	MSC 3	MSC 4	MSC 5	QC	TC	ANSI	UNIX V
	▲	▲	▲	▲	▲	▲	▲

PURPOSE Use *puts* to output a string to the standard output file *stdout*.

SYNTAX `int puts(const char *string);`

`const char *string;`   String to be output

EXAMPLE CALL `puts("Do you really want to quit? ");`

INCLUDES `#include <stdio.h>`   For function declaration

DESCRIPTION The *puts* function writes the string specified in the argument *string* to the standard output file *stdout*—by default, the screen. The string's terminating null character is replaced by a newline (\n) in the output.

RETURNS In Microsoft C 5.0 and 5.1, *puts* returns a zero if successful. In case of an error, it returns a nonzero value. In earlier versions, when all is well, *puts* returns the last character it wrote. Otherwise, it returns EOF to indicate error.

SEE ALSO `fgets`   To read a line from a file

`fputs`   To write a string to a file

`gets`   To read a line from the standard input, *stdin*

EXAMPLE Use *puts* to write a message to the screen, assuming that *stdout* has not been redirected.

```
#include <stdio.h>
char message[81] =
        "Failure reading drive C\nAbort, Retry, Fail?";
main()
{
    puts(message);
}
```

putw

COMPATIBILITY	MSC 3	MSC 4	MSC 5	QC	TC	ANSI	UNIX V
	▲	▲	▲	▲	▲		▲

PURPOSE Use *putw* to write word (a binary value of type *int*) into a file opened for buffered binary writing.

SYNTAX `int putw(int intval, FILE *file_pointer);`

`int intval;` Integer value to be written to file

`FILE *file_pointer;` Pointer to FILE data structure associated with file from which a word is read

EXAMPLE CALL `putw(int_value, outfile);`

INCLUDES `#include <stdio.h>` For function declaration and definition of FILE

DESCRIPTION The *putw* function writes the binary value of the integer argument *intval* at the current position in the file specified by the argument *file_pointer*. As this is a 2-byte value on most MS-DOS machines the file pointer is updated accordingly.

RETURNS The *putw* function returns the integer value it wrote. A return value equal to the constant EOF defined in *stdio.h* may indicate an error. However, since EOF is also a valid integer, you should call *ferror* to determine if an error had actually occurred.

COMMENTS The *putw* function is provided only for compatibility with previous Microsoft C libraries. A program that uses this function may have problems when ported to a new system, because the size of integers and the ordering of the bytes within it (which one is most significant and which is least significant) vary among microprocessors.

SEE ALSO getw To read a word from a file

EXAMPLE Open a file in the binary write (*wb*) mode. Use *putw* to write some words to the file. Since the words are hexadecimal representations of a string, you can use the DOS TYPE command on the file to see how this works.

```
#include <stdio.h>
/* The string "Hi There\n" in hexadecimal. Because of
 * byte-ordering conventions they may not look obvious.
 * By the way, here are the ASCII codes:
 * H = 48, i = 69, blank = 20, T = 54, h = 68, e = 65,
```

 Input and Output Routines

```
     *     and r = 72
     */
int words[] = {0x6948, 0x5420, 0x6568, 0x6572, 0x0A0D};
int numw = sizeof(words)/sizeof(int);
main()
{
    int i;
    FILE *infile;
    char filename[81];
    printf("Enter name of a file to write to: ");
    gets(filename);
/* Open the file for reading */
    if ( (infile = fopen(filename, "wb")) == NULL)
    {
        printf("fopen failed.\n");
        exit(0);
    }
/* Write the words to the file */
    for (i=0; i<numw; i++)
    {
        if( putw(words[i], infile) == EOF)
        {
/* Check if there was a real error */
            if(ferror(infile) != 0)
            {
                printf("File: %s write error\n",
                    filename);
                exit(0);
            }
        }
    }
/* Ask user to type file out and check */
    printf("To see results use 'TYPE %s'\n", filename);
}
```

Stream I/O

rewind

COMPATIBILITY	MSC 3	MSC 4	MSC 5	QC	TC	ANSI	UNIX V
	▲	▲	▲	▲	▲	▲	▲

PURPOSE Use the *rewind* function to set the current read or write position associated with a file opened for buffered I/O to the beginning of the file.

SYNTAX `void rewind(FILE *file_pointer);`

rewind

    FILE *file_pointer;   Pointer to FILE data structure associated with file whose
                  current position is to be set to the beginning of the file

EXAMPLE CALL rewind(input_file);

INCLUDES #include <stdio.h>   For function declaration and definition of FILE

DESCRIPTION The *rewind* function sets the current read or write position of the file specified by the argument *file_pointer* to the beginning of the file and clears the
end-of-file or error indicator.

COMMON USES The *rewind* function is used to go to the beginning of a file which can also be
achieved by calling *fseek* with the proper arguments. However, *fseek* will not
clear the error indicator.

SEE ALSO fseek   To set the current position indicator of a file

EXAMPLE Open a file using *fopen* for reading. Read and display a line. Now call *rewind*
to go back to the beginning and read a line again. The two lines should be
identical.

```
#include <stdio.h>
main()
{
    FILE *infile;
    char filename[80], buffer[81];
    printf("Enter name of a text file: ");
    gets(filename);
/* Open the file for reading */
    if ( (infile = fopen(filename, "r")) == NULL)
    {
        printf("fopen failed.\n");
        exit(0);
    }
/* Read and display a line */
    fgets(buffer, 80, infile);
    printf("Line read (before rewind): %s", buffer);
/* Rewind and read a line again */
    rewind(infile);
    fgets(buffer, 80, infile);
    printf("Line read (after rewind) : %s", buffer);
}
```

 **Input and Output Routines**

rmtmp

COMPATIBILITY	MSC 3	MSC 4	MSC 5	QC	TC	ANSI	UNIX V
	▲	▲	▲	▲			▲

PURPOSE Use *rmtmp* to close all temporary files created by *tmpfile* and delete them from the current working directory.

SYNTAX `int rmtmp(void);`

EXAMPLE CALL `number_removed = rmtmp();`

INCLUDES `#include <stdio.h>`   For function declaration

DESCRIPTION The *rmtmp* function first looks for all temporary files in the current working directory that were created earlier by *tmpfile*. It then closes and deletes each file.

RETURNS The *rmtmp* function returns the total number of temporary files it closed and deleted.

COMMENTS If you change the current working directory (for example, by calling the DOS function 3Bh via *intdosx*) after calling *tmpfile*, *rmtmp* will not be able to delete the temporary file created in the previous directory. Even those files, however, are automatically deleted when the program terminates normally.

SEE ALSO `tmpfile`   To open a temporary file in the current working directory

EXAMPLE Call *rmtmp* to open three temporary files and then call *rmtmp* to close and delete them. Display the number reported by *rmtmp* to confirm that three files were removed.

```
#include <stdio.h>
main()
{
    int i, numrm;
    FILE *tfile;
    for(i=0; i<3; i++)
    {
        if ((tfile = tmpfile()) == NULL)
            perror("rmtmp failed");
        else printf("Temp file %d created\n", i+1);
    }
/* Now remove these files */
    numrm = rmtmp();
    printf("%d files removed by rmtmp\n", numrm);
}
```

rmtmp

Stream I/O
scanf

COMPATIBILITY	MSC 3	MSC 4	MSC 5	QC	TC	ANSI	UNIX V
	▲	▲	▲	▲	▲	▲	▲

PURPOSE Use *scanf* to read character strings from the standard input file *stdin* and convert the strings to values of C variables according to specified formats. As an example, you can use *scanf* to read a value into a short integer from the standard input.

SYNTAX

```
int scanf(const char *format_string,...);
```

```
const char *format_string;
```
          Character string that describes the format to be used

`...`   Variable number of arguments representing addresses of variables whose values are being read

EXAMPLE CALL

```
scanf(" %d:%d:%d", &hour, &minute, &second);
```

INCLUDES

```
#include <stdio.h>
```
          For function declaration

DESCRIPTION The *scanf* function accepts a variable number of arguments, which it interprets as addresses of C variables, and reads character strings from *stdin*, representing their values. It converts them to their internal representations using formatting commands embedded in the argument *format_string* which must be present in a call to *scanf*.

The interpretation of the variables depends on the *format_string*. The formatting command for each variable begins with a percentage sign and can contain other characters as well. A whitespace character (a blank space, a tab, or a newline) may cause *scanf* to ignore whitespace characters from *stdin*. Other nonwhitespace characters, excluding the percentage sign, cause *scanf* to ignore each matching character from the input. It begins to interpret the first nonmatching character as the value of a variable that is being read.

For each C variable whose address is included in the argument list to *scanf*, there must be a format specification embedded in the *format_string*. The format specification for each variable has the following form:

Format Specification for *scanf* in Microsoft C

%[*][Width][Addressing_mode][Size][Type]

Table 15-13 summarizes the purpose of each field in the format specification used by *scanf*. Further details are provided in Table 15-14.

 **Input and Output Routines**

Table 15-13. *Fields in a Format Specification for* scanf

Field	Explanation
% (Required)	Indicates the beginning of a format specification. Use %% to read a percentage sign from the input.
* (Optional)	The characters representing the value are read according to the format specification, but the value is not stored. It is not necessary to give an argument corresponding to this format specification.
Width (Optional)	A positive value specifying the maximum number of characters to be read for the value of this variable.
Addressing_ mode (Optional)	This field is specific to Microsoft C 4.0 and above. Either F (for "far") or N (for "near") can be used here to override the default addressing mode of the memory model being used. As an example, use F in this field when reading the value of a far integer in a small memory model program.
Size (Optional)	A character that modifies the *Type* field which comes next. One of the characters h, l, or L appears in this field to differentiate between short and long integers and between float and double. Shown below is a sumary of this field:

Prefix	When to Use
h	Use when reading integers using *Type* d, i, o, x, or X to indicate that the argument is a short integer. Also, use with *Type* u to indicate that the variable being read is an unsigned short integer.
l	Use when reading integers or unsigned integers with a *Type* field of d, i, o, x, X, or u to specify that the variable to be read is a long integer. Also use with floating-point variables (when the *Type* field is e, E, g, or G) to specify a double, rather than a float.

Field	Explanation
Type (Required)	A letter that indicates the type of variable being read. Table 15-14 lists the characters and their meanings.

The most important among these fields is the *Type* field which tells *scanf* the type of C variable into which it must convert the input characters. Table 15-14 lists the characters that can appear in the *Type* field and the kind of C variable each one signifies.

Table 15-14. Type *Field in Format Specification for* scanf

Type	Expected Input	Type of Argument
c	Single character. Whitespace characters (space, tab, or newline) will be read in this format.	Pointer to char
d	Decimal integer.	Pointer to int
D	Decimal integer.	Pointer to long
e E f g G	Signed value in the scientific format, for example, −1.234567e+002 and 9.876543e−002 or in the format (sign)(digits).(digits), for example, −1.234567 and 9.876543.	Pointer to float
i	Decimal, hexadecimal, or octal integer.	Pointer to int
I	Decimal, hexadecimal, or octal integer.	Pointer to long

Table 15-14. *(cont.)*

Type	Expected Input	Type of Argument
n	This is not really a reading format. The argument corresponding to this format is a pointer to an integer. Before returning, the *scanf* function stores in this integer the total number of characters it has read from the input file or the input file's buffer in this integer.	
o	Octal digits without any sign.	Pointer to int
O	Octal digits without any sign.	Pointer to long
p	Hexadecimal digits in the form *SSSS:OOOO* using uppercase letters. This format is only available in Microsoft C versions 4.0 and 5.0 under MS-DOS.	
s	Character string.	Pointer to an array of characters large enough to hold input string plus a terminating null
u	Unsigned decimal integer.	Pointer to unsigned int
U	Unsigned decimal integer.	Pointer to unsigned long
x	Hexadecimal digits.	Pointer to int
X	Hexadecimal digits.	Pointer to long

Normally, strings read using the %s format are assumed to be delimited by blank spaces. When you want to read a string delimited by any character other than those in a specific set, you can specify the set of characters within brackets and use this in place of the s in the format specification. If the first character inside the brackets is a caret (^), the set shows the characters that terminate the string. Thus, for example, %[^'\"] reads a string delimited by single or double quote characters.

Strings can be read and stored without the terminating null character by using the %[decimal number]c format in which the *decimal number* denotes the number of characters being read into the character string.

RETURNS The *scanf* function returns the number of input items that were successfully read, converted, and saved in variables. A return value equal to the constant EOF (defined in *stdio.h*) means that an end-of-file was encountered during the read operation.

COMMENTS Use two signs when you need to read a percentage sign. Note that several features of *scanf* in Microsoft C library are nonstandard extensions. In particular, should you want your application program to be portable across multiple systems, avoid the N and F addressing mode modifiers and the p and n formats for reading pointers.

SEE ALSO fscanf   Formatted read from any buffered file

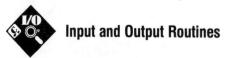

Input and Output Routines

sscanf   For formatted reading from a string

cscanf   Formatted, unbuffered input from console

EXAMPLE Write a C program that reads the amount of principal, the interest rate, and the number of months to maturity of a certificate of deposit. Use *scanf* to read in the values. Now compute the amount at maturity and print it out.

```c
#include <stdio.h>
#include <math.h>
main()
{
    int num_months;
    double interest_rate, principal, final_amount;
/* Ask user to enter all necessary amounts */
    printf("Enter amount of principal, annual interest \
rate:");
    scanf(" %lf %lf", &principal, &interest_rate);
    printf("Enter number of months before deposit \
matures:");
    scanf(" %d", &num_months);
/* Compute amount at maturity and print value */
    final_amount = principal *
                    pow((1.0 + interest_rate/12.0/100.0),
                        (double)num_months);
        printf("$%.2f @%.2f%% annual rate yields $%.2f \
after %d months\n", principal, interest_rate,
                    final_amount, num_months);
}
```

Stream I/O
setbuf

COMPATIBILITY	MSC 3	MSC 4	MSC 5	QC	TC	ANSI	UNIX V
	▲	▲	▲	▲	▲	▲	▲

PURPOSE Use the *setbuf* function to assign your own buffer instead of the system-allocated one for use by a file that has been opened for buffered I/O.

SYNTAX `void setbuf(FILE *file_pointer, char *buffer);`

`FILE *file_pointer;`   Pointer to FILE data structure associated with file whose buffer is being set

`char *buffer;`   Pointer to buffer (or NULL if no buffering is to be done)

EXAMPLE CALL `setbuf(infile, mybuffer);`

INCLUDES #include <stdio.h>   For function declaration and definition of FILE

DESCRIPTION The *setbuf* function sets the buffer to be used during I/O involving the file specified by the argument *file_pointer* which must have been returned earlier by *fopen*. If the pointer to buffer given in the argument *buffer* is NULL, *setbuf* turns off buffering for that file. If the pointer is not NULL, it should point to an allocated array of characters BUFSIZ bytes long, where BUFSIZ is a constant defined in *stdio.h* (the declared value is 512). This buffer is used for all subsequent I/O operations with the file specified by the argument *file_pointer*.

COMMENTS While *setbuf* merely lets you switch the buffer used for file I/O to one allocated by you, the companion function *setvbuf* enables you to control the size of the buffer and the level of buffering as well. For example, you would use *setvbuf* if you wanted to read data in chunks larger than the default 512-byte size of the buffer normally used by Microsoft C.

SEE ALSO setvbuf   To assign your own buffer with specific size and to control level of buffering during I/O to a file

EXAMPLE Use *setbuf* to assign your own buffer, at least BUFSIZ characters long, to a file that you have opened with *fopen* for read operations. Now read a character using *fgetc* to initiate a read operation and fill the buffer. Print the buffer to see the effect.

```
#include <stdio.h>
main()
{
    FILE *infile;
    char filename[81], buffer[BUFSIZ+1];
    printf("Enter name of a text file: ");
    gets(filename);
/* Open the file for reading */
    if ( (infile = fopen(filename, "r")) == NULL)
    {
        printf("fopen failed.\n");
        exit(0);
    }
/* Set up a new buffer for the file */
    setbuf(infile, buffer);
/* Now read in a single character -- this should fill
 * up the buffer
 */
    fgetc(infile);
    buffer[BUFSIZ] = '\0';    /* Make it a C string */
    printf("After reading one character from file \
buffer has:\n%s\n", buffer);
}
```

 Input and Output Routines

setvbuf

COMPATIBILITY	MSC 3	MSC 4	MSC 5	QC	TC	ANSI	UNIX V
	▲	▲	▲	▲	▲	▲	▲

PURPOSE Use the *setvbuf* function to assign a buffer of a specific size to a file open for buffered I/O. You can also control the type of buffering to be used or turn off buffering for the specified file.

SYNTAX
```
int setvbuf(FILE *file_pointer, char *buffer, int buf_type,
                                            size_t buf_size);
```

FILE *file_pointer;   Pointer to FILE data structure associated with file whose buffer is being set

char *buffer;   Pointer to buffer (or NULL if no buffering requested)

int buf_type;   Type of buffering desired (see table below for values)

size_t buf_size;   Size of buffer in bytes, if any assigned

EXAMPLE CALL `setvbuf(infile, buffer, _IOFBF, 120);`

INCLUDES `#include <stdio.h>`   For function declaration and definition of FILE and *size_t* data types

DESCRIPTION The *setvbuf* function sets the buffer and the level of buffering for the file specified by the argument *file_pointer* which must have been returned earlier by *fopen*.

First *setvbuf* checks the argument *buf_type* to see the type of buffering requested. This argument can have one of the values shown in the table, each of which indicates a level of buffering.

Type	Interpretation
_IOFBF	Bytes will be read until buffer is completely filled. This is called "full buffering."
_IOLBF	Each line read from the input stream is buffered. In this "line buffering" mode the reading stops when a whole line has been read.
_IONBF	No buffering is done.

If the argument *buf_type* is _IONBF, the other arguments are ignored and the internal flags are set so that no buffering is done for the file indicated by *file_pointer*. If the argument *buf_type* is either _IOFBF or _IOLBF, the

setvbuf

buffering option is first saved internally. Then *setvbuf* checks if the pointer to the buffer specified in the argument *buffer* is a NULL. If it is, *setvbuf* turns off buffering in version 4.0 of Microsoft C, but in versions 5.0 and 5.1 it allocates a buffer using the size specified in the argument *buf_size*. (To turn off buffering in 5.0 and 5.1, use buffer type _IONBF). If the argument *buffer* is not NULL, it should be a buffer of size *buf_size* bytes allocated by you. This is set by *setvbuf* as the buffer for the specified file.

COMMON USES The *setvbuf* function gives you control over the amount of buffering and the actual buffer to be used by a file.

RETURNS If successful, *setvbuf* returns a zero. In cases of bad parameters or other errors, the return value is nonzero.

COMMENTS If you only want to switch to a buffer of your own and not to change any other features of buffered I/O, *setbuf* is a much simpler function to use.

SEE ALSO setbuf   To assign your own buffer of fixed size to a file

EXAMPLE Open a file using *fopen* for reading. Use *setvbuf* to assign a 120-byte buffer for the file and to specify buffer type _IOFBF. Now read a character from the file using *fgetc*, and print the buffer out using *putchar*. You will notice that because of buffering during read, the first 120 characters of the file are now in the buffer, even though you only read a single character.

```
#include <stdio.h>
main()
{
    FILE *infile;
    char filename[81], buffer[121];
    printf("Enter name of a text file: ");
    gets(filename);
/* Open the file for reading */
    if ( (infile = fopen(filename, "r")) == NULL)
    {
        printf("fopen failed.\n");
        exit(0);
    }
/* Set up a new buffer for the file */
    if (setvbuf(infile, buffer, _IOFBF, 120) != 0)
    {
        perror("setvbuf failed");
    }
    else
    {
        fgetc(infile);
        buffer[120] = '\0';
        printf("After reading one character buffer \
```

 Input and Output Routines

```
has:\n%s\n", buffer);
    }
}
```

COMPATIBILITY	MSC 3	MSC 4	MSC 5	QC	TC	ANSI	UNIX V
	▲	▲	▲	▲	▲	▲	▲

PURPOSE Use the *sprintf* function to format and write the values of C variables to a string.

SYNTAX `int sprintf(char *p_string, const char *format_string,...);`

`char *p_string;`   Pointer to an array of characters where *sprintf* sends its formatted output

`const char *format_string;`   Character string that describes the format to be used

`...`   Variable number of arguments depending on the number of items being printed

EXAMPLE CALL `sprintf(buffer, "FY 88 Profit = %.2f\n", profit);`

INCLUDES `#include <stdio.h>`   For function declaration

DESCRIPTION The *sprintf* function accepts a variable number of arguments, converts their values to characters, and stores these characters in the buffer whose address is specified in the argument *p_string*. The performance of *sprintf* is identical to that of *fprintf* and *printf* except that *sprintf* sends its output to a character buffer instead of a file. After formatting and storing the characters in the buffer *p_string*, *sprintf* appends a null character to make the buffer a C string.

As in *printf*, the conversion of values of variables to character strings is done according to formatting commands given in a character string *format_string*. The available formatting commands and options are described in detail in the reference pages on *printf*. In particular, Tables 15-9, 15-10, 15-11, and 15-12 tabulate the characters that appear in the format commands (which always begin with the character %). By the way, to actually print a percent sign (instead of having it interpreted as a formatting command), use two percent signs in a row.

COMMON USES A common use of *sprintf* is to prepare formatted strings for use by such other output routines as *_outtext* in the graphics library that do not have any formatting capabilities.

sprintf

RETURNS　The *sprintf* function returns the number of characters it has stored in the buffer, excluding the terminating null character.

SEE ALSO

printf　　　For printing to *stdout* and for detailed information on formats

vprintf　　　Printing to *stdout* using a pointer to a list of arguments

fprintf, vfprintf　　　For formatted printing to a file

vsprintf　　　Another routine for formatted output to a string

EXAMPLE　Use *fprintf* to prepare a formatted string showing the value of a C variable. Display the string with *printf*.

```
#include <stdio.h>
int     i     = 100;
double  x     = 1.23456;
main()
{
    int numout;
    char outbuf[81];
    numout = sprintf(outbuf, "The value of i = %d and \
the value of x = %g\n", i, x);
    printf("sprintf wrote %d characters and the buffer \
contains:\n%s", numout, outbuf);
}
```

Stream I/O
sscanf

COMPATIBILITY	MSC 3	MSC 4	MSC 5	QC	TC	ANSI	UNIX V
	▲	▲	▲	▲	▲	▲	▲

PURPOSE　Use *sscanf* to read characters from a buffer and to convert and store them in C variables according to specified formats.

SYNTAX　`int sscanf(const char *buffer, const char *format_string,...);`

const char *buffer;　　　Pointer to buffer from which characters will be read and converted to values of variables

const char *format_string;　　　Character string that describes the format to be used

...　　　Variable number of arguments representing addresses of variables whose values are being read

EXAMPLE CALL　`sscanf(buffer, "Name: %s Age: %d", name, &age);`

 **Input and Output Routines**

INCLUDES #include <stdio.h>   For function declaration

DESCRIPTION The *sscanf* function reads a stream of characters from the buffer specified in the argument *buffer* and converts them to values according to format specifications embedded in the argument *format_string*. It then stores the values in C variables whose addresses are provided in the variable length argument list.

The optional arguments following the *format_string* are addresses of C variables whose values are being read. Each address has a corresponding format specification in the argument *format_string*. The format specification always begins with a percent sign, and the formatting commands are identical to the ones used with the function *scanf*. A detailed list of the formats is provided in the reference pages on *scanf*.

COMMON USES The *sscanf* function is handy for in-memory conversion of characters to values. You may often find it convenient to read in strings using either *gets* or *fgets* and then extract values from the string by using *sscanf*.

RETURNS The *sscanf* function returns the number of fields that were successfully read, converted, and assigned to variables. If the string ends before completing the read operation, the return value is the constant EOF, defined in the include file *stdio.h*.

SEE ALSO scanf   Formatted reading from *stdin*

fscanf   For formatted, buffered reading from a file

cscanf   Formatted, unbuffered input from console

EXAMPLE Suppose you have a program that lets the user set the value of a variable by a command of the form "name = value" (i.e., the name is separated from the value by one or more blanks surrounding an equal sign). One way to implement this is to read the entire line into an internal buffer using *gets*. You can then use *sscanf* to separate the variable name and its value. As you can see from the example below, the features of *sscanf* provide easy ways of implementing such user-friendly features as this.

```
#include <stdio.h>
main()
{
    double value;
    char buffer[81], name[81];
    printf("Enter value of variable as \
\"name=<value>\":");
    gets(buffer);
/* Now use sscanf to separate name and value */
    sscanf(buffer, " %[^=] = %lf", name, &value);
/* Display result to user */
    printf("Value of variable named %s is set to %f\n",
```

sscanf

```
        name, value);
}
```

Stream I/O

tempnam

COMPATIBILITY	MSC 3	MSC 4	MSC 5	QC	TC	ANSI	UNIX V
		▲	▲	▲			▲

PURPOSE Use the *tempnam* function to generate a temporary file name for your application. The file name uses the default directory name from the MS-DOS environment variable TMP, if it is defined, and has a specified prefix.

SYNTAX `char *tempnam(char *dir_name, char *file_prefix);`

`char *dir_name;`   Pointer to string with the directory name to be used if environment variable TMP is undefined

`char *file_prefix;`   Pointer to string with prefix characters for the file name

EXAMPLE CALL `tfilename = tempnam(NULL, "mscb");`

INCLUDES `#include <stdio.h>`   For function declaration

DESCRIPTION The *tempnam* function generates a file name in the following manner. It first checks if the MS-DOS environment variable TMP is defined. If TMP is defined, *tempnam* uses that as the directory portion of the file name. If TMP is undefined, and the argument *dir_name* is not NULL, the string from this argument is chosen as the directory name. If none of this works, the defined constant *P_tmpdir* in the include file *stdio.h* provides the directory name. If the directory name cannot be derived from any of these sources, the file name will not have a specific directory name, which means that when you create the file, it will be in the current working directory.

Following this process, *tempnam* creates the rest of the file name by appending up to five digits having a maximum value of 65,535 to the prefix provided in the argument *file_prefix*. (The prefix together with the digits may not exceed eight characters in length.) If a file with that name already exists, *tempnam* creates another name by incrementing the last digit in the file name. It continues this until a unique file name is found or until no more file names can be generated.

The *tempnam* function actually allocates the storage necessary to hold the file name it generates. You must deallocate the space by calling *free*.

 **Input and Output Routines**

COMMON USES The *tempnam* function is a handy tool, similar to *tmpnam*, for constructing temporary file names. It is more useful than the latter because of its increased control over generation of parts of the file name.

RETURNS The *tempnam* function returns a pointer to the name generated. If the generated name is not unique or if a file name could not be created with the specified prefix (for example, when a file with the same name already exits), *tempnam* returns a NULL.

COMMENTS If you do not care about the file name and simply want to open a temporary file for storing transient data in your application, you may be able to get by with *tmpfile*. Remember that when using *tmpnam* or *tempnam*, you have to explicitly open the temporary file (and delete it too).

Note that *tempnam* accepts a prefix whose length is more than the number of characters allowed in an MS-DOS file name (11 characters including extension) and returns it as a name; the burden is on you to ensure that the file name meets MS-DOS requirements.

SEE ALSO

tempnam   To create a temporary file name with a prefix in a different directory

tempfile   To open a temporary file in current working directory

EXAMPLE Call *tempnam* to generate a temporary file name and print the name. Allow the user to enter the prefix. You will see that *tempnam* accepts a prefix much longer than a valid MS-DOS file name.

```
#include <stdio.h>
main()
{
    char *tfilename, prefix[80];
    printf("Enter a prefix for the file name: ");
    tfilename = tempnam(NULL, prefix);
    if (tfilename == NULL)
    {
        perror("tempnam failed");
    }
    else
    {
        printf("Temporary file name: %s\n", tfilename);
    }
}
```

tempnam

Stream I/O
tmpfile

COMPATIBILITY	MSC 3	MSC 4	MSC 5	QC	TC	ANSI	UNIX V
		▲	▲	▲		▲	▲

PURPOSE Use *tmpfile* to open a temporary file in the current directory for buffered binary read/write operations.

SYNTAX `FILE *tmpfile(void);`

EXAMPLE CALL `p_tfile = tmpfile();`

INCLUDES `#include <stdio.h>`   For function declaration and definition of FILE data type

DESCRIPTION The *tmpfile* function opens a temporary file in the current working directory. The file is opened in the mode *w+b* which means binary read and write operations can be performed on this file. You have no access to the name of the file that is created nor is the file available to you after a normal exit from the program. The file is automatically deleted when your program terminates normally or when you close the file. You can delete all such files by calling *rmtmp*.

COMMON USES The *tmpfile* function is a convenient way of opening temporary work files in an application.

RETURNS The *tmpfile* function returns a pointer to the FILE data structure of the temporary file it opens. In case of error, the return pointer will be NULL.

COMMENTS Unlike *tmpnam* and *tempnam*, which simply generate the file name, a file is opened by *tmpfile* and the file is truly temporary because it is deleted when the program ends.

SEE ALSO `rmtmp`   To delete all temporary files in current working directory

EXAMPLE Call *tmpfile* to open a temporary file and write the contents of a buffer to the file. Unfortunately, the file will be gone when you exit the program, so there will be no evidence of the temporary file. Nor is the file name available for printing.

```
#include <stdio.h>
char    message[80] = "Testing tmpfile.... ";
main()
{
    FILE *tfile;
    if ((tfile = tmpfile()) == NULL)
    {
```

 Input and Output Routines

```
            perror("tmpfile failed");
    }
    else
    {
        printf("Temporary file successfully opened.\n");
        printf("Wrote %d characters to file\n",
            fwrite((void *)message, sizeof(char), 80,
                tfile));
        printf("File will be gone when you exit.\n");
    }
}
```

tmpnam

COMPATIBILITY	MSC 3	MSC 4	MSC 5	QC	TC	ANSI	UNIX V
		▲	▲	▲		▲	▲

PURPOSE Use the *tmpnam* function to generate a temporary file name for your application.

SYNTAX `char *tmpnam(char *file_name);`

`char *file_name;`   Pointer to string where file name will be returned

EXAMPLE CALL `tmpnam(tfilename);`

INCLUDES `#include <stdio.h>`   For function declaration

DESCRIPTION The *tmpnam* function generates a file name by appending six digits to the directory name defined by the constant *P_tmpdir* in the include file *stdio.h*. This null-terminated file name is returned in a buffer, which must be allocated by you and whose address must be passed to *tmpnam* in the argument *file_name*. The size of the buffer that holds the file name must be at least equal to the constant *L_tmpnam*, which is defined in *stdio.h* to be eight digits plus the length of the directory name *P_tmpdir*. The default directory name is set to \\, (i.e., all temporary files will be at the root directory). You should call *tempnam* if you want to generate arbitrary file names in a separate directory and with specific prefix characters of your choice. You can generate up to *TMP_MAX* (defined in *stdio.h* to be 32,767) unique file names with *tmpnam*.

If the argument *file_name* is NULL, the generated file name is stored internally by *tmpnam* and a pointer to this name is returned by *tmpnam*. This name is preserved until another call is made to this function. So you can get by with a NULL argument to *tmpnam* and simply use the pointer returned by it as long as you use this name before the next call to *tmpnam*.

COMMON USES The *tmpnam* function is a handy tool if your application generates temporary files.

RETURNS The *tmpnam* function returns a pointer to the name generated. If the generated name is not unique, it returns a NULL.

COMMENTS You are responsible for opening the file using the file name generated by *tmpnam*. You can use *tmpfile* to directly open a temporary file.

SEE ALSO

tempnam   To create a temporary file name with a prefix in a different directory

tmpfile   To open a temporary file in the current working directory

EXAMPLE Call *tmpnam* to generate a temporary file name and print this name. Note that we do not allocate any storage for the string itself; we use the pointer returned by *tmpnam*.

```
#include <stdio.h>
main()
{
    char *tfilename;
    tfilename = tmpnam(NULL);
    if (tfilename == NULL)
    {
        perror("tmpnam failed");
    }
    else
    {
        printf("Temporary file name: %s\n", tfilename);
    }
}
```

Stream I/O
ungetc

COMPATIBILITY	MSC 3	MSC 4	MSC 5	QC	TC	ANSI	UNIX V
	▲	▲	▲	▲	▲	▲	▲

PURPOSE Use *ungetc* to place any character, except the constant EOF, in the buffer associated with a file opened for buffered input.

SYNTAX `int ungetc(int c, FILE *file_pointer);`

`int c;`   Character to be placed in the file's buffer

 Input and Output Routines

　　　　　　　　`FILE *file_pointer;`　　Pointer to FILE data structure associated with file in whose
　　　　　　　　　　　　　　　　　　　　buffer the character is placed

EXAMPLE CALL　`ungetc(last_char, infile);`

INCLUDES　`#include <stdio.h>`　　For function declaration and definition of FILE data type

DESCRIPTION　The *ungetc* function places the character given in the integer argument *c* in
the buffer associated with the file specified by the argument *file_pointer* so
that the next read operation on that file starts with that character. You must
read at least once before attempting to place a character in a file's buffer;
otherwise, the buffer is not in a usable state. Also, *ungetc* ignores any attempt
to push the constant EOF.

　　　　Since *ungetc* places the character in the file's buffer, any operation that
tampers with the buffer or the file's current position (for example, *fflush*,
fseek, *fsetpos* or *rewind*) may erase the character.

　　　　The *ungetc* function affects the file's current position differently for different translation modes. In the text mode the current position remains as it
was before the call to *ungetc*. Thus the file's position is undefined until the
pushed character is read back or discarded. In the binary mode the file's position is decremented after each call to *ungetc*. Once the file's position reaches
zero, however, the value becomes undefined after calls to *ungetc*.

COMMON USES　The *ungetc* function is used to reject an invalid character that has just been
read. The character can be placed back in the input buffer and then displayed
by an error-reporting routine.

RETURNS　If there are no errors, *ungetc* returns the character it pushed back. Otherwise,
it returns the constant EOF to indicate an error.

SEE ALSO　`getc`　　Macro to read a character from a file

　　　　　　`getchar`　　Function to read a character from *stdin*

　　　　　　`fputc, fputchar,`
　　　　　　`putc, putchar`　　To write a character to a file

EXAMPLE　Write a program that asks the user to enter an integer. Use *getchar* to read the
digits and accumulate them into an integer. Once a nondigit is reached (use
the macro *isdigit* to check), put that character back in the buffer by calling
ungetc. Now print a message showing the integer value and indicating the
first noninteger character that the user typed. This is a classic use of *ungetc*.

```
#include <stdio.h>
#include <ctype.h>        /* For the macro isdigit() */
main()
{
    int intval = 0, c;
```

ungetc

```
    char buff[81];
/* Ask user to type in an integer */
    printf("Enter an integer followed by some other \
characters:");
    while ( (c = getchar()) != EOF && isdigit(c) )
    {
        intval = 10*intval + c - 48; /* 0 is ASCII 48 */
    }
/* Push back the first non-digit read from stdin */
    if (c != EOF) ungetc(c, stdin);
/* Print message to user */
    printf("Integer you entered = %d.\n\
Rest of the string beginning at the first non-integer \
in buffer: %s\n", intval, gets(buff));
}
```

Stream I/O
vfprintf

COMPATIBILITY	MSC 3	MSC 4	MSC 5	QC	TC	ANSI	UNIX V
		▲	▲	▲	▲	▲	▲

PURPOSE Use *vfprintf* to write formatted output to a file, just as *fprintf* does, except that *vfprintf* accepts a pointer to the list of variables rather than the variables themselves, allowing a number of items to be printed.

SYNTAX
```
int vfprintf(FILE *file_pointer, const char *format_string,
                                 va_list arg_pointer);
```

FILE *file_pointer;   Pointer to FILE data structure of the file to which the output goes

const char *format_string;   Character string that describes the format to be used

va_list arg_pointer;   Pointer to a list containing a variable number of arguments being printed

EXAMPLE CALL vfprintf(stderr, p_format, p_arg);

INCLUDES #include <stdio.h>   For function declaration

#include <stdarg.h>   When writing for ANSI compatibility (defines va_list)

#include <varargs.h>   When writing for UNIX System V compatibility (defines va_list)

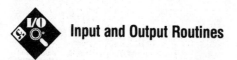 **Input and Output Routines**

DESCRIPTION   The *vfprintf* function accepts a pointer to a list of a number of arguments in *arg_pointer*, converts their values to characters, and writes them to the file specified by the argument *file_pointer*.

The only difference between *fprintf* and *vfprintf* is that *fprintf* accepts its arguments directly, whereas *vfprintf* accepts a pointer to a list of a variable number of arguments. The format used to print the variables is given in the argument *format_string*, a character string with embedded format commands that begin with a percent sign. Detailed information on the format specification appears in the reference pages on *printf* (see Tables 15-9, 15-10, 15-11, and 15-12).

COMMON USES   The *vfprintf* is useful for printing values of arguments in routines that accept arguments of varying length. An example would be a customized error handler that accepts a list of arguments and prints them out.

RETURNS   The *vfprintf* function returns the number of characters it has printed, excluding the terminating null character.

SEE ALSO   printf   For printing to *stdout* and for detailed information on formats

vprintf   Printing to *stdout* using a pointer to a list of arguments

fprintf   For formatted printing to a file

sprintf, vsprintf   For formatted output to a string

va_start, va_arg, va_end   Macros for accessing variable-length argument lists

EXAMPLE   Write a routine to send error messages to *stderr*. The routine should accept a variable number of arguments, the first of which is a format string followed by one or more arguments, just like *fprintf* accepts. The routine, which in this example conforms to the UNIX System V standard of handling variable arguments, prints the arguments using the given format. Test the routine using a simple main program.

```
#include <stdio.h>
#include <varargs.h>        /* UNIX Sys V standard */
char filename[80] = "EXAMPLE.EXE";
main()
{
        int line_no = 131;
/* Call the error handler to print an error message.
 * First just a single line. Then a more detailed
 * message with more arguments.
 */
        my_errmsg("Syntax error\n");

        my_errmsg("File: %s at line_no %d\n", filename,
```

vfprintf

```
                        line_no);
}
/*-------------------------------------------------*/
/*   my_errmsg: accepts variable number of arguments
 *               and prints their values to stderr
 */
my_errmsg(va_alist)
va_dcl
{
    char *p_format;
    va_list p_arg;
/* Use va_start followed by va_arg macros to get to the
 * start of the variable number of arguments. This will
 * alter the pointer p_arg to point to the list of
 * variables to be printed.
 */
    va_start(p_arg);
    p_format = va_arg(p_arg, char*);
    vfprintf(stderr, p_format, p_arg);
/* Use the va_end macro to reset the p_arg to NULL */
    va_end(p_arg);
}
```

Stream I/O
vprintf

COMPATIBILITY	MSC 3	MSC 4	MSC 5	QC	TC	ANSI	UNIX V
		▲	▲	▲	▲	▲	▲

PURPOSE   Use *vprintf* to write formatted output to *stdout* (that is, perform the same functions as *printf*) when you have only a pointer to the list of variables to be printed, rather than the variables themselves. This allows a variable number of arguments to be printed.

SYNTAX   `int vprintf(const char *format_string, va_list arg_pointer);`

`const char *format_string;`   Character string that describes the format to be used

`va_list arg_pointer;`   Pointer to a list containing a variable number of arguments that are being printed

EXAMPLE CALL   `vprintf(p_format, p_arg);`

INCLUDES   `#include <stdio.h>`   For function declaration

 **Input and Output Routines**

```
#include <stdarg.h>          When writing for ANSI compatibility (defines va_list)

#include <varargs.h>         When writing for UNIX System V compatibility (defines va_
                             list)
```

DESCRIPTION   The *vprintf* function accepts a pointer to a list of a variable number of arguments in *arg_pointer*, converts their values to characters, and writes them to the preopened file *stdout*. Except for accepting a pointer to a list of arguments rather than using the arguments themselves, *vprintf* works as *fprintf* and *printf* do. The argument *format_string* is a character string with embedded format commands that begin with a percent sign. Their meaning is explained in the reference pages on *printf* (see Tables 15-9, 15-10, 15-11, and 15-12).

COMMON USES   The *vprintf* is necessary when you have a list of arguments available and want to print them out. A common example is a customized error handler that accepts a list of arguments.

RETURNS   The *vprintf* function returns the number of characters it has printed, excluding the terminating null character.

SEE ALSO   printf   For printing to *stdout* and for detailed information on formats

fprintf, vfprintf   For formatted printing to a file

sprintf, vsprintf   For formatted output to a string

va_start, va_arg, va_end   Macros for accessing variable-length argument lists

EXAMPLE   Write an error-handling routine, conforming to the proposed ANSI C standards, that takes a variable number of arguments and prints an error message that includes the values of the passed parameters. Use *vprintf* to do the printing in the error handler. Write a sample main program to demonstrate the use of the error handler.

```
#include <stdio.h>
#include <stdarg.h>        /* ANSI C compatible */
void error_handler(char *,...);
char filename[80] = "COMMAND.COM";
main()
{
    int offset = 0x232A;
/* Call the error handler to print an error message.
 * First just a single line. Then a more detailed
 * message with more arguments.
 */
    error_handler("System error\n");
    error_handler("File %s at offset %X\n",
```

vprintf

```
                            filename, offset);
        }
        /*--------------------------------------------------*/
        /*  error_handler: accepts variable number of arguments
         *                  and prints messages
         */
        void error_handler(char *my_format,...)
        {
            va_list arg_pointer;
        /* Use va_start macro to get to the start of the
         * variable number of arguments. This will alter the
         * pointer arg_pointer to point to the list of
         * variables to be printed.
         */
            va_start(arg_pointer, my_format);
            vprintf(my_format, arg_pointer);
        /* Use the va_end macro to reset the arg_pointer */
            va_end(arg_pointer);
        }
```

Stream I/O
vsprintf

COMPATIBILITY	MSC 3	MSC 4	MSC 5	QC	TC	ANSI	UNIX V
		▲	▲	▲	▲	▲	▲

PURPOSE Use *vsprintf* to write formatted output to a string (that is, perform the same function as *sprintf*), except that *vsprintf* uses a pointer to a list of variables rather than the variables themselves. Thus a variable number of arguments can be formatted.

SYNTAX
```
int vsprintf(char *p_string, const char *format_string,
                                va_list arg_pointer);
```

`char *p_string;`   Pointer to an array of characters where *vsprintf* sends its formatted output

`const char *format_string;`   Character string that describes the format to be used

`va_list arg_pointer;`   Pointer to a list containing a variable number of arguments that are being printed

EXAMPLE CALL `vsprintf(err_msg, p_format, p_arg);`

INCLUDES `#include <stdio.h>`   For function declaration

 **Input and Output Routines**

```
#include <stdarg.h>        When writing for ANSI compatibility (defines va_list)

#include <varargs.h>       When writing for UNIX System V compatibility (defines va_
                           list)
```

DESCRIPTION   The *vsprintf* function accepts a pointer to a list of a variable number of arguments in *arg_pointer*, prepares a formatted character string, and saves the
string in the area of memory whose address is given in the argument *p_
string*. In so doing, it functions exactly as *sprintf* does, except that *vsprintf*
accepts a pointer. The conversion of a variable's value to a character string is
done according to the format string in the argument *format_string*, which is
an ordinary text string containing embedded format commands beginning
with a percent sign. Detailed information on format specification appears in
the reference pages on *printf* (see Tables 15-9, 15-10, 15-11, and 15-12). On return from *vsprintf*, the *p_string* will be a standard C string.

COMMON USES   The *vsprintf* function is useful in preparing a string with the values of the
arguments in routines that accept variable-length arguments. This string may
be used by other output routines (such as *_outtext* in the graphics library,
which does not have any formatting capability). An example of such a routine
would be an error handler that accepts a list of arguments and prints them out
in the graphics mode using *_outtext*.

RETURNS   The *vsprintf* function returns the number of characters it has printed, excluding the terminating null character.

SEE ALSO   printf   For printing to *stdout* and for detailed information on formats

vprintf   For printing to *stdout* using a pointer to a list of arguments

fprintf, vfprintf   For formatted printing to a file

sprintf   For formatted output to a string

va_start, va_arg, va_end   Macros for accessing variable-length argument lists

EXAMPLE   Write an error handler, conforming to the ANSI C standard, to display error
messages in a graphics display using *_outtext*. The routine should accept a
variable number of arguments, the first of which is a format string followed
by one or more arguments, as would be used with *printf*. The routine should
then use *vsprintf* to prepare a string with the values of the arguments in the
given format. Test the routine with a simple main program.

```
#include <stdio.h>
#include <stdarg.h>                /* ANSI C compatible  */
#include <graph.h>
#define RED    4L /* "long" constant for _setbkcolor */
#define YELLOW 14 /* Text color number 14 is yellow  */
```

vsprintf

```c
void error_handler(char *,...);
char filename[80] = "COMMAND.COM";
main()
{
    int offset = 0x232A;
/* Assume we are already in text mode                    */
    _clearscreen(_GCLEARSCREEN);     /* Clear  screen */
    _settextwindow(10,10,15,70); /* Define text window*/
    _setbkcolor(RED);         /* Set background to red    */
    _clearscreen(_GWINDOW); /* clear out text window  */

/* Once a text window is defined all text positions are
 * relative to upper left corner of the window. Notice
 * that this can be used for pop-up menus.
 */
    _settextposition(1,1);      /* Set text position   */
    _settextcolor(YELLOW);      /* Set text color      */
/* Call the error handler to print an error message.
 * First just a single line. Then a more detailed
 * message with more arguments.
 */
    error_handler("System error\n");
    error_handler("File %s at offset %X\n", filename,
                  offset);
}
/*--------------------------------------------------------*/
/*  error_handler: accepts variable number of arguments
 *                 and prints messages
 */
void error_handler(char *my_format,...)
{
    va_list arg_pointer;
    char buffer[80];    /* Buffer for text string */
/* Use va_start macro to get to the start of the
 * variable number of arguments. This will alter the
 * pointer arg_pointer to point to the list of
 * variables to be printed.
 */
    va_start(arg_pointer, my_format);
    vsprintf(buffer, my_format, arg_pointer);
/* Now display the message by calling _outtext    */
    _outtext(buffer);
/* Use the va_end macro to reset the arg_pointer */
    va_end(arg_pointer);
}
```

Input and Output Routines

close

COMPATIBILITY	MSC 3	MSC 4	MSC 5	QC	TC	ANSI	UNIX V
	▲	▲	▲	▲	▲		▲

PURPOSE Use *close* to close a file specified by a valid handle, an integer returned by a prior call to *open*.

SYNTAX `int close(int handle);`

`int handle;`   Handle of an open file

EXAMPLE CALL `close(handle);`

INCLUDES `#include <io.h>`   For function declaration

DESCRIPTION The *close* function closes the file specified by the argument *handle*. The *handle* must be the integer returned by a previous call to the function *open* or *creat*.

RETURNS If the file is successfully closed, *close* returns a 0. Otherwise, it returns a value of −1 to indicate error and sets the global variable *errno* to the constant EBADF, indicating an invalid file handle.

SEE ALSO open   To open a file for unformatted, unbuffered I/O

fopen, fclose   File opening and closing for buffered I/O

EXAMPLE Illustrate the use of *close* by attempting to close a file that is not open. Use *perror* to print the error message returned by the system.

```
#include <stdio.h>
#include <io.h>
main()
{
/* Call close with an invalid file handle. Handles 0
 * thru 4 are in use by stdin, stdout, stderr, stdaux
 * and stdprn. So, let's use handle 5.
 */
    printf("Attempting to close file handle 5...\n");
    if ( close(5) != 0)
    {
        perror("Close failed");
    }
}
```

Low-level I/O
creat

COMPATIBILITY	MSC 3	MSC 4	MSC 5	QC	TC	ANSI	UNIX V
	▲	▲	▲	▲	▲		▲

PURPOSE Use *creat* to make a new file or truncate an existing file. The file is specified by its name which may include a path specification.

SYNTAX `int creat(char *filename, int pmode);`

`char *filename;`   File name and path specification

`int pmode;`   Permission settings for the file, indicating whether reading, writing, or both are permitted

EXAMPLE CALL `handle = creat("temp.dat", S_IREAD¦S_IWRITE);`

INCLUDES `#include <io.h>`   For function declaration

`#include <sys\types.h>`   For definition of data types used in ⟨sys\stat.h⟩

`#include <sys\stat.h>`   For definition of constants to specify permission settings of a file

DESCRIPTION The *creat* function first checks whether the file named *filename* exists. If it does, the file is truncated, opened for writing and the previous contents of the file are destroyed. If the file does not exist, a new one is created. The argument *filename* includes the directory specification as well as the name of the file. If no directory specification is present, the file is created in the current working directory. Thus if the *filename* is *"c:\\temp\\test.dat"* the file is created in directory \TEMP of drive C, even if the current directory is something else.

The integer argument *pmode* specifies the newly created file's permission setting, which is applied to the file when it is closed. The permission setting is given in terms of predefined constants. The permission settings given in *pmode* are validated against the current default settings defined by *umask*. Consult the reference pages on *umask* for this validation process. The possible values of *pmode* are given in Table 15-16.

RETURNS If the file is successfully created (or truncated), *creat* returns a valid handle to the file. In case of error, it returns a −1 and sets the global variable *errno* to one of the constants defined in the file *errno.h*. These are defined in the table below.

 **Input and Output Routines**

Error Constant	Meaning
EACCES	Cannot access file. This means the given file name refers to a directory, or the file is read only, or file-sharing is enabled and sharing mode does not allow the operation being attempted.
EMFILE	No more file handles available. This means you have hit the MS-DOS enforced limit of 20 files that a single process can open simultaneously.
ENOENT	File was not found or a directory corresponding to the path specification in the file name is nonexistent.

COMMENTS The *creat* function is included to preserve compatibility with libraries in earlier versions of Microsoft C. The function of *creat* is provided by *open* with the flags O_CREAT and O_TRUNC. Microsoft recommends that you use *open* to create files, instead of *creat*.

SEE ALSO open   To open a file for unformatted, unbuffered I/O

umask   To specify default permission setting

EXAMPLE Write a C program that prompts the user for a file name and then uses *creat* to open that file with both read and write permission settings. Use *perror* to inform the user of errors.

```
#include <stdio.h>
#include <sys\types.h>
#include <sys\stat.h>
#include <io.h>

main()
{
    int handle;
    unsigned char filename[81];

/* Ask user for file name */
    printf("Enter name of file to be created: ");
    gets(filename);
    if ( (handle = creat(filename, S_IREAD|S_IWRITE))
        == -1)
    {
        perror("Error creating file!");
    }
    else
    {
        printf("\nFile %s created\n", filename);
    }
}
```

creat

Low-level I/O
dup

COMPATIBILITY	MSC 3	MSC 4	MSC 5	QC	TC	ANSI	UNIX V
	▲	▲	▲	▲	▲		▲

PURPOSE Use *dup* to create a second handle for a file that is already open and has a valid handle.

SYNTAX `int dup(int handle);`

`int handle;`   Handle of an open file

EXAMPLE CALL `new_handle = dup(old_handle);`

INCLUDES `#include <io.h>`   For function declaration

DESCRIPTION The *dup* function assigns another handle to a file that is already open and has a valid handle. The current handle must be given in the argument *handle*. The creation of a duplicate handle counts as a new open file and is subject to the 20-file limit imposed by MS-DOS.

COMMON USES In UNIX systems, *dup* is used to perform I/O with an interprocess communication mechanism called "pipes."

RETURNS If a new handle is successfully created, *dup* returns the duplicate handle. Otherwise, it returns a value of −1 to indicate error and sets the global variable *errno* to either EMFILE if no more file handles are possible or to EBADF, indicating that the argument *handle* is not a valid file handle.

SEE ALSO open   To open a file for unformatted, unbuffered I/O

creat   To create a new file and open it for unformatted, unbuffered I/O

EXAMPLE Create a new handle for *stdout* that is assigned the handle 1 when the program starts running. Write a string to the new handle to show that indeed the new handle refers to stdout.

```
#include <stdio.h>
#include <io.h>
char message[] =
"Testing dup. This should appear on stdout\n";
main()
{
    int newhandle;
/* By default, stdout has handle 1.
 * create another handle for stdout
```

 Input and Output Routines

```
*/
    if((newhandle = dup(1)) == -1)
    {
            perror("dup on handle 1 failed!");
    }
    else
    {
            printf("New handle for stdout is %d\n", newhandle);
            write(newhandle, message, sizeof(message));
    }
}
```

Low-level I/O

dup2

COMPATIBILITY	MSC 3	MSC 4	MSC 5	QC	TC	ANSI	UNIX V
	▲	▲	▲	▲	▲		▲

PURPOSE Use *dup2* to force a second file handle to refer to the same file as a first one. The first handle must be a valid one, associated with a file that is already open.

SYNTAX `int dup2(int handle1, int handle2);`

`int handle1;`   Handle of an open file

`int handle2;`   Another handle that will become associated with the same file as *handle1*

EXAMPLE CALL `dup2(oldhandle, newhandle);`

INCLUDES `#include <io.h>`   For function declaration

DESCRIPTION The *dup2* function forces *handle2* to refer to the same file as *handle1*, a valid handle to a file that is currently open. If *handle2* also refers to an open file, that file is closed and *handle2* is then assigned to the file associated with *handle1*. After successful return from *dup2*, either handle may be used to refer to the file.

COMMON USES The *dup2* function is used to redirect the standard input and output streams, *stdin* and *stdout*.

RETURNS If *handle2* is successfully assigned to the file associated with *handle1*, *dup2* returns a 0. Otherwise, it returns a -1 to indicate error and sets the global variable *errno* to either EMFILE if no more file handles are possible or to the constant EBADF, indicating that *handle1* is not a valid file handle.

dup2

SEE ALSO   open   To open a file for unformatted, unbuffered I/O

          creat   To create a new file and open it for unformatted, unbuffered I/O

EXAMPLE   Use *dup2* to write a program that redirects *stdout* to a file of your choice. Open a file and use *dup2* to assign *handle1* (the usual handle for *stdout*) to the newly opened file (use the macro *fileno* to find this). Now write some messages to *stdout* and they should go to the file. Remember to flush the buffers, close the file, and reassign handle 1 to *stdout*.

```
#include <stdio.h>
#include <io.h>
main()
{
    int saved_handle;
    char filename[81];
    FILE *new_stdout;
/* Ask for filename to which stdout will be assigned */
    printf("Enter filename to which stdout will be \
assigned:");

    gets(filename);
    if((new_stdout = fopen(filename, "w")) == NULL)
    {
            perror("fopen failed");
            exit(1);
    }
/* First duplicate the handle for stdout so that we can
 * reset things at the end
 */
    if((saved_handle = dup(1)) == -1)
    {
            perror("dup failed on handle 1!");
            exit(1);
    }
/* Get the handle of the new file using 'fileno' and
 * assign handle 1 (stdout) to it by calling dup2
 */
    if(dup2(fileno(new_stdout), 1) == -1)
    {
            perror("dup2 failed to assign handle 1!");
    }
    else
    {
            printf("New handle for stdout is %d\n",
                fileno(new_stdout));
        printf("Testing dup2. \
This should be in file: %s\n", filename);
```

 Input and Output Routines

```
/* Flush to send output to open file */
        fflush(stdout);
/* Reassign stdout to handle 1 before exiting */
        fclose(new_stdout);
        dup2(saved_handle, 1);
        printf("Enter 'TYPE %s' to see result\n",
                filename);
    }
}
```

eof

COMPATIBILITY	MSC 3	MSC 4	MSC 5	QC	TC	ANSI	UNIX V
	▲	▲	▲	▲	▲		

PURPOSE Use the *eof* function to determine whether end-of-file has been reached in a file specified by its handle.

SYNTAX `int eof(int handle);`

`int handle;`   Handle of an open file

EXAMPLE CALL `if(eof(handle) != 0) printf("File ended!\n");`

INCLUDES `#include <io.h>`   For function declaration

DESCRIPTION The *eof* function checks whether the file specified by the argument *handle* is at the end-of-file. The analogous function for stream I/O is *feof*. Many low-level I/O routines return a −1 to indicate an error. Since low-level I/O routines are used primarily to read binary data and a data byte could very well contain a −1 (FF in hexadecimal), a function such as *eof* is necessary to determine if the file actually ended or you simply read a byte containing the value −1.

RETURNS For a valid file handle, *eof* returns a 1 to indicate an end-of-file and a 0 when not. If the specified file handle is invalid, it returns a −1 and sets the global variable *errno* to the constant EBADF.

SEE ALSO `feof, ferror`   To determine end-of-file and error conditions for files opened for buffered I/O

EXAMPLE Write a program that opens up the file *autoexec.bat* in the root directory of drive C and reads it, 80 bytes at a time, until end-of-file is reached. Use the *eof* function to test for end-of-file. Display the data read.

eof

```
#include <stdio.h>
#include <io.h>
#include <fcntl.h>
main()
{
    int fhandle, total=0, count;
    unsigned char buffer[80];
/* Open the file "autoexec.bat." Note the two '\' */
    if ( (fhandle = open("c:\\autoexec.bat",
                          O_RDONLY)) == -1)
    {
        printf("open failed");
            exit(1);
    }
    printf("Contents of c:autoexec.bat:\n");
    while ( !eof(fhandle))            /* Read until EOF */
    {
        if ((count = read(fhandle, buffer, 80)) == -1)
        {
            perror("read error");
            break;   /* exit from while loop */
        }
        total += count;
        write(1, buffer, count);
    }
    printf("=== %d bytes read ===\n", total);
}
```

Low-level I/O
lseek

COMPATIBILITY	MSC 3	MSC 4	MSC 5	QC	TC	ANSI	UNIX V
	▲	▲	▲	▲	▲		▲

PURPOSE Use the *lseek* function to move to a new position in a file opened for unbuffered and unformatted I/O.

SYNTAX `long lseek(int handle, long offset, int origin);`

`int handle;`   Handle associated with file whose current position is to be set

`long offset;`   Offset of new position (in bytes) from origin

`int origin;`   Constant indicating the position from which to offset

EXAMPLE CALL `lseek(fhandle, 512L, SEEK_SET); /* Skip 512 bytes */`

 Input and Output Routines

INCLUDES   #include <stdio.h>   For definition of constants used to specify "origin"

#include <io.h>   For function declaration

DESCRIPTION   The *lseek* function sets the current read or write position of the file specified by the argument *handle* to a new value indicated by the arguments *offset* and *origin*. The *offset* is a long integer indicating how far away the new position is from a specific location given in *origin*. The *origin,* defined in *stdio.h*, must be one of the constants shown in the table.

Origin	Interpretation
SEEK_SET	Beginning of file
SEEK_CUR	Current position in the file
SEEK_END	End of file

The file position may be set anywhere in the file except before the beginning of the file.

COMMON USES   The *lseek* function is used when reading unformatted data from files in a random manner. For example, an application may create a data file with a specific format, say, a header of 512 bytes followed by actual data. When reading from such a file, you can use *lseek* to jump over the header and retrieve specific pieces of information with *read*.

RETURNS   When successful, *lseek* returns the offset of the current position from the beginning of the file. In case of error, the return value is −1 and the global variable *errno* is set to either EBADF, indicating that the file handle is invalid, or to EINVAL if an attempt is made to set position before the beginning of the file. If the handle is associated with a device for which setting the current position does not make sense, the return value is meaningless.

SEE ALSO   tell   To get the offset of the current position in a file in number of bytes from the beginning

fseek   Counterpart of *lseek* for files opened for buffered I/O

EXAMPLE   Open a file, *autoexec.bat*, in your system and go to the end of the file using *lseek* with SEEK_END as origin. Report the value returned by *lseek*. This is the size of the file in bytes. Now move back 20 bytes and read the last 20 bytes in the file. Display the characters read.

```
#include <stdio.h>
#include <io.h>
#include <fcntl.h>
```

lseek

```
main()
{
    int fhandle, count;
    long curpos;
    unsigned char buffer[20];
/* Open the file "autoexec.bat." */
    if ( (fhandle = open("c:\\autoexec.bat",
                  O_RDONLY)) == -1)
    {
            printf("open failed");
                    exit(1);
    }
/* Go to end of file using "lseek" and SEEK_END */
    curpos = lseek(fhandle, 0L, SEEK_END);
    printf("End of file in 'autoexec.bat' is %ld bytes \
from beginning\n", curpos);
/* Move back 20 bytes, read the last 20 bytes
 * and print the characters that were read in.
 */
    lseek(fhandle, -20L, SEEK_CUR);
    if ((count = read(fhandle, buffer, 20)) == -1)
    {
            perror("read error");
            exit(1);
    }
    printf("The last 20 characters in 'autoexec.bat' are:\n");
    write(1, buffer, count);
}
```

Low-level I/O

open

COMPATIBILITY	MSC 3	MSC 4	MSC 5	QC	TC	ANSI	UNIX V
	▲	▲	▲	▲	▲		

PURPOSE Before performing any read or write operations, use *open* to open a file for unbuffered and unformatted I/O operations.

SYNTAX `int open(char *filename, int oflag [, int pmode]);`

`char *filename;`   Name of file to be opened, including drive and directory specification

`int oflag;`   Integer formed by bitwise OR of predefined constants that indicate the types of operations allowed on that file

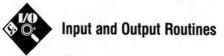 **Input and Output Routines**

int pmode; Optional argument to specify whether reading, writing, or both are permitted

EXAMPLE CALL filehandle = open("temp.dat", O_WRONLY|O_CREAT, S_IWRITE);

INCLUDES #include <io.h> For function declaration

#include <fcntl.h> For definition of constants to indicate valid operations

#include <sys\types.h> For definition of data types used in <sys\stat.h>

#include <sys\stat.h> For definition of constants to specify permission settings of a file

DESCRIPTION The *open* function opens the file specified in the argument *filename*. The type of operations you intend to perform on the file once it is opened must be indicated by the argument *oflag*. This is an integer formed by the bitwise OR of the constants shown in Table 15-15. The constants are defined in the include file *fcntl.h*.

Table 15-15. *Constants Indicating Type of Operations Allowed on File*

Constant	Interpretation
O_APPEND	Writing always occurs at the end of the file.
O_BINARY	File is opened in the binary, or untranslated, mode. This is the same binary mode used with *fopen*; see its reference pages for more explanation.
O_CREAT	Creates and opens a file for writing if the named file does not exist.
O_EXCL	Returns an error value if file already exists and O_CREAT was specified.
O_RDONLY	File is opened for reading only. When O_RDONLY is given, O_WRONLY and O_RDWR are disallowed.
O_RDWR	File is opened for both reading and writing. When O_RDWR is given, O_RDONLY and O_WRONLY are disallowed.
O_TEXT	File is opened in text, or translated, mode. This is the same text mode used with *fopen*; see its reference pages for elaboration.
O_TRUNC	Opens an existing file and truncates it to zero length, destroying its current contents. The file must have write permission for this to succeed.
O_WRONLY	File is opened for writing only. When O_WRONLY is used, O_RDONLY and O_RDWR are not allowed.

The third argument to *open*, *pmode*, you only need it when requesting the creation of a new file by using the flag O_CREAT. If the file does not exist, the value of *pmode* is used to set the permission of the newly created file. Table 15-16 shows the possible values of the argument *pmode*. These constants are defined in the header file *sys\stat.h*. As you can see in the table, a file in MS-DOS always has read permission. The permission setting indicated by the *pmode* argument is modified by the permission mask that you can set with *umask*. Consult its reference pages to see how this is done.

open

Table 15-16. *Permission Settings for Newly Created Files*

Constant	Interpretation
S_IWRITE	Both reading and writing permitted.
S_IREAD	Only reading permitted.
S_IREAD ¦ S_IWRITE	Both reading and writing permitted.

Microsoft warns users of a bug under MS-DOS versions 3.0 and above that can occur when file-sharing is enabled. The sharing is enabled by executing SHARE.EXE, which comes with these versions of MS-DOS. Once this is done and a file is opened with *oflag* set to O_CREAT¦O_READONLY or O_CREAT¦O_WRONLY, DOS prematurely closes the file during any system calls made within *open*. The suggested remedy is to open the file with *pmode* equal to S_IWRITE. Then, after closing the file you can call *chmod* to change the permission back to *S_IREAD*. Another remedy is to open the file with *pmode* set to S_IREAD and *oflag* equal to O_CREAT¦O_RDWR.

COMMON USES The *open* function is used to open a file before performing any unbuffered and unformatted I/O (see the tutorial section) operations on it.

RETURNS If the file is successfully opened, *open* returns the file handle, an integer to be used in subsequent I/O operations on the file using the functions *read* and *write*. In case of an error, *open* returns a -1. At the same time, the global variable *errno* is set to one of the constants shown in Table 15-17 and defined in *errno.h*.

Table 15-17. *Error Codes Returned by* open

Error Constant	Meaning of Error Value
EACCES	Cannot access file. This means the file name refers to a directory, or an attempt was made to open a read-only file for write operations, or file-sharing is enabled and sharing mode does not allow the operation being attempted.
EINVAL	Invalid or conflicting open mode and permissionsetting.
EEXIST	This error is returned when the flags O_CREAT and O_EXCL are specified but the file already exists.
EMFILE	No more file handles available. This means you have hit the MS-DOS 20-file limit that a single process can open simultaneously.
ENOENT	File was not found or a directory corresponding to the path specification in the file name is nonexistent.

SEE ALSO

close   To close a file opened by *open*

fopen   To open a file for buffered I/O

EXAMPLE Write a program that prompts for a file name and opens that file for write operations. Use the O_CREAT and the O_EXCL operation flags to ensure that an existing file is not destroyed.

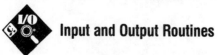 **Input and Output Routines**

```
#include <stdio.h>
#include <io.h>
#include <fcntl.h>
#include <sys\types.h>
#include <sys\stat.h>

main()
{
    int handle;
    char filename[81];
    printf("Enter name of a file to open: ");
    gets(filename);
/* Open the file for write operations.
 * Don't overwrite existing file.
 */
    if ((handle = open(filename, O_WRONLY|O_CREAT|O_EXCL,
                  S_IREAD|S_IWRITE))  == -1)
    {
/* Use perror to print the message so that we also see
 * the error message corresponding to the value of
 * 'errno'
 */
            perror("Open failed! ");
    }
    else
    {
            printf("File %s opened successfully\n",filename);
/* In an actual program we will use the file for I/O.
 * Here we simply exit.
 */
    }
}
```

Low-level I/O
read

COMPATIBILITY	MSC 3	MSC 4	MSC 5	QC	TC	ANSI	UNIX V
	▲	▲	▲	▲	▲		▲

PURPOSE Use *read* to retrieve a specified number of bytes of data, without any formatting, from the current position in a file that has been opened for unformatted I/O.

SYNTAX `int read(int handle, char *buffer, unsigned count);`

`int handle;`   Handle of file from which data will be read

`char *buffer;`   Pointer to buffer into which data will be copied

`unsigned count;`   Number of bytes to be read

read

EXAMPLE CALL
```
if ((bytes_read = read(fhandle, bigbuffer, 60000)) == -1)
                perror("read error");
```

INCLUDES   `#include <io.h>`   For function declaration

DESCRIPTION   The *read* function copies the number of bytes specified in the argument *count* from the file whose handle is in the integer argument *handle* to the array of characters, *buffer*. Reading starts at the current position, which is incremented when the operation is completed. If the file is opened in the text mode, each CR-LF pair read from the file is replaced by a newline character in the *buffer*, and a Control-Z character is interpreted as end-of-file.

RETURNS   The *read* function returns the number of bytes actually read from the file. In case of an error, *read* returns −1 and sets *errno* to EBADF to indicate an invalid file handle or that the file was not opened for writing. In MS-DOS 3.0 and higher, read errors may occur due to a locked file.

COMMENTS   Since *read* returns an signed integer, the return value should be converted to *unsigned int* when reading more than 32 K of data from a file or the return value will be negative. Because the number of bytes to be read is specified in an unsigned integer argument, you could theoretically read 65,535 bytes at a time. But, 65,535 (or FFFFh) also means −1 in signed representation so when reading 65,535 bytes the return value indicates an error. The practical maximum then is 65,534.

SEE ALSO   `creat, open, sopen`   To create and open new files for unformatted I/O

`write`   To write a specified number of bytes to a file

EXAMPLE   Write a program that opens a file, say, "autoexec.bat," in the root directory of drive C, reads 60,000 bytes from it, and displays the number of bytes read.

```
#include <stdio.h>
#include <io.h>
#include <fcntl.h>
static char bigbuffer[60000];
main()
{
        int fhandle, total=0;
        unsigned int bytes_read;

/* Open the file "autoexec.bat." Note that we need two '\'  */
        if ( (fhandle = open("c:autoexec.bat",
                            O_RDONLY)) == -1)
        {
            printf("open failed");
            exit(1);
        }
        printf(
```

 Input and Output Routines

```
        "Attempting to read 60000 bytes from c:autoexec.bat:\n");
        if ((bytes_read = read(fhandle, bigbuffer, 60000)) == -1)
        {
            perror("read error");
            exit(1);
        }
        printf("Only %u bytes read. Here's what was read:\n",
                bytes_read);
        write(1, bigbuffer, bytes_read);
}
```

Low-level I/O

sopen

COMPATIBILITY	MSC 3	MSC 4	MSC 5	QC	TC	ANSI	UNIX V
	▲	▲	▲	▲	▲		

PURPOSE Use *sopen* to open a file for shared, unbuffered, and unformatted I/O operations. File-sharing is ignored if SHARE.EXE has not been run. Note that SHARE.EXE (or SHARE.COM), commands that facilitate use of MS-DOS systems in local area networks, is present only in MS-DOS versions 3.0 and higher.

SYNTAX `int sopen(char *filename, int oflag, int shflag [, int pmode]);`

`char *filename;`   Name of file to be opened, including drive and directory specification

`int oflag;`   Integer formed by bitwise OR of predefined constants that indicate the types of operations allowed on file being opened

`int shflag;`   Integer formed by bitwise OR of predefined constants that indicate the modes of sharing to be enabled

`int pmode;`   Optional argument to specify whether reading, writing, or both are permitted

EXAMPLE CALL `fhandle = sopen("c:\\autoexec.bat", O_RDONLY, SH_DENYRW);`

INCLUDES `#include <io.h>`   For function declaration

`#include <share.h>`   For definition of constants to indicate modes of sharing

`#include <fcntl.h>`   For definition of constants to indicate valid operations

`#include <sys\types.h>`   For definition of data types used in ⟨sys\stat.h⟩

`#include <sys\stat.h>`   For definition of constants to specify permission settings of a file

sopen

DESCRIPTION   The *sopen* function opens the file specified in the argument *filename*. The type of operations you intend to perform on the file once it is opened must be indicated by the argument *oflag*, an integer formed by the bitwise OR of constants shown in Table 15-15. The constants are defined in the include file *fcntl.h*.

The argument *shflag* is used to specify the level of sharing enabled. It is specified by bitwise OR of an appropriate combination of constants defined in the file *share.h* and shown in Table 15-18. The argument is ignored if you have not enabled file-sharing by running SHARE.EXE (or SHARE.COM).

Table 15-18. *Constants that Indicate Level of File-Sharing*

Constant	Interpretation
SH_COMPAT	No other process is allowed to access the file. This is called the "compatibility mode" and the same process can open the file any number of times in this mode. This is how DOS normally operates, hence the name.
SH_DENYRW	A single process has exclusive read and write access to the file. The process must close the file before opening it again.
SH_DENYWR	No other process can access the file for writing.
SH_DENYRD	No other process can access the file for reading.
SH_DENYNO	Any process may access the file for both reading and for writing.

The last argument to *sopen*, *pmode*, is necessary only when requesting the creation of a new file by the flag O_CREAT. If the file does not already exist, the value of *pmode* is used to set the permission of the newly created file. Table 15-16 shows the various values of the argument *pmode*. As you can see in Table 15-16, an MS-DOS file always has read permission. The permission setting indicated by the *pmode* argument is modified by the permission mask set by calling *umask*. Consult the reference pages on *umask* to see how this is done. These *pmode* constants are defined in the header file *sys\stat.h*.

Microsoft warns users of a bug under MS-DOS versions 3.0 and above that can occur when opening a file with *sopen* with file-sharing enabled. File-sharing is enabled by executing SHARE.EXE which comes with these versions of MS-DOS. Once this is done and a file is opened with *oflag* set to O_CREAT|O_READONLY or O_CREAT|O_WRONLY and *sh_flag* set to SH_COMPAT, DOS prematurely closes the file during any system calls made within *sopen* or it will generate a "sharing violation" interrupt (number 24h). The suggested remedy is to sopen the file with *pmode* set to S_IWRITE. Then, after closing the file you can call *chmod* to change the permission back to S_IREAD. Another remedy is to sopen the file with *pmode* set to S_IREAD and *oflag* equal to O_CREAT|O_RDWR and *shflag* set to SH_COMPAT. Starting with Microsoft C 5.1, under OS/2, *sopen* enables you to open files for sharing by multiple processes.

COMMON USES   The *sopen* function is used to open files for sharing in networks. It works in the same way as *open* except that it can also specify the level of file-sharing allowed.

 **Input and Output Routines**

RETURNS   If the file is successfully opened, *sopen* returns the file handle, an integer to be used in subsequent I/O operations on the file using the functions *read* and *write*. In case of an error, *sopen* returns a −1. At the same time, the global variable *errno* is set to one of the constants shown in Table 15-17 and defined in *errno.h*:

COMMENTS   File-sharing modes work properly only with unbuffered files. So you should not call *fdopen* to associate a FILE data structure and enable buffering for a file opened by *sopen*.

SEE ALSO   close   To close a file opened by *sopen*

fopen   To open a file for buffered I/O

EXAMPLE   If you are running MS-DOS version 3.0 or higher, install file-sharing by typing SHARE to run the program SHARE.EXE distributed with DOS. Now open a file, *autoexec.bat*, by calling *sopen* with the "share flag" equal to SH _DENYRW. Try to open the file once more. If it fails, you have not installed file-sharing. On the other hand, if SHARE has been run, this second call will fail because the file is already open and no one has permission to read or write (not even the same process!).

```
#include <stdio.h>
#include <io.h>
#include <fcntl.h>
#include <share.h>
main()
{
    int fhandle1, fhandle2;

/* Open the file "autoexec.bat." */
    if ( (fhandle1 = sopen("c:\\autoexec.bat",
                    O_RDONLY, SH_DENYRW)) == -1)
    {
        perror("open failed");
        exit(1);
    }
    printf("AUTOEXEC.BAT opened once. Handle = %d\n",
            fhandle1);
/* Now open again */
    if ( (fhandle2 = sopen("c:autoexec.bat",
                    O_RDONLY, SH_DENYRW)) == -1)
    {
        perror("open failed");
        printf("SHARE installed\n");
        exit(1);
    }
    printf("AUTOEXEC.BAT opened again. Handle = %d\n",
            fhandle2);
```

sopen

```
    printf("SHARE has not been installed\n");
}
```

Low-level I/O
tell

COMPATIBILITY	MSC 3	MSC 4	MSC 5	QC	TC	ANSI	UNIX V
	▲	▲	▲	▲	▲		

PURPOSE Use *tell* to determine the current position in a file specified by its handle.

SYNTAX `long tell(int handle);`

`int handle;`   Handle of an open file

EXAMPLE CALL `curpos = tell(filehandle);`

INCLUDES `#include <io.h>`   For function declaration

DESCRIPTION The *tell* function returns the current position in the file specified by the argument *handle*. The position is returned as the number of bytes from the beginning of the file.

RETURNS For a valid file handle, *tell* returns the current position as a long integer value containing the byte offset of the current location in the file from its beginning. If the specified file handle is invalid, it returns a −1 and sets the global variable *errno* to the constant EBADF. If the handle refers to a device for which the file position cannot be set arbitrarily, the value returned by *tell* is meaningless.

SEE ALSO `lseek`   To set the current position in a file opened for unformatted I/O

`ftell`   Counterpart of *tell* for files opened for buffered I/O

EXAMPLE Write a program that opens a file and uses *tell* to report the current position in the file. Now read 80 bytes from the file using *read*. Check and report the position again after the read.

```
#include <stdio.h>
#include <io.h>
#include <fcntl.h>
main()
{
    int fhandle, count;
    long curpos;
```

 Input and Output Routines

```
        unsigned char buffer[80];
/* Open the file "autoexec.bat." */
    if ( (fhandle = open("c:\\autoexec.bat",
                            O_RDONLY)) == -1)
    {
            printf("open failed");
            exit(1);
    }
/* Display current position using "tell" */
    curpos = tell(fhandle);
    printf("Currently at position %ld \
in 'autoexec.bat'\n", curpos);
/* Now read 80 bytes and check position again */
    if ((count = read(fhandle, buffer, 80)) == -1)
    {
            perror("read error");
            exit(1);
    }
    printf("Read following 80 characters:\n");
    write(1, buffer, count);
    curpos = tell(fhandle);
    printf("\nNow at position: %ld bytes from beginning\n",
                curpos);
}
```

Low-level I/O
write

COMPATIBILITY	MSC 3	MSC 4	MSC 5	QC	TC	ANSI	UNIX V
	▲	▲	▲	▲	▲		▲

PURPOSE Use _write_ to save a specified number of bytes of data, without any formatting, at the current position in a file opened for unformatted I/O.

SYNTAX `int write(int handle, char *buffer, unsigned count);`

`int handle;` Handle of file to which data will be written

`char *buffer;` Pointer to array of characters representing data to be written

`unsigned count;` Number of bytes to be written

EXAMPLE CALL `write(handle, data_buffer, 1024);`

INCLUDES `#include <io.h>` For function declaration

DESCRIPTION   In a file opened by a call to *open* for writing or appending, the *write* function copies the number of bytes specified in the argument *count* from the array at *buffer* to the file whose handle is in the integer argument *handle*. The writing of the data begins at the current position in the file and the current position is appropriately incremented after writing out the data. If the file is opened for appending, the writing will always take place at the end of the file.

If the file is opened in text mode, each newline character in the data is replaced by a CR-LF pair in the file. Note that *write* treats a Control-Z character as the logical end-of-file.

RETURNS   The *write* function returns the number of bytes actually written to the file. If, for example, the disk space runs out before all the data is written, the return value may be something less than *count*. A return value of −1 indicates an error. The value in the global variable *errno* will contain an error code; if it is equal to the constant EBADF, the error was caused by giving either an invalid file handle or one for a file not opened for writing. If the system runs out of disk space, *errno* is set to the constant ENOSPC.

COMMENTS   When writing more than 32 K of data to a file, you receive the value returned by *write* in an *unsigned int* variable; otherwise an *int* shows a negative value. A consequence of returning a −1 to indicate error is that you can write no more than 65,534 bytes to a file at a time and still be able to tell if an error has occurred because 65,535 (or FFFF in hexadecimal) is also the representation of −1 in the microprocessor.

SEE ALSO   creat, open, sopen   To create and open new files for unformatted I/O

write   To write a specified number of bytes to a file

EXAMPLE   Open a file for write operations and write a large number of bytes to the file. Report the value returned by *write*. Initialize the buffer to be written with a test message that ends with a Control-Z (\032) so you can type the file with the TYPE command and have the printing stop after that because it interprets Control-Z as the end-of-file.

```
#include <stdio.h>
#include <sys\types.h>
#include <sys\stat.h>
#include <fcntl.h>
#include <io.h>
/* Initialize array with a string plus Control-Z to
 * mark end of file.
 */
static char bigbuffer[60000]="Testing write\n\032";
main()
{
    unsigned bytes_written;
    int filehandle;
```

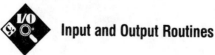 **Input and Output Routines**

```
        char filename[81];
        printf("Enter name of file to be opened for \
writing:");
        gets(filename);
/* Open the file for write operations.
 * Don't overwrite existing file.
 */
        if ((filehandle = open(filename,
        O_WRONLY|O_CREAT|O_EXCL, S_IREAD|S_IWRITE)) == -1)
        {
            perror("Open failed! ");
            exit(1);
        }
/* Now write out 60,000 bytes of data.
 * Most of it'll be junk.
 */
        if((bytes_written = write(filehandle, bigbuffer,
                            60000)) == -1)
        {
            perror("write failed");
        }
        else
        {
            printf("%u bytes written to file: %s\n",
                    bytes_written,  filename);
            printf("Use 'TYPE %s' to see result\n",
                    filename);
        }
    }
}
```

Console and Port I/O

cgets

COMPATIBILITY	MSC 3	MSC 4	MSC 5	QC	TC	ANSI	UNIX V
	▲	▲	▲	▲	▲		

PURPOSE Use *cgets* to read a string of characters from the keyboard. The line is read until a newline character is reached and replaced by a null character, which generates a C string. You must allocate the buffer in which the string is stored. Store as the first byte the maximum number of characters to be read.

SYNTAX `char *cgets(char *buffer);`

`char *buffer;` Buffer where string will be stored

EXAMPLE CALL `cgets(user_input);`

INCLUDES `#include <conio.h>` For function declaration

DESCRIPTION The *cgets* function begins by reading the value in the first character of the buffer whose address is given in the argument *buffer*. The function uses that as the maximum number of characters to be read. It accepts keystrokes and stores them in *buffer* starting at the third location (i.e., *buffer2*). The reading from the keyboard continues until a newline character is encountered or until the specified maximum number of characters has been read. Then *cgets* replaces the newline character with a null character and returns after storing in *buffer1* the number of characters it read. Note that the buffer whose address is given in the argument *buffer* must have enough room to hold all the characters, including the null character and the additional two bytes used to store the two lengths.

RETURNS The *cgets* function returns a pointer to the beginning of the string (i.e., the location *buffer2*).

SEE ALSO cputs   To write a string to the console

EXAMPLE Use *cgets* to read a line from the console. Display the line using *cprintf*.

```
#include <conio.h>
main()
{
    int numread;
    char string[82], *input;
    string[0] = 80;       /* Max no. of characters */
    cprintf("Enter a line: ");
    input = cgets(string);
    numread = string[1];   /* Number of chars read*/
    cprintf("\nYou entered: %d characters. \
The string is \r\n%s\r\n", numread, input);
}
```

Console and Port I/O
cprintf

COMPATIBILITY	MSC 3	MSC 4	MSC 5	QC	TC	ANSI	UNIX V
	▲	▲	▲	▲	▲		

PURPOSE Use *cprintf* to convert the values of C variables into a character string according to specified formats and print the string on the display. This function provides the function of *printf* for console output operations.

SYNTAX `int cprintf(char *format_string, ...);`

`char *format_string;`   Character string that describes the format to be used

`...`   Variable number of arguments depending on the number of items being printed

 Input and Output Routines

EXAMPLE CALL `cprintf("File %s has %d bytes of data\n", fname, size);`

INCLUDES `#include <conio.h>`   For function declaration

DESCRIPTION The *cprintf* function accepts a variable number of arguments and formats and prints them to the console. The format to be used for each variable is specified in *format_string*, an array of characters with embedded formatting commands that start with a percentage sign. The reference pages on *printf* describe in detail the formatting options available.

Note that *cprintf* does not translate the newline character (\n) to a CR-LF combination, instead \n is interpreted as a linefeed and \r should be used to indicate a carriage return.

RETURNS The *cprintf* function returns the number of characters it has printed on the console.

SEE ALSO `printf`   For printing to *stdout* and for detailed information on formats

EXAMPLE Use *cprintf* to display a formatted table of the cubes of the numbers from 1 to 10 on the screen.

```
#include <conio.h>
main()
{
    int i;
    cprintf("Table of cubes\r\n");
    for(i=1; i<11; i++)
    {
        cprintf("The cube of %2d is %4d\r\n", i, i*i*i);
    }
}
```

Console and Port I/O

cputs

COMPATIBILITY	MSC 3	MSC 4	MSC 5	QC	TC	ANSI	UNIX V
	▲	▲	▲	▲	▲		

PURPOSE Use *cputs* to write a string to the display. No newline character is sent after the string.

SYNTAX `int cputs(char *string);`

`char *string;`   String to be output

EXAMPLE CALL `cputs("Are you sure (Y/N)? ");`

INCLUDES `#include <conio.h>`   For function declaration

DESCRIPTION The *cputs* function writes the string specified in the argument *string* to the display. Unlike *puts*, *cputs* does not automatically send a newline character after writing the string to the display.

RETURNS In Microsoft C version 5.0, and 5.1, *cputs* returns a zero if successful and a nonzero value in case of error. In earlier versions, *cputs* has no return value.

SEE ALSO cgets   To read a line from the console

EXAMPLE Use *cputs* to write a message to the screen.

```
#include <stdio.h>
char message[81] =
        "Insert the 'Upgrade 1.1' disk into drive A:\n";
main()
{
    cputs(message);
}
```

Console and Port I/O

cscanf

COMPATIBILITY	MSC 3	MSC 4	MSC 5	QC	TC	ANSI	UNIX V
	▲	▲	▲	▲	▲		

PURPOSE Use *cscanf* to read characters directly from the keyboard, convert them into values using specified formats, and store the values in C variables.

SYNTAX `int cscanf(char *format_string,...);`

`char *format_string;`   Character string that describes the format to be used

`...`   Variable number of arguments representing addresses of variables whose values are being read

EXAMPLE CALL `cscanf(" %d/%d/%d", &month, &day, &year);`

INCLUDES `#include <conio.h>`   For function declaration

DESCRIPTION The *cscanf* function reads an unbuffered stream of characters directly from the keyboard and converts them to values according to the format specifications embedded in the argument *format_string*. It then stores the values in C variables whose addresses are provided in the rest of the variable-length argument list. Each variable must have a corresponding formatting command in *format_string*. The format specification for a variable always begins with a percentage sign and the formatting options are the same as the ones available with the function *scanf*. (See its reference pages for a detailed list of the specifications.)

 Input and Output Routines

RETURNS The *cscanf* function returns the number of fields that were successfully read, converted, and assigned to variables. The count excludes items that were read but not assigned to any variable. The constant EOF is returned in case of an end-of-file during the read.

SEE ALSO

scanf   Formatted reading from *stdin*

fscanf   For formatted, buffered reading from a file

sscanf   Formatted reading from a string

EXAMPLE Use *cscanf* with the %p format to read a memory address from the keyboard. The address is of the form *SSSS:OOOO* in which the S and O are uppercase hexadecimal digits. Now dump out, as ASCII characters, the values in the 25 bytes following that memory address. Try the address *F000:E000* for an interesting result. (How about extending this to a small tool to examine memory in various formats—say, hexadecimal digits or integers?)

```
#include <conio.h>
main()
{
    int i;
    char far *far_ptr;
    cprintf("Enter memory address to dump in the form \
SSSS:0000\r\n(Try F0000:E0000)    ");
    cscanf(" %p", &far_ptr);
    cprintf("Dump of 25 bytes at %p\r\n", far_ptr);
    for(i=0; i<25; i++)
    {
            cprintf("%Fc", *(far_ptr+i));
    }
}
```

Console and Port I/O
getch

COMPATIBILITY	MSC 3	MSC 4	MSC 5	QC	TC	ANSI	UNIX V
	▲	▲	▲	▲	▲		

PURPOSE Use the *getch* function to read a character from the keyboard without echoing it to the display.

SYNTAX int getch(void);

EXAMPLE CALL in_char = getch();

INCLUDES #include <conio.h>   For function declaration

getch

DESCRIPTION The *getch* function reads a character from the console without any buffering and the character is not echoed to the screen. Typing CONTROL-C during a call to *getch* generates the 8086 software interrupt number 23h.

COMMON USES The *getch* function is useful in implementing user interfaces in which the user hits a single key to indicate a choice and the choice is acted on as soon as the key is pressed.

RETURNS The *getch* function returns the character read from the keyboard.

SEE ALSO

getche   To read a keystroke and echo it to the display

getchar   For buffered read from *stdin*

EXAMPLE Write a small C program enabling the user to hit any key to exit. Use *getch* to read the keystroke and exit as soon as it's done.

```c
#include <stdio.h>
#include <conio.h>

main()
{
    printf("Hit any character to exit:");
    getch();  /* Ignore character being read */
}
```

Console and Port I/O

getche

COMPATIBILITY	MSC 3	MSC 4	MSC 5	QC	TC	ANSI	UNIX V
	▲	▲	▲	▲	▲		

PURPOSE Use the *getche* function to read a character from the keyboard and echo it to the display.

SYNTAX `int getche(void);`

EXAMPLE CALL `in_char = getche();`

INCLUDES `#include <conio.h>`   For function declaration

DESCRIPTION The *getche* function reads a character from the keyboard without any buffering and echoes the character to the screen. Typing CONTROL-C during a call to *getche* generates software interrupt number 23h.

RETURNS The *getche* function returns the character read from the keyboard.

SEE ALSO

getch   To read a keystroke without echoing it to the display

getchear   For buffered read from *stdin*

 Input and Output Routines

EXAMPLE Write a program to read characters from the keyboard until a carriage return or until 80 characters have been read. Convert uppercase letters to lowercase and print the string entered. Note that you have to compare the value returned by *getche* with \r to confirm that it is a carriage return (comparing it with \n will not work).

```
#include <conio.h>

main()
{
    int i, c;
    char buffer[81];
    cprintf("Enter a line:");
    for(i=0; i<80; i++)
    {
        if((buffer[i] = tolower(getche())) == '\r')
            break;
    }
    buffer[i] = '\0';
    cprintf("\nYou entered: %s", buffer);
}
```

Console and Port I/O

inp

COMPATIBILITY	MSC 3	MSC 4	MSC 5	QC	TC	ANSI	UNIX V
	▲	▲	▲	▲	inportb		

PURPOSE Use *inp* to read a byte from a specific I/O port whose address you provide as an argument. For example, you can use *inp* read from port 21h to determine which interrupt numbers are currently acknowledged by the 8259A programmable interrupt controller.

SYNTAX int inp(unsigned port);

unsigned port;   Address of the port from which a byte is to be read

EXAMPLE CALL byte_read = inp(0x3f8);

INCLUDES #include <conio.h>   For function declaration

DESCRIPTION The *inp* function uses the assembly language instruction IN to read a byte of data from the port address specified in the argument *port*.

COMMON USES The *inp* function is used to control input/output devices. The control circuitry of these devices has registers which are accessible through the IN and OUT instructions of the 8086 microprocessor family. The *inp* function is a C language interface to the IN instruction.

RETURNS The *inp* function returns the byte read from the port.

COMMENTS Everyone knows that in the IBM PC world, we are supposed to use DOS or BIOS to talk to the I/O devices (keyboard, video display, etc.). DOS and BIOS lack adequate support, however, for several important peripherals including the serial port and the speaker. In these cases you must access the device's registers using appropriate port addresses and the functions *inp* and *outp* come in handy.

SEE ALSO

inpw   To read a word from a port address

outp, outpw   To write to an I/O port

EXAMPLE The PC's peripheral devices get the microprocessor's attention by generating interrupts that are fielded by an integrated circuit (the Intel 8259A program-mable interrupt controller). The 8259A looks at the bits in a register, reached via port number 21h, to decide which interrupts go on to the CPU. Read the contents of this register using the *inp* function and display the contents in hexadecimal format.

```c
#include <stdio.h>
#include <conio.h>
#define PORT_8259    0x21

main()
{
    int int_ack_status;
/* Read 8259's status */
    int_ack_status = inp(PORT_8259);
    printf("Current contents of register at \
port 21h: %X\n", int_ack_status);
}
```

Console and Port I/O
inpw

PURPOSE Use *inpw* to read a 16-bit word from a specific I/O port. For example, you can use *inpw* to read two adjacent ports at once.

SYNTAX unsigned int inpw(unsigned port);

unsigned port;   Address of the port from which a word is to be read

EXAMPLE CALL word_8259 = inpw(0x20);

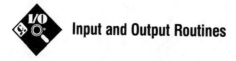 **Input and Output Routines**

INCLUDES   `#include <conio.h>`   For function declaration

DESCRIPTION   The *inpw* function uses the assembly language instruction IN to read a word (2 bytes) of data from the port address specified in the argument *port*.

COMMON USES   The *inpw* function is useful in reading two adjacent ports at once.

RETURNS   The *inpw* function returns an unsigned integer containing the 16-bit word it read from the port address.

SEE ALSO   `inp`   To read a byte from a port address

`outp, outpw`   To write to an I/O port

EXAMPLE   The Intel 8259A programmable interrupt controller schedules and sometimes blocks interrupt signals generated by peripheral devices and meant for the microprocessor. The 8259A is programmed through two registers at port addresses 20h and 21h. Use *inp* to read the contents of each register and display them. Then, using the *inpw* function, read both registers simultaneously and display the contents in hexadecimal format. Compare these with the values you read individually.

```
#include <stdio.h>
#include <conio.h>
#define PORT_8259_20    0x20
#define PORT_8259_21    0x21

main()
{
    unsigned int word_8259;
    int p20, p21;
/* Read both ports of the 8259A */
    word_8259 = inpw(PORT_8259_20);
/* Now read them individually */
    p20 = inp(PORT_8259_20);
    p21 = inp(PORT_8259_21);
    printf("Current contents of register \
at port 20h: %X\n", p20);
    printf("Current contents of register \
at port 21h: %X\n", p21);
    printf("Result of reading with inpw at \
port 20h:  %X\n", word_8259);
}
```

inpw

Console and Port I/O
kbhit

COMPATIBILITY	MSC 3	MSC 4	MSC 5	QC	TC	ANSI	UNIX V
	▲	▲	▲	▲	▲		

PURPOSE Use the console I/O function *kbhit* to check whether any keystrokes are waiting to be read. Since *kbhit* does not wait for a key to be pressed, it is ideal for applications in which you can continue with your normal processing until the user interrupts by hitting a key.

SYNTAX `int kbhit(void);`

EXAMPLE CALL
```
/* Do your thing until user presses a key */
while( !kbhit() ) do_your_thing();
```

INCLUDES `#include <conio.h>`   For function declaration

DESCRIPTION The *kbhit* function checks if any keystrokes are in the keyboard buffer waiting to be read.

COMMON USES The *kbhit* function is useful in writing applications where you can continue doing whatever your program is meant to do until the user actually hits a key. All you have to do is keep checking for any keystroke using *kbhit* every so often (such as at the beginning of an outer loop) and perform a read only when a keystroke is waiting.

RETURNS If a key was pressed, *kbhit* returns a nonzero value. Otherwise, it returns a zero.

COMMENTS The *kbhit* function is one function in the Microsoft C library that you cannot do without if you want to develop an event-driven application. Consider for example, an application such as a "terminal emulator." This will have a main loop where you must respond to two types of events (at least): characters arriving from the serial port and characters being entered from the keyboard. If you attempted to handle the keyboard events by using a function such as *getch*, you would soon discover that the program will keep waiting in that function until a character is actually entered and other events, such as serial input, would be lost. With *kbhit*, however, you are able to check and move on if nothing was hit on the keyboard.

EXAMPLE The graphics function *_putimage* can be used to perform rudimentary animation. Modify the example shown in the reference pages on *_putimage* to move the small stick figure on the screen continuously until the user hits a key. Use *kbhit* in an endless loop to achieve this.

```
#include <stdio.h>
#include <malloc.h>
```

 **Input and Output Routines**

```
#include <graph.h>
#define YELLOW 14
main()
{
    char far *image;                    /* Storage for image */
    char buffer[80];
    short x=0, y=0;
    unsigned numbytes, c = 0;
/* Assume EGA. Put in high-resolution graphics mode */
    if (_setvideomode(_ERESCOLOR) == 0)
    {
/* Error setting mode */
        printf("Not EGA hardware\n");
        exit(0);
    }
/* Draw a small stick figure to save */
    _setcolor(YELLOW);
    _ellipse(_GFILLINTERIOR,0,0,10,10);
    _moveto(5,10);
    _lineto(5,20);
    _lineto(0,30);
    _moveto(10,30);
    _lineto(5,20);
    _moveto(0,15);
    _lineto(0,10);
    _lineto(10,15);
/* Determine storage needed for entire screen and
 * display result.
 */
    numbytes = (unsigned int)_imagesize(0,0,10,30);
/* Allocate buffer for image */
    if ((image = (char far *) malloc(numbytes))
        == (char far *)NULL)
    {
        _setvideomode(_DEFAULTMODE);
        printf("Not enough memory for image storage\n");
        exit(0);
    }
    _getimage(x,y,10,30,image); /* Save the image */
/* Now clear screen and draw saved image at several
 * screen locations.
 */
    _clearscreen(_GCLEARSCREEN);
    _settextposition(1,1);
    _outtext("Demonstrating animation with _putimage");
    _settextposition(20,1);
    _outtext("Hit any key to exit:");
    _setlogorg(320,175);
```

kbhit

```
    _putimage(x,y,image,_GXOR);
/* Using kbhit and _putimage, perform animation
 * until user hits a key.
 */
    while( !kbhit() )
    {
/* Erase at last position */
        _putimage(x,y,image,_GXOR);
        y += 2;
        x += 2;
        if(x > 300) x = -300;
        if(y > 200) y = -100;
/* Redraw at new position */
        _putimage(x,y,image,_GXOR);
    }
/* Restore original mode */
    _setvideomode(_DEFAULTMODE);
}
```

Console and Port I/O

outp

COMPATIBILITY	MSC 3	MSC 4	MSC 5	QC	TC	ANSI	UNIX V
	▲	▲	▲	▲	outportb		

PURPOSE Use *outp* to write a byte to a specified I/O port. For example, you can use *outp* to generate sound on the IBM PC by sending appropriate data to the Intel 8255 programmable peripheral interface chip via port address 61h.

SYNTAX `int outp(unsigned port, int byte);`

`unsigned port;`   Address of the port to which the byte is sent

`int byte;`   Byte to be written to the port

EXAMPLE CALL `outp(0x43, 0xb6);`

INCLUDES `#include <conio.h>`   For function declaration

DESCRIPTION The *outp* function uses the assembly language instruction OUT to send a byte of data from the argument *byte* to the port address specified in the argument *port*.

COMMON USES Use the *outp* function in conjunction with *inp* to access registers in input/output devices. The *outp* function is a C language interface to the OUT instruction.

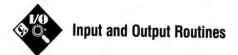 **Input and Output Routines**

RETURNS   The *outp* function returns the byte it sent to the port.

COMMENTS   Some peripheral devices such as the speaker and the serial ports are not adequately supported in the IBM PC's BIOS. In particular, the speaker is accessible only through the IN and OUT instructions; the Microsoft C library functions *inp* and *outp* are invaluable in such a situation.

SEE ALSO   outpw   To write a 16-bit word to a port address

inp, inpw   To read from an I/O port

EXAMPLE   The IBM PC's speaker can be used to generate a tone by programming it via the 8255 chip at port address 61h and using the system timer (Intel 8254 chip) to control the speaker. Here is how it works. First you will set up the timer as an oscillator by sending the data byte B6h to the port 43h. Then you compute the ratio of the frequency of sound you want and the frequency of the timer's clock frequency (1.19 MHz). Write this value to port 42h. Tell the 8255 chip to drive the speaker under the control of the timer by reading the port 61h and writing the value back with the first two bits set to 1 (perform a logical OR with 3). This gets the sound going. Let the sound continue as long as you wish. Shut the speaker off by reading port 61h again and setting bits 0 and 1 to 0.

```
#include <conio.h>

#define TIMER_FREQ    1193180L /* Timer freq = 1.19 MHz */
#define TIMER_COUNT   0x42     /* 8253 timer -- count       */
#define TIMER_MODE    0x43     /* 8253 timer control port   */
#define TIMER_OSC     0xb6     /*To use timer as oscillator */
#define OUT_8255      0x61     /* 8255 PPI output port adrs */
#define SPKRON        3        /* Bit 0 = control spkr by timer*/
                              /* Bit 1 = speaker on/off       */

main()
{
        unsigned freq, status, ratio, part_ratio;
        char input[81];
        cprintf("Enter frequency in Hz \
(between 100 and 15000):");
        cscanf("%hu", &freq);
/* First read and save status of the 8255 chip */
        status = inp (OUT_8255);
/* Put timer in oscillator mode */
        outp (TIMER_MODE, TIMER_OSC);
        ratio = (unsigned)(TIMER_FREQ/freq);
        part_ratio = ratio & 0xff; /* low byte of ratio    */
        outp(TIMER_COUNT, part_ratio);
        part_ratio = (ratio >> 8) & 0xff; /* high byte     */
        outp(TIMER_COUNT, part_ratio);
```

```
/* Finally turn on speaker */
        outp (OUT_8255, (status | SPKRON));

/* Ask user to indicate when to stop the
 * annoying tone...
 */
        cprintf("\nHit return to exit:");
        cgets(input);

/* Now turn off speaker */
        status = inp (OUT_8255); /* get current status */
/* Turn speaker off */
        outp (OUT_8255, (status & ~SPKRON));
}
```

Console and Port I/O
outpw

COMPATIBILITY	MSC 3	MSC 4	MSC 5	QC	TC	ANSI	UNIX V
			▲	▲	outport		

PURPOSE Use the *outpw* function to write a 16-bit word to a specified I/O port address. For example, you can use *outpw* to send 2-bytes simultaneously to the control registers in your enhanced graphics adapter when programming it directly for graphics.

SYNTAX `int outpw(unsigned port, unsigned word);`

`unsigned port;` Address of the port to which the word is sent

`unsigned word;` Word to be written to the port

EXAMPLE CALL `outpw(0x3ce, (2<<8) | 0x5); /* Put EGA in write mode 2 */`

INCLUDES `#include <conio.h>` For function declaration

DESCRIPTION The *outpw* function uses the assembly language instruction OUT to send a 16-bit word given in the argument *word* to the port address specified by the argument *port*.

COMMON USES The *outpw* function, introduced in Microsoft C 5.0, allows you to send 2 bytes of data to two adjacent I/O ports by a single function call. As shown in the example, this comes in handy when programming the EGA.

RETURNS The *outpw* function returns the word it sent to the port.

COMMENTS Each I/O address on the IBM PC provides access to an 8-bit register. If you use

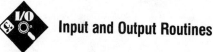

Input and Output Routines

outpw to send 2 bytes to, say, I/O address 3CEh, the first byte goes to the register at 3CEh and the second byte goes to the adjoining register at 3CFh. Thus when programming a peripheral such as the EGA, to which you often send specific data to two registers with addresses next to each other, it's advantageous to use *outpw*.

SEE ALSO outp   To write a byte to a port address

inp, inpw   To read from an I/O port

EXAMPLE The EGA can be programmed in its 640×350 high-resolution mode by manipulating the registers directly and sending data to its video memory. The programming involves sending a "register select" command to an I/O port followed by the register number to the next port. This can be achieved by a single call to *outpw*. The example below, meant to draw a rectangle filled with color, illustrates this.

```
#include <stdio.h>
#include <dos.h>

#define EGA_RAM ((unsigned char far *)0xA0000000)
#define MAX_GR_COLS  640
#define MAX_GR_ROWS  350
#define MAX_COL_BYTES (MAX_GR_COLS/8)

#define BIOS_VIDEO 0x10
#define SETMODE      0     /* BIOS Service: set video mode*/
#define EGAMODE     16     /* EGA mode for high resolution*/

#define EGA_GR12 0x3ce /* Port to select register     */
#define EGA_GR_MODE 0x5 /* Register no. for write mode*/

/* The box size and the color */
#define XSTART  120
#define YSTART  120
#define XSIZE   280
#define YSIZE   200
#define COLOR   2

static union REGS xr, yr;
static char far *videoram;

main()
{
    int ynum, bytecount, startadrs, startbyte, stopbyte,
        horbytes, skipbytes;
    unsigned temp, egacommand;
```

```
/* Use BIOS to put EGA in high-res graphics mode */
    xr.h.ah = SETMODE;
    xr.h.al = EGAMODE;
    int86 (BIOS_VIDEO, &xr, &yr);


/* Compute starting address */
    startbyte = XSTART/8;
    startadrs = 80*YSTART + startbyte;
    videoram = EGA_RAM + startadrs;
    skipbytes = MAX_COL_BYTES;


/* Put EGA in write mode 2. Use outpw. The following
 * code is  equivalent to 2 lines:
 *           outp (EGA_GR12, EGA_GR_MODE);
 *           outp (EGA_GR_PORT, 2);
 */

    egacommand = (2<<8) ¦ EGA_GR_MODE;
    outpw(EGA_GR12, egacommand);


    stopbyte = (XSTART + XSIZE - 1)/8;
    horbytes = stopbyte - startbyte;
    skipbytes = MAX_COL_BYTES - horbytes;


/* We already have the proper graphics mode settings */
        for (ynum = 0; ynum < YSIZE; ynum++)
        {
            for (bytecount = 0; bytecount < horbytes;
                bytecount++)
            {
/* Fill in 8 bits at a time.
 * First read to latch in bytes.
 */
                temp = *videoram;
/* Now write out pixel value to all 8 bits at once */
                *videoram = COLOR;
                videoram++;
            }
/* Skip to next row */
            videoram += skipbytes;
        }


/* Reset graphics environment back to BIOS standard */
    egacommand = EGA_GR_MODE;
    outpw(EGA_GR12, egacommand);
}
```

Input and Output Routines

putch

COMPATIBILITY	MSC 3	MSC 4	MSC 5	QC	TC	ANSI	UNIX V
	▲	▲	▲	▲	▲		

PURPOSE Use the *putch* function to write a single character to the display without intermediate buffering.

SYNTAX `int putch(int c);`

`int c;`   Character to be written

EXAMPLE CALL `putch('>');`

INCLUDES `#include <conio.h>`   For function declaration

DESCRIPTION The *putch* function writes the character *c* to the display.

RETURNS In Microsoft C versions 5.0 and 5.1, *putch*, when successful, returns the character it wrote. Otherwise it returns the constant EOF (defined in *stdio.h*).

SEE ALSO `getch, getche`   For unbuffered read from the keyboard

EXAMPLE Use *putch* to write a line (maximum length of 80 characters) to the standard output.

```
#include <stdio.h>
char buffer[81] = "Testing putch...\n";
main()
{
    int i;
/* Write characters to display until we reach the null */
    for(i=0; i<81 && buffer[i] != '\0'; i++)
    {
        putch(buffer[i]);
    }
}
```

ungetch

COMPATIBILITY	MSC 3	MSC 4	MSC 5	QC	TC	ANSI	UNIX V
	▲	▲	▲	▲	▲		

PURPOSE Use the *ungetch* function to place a single character in the keyboard buffer so that it is the next character read from the console. You cannot place more than one character before the next read.

SYNTAX

```
int ungetch(int c);
```

```
int c;          Character to be placed in the keyboard buffer
```

EXAMPLE CALL

```
ungetch(last_char);
```

INCLUDES

```
#include <conio.h>          For function declaration
```

DESCRIPTION

The *ungetch* function places the character given in the integer argument *c* into the keyboard buffer so that the next console read operation returns that character. You can place only one character in the buffer before reading and the character must not be equal to the constant EOF defined in *stdio.h*.

RETURNS

If there are no errors, *ungetch* returns the character it pushed back. Otherwise, it returns the constant EOF to indicate an error—which is why you should not try to push back EOF.

SEE ALSO

```
getch, getche          To read a character from the console
```

EXAMPLE

Write a program that asks the user to enter an integer. Use *getche* to read the digits and accumulate them into an integer. Once you reach a nondigit (use the macro *isdigit* to check), put that character back into the console by calling *ungetch*. Now print a message showing the integer value and indicating the first noninteger character typed.

```
#include <stdio.h>
#include <conio.h>
#include <ctype.h>   /* For the macro isdigit() */
main()
{
    int intval = 0, c;
    char buff[81];
/* Ask user to type in an integer */
    printf("Enter an integer followed by some other \
characters:");
    while ( (c = getche()) != EOF && isdigit(c) )
    {
        intval = 10*intval + c - 48; /* 0 is ASCII 48 */
    }
/* Push back the first non-digit read from stdin */
    if (c != EOF) ungetch(c);
/* Print message to user */
    printf("\nInteger you entered = %d.\n\
First non-integer encountered: %c\n", intval, getch());
}
```

 **Input and Output Routines**

Introduction

All IBM-compatible MS-DOS machines come with a basic input/output system (BIOS) built into the read-only memory (ROM). This is a set of rudimentary I/O routines for accessing peripheral devices such as the keyboard, display, printer, serial port, and floppy or hard disk, among many others. In addition to the built-in ROM BIOS, MS-DOS itself has a host of standard utility functions that also perform I/O and provide access to the DOS file system. Essentially, you can count on both of these sets of services being present on every IBM PC or compatible that uses MS-DOS as its operating system. The DOS services are more portable than the BIOS ones because the BIOS code in PC-compatibles is only a functional copy of the original IBM BIOS, whereas the MS-DOS routines are part of the operating system software which is consistent across all machines. In general, however, programs that use DOS or BIOS calls to perform various I/O functions are likely to work properly in all IBM-compatible computers. Programs that directly access hardware using I/O port addresses or video memory addresses obtain the greatest processing speed, but may not work on all PC compatibles. Thus it is advantageous to be able to use these portable DOS and BIOS services in your programs whenever there are no overriding performance considerations.

The Microsoft C library includes a set of functions that provide access to the BIOS and DOS services from your C programs. These functions for making *system calls* enable you to harness the full potential of the PC without having to write, in most cases, even a single line of code in 8086 assembly language.

The *system calls* routines, with names prefixed by ``_dos_'' and ``_bios_'' were introduced in Microsoft C 5.0 and are specific to Microsoft C. Unfortunately, every C compiler for the IBM PC has a different name for each of these routines. However, the basic set of *int86, int86x, intdos,* and *intdosx* appear to be present in most C compilers for the IBM PC.

We should also point out that many of the services offered by the system calls category are duplicated elsewhere in the Microsoft C library. Entire categories of portable routines exist for memory allocation, file I/O, and date/time information. For these tasks, you are better off using the standard library routines because they are much more portable than the DOS and BIOS calls. In general, use the most portable routine that provides acceptable performance.

Concepts: Basics of BIOS and DOS Interface

C programmers are familiar with the concept of compiling groups of functions to generate object code and using the linker to construct an executable file. In such a situation, you normally invoke a routine's code by a C function call. The parameters that you pass to the function are transferred via the stack.

Now consider the case of BIOS and DOS functions. These routines are also in compiled object code form, but you cannot link with them because the addresses of the routines are not known to you. (Even if they were, it would pose a problem if they changed in future revisions of the BIOS and DOS.) A more fundamental access mechanism is needed, a method that can be counted on to work on every PC irrespective of where the actual object code of the BIOS and DOS functions reside. The assembly language instruction INT which generates a software interrupt on an 8086 microprocessor provides the solution.

SOFTWARE INTERRUPTS ON 8086 MICRO-PROCESSORS In a PC, an "interrupt" refers to a mechanism that hardware devices use to get the attention of the microprocessor that they service. The 8086 microprocessor keeps a table of function addresses called an "interrupt vector table" in the memory. When the microprocessor receives an interrupt signal, it first saves the contents of the internal registers and the address of the code it was executing at that moment. Next it determines the interrupt number from the interrupt signal and locates that entry in the interrupt vector table. Then it jumps to that function address and begins executing the code there, which presumably satisfies the needs of the device that generated the interrupt signal in the first place. The microprocessor returns to the code it was executing when it was interrupted as soon as it executes the assembly language instruction IRET. Thus the function that handles or services the interrupt must end with an IRET (see Figure 16-1).

Software interrupts behave in the same way as hardware interrupts, except that they are generated by an assembly language of the form *INT ⟨int_number⟩* where *⟨int_number⟩* is the interrupt number we want generated. If we write a routine to perform a task, end it with an IRET instruction, and place its address in the entry corresponding to the *⟨int_number⟩* in the interrupt vector table, the routine can be invoked by executing the instruction *INT ⟨int_number⟩*, which is precisely how the BIOS and DOS functions are made available to assembly language programmers. Parameters are passed from C to these routines by placing them in the microprocessor's registers, and results are returned through the registers also. Since the routines in

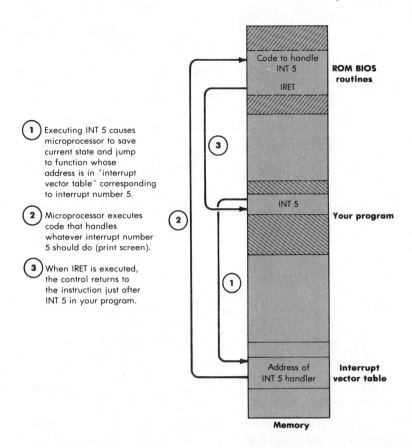

① Executing INT 5 causes microprocessor to save current state and jump to function whose address is in "interrupt vector table" corresponding to interrupt number 5.

② Microprocessor executes code that handles whatever interrupt number 5 should do (print screen).

③ When IRET is executed, the control returns to the instruction just after INT 5 in your program.

Figure 16-1. *Accessing BIOS and DOS functions via software interrupts*

the system calls category allow us to make software interrupts, they allow access to the BIOS and DOS functions.

Typically, a single interrupt number provides access to an entire category of service, with the specific service selected by a value in a register. For example, interrupt number 21h provides access to almost a hundred functions embedded in MS-DOS. The exact function to be invoked is specified by a function number placed in the AH register.

SOFTWARE INTERRUPTS FROM MICROSOFT C

Microsoft C provides the routines *int86* and *int86x* for generating arbitrary software interrupts. These routines accept the register settings in a "union" (see Chapter 1) named REGS, which is defined in the include file *dos.h* and is the overlay of two structures, one named *x* of type WORDREGS and the other named *h* of type BYTEREGS (see Figure 16-2). This arrangement means that the member *x* in the "union" REGS provides access to the 16-bit word registers AX, BX, CX, and DX, while the member *h* is used for accessing the corresponding 8-bit halves, AH, AL, BH, BL, CH, CL, DH, and DL. The segment registers ES, CS, SS, and DS are passed via a "structure" named SREGS, which is also defined in *dos.h*.

To pass register values you have to declare data items of type REGS and

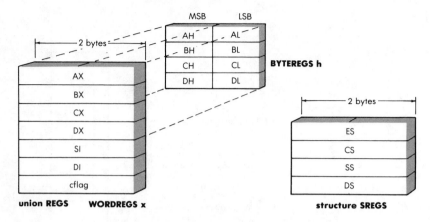

Figure 16-2. *Union REGS and structure SREGS*

SREGS and set the internal fields of these structures to the desired register values. The interface routine in the C library loads the registers from these data structures before generating the software interrupt necessary to access the desired BIOS or DOS service. Upon return from the interrupt, the interface routine copies the register values into another structure which you also allocate and whose address you pass to the routine. This allows the program to obtain the results or error codes returned by the service called.

Table 16-1 shows the interrupt numbers for the BIOS services. Table 16-2 lists the DOS services according to function number. The DOS services all use interrupt number 21h, with a function number specified in the AH register. Each of these tables shows the specific Microsoft C routines that provide access to a particular service. For more information on a particular routine, consult the appropriate reference page. If no special Microsoft C routine exists, you can use the general-purpose interrupt routines *int86x* or *intdosx* to access the service. In this case, you can find further details in reference books on MS-DOS (Duncan[3] and IBM PC (Norton[5], Smith[6]) listed under *Further Reading*.

Table 16-1. *Interrupts to Access ROM BIOS Routines*

Interrupt Number (Hex)	Purpose	Microsoft C 5.1 Interface Routine
05	Print screen	N/A
10	Video I/O	N/A
11	Equipment determination	_bios_equiplist
12	Memory size determination	_bios_memsize
13	Diskette I/O (and hard disk I/O on AT, XT and PS/2)	_bios_disk
14	I/O with RS-232C serial communications port	_bios_serialcom
15	Cassette I/O (and system services on AT, XT, and PS/2)	N/A
16	Keyboard I/O	_bios_keybrd

Table 16-1. *(cont.)*

Interrupt Number (Hex)	Purpose	Microsoft C 5.1 Interface Routine
17	Printer I/O	_bios_printer
18	Access ROM-resident BASIC	N/A
19	Bootstrap loader to load operating system from disk	N/A
1A	Time of day	_bios_timeofday
1B	Keyboard break address	N/A
1C	Timer tick	N/A

Table 16-2. *MS-DOS Interface Routines*

Function Number (Hex)	Action	Microsoft C 5.1 DOS Interface
00	Terminates program and returns to DOS.	
01	Reads a character from keyboard (AL has character).	
02	Displays character in DL on screen.	
03	Reads character from AUX into AL.	
04	Writes character in DL to AUX.	
05	Sends character in DL to printer port.	
06	Performs direct console I/O (DL = FF means input).	
07	Directly inputs a character from STDIN.	
08	Reads a character from keyboard without echoing it.	
09	Prints a string ending in a $.	
0A	Reads characters from keyboard into a buffer.	
0B	Checks status of STDIN.	
0C	Clears keyboard buffer.	
0D	Resets disk and flushes all disk buffers.	
0E	Sets the default disk drive.	
0F	Opens a disk file (requires File Control Block *[FCB]*).	
10	Closes a disk file (specified by FCB).	
11	Searches for first occurrence of a file using FCB.	
12	Searches for next occurrence of a file using FCB.	
13	Deletes file specified by an FCB.	
14	Reads a disk file sequentially.	
15	Writes sequentially to a disk file.	
16	Creates a disk file.	
17	Renames a disk file.	
18	Reserved.	
19	Returns default disk drive number in AL.	_dos_getdrive
1A	Sets up a disk transfer area (DTA) address.	
1B	Returns allocation information about default disk drive.	
1C	Returns allocation information of a specific drive.	

Table 16-2. *(cont.)*

Function Number (Hex)	Action	Microsoft C 5.1 DOS Interface
1D	Reserved.	
1E	Reserved.	
1F	Reserved.	
20	Reserved.	
21	Reads a record from disk (random access).	
22	Writes a record to disk (random access).	
23	Returns file size in FCB, if file found.	
24	Sets up record number for random access read/write.	
25	Sets up a new interrupt vector.	_dos_setvect
26	Creates a Program Segment Prefix (PSP).	
27	Reads a block of records from disk (random access).	
28	Writes a block of records to disk (random access).	
29	Parses a file name.	
2A	Returns current date (DL = day, DH = month, CX = year).	_dos_getdate
2B	Sets the current date.	_dos_setdate
2C	Returns the current time.ta_dos_gettime	
2D	Sets the current time.	_dos_settime
2E	Sets verify flag on or off.	
2F	Returns the address of disk transfer area (DTA).	
30	Returns version of DOS.	
31	Terminates program but leaves it intact in memory.	_dos_keep
32	Used internally by DOS to get drive parameter block.	
33	Gets or sets Control-Break flag.	
34	Used internally by DOS to get a pointer to a byte that indicates when DOS is in a "critical section" (when flag is set, it is not safe to call DOS functions; this feature is used by many TSR utilities). This is not officially documented by Microsoft.	
35	Returns the interrupt vector for a specific interrupt.	_dos_getvect
36	Returns information about total and unused space on a specified disk drive.	_dos_getdiskfree
37	Used internally (switch character and device availability). This is not officially documented by Microsoft.	
38	Gets or sets country-dependent information.	
39	Creates a subdirectory.	
3A	Removes a subdirectory.	
3B	Changes the current directory.	
3C	Creates a named disk file and returns handle in AX.	_dos_creat
3D	Opens a named disk file and returns handle in AX.	_dos_open
3E	Closes a file specified by a handle.	_dos_close

Table 16-2. *(cont.)*

Function Number (Hex)	Action	Microsoft C 5.1 DOS Interface
3F	Reads a number of bytes from a disk file specified by a handle.	_dos_read
40	Writes a number of bytes to a disk file specified by a handle.	_dos_write
41	Deletes a named disk file.	
42	Moves the read/write pointer of a file specified by a handle.	
43	Gets or sets the attributes of a file. (Attributes determine if a file is hidden, read-only, and so on.)	_dos_getfileattr
44	Provides device driver control (IOCTL).	
45	Creates a duplicate file handle.	
46	Forces a new file handle to point to the same file as an existing handle.	
47	Returns current directory name.	
48	Allocates a specified number of paragraphs of memory and returns the segment address of the allocated memory.	_dos_allocmem
49	Releases a previously allocated block of memory.	_dos_freemem
4A	Adjusts the size of a previously allocated block of memory.	
4B	Loads and/or executes a program.	
4C	Terminates a program and returns an exit code.	
4D	Returns exit code of a subprogram.	
4E	Searches for first occurrence of a named file.	_dos_findfirst
4F	Searches for next occurrence of a named file.	_dos_findnext
50	Used internally to set new PSP segment.	
51	Used internally to get current PSP segment.	
52	Used internally by DOS to get list of disks.	
53	Used internally by DOS to translate the BIOS parameter block.	
54	Returns the verify flag in AH.	
55	Used internally by DOS to create a PSP.	
56	Renames a file.	
57	Gets or sets the modification time and date of a disk file specified by its handle.	_dos_getftime
58	Gets or sets the memory allocation strategy to be used by DOS. (*DOS 3.X only*).	
59	Returns extended error information (*DOS 3.X only*).	dosexterr
5A	Creates a temporary file (*DOS 3.X only*).	
5B	Creates a new file (*DOS 3.X only*).	_dos_creatnew
5C	Locks or unlocks a file for shared access (*DOS 3.X only*).	
5D	Used internally by DOS.	

Table 16-2. *(cont.)*

Function Number (Hex)	Action	Microsoft C 5.1 DOS Interface
5E	Returns machine name and printer set up (*DOS 3.X only*).	
5F	Gets list of device redirections in Microsoft network (*DOS 3.X only*).	
60	Used internally by DOS.	
61	Reserved.	
62	Returns the PSP (Program Segment Address) (*DOS 3.X only*).	
63	Returns lead byte table (*DOS 2.25 only*).	
64	Reserved.	
65	Returns extended country information (*DOS 3.3 only*).	
66	Gets or sets global page table (*DOS 3.3 only*).	
67	Sets the maximum number of file handles (must be less than 255). This breaks the "20 open file per process" limit of DOS 3.2 and lower. (*DOS 3.3 only*).	
68	Writes all buffered data meant for a file to the disk (*DOS 3.3 only*).	

Notes on BIOS and DOS Services

The functions in the system calls category allow you to use virtually all routines in the IBM PC ROM BIOS as well as all functions in DOS that are accessible via interrupt number 21h. Table 16-3 lists the Microsoft C routines that provide access to the system services, grouped according to the tasks they perform. The BIOS routines are not listed because each one performs a distinct task. Table 16-4 shows the routines that are part of the BIOS interface.

Table 16-3. *Microsoft C 5.1 System Interface Routines by Task*

Task	Routines
Generate 8086 software interrupt	int86, int86x
Call any DOS function	bdos, intdos, intdosx
Get segment and offset addresses	FP_OFF, FP_SEG, segread
Perform file I/O using DOS(see I/O routines in Chapter 15)	_dos_close, _dos_creat, _dos_creatnew, _dos_open, _dos_read, _dos_write
Find and alter file information	_dos_findfirst, _dos_findnext, _dos_getdiskfree, _dos_getdrive, _dos_getfileattr, _dos_getftime, _dos_setfileattr, _dos_setftime

Table 16-3. *(cont.)*

Task	Routines
Handle interrupts	_chain_intr, _disable, _dos_getvect, _dos_setvect, _enable
Allocate and free memory (see Chapter 5 for others)	_dos_allocmem, _dos_freemem, _dos_setblock
Get or set date and time (see Chapter 12)	_dos_getdate, _dos_gettime, _dos_setdate, _dos_settime
Handle hardware and other errors	dosexterr, _harderr, _hardresume, _hardretn

Table 16-4. *BIOS Interface Routines in Microsoft C 5.1*

Routine	Interrupt Number (Hex)	Purpose of Routine
_bios_disk	13	Access physical sectors in floppy and hard disk (hard disk only on XT, AT, and PS/2)
_bios_equiplist	11	Obtain a list of peripherals attached to the PC
_bios_keybrd	16	Read character from keyboard and query the status of function, Alt and Shift keys
_bios_memsize	12	Determine amount of memory in the system
_bios_printer	17	Send character to parallel printer port and determine status of printer
_bios_serialcom	14	Perform I/O with RS-232C serial port (initialize port, send and receive a character)
_bios_timeofday	1A	Read and set current clock setting (also, access the real-time clock in AT, XT, and PS/2)

MICROSOFT C INTERFACE TO DOS AND BIOS SERVICES

Microsoft C provides three ways to access the DOS services (see Figure 16-3). The first approach is to use the general software interrupts, *int86* and *int86x*, and call DOS directly using interrupt number 21h. The second method uses the generic DOS interrupt routines *bdos*, *intdos*, and *intdosx*. The third method is to use the specific DOS system calls (the routines in Table 16-5 whose names begin with *_dos_*).

BIOS services are accessed by two methods: via the general-purpose interrupt routines or by calling a specific BIOS interface routine listed in Table 16-4.

To call a DOS or BIOS service using the general-purpose interrupt routine, you set up the registers by using a "union" REGS data type and then provide the interrupt number to *int86* (or *int86x* if the service requires the use of the DS and ES registers). For DOS, the interrupt number is always 21h. Different services are accessed by placing the DOS function number in the AH register. Other register values depend on the DOS function being called. For example, the DOS time function (number 2Ch) may be called as follows:

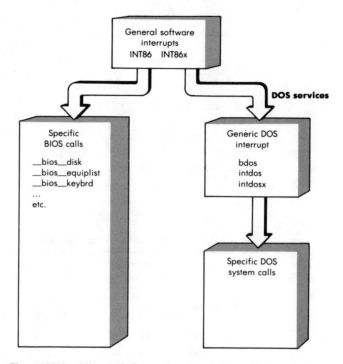

Figure 16-3. *Microsoft C Interface for BIOS and DOS services*

```
#include <stdio.h>
#include <dos.h>
#define DOS_GETTIME 0x2c
main()
{
    union REGS xr, yr;
    xr.h.ah = DOS_GETTIME;
    int86(0x21, &xr, &yr);
    printf("Current time is %.2d:%.2d:%.2d\n",
            yr.h.ch, yr.h.cl, yr.h.dh);
}
```

The *dos.h* include file is necessary for the definition of the union REGS. If we were to use the *intdos* interface (we do not have to use *intdosx* because the service does not need anything in the segment registers), the line containing the call to *int86* in our example would be replaced by:

```
intdos(&xr, &yr);
```

Lastly, if we make use of the interface routine *_dos_gettime* provided specifically for accessing the system time, the example becomes:

```
#include <stdio.h>
#include <dos.h>
main()
{
    struct dostime_t time;
    _dos_gettime(&time);
    printf("Current time: %d:%d:%d.%d\n", time.hour,
            time.minute, time.second, time.hsecond);
}
```

This use of the function is more natural to C programmers because it does not involve the use of the 8086 specific data structures (REGS and SREGS).

The general-purpose interrupt routines, *int86* and *int86x*, are important because they enable you to generate *any* software interrupt on the PC. Consequently, every BIOS and DOS function shown in Tables 16-1 and 16-2 can be invoked with one of these two routines. The difference between them is that plain *int86* allows you to set all registers except the segment registers while *int86x* also lets you specify new values for the segment registers (only the DS and ES segment registers can be set to new values because CS contains the segment address of our code while SS holds the current stack segment address).

Despite their versatility, there is one drawback to the *int86* and *int86x* functions. To use them effectively, you have to know what each interrupt number accesses and its relevant register settings. The *intdos* and *intdosx* are versions of *int86* and *int86x* that are set to generate interrupt number 21h. Thus these two routines can access any one of the hundred or so DOS functions. Like the *int86* pair, *intdosx* enables you to specify new values for the segment registers DS and ES and *intdos* uses the default settings of DS and ES.

Many DOS and BIOS functions require that you specify both the segment address and the offset of a data item. You can get these values by using the macros FP_SEG and FP_OFF, respectively. The function *segread* lets you get the current values of the segment registers DS, ES, CS, and SS.

ACCESSING THE BIOS SERVICES

The BIOS has a relatively small number of functions that provide access to the following peripherals:

- ▶ disk (hard disk and diskette)
- ▶ keyboard
- ▶ video
- ▶ printer
- ▶ serial communications port
- ▶ system timer

Table 16-1 lists interrupt numbers that are used with the INT instruction to invoke the BIOS services. The Microsoft C 5.1 library provides interface routines for most of these interrupts. These interface routines are included in the table. Each routine is described in detail in its reference page and is also summarized in Table 16-4. Note in Table 16-1 that no explicit interface is included for the video services accessed via interrupt number 10h. This is not applicable in versions 5.0 and 5.1 of Microsoft C because there is an entire category of graphics routines (see Chapters 17, 18, and 19) available. You can still use *int86* to call the BIOS video routines.

Specific Interface Routines for BIOS

Table 16-4 summarizes the routines that call BIOS functions. In Table 16-1, we listed the interrupt numbers used to access the ROM BIOS services. Accessing the services through the interrupt number however, requires you to set up the registers using the REGS and SREGS data structures and then use either *int86* or *int86x* to generate the interrupt. The BIOS interface routines listed in Table 16-4 simplify the task. They are easier to use because they accept normal C arguments and return values normally rather than use the REGS and SREGS structures. They also have descriptive names. Table 16-4 also shows the interrupt number to which the function provides an interface. The interrupt numbers are provided as cross references to entries in Table 16-1.

ACCESSING THE DOS SERVICES

Compared to the BIOS, MS-DOS services are far more numerous. They generally affect the file system, memory management, process management, and input and output functions. Unlike the BIOS, all MS-DOS functions are accessible via the *INT 21h* instruction with the exact function specified in the AH register. In Table 16-2 we list the most common DOS functions. The function number shown in the table has to be put in the AH register before generating interrupt 21h. In certain cases, Microsoft C 5.1 provides a special purpose routine for accessing that DOS function and these are also listed in the table. Consult the reference page for specific routines for further information. Table 16-3 also summarizes all the DOS interface routines in Microsoft C 5.1. Short summaries of some important DOS services follow.

Access to the MS-DOS File System

A large percentage of the DOS interface routines provide access to the MS-DOS file system. You can find substitutes for each of the routines for performing file I/O. These substitutes are more portable and are described in Chapter 15. There is, however, no substitutes for the routines that allow you to get and set file attributes and let you search for files in the directory (*_dos_findfirst* and *_dos_findnext*). For these tasks, the DOS interface is very useful.

Servicing Interrupts

When we discussed hardware interrupts we mentioned installing a function in the interrupt vector table to process whatever a particular hardware interrupt requires. There are a few hidden treasures in Microsoft C 5.1 and its library that can help you write an interrupt handler entirely in C. The first of these is the newly introduced *interrupt* attribute for functions (see Chapter 1 for details) which causes the compiler to push all registers upon entry to the function and to use an IRET instruction for exiting the function. The other treasures are the library routines *_disable* and *_enable*, which are C equivalents of the assembly language instructions CLI and STI, respectively. Last but not least are the routines *_dos_getvect* and *_dos_setvect* for retrieving and setting particular entries in the interrupt vector table. Using these new features, you can write routines that, as an example, can perform interrupt-driven I/O with the serial port on the PC.

Memory Allocation and Time
You also get to access the DOS functions for memory allocation and for getting or setting the date and the time. These routines are redundant, though, because there is an assortment of memory allocation (Chapter 5) and time (Chapter 12) routines in the Microsoft C library.

Error Handling
Hardware errors on the PC cause an interrupt 24h to be generated. There are three routines, _harderr, _hardresume, and _hardretn, to help you set up an appropriate handler for this interrupt. By the way, the normal handler for this interrupt is the originator of the infamous message, "Abort, Retry, Ignore?"

Specific Interface Routines for DOS
Table 16-5 lists the Microsoft C 5.1 routines that are meant as gateways to a few selected DOS functions. These *DOS interface* routines make it easier to pass arguments and receive return values. Each routine in Table 16-5 also has an entry showing the DOS function number for which the routine serves as an interface. If you have the need to use one of the DOS functions listed in Table 16-2 for which no simple interface routine exists, you can access the function using the *intdos* and *intdosx* routines. The function number to be placed in the AH register (of a REGS structure) and you have to consult a DOS manual for details on the input and output parameters for the DOS function you want to call.

Table 16-5. *MS-DOS Interface Routines in Microsoft C 5.1*

Routine	DOS Function Number (Hex)	Purpose of Routine
bdos	—	Access any DOS function that makes use of only AL and DX registers.
_dos_allocmem	48	Allocate a specified number of paragraphs of memory.
_dos_close	3E	Close a file specified by a handle.
_dos_creat	3C	Create and truncate a file of given name (a string) and get a handle back (deletes existing file of same name).
_dos_creatnew	5B	Like _dos_creat, but _dos_creatnew fails if named file already exists.
_dos_findfirst	4E	Find the first occurrence of a named file (a string). Requires a disk transfer area (DTA) which can be set up by function 1Ah.
_dos_findnext	4F	For a file name containing wildcard characters (* or ?), finds the next occurrence of a file of that name.

Table 16-5. *(cont.)*

Routine	DOS Function Number (Hex)	Purpose of Routine
		Assumes _dos_findfirst was called and it found a file.
_dos_freemem	49	Free a block of memory.
_dos_getdate	2A	Get the current date (day, month, and year)
_dos_getdiskfree	36	Get the total number of clusters and the number available for use on a disk drive. The number of bytes per cluster is also returned. So the total storage capacity of a disk and the amount free can be computed easily.
_dos_getdrive	19	Get the current drive (0 means A, 1 means B, and so on).
_dos_getfileattr	43	Get the attribute of a file. This tells us if the file is read only, hidden, a system file, a volume label, a subdirectory, or changed since last backup.
_dos_getftime	57	Get the time and date a file was last modified (file specified by handle).
_dos_gettime	2C	Get the current time in hours, minutes, seconds, and hundredths of a second. (Note that system time is updated 18.2 times a second.)
_dos_getvect	35	Get the contents of the interrupt vector table for a specified interrupt number.
_dos_keep	31	Terminate current program but leave it intact in memory (used to install the "terminate-but-stay-resident" or TSR utilities).
_dos_open	3D	Open a named file for a specific type of access and obtain a 16-bit handle to uniquely identify the open file.
_dos_read	3F	Read a specified number of bytes from a file into a buffer in memory.
_dos_setblock	4A	Change the size of a previously allocated block of memory.
_dos_setdate	2B	Set the system date.
_dos_setdrive	0E	Set the default disk drive (specified by a number, 0 means A, 1 means B, and so on).
_dos_setfileattr	43	Alter the current attribute of a file (see _dos_getfileattr).
_dos_setftime	57	Set the modification time of a file (file specified by handle).
_dos_settime	2D	Set the current system time.
_dos_setvect	25	Set the entry in the interrupt vector table corresponding to a given interrupt number. The new value should be the address of a routine designed to handle that interrupt number.
_dos_write	40	Write a specified number of bytes from a buffer to an open file (need handle).
dosexterr	59	Get detailed error information about the last error that

Table 16-5. *(cont.)*

Routine	DOS Function Number (Hex)	Purpose of Routine
		occurred during an "INT 21h" instruction. The information is returned in the registers and you will have to consult a DOS reference guide for exact meaning of the values that are returned.
intdos	any	Call any DOS function by placing function number in AH (using the REGS union). Not useful for those functions that require the use of DS and ES segment registers.
intdosx	any	Used to call any DOS function including those requiring the use of DS and ES segment registers.

MISCELLANEOUS INTERFACE ROUTINES

In addition to the BIOS and DOS interface routines, the system calls category of the Microsoft C 5.1 library also includes routines for obtaining register values of the 8086 microprocessor, handling hardware errors in the MS-DOS system, enabling and disabling interrupts, and installing interrupt handlers. We discussed these features in our overview of the system call routines. They are detailed in Table 16-6. Note that *int86* and *int86x* are considered basic system interface routines because their primary purpose is to generate software interrupts in the 8086 microprocessor. Thus, all the ROM BIOS and DOS functions can be accessed using the *int86* and *int86x* routines.

Table 16-6. *Interface Routines in Microsoft C 5.1*

Routine	Interrupt Number (Hex)	Purpose of Routine
_chain_intr	none	Chain one interrupt handler to another, allowing you to jump unconditionally to a function.
_disable	none	Execute a CLI instruction thus disabling all interrupts.
_enable	none	Execute an STI instruction to enable interrupts again.
FP_OFF	none	Return the offset address of a far pointer (see Chapter 2).
FP_SEG	none	Return the segment address of a far pointer (see Chapter 2).
_harderr	24	This does not generate the interrupt number 24h; rather this function sets the interrupt vector entry for 24h to a given function address. Since the system generates an interrupt 24h when a hardware error occurs, this function is meant to handle fatal hardware errors. Can you guess what the default function does? (Hint: Type DIR A: without placing a diskette in drive A.)
_hardresume	none	Return to MS-DOS after a hardware error (or interrupt 24h).
_hardretn	none	Return to application where hardware error (or interrupt 24h) occurred.
int86	any	Call any function accessible by a software interrupt. Not

Table 16-6. *(cont.)*

Routine	Interrupt Number (Hex)	Purpose of Routine
		useful for those functions that require the use of DS and ES segment registers.
int86x	any	Used to call any function, including those requiring the use of DS and ES segment registers.
segread	none	Obtain the current contents of the segment registers CS, DS, ES, and SS.

Cautions

▶ The system calls category of the Microsoft C 5.1 library contains routines that allow you to perform tasks that are often intimately tied to hardware. To use these functions effectively, it is necessary to understand the basic operation of the IBM PC hardware as well as that of MS-DOS.

▶ Programs that depend on the system calls functions run on MS-DOS machines only and are not portable to other systems.

▶ If you are not familiar with the interrupt concept, the physical layout of a diskette, or the DOS file system, consult the references suggested at the end of this tutorial.

▶ Note that the Microsoft C library has other file I/O routines that use handles to access files. Although they may seem similar, you should not mix the DOS file I/O calls with those from the Input and Output category (see Chapter 15). In fact, there is no reason to use the file I/O routines in this section because the regular C library I/O routines are more functional than those in the system calls category. Besides, the I/O routines listed in Chapter 15 are portable because many of them are part of the proposed ANSI standard definition of C.

Further Reading

The number of system features and peripherals that you can access and manipulate using the system call routines is quite large. Although a detailed discussion of all the things you can do with these interface routines is beyond the scope of this book, there are quite a few resources that can help you.

The recent book by Lafore[1] is an excellent book for anyone learning C on the IBM PC. In the course of teaching the language, it also goes over the basics of the ROM BIOS routines. Prata's book[2] covers the same ground in a more advanced manner. For detailed information on MS-DOS, the book by

Duncan[3] is ideal. The developer's guide by Angermeyer and Jaeger[4] has an excellent discussion of the physical layout of diskettes and of the DOS file system. The ROM BIOS functions are discussed in depth by Norton[5] and information specific to the IBM PC/AT appears in Smith's book[6].

1. Robert Lafore, The Waite Group, *Microsoft C Programming for the IBM*, Howard W. Sams & Company, Indianapolis, IN, 1987, 681 pages.

2. Stephen Prata, The Waite Group, *Advanced C Primer++*, Howard W. Sams & Company, Indianapolis, IN, 1986, 502 pages.

3. Ray Duncan, *Advanced MS-DOS*, Microsoft Press, Redmond, WA, 1986, 468 pages.

4. John Angermeyer and Kevin Jaeger, The Waite Group, *MS-DOS Developer's Guide*, Howard W. Sams & Company, Indianapolis, IN, 1987, 440 pages.

5. Peter Norton, *The Peter Norton Programmer's Guide to the IBM PC*, Microsoft Press, Redmond, WA, 1985, 426 pages.

6. James T. Smith, *The IBM PC AT Programmer's Guide*, Prentice-Hall, New York, NY, 1986, 277 pages.

bdos

COMPATIBILITY	MSC 3	MSC 4	MSC 5	QC	TC	ANSI	UNIX V
	▲	▲	▲	▲	▲		

PURPOSE Use the *bdos* function to call a subset of the DOS functions that can be invoked by an INT 21h instruction. You can use *bdos* to call only those DOS functions that require no arguments or that take arguments in the *DX* and the *AL* registers only. For example, you can use *bdos* with function number 1 to read a character from the keyboard. The returned character will be in the low-order byte of the return value. In contrast to the more general-purpose *intdos* and *intdosx*, the *bdos* function is a simplified way to access a small set of DOS functions.

SYNTAX
```
int bdos (int funcno, unsigned dx_val, unsigned al_val);

int funcno;          DOS function number

unsigned dx_val;        DX register value

unsigned al_val;        AL register value
```

EXAMPLE CALL
```
bdos(2, q', 0);  /* Use DOS function 2 to display 'q' */
```

INCLUDES
```
#include <dos.h>      For function declaration
```

DESCRIPTION The function *bdos* provides simplified access by an INT 21h instruction to the set of DOS functions requiring no arguments or taking arguments in the *DX* and *AL* registers only. This function first copies the values from the unsigned integer arguments *dx_val* and *al_val* into the system's *DX* and *AL* registers, respectively. Then it invokes the DOS function number *funcno* with an *INT 21h* instruction. At the end of the DOS call, *bdos* returns the contents of the *AX* register. The meaning of this value depends on the DOS service requested in *funcno* (see the tutorial section).

COMMON USES The *bdos* function is used to read characters from the keyboard and write characters to the screen using the MS-DOS interface. The advantage of using these services is that your programs will be compatible with all MS-DOS computers.

The *intdos* and *intdosx* functions are more general gateways to the DOS functions, but *bdos* is simpler to use. Of course, you cannot use *dos* if the function being called requires that you provide arguments in registers other than DX and AL.

RETURNS The return value is the content of the *AX* register at the end of the DOS call. For example, if the DOS call returns a value in *AL*, you can get this value by ignoring the high-order byte of the return value.

 **System Calls**

COMMENTS Note that the *intdosx* function provides a more versatile gateway to the DOS functions because it enables you to set up all register values before calling DOS via INT 21h. You should use *bdos* only when the specific conditions described above are met.

SEE ALSO `intdosx, intdos` More general mechanism to access DOS functions

`Table 16-5` Simplified access to several DOS functions

EXAMPLES Read a character from the keyboard using DOS function 1. The character is returned in the *AL* register. Remember that *bdos* returns the value of the *AX* register.

```
#include <stdio.h>
#include <dos.h>
/* DOS function to read from keyboard */
#define DOS_KBDIN 1
main()
{
    unsigned int ch_read;
/* Nothing needs to be specified for DX and AL. Use 0's
 * Also, zero out the high-order byte by bitwise AND
 * with FFh
 */
    ch_read = bdos(DOS_KBDIN, 0, 0) & 0xff;
    printf("\nCharacter read = %c\n", ch_read);
}
```

Use DOS function number 2 to display on your monitor a character placed in the *DL* register (perhaps a character you just read from the keyboard). The return value has no meaning in this case.

```
#include <stdio.h>
#include <dos.h>
#define DOS_KBDIN    1
#define DOS_DISPCHAR 2
main()
{
    unsigned int ch_read;
/* First read a character. (see previous example) */
    ch_read = bdos(DOS_KBDIN, 0, 0) & 0xff;

/* Now display the character. DX is the character.
 * Nothing is needed in AL.
 */
    printf("\nHere's what you typed: ");
    bdos(DOS_DISPCHAR, ch_read, 0);
}
```

bdos

__bios__disk

COMPATIBILITY	MSC 3	MSC 4	MSC 5	QC	TC	ANSI	UNIX V
			▲	▲	biosdisk		

PURPOSE Use the *_bios_disk* function to perform *raw* disk I/O operations on the PC's 5¼-inch disk drive by using BIOS. For example, you can use *_bios_disk* to read and write physical sectors from the disk, to determine the status of the floppy disk drive, and even format a disk (if you are writing an alternative to the DOS FORMAT command).

Since this function allows you to perform low-level disk I/O directly, you should use it with caution because it can destroy data and damage the existing MS-DOS file system on your disk.

SYNTAX `unsigned _bios_disk (unsigned service, struct diskinfo_t *info);`

`unsigned service;`   Service code

`struct diskinfo_t *info;`   Disk information

EXAMPLE CALL `_bios_disk(_DISK_READ, &info);`

INCLUDES `#include <bios.h>`   For service codes and definition of structure *diskinfo_t*

DESCRIPTION The *_bios_disk* function, introduced in version 5.0 of Microsoft C, is a gateway to a set of ROM BIOS routines that provide access to the PC's disk drive via software interrupt number 13h. It provides a cleaner calling convention than is achieved by generating an INT 13h using the *int86x* function. The *_bios_disk* function performs the task requested in the argument *service code*. It expects information about the disk drive (for example, the head number, track number, etc.) in a C structure whose address must be provided in the argument *diskinfo*.

This structure data type, named *diskinfo_t*, having the layout shown below, is declared in the *include* file *bios.h*.

```
struct diskinfo_t
{
        unsigned drive;     /* Drive number (0 or 1)                 */
        unsigned head;      /* Head number (0 or 1) or which side?   */
        unsigned track;     /* Track number                          */
        unsigned sector;    /* Start sector number                   */
        unsigned nsectors;  /* Number of sectors for which requested */
                            /* service is to be performed            */
        void far *buffer;   /* Pointer to buffer in memory for use   */
                            /* during requested service              */
};
```

As shown in Table 16-7, the valid range of values for number of sectors and tracks depends on the type of disk.

 **System Calls**

Table 16-7. *Tracks and Sectors of 5¼-Inch Disks*

Disk Capacity	Drive Capacity	Valid Track Number	Valid Sector Number
320 K	320/360 K	0 through 39	1 through 8
360 K	320/360 K	0 through 39	1 through 9
320 K	1.2 Mb (AT)	0 through 39	1 through 8
360 K	1.2 Mb (AT)	0 through 39	1 through 9
1.2 Mb	1.2 Mb (AT)	0 through 79	1 through 15

Enough memory must be allocated for the buffer used by _bios_disk. For example, since a single sector in an IBM PC disk can hold 512 bytes, to read n sectors the buffer size must be at least $n \times 512$ bytes.

The service requested from _bios_disk can be specified by using the mnemonic service names for the six services defined in the *bios.h* header file. These are summarized in Table 16-8.

Table 16-8. *Disk Service Codes Accepted by* _bios_

Service	Function Performed	Fields of diskinfo_t Used
_DISK_RESET	Resets the floppy disk controller, so that status is set to zero to indicate that no error has occurred. Useful for resetting after an error.	None
_DISK_STATUS	Gets status of last disk operation. See description of *Returns* below for details of the status code.	
_DISK_READ	Reads specified number of sectors into buffer in memory. Return value indicates error, if any.	drive, head, track, sector, nsectors, buffer
_DISK_WRITE	Writes data from the memory buffer to specified number of sectors on the disk. This is the reverse of the _DISK_READ service.	drive, head, track, sector, nsectors, buffer
_DISK_VERIFY	First verifies that specified sectors exist and can be read. Then a cyclic redundancy check (CRC) is performed to verify that data in these sectors is correct. Since the stored data includes a CRC value it is possible to tell if any data has been corrupted. This service is similar to _DISK_READ except that the memory buffer is not used. Return value indicates error, if any.	drive, head, track, sector, nsectors
_DISK_FORMAT	Formats one track on one side (head) of the disk. This is similar to _DISK_WRITE except that sector information is not used. For proper formatting, the buffer pointer must point to a data area that contains four byte codes that describe the layout and the size of the sectors in that track.	

_bios_disk

COMMON USES This function is useful for developing disk utilities that allow the user to read and examine individual sectors and format disks, perhaps providing an alternative to the DOS FORMAT command with a nicer user interface. There are several commercial utility packages that allow you to "unerase" files and change file attributes, for example, to let you mark a file "hidden" so that it does not show up on directory listings. You can develop a similar function on your own by using the *_bios_disk* function.

RETURNS The *_bios_disk* function returns the contents of the *AX* register at the end of the call. Since it uses an INT 13h call, after a read, write, or verify operation, *AL* contains the total number of sectors for which the operation was to have been performed, while an 8-bit status code indicating success or cause of failure is returned in *AH*. When the operation is completed successfully, *AH* is zero. Thus, a good way to tell whether there has been an error is to compare the value returned by *_bios_disk* with the *nsectors* field of the *info* data structure. If they are equal, the operation went well. Otherwise the high-order byte of the return value contains the error code. The error codes are summarized in Table 16-9 (these error codes are also defined in the BIOS listings in the *IBM PC Technical Reference Manual*).

Table 16-9. *Error Codes Returned by _bios_disk*

Contents of the High-Order Byte of Return Value (Hex)	Meaning of Error Code
01	Command not known to disk I/O system.
02	Could not find address marks that identify the side, track, sector, and sector size on soft-sectored disks.
03	Could not write because disk is write-protected.
04	Could not find specified sector.
05	Reset failed.
08	Data transfers can occur directly between the disk and the PC's memory in an interrupt-driven approach. This is known as Direct Memory Access (DMA) and there are DMA controller chips on the PC to perform this task. This error code means that some data was lost during a DMA transfer.
09	DMA transfers (see error code 8) are not allowed to write to memory across a 64-K boundary. This error indicates that there was an attempt to do this.
10	The disk controller stores a cyclic redundancy check (CRC) value for each sector of data. During a read operation it can compute the CRC value again and conclude whether the data has been corrupted. This error code tells us that the CRC check indicates an error.
20	Disk controller failed.
40	Could not move to requested track.
80	Disk drive timed out or failed to respond because the door is open or the drive motor has not come up to speed yet. A retry is recommended.

 **System Calls**

COMMENTS To make effective use of this function, you need a good understanding of how the MS-DOS file system is related to the physical tracks and sectors. Its use also calls for some care since the capability of formatting and writing data directly to sectors of a disk makes it possible to inadvertently damage existing files and, worse, destroy crucial sectors with information about how the sectors are allocated to files (e.g., the File Allocation Table [FAT]). Consult a book such as *MS-DOS Developer's Guide* by Angermeyer and Jaeger for detailed information on these topics.

SEE ALSO int86x More general mechanism to access BIOS functions

EXAMPLE Under MS-DOS, on double-sided double-density (9-track, 40-sector, 360-K) disks the directory entries begin at Track 0, Sector 6. A 512-byte sector has 16 directory entries, each 32 bytes long. The first 11 bytes of a directory entry contain the name of the file (8-character name followed by 3-character extension). Use _bios_disk to read the first directory sector from this disk and display the first 10 names found in it. By the way, if you have erased files or the disk is newly formatted, you may see some strange file names—this is perfectly normal. Also, if your disk has a volume name, it will be the first file name displayed.

```
#include <stdio.h>
#include <dos.h>
#include <bios.h>
#define DOS_DISPCHAR 2
main()
{
    int i, j, retry, strt;
    unsigned ch_out, status = 0;
    char buf[512];
    void far *pbuf;
    struct diskinfo_t info;

/* Set up diskette information and buffer pointer */
    pbuf = (void far *)(&buf[0]);
    info.buffer = pbuf;
    info.drive = 0;  /* Drive A, use 1 for drive B */
    info.head = 0;
    info.track = 0;
    info.sector = 6;  /* Location of first directory
                         entry for DSDD diskettes */
    info.nsectors = 1;

/* Read sector making up to 3 retries. Retries are
 * necessary to make sure that any error is not due to
 * motor start-up delay. See explanation for error code
 * 80h above.
 */
```

_bios_disk

```
for (retry = 0; retry <= 3; retry++)
{
    if ((status = _bios_disk(_DISK_READ, &info))
        == info.nsectors)
    {
        printf("Read OK.\n");
        printf("First 10 directory entries are:\n");
        for (i=0; i<10; i++)
        {
            strt = 32*i; /* Each entry is 32-bytes */
            /* Each name is 11 bytes */
            for (j=0; j<11; j++)
            {
                ch_out = buf[strt+j];
                bdos(DOS_DISPCHAR, ch_out, 0);
            }
            printf("\n");
        }
        exit(0);
    }
}

/* Read failed despite 3 retries. Report error */
    printf("Error reading from diskette! status=%x\n",
        status);
}
```

__bios__equiplist

COMPATIBILITY	MSC 3	MSC 4	MSC 5	QC	TC	ANSI	UNIX V
			▲	▲	biosequip		

PURPOSE Use *_bios_equiplist* to get information about the hardware and peripherals in the user's PC. The list of equipment is returned in coded form in a single unsigned integer, whose bit values are shown in Table 16-10.

SYNTAX unsigned _bios_equiplist (void);

EXAMPLE CALL equip_flag = _bios_equiplist();

INCLUDES #include <bios.h>   For declaration of function

DESCRIPTION The *_bios_equiplist* function uses the BIOS interrupt 11h to get a list of hardware and peripherals currently installed in the PC. The combination of bits in the return value indicates the presence or absence of the hardware and peripherals specified in Table 16-10.

 **System Calls**

RETURNS   This function returns the contents of the *AX* register of BIOS interrupt 11h. The bits of the return value are interpreted as shown in Table 16-10. Note that bit 0 is the least significant bit.

Table 16-10. *Meaning of Bits in Value Returned by* __bios__equiplist

Bits	Meaning
0	1 = one or more disk drives attached, 0 means no disk drives.
1	1 = a math coprocessor is present.
2–3	Size of system memory in units of 4 K.
4–5	Initial video mode (00 = unused, 01 = 40 × 25 black and white text with color card, 10 = 80 × 25 black and white text with color card, 11 = 80 × 25 text on monochrome card).
6–7	Number of disk drives installed (00 = 1, 01 = 2). Only floppy disk drives are reported.
8	Set to 0 only if a Direct Memory Access (DMA) chip is present.
9–11	Number of RS 232C serial ports in the system.
12	1 = a game adapter is installed.
13	1 = a serial printer is attached.
14–15	Number of printers attached to system.

COMMENTS   This function is of limited usefulness. For example, bits 4 and 5 indicate the initial video mode, but not the current mode. The function does, however, provide such basic information as the number of RS232 serial ports, the number of disk drives, and the number of printers attached to the PC.

SEE ALSO   int86   For another way of generating BIOS interrupt 11h

EXAMPLE   Use the *__bios__equiplist* to obtain the number of disk drives, the number of serial ports, and the number of printers on the user's system and to determine if a math coprocessor is available. This approach can be used to ensure that the user's system has the minimal configuration necessary to run a program or to allow a program to use optional hardware.

```
#include <stdio.h>
#include <bios.h>
main()
{
    unsigned elist, d_drives=0, s_ports=0, printers=0;
    elist = _bios_equiplist();
/* Extract each item from the return value */
    if(elist & 0x0001)
    {
        d_drives = ((elist & 0x00c0) >> 6) + 1;
    }
```

__bios__equiplist

```
s_ports = (elist & 0x0e00) >> 9;
printers = (elist & 0xc000) >> 14;
printf("This system ");
if((elist & 0x0002)>>1)
{
    printf("has a math co-processor, ");
}
printf("%d diskette drives,\n", d_drives);
printf("%d serial ports and %d printers\n",
        s_ports, printers);
}
```

__bios__keybrd

COMPATIBILITY	MSC 3	MSC 4	MSC 5	QC	TC	ANSI	UNIX V
			▲	▲	bioskey		

PURPOSE   Use _bios_keybrd to access the BIOS routines for keyboard I/O. You can use it to read the next available character, to check if a character is waiting to be read, and to check if the special keys such as ALT, CTRL, and SHIFT are being pressed.

SYNTAX   `unsigned _bios_keybrd (unsigned service);`

`unsigned service;`   Keyboard function requested

EXAMPLE CALL   `ch_read = _bios_keybrd(_KEYBRD_READ) & 0xff;`

INCLUDES   `#include <bios.h>`   For definition of function and service codes

DESCRIPTION   The _bios_keybrd routine accesses the BIOS keyboard services by generating 8086 interrupt number 16h. The service to be performed is specified by one of the mnemonic constants that are defined in *bios.h*. The service names and the tasks they perform are summarized in Table 16-11.

Table 16-11. *Services Offered by* __bios__keybrd

Name	Service Performed
_KEYBRD_READ	Reads next available character from the keyboard buffer. Waits for a character if necessary. (See *Returns* for more information.)
_KEYBRD_READY	Checks the keyboard buffer for characters waiting to be read. (See *Returns* for explanation.)
_KEYBRD_SHIFTSTATUS	Returns current status of the SHIFT, CTRL, and ALT keys and indicates whether the SCROLL LOCK, NUM LOCK, and CAPS LOCK indicators are on.

 **System Calls**

RETURNS   After the call _*bios_keybrd(_KEYBRD_READ)*, the low-order byte of the return value contains the ASCII code of the character just read, and the high-order byte has the *scan code*—a unique byte generated by the keyboard when a key is either pressed or released. (See the *IBM PC Technical Reference Manual* for a list of the scan codes for its keyboard.) The character read is removed from the buffer.

The _*KEYBRD_READY* service returns a zero if the keyboard buffer is empty. Otherwise it returns the character in the same way that _*KEYBRD _READ* does, but it does not remove the character from the buffer.

The _*KEYBRD_SHIFTSTATUS* service returns in the low-order byte of the return value the current settings of the three LED indicators (CAPS LOCK, NUM LOCK, and SCROLL LOCK) and whether any of the SHIFT, ALT, or CTRL keys are being pressed. As shown in Table 16-12, one bit is used to represent each status.

Table 16-12. *Interpreting SHIFT Status Byte Returned by _bios_keybrd*

Bit	Interpretation When Bit Is a 1
0	Right SHIFT key pressed.
1	Left SHIFT key pressed.
2	CTRL key pressed.
3	ALT key pressed.
4	Scroll Lock indicator is ON.
5	Num Lock indicator is ON.
6	Caps Lock indicator is ON.
7	In INSERT mode.

COMMENTS   The _*KEYBRD_READY* service is very helpful when you want to continue doing something until the user presses a key. You can do your work in a loop, using this service to see if a key has been pressed. Since this service does not wait for a character to be typed, you can continue the work but respond quickly to the user's keystrokes. The *kbhit* function also provides this service and is easier to use.

SEE ALSO   int86   Alternate ways to access BIOS keyboard functions using interrupt 16h

kbhit   Another way to check for a keypress

EXAMPLE   Use the _KEYBRD_READY service to check if a key has been pressed. If not, keep updating a count until a key is pressed or the count is 50000.

```
#include <stdio.h>
#include <bios.h>

main()
```

_bios_keybrd

```
{
    unsigned count=0, ch_hit=0;
    while(count<50000)
    {
        if(_bios_keybrd(_KEYBRD_READY))
        {
/* Read the keystroke and mask out the high byte */
            ch_hit = _bios_keybrd(_KEYBRD_READ) & 0xff;
            printf("You entered: %c\n", ch_hit);
        }
        count++;
    }
    printf("Count is %d\n", count);
}
```

__bios__memsize

COMPATIBILITY	MSC 3	MSC 4	MSC 5	QC	TC	ANSI	UNIX V
			▲	▲	biosmemory		

PURPOSE Use *_bios_memsize* to determine the amount of memory in the PC. A program can use this to check if there is enough memory for it to run.

SYNTAX `unsigned _bios_memsize (void);`

EXAMPLE CALL `total_kilobytes = _bios_memsize();`

INCLUDES `#include <bios.h>`   For declaration of function

DESCRIPTION This function gets the amount of memory in the system by using BIOS interrupt 12h.

RETURNS The return value is the total memory in the system in 1-K (1,024 bytes) blocks.

EXAMPLE Check the amount of memory on the system using *_bios_memsize*.

```
#include <bios.h>
main()
{
    unsigned memsize;
    memsize = _bios_memsize();
    printf("This system has %dK memory.\n", memsize);
}
```

 **System Calls**

__bios__printer

COMPATIBILITY	MSC 3	MSC 4	MSC 5	QC	TC	ANSI	UNIX V
			▲	▲	biosprint		

PURPOSE Use *_bios_printer* to initialize the printer, determine its status, and send characters to it.

SYNTAX `unsigned _bios_printer (unsigned service,`
`                                    unsigned printer, unsigned data);`

`unsigned service;`   Printer function requested

`unsigned printer;`   Printer port, 0=LPT1 and 1=LPT2

`unsigned data;`   Character being sent to printer

EXAMPLE CALL `_bios_printer(_PRINTER_WRITE, LPT1, 'x');`

INCLUDES `#include <bios.h>`   For definition of function codes

DESCRIPTION The *_bios_printer* function is an interface to the BIOS printer routines accessible through software interrupt 17h. The routine performs the service indicated by the argument *service* on the printer port selected by the argument *printer*, using the *data* where needed. Request the service by using the constants that are defined in *bios.h*. Table 16-13 shows these service codes.

Table 16-13. *Service Codes for __bios__printer*

Name	Service Performed
_PRINTER_STATUS	Returns status of the printer. (See *Returns* for meaning.)
_PRINTER_INIT	Initializes printer connected to specified port. Note that *printer* = 0 means LPT1 and 1 means LPT2 and so on. The value of *data* is ignored. The status is returned.
_PRINTER_WRITE	Sends the low-order byte of *data* to the printer and returns the status after the operation.

RETURNS The low-order byte of the return value represents the status of the printer. The meanings of the bits are shown in Table 16-14.

SEE ALSO `int86`   For another way to access the BIOS printer services

EXAMPLE Use *_bios_printer* to initialize a printer at port LPT1: and print a line if the printer is ready.

```
#include <stdio.h>
#include <bios.h>
#define LPT1 0
char str[] = "\rTesting BIOS priniting routine\n\r";
main()
{
    unsigned status, data;
    int i;
    status = _bios_printer(_PRINTER_INIT, LPT1, data);
    for (i=0; str[i] != '\0'; i++)
    {
        data = str[i];
        _bios_printer(_PRINTER_WRITE, LPT1, data);
    }
}
```

Table 16-14. *Interpreting Status Byte of Printer*

Bit	Interpretation when Bit Is a 1
0	Printer has timed out.
1	Not used.
2	Not used.
3	I/O error has occurred.
4	Printer is selected for output.
5	Printer is out of paper.
6	Acknowledgment from printer.
7	Printer not busy (if bit is 0, printer is busy).

__bios__serialcom

COMPATIBILITY	MSC 3	MSC 4	MSC 5	QC	TC	ANSI	UNIX V
			▲	▲	bioscom		

PURPOSE Use *_bios_serialcom* to access the RS232 serial ports (either COM1 or COM2) of the PC. You can use this function to perform "polled" I/O, set communications parameters (for example, baud rate, parity, etc.), and check the status of the port.

SYNTAX unsigned _bios_serialcom (unsigned service, unsigned port, unsigned data);

unsigned service;   Service requested

System Calls

unsigned port;   Serial port number, 0=COM1 and 1=COM2

unsigned data;   Character to be sent or communications parameters

EXAMPLE CALL   ch_rcvd = 0xff & _bios_serialcom(_COM_RECEIVE, COM1, 0);

INCLUDES   #include <bios.h>   For definition of function codes

DESCRIPTION   This function lets you use the services offered by the BIOS routines normally accessible by interrupt number 14h. Only the ports COM1 and COM2 can be handled by this routine. The argument *port* specifies the port number: a 0 means COM1 and a 1 indicates COM2. The function performs the service requested in the argument *service* using the *data* where necessary. The service codes, defined in *bios.h*, are shown in Table 16-15. They can be used as the *service* argument.

Table 16-15. *Service Codes for* _bios_serialcom

Name	Service Performed
_COM_INIT	Initializes the serial port using the communications parameters given in *data*. (See Table 16-16 for the parameters.)
_COM_SEND	Sends the character in the low-order byte of *data* over the serial port *port*.
_COM_RECEIVE	Receives a character from *port* and returns it in the low-order byte of the return value.
_COM_STATUS	Returns the current status of the port. (See *Returns* for more details.)

Several communications parameters must be initialized before using the serial port: word length; number of bits that make one character; number of stop bits, indicating the end of a character; parity to be used; and baud rate, indicating how fast the port sends the bits that make up a single character. The *_bios_serialcom* function makes specifying the parameters simple: pick a constant from each of the four categories shown in Table 16-16 and logically OR them together to construct the unsigned argument *data*. For example, if you select an 8-bit word length, 1 stop bit, no parity, and a baud rate of 300 baud, you would use

(_COM_CHR8 | _COM_STOP1 | _COM_NOPARITY | _COM_300)

as the *data* argument with the service code _COM_INIT (the bar separating the values is the bitwise OR operator).

COMMON USES   The *_bios_serialcom* function is useful for simple polled I/O from the serial port at baud rates of up to 300 baud. Beyond this rate, the characters arrive so fast that your program cannot keep up. For higher performance, it is necessary to use an interrupt-driven approach in which the serial port invokes an

_bios_serialcom

Table 16-16. *Constants for Selecting Communications Parameters*

Category Name	List of Constants	Communications Parameter Setting
Word length	_COM_CHR7	7 bits per character
	_COM_CHR8	8 bits per character
Stop bits	_COM_STOP1	1 stop bit
	_COM_STOP2	2 stop bits
Parity	_COM_NOPARITY	No parity bit
	_COM_EVENPARITY	Even parity—parity bit is such that total number of 1s is even
	_COM_ODDPARITY	Odd parity—parity bit is such that total number of 1s is odd.
Baud rate	_COM_110	110 baud
	_COM_150	150 baud
	_COM_300	300 baud
	_COM_600	600 baud
	_COM_1200	1200 baud
	_COM_2400	2400 baud
	_COM_4800	4800 baud
	_COM_9600	9600 baud

interrupt handler when it needs attention. (See Chapter 13 of *MS-DOS Papers* by The Waite Group for an example of an interrupt-driven serial I/O package.)

RETURNS The high-order byte of the return value represents the status of the communications port. The meanings of the specific bits are shown in Table 16-17. For the _COM_SEND service, the low-order byte of the return value should contain the character just sent out. As is shown in the table, if bit 15 is set, the character was not sent because the port was not ready within a specified period of time. When reading a character from the serial port using the _COM_RECEIVE service, the low-order byte of the return value is the character just read, provided none of the bits in the high-order byte is set. If any bit in the high-order byte is set, an error has occurred and the cause of the error is indicated by the bit that is set.

Table 16-17. *Interpreting Status of Serial Port*

Bit	Interpretation when Bit Is a 1
8	Received data is ready.
9	Data overrun error occurred (a character was received before the last one was read).
10	Parity error occurred.
11	Framing error occurred (the end of a character was not recognized properly).
12	"Break" signal was detected (meaning that the signal on the receive line went dead for a while).
13	Register that holds a character to be transmitted is empty.
14	Shift register that moves the character out for transmission is empty.
15	Serial port has timed out.

 **System Calls**

For the _COM_INIT and _COM_STATUS services the low-order byte contains the status of the modem. The meanings of the bits in this case are shown in Table 16-18.

Table 16-18. *Modem Status*

Bit	Interpretation when Bit Is a 1
0	Change in "Clear To Send" signal (see bit 4).
1	Change in "Data Set Ready" signal (see bit 5).
2	Trailing edge ring indicator.
3	Change detected in quality of signal in the receive line.
4	Clear To Send (meaning modem is ready to receive data from the serial port).
5	Data Set Ready (meaning modem is connected to phone line).
6	Modem is receiving a "ring" voltage (meaning an incoming telephone call is detected).
7	Signal detected in the receive line.

SEE ALSO   int86   For access to the BIOS serial I/O services through 8086 software interrupt number 14h

EXAMPLE   Use *_bios_serialcom* to set up the serial port at 300 baud, 8-bit word length, 1 stop bit, and no parity. If you have a Hayes-compatible modem connected, once you have set the port, you can try conversing with it. For example, if you type AT, the modem should answer back with an OK (if there is no response try typing ATE1V1 to set up the modem properly). Assume that you are using the COM1 port.

```
#include <stdio.h>
#include <bios.h>
#define COM1 0
main()
{
    int ch_hit;
    unsigned service, data, status;
    data = (_COM_CHR8 | _COM_STOP1 |_COM_NOPARITY |
            _COM_300);
    _bios_serialcom(_COM_INIT, COM1, data);
    printf("Connecting to serial port 1. \
Type 'q' to exit\n");

    while(1)
    {
/* First see if "DATA READY" flag is set. If yes read
 * character from serial port.
 */
        status = 0x100 &
```

__bios__serialcom

588 *Files and I/O*

```
            _bios_serialcom(_COM_STATUS, COM1, 0);
        if (status == 0x100)
        {
/* If there is a character, get it and display it */
            ch_hit = 0xff &
                _bios_serialcom(_COM_RECEIVE, COM1, 0);
            printf("%c", ch_hit);
        }


/* Now check if any key has been pressed */
        if(_bios_keybrd(_KEYBRD_READY))
        {
/* If yes, read the keyboard buffer */
            ch_hit = _bios_keybrd(_KEYBRD_READ) & 0xff;
            if((ch_hit == 'q') || (ch_hit == 'Q'))
            {
/* Exit if it's a 'q' or a 'Q' */
                printf("Exiting...\n");
                exit(0);
            }


/* Else, wait until "transmit holding register empty"
 * flag is set. Once it's set, send out character to
 * serial port.
 */
            status = 0x2000 &
                _bios_serialcom(_COM_STATUS, COM1, 0);
            while (status != 0x2000)
            {
                status = 0x2000 &
                _bios_serialcom(_COM_STATUS, COM1, 0);
            }
            _bios_serialcom(_COM_SEND, COM1, ch_hit);
            if ((status & 0x8000) == 0x8000)
            {
                printf("Error sending: %c\n", ch_hit);
            }
        }
    }
}
```

System Calls

__bios__timeofday

COMPATIBILITY	MSC 3	MSC 4	MSC 5	QC	TC	ANSI	UNIX V
			▲	▲	biostime		

PURPOSE Use the _bios_timeofday function to retrieve or set the current system clock count on the PC. The clock count is incremented 18.2 times a second, so you can use this function to wait for a specified number of seconds, albeit with a resolution of 1/18.2 second (or about 55 milliseconds) only.

SYNTAX unsigned _bios_timeofday (unsigned service, long *clockcount);

unsigned service;   Service requested

long *clockcount;   Timer clock counts

EXAMPLE CALL _bios_timeofday(_TIME_GETCLOCK, &clock_count);

INCLUDES #include <bios.h>   For definition of service codes

DESCRIPTION The _bios_timeofday function invokes the ROM BIOS time-of-day interrupt (number 1Ah) to get the current clock count or to reset the clock count to a new value. Incremented 18.2 times a second, the count can serve as a timer with a resolution of 1/18.2 second (or 55 milliseconds). The service requested is specified by using a constant defined in *bios.h*. Table 16-19 explains the use of the service codes.

Table 16-19. *Service Codes for* __bios__timeofday

Name	Service Performed
_TIME_GETCLOCK	Copies the current value of the clock count into the long integer that *clockcount* points to. The function returns 1 if midnight has passed since the clock was last read or set; otherwise the return value is 0.
_TIME_SETCLOCK	Sets the current system clock count to the value specified in the long integer that *clockcount* points to. The return value is unspecified.

COMMON USES This function is useful in writing delay routines that wait for a specified number of seconds before returning.

RETURNS The return value is defined only when *service* is _TIME_GETCLOCK. In this case, a return value of 1 indicates that midnight has passed since the last time the clock was read.

COMMENTS One drawback of using _bios_timeofday as a timer is the coarseness of the clock counts which are updated once every 55 milliseconds only.

SEE ALSO   int86   For general purpose access to BIOS INT 1Ah services

EXAMPLE   Write a routine that uses *_bios_timeofday* to wait for a specified number of seconds before exiting.

```
#include <stdio.h>
#include <bios.h>

main()
{
    long oldcount, newcount;
    int ticks;
    printf("How many seconds to wait? ");
    scanf("%d", &ticks);
    ticks *= 18.2;
    _bios_timeofday(_TIME_GETCLOCK, &oldcount);
    newcount =oldcount;
    while ((newcount-oldcount) < ticks)
    {
        _bios_timeofday(_TIME_GETCLOCK, &newcount);
    }
    printf("\nWaited for %d clock ticks\n", ticks);
}
```

__chain__intr

COMPATIBILITY	MSC 3	MSC 4	MSC 5	QC	TC	ANSI	UNIX V
			▲	▲			

PURPOSE   Use *_chain_intr* to jump from one interrupt handler to another. For example, you can write your own interrupt handler for a particular interrupt and after performing the tasks you want done, you can call *_chain_intr* to jump to the interrupt handler originally installed.

SYNTAX   `void _chain_intr (void (interrupt far *handler)());`

       `interrupt far *handler;`   Far pointer to the handler, a function of type *interrupt*

EXAMPLE CALL   `void (interrupt far *old_handler)();`
                      `_chain_intr(old_handler);`

INCLUDES   `#include <dos.h>`   For declaration of function

DESCRIPTION   The *_chain_intr* function simply jumps to the address of the interrupt handler specified in the argument *handler*, which is a far pointer to an interrupt

System Calls

handler. The handler is a function of type *interrupt*, a keyword introduced in version 5.0 to allow writing interrupt handlers in C. (See Chapter 1 for more information on the *interrupt* attribute.)

   If you want to chain the existing interrupt handler to the one you are writing, you can first get the address of the old handler by calling the function *_dos_getvect*. Then in your own interrupt handler, after completing all processing, you can perform the chaining by invoking *_chain_intr* with the old handler's address as the argument.

COMMON USES   This function is useful in writing interrupt handlers in Microsoft C 5.0 and 5.1. When you want something extra done during a certain interrupt and yet want to retain all the old functions, you can install your own interrupt handler for that interrupt only and chain to the old interrupt vector from within your handler.

COMMENTS   You need an understanding of the 8086 interrupt mechanism before you can make effective use of this function. See the tutorial section for some background information and further references.

SEE ALSO   _dos_getvect   To get the address of the current interrupt handler for an interrupt

   _dos_setvect   To install a new interrupt vector

   _dos_keep   To install "terminate and stay resident" programs

EXAMPLE   Use the *_dos_getvect* function to get and save the current address of the interrupt handler for the BIOS video interrupts (number 10h). Now install your own interrupt handler using *_dos_setvect*. In your interrupt handler, chain to the old handler by using the *_chain_intr* function. Try something with the video interrupt to see if this scheme works. For example, you can use the function that allows you to change the cursor shape and see if everything works. Before exiting, reset the interrupt vector to its original state. (Notice the use of the *_disable* and *_enable* pair to ensure that nothing goes wrong while we are taking over an interrupt vector.)

```
#include <stdio.h>
#include <dos.h>
#define BIOS_VIDEO 0x10
void interrupt far vio_handler(void);
void (interrupt far *old_handler)();
main()
{
    union REGS xr, yr;
    unsigned c;
    unsigned intno = BIOS_VIDEO;
    old_handler = _dos_getvect(intno);
/* Print out address of old handler using %p format */
    printf("\nThe address of the old handler is : %p\n",
```

_chain_intr

```
                    old_handler);
/* Install the new handler named vio_handler
 * Disable interrupts when changing handler
 */
    _disable();
    _dos_setvect(intno, vio_handler);
    _enable();
    printf("Installed new handler: %p\n", vio_handler);
/* Do some video I/O -- change cursor to a solid block*/
    xr.h.ah = 1;
    xr.h.ch = 0;
    xr.h.cl = 8;
    int86(BIOS_VIDEO, &xr, &yr);
/* Quit when user says so */
    printf("Hit q to quit: ");
    while ((c=getch()) != 'q'); /* Keep looping till 'q'*/
/* Reset vector. Disable interrupts when doing this    */
    _disable();
    _dos_setvect(intno, old_handler);
    _enable();
}
/*-------------------------------------------------*/
void interrupt far vio_handler()
{
/* Our handler simply chains to the old_handler using
 * the library routine _chain_intr.
 */
    _chain_intr(old_handler);
}
```

__disable

COMPATIBILITY	MSC 3	MSC 4	MSC 5	QC	TC	ANSI	UNIX V
			▲	▲	disable		

PURPOSE Use the __disable function to turn off interrupts on the 8086 microprocessor by a CLI instruction. You may, for example, want to turn off interrupts when installing a new handler for an interrupt. Remember to call __enable to turn interrupts back on as soon as possible.

SYNTAX void _disable(void);

EXAMPLE CALL _disable();

INCLUDES #include <dos.h>   For function declaration

 **System Calls**

DESCRIPTION The _disable function executes an 8086 *CLI* instruction.

COMMON USES The _disable function is useful when interrupts have to be turned off in critical sections of a program. Such cases typically arise in programs that install or remove interrupt handlers (see the tutorial section).

COMMENTS The _disable function was not present in earlier versions of Microsoft C (3.0 or 4.0). The addition of this function greatly enhances your capability to write software with interrupt handlers almost entirely in C, but you must be careful because of its intimate ties to the hardware. You should understand the interrupt mechanism of the 8086 microprocessor before using this function. In particular, the system clock is updated by interrupts so disabling interrupts for long periods of time interferes with the time-keeping. This function is a good example of the low-level access to hardware afforded by Microsoft C on the IBM PC.

SEE ALSO _enable   To enable 8086 interrupts

EXAMPLE See the example in the reference page on _dos_setvect for a sample usage of _disable.

__dos__allocmem

COMPATIBILITY	MSC 3	MSC 4	MSC 5	QC	TC	ANSI	UNIX V
			▲	▲	allocmem		

PURPOSE Use _dos_allocmem to allocate memory in 16-byte chunks (called "paragraphs") from a pool maintained by DOS. Remember to free the memory using the companion function _dos_freemem when you no longer need it.

SYNTAX unsigned _dos_allocmem (unsigned npara, unsigned *segadd);

unsigned npara;   Number of 16-byte paragraphs to be allocated

unsigned *segadd;   Segment address of allocated memory

INCLUDES #include <dos.h>   For declaration of function

DESCRIPTION The _dos_allocmem function calls the DOS function 48h to allocate the paragraphs of memory requested in the argument *npara* and return the segment address of the block through the unsigned integer to which the argument *segadd* points. If the requested amount of memory could not be allocated, _dos_allocmen sets *segadd* to the maximum available memory size (in paragraphs). The offset is always zero. The address of the allocated memory should be saved for use in freeing the block later with _dos _freemem.

RETURNS　This function returns zero if memory was successfully allocated. If unsuccessful, the return value is an MS-DOS error code (see the reference page on *dosexterr* for a list of codes) and the global variable *errno* is set to the constant ENOMEM, indicating that not enough memory is available.

COMMENTS　The _dos_allocmem and _dos_freemem functions are MS-DOS specific. Other memory allocation functions (for example, *malloc, calloc, free*) are more portable (for example, when moving your program to UNIX). It is interesting to note that the standard allocation routines use a memory pool that the Microsoft C startup routine gets by requesting a chuck of memory from DOS using the same DOS function that _dos_allocmem invokes.

SEE ALSO　_dos_freemem　　　　To free up memory allocated by _dos_allocmem

　　　　_dos_setblock　　　　To alter the size of the chunk allocated by _dos_allocmem

　　　　alloca, calloc, halloc, malloc　　　Other memory allocation routines

EXAMPLE　Use the _dos_allocmem to allocate 5 paragraphs of memory, enough to hold 80 characters. Store a string in the allocated buffer, print the string, and free the allocated buffer.

```
#include <stdio.h>
#include <dos.h>
#include <memory.h>
#define DOS_PRTSTR 0x09
char str[80]="Testing _dos_allocmem...\n$";
main()
{
    union REGS xr;
    struct SREGS sr;
    char far *stradd;
    unsigned int segadd;
    stradd = (char far *)(&str[0]);
    if (_dos_allocmem(5, &segadd) != 0)
    {
        printf("Memory allocation failed!\n");
        exit(0);
    }
/* Copy string into allocated memory using movedata */
    movedata(FP_SEG(stradd),FP_OFF(stradd),
            segadd, 0, 80);
    sr.ds = segadd;
    xr.x.dx = 0;
    xr.h.ah = DOS_PRTSTR;
```

 **System Calls**

```
        intdosx(&xr, &xr, &sr);

    /* Free memory before exiting */
        _dos_freemem(segadd);
    }
```

__dos__close

COMPATIBILITY	MSC 3	MSC 4	MSC 5	QC	TC	ANSI	UNIX V
			▲	▲	_close		

PURPOSE Use _dos_close to close a file that you opened by calling _dos_open or that you created by using _dos_creat or _dos_creatnew.

SYNTAX unsigned _dos_close (int filehandle);

int filehandle;　　The file handle or identifier

EXAMPLE CALL _dos_close(handle);

INCLUDES #include <dos.h>　　For declaration of function

DESCRIPTION The _dos_close function calls DOS function 3Eh to close the file specified by the identifying number, or handle, in the argument *filehandle*. The file handle must be the one returned when the file was opened by _dos_open or created by _dos_creat or _dos_creatnew. The _dos_close operation involves flushing (writing) to the disk internal MS-DOS buffers associated with that file, closing the file, and releasing the handle for reuse. The date stamp, the time stamp, and the file size are also updated.

RETURNS This function returns zero if successful; otherwise, it returns the MS-DOS error code and sets the global variable *errno* to the constant EBADF, indicating that the file handle is invalid.

COMMENTS The functions *open* and *close* offer a more portable means of achieving the same result as this DOS-specific function.

SEE ALSO _dos_open　　To open an existing file using a DOS call

_dos_creat,
_dos_creatnew　　To create a new file

open, close　　Portable versions of similar file opening and closing functions

EXAMPLE Use _dos_close to close a file opened by _dos_open.

__dos__close

```
#include <stdio.h>
#include <fcntl.h>
#include <dos.h>
main()
{
    char fname[40], *p_fname;
    int filehandle;

    printf("Enter name of file to open using \
_dos_open: ");
    p_fname = gets(fname);

/* Open the file using _dos_open */
    if (_dos_open(p_fname, O_RDONLY, &filehandle) != 0)
    {
        printf("Error opening file: %s\n", fname);
        exit(0);
    }
    printf("File %s opened.\n", fname);

/* Now close file */
    if (_dos_close(filehandle) != 0)
    {
        perror("Error closing file with _dos_close");
        exit(0);
    }
    printf("File %s closed.\n", fname);
}
```

__dos__creat

COMPATIBILITY	MSC 3	MSC 4	MSC 5	QC	TC	ANSI	UNIX V
			▲	▲	_creat		

PURPOSE   Use *_dos_creat* to create a new file or to truncate an existing file to zero length.

SYNTAX   unsigned _dos_creat (char *filename, unsigned attribute,
                                         int *filehandle);

char *filename;   File name, including path

unsigned attribute;   Attributes of the file

int *filehandle;   Pointer to location where the handle, or identifier, is returned

 **System Calls**

EXAMPLE CALL   _dos_creat("c:\\tmptmp001", _A_NORMAL, &filehandle);

INCLUDES   #include <dos.h>   For declaration of function and definition of attribute names

DESCRIPTION   The _dos_creat function calls the DOS function 3Ch to create the file whose name (including the DOS pathname) is specified by the argument *filename* and whose attributes are in the argument *attribute*. If the file already exists, it is truncated to zero length and its old attributes are retained.

The attribute indicates whether a file is read-only, whether it is hidden, and so on. You specify the attribute by using the bitwise OR of attribute names picked from Table 16-20. The attribute constants are defined in *dos.h*. Once the file is successfully opened, an identifying number, or handle, is returned in the location whose address is specified in the argument *filehandle*.

Table 16-20. *Interpretation of File Attribute Constants*

Name	Interpretation of Attribute
_A_NORMAL	Normal file without any read or write restrictions.
_A_RDONLY	File cannot be opened for write operations.
_A_HIDDEN	File will not show up on directory search.
_A_SYSTEM	File is marked as a system file and will be excluded from normal directory searches.
_A_VOLID	Volume name; can exist only in root directory.
_A_SUBDIR	Subdirectory name (meaning the file is a subdirectory).
_A_ARCH	If set, file will be archived by MS-DOS *BACKUP* command. This attribute is set after any changes to the file.

RETURNS   This function returns zero if successful; otherwise, it returns the MS-DOS error code and sets the global variable *errno* to one of the constants shown in Table 16-21.

Table 16-21. *Error Codes Returned by _dos_creat*

Error Code	Interpretation
ENOENT	Path not found.
EMFILE	Too many files open (limit is 20 for a process).
EACCES	Access denied. (For example, the file exists and cannot be overwritten or the root directory is full.)

COMMENTS   The *creat* function provides a more portable means of achieving the same result as does this DOS-specific function.

Under MS-DOS, the maximum number of concurrently open files for a single process is 20.

_dos_creat

SEE ALSO   _dos_close   To close a file

_dos_creatnew   To create a new file but not overwrite existing ones

creat   Portable versions of similar file creation function

EXAMPLE   Use *_dos_creat* to create a file. Close the file by calling *_dos_close*.

```c
#include <stdio.h>
#include <dos.h>
main()
{
    char fname[40], *p_fname;
    int filehandle;

    printf("Enter name of file to create using \
_dos_creat: ");
    p_fname = gets(fname);

/* Create the file using _dos_creat */
    if (_dos_creat(p_fname, _A_NORMAL,
                             &filehandle) != 0)
    {
        perror("Error creating file");
        exit(0);
    }
    printf("File %s created.\n", fname);

/* Now close file */
    if (_dos_close(filehandle) != 0)
    {
        perror("Error closing file with _dos_close");
        exit(0);
    }
    printf("File %s closed.\n", fname);
}
```

System Calls

__dos__creatnew

COMPATIBILITY	MSC 3	MSC 4	MSC 5	QC	TC	ANSI	UNIX V
			▲	▲	creatnew		

PURPOSE Use *_dos_creatnew* to create a new file. Unlike *_dos_creat*, this function does not overwrite an existing file.

SYNTAX
```
unsigned _dos_creatnew (char *filename, unsigned attribute,
                                          int *filehandle);
```

char *filename;   File name, including path

unsigned attribute;   Attributes of the file

int *filehandle;   Pointer to location where the handle, or identifier, is returned

EXAMPLE CALL `_dos_creatnew("c:\\mscb\\toc.1", _A_NORMAL, &filehandle);`

INCLUDES `#include <dos.h>`   For declaration of function and definition of attribute names

DESCRIPTION The *_dos_creatnew* function calls the DOS function 5Bh to create the file whose name (including the full DOS pathname) is specified by the argument *filename* and whose attributes are in the argument *attribute*. This function fails if the file already exists.

The attribute indicates whether a file is read-only, hidden, and so on. You can specify the attribute by using the bitwise OR of attribute names picked from Table 16-21. The attribute constants are defined in *dos.h*.

Once the file is successfully opened, an identifying number, or handle, is returned in the location whose address is specified in the argument *filehandle*.

RETURNS This function returns zero if successful, otherwise, it returns the MS-DOS error code and sets the global variable *errno* to one of the constants shown in Table 16-22.

Table 16-22. *Error Codes Returned by* __dos__creatnew

Error Code	Interpretation
ENOENT	Path not found.
EMFILE	Too many files open (limit is 20 for a process).
EACCES	Access denied (for example, an attempt to create a file in a full root directory).
EEXIST	File already exists.

SEE ALSO   `_dos_close`   To close a file

`_dos_creat`   To create a new file or to overwrite existing ones

`creat`   Portable versions of similar file creation function

EXAMPLE   Use *_dos_creatnew* to create a new file. Close the file by calling *_dos_close*.

```
#include <stdio.h>
#include <dos.h>
main()
{
    char fname[40], *p_fname;
    unsigned status;
    int filehandle;

    printf("Enter name of file to create: ");
    p_fname = gets(fname);

/* Create the file using _dos_creat */
    if((status = _dos_creatnew(p_fname, _A_NORMAL,
        &filehandle) != 0))
    {
        printf("Error creating file: %s\n", fname);
        if(status == EEXIST)
                printf("File already exists!\n");
        exit(0);
    }
    printf("File %s created.\n", fname);

/* Now close file */
    if (_dos_close(filehandle) != 0)
    {
        printf("Error closing file with _dos_close\n");
        exit(0);
    }
    printf("File %s closed.\n", fname);
}
```

System Calls

__dos__findfirst

COMPATIBILITY	MSC 3	MSC 4	MSC 5	QC	TC	ANSI	UNIX V
			▲	▲	findfirst		

PURPOSE   Use _dos_findfirst to find the first file whose name and attributes match the specified values. Since the specified name can have wildcard characters (* and ?), this function can find, for example, the first file with a .C extension by searching for all *.C files.

SYNTAX
```
unsigned _dos_findfirst(char *filename, unsigned attribute,
                                   struct find_t *fileinfo);
```

char *filename;   File name to search for including path

unsigned attribute;   File attributes to match

struct find_t *fileinfo;   Structure to hold results of search

EXAMPLE CALL
```
/* Search volume name */
_dos_findfirst("\*.*", _A_VOLID, &fileinfo);
```

INCLUDES   `#include <dos.h>`   For declaration of function and definition of attribute names

DESCRIPTION   The _dos_findfirst function calls the DOS function 4Eh to get the information about the first file whose name matches the one in the character string *filename* and whose attributes are identical to those given in the argument *attribute*. The file name can have the * and ? wildcard characters.

Specify the attribute to be matched by using a value created by the bitwise OR of attribute names picked from Table 16-21. These attribute constants are defined in *dos.h*.

The results of the search are returned in a structure of type *find_t*, which is defined in *dos.h*. A pointer to one structure must be provided in the argument *fileinfo*. The layout and C declaration of *dos.h* are shown below.

```
struct find_t
{
    char     reserved[21];  /* Reserved for use by MS-DOS */
    char     attrib;        /* Attribute byte of file    */
    unsigned wr_time;       /* Time of last file update  */
    unsigned wr_date;       /* Date of last file update  */
    long     size;          /* File's length in bytes    */
    char     name[13];      /* Null-terminated file name */
};
```

After the function returns successfully, the field *name* contains the null-terminated name (not the entire path, just the file name and extension) of the first file that met the search criteria. The attribute of this file is copied into the field *attrib*. The date and time of last write to this file are in *wr_date* and *wr_time*. Finally, the long integer field *size* contains the length of the file in bytes.

COMMON USES This function is commonly used with its companion *_dos_findnext* to find all occurrences of a file name with a wildcard specification such as all *.C* files.

RETURNS The function returns zero if successful; otherwise, it returns the MS-DOS error code and sets the global variable *errno* to the constant ENOENT, indicating that the file could not be found.

SEE ALSO _dos_findnext   To get the next file that also meets search criteria

EXAMPLE Use *_dos_findfirst* to find the volume name. You have to specify a search name \ *.* and an attribute of _A_VOLID to do this.

```
#include <stdio.h>
#include <dos.h>
main()
{
    struct find_t fileinfo;

    if (_dos_findfirst("\*.*", _A_VOLID,
                                &fileinfo) != 0)
    {
        printf("Unsuccessful _dos_findfirst call!\n");
        exit(0);
    }
    printf("The volume name is: %s\n",
            fileinfo.name);
}
```

__dos__findnext

COMPATIBILITY	MSC 3	MSC 4	MSC 5	QC	TC	ANSI	UNIX V
			▲	▲	findnext		

PURPOSE Use *_dos_findnext* right after *_dos_findfirst* to find the remaining instances of files whose names and attributes match the values used during the *_dos_findfirst* call. You call *_dos_findnext* only if the file name specified in the call to *_dos_findfirst* contained one or more wildcard characters (* and ?). You can use this function to find, for example, all the files with a .C extension by searching for all *.C* files.

 **System Calls**

SYNTAX	`unsigned _dos_findnext(struct find_t *fileinfo);`
	`struct find_t *fileinfo;` Structure to hold results of search
EXAMPLE CALL	`_dos_findnext(&fileinfo);`
INCLUDES	`#include <dos.h>` For declaration of function

DESCRIPTION The *_dos_findnext* function calls the DOS function 4Fh to find the next file whose name and attributes are identical to those given in the call to the *_dos _findfirst* function. The results of the search by *_dos_findnext* are returned in a structure of type *find_t*. You provide a pointer to a structure of this type in the argument *fileinfo* when calling *_dos_findnext*. The structure *find_t* is defined in *dos.h*; its layout and C declaration are shown in the description of the companion function *_dos_findfirst*.

After the function returns successfully, the field *name* contains the null-terminated name (not the entire path, just file name and extension) of the next file that met the search criteria. The attribute of this file is copied into the field *attrib* of the *find_t* structure. The date and time of the last write operation on this file are in *wr_date* and *wr_time*. Finally, *size* contains the length of the file in bytes.

COMMON USES This function is called in a loop right after *_dos_findfirst* to find the remaining occurrences of a file with a wildcard specification such as all *.C* files.

RETURNS The function returns zero if successful; otherwise, it returns the MS-DOS error code and sets the global variable *errno* to the constant ENOENT indicating that the search failed.

SEE ALSO `_dos_findfirst`   To begin the search and find the first file that meets the search criteria

EXAMPLE Use *_dos_findnext* to find all files with a *.C* extension. You need to call *_dos_findfirst* to set up the search and get the first file that matches the specified name and attribute.

```
#include <stdio.h>
#include <dos.h>
main()
{
    int count;
    long totalsize;
    struct find_t fileinfo;
    if (_dos_findfirst("*.c", _A_NORMAL, &fileinfo)
        != 0)
    {
        printf("Unsuccessful _dos_findnext call!\n");
        exit(0);
```

__dos__findnext

```
    }
    printf("Listing of *.c files:\n");
    printf("%s     %d bytes\n", fileinfo.name,
                                fileinfo.size);
    count = 1;
    totalsize = fileinfo.size;
    while (_dos_findnext(&fileinfo) == 0)
    {
        count++;
        totalsize += fileinfo.size;
/* Now print the name and size of each matching file */
        printf("%s     %d bytes\n",
                fileinfo.name, fileinfo.size);
    }
    printf("\n%d files %d bytes.\n", count, totalsize);
}
```

__dos__freemem

COMPATIBILITY	MSC 3	MSC 4	MSC 5	QC	TC	ANSI	UNIX V
			▲	▲	freemem		

PURPOSE Use *_dos_freemem* to free memory allocated with the *_dos_allocmem* function. Use the segment address returned by *_dos_allocmem* to indicate which chunk of memory you are freeing.

SYNTAX unsigned _dos_freemem (unsigned segadd);

unsigned segadd;   Segment address of allocated memory

EXAMPLE CALL _dos_freemem(segment);

INCLUDES #include <dos.h>   For declaration of function

DESCRIPTION The *_dos_freemem* function calls DOS function 49h to free memory allocated with the *_dos_allocmem* function. The segment address of the block freed is specified through the unsigned integer *segadd*. The offset is always zero. This should be the same segment address that was returned by *_dos_allocmem* when the memory was allocated.

RETURNS This function returns zero if memory was successfully released. Otherwise, the return value is the MS-DOS error code and the global variable *errno* is set to the constant ENOMEM, indicating a bad segment value.

 **System Calls**

SEE ALSO	_dos_allocmem	The corresponding routine to allocate memory; also shows how to use *_dos_freemem*
	_dos_setblock	To alter the size of the chunk allocated by *_dos_allocmem*
	ffree, free, hfree, nfree	Other routines that release memory

EXAMPLE Use *_dos_allocmem* to allocate 10 paragraphs of memory. Next call *_dos_freemem* to free this block of memory.

```
#include <stdio.h>
#include <dos.h>
main()
{
    unsigned segadd;
    if (_dos_allocmem(10, &segadd) != 0)
    {
        perror("Memory allocation failed");
        exit(0);
    }
    printf("10 paragraphs of memory allocated \n\
at segment address: %u\n", segadd);
/* Free memory before exiting */
    if(_dos_freemem(segadd) != 0)
    {
        perror("_dos_freemem failed");
    }
    else
    {
        printf("The memory is released now.\n");
    }
}
```

__dos__getdate

COMPATIBILITY	MSC 3	MSC 4	MSC 5	QC	TC	ANSI	UNIX V
			▲	▲	getdate		

PURPOSE Use *_dos_getdate* to get the current system date, as maintained by DOS.

SYNTAX `void _dos_getdate (struct dosdate_t *date);`

`struct dosdate_t *date;` Pointer to a structure that holds the components of date

EXAMPLE CALL `_dos_getdate(&date);`

INCLUDES   `#include <dos.h>`   For definition of the structure *dosdate_t*

DESCRIPTION   The *_dos_getdate* function calls DOS function 2Ah to get the current system date. The components of the date—the day, month, year, and day of the week—are stored in fields of the structure type *dosdate_t*, which is defined in *dos.h*. The layout of this structure and its C declaration are shown below.

```
struct dosdate_t
{
    unsigned char day;          /* day of the month (range 1-31) */
    unsigned char month;        /* month (range 1-12)            */
    unsigned int year;          /* year (range 1980-2099)        */
    unsigned char dayofweek;    /* Day of the week 0-6, 0=Sunday */
};
```

SEE ALSO   `_dos_setdate`   The corresponding routine that sets the system date

`_dos_gettime, _dos_settime`   To get and set the system time

`_strdate, _strtime,`
`gmtime, localtime,`
`mktime, time`   Other date and time services

EXAMPLE   Use the *_dos_getdate* to get and display the current system date.

```
#include <stdio.h>
#include <dos.h>
main()
{
    struct dosdate_t date;
    _dos_getdate(&date);
    printf("Date: %d/%d/%d\n", date.month, date.day,
            date.year -1900);
}
```

__dos__getdiskfree

COMPATIBILITY	MSC 3	MSC 4	MSC 5	QC	TC	ANSI	UNIX V
			▲	▲	getdfree		

PURPOSE   Use *_dos_getdiskfree* to determine the total capacity of a disk, as well as the amount of free space.

SYNTAX   `unsigned _dos_getdiskfree(unsigned drive, struct diskfree_t *dfinfo);`

 **System Calls**

unsigned drive;   Drive number: 0=default, 1=A, 2=B

struct diskfree_t *dfinfo;   Structure to hold information on disk space

EXAMPLE CALL   _dos_getdiskfree (0, &dfinfo);

INCLUDES   #include <dos.h>   For declaration of structure *diskfree_t*

DESCRIPTION   The _dos_getdiskfree function calls the DOS function 36h to retrieve information on the total and free disk space available on the drive specified by the argument *drive*. If the argument is a zero, information about the current default drive is returned; a value of 1 means drive A, 2 means B, and so on.

The requested information is returned in a structure of type *diskfree_t* whose address is specified in the argument *dfinfo*. The data structure is declared in *dos.b*. Its layout and C declaration are shown below.

```
struct diskfree_t
{
    unsigned total_clusters;
    unsigned avail_clusters;
    unsigned sectors_per_cluster;
    unsigned bytes_per_sector;
};
```

The information about disk space is returned as number of "clusters" on the disk and the number not in use. These values are in the fields *total_clusters* and *avail_clusters*. Since a cluster is a collection of sectors, by using the value given in *sectors_per_cluster* and the value from the field *bytes_per _sector*, we can compute in bytes the total disk space and the unused amount.

COMMON USES   This function can be used to verify that there is enough free space on the current disk before attempting a critical operation such as saving a file.

RETURNS   The function returns a zero if successful. In case of an error, it returns a nonzero and the global variable *errno* is set to EINVAL, indicating an invalid drive number.

SEE ALSO   _dos_getdrive, _dos_setdrive   To get information about the current default drive or to change the current default

EXAMPLE   Use _dos_getdiskfree to display the total capacity of your drive in bytes and the amount not in use.

```
#include <stdio.h>
#include <dos.h>
main()
{
```

_dos_getdiskfree

```
      unsigned long total_space, free_space,
                    bytes_per_cluster;
      struct diskfree_t dfinfo;
      if(_dos_getdiskfree (0, &dfinfo) !=0)
      {
          printf("Error in _dos_getdiskfree\n");
          exit(0);
      }
      bytes_per_cluster = dfinfo.sectors_per_cluster *
                          dfinfo.bytes_per_sector;
      total_space = dfinfo.total_clusters *
                    bytes_per_cluster;
      free_space = dfinfo.avail_clusters *
                   bytes_per_cluster;
      printf ("%ld bytes free out of %ld bytes of total \
  space.\n", free_space, total_space);
  }
```

__dos__getdrive

COMPATIBILITY	MSC 3	MSC 4	MSC 5	QC	TC	ANSI	UNIX V
			▲	▲	getdisk		

PURPOSE   Use *_dos_getdrive* to determine the current default drive number.

SYNTAX   void _dos_getdrive (unsigned *driveno);

unsigned *driveno;   Pointer to location where current default drive number is to be returned

EXAMPLE CALL   _dos_getdrive(&drive_number);

INCLUDES   #include <dos.h>   For declaration of function

DESCRIPTION   The *_dos_getdrive* function calls the DOS function 19h to get the current default drive number. Before returning, it loads the drive number into the location whose address is in the argument *driveno*. The returned drive number is interpreted as follows: a 1 means drive A, a 2 means drive B, and so on.

COMMON USES   When you create a file or perform file I/O, DOS assumes you are referring to the file on the current default drive if a drive is not explicitly specified. The drive number returned by *_dos_getdrive* gives this default drive.

SEE ALSO   _dos_setdrive   To change the current default drive number

 **System Calls**

EXAMPLE Use *_dos_getdrive* to show the current default drive number.

```
#include <stdio.h>
#include <dos.h>
main()
{
    unsigned drive;
    _dos_getdrive(&drive);
    printf ("The current drive is: %c\n", drive+'A'-1);
}
```

__dos__getfileattr

COMPATIBILITY	MSC 3	MSC 4	MSC 5	QC	TC	ANSI	UNIX V
			▲	▲			

PURPOSE Use *_dos_getfileattr* to get the attributes of a file. For example, you can determine if a file is a normal file or a subdirectory by using this function.

SYNTAX `unsigned _dos_getfileattr(char *filename, unsigned *attribute);`

`char *filename;`   File name, including path

`unsigned *attribute;`   Location to store attributes

EXAMPLE CALL `_dos_getfileattr("c:\\autoexec.bat", &attribute);`

INCLUDES `#include <dos.h>`   For declaration of function and definition of attribute names

DESCRIPTION The *_dos_getfileattr* function calls DOS function 43h to get the attributes of the file whose name is in the character string *filename*. The argument *attribute* points to an unsigned integer whose low-order byte contains the attribute upon return.

The attribute indicates whether a file is read only, whether it is a subdirectory, and so on. You can test for an exact combination of attributes by comparing the returned attribute with the bitwise OR of attribute names picked from Table 16-20. The attribute constants are defined in *dos.h*.

Sometimes it is necessary to check only if a file has a certain attribute set. For example, if you want to determine whether a file has the archive attribute (_A_ARCH) set, you can do so by first performing a bitwise AND of the returned attribute value with _A_ARCH and comparing the result for equality with _A_ARCH. If the test succeeds, the attribute is set.

RETURNS The function returns zero if successful; otherwise, it returns the MS-DOS error code and sets the global variable *errno* to the constant ENOENT indicating that the file could not be found.

__dos__getfileattr

SEE ALSO   `_dos_setfileattr`   To change the attributes of a file

EXAMPLE   Use *_dos_getfileattr* to check if a file whose name is provided by the user is a subdirectory.

```c
#include <stdio.h>
#include <dos.h>
main()
{
    unsigned attribute;
    char filename[80], *p_fname;
    printf("Enter filename: ");
    p_fname = gets(filename);
    if (_dos_getfileattr(p_fname, &attribute) != 0)
    {
        printf("Error in _dos_getfileattr call!\n");
        exit(0);
    }
    if ( (attribute & _A_SUBDIR) == _A_SUBDIR )
    {
        printf("%s is a subdirectory.\n", filename);
    }
    else
    {
        printf("%s is NOT a subdirectory.\n", filename);
    }
}
```

__dos__getftime

COMPATIBILITY	MSC 3	MSC 4	MSC 5	QC	TC	ANSI	UNIX V
			▲	▲	getftime		

PURPOSE   Use *_dos_getftime* to get the date and time a file was last modified. To request this information, you need a handle returned by a function such as *_dos_open* or *_dos_creat*.

SYNTAX
```c
unsigned _dos_getftime(int filehandle, unsigned *date,
                                       unsigned *time);
```

`int filehandle;`   The file handle, or identifier

`unsigned *date;`   Pointer to location to hold date information

`unsigned *time;`   Pointer to location to hold time information

 **System Calls**

EXAMPLE CALL   `_dos_getftime(handle, &date, &time);`

INCLUDES   `#include <dos.h>`   For declaration of function

DESCRIPTION   For each file, DOS records the time and date the file was last modified: the information you get when you type the DIR command. The information is maintained in coded form. The date is stored in a 16-bit word whose bits are interpreted as follows:

Bits	Contents
0–4	Day of the month (value between 1 and 31).
5–8	Month (value between 1 and 12).
9–15	Years since 1980 (for example, 1988 is stored as 8).

The last update time of the file is also maintained in a 16-bit word:

Bits	Contents
0–4	Number of 2-second increments (value between 0 and 29).
5–10	Minutes (value between 0 and 59).
11–15	Hours (value between 0 and 23).

The _dos_getftime function calls the DOS function 57h to return the date and time information of the file specified by the identifying number, or handle, in the argument *filehandle*. The date and time information is returned in locations whose addresses are given in the arguments *date* and *time*. The file handle must be one returned when the file was opened by _dos_open or created by _dos_creat or _dos_creatnew.

RETURNS   This function returns zero if successful; otherwise, it returns the MS-DOS error code and sets the global variable *errno* to the constant EBADF, indicating that the file handle is invalid.

SEE ALSO   `_dos_setftime`   To change the date and time stamp of a file

`_dos_open`   To open an existing file using a DOS call

`_dos_creat, _dos_creatnew`   To create a new file

EXAMPLE   Use _dos_open to open a file and then call _dos_getftime to display its date and time stamp.

_dos_getftime

```c
#include <stdio.h>
#include <fcntl.h>
#include <dos.h>
main()
{
    char fname[40], *p_fname;
    int filehandle;
    unsigned date, time, day, month, year,
             hour, minute, second;

    printf("Enter name of an existing file: ");
    p_fname = gets(fname);

/* Open the file using _dos_open */
    if (_dos_open(p_fname, O_RDONLY, &filehandle) != 0)
    {
        printf("Error opening file: %s\n", fname);
        exit(0);
    }
    printf("File %s opened.\n", fname);

/* Get file's date and time stamp */
    _dos_getftime(filehandle, &date, &time);

/* Now decipher the return values */
    second = 2 * (time & 0x1f);
    minute = (time >> 5) & 0x3f;
    hour = (time >> 11) & 0x1f;
    day = date & 0x1f;
    month = (date >> 5) & 0xf;
/* NOTE: year is relative to 1980.
 * So we are adding 80.
 */
    year = ((date >> 9) & 0x7f) + 80;
    printf("File: %s  Date: %d-%d-%d Time: %.2d:%.2d:\
%.2d\n", fname, month, day, year, hour, minute, second);

/* Now close file */
    if (_dos_close(filehandle) != 0)
    {
        printf("Error closing file with _dos_close\n");
        exit(0);
    }
    printf("File %s closed.\n", fname);
}
```

 **System Calls**

__dos__gettime

COMPATIBILITY	MSC 3	MSC 4	MSC 5	QC	TC	ANSI	UNIX V
			▲	▲	gettime		

PURPOSE Use _dos_gettime to get the current system time.

SYNTAX `void _dos_gettime (struct dostime_t *time);`

`struct dostime_t *time;`   Pointer to a structure that holds the components of time

EXAMPLE CALL `_dos_gettime(&time_info);`

INCLUDES `#include <dos.h>`   For definition of the structure *dostime_t*

DESCRIPTION The _dos_gettime function calls DOS function 2Ch to get the system time whose components—the hour, minute, second, and hundredth of a second—are stored in fields of the structure type *dostime_t*, which is defined in *dos.h*. The layout and C declaration of the structure *dostime_t* are shown below.

```
struct dostime_t
{
    unsigned char hour;     /* Hour (range 0-23)                   */
    unsigned char minute;   /* Minutes (range 0-59)                */
    unsigned char second;   /* Seconds (range 0-59)                */
    unsigned char hsecond;  /* Hundredth of a second (range 0-99) */
};
```

SEE ALSO `_dos_settime`   The corresponding routine that sets the system time

`_dos_getdate,`
`_dos_setdate`   To get and set the system date

`_strdate, _strtime,`
`gmtime, localtime,`
`mktime, time`   Other date and time services

EXAMPLE Use _dos_gettime to display the current system time.

```
#include <stdio.h>
#include <dos.h>
main()
{
    struct dostime_t time;
    _dos_gettime(&time);
    printf("Current time: %d:%d:%d.%d\n", time.hour,
```

```
                        time.minute, time.second, time.hsecond);
        }
```

__dos__getvect

COMPATIBILITY	MSC 3	MSC 4	MSC 5	QC	TC	ANSI	UNIX V
			▲	▲	getvect		

PURPOSE Use *__dos__getvect* to get the current value of the interrupt vector for a specific interrupt number. The interrupt vector is the address of the routine that is invoked when the interrupt occurs.

SYNTAX `void (interrupt far *_dos_getvect (unsigned intno))();`

`unsigned intno;`   Interrupt number whose handler's address is returned

EXAMPLE CALL
```
void (interrupt far *int_handler)();
int_handler = _dos_getvect(int_number);
```

INCLUDES `#include <dos.h>`   For declaration of function

DESCRIPTION The *__dos__getvect* function calls the DOS function 35h to retrieve the address of the current interrupt handler for the interrupt specified in the argument *intno*.

COMMON USES This function is commonly used to get the address of the interrupt handler before setting it to a new value by calling the companion function *__dos__setvect*. Another use of this function is to get the address of certain tables that BIOS and DOS lets you access via interrupt vectors.

RETURNS The return value is a far pointer to the interrupt handler, which is a function of type *interrupt*, a keyword introduced in version 5.0 to allow writing interrupt handlers in C (see Chapter 1 for more details).

SEE ALSO `_dos_setvect`   To install a new interrupt handler

EXAMPLE Use the *__dos__getvect* function to report the current interrupt vector corresponding to an interrupt number entered by the user. Try the interrupt number 18 (the vector to ROM-resident BASIC. On a PC-AT the vector should be F600:0000. On other machines, the technical reference guide may list the vector for resident BASIC.)

```
#include <stdio.h>
#include <dos.h>
    :
```

 **System Calls**

```
main()
{
    void (interrupt far *int_handler)();
    unsigned intno;
    printf("Enter interrupt number in hexadecimal \
format: ");
    scanf(" %x", &intno);
    int_handler = _dos_getvect(intno);
/* Print out address of handler using the %p format */
    printf("\nThe address of the handler is : %p\n",
            int_handler);
}
```

__dos__keep

COMPATIBILITY	MSC 3	MSC 4	MSC 5	QC	TC	ANSI	UNIX V
			▲	▲	keep		

PURPOSE Use _dos_keep to install "terminate-and-stay-resident" (TSR) programs.

SYNTAX `void _dos_keep(unsigned status, unsigned memsize);`

`unsigned status;` Status code to be returned to calling process

`unsigned memsize;` Size of memory needed by TSR program, in 16-byte paragraphs

EXAMPLE CALL `_dos_keep(0, programsize_in_paragraphs);`

INCLUDES `#include <dos.h>` For declaration of function

DESCRIPTION The _dos_keep function calls DOS function 31h to install the current program in memory, reserving the number of paragraphs specified in the argument *memsize*. Then it exits the program, returning the value specified in *status* to its parent (normally DOS). The return code is analogous to the code used with the *exit* routine. As in *exit*, a *status* equal to zero means there were no errors. Other values signify errors.

COMMON USES This function can be used to install your own memory-resident interrupt handler in the system.

COMMENTS It is not clear how you can set the argument *memsize* in the call to _dos_keep. One approach is to use your knowledge of the layout of the program in memory. The global variable _psp provides the segment address of the *program segment prefix*, which is where the program starts. The end of the program is the top of the stack. We can get the stack segment address (SS) by using *segread*. If we can also get the current stack pointer (SP), a good estimate of the program's size is:

```
prog_size = SS + (SP + safety_margin)/16 - _psp;
```

where *safety_margin* is a small number of bytes (around 100) to account for uncertainties in our estimate. The division by 16 is necessary to convert the stack pointer to paragraphs. One way to get the stack pointer is to use *alloca* to allocate some memory from the stack. The returned pointer, cast as an unsigned integer, can serve as SP in our formula for the program size.

You should gain some familiarity with the concepts of "terminate-and-stay-resident" programs before using the *_dos_keep* function.

SEE ALSO
_dos_getvect, _dos_setvect	To retrieve current interrupt vector and install a new one
_chain_intr	To jump from one interrupt handler to another

EXAMPLE See the March 1988 issue of *Computer Language* (pp. 67–76) for an article by Al Stevens, "Writing Terminate-and-Stay-Resident Programs, Part II: Microsoft C and QuickC," in which he shows how to use *_dos_keep* to write a TSR utility entirely in Microsoft C.

__dos__open

COMPATIBILITY	MSC 3	MSC 4	MSC 5	QC	TC	ANSI	UNIX V
			▲	▲	_open		

PURPOSE Use *_dos_open* to open an existing file.

SYNTAX
```
unsigned _dos_open (char *filename, unsigned mode,
                    int *filehandle);
```

char *filename;	File name, including path
unsigned mode;	Permissions for operations to be performed on the file
int *filehandle;	Pointer to location where the file handle, or identifier, is returned

EXAMPLE CALL `_dos_open(fname, SH_COMPAT|O_RDONLY, &filehandle);`

INCLUDES
#include <dos.h>	For declaration of function
#include <fcntl.h>	For definition of permission mode names

 **System Calls**

DESCRIPTION   The *_dos_open* function calls DOS function 3Dh to open the file whose name (including the pathname) is specified by the argument *filename*. The operations that can be performed on the file are indicated by the argument *mode*: how the file can be accessed, how much sharing is allowed, and whether the file can be inherited by a child process. The argument is specified by a value created by the bitwise OR of mode names picked from Table 16-23. At most, you should pick one name from each category. These names are defined in the include file *fcntl.h*.

Table 16-23. *Modes in which Files Can Be Opened*

Category Name	Mode Name	Interpretation
Access	O_RDONLY	Only reading allowed.
	O_WRONLY	Only writing allowed.
	O_RDWR	Both reading and writing allowed.
Sharing	SH_COMPAT	No other process can access the file. This is called the "compatibilty mode" and the same process can open the file any number of times. This is how DOS normally operates.
	SH_DENYRW	No one else can read from or write to this file.
	SH_DENYWR	No one else can write to this file.
	SH_DENYRD	No one else can read from this file.
	SH_DENYNONE	File is completely shareable.
Inheritance	O_NOINHERIT	File will not be inherited by any child process.

Once the file is successfully opened, an identifying number, or handle, is returned in the location whose address is specified in the argument *filehandle*.

RETURNS   This function returns zero if successful; otherwise, it returns the MS-DOS error code (see *dosexterr*) and sets the global variable *errno* to one of the constants shown in Table 16-24.

Table 16-24. *Error Codes Set by* _dos_open

Error Code	Interpretation
EINVAL	Either access mode value is invalid or a sharing mode value is specified when file-sharing routines are not loaded.
ENOENT	File not found.
EMFILE	Too many files open (limit is 20 for a process).
EACCES	Access was denied (for example, trying to open a read-only file for writing).

COMMENTS   The functions *open* and *close* offer a more portable means of achieving the same result as this DOS-specific function.

Under MS-DOS, the maximum number of open files for a single process is 20.

_dos_open

SEE ALSO `_dos_close` To close a file opened by *_dos_open*

`_dos_creat, _dos_creatnew` To create a new file

`open, close` Portable versions of similar file opening and closing functions

EXAMPLE Use *_dos_open* to open a file. Close the file by calling *_dos_close*.

```
#include <stdio.h>
#include <fcntl.h>
#include <dos.h>
main()
{
    char fname[40], *p_fname;
    int filehandle;

    printf("Enter name of file to open using \
_dos_open: ");
    p_fname = gets(fname);

/* Open the file in "compatibilty mode" and for reading
 *  only
 */
    if (_dos_open(p_fname, SH_COMPAT|O_RDONLY,
        &filehandle) != 0)
    {
        printf("Error opening file: %s\n", fname);
        exit(0);
    }
    printf("File %s opened.\n", fname);

/* Now close file */
    if (_dos_close(filehandle) != 0)
    {
        printf("Error closing file with _dos_close\n");
        exit(0);
    }
    printf("File %s closed.\n", fname);
}
```

 **System Calls**

__dos__read

COMPATIBILITY	MSC 3	MSC 4	MSC 5	QC	TC	ANSI	UNIX V
			▲	▲	_read		

PURPOSE Use __dos_read_ to read a specified number of bytes from a file into a buffer. To call this function, you need a handle returned by a function such as __dos _open_ or __dos_creat_ or __dos_creatnew_.

SYNTAX
```
unsigned _dos_read(int filehandle, void far *buffer,
                     unsigned readcount, unsigned *bytes_read);
```

`int filehandle;`   The file handle or identifier

`void far *buffer;`   Pointer to buffer where the data read from the file is stored

`unsigned readcount;`   Number of bytes to be read

`unsigned *bytes_read;`   Pointer to location that contains the number of bytes read

EXAMPLE CALL `_dos_read(filehandle, pbuf, 80, &bytes_read);`

INCLUDES `#include <dos.h>`   For declaration of function

DESCRIPTION The __dos_read_ function calls DOS function 3Fh to transfer the number of bytes requested in the argument _readcount_ from the current position in the file to the locations accessed through the pointer _buffer_. Upon return, the location, whose address is in _bytes_read_, contains the number of bytes read. The file from which you want to read is specified by the identifying number, or handle, in the argument _filehandle_.

RETURNS This function returns zero if successful. Otherwise, it returns the MS-DOS error code and sets the global variable _errno_ either to the constant EBADF, indicating that the file handle is invalid, or to EACCES, indicating that access was denied (the file probably is not open for read access).

COMMENTS The function _read_ offers a more portable means of achieving the same result as this DOS-specific function.

SEE ALSO

`_dos_write`   To write a buffer to a file

`read, write`   Portable versions of similar read and write functions

`_dos_open`   To open an existing file using a DOS call

`_dos_close`   To close a file

`_dos_creat, _dos_creatnew`   To create a new file

EXAMPLE Use *_dos_open* to open an existing text file and then call *_dos_read* to read the first 80 characters into a buffer. Display the contents of the buffer. Finally close the file using *_dos_close*.

```c
#include <stdio.h>
#include <fcntl.h>
#include <dos.h>
main()
{
    char fname[40], *p_fname;
    char buffer[80];
    void far *pbuf;
    int filehandle;
    unsigned bytes_read;
    pbuf = (void far *)(&buffer[0]);
    printf("Enter name of an existing file: ");
    p_fname = gets(fname);

/* Open the file using _dos_open */
    if (_dos_open(p_fname, O_RDONLY, &filehandle) != 0)
    {
        printf("Error opening file: %s\n", fname);
        exit(0);
    }
    printf("File %s opened.\n", fname);

/* Now read the first 80 bytes */
    if (_dos_read(filehandle, pbuf, 80, &bytes_read)
        == 0)
    {
        printf("%d bytes read\n", bytes_read);
        printf("The bytes read are:\n%s\n", buffer);
    }

/* Now close file */
    if (_dos_close(filehandle) != 0)
    {
        printf("Error closing file with _dos_close\n");
        exit(0);
    }
    printf("File %s closed.\n", fname);
}
```

 **System Calls**

__dos__setblock

COMPATIBILITY	MSC 3	MSC 4	MSC 5	QC	TC	ANSI	UNIX V
			▲	▲	setblock		

PURPOSE Use *_dos_setblock* to adjust the size of a block of memory allocated by *_dos_allocmem*.

SYNTAX
```
unsigned _dos_setblock (unsigned newsize, unsigned segadd,
                        unsigned *maxavail);
```

`unsigned newsize;`   New size of block in units of 16-byte paragraphs

`unsigned segadd;`   Segment address of block

`unsigned *maxavail;`   Pointer to location that upon failure is set to the maximum number of paragraphs available

EXAMPLE CALL `_dos_setblock (5, segadd, &maxsize);`

INCLUDES `#include <dos.h>`   For declaration of function

DESCRIPTION The *_dos_setblock* function calls DOS function 4Ah to enlarge the size of a block of memory allocated by *_dos_allocmem*. The argument *newsize* specifies the desired size of the block in paragraph (16-byte) units, *segadd* (segment address of the block previously returned by *_dos_allocmem*), and *maxavail* (pointer to an unsigned integer that, in case of failure, contains the maximum number of paragraphs available).

RETURNS This function returns zero if memory was successfully allocated. Otherwise, the return value is the MS-DOS error code and the global variable *errno* is set to the constant ENOMEM, indicating that the segment address of the block was not valid.

If the MS-DOS error code returned by *_dos_setblock* is 8, insufficient memory was available to satisfy the request. In this case, the maximum available block size (in paragraphs) is returned in the location whose address is in the argument *maxavail*.

COMMENTS The *_dos_setblock* function is analogous to the standard library routine *realloc*. Of course, *_dos_setblock* must be used only to enlarge or shrink blocks allocated by its counterpart, *_dos_allocmem*.

SEE ALSO

`_dos_allocmem`   The corresponding routine that allocated the memory in the first place

`_dos_freemem`   To free memory allocated by *_dos_allocmem*

`realloc`   Other memory block resizing routines

__dos__setblock

EXAMPLE Use _dos_allocmem to allocate 1 paragraph of memory. Now use _dos
_setblock to enlarge the block size to 5 paragraphs in order to store 80 charac-
ters. Store a string in the new buffer and print the string out. Finally, free the
allocated buffer.

```
#include <stdio.h>
#include <dos.h>
#include <memory.h>
char str[80]="Testing _dos_allocmem...\n$";
main()
{
    union REGS xr;
    struct SREGS sr;
    char far *stradd;
    unsigned int segadd, maxsize;
    stradd = (char far *)(&str[0]);
    if (_dos_allocmem(1, &segadd) != 0)
    {
        printf("Memory allocation failed!\n");
        exit(0);
    }
    if (_dos_setblock (5, segadd, &maxsize) != 0)
    {
        printf("_dos_setblock failed!\n");
        printf("Maximum size possible = %d \
paragraphs\n", maxsize);
        exit(0);
    }
/* Use movedata to copy the string to allocated memory*/
    movedata(FP_SEG(stradd),FP_OFF(stradd), segadd,
            0, 80);
    sr.ds = segadd;
    xr.x.dx = 0;
    xr.h.ah = DOS_PRTSTR;
    intdosx(&xr, &xr, &sr);

/* Free memory before exiting */
    _dos_freemem(segadd);
}
```

System Calls

__dos__setdate

COMPATIBILITY	MSC 3	MSC 4	MSC 5	QC	TC	ANSI	UNIX V
			▲	▲	setdate		

PURPOSE Use *__dos__setdate* to change the current system date.

SYNTAX `unsigned _dos_setdate (struct dosdate_t *date);`

`struct dosdate_t *date;`   Pointer to a structure that holds the components of date

EXAMPLE CALL `_dos_setdate(&date_info);`

INCLUDES `#include <dos.h>`   For definition of the structure *dosdate__t*

DESCRIPTION The *__dos__setdate* function calls DOS function 2Bh to set the system date whose components—the day, month, year, and day of the week—should be specified by placing appropriate values in fields of the structure type *dosdate__t*, which is defined in *dos.h*. The C declaration of the structure is shown below.

```
struct dosdate_t
{
    unsigned char day;          /* day of the month (range 1-31) */
    unsigned char month;        /* month (range 1-12)            */
    unsigned int year;          /* year (range 1980-2099)        */
    unsigned char dayofweek;    /* Day of the week 0-6, 0=Sunday */
};
```

RETURNS This function returns a zero if the operation is successful. Otherwise, it returns a nonzero value and sets the global variable *errno* to the constant *EINVAL*, which means an invalid value was specified.

SEE ALSO `_dos_getdate`   The corresponding routine that returns the system date

`_dos_gettime, _dos_settime`   To get and set the system time

`_strdate, _strtime,`
`gmtime, localtime,`
`mktime, time`   Other date and time services

EXAMPLE Use *__dos__setdate* to change the system date.

```
#include <stdio.h>
#include <dos.h>
main()
{
```

```
    unsigned month, day, year;
    struct dosdate_t date;
    printf ("Enter new date in the form MM/DD/YY:");
    scanf("%d/%d/&d", &month, &day, &year);
    date.day = day;
    date.month = month;
    date.year = year + 1900;
    if (_dos_setdate(&date) != 0)
    {
        printf("Error setting date!\n");
    }
    else
    {
        printf("New date: %d/%d/%d\n", date.month,
            date.day, date.year -1900);
    }
}
```

__dos__setdrive

COMPATIBILITY	MSC 3	MSC 4	MSC 5	QC	TC	ANSI	UNIX V
			▲	▲	setdisk		

PURPOSE   Use *_dos_setdrive* to change to a new default drive number. For example, you can use this function to make drive A the default drive after starting your program from drive C.

SYNTAX   `void _dos_setdrive (unsigned driveno, unsigned *maxdrives);`

`unsigned driveno;`   New default drive number

`unsigned *maxdrives;`   Total number of logical drives

EXAMPLE CALL   `_dos_setdrive(1, &maxdrives); /* New drive is A: */`

INCLUDES   `#include <dos.h>`   For declaration of function

DESCRIPTION   The *_dos_setdrive* function calls DOS function 0Eh to set the current default drive to one specified by the argument *driveno*, interpreted as follows: 1 means drive A, 2 means drive B, and so on.

   The total number of logical drives in the system is returned in the unsigned integer variable whose address is in the argument *maxdrives*.

COMMON USES   MS-DOS uses the concept of "current default drive" when locating files. If all of your file I/O will be from a certain disk drive, you can use the *_dos_setdrive* function to set the default drive before performing any file I/O.

 **System Calls**

COMMENTS There is no return value, so the only way of knowing that this function worked is to call *_dos_getdrive* immediately afterwards to verify that the current default drive has indeed been changed.

SEE ALSO _dos_getdrive   To get the number of the current default drive

EXAMPLE Use *_dos_setdrive* to change the default drive number to one requested by the user. Call *_dos_getdrive* to verify that the new default is in effect.

```
#include <stdio.h>
#include <ctype.h>
#include <dos.h>
main()
{
    char ch_in;
    unsigned drive, maxdrives;
    printf("Enter new drive name (A, B etc):";
    scanf("%c", ch_in);
/* Convert the letter into a number, 0 for A, 1 for B */
    drive = toupper(ch_in) - 'A' + 1;
    _dos_setdrive(drive, &maxdrives);
    _dos_getdrive(&drive);
    printf ("The current drive is: %c\n", drive+'A'-1);
    printf ("There are %d logical drives on the \
system\n", maxdrives);
}
```

__dos__setfileattr

COMPATIBILITY	MSC 3	MSC 4	MSC 5	QC	TC	ANSI	UNIX V
			▲	▲			

PURPOSE Use *_dos_setfileattr* to change the attributes of a file. For example, you can hide a file so that it does not show up on a MS-DOS DIR command.

SYNTAX unsigned _dos_setfileattr(char *filename, unsigned attribute);

char *filename;   File name, including path

unsigned attribute;   New attributes

EXAMPLE CALL _dos_setfileattr("secret.dat", _A_HIDDEN); /* Hide file */

INCLUDES #include <dos.h>   For declaration of function and definition of attribute names

DESCRIPTION The *_dos_setfileattr* function calls DOS function 43h to alter the attributes of the file whose name is in the character string *filename*. The new attributes for the file are specified in the argument *attribute*. You can select a combination of attributes by specifying a value created by the bitwise OR of attribute names picked from Table 16-20. These attribute constants are defined in *dos.h*.

RETURNS The return value is zero if successful. Otherwise, the function returns the MS-DOS error code and sets the global variable *errno* to the constant ENOENT, indicating that the file could not be found.

SEE ALSO _dos_getfileattr   To determine the current attributes of a file

EXAMPLE Use *_dos_setfileattr* to hide a file whose name is provided by the user. (You can write a similar program to make the file appear again).

```
#include <stdio.h>
#include <dos.h>
main()
{
    char filename[80], *p_fname;
    printf("Enter name of file to hide: ");
    p_fname = gets(filename);
    if (_dos_setfileattr(p_fname, _A_HIDDEN) != 0)
    {
        printf("Error in _dos_setfileattr call!\n");
        exit(0);
    }
    printf("%s is now hidden. Try DIR to verify.\n",
            filename);
}
```

__dos__setftime

COMPATIBILITY	MSC 3	MSC 4	MSC 5	QC	TC	ANSI	UNIX V
			▲	▲	setftime		

PURPOSE Use *_dos_setftime* to change the date and time stamp of a file. Before calling this function, you need a handle returned by a function such as *_dos_open* or *_dos_creat*.

SYNTAX unsigned _dos_setftime(int filehandle, unsigned date,
                                unsigned time);

int filehandle;   The file handle, or identifier

System Calls

　　　unsigned date;　　　Date information in packed form

　　　unsigned time;　　　Time information in packed form

EXAMPLE CALL　_dos_setftime(filehandle, date, time);

INCLUDES　#include <dos.h>　　　For declaration of function

DESCRIPTION　The _dos_setftime_ function calls DOS function 57h to change the date and time stamp of the file specified by the identifying number, or handle, in the argument *filehandle*. The date and time information is entered in the arguments *date* and *time*. The handle must be one returned when the file was opened by _dos_open_ or created by _dos_creat_ or _dos_creatnew_.

　　　The date and time stamps indicate when the file was last modified. You can decode the stamps by consulting the figure shown in the description of _dos_getftime_. The example below illustrates how you can prepare the date and time information for this function. Note that the value stored in the year field should be relative to 1980 (i.e., it is the current year minus 1980).

RETURNS　This function returns zero if successful; otherwise, it returns the MS-DOS error code and sets the global variable *errno* to the constant EBADF, indicating that the file handle is invalid.

SEE ALSO　_dos_getftime　　　To get the date and time stamp of a file

　　　_dos_open　　　To open an existing file using a DOS call

　　　_dos_creat, _dos_creatnew　　　To create a new file

EXAMPLE　Use _dos_open_ to open a file and then call _dos_setftime_ to store a new date and time stamp. Use _dos_getftime_ to verify that the date and time stamps have indeed changed.

```
#include <stdio.h>
#include <fcntl.h>
#include <dos.h>
main()
{
    char fname[40], *p_fname;
    int filehandle;
    unsigned date, time, day, month, year,
             hour, minute, second;

    printf("Enter name of an existing file: ");
    p_fname = gets(fname);

/* Open the file using _dos_open */
    if (_dos_open(p_fname, O_RDONLY, &filehandle) != 0)
```

__dos__setftime

```
      {
          printf("Error opening file: %s\n", fname);
          exit(0);
      }
      printf("File %s opened.\n", fname);

/* Ask for new date and time stamp: */
      printf("Enter new date in the format MM-DD-YY:");
      scanf("%u-%u-%u", &month, &day, &year);
      printf("Enter new time in the format HH:MM:SS ");
      scanf("%u:%u:%u", &hour, &minute, &second);

/* Pack date and time information into single words */
      date = (((year - 80) << 9) | (date << 5)) | day;
      time = ((hour << 11) | (minute << 5)) | second;

/* Set the date and time stamp */
      _dos_setftime(filehandle, date, time);

/* Get file's date and time stamp to verify the new
 * date and time
 */
      _dos_getftime(filehandle, &date, &time);

/* Now decipher the return values */
      second = time & 0x1f;
      minute = (time >> 5) & 0x3f;
      hour = (time >> 11) & 0x1f;
      day = date & 0x1f;
      month = (date >> 5) & 0xf;
/* NOTE: year is relative to 1980. So we are adding 80*/
      year = ((date >> 9) & 0x7f) + 80;
      printf("File: %s  Date: %d-%d-%d Time: %.2d:%.2d:\
%.2d\n", fname, month, day, year, hour, minute, second);

/* Now close file */
      if (_dos_close(filehandle) != 0)
      {
          printf("Error closing file with _dos_close\n");
          exit(0);
      }
      printf("File %s closed.\n", fname);
}
```

 **System Calls**

__dos__settime

COMPATIBILITY	MSC 3	MSC 4	MSC 5	QC	TC	ANSI	UNIX V
			▲	▲	settime		

PURPOSE Use _dos_settime to change the current system time.

SYNTAX unsigned _dos_settime (struct dostime_t *time);

struct dostime_t *time;   Pointer to a structure that holds the components of time

EXAMPLE CALL _dos_settime(&time_info);

INCLUDES #include <dos.h>   For definition of the structure dostime_t

DESCRIPTION The _dos_settime function calls DOS function 2Dh to set the current system time whose components—the hour, minutes, seconds, and hundredths of a second—are loaded in appropriate fields of the structure type dostime_t, which is defined in dos.h. The layout of this structure along with the C declaration of the internal fields are shown below:

```
struct dostime_t
{
    unsigned char hour;    /* Hour (range 0---23)                    */
    unsigned char minute;  /* Minutes (range 0---59)                 */
    unsigned char second;  /* Seconds (range 0---59)                 */
    unsigned char hsecond; /* Hundredths of a second (range 0---99) */
};
```

RETURNS This function returns a zero if the operation is successful. Otherwise, it returns a nonzero value and sets the global variable errno to the constant EINVAL, which means an invalid value was specified.

SEE ALSO _dos_gettime   The corresponding routine that returns the system time

_dos_getdate,
_dos_setdate   To get and set the system date

_strdate, _strtime,
gmtime, localtime,
mktime, time   Other date and time services

EXAMPLE Use the _dos_settime to change the current system time.

```
#include <stdio.h>
#include <dos.h>
main()
```

```
{
    unsigned hour, minute, second;
    struct dostime_t time;
    printf ("Enter new time in the form HH:MM:SS:");
    scanf("%d:%d:&d", &hour, &minute, &second);
    time.hour = hour;
    time.minute = minute;
    time.second = second;
    if (_dos_settime(&time) != 0)
    {
        printf("Error setting time!\n");
    }
    else
    {
        printf("New time: %d:%d:%d.%d\n", time.hour,
            time.minute, time.second, time.hsecond);
    }
}
```

__dos__setvect

COMPATIBILITY	MSC 3	MSC 4	MSC 5	QC	TC	ANSI	UNIX V
			▲	▲	setvect		

PURPOSE Use _dos_setvect to install a new interrupt vector for a specific interrupt number. The interrupt vector is the address of the routine that is invoked when the interrupt occurs.

SYNTAX
```
void _dos_setvect (unsigned intno,
                   void(interrupt far *handler)());
```

`unsigned intno;`   Interrupt number whose vector is being set

`interrupt far *handler;`   Far pointer to the new handler, a function of type *interrupt*

EXAMPLE CALL
```
void interrupt far our_handler(void);
_dos_setvect(int_number, our_handler);
```

INCLUDES `#include <dos.h>`   For declaration of function

DESCRIPTION The _dos_setvect function calls the DOS function 25h to install the address of the interrupt handler specified in the argument *handler* as the new vector for the interrupt number specified in the argument *intno*. The argument *handler* is a far pointer to the interrupt handler, a function of type *interrupt*,

 **System Calls**

which is a keyword introduced in version 5.0 to allow writing interrupt handlers in C (see Chapter 1 for a discussion of the *interrupt* keyword).

COMMON USES   This function is often used to install a new interrupt handler. For example, if you were writing an interrupt-driven I/O routine for the serial port you could use this routine to install your handler in place of the default handler.

COMMENTS   It is good practice to save the interrupt vector before installing a new one. That way you can restore the system to its original status when your program exits.

SEE ALSO   _dos_getvect   To get the address of the current interrupt handler

EXAMPLE   In the IBM PC, interrupt 1Ch is generated at every clock tick. These clock ticks occur about 18.2 times a second and are used to maintain the time in the system. You can hook your routine onto this interrupt and have the routine executed at every clock tick. Write a routine using *_dos_getvect* and *_dos_setvect* to install your own interrupt handler for interrupt 1Ch. You can increment a counter in the interrupt handler to show that the program worked.

```
#include <stdio.h>
#include <dos.h>
#define TIMER_TICK 0x1c
unsigned long tickcount = 0;
void interrupt far our_handler(void);
main()
{
    unsigned c;
    void (interrupt far *old_handler)();
    unsigned intno = TIMER_TICK;
    old_handler = _dos_getvect(intno);
/* Print out address of old handler using the %p
 * format
 */
    printf("\nThe address of the old handler is : %p\n",
            old_handler);
/* Install the new handler named our_handler
 * Disable interrupts when changing handler
 */
    _disable();
    _dos_setvect(intno, our_handler);
    _enable();
    printf("Installed new handler: %p\n", our_handler);
    printf("Hit q to quit: ");
    while ((c=getch()) != 'q'); /* Keep looping till 'q'*/
/* Reset vector and print the tickcount. Again disable
 * interrupts when doing this.
```

_dos_setvect

```
*/
    _disable();
    _dos_setvect(intno, old_handler);
    _enable();
    printf("The tick counter is now: %ld\n", tickcount);
}
/*---------------------------------------------------*/
void interrupt far our_handler()
{
/* Our handler simply increments a counter. But this
 * will be proof enough that the handler works because
 * we are not calling it explicitly in the main program
 * and the only way it gets called is via INT 1Ch.
 */
    tickcount++;
}
```

__dos__write

COMPATIBILITY	MSC 3	MSC 4	MSC 5	QC	TC	ANSI	UNIX V
			▲	▲	_write		

PURPOSE Use *_dos_write* to write a specified number of bytes from a buffer into a file at its current location. Before calling this function, you need a handle returned by a function such as *_dos_open* or *_dos_creatnew* or *_dos_creat*. DOS function 42h can be used to move the current location in a file.

SYNTAX
```
unsigned _dos_write(int filehandle, void far *buffer,
                unsigned writecount, unsigned *bytes_written);
```

`int filehandle;`   The file handle, or identifier

`void far *buffer;`   Pointer to buffer where the data read from the file is stored

`unsigned writecount;`   Number of bytes to be written

`unsigned *bytes_written;`   Pointer to location that contains the actual number of bytes written

EXAMPLE CALL `_dos_write(filehandle, pbuf, 80, &bytes_written);`

INCLUDES `#include <dos.h>`   For declaration of function

DESCRIPTION The *_dos_write* function calls DOS function 40h to transfer the number of bytes specified in the argument *writecount* from the memory locations ac-

 **System Calls**

cessed through the pointer *buffer* into the file whose handle, or identifying number, is given in the argument *filehandle*. The data is written at the current position of the file pointer, which is updated when the writing is complete. Upon return, the location whose address is in *bytes_written* contains the number of bytes written to the file.

RETURNS This function returns zero if successful. Otherwise, it returns the MS-DOS error code and sets the global variable *errno* either to the constant EBADF, indicating that the file handle is invalid, or to EACCES, indicating that access was denied (the file probably is not open for write access).

COMMENTS The function *write* offers a more portable means of achieving the same result as this DOS-specific function.

SEE ALSO

_dos_read   To read from a file

read, write   Portable versions of similar read and write functions

_dos_open   To open an existing file using a DOS call

_dos_close   To close a file

_dos_creat,
_dos_creatnew   To create a new file

EXAMPLE Use *_dos_open* to open an existing text file. Use *_dos_write* to write an extra line at the beginning of the file. Finally, close the file using *_dos_close*.

```
#include <stdio.h>
#include <fcntl.h>
#include <dos.h>
char buffer[80] = "Testing _dos_write ........ ";
main()
{
    char fname[40], *p_fname;
    void far *pbuf;
    int filehandle;
    unsigned bytes;
    pbuf = (void far *)(&buffer[0]);
    printf("Enter name of an existing file: ");
    p_fname = gets(fname);

/* Open the file using _dos_open */
    if (_dos_open(p_fname, O_RDWR, &filehandle) != 0)
    {
        printf("Error opening file: %s\n", fname);
        exit(0);
    }
```

__dos__write

```
        printf("File %s opened.\n", fname);

/* Now write out buffer */
    if (_dos_write(filehandle, pbuf, 80, &bytes) == 0)
    {
        printf("%d bytes written\n", bytes);
    }

/* Now close file */
    if (_dos_close(filehandle) != 0)
    {
        printf("Error closing file with _dos_close\n");
        exit(0);
    }
    printf("File %s closed.\n", fname);
}
```

dosexterr

COMPATIBILITY	MSC 3	MSC 4	MSC 5	QC	TC	ANSI	UNIX V
	▲	▲	▲	▲	▲		

PURPOSE On MS-DOS 3.0 or higher, use *dosexterr* after an error return from a DOS function call to obtain detailed information on the cause of error and possible remedial action.

SYNTAX `int dosexterr (struct DOSERROR *errbuf);`

`struct DOSERROR *errbuf;`   Pointer to structure that contains information on return

EXAMPLE CALL `dosexterr(&errbuf);`

INCLUDES `#include <dos.h>`   For declaration of function and declaration of the structure type DOSERROR

DESCRIPTION The *dosexterr* function calls DOS function 59h to get detailed information on the cause of an unsuccessful call to a DOS function (INT 21h). The information about the error is returned in a structure of type DOSERROR, and a pointer to one such structure must be passed in the argument *errbuf*. The DOSERROR structure is defined in *dos.h* and its C declaration is shown below.

```
struct DOSERROR
{
    int  exterror;  /* Extended error code */
    char class;     /* Error class         */
```

 **System Calls**

```
      char action;    /* Recommended action */
      char locus;     /* Error locus -- device
                         where it occurred */
};
```

The interpretation of the *exterror* field in this structure is given in Table 16-25. For more detailed information on this and the other fields consult the *Microsoft MS-DOS Programmer's Reference Manual* available from Microsoft Corporation.

Table 16-25. *Extended Error Codes from* dosexterr

Value of *exterror* (hex)	Interpretation
0	No error in previous DOS function call
1	Invalid function number
2	File not found
3	Path not found (bad drive or directory name)
4	Too many open files
5	Access denied
6	Invalid file handle
7	Memory control blocks destroyed
8	Insufficient memory
9	Invalid memory block address
A	Invalid environment
B	Invalid format
C	Invalid access code
D	Invalid data
E	— Reserved —
F	Invalid disk drive
10	Attempt to remove current directory
11	Not the same device
12	No more files
13	Disk write protected
14	Unknown unit
15	Drive not ready
16	Unknown command
17	CRC error in data
18	Bad request structure length
19	Seek error
1A	Unknown medium
1B	Sector not found
1C	Printer out of paper
1D	Write fault
1E	Read fault

dosexterr

Table 16-25. *(cont.)*

Value of *exterror* (hex)	Interpretation
1F	General failure
20	Sharing violation
21	Lock violation
22	Invalid disk change
23	File Control Block (FCB) unavailable
24-4F	— Reserved —
50	File already exists
51	— Reserved —
52	Cannot make directory
53	Failed during critical error interrupt (INT 24h)

RETURNS   The return value is identical to the field *exterror* which is the value of the *AX* register.

SEE ALSO   perror   To print an error message

EXAMPLE   Try to close a nonexistent file using a DOS function call. Then call *dosexterr* to get the error code. You should get a report that *exterror* is 6, which means the file handle is invalid.

```
#include <stdio.h>
#include <dos.h>

main()
{

    struct DOSERROR errbuf;
/* Try closing a non-existent file */
    if (_dos_close(1000) != 0)
    {
        printf("Error closing file.\n");
        dosexterr(&errbuf);
        printf("exterror=%x, class=%x, action=%x, \
locus=%x\n", errbuf.exterror, errbuf.class,
        errbuf.action, errbuf.locus);
    }
}
```

System Calls

__enable

COMPATIBILITY	MSC 3	MSC 4	MSC 5	QC	TC	ANSI	UNIX V
			▲	▲	enable		

PURPOSE Use *_enable* to allow the 8086 microprocessor to acknowledge interrupts. Call *enable* after turning off interrupts by calling *_disable*.

SYNTAX `void _enable(void);`

EXAMPLE CALL `_enable();`

INCLUDES `#include <dos.h>`   For declaration of function

DESCRIPTION The *_enable* function executes an 8086 *STI* instruction.

COMMON USES The *_enable* function is used in conjunction with *_disable* to protect a section of code from being interrupted. You do not need the *_enable* function for routine programming chores, but its availability enables you to write such exotic programs as interrupt handlers in Microsoft C (see the tutorial section for a description of interrupt handlers).

SEE ALSO `_disable`   To disable 8086 interrupts

EXAMPLE See the example in the reference page on *_dos_setvect* for sample usage.

FP__OFF

COMPATIBILITY	MSC 3	MSC 4	MSC 5	QC	TC	ANSI	UNIX V
	▲	▲	▲	▲	▲		

PURPOSE *FP_OFF* is a C macro to get the 16-bit offset portion of the address of any data element. The macro expects a long (32-bit) pointer to a memory location, such as the beginning of an array or a C structure. For example, you can see *FP_OFF* to get the offset of a string that you want to display using the DOS function 9h. Using the *FP_OFF* macro is the only way to get the offset of a data element in a C program.

SYNTAX `unsigned int FP_OFF(char far *address);`

`char far *address;`   Long pointer to memory location

EXAMPLE CALL `offset_buf = FP_OFF(p_buf); /* p_buf is a far pointer */`

INCLUDES `#include <dos.h>`   For definition of the macro

DESCRIPTION The *FP_OFF* function, implemented as a macro, accepts a 2-bit pointer as an argument and returns the 16-bit offset portion of the pointer. When using *FP_OFF*, the argument *address* must be of type *(char far *)*.

COMMON USES *FP_OFF* is commonly used with its counterpart *FP_SEG* to generate 16-bit offset and segment addresses of strings and functions for use in DOS function calls.

RETURNS *FP_OFF* returns the offset as an unsigned 16-bit integer.

SEE ALSO FP_SEG   For segment address

EXAMPLE Use *FP_OFF* to get the offset of a string. You'll need this, for example, when printing a string using DOS function 9h so that you can pass the offset address to the print function.

```
#include <stdio.h>
#include <dos.h>
char sample[] = "Test string";
main()
{
    char far *ps;
    unsigned off_sample;
/* Cast the address of the first character as a far
 * pointer
 */
    ps = (char far *)&sample[0];
    off_sample = FP_OFF(ps);
    printf("The offset of the string is: %d\n",
            off_sample);
}
```

FP__SEG

COMPATIBILITY	MSC 3	MSC 4	MSC 5	QC	TC	ANSI	UNIX V
	▲	▲	▲	▲	▲		

PURPOSE Use the *FP_SEG* macro to get the segment address of a memory location. The macro expects a long (32-bit) pointer to a memory location. For example, you can use *FP_SEG* to get the segment address of a string that you want to display using the DOS function 9h. You must use *FP_SEG* whenever a BIOS or DOS call requires the segment address of a data element.

SYNTAX unsigned FP_SEG(char far *address);

          char far *address;   Long pointer to memory location

 **System Calls**

EXAMPLE CALL segadd_buf = FP_SEG(p_buf); /* p_buf is a far pointer */

INCLUDES #include <dos.h>   For definition of the macro

DESCRIPTION The *FP_SEG* function, implemented as a macro, accepts a 32-bit pointer as an argument and returns the segment address of the pointer. When using *FP_OFF*, the argument *address* must be of type *(char far *)*.

COMMON USES *FP_SEG* is commonly used with its counterpart *FP_OFF* to generate segment and offset addresses of strings and functions for use in DOS function calls.

RETURNS *FP_SEG* returns the offset as an unsigned 16-bit integer.

SEE ALSO FP_OFF   For the offset address

EXAMPLE Use *FP_SEG* to get the segment address of a string. For example, if you want to print the string using DOS function 9h, you will need to specify the offset and the segment address of the string. You can use the *FP_SEG* macro in this case.

```
#include <stdio.h>
#include <dos.h>
char sample[] = "Test string";
main()
{
    char far *ps;
    unsigned seg_sample;
/* Cast the address of the first character as a far
 * pointer
 */
    ps = (char far *)&sample[0];
    seg_sample = FP_SEG(ps);
    printf("The segment address of the string is: %d\n",
                                        seg_sample);
}
```

FP_SEG

__harderr

COMPATIBILITY	MSC 3	MSC 4	MSC 5	QC	TC	ANSI	UNIX V
			▲	▲	harderr		

PURPOSE Use *__harderr* to install a new handler for interrupt 24h (critical error) to call a routine whose address you will pass to *__harderr* as an argument. This interrupt occurs on hardware errors during such I/O operations as trying to read from a disk with the drive door open.

SYNTAX
```
void _harderr (void (far *funcptr)());
```
```
void (far *funcptr)();
```
Far pointer to the function that will be called by the new INT 24h handler

EXAMPLE CALL
```
void far harderror_handler(unsigned, unsigned,
                           unsigned far *);
_harderr(harderror_handler);
```

INCLUDES `#include <dos.h>` For declaration of function

DESCRIPTION The *__harderr* function installs a new handler for interrupt 24h to handle a critical error, which usually occurs when hardware malfunctions. The address of the routine to be called is specified in the argument *funcptr*. The installed handler will call the specified function with three arguments in the following manner:

```
(* funcptr)(unsigned deverror, unsigned errcode,
                          unsigned far *devhdr);
```

where *deverror* and *errcode* are unsigned integers containing, respectively, the *AX* and *DI* register values that MS-DOS passes to the INT 24h handler. The *devhdr* argument is a far pointer to a "device header" structure containing descriptive information about the device on which the error occurred. The routine you want called should not alter anything in this device header.

The value in the low-order byte of the argument *errcode* indicates the type of error that occurred. Table 16-26 shows the interpretation of the error code.

If the error occurred during disk I/O, bit 15 (the most significant bit) of the *deverror* argument is set to 0 and the *deverror* provides detailed information about the disk error. The bits and their meanings are shown in Table 16-27. The low-order byte of *deverror* contains the drive number where the error occurred. A 0 indicates drive A, a 1 means drive B, and so on.

If bit 15 of *deverror* is a 1, the error did not occur during disk I/O, and you have to look elsewhere to find the cause. A word located at offset 4 in the device header contains further information about where the error occurred. Access it as an unsigned integer at the address *devhdr+4*. Table 16-28 tells you how to interpret the source of the error in this case.

 **System Calls**

Table 16-26. *Error Codes Indicated by Low Byte of errcode*

Error Code (hexadecimal)	Meaning
0	Attempted to write to a write-protected disk
1	Unknown unit (source of error not known)
2	Drive not ready
3	Unknown command
4	Cyclic Redundancy Check (CRC) indicates error in data
5	Length of "drive request structure" is bad
6	Seek error
7	Unknown media type
8	Sector not found
9	Printer out of paper
A	Write fault
B	Read fault
C	General failure

Table 16-27. *Disk Error Information in Critical Error Handler*

Bit	Meaning
15	If 0, it's a disk error. IGNORE rest if this bit is 1.
14	— Not used —
13	If 0, "Ignore" response is not allowed.
12	If 0, "Retry" response is not allowed,
11	If 0, "Abort" response is not allowed.
9–10	Indicates area where error occurred:
	00 MS-DOS
	01 File Allocation Table (FAT)
	10 Directory
	11 Data area
8	If 1, it's a write error. 0 means read error.

Table 16-28. *Source of Nondisk I/O Error*

Bits of the Word at (devhdr + 4)	Source of Error
15	0 = Bad memory image of FAT.
	1 = Error in a character device, interpret error source from bits 0 through 3 of word at address *devhdr*.
	0001 = Error in standard input.
	0010 = Error in standard output.
	0100 = Error in null device.
	1000 = Error in clock device.

__harderr

In the function, whose pointer you are specifying in the argument *funcptr*, you can also make certain MS-DOS function calls. Specifically, you can issue calls to DOS functions 01 through 0Ch and function 59h. Note, however, that many C library routines cannot be used within this function because they call MS-DOS functions to do their job.

If you want to return to MS-DOS, end this function with a *return* or a call to _*hardresume*. You can return to the program where the error occurred by issuing a call to _*hardretn*.

COMMON USES   This function, introduced in Microsoft C 5.0, is useful in writing robust application programs in which user mistakes do not require aborting from the application.

COMMENTS   It is a good idea to install your own critical error handler; the default MS-DOS handler is somewhat crude and often causes the current application to abort. The availability of this function makes it easy to develop the error handler entirely in C.

SEE ALSO

_hardresume	To return to DOS from the error handler
_hardretn	To return to the program where the error originally occurred
_dos_getvect	To retrieve an existing interrupt vector
_dos_setvect	To install a new interrupt vector
_chain_intr	To jump from one interrupt handler to another
_dos_keep	To install "terminate and stay resident" programs

EXAMPLE   Write a critical error handler that checks for a "drive not ready" error that occurs, for example, when you try to find the disk space on drive A when the drive is empty. Let the handler print a message asking the user to insert a disk and continue when the user strikes an appropriate key. Assume that current default drive is not A. Notice the global flag indicating when a critical error occurs so that we can tell when the call to _*dos_getdiskfree* fails because of a "drive not ready" error.

```
#include <stdio.h>
#include <dos.h>
/* Prototype of our critical error handler */
void far harderror_handler(unsigned, unsigned,
                           unsigned far *);
unsigned char far error_flag = 0;
main()
{
    unsigned drivea =1;
    unsigned long total_space, free_space,
```

System Calls

```
                          bytes_per_cluster;
        struct diskfree_t dfinfo;
/* Install our critical error handler */
        _harderr(harderror_handler);
        printf("We will check our critical error handler.\n\
Make sure drive A: is empty. Hit any key to continue: ");
        getch();
/* Try an operation on drive A: */
        _dos_getdiskfree (drivea, &dfinfo);


/* If error_flag is set call _dos_getdiskfree again */
        if(error_flag) _dos_getdiskfree(drivea, &dfinfo);


/* Compute space statistics and display result */
        bytes_per_cluster = dfinfo.sectors_per_cluster *
                            dfinfo.bytes_per_sector;
        total_space = dfinfo.total_clusters *
                      bytes_per_cluster;
        free_space = dfinfo.avail_clusters *


                     bytes_per_cluster;
        printf ("\n%ld bytes free out of %ld bytes of \
total space.\n", free_space, total_space);
}
/*----------------------------------------------------*/
#define DRIVE_NOT_READY 2
void far harderror_handler(unsigned deverror,
                           unsigned errorcode,
                           unsigned far *devhdr)
{
        char dletter;
/* Set a flag to let our program know about the error */
        error_flag = 1;
/* Check if this is a "drive not ready" error */
        if ((errorcode & 0xff) == DRIVE_NOT_READY)
        {
/* Find out which drive, it's in low byte of deverror */
            dletter = 'A' + (deverror & 0xff);
/* Ask user to insert a diskette into the drive */
            printf("\nDrive %c is not ready.\n\
Please insert a diskette and hit any key to continue:",
                   dletter);
            getch();  /* Read key before returning */
/* Use _hardretn to go back to your program      */
            _hardretn(-1);
        }
        else
        {
```

__harderr

```
/* Unknown error, print message and abort program */
        printf("Unknown critical error. Aborting...\n");
        _hardresume(_HARDERR_ABORT);
    }
}
```

__hardresume

COMPATIBILITY	MSC 3	MSC 4	MSC 5	QC	TC	ANSI	UNIX V
			▲	▲	hardresume		

PURPOSE Use *_hardresume* to return to MS-DOS from your own critical error handler, which can be installed by calling the function *_harderr*.

SYNTAX `void _hardresume (int returncode);`

`int returncode;`   Tells DOS how the handler is returning

EXAMPLE CALL `_hardresume(_HARDERR_ABORT);`

INCLUDES `#include <dos.h>`   For declaration of function and for return code constants

DESCRIPTION The *_hardresume* function is used to return to DOS from a routine that you install to process interrupt 24h, which is triggered by critical hardware errors that might occur during an I/O request. The installation of the handler is done by passing its address to the function *_harderr*.

The argument *returncode* tells *_hardresume* what to do upon returning to DOS. Use one of the predefined constants given in table 16-29 to specify the action. These constants are defined in *dos.h*.

Table 16-29. *Error Codes Used by* __hardresume

Return Code Constant	Action Taken by MS-DOS
_HARDERR_IGNORE	Ignores the error.
_HARDERR_RETRY	Retries the operation that caused the error.
_HARDERR_ABORT	Aborts the program by invoking INT 23h.
_HARDERR_FAIL	Causes the MS-DOS system call in progress to fail (only under MS-DOS 3.0 and higher).

COMMENTS This function, introduced in Microsoft C 5.0, is used only in a user-installed critical error handler and is not intended for any other use.

 **System Calls**

SEE ALSO   _hardretn   To return to the application program from the error handler

_chain_intr   To jump from one interrupt handler to another

EXAMPLE   The example of the use of _*harderr* also includes the use of _*hardresume*.

__hardretn

COMPATIBILITY	MSC 3	MSC 4	MSC 5	QC	TC	ANSI	UNIX V
			▲	▲	hardretn		

PURPOSE   Use _*hardretn* to return to the application program from your own critical error handler, which can be installed by calling the function _*harderr*.

SYNTAX   void _hardretn (int errorcode);

int errorcode;   MS-DOS error code returned to application program

EXAMPLE CALL   _hardretn(-1);

INCLUDES   #include <dos.h>   For declaration of function

DESCRIPTION   The _*hardretn* function is used to return directly to an application program from an error-handling routine designed to process critical hardware errors that might occur during an I/O request. This routine should be installed as the handler for interrupt 24h by passing its address to the function _*harderr*.

A call to _*hardretn* forces a return to the application program just past the point where the erroneous I/O request occurred. When invoking _*hardretn*, the argument *errorcode* should be an MS-DOS error code appropriate for the I/O operation during which the error occurred. The application program should have code to deal with a returned error condition.

If the number of the DOS function during which the error occurred is 38h or higher, the _*hardretn* function loads AX with the value of *errorcode* before forcing the return. Since integer and unsigned return values from C functions are passed in the AX register, this fools the application program into thinking that a DOS error occurred (instead of a hardware error).

If the hardware error occurred during a DOS I/O function numbered 37h or lower, the return value seen by the application program is FFh. No error code is returned to the application if the error occurs during a DOS function that does not have a way of returning an error condition. In these cases the argument *errorcode* is ignored.

COMMENTS   This function, introduced in Microsoft C 5.0, is used only in a user-installed critical error handler and is not intended for any other use.

SEE ALSO _hardresume   To return to DOS from the error handler

_chain_intr   To jump from one interrupt handler to another

EXAMPLE The example of the use of *_harderr* also shows how *_hardretn* is used.

int86

COMPATIBILITY	MSC 3	MSC 4	MSC 5	QC	TC	ANSI	UNIX V
	▲	▲	▲	▲	▲		

PURPOSE Use the *int86* function to invoke any BIOS and DOS service routines that can be accessed by generating an 86 software interrupt of specified number. Use int86 when the function you are calling via interrupt does not require that you pass an argument through the segment registers DS and ES or when you are using a memory model that does not require that you specify the segment registers to access data. For example, you can use *int86* to call the ROM BIOS video function to position the cursor on the screen. The *int86* function uses the REGS data structure to pass register values back and forth (see the tutorial section).

SYNTAX `int int86( int intno, union REGS *inregs, union REGS *outregs);`

`int intno;`   Interrupt number

`union REGS * inregs;`   Input registers

`union REGS * outregs;`   Output registers

EXAMPLE CALL `int86(0x10, &inregs, &outregs);`

INCLUDES `#include <dos.h>`   For definition of REGS

DESCRIPTION The *int86* function first copies the values for the registers from the C structure *inregs* into the corresponding registers in the microprocessor. Then it generates the software interrupt number *intno* via the INT instruction. After returning from the interrupt, the function copies the contents of the 8086 registers and the system carry flag into corresponding elements in the C structure *outregs*.

The arguments *inregs* and *outregs* are the union of two structures and are defined in the include file *dos.h* (see the tutorial section). Examples below illustrate how the register values are specified.

COMMON USES Prior to Microsoft C 5.0, the most common use of the *int86* function was to access the BIOS functions on the PC, enabling you to move the cursor, read the keyboard, perform screen I/O, and so on. In versions 5.0 and 5.1 of the

 **System Calls**

compiler, however, a number of simpler routines are set up to access individual BIOS and DOS functions. Still, the *int86* function has its place. Since its underlying function is to generate software interrupts, you can use it to initiate any interrupt you want and consequently access any function that can be invoked by an interrupt. See Tables 16-1 and 16-2 for a list of all BIOS and DOS functions that can be called by software interrupts.

RETURNS   The AX register contains the return value after the interrupt return. An error is indicated by a nonzero value in *outregs.cflag*. The global variable *_doserrno* is set to an error code that tells you what caused the error. See Table 16-25 for list of error codes.

COMMENTS   The arguments required by the actual DOS or BIOS function invoked by the interrupt determine whether the segment registers DS and ES need to be loaded before executing the interrupt. For example, if register DX is supposed to contain the offset of a data element and you are using the large model, you can set the data segment register DS to point to your data area. In this case, you would use the *int86x* function for the interrupt because it allows you to load the DS register with a new value before making the software interrupt.

SEE ALSO   int86x   For software interrupts that require that you set up segment registers DS and ES

bdos, intdos, intdosx   To make a MS-DOS system call with an INT 21H instruction

Table 16-4   Simplified access to several BIOS functions

Table 16-5   Simplified access to specific MS-DOS functions

EXAMPLES   Write a routine that uses the BIOS video services to position the cursor at column "col" and row number "row" on the screen. Note that (0,0) is the upper left corner of the screen.

```
#include <dos.h>
#define BIOS_VIDEO 0x10

void putcursor(row, col)
int row, col;
{
    union REGS xr;

    xr.h.ah = 2;      /* Function number to set cursor */
    xr.h.dh = row;
    xr.h.dl = col;

    xr.h.bh = 0;      /* Assume video page 0           */
                      /* Use xr for both input/output  */
    int86(BIOS_VIDEO, &xr, &xr);
}
```

int86

On an IBM PC, when you press the SHIFT and PrtSc keys together, the keyboard generates interrupt 5. The BIOS already includes a routine to print the screen when this interrupt occurs. Use int86 to print the screen by initiating interrupt 5.

```
#include <stdio.h>
#include <dos.h>
#define BIOS_PRNTSCR  5

union REGS xr;
main()
{
    printf("Test: Printing screen\n");
    int86(BIOS_PRNTSCR, &xr, &xr);
}
```

A large number of DOS functions are available via 8086 interrupt 21h. By specifying function 2Ah in AH, you can get the current date with the day in DL, month in DH, and year in CX. The program below shows how:

```
#include <stdio.h>
#include <dos.h>

#define DOS_GETDATE 0x2a
#define DOS_INT     0x21

static char *months[] = { "---", "JAN", "FEB", "MAR", "APR",
    "MAY", "JUN", "JUL", "AUG", "SEP", "OCT", "NOV", "DEC"};

main()
{
    union REGS xr, yr;
    xr.h.ah = DOS_GETDATE;
    int86 (DOS_INT, &xr, &yr);
    printf("Today's date is: %.2d-%s-%.4d\n",
            yr.h.dl, months[yr.h.dh], yr.x.cx);
}
```

If you have an Enhanced Graphics Adapter (EGA), the BIOS video interrupt (interrupt 10h with AH = 12h and BL = 10h) lets you find out how much physical memory is available on the graphics adapter and which video mode it is in. Write a routine using *int86* to get this information about the EGA.

```
#include <stdio.h>
```

 **System Calls**

```
#include <dos.h>
static union REGS xr, yr;
#define BIOS_VIDEO 0x10
main()
{
/* Set up registers as needed by BIOS video function. */
    xr.h.ah = 0x12;
    xr.h.bl = 0x10;
    int86 (BIOS_VIDEO, &xr, &yr);

/* Upon return values are in structure yr */
    if (yr.h.bh == 0) printf("EGA in color mode\n");
    if (yr.h.bh == 1) printf("EGA in mono mode\n");
    printf("Memory size: ");
    switch (yr.h.bl)
    {
        case 0: printf("64K\n");
                break;
        case 1: printf("128K\n");
                break;
        case 2: printf("192K\n");
                break;
        case 3: printf("256K\n");
                break;
    }
}
```

int86x

COMPATIBILITY	MSC 3	MSC 4	MSC 5	QC	TC	ANSI	UNIX V
	▲	▲	▲	▲	▲		

PURPOSE Use the *int86x* function to generate an 8086 software interrupt of specified number. Use *int86x* when the function called by the interrupt requires arguments placed in the segment registers DS and ES or when you are using a memory model that requires that you specify the segment registers to access data. For example, you can use *int86x* with interrupt 21h to access the MS-DOS function 3Bh, which allows you to change the current directory from your program. The *int86x* function uses the REGS and SREGS structures as shown below.

SYNTAX
```
int int86x(int intno, union REGS *inr, union REGS *outr,
        struct SREGS *segr);

int intno;        Interrupt number
```

```
union REGS *inr;        Input registers

union REGS *outr;        Output registers

struct SREGS *segr;        Segment registers
```

EXAMPLE CALL   `int86x(0x21, &inregs, &outregs, &segregs);`

INCLUDES   `#include <dos.h>`   For definition of REGS and SREGS

DESCRIPTION   The *int86x* function first copies the values of the registers from the C structure *inr* into the corresponding registers in the microprocessor. It saves the DS register and then copies new values from the *segr* structure into DS and ES. After that, it generates the software interrupt *intno* via the INT instruction. After returning from the interrupt, *int86x* copies the contents of the 8086 registers and the system carry flag into corresponding elements in the C structure *outr*. It also restores the DS register before returning.

The arguments *inr* and *outr* are the union of two structures. This and the structure SREGS are defined in the include file *dos.h* (see the tutorial section). The examples below illustrate how the register values are specified.

COMMON USES   The most common use of the *int86x* function is to access the MS-DOS and BIOS functions on the PC, especially those that either accept arguments or return values via the segment registers DS and ES. The BIOS and DOS functions, for example, allow you to read from the floppy disk, change current directory, and print a string. Since the underlying function of *int86x* is to make software interrupts, you can use it to initiate any interrupt you want and consequently access anything on the PC that is reached by an interrupt. This includes all DOS services as well. See Tables 16-1 and 16-2 for a list of all significant DOS and BIOS functions invoked by software interrupts.

RETURNS   The register AX contains the return value after the interrupt return. An error is indicated by a nonzero value in *outr.cflag*. The global variable *_doserrno* is set to an error code that tells you what caused the error. See Table 16-25 for a list of error codes.

COMMENTS   The arguments required by the actual function invoked by the interrupt determine whether the segment registers DS and ES need to be loaded before executing the interrupt. You must use *int86x* whenever arguments have to be passed through DS and ES.

The *int86x* function is the most general interface to the BIOS and MS-DOS services. The Microsoft C run-time library includes several special functions designed as gateways to specific DOS and BIOS calls. Note, however, that *every* interrupt service on the PC is accessible via *int86x*.

SEE ALSO   `int86`   For software interrupts that do not require that you set up segment registers DS and ES

System Calls

bdos, intdos, intdosx   To make an MS-DOS system call with an INT 21H
                               instruction

Table 16-4   Simplified access to several BIOS functions
Table 16-5   Simplified access to specific MS-DOS functions

EXAMPLES Change the current directory by calling DOS function 3Bh with *int86x*. Use
the *FP_OFF* and FP_SEG macros to find offset and segment addresses of
strings that have to be passed to the DOS function 3Bh.

```
#include <stdio.h>
#include <dos.h>
/* Interrupt number for DOS functions */
#define DOS_INT 0x21
/* DOS "change directory" function     */
#define DOS_CHDIR 0x3b
/* Buffer to hold path name            */
static char buff[80];
main()
{
/* Far pointer to directory name string*/
    char far *dirname;
/* Set up the structure for registers  */
    union REGS xr;
    struct SREGS sr;
    printf("Enter pathname: ");
    gets(buff);
 /* Set up far pointer to name*/
    dirname = &buff[0];
    xr.h.ah = DOS_CHDIR;
/* Offset of string to DX     */
    xr.x.dx = FP_OFF(dirname);
/* Segment of string to DS    */
    sr.ds = FP_SEG(dirname);
    int86x(DOS_INT, &xr, &xr, &sr);
}
```

Use *int86x* to access the MS-DOS function 9h, accessible via interrupt 2ih, to
print a string terminated with a $. Use the *FP_SEG* and *FP_OFF* functions to
get the segment and offset addresses of the string to be printed.

```
#include <dos.h>
#define DOS_INT     0x21
/* DOS "print string" function */
#define DOS_PRTSTR  0x9
```

int86x

```
char str[]="Testing String Print Function$";
main()
{
    union  REGS  xr;
    struct SREGS sr;

    xr.h.ah = DOS_PRTSTR;
/* Offset string to DX          */
    xr.x.dx = FP_OFF(str);
/* Segment of string to DS      */
    sr.ds = FP_SEG(str);
    int86x(DOS_INT, &xr, &xr, &sr);
}
```

intdos

COMPATIBILITY	MSC 3	MSC 4	MSC 5	QC	TC	ANSI	UNIX V
	▲	▲	▲	▲	▲		

PURPOSE Use the *intdos* function to access the popular set of MS-DOS system utility routines that are normally called via 8086 software interrupt 21h. Use *intdos* when the DOS function does not require that you exchange any arguments through the segment registers DS and ES or when you are using a memory model that does not require that you specify the segment registers to access data. For example, you can use intdos with function 19h to get the current disk drive number.

Since the *int86* function can generate any software interrupt, you can duplicate the effect of *intdos* by calling *int86* with interrupt 21h. The only advantage of the *intdos* function is its shorter list of arguments.

SYNTAX `int intdos( union REGS *inregs, union REGS *outregs);`

`union REGS *inregs;`   Input registers

`union REGS *outregs;`   Output registers

EXAMPLE CALL `intdos(&inregs, &outregs);`

INCLUDES `#include <dos.h>`   For definition of REGS

DESCRIPTION The *intdos* function first copies the values of the registers from the C structure *inregs* into the corresponding registers in the microprocessor. Then it generates the software interrupt 21h to access the MS-DOS system functions. After returning from the interrupt, *intdos* copies the contents of the 8086 reg-

 **System Calls**

isters and the system carry flag into corresponding elements in the C structure *outregs*. The task performed by DOS depends on the function number specified in the AH register.

The arguments *inregs* and *outregs* are the union of two structures and are defined in the include file *dos.h* (see the tutorial section). The examples below illustrate how the register values are specified.

COMMON USES The *intdos* function is used to access the MS-DOS system routines that are accessible through an INT 21h instruction. These routines, for example, allow you to read the keyboard, write to the screen, and manipulate DOS directories and files. Table 16-2 gives a complete list of all DOS functions.

RETURNS The register AX contains the return value after the interrupt return. An error is indicated by a nonzero value in the *outregs* field *.cflag*. The global variable *_doserrno* is set to an error code that tells you what caused the error. See Table 16-25 for a list of error codes.

COMMENTS The arguments required by the MS-DOS function invoked by *intdos* determine whether the segment registers DS and ES need to be loaded before calling this function. For example if register DX is supposed to contain the offset of a data element and you are using the large model, you can set the data segment register DS to point to your data area. In this case, you would use the *intdosx* function because it allows you to load the DS register with a new value before invoking the DOS function.

SEE ALSO int86, int86x   For other software interrupts

intdosx   To access MS-DOS functions that require arguments in segment registers DS and ES

bdos   To access those MS-DOS routines that take arguments in the DX and AL registers only

Table 16-5   These functions provide simplified access to specific MS-DOS services

EXAMPLES MS-DOS function 19h returns the default drive number in the *AL* register. Access this function via *intdos* and get the current drive number (0 means A, 1 means B, 2 means C, and so on).

```c
#include <stdio.h>
#include <dos.h>
#define DOS_GETDRIVE 0x19
union REGS xr;
main()
{
    xr.h.ah = DOS_GETDRIVE;
    intdos(&xr, &xr);
```

intdos

```
/* Adding 65 to the value gives us the drive letter */
    printf("Current drive: %c\n", xr.h.al+65);
}
```

DOS function 2Ch returns the current time with the hours in *CH*, minutes in *CL*, and the seconds in *DH*. Use *intdos* to get the current time and display it.

```
#include <stdio.h>
#include <dos.h>
#define DOS_GETTIME 0x2c
main()
{
    union REGS xr, yr;
    xr.h.ah = DOS_GETTIME;
    intdos(&xr, &yr);
    printf("Current time is %.2d:%.2d:%.2d\n",
            yr.h.ch, yr.h.cl, yr.h.dh);
}
```

intdosx

COMPATIBILITY	MSC 3	MSC 4	MSC 5	QC	TC	ANSI	UNIX V
	▲	▲	▲	▲	▲		

PURPOSE Use the *intdosx* function to access any MS-DOS system function, even those that require arguments in the segment registers DS and ES (*intdos* cannot handle these cases). You must use *intdosx* when the DOS function requires arguments exchanged through the segment registers *DS* and *ES* or when you are using a memory model that requires that you specify the segment registers in order to access data. For example, you can use *intdosx* with function 39h to create a subdirectory.

SYNTAX
```
int intdosx(union REGS *inr, union REGS *outr,
            struct SREGS *segr);
```

```
union REGS *inr;          Input registers

union REGS *outr;         Output registers

struct SREGS *segr;       Segment registers
```

EXAMPLE CALL
```
intdosx(&inregs, &outregs, &segregs);
```

 **System Calls**

INCLUDES   `#include <dos.h>`   For definition of REGS and SREGS

DESCRIPTION   The *intdosx* function copies the values of the registers from the C structure *inr* into the corresponding registers in the microprocessor. It saves the DS register and then copies new values from segr into DS and ES. After that, it calls DOS by an INT 21h instruction. After returning from DOS, *intdosx* copies the contents of the 8086 registers and the system carry flag into corresponding elements in the C structure *outr*. It also restores the DS register before returning. The actions performed by DOS depend on the function number specified in the AH register.

The arguments *inr* and *outr* are the union of two structures. This and the structure SREGS are defined in the include file *dos.h* (see the tutorial section). The examples below illustrate how the register values are specified.

COMMON USES   The *intdosx* function is used to call MS-DOS functions on the PC, especially those that either accept arguments or return values via the segment registers DS and ES. The DOS functions, for example, allow you to read from the floppy disk, change the current directory, and create a subdirectory. See Table 16-2 for a list of all DOS functions that can be called by software interrupts.

RETURNS   The register AX contains the return value after the interrupt return. An error is indicated by a nonzero value in *outr.cflag*. The global variable *_doserrno* is set to an error code that tells you what caused the error. See Table 16-25 for a list of error codes.

COMMENTS   The arguments required by the DOS function invoked by *intdosx* determine whether the segment registers DS and ES need to be loaded before calling *intdosx*. You must use *intdosx* whenever parameters are exchanged through the segment registers DS and ES.

The *intdosx* function is a general interface to the MS-DOS functions. The Microsoft C run-time library includes several special functions designed as gateways to specific DOS calls. Note, however, that every DOS function on the PC is accessible via *intdosx*.

SEE ALSO   `int86,`
`int86x`   To generate any 8086 software interrupt

`intdos`   For MS-DOS calls that do not require that you set up segment registers DS and ES

`bdos`   To access those MS-DOS routines that take arguments in the DX and AL registers only

Table 16-5   These functions provide simplified access to specific MS-DOS services

EXAMPLES   Use the MS-DOS function 39h to create a subdirectory in the current directory. The segment and offset of the subdirectory name should be specified via the registers DS and DX, respectively.

intdosx

```
#include <stdio.h>
#include <dos.h>

#define  DOS_MAKEDIR 0x39

union REGS xr;
struct SREGS sr;

main()
{
    char pathname[80];
    printf("Enter name of subdirectory: ");
    gets(pathname);

    xr.h.ah = DOS_MAKEDIR;
    sr.ds = FP_SEG(pathname);
    xr.x.dx = FP_OFF(pathname);
    intdosx(&xr, &xr, &sr);

    if (xr.x.cflag == 1)
    {
        printf("\nError creating subdirectory\n");
    }
}
```

Use DOS function Ah to read a line from the keyboard up to and including a carriage return. The line is stored in a buffer whose segment address must be in DS and the offset in DX. The first byte of the buffer contains the maximum number of characters to be read. On return, the second byte has the number of characters read.

```
#include <stdio.h>
#include <dos.h>
#define DOS_BUFIN 0x0a
static char buffer[82] = {80, 0};
main()
{
    union REGS xr;
    struct SREGS sr;
    int numchars;
    char far *pbuf;
    pbuf = (char far *)(&buffer[0]);
    printf("Enter a line: ");
    sr.ds = FP_SEG(pbuf);
    xr.h.ah = DOS_BUFIN;
    xr.x.dx = FP_OFF(pbuf);
```

System Calls

```
    intdosx(&xr, &xr, &sr);
/* The number of characters not counting the carriage
 * return
 */
    numchars = buffer[1];
/* Make it an ASCIIZ string by adding a 0 at the end*/
    buffer[numchars+2] = '\0';
    printf("\nYou typed %d characters\n", numchars);
    printf("The string is: %s", buffer+2);
}
```

segread

COMPATIBILITY	MSC 3	MSC 4	MSC 5	QC	TC	ANSI	UNIX V
	▲	▲	▲	▲	▲		

PURPOSE Use the *segread* function to retrieve the values of the 8086 segment registers CS, DS, ES, and SS from C programs. For example, you may want to read and save the value of ES before it is altered during a call to *int86x* or *intdosx* or you may want to check the segment register values to debug your C program.

SYNTAX `void segread (struct SREGS *segregs);`

`struct SREGS *segregs;`   C structure to hold segment registers

EXAMPLE CALL `segread(&segregs);`

INCLUDES `#include <dos.h>`   For definition of SREGS

DESCRIPTION The *segread* function copies the current values of the 8086 segment registers into the C structure *segregs* which has one unsigned integer variable for each segment register. These variables are named *cs, ds, es,* and *ss.* Starting with Microsoft C 5.1, under OS/2, the segment register values are selector values (see *Inside OS/2* by Gordon Letwin, Microsoft Press, 1988, for OS/2 terminology and features).

COMMON USES This function is commonly used to save the value of ES before calling *int86x* or *intdosx* since ES is frequently used by BIOS routines.

COMMENTS The segment register values are usually of no concern to C programmers except when accessing system-level functions.

SEE ALSO `int86x, intdosx`   For 8086 software interrupts that may require you to set up segment registers DS and ES

segread

EXAMPLE   Use the *segread* function to display the values of the 8086 segment registers.

```
#include <stdio.h>
#include <dos.h>
struct SREGS sr;

main()
{
    segread(&sr);
    printf("Currently cs = %x, ds = %x, es = %x, ss = %x\n",
            sr.cs, sr.ds, sr.es, sr.ss);
}
```

System Calls

V Graphics

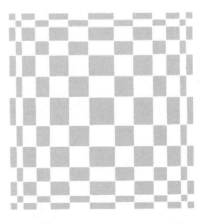

Chapter *17* ***Graphics Modes, Coordinates, and Attributes***

Introduction

Increasingly, graphics user interfaces are the norm for PC-based applications, as the older text-based DOS makes way for OS/2 with its promise of a bit-mapped window-oriented interface. An application also needs good text output capabilities to be competitive with others. Even though we recognize the need, the task of programming a user interface with good graphics as well as text capabilities remains a particularly complicated business in the PC world because of the variety of graphics adapters and the various displays that can be used with these adapters. Adding to this complexity is the IBM PC's limited support for video I/O in the ROM BIOS (see Chapter 16). This meant that, until recently, creating an effective screen-oriented program involved writing many parts of the program in assembly language. All this has changed in Microsoft C 5.1—thanks to the addition of 43 graphics routines to the library. These routines make the task of creating graphics-based programs much simpler by providing all the basic capabilities needed. For example, there are routines to determine the video equipment and set an appropriate video mode. You can select colors, line styles, and fill patterns; draw primitive shapes such as straight line, rectangle, arc, and ellipse; mix text and graphics on the screen; and even perform animation by saving and restoring screen images.

In the next three chapters of the book we describe these graphics library routines. This chapter presents the information you need to get started with the Microsoft C graphics library. In Chapter 18 we describe the drawing and animation routines, and in Chapter 19, the routines for text output.

We will start with a discussion of the options available for graphics programming on the PC, the video modes in which the common graphics adapters operate, and the coordinate systems used in the Microsoft C graphics library. We will then describe the library routines that let you control the modes and attributes of the Microsoft C graphics programming model. We will limit discussion of the graphics hardware to those aspects that directly affect graphics programming, so we will present information on number of

661

colors and resolutions, but skip unnecessary details such as scan rate of monitors and screen sizes.

Basics of PC Graphics

In the IBM PC (and compatibles) screen output relies on two components: the display adapter and the display monitor. As shown in Figure 17-1, the "adapter" is a hardware card that you plug into one of the slots inside the PC and the "monitor" is the display screen where the actual characters and graphics appears.

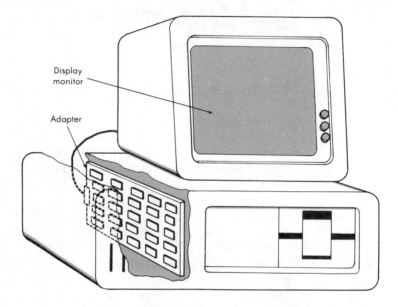

Display
monitor

Adapter

Figure 17-1. *Display hardware in IBM PC*

Whether we can display graphics on a monitor or not depends entirely on the adapter. A monitor is capable of displaying an array of dots known as "pixels." Characters displayed on a monitor are built with a pattern of pixels which is sent to the monitor by the adapter. The ability to display graphics, therefore, depends on the type of adapter.

ADAPTERS AND MONITORS FOR THE IBM PC There are three standard display adapters in the IBM PC marketplace: Monochrome Display Adapter (MDA), Color Graphics Adapter (CGA), and the Enhanced Graphics Adapter (EGA). A fourth adapter, Hercules Graphics Card (HGC), is a monochrome graphics adapter capable of displaying graphics on the monochrome monitor. Three monitors are available: the monochrome display, the color display, and the enhanced color display.

The MDA is the display adapter used in the original IBM PC. It can display 80 characters (columns) by 25 lines (rows) of text output (no graphics) on the monochrome display. The HGC displays text too, like the MDA, but it can also display graphics on the monochrome monitor at a resolution of 720 pixels horizontally and 348 pixels vertically. (Another way of saying this is that the HGC has a resolution of 720×348. From now on we will express resolutions like this.)

The CGA can also display text as well as graphics, and it does so in color on a color display monitor. Specifically, the CGA can display text using a combination of any 1 of 16 foreground colors and 1 of 8 background colors. Graphics can be displayed in 4 colors with 320×200 resolution. If you choose 2-color (black and white) graphics, the resolution goes up to 640×200. We will soon explain this trade-off between number of colors and resolution.

The EGA, introduced by IBM in 1984, moves towards higher resolution graphics and more colors. It displays text and graphics in color on an enhanced color display monitor. To retain compatibility with earlier hardware, the EGA is provided with operational modes in which it can display text on a monochrome monitor and emulate a CGA. In its highest resolution mode, the EGA can generate graphics output in 16 colors with 640×350 resolution.

DISPLAY SYSTEMS
IN IBM PS/2

With the new PS/2 systems, IBM introduced two new adapters: the Multi Color Graphics Array (MCGA) and the Video Graphics Array (VGA). The VGA is a successor to the EGA. In one video mode (mode 12h), the VGA offers 640×480 resolution graphics with 16 colors out of a possible 256 simultaneous colors. The VGA can also provide 320×200 resolution graphics with 256 colors (mode 13h). The MCGA is similar to the CGA, but it has a 2-color 640×480 mode. It is available on the PS/2 Model 30, which has a PC-compatible bus. The VGA is built into all other PS/2 models. These two adapters are designed to drive an "analog monitor," as opposed to the "digital" ones that are used with MDA, CGA, and EGA in the PC. As its name implies, a digital monitor uses a fixed number of on/off signals. For example, the enhanced color display monitor accepts the six on/off signals: red, green, and blue and intensified versions of each, so it is capable of displaying 64 distinct colors ($2^6 = 64$), but it is actually limited to 16 of these because there are only 4 bits of storage for each pixel in the video memory on the display adapter). In an analog monitor, the three red, green, and blue signals can vary continuously instead of being on or off. This allows continuously varying shades of colors. Inside the MCGA and VGA adapters, the colors are still represented digitally. For example, in MCGA, red, green, and blue are each represented by 6-bit values. A Digital-to-Analog Converter (DAC) converts these digital values to analog signals before they are fed to the monitor.

As you can see, in graphics programming on the PC and PS/2 we have to deal with quite a few combinations of adapters and monitors. So any help in the form of library routines that can be called from C is greatly appreciated. This is exactly what the graphics library in Microsoft C 5.1 does.

PROGRAMMING
THE DISPLAY
ADAPTERS

Like most peripheral devices in the IBM PC and PS/2, the display adapters are programmed via 8-bit registers that are accessible by input port addresses (see the tutorial in Chapter 15 for a description of port I/O routines in Microsoft C). In addition to these control registers, all PC display adapters share one common property: they are "memory mapped." Each pixel on the display screen corresponds to 1 or more bits in a memory location (in the video adapter) accessible just like the rest of the memory locations in the system. This "video memory," or video RAM, is physically present on the display adapter but it has addresses that map into the normal address space of the microprocessor. The circuitry in the adapter reads values from the video RAM and displays the pixels on the monitor. Thus you can show text and graphics on the monitor by directly manipulating the video RAM, provided you know how it is organized. The method of storing information in the video memory depends on whether text or graphics is being displayed.

In text display modes, a rectangular grid of pixels is used to display one character. Each character is stored using two bytes: one for the 8-bit code of the character and the other to store the display attributes for that character. These attributes determine such characteristics as the colors of the character and of the background pixels and whether the character is blinking. The exact pattern of pixels necessary to draw each character is stored in a separate table in memory. These patterns are referred to as "fonts."

In graphics modes, the number of bits necessary to represent a pixel depends on the number of colors to be displayed. For a black and white monitor, each pixel is either on or off, so a single bit is enough to store all the information necessary to display a pixel. By the same token, to display 16 colors we need 4 bits of storage per pixel. The maximum number of colors that can be displayed is given by 2^n where n is the number of bits per pixel. Since the amount of memory on the adapter is fixed, there is always a trade-off between the number of on-screen pixels and the number of colors.

The physical organization of the video RAM varies quite a bit from one adapter to another, and the details (especially in EGA and VGA) can be overwhelming even for a simple program. The Microsoft C graphics routines eliminate the need to learn the detailed organization of the video memory and display adapters.

BIOS VIDEO ROUTINES

The BIOS routines which reside in the read-only memory (ROM) of every PC provide a portable way to program the video adapters. Using software interrupt 10h (see the tutorial in Chapter 16), you can invoke a set of functions that allow setting the video mode and reading and writing pixel values. A number of video modes for text or graphics output are available in the BIOS video routines, each suitable for a specific monitor (if that adapter supports multiple monitor types). In a text mode you can write a character to the screen with an associated attribute to control its appearance. In a graphics mode, you are limited to either writing a pixel or reading the value of a single point on the screen. BIOS is adequate for basic display programming. But for very fast screen drawing, especially in graphics modes, directly writing to the video memory may be preferred, even at the expense of loss of portability of the code.

THE MICROSOFT C SOLUTION

Where does the Microsoft C graphics library fit in this picture? The Microsoft graphics routines perform better than the the BIOS video routines and they provide many more basic capabilities than does BIOS interrupt 10h. Additionally, the Microsoft C graphics library routines are much easier to use than the BIOS routines, which must be invoked via software interrupts. To use the graphics library, you do not have to know the implementation details of the routines, but you do have to understand the graphics "model" used by Microsoft.

The Microsoft C 5.1 Graphics Model

The Microsoft C graphics model is the collection of such concepts as coordinates, colors, palettes, line styles, fill masks, and primitive shapes that the library uses. Many of the ideas have their roots in the hardware, and we will make these connections clear as the concepts are discussed.

DISPLAY SCREEN AND THE COORDINATE SYSTEMS

As shown in Figure 17-2, in text modes the entire screen is viewed as a grid of cells, usually 25 rows by 80 columns. Each cell can hold a character with certain foreground and background colors if the monitor is capable of displaying colors. A location on the screen is expressed in terms of rows and columns with the upper left hand corner corresponding to (0,0), the column numbers increasing from left to right and the row numbers increasing vertically downwards.

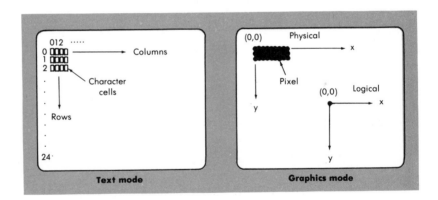

Figure 17-2. *Coordinate frames in text and graphics modes*

In graphics modes, the screen is seen as a matrix of pixels each capable of displaying one or more colors. Depending on the graphics mode and display adapter, the width and height of this matrix, in pixels, can be one of the following: 320×200 (CGA 4-color mode and VGA 256-color mode), 640×200 (CGA 2-color mode), 640×350 (EGA 16-color mode), or 640×480 (VGA 16-color mode). The Microsoft C graphics library uses two coordinate systems: one "physical" and the other "logical." Initially, both coordinate systems coincide with each other. Both have their origin at the upper left hand corner of the physical screen with the x-axis positive to the right and the y-axis positive going downwards, as shown in Figure 17-2.

The physical coordinate frame is permanently affixed to the display screen, but the logical system's origin can be moved. Figure 17-2 shows the logical coordinate system located at the middle of the physical screen.

All graphics functions in the library work with logical coordinates so the graphics output can be easily translated (shifted) on the screen by redefining the logical origin. A call that draws a rectangle with its upper left corner at logical (0,0) will be drawn at a new location on the screen if we move the logical origin (using *_setlogorg*) and issue the call to draw the rectangle again.

VIDEO MODES The video modes used in the Microsoft graphics library are directly linked to the BIOS video function modes, which determine whether the hardware should be configured for text output only or for both graphics and text output. The mode also specifies the number of colors and the graphics resolution of the screen.

Table 17-1 shows the video mode constants known to the graphics library. The adapter that supports each video mode is also listed in the table. The mode constants are defined in the header file *graph.h*. You use these constants when selecting a video mode with a call to *_setvideomode*.

Table 17-1. *Video Modes in Microsoft C Graphics Library*

Mode Constant	Interpretation	Adapter
_DEFAULTMODE	Default mode for the current hardware configuration	—
_TEXTBW40	40 × 25 text in 16 shades of grey	CGA
_TEXTC40	40 × 25 text in 16 or 8 colors	CGA
_TEXTBW80	80 × 25 text in 16 shades of grey	CGA
_TEXTC80	80 × 25 text in 16 or 8 color	CGA
_MRES4COLOR	320 × 200 graphics in 4 color	CGA
_MRESNOCOLOR	320 × 200 graphics in 4 shades of grey	CGA
_HRESBW	640 × 200 graphics in black and white	CGA
_TEXTMONO	80 × 25 text in black and white	Monochrome Adapter
_MRES16COLOR	320 × 200 graphics in 16 colors	EGA
_HRES16COLOR	640 × 200 graphics in 16 colors	EGA
_ERESNOCOLOR	640 × 350 graphics in black and white	EGA
_ERESCOLOR	640 × 350 graphics in 4 or 16 colors	EGA
_VRES2COLOR	640 × 480 graphics in black and white	VGA
_VRES16COLOR	640 × 480 graphics in 16 colors	VGA
_MRES256COLOR	320 × 200 graphics in 256 colors	VGA
_HERCMONO	720 × 348 graphics in black and white	HGC

SELECTING A As mentioned earlier, one of the problems in developing graphics software
VIDEO MODE for the IBM PC is the diversity of hardware configurations that your software

encounters once it is out of your hands. One common trend among developers seems to be to use what we call the "least common denominator" approach—make use of the lowest resolution video mode (usually a CGA mode) that is guaranteed to be emulated on most other adapters. While this works, it is also disheartening to see the advanced capabilities of the EGA and VGA adapters going to waste for want of software that supports them. The situation is improving gradually and if you are developing an application using the Microsoft C 5.1 graphics library, you can make use of its facilities to utilize the best video mode the hardware can support. Here's the procedure to follow. Call _getvideoconfig and check which adapter and monitor the system has. Based on this information, choose the best video mode that suits your application. For example, if you find an EGA with 128 K or more video memory attached to an enhanced color display, you can choose the _ERESCOLOR mode, which allows 16 color graphics with 640×350 resolution. On the other hand, with a CGA, you might settle for the 640×200 black and white mode (_HRESBW). If your program must operate in a graphics mode and the _getvideoconfig routine reports an MDA, which cannot display graphics, you can print an error message and exit.

Once you decide on a mode, use _setvideomode to put the display adapter in that mode. Call _getvideoconfig again to get such details as screen resolution, number of colors, and number of video pages available for this mode. At this point, your application can display graphics and text output. Remember the parameters such as graphics position, text position, line style, fill mask, and others that the graphics library uses during its operation. Set these to appropriate values before calling graphics or text output routines. We will discuss these attributes and parameters later.

When your application is ready to exit, call _setvideomode with the argument _DEFAULTMODE. This restores the hardware to its initial configuration. Here is how the skeleton of a graphics application looks:

```
#include <graph.h>    /* Graphics program always need this */
    :
    :
struct videoconfig video_info;
short videomode = _HRESBW;
    :
    :
_getvideoconfig(&video_info);  /* Call to find adapter */
switch (video_info.adapter)
{
    case _MDPA:
        printf("This program needs a graphics adapter.\n");
        exit(0);

    case _CGA:
        videomode = _HRESBW;      /* 2 color 640x200 CGA mode */
        break;
```

```
            case _EGA:
                videomode = _ERESCOLOR;   /* 16 color 640x350 EGA mode */
                break;

            case _VGA:
                videomode = _VRES16COLOR; /* 16 color 640x480 VGA mode */
                break;
        }
/* Set adapter to selected mode */
        _setvideomode(videomode);
/* Call _getvideoconfig again to find resolution and colors of
 * this mode.
 */
        _getvideoconfig(&video_info);
/* Set color, line style, fill mask and draw the graphics you want */
        :
        :
/* Restore original mode */
        _setvideomode(_DEFAULTMODE);
        :
        :
```

COLORS AND PALETTES

Any color can be represented by a combination of the primary colors: red (R), green (G), and blue (B). In a digital scheme, a fixed number of bits are used to represent the permissible levels in each component of the RGB signal: a total of 2^6 (each combination of R, G, and B is a color). Even though an analog monitor has an infinite number of possible colors, we do not have an infinite number of levels in the RGB signal. In the VGA, for example, each component of RGB is represented by an 8-bit value of which the two high-order bits are always zero. Thus each component has a 6-bit value or 64 levels. This means we can have a total of $64 \times 64 \times 64 = 262,144$ (or 256 K) possible colors in the VGA. Although an adapter may be able to "understand" 256-K color values, we will need a lot of video memory to display these colors because, with 6 bits per primary color, the RGB value at each pixel will require at least 18 bits (3×6 bits) of storage.

With 4 bits of storage for each pixel (as in EGA and VGA mode 12h), the value stored at each video memory location corresponding to a pixel can be any value from 0 to 15 ($2^4 - 1$). Suppose the monitor is capable of accepting 64 (a 6-bit value) different colors and the display adapter is designed to generate the 6-bit value. How should the 4-bit value in a pixel be mapped into a 6-bit value sent to the monitor? The solution is to use a "palette," a table with as many entries as there are possible pixel values (16) and each pixel value has an entry showing one of the possible colors (a number from 0 to 63). The adapter uses the pixel value to look up the color it must send to the monitor. Figure 17-3 illustrates the concept of pixel values mapped to colors via the palette. Figure 17-3 also shows the video memory organized as four bit planes.

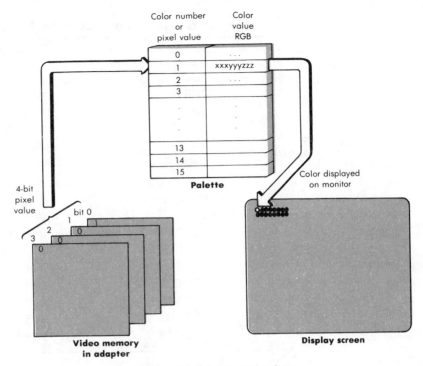

Figure 17-3. *Colors and palettes*

The pixel value, or "color number," refers to the contents of the bits in the video memory corresponding to a pixel. The "color value" is the digital signal (even an analog monitor receives a digital signal that has been converted to analog form using a Digital-to-Analog Converter) that causes a monitor to display a specific color from the current palette. Stated another way, the color number or pixel value is what is stored at a memory location corresponding to a pixel and the color value denotes an RGB signal level that causes the monitor to display a specific color by use of the palette.

The pixel value of 0 has a special significance in the display adapters. All display adapters treat pixels containing a 0 as part of the background. Thus on adapters like EGA and VGA, where the current palette can be redefined, if you change the mapping of pixel value 0 in the palette, the background will change color. For example, *_remappalette(0, _BLUE);* changes the background to blue (constants for common color values are defined in the file *graph.h* and listed in Table 17-2).

Palettes in CGA

The palettes are predefined in CGA. When operated in the text modes _TEXTC40 and _TEXTC80, up to 16 colors can be displayed and the palette is fixed as shown in Table 17-3. Note that in the table, we have used descriptive names instead of color values. The graphics modes _MRES4COLOR and _MRESNOCOLOR are supported by the CGA as well as the EGA. The _MRES4COLOR mode is designed to be used with color monitors and provides four predefined palettes, each with four colors (color 0 in each palette is the background color and can be separately selected). The colors 1 through 3 of these four palettes are shown in Table 17-4.

Table 17-2. *Color Constants and Their Values*

Color Constant	Hexadecimal Value
_BLACK	0x000000L
_BLUE	0x2a0000L
_GREEN	0x002a00L
_CYAN	0x2a2a00L
_RED	0x00002aL
_MAGENTA	0x2a002aL
_BROWN	0x00152aL
_WHITE	0x2a2a2aL
_GRAY	0x151515L
_LIGHTBLUE	0x3F1515L
_LIGHTGREEN	0x153f15L
_LIGHTCYAN	0x3f3f15L
_LIGHTRED	0x15153fL
_LIGHTMAGENTA	0x3f153fL
_LIGHTYELLOW	0x153f3fL
_BRIGHTWHITE	0x3f3f3fL

Table 17-3. *CGA Palette in Text Modes*

Pixel Value	Maps to Color
0	Black
1	Blue
2	Green
3	Cyan
4	Red
5	Magenta
6	Brown
7	White
8	Dark grey
9	Light blue
10	Light green
11	Light cyan
12	Light red
13	Light magenta
14	Yellow
15	Bright white

The _MRESNOCOLOR mode is meant for use with monochrome displays that can produce shades of gray. When used with color displays, this mode also allows a set of palettes. On an IBM EGA with an enhanced color display, both _MRES4COLOR and _MRESNOCOLOR modes use the same palettes as those shown in Table 17-4. However, the palettes may differ on EGA clones because of the differences in emulating the CGA modes in the EGA hardware. Use the _selectpalette function to choose a CGA palette. For example, _selectpalette(0) selects palette 0.

Table 17-4. *The Four Palettes in* _MRES4COLOR *Mode*

Palette Number	Pixel Value		
	1	**2**	**3**
0	Green	Red	Brown
1	Cyan	Magenta	Light Gray
2	Light Green	Light Red	Yellow
3	Light Cyan	Light Magenta	White

Palettes in EGA and VGA

On the EGA and the VGA, the default definition of the palette in the 16 color modes coincides with that shown in Table 17-3. However, you can redefine the palette in EGA and VGA. The Microsoft C graphics library has a predefined set of color values which are shown in Table 17-2. Use these names when redefining palettes for EGA and VGA. The names of the colors in Table 17-2 are self-explanatory. Notice that each value has 6 hexadecimal digits, so each consists of 3 bytes. The color value is constructed by laying out these 3 bytes one after another. The least significant byte (the rightmost) denotes the intensity of the red component of the color. The byte in the middle contains the amount of green and the most significant byte (the leftmost) represents the amount of blue.

Use the _remapallpalette function to redefine pixel values on the EGA and VGA. A single pixel value can be mapped to a new color with a call to _remappalette. For example, _remappalette(1, _RED) maps pixel value 1 to the color red.

VIDEO PAGES
Although all PC displays are memory-mapped, the actual amount of video memory necessary for all pixels depends on the video mode. In some modes, there is enough video memory for all the screen pixels several times over. This allows multiple "video pages"; each area of memory sufficient to hold a full screen is a page. Only one page is displayed, but the adapter allows switching from one page to another. Since this "flipping of the video page" happens very fast, it can used to your advantage in your programs to provide very fast screen updates. The trick is to prepare the entire screen in a video page that is not being shown and then switch to that video page to display its contents on the screen.

The number of video pages available in an adapter depends on the amount of video memory on the adapter and the mode in which the adapter is being operated. For example, the CGA with 16 K of video RAM supports up to four video pages in the text mode _TEXTC80. On the other hand, an EGA with 256 K of video RAM can have two video pages even in the high-resolution graphics mode _ERESCOLOR (see the reference pages on _setactivepage for an example program showing page flipping on the EGA in the 640×350 16-color mode).

The video pages are numbered starting at 0 and initially both active and visual pages are 0. You can select a new active page by calling _setactivepage and display another page with the call _setvisualpage. For example, _setvisualpage(1) will begin displaying video page 1 on the screen.

CURRENT POSITIONS, LINE STYLES, AND FILL MASKS

The drawing and text output routines in the graphics library rely on several internally maintained attributes and parameters. Table 17-5 summarizes these parameters including the name of the relevant functions in the library. By the way, the functions themselves are further categorized in the next section. The functions are described in detail in the reference pages that follow this tutorial.

Table 17-5. *Parameters Maintained by the Graphics Library Routines*

Parameter	Meaning
Active Page	When there is enough memory for more than one video page, the active page denotes the portion of video memory where all current graphics and text output goes. TO SET: use _setactivepage TO GET: cannot get
Background Color	This is the color that will appear in the background color. In text mode, it is specified by a color number. In graphics mode, the background color is given as a color value and involves redefining color 0 in the palette. TO SET: use _setbkcolor TO GET: use _getbkcolor
Clipping Region	The clipping region is a rectangle on the screen specified by the physical coordinates of its upper left and lower right corners. All graphics output (not text) falling outside this rectangle is clipped and will not appear on the screen. TO SET: use _setcliprgn TO GET: cannot get
Fill Mask	When filling an area with a color, the fill mask determines the pattern used in the fill operation. As shown in Figure 17-4, the fill mask is specified by an 8-byte bit pattern. This is viewed as an 8 × 8 array of bits. The area being filled is also subdivided into 8 × 8 blocks of pixels. The fill mask is then applied to each 8 × 8 block as follows: wherever a 1 appears in the mask, the corresponding pixel on the screen is set to the current graphics color; a 0 in the mask leaves the corresponding screen pixel unchanged. TO SET: use _setfillmask TO GET: use _getfillmask
Graphics Color	This is the color number or pixel value to be used for all subsequent graphics output that uses color (for example, line drawing by _lineto).

Table 17-5. *(cont.)*

Parameter	Meaning
	TO SET: use _setcolor
	TO GET: use _getcolor
Graphics Position	This is a pixel position in logical (x,y) coordinates representing the location where subsequent graphics output starts. The graphics drawing functions update this position as they generate output to the screen.
	TO SET: use _moveto
	TO GET: use _getcurrentposition
Line Style	When drawing a line in the graphics mode, the line style determines the appearance of the line on the screen. The line style is specified by a 16-bit unsigned integer. As shown in Figure 17-4, the line style value is viewed as an array of 16 bits. The line being drawn on the screen is also subdivided into 16-pixel chunks. The line style is applied as follows: if a bit is 1, the corresponding screen pixel is set to the current color; if a bit is 0, the corresponding pixel on the screen is left unchanged.
	TO SET: use _setlinestyle
	TO GET: use _getlinestyle
Logical Origin	The physical coordinates of the point where the origin of the logical coordinate axes is currently located. Logical coordinates are used in graphics mode only.
	TO SET: use _setlogorg
	TO GET: use _getphyscoord(0,0)
Text Color	This is a color number (or pixel value) used by the text output routine _outtext as the color of the text it sends to the screen.
	TO SET: use _settextcolor
	TO GET: use _gettextcolor
Text Position	This is a character position in (row, column) coordinates representing the location where subsequent text output starts. The text output function _outtext updates this position as it writes to the screen.
	TO SET: use _settextposition
	TO GET: use _gettextposition
Text Window	A rectangular region specified in terms of the text coordinates (row and column) of the window's upper left and lower right corners. All text output is confined in this window.
	TO SET: use _settextwindow
	TO GET: cannot get
Video Mode	This is the current video mode.
	TO SET: use _setvideomode
	TO GET: use _getvideoconfig
Visual Page	When there is enough display memory on the adapter for more than one video pages, the visual page denotes the portion of video memory that is currently being mapped to the display screen.
	TO SET: use _setvisualpage
	TO GET: cannot get

ROUTINES TO CONTROL MODES AND ATTRIBUTES The 21 routines in the graphics library are useful for setting modes and attributes as well as getting their current values. Table 17-6 is a list of these routines organized according to attributes each one controls (an alphabetically arranged list of the routines appears in Table 17-7).

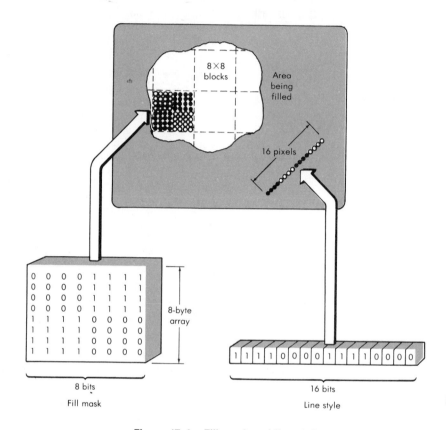

Figure 17-4. *Fill mask and line style*

Table 17-6. *Mode and Attribute Control Routines by Task*

Task	Routines
Determine available display hardware, the current video mode, and its capabilities.	_getvideoconfig
Set video mode.	_setvideomode
Set up clipping region and viewport.	_setcliprgn, _setviewport
Manipulate coordinate systems.	_getlogcoord, _getphyscoord, _setlogorg
Control colors and palettes.	_getbkcolor, _getcolor, _remapallpalette, _remappalette, _selectpalette, _setbkcolor, _setcolor
Control fill pattern and line style.	_getfillmask, _getlinestyle, _setfillmask, _setlinestyle

Table 17-6. *(cont.)*

Task	Routines
Control video pages.	_setactivepage, _setvisualpage
Cursor control in graphics mode.	_displaycursor

Table 17-7. *Mode and Attribute Control Routines*

Routine	Description
_displaycursor	Turns cursor on or off in graphics mode.
_getbkcolor	Gets current background color.
_getcolor	Gets current color for graphics output.
_getfillmask	Gets current fill mask.
_getlinestyle	Gets current line style.
_getlogcoord	Converts physical coordinates to logical ones.
_getphyscoord	Converts logical coordinates to physical ones.
_getvideoconfig	Gets information about the current video configuration.
_remapallpalette	Redefines entire palette in EGA or VGA.
_remappalette	Redefines a pixel value in the palette (EGA or VGA only)
_selectpalette	Selects a predefined CGA palette.
_setactivepage	Selects a video page to be the page where all current output goes.
_setbkcolor	Sets a new background color.
_setcliprgn	Defines a rectangular area of the screen as the clipping region (output outside this area is not displayed).
_setcolor	Sets the color to be used by subsequent graphics output.
_setfillmask	Defines a new fill pattern used when filling a region.
_setlinestyle	Defines a new line style.
_setlogorg	Relocates the origin of the logical coordinate system on the screen.
_setvideomode	Selects a video mode.
_setviewport	Sets up a rectangular clipping region and moves the logical origin to the upper left corner of the region.
_setvisualpage	Selects a video page as the one to be displayed on the screen.

Further Reading

Although a graphics library hides much of the detail of the display hardware, it is necessary to know about the inner working of the adapter in order to make the graphics application work right. Here are some references that can help you get familiar with PC graphics.

Norton's guide[1] discusses the basics of video and gives details of the CGA and MDA. (The EGA and VGA are only beginning to be discussed in books. Coverage in popular journals[2] remains a good source for information on these adapters.) The recent book by Wilton[3] is an excellent reference on PC and PS/2 video programming, complete with sample assembly language routines that can be called from Microsoft C. Kliewer's book[4] can also serve as an EGA/VGA programmer's reference, although it does not have the depth and details of Wilton's text. Also, Lafore[5] covers CGA and EGA programming in his book.

Hansen's book[6] shows the development of a library of utility functions, including a set for screen display. He also shows several tricks used to determine the display hardware in a system and a way to write to the CGA memory without generating "snow" on the screen.

The book by Rochkind[7], the author of the PC editor EDIX, is devoted solely to the subject of developing a portable text-oriented display package. It has an excellent presentation of the gradual development of a modular display library that can help you manage any types of displays effectively.

On the graphics side, Johnson[8] presents the development of an EGA-based graphics package with complete source listings.

1. Peter Norton, *The Peter Norton Programmer's Guide to the IBM PC*, Microsoft Press, Redmond, WA, 1985, 426 pages.

2. Charles Petzold, "Exploring the EGA, Part I and II," *PC Magazine*, August 1986, 367–384 and September 1986, 287–313.

3. Richard Wilton, *Programmer's Guide to PC & PS/2 Video Systems*, Microsoft Press, Redmond, WA, 1987, 531 pages.

4. Bradley D. Kliewer, *EGA/VGA A Programmer's Reference Guide*, Intertext Publications, Inc., New York, NY, 1988, 269 pages.

5. Robert Lafore, The Waite Group, *Microsoft C Programming for the IBM*, Howard W. Sams & Company, Indianapolis, IN, 1987, 681 pages.

6. Augie Hansen, *Proficient C*, Microsoft Press, Redmond, WA, 1987, 492 pages.

7. Marc J. Rochkind, *Advanced C Programming for Displays*, Prentice-Hall, Englewood Cliffs, NJ, 1988, 331 pages.

8. Nelson Johnson, *Advanced Graphics in C*, Osborne McGraw-Hill, Berkeley, CA, 1987, 670 pages.

__displaycursor

COMPATIBILITY	MSC 3	MSC 4	MSC 5	QC	TC	ANSI	UNIX V
			▲	▲			

PURPOSE Use _displaycursor to turn the solid cursor on or off while in the graphics mode.

SYNTAX `short far _displaycursor(short on_off);`

`short on_off;`   Selected display mode of cursor

EXAMPLE CALL `_displaycursor(_GCURSOROFF);`

INCLUDES `#include <graph.h>`   For function declaration and definition of mode names

DESCRIPTION The _displaycursor function allows you to turn a solid cursor on or off during the graphics mode. By default, this cursor is not displayed when you first enter a graphics mode. The cursor state is specified in the short integer argument on_off. You can specify one of the following constants as the value of on_off.

_GCURSORON   Turn cursor on.

_GCURSOROFF   Turn cursor off.

These constants are defined in the header file *graph.h*.

RETURNS The return value is the previous value of the cursor state (i.e., it is either _GCURSOROFF or _GCURSORON depending on whether the cursor was off or on before calling this function).

COMMENTS In the graphics mode, when text is printed using the routine _outtext, you may sometimes wish to turn the cursor on. When prompting for some input, for example, you can get the user's attention to the prompt by having the cursor on.

EXAMPLE If you have an EGA with an enhanced color monitor, write a C program using _setvideomode to put the adapter in the graphics mode and then turn the cursor on and off to illustrate the effect.

```
#include <stdio.h>
#include <graph.h>
main()
{
    char str[80];
    _setvideomode(_ERESCOLOR);
    _displaycursor(_GCURSORON);
    _settextposition(1,1);
```

```
        _outtext("Cursor is on now. \
Enter a string and see how it feels:");
        gets(str);
        _displaycursor(_GCURSOROFF);
        _settextposition(2,1);
        _outtext("Now the cursor is off. \
Type a string to see the difference.");
        gets(str);
        _settextposition(3,1);
        _outtext("Hit any key to reset to original mode:");
        getch();
        _setvideomode(_DEFAULTMODE);
}
```

__getbkcolor

COMPATIBILITY	MSC 3	MSC 4	MSC 5	QC	TC	ANSI	UNIX V
			▲	▲	getbkcolor		

PURPOSE Use the *_getbkcolor* function to get the value of the current background color. The meaning of the returned value depends on the current video mode.

SYNTAX `long far _getbkcolor(void);`

EXAMPLE CALL `bcolor = _getbkcolor();   /* Retrieve background color */`

INCLUDES `#include <graph.h>`   For function declaration

DESCRIPTION The *_getbkcolor* function returns the pixel value for those pixels that are part of the background. The return value is interpreted according to the current video mode. In text modes, the background pixels contain a color number from the current palette. In graphics modes, the background pixels always contain a 0. For example, in the EGA, color number 4 in the default palette is red. So when the EGA is in text mode, the form *_setbkcolor(4L)* followed by a call to *_clearscreen* sets the screen background to red (see the example below). If you call *_getbkcolor* after this, the return value will be 4.

On the other hand, in the graphics mode, to set the background to red, we have to make a call of the form *_setbkcolor(_RED)*, where _RED is a predefined constant value (see the reference pages on *_setbkcolor*). The background immediately becomes red. A call to *_getbkcolor*, however, will not return the value of the constant _RED. It will, instead, return 0.

COMMON USES The *_getbkcolor* function is useful in determining the background color number in text modes.

Graphics Modes, Coordinates, and Attributes

RETURNS The _getbkcolor_ function returns a long integer that has the value of background pixels.

SEE ALSO _setbkcolor   To change the current background color

EXAMPLES Suppose you are in a text mode. Set a new background color by calling _setbkcolor_ and make it visible by calling _clearscreen_. Now call _getbkcolor_ to check the current background color.

```
#include <stdio.h>
#include <graph.h>
/* Need a "long" constant for _setbkcolor   */
#define RED 4L
main()
{
    long bcolor;      /* for current background color */
    _setbkcolor(RED); /* Set background color to red */
    _clearscreen(_GCLEARSCREEN); /* make it effective*/
    bcolor = _getbkcolor(); /* Retrieve backgnd color*/
    printf("Current background color is: %d\n\n",
            bcolor);
    printf("Use the DOS command MODE CO80 to reset \
display\n");
}
```

Assuming an EGA environment, enter a high-resolution graphics mode and change the background color to blue by calling _setbkcolor_ (use the predefined _BLUE). Now call _getbkcolor_ to get the value and show it to the user. You will see that it is zero.

```
#include <stdio.h>
#include <graph.h>
main()
{
    long bcolor;
    char buffer[80];
/* Enter hi-resolution graphics mode on EGA */
    if (_setvideomode(_ERESCOLOR) == 0)
    {
/* Error setting mode */
        printf("Mode not supported by hardware\n");
        exit(0);
    }
/* Set background to _BLUE, then get value */
    _setbkcolor(_BLUE);
    bcolor = _getbkcolor();
```

_getbkcolor

```
    _settextposition(1,1);
    _outtext("Demonstrating _getbkcolor\n");
    sprintf(buffer,"Current background color is: %d",
            bcolor);
    _settextposition(2,1);
    _outtext(buffer);

/* Restore original mode */
/* Give user a chance to see the result */
    _settextposition(40,1);
    _outtext("Hit any key to exit:");
    getch();
    _setvideomode(_DEFAULTMODE);
}
```

__getcolor

COMPATIBILITY	MSC 3	MSC 4	MSC 5	QC	TC	ANSI	UNIX V
			▲	▲	getcolor		

PURPOSE Use the _getcolor_ function to obtain the current color number. The current color can be set by calling _setcolor_.

SYNTAX `short far _getcolor(void);`

EXAMPLE CALL `current_color = _getcolor();`

INCLUDES `#include <graph.h>` For function declaration

DESCRIPTION The _getcolor_ function is used to get back the current color number used by all line-drawing and fill routines. Until a color is set, the default value is the highest numbered color from the current palette (see the tutorial for an explanation of palettes).

COMMON USES The _getcolor_ function gets the current color value and saves it so that it may be restored to its original value before exiting the program.

RETURNS The _getcolor_ function returns the current color number.

SEE ALSO `_setcolor` To change to a new color

EXAMPLE Get the current color and draw a line to show what color it is. Then change to a new color and verify that the change occurred by calling _getcolor_.

Graphics Modes, Coordinates, and Attributes

```c
#include <stdio.h>
#include <graph.h>
#define RED  4     /* Color number 4 is red  */

main()
{
    int i;
    short y = 60;
    char buffer[80];
/* Enter hi-resolution graphics mode on EGA */
    if (_setvideomode(_ERESCOLOR) != 0)
    {
        _settextposition(1,1);
        _outtext("Demonstrating _getcolor");
/* Get current color number */
        sprintf(buffer,"Current color: %d",
                _getcolor());
        _settextposition(2,1);
        _outtext(buffer);
        _moveto(0,y);
        _lineto(500,y);
        y += 40;
/* Select a new color and verify by calling _getcolor */
        _setcolor(RED);
        sprintf(buffer,"New color: %d (should be 4)",
                _getcolor());
        _settextposition(6,1);
        _outtext(buffer);
        _moveto(0,y);
        _lineto(500,y);
/* Restore original mode */
/* Give user a chance to see the result */
        _settextposition(40,1);
        _outtext("Hit any key to exit:");
        getch();
        _setvideomode(_DEFAULTMODE);
    }
    else
    {
/* Error setting mode */
        printf("Mode not supported by hardware\n");
    }
}
```

_getcolor

__getfillmask

COMPATIBILITY	MSC 3	MSC 4	MSC 5	QC	TC	ANSI	UNIX V
			▲	▲	getfillpattern		

PURPOSE Use *_getfillmask* to retrieve the 8 bytes that define the current 8×8 mask used by the routines *_floodfill, _rectangle, _ellipse,* and *_pie* that fill an area with the current color. (See the description of *_setfillmask* for an explanation of how the fill mask is used.)

SYNTAX `unsigned char far * far _getfillmask(unsigned char far *fillmask);`

`unsigned char far *fillmask;`   8×8 bit pattern that determines how the filled area looks

EXAMPLE CALL `p_mask = _getfillmask(current_mask);`

INCLUDES `#include <graph.h>`   For function declaration

DESCRIPTION The *_getfillmask* function is used to retrieve the 8×8 pattern of bits that serves as the current mask to be used by the routines *_floodfill, _rectangle, _ellipse,* and *_pie* to fill an area with the current color.
     The fill pattern is returned in eight characters whose address is provided to *_getfillmask* in the argument *fillmask*. The reference page on *_setfillmask* explains how to interpret the fill mask.

COMMON USES This function gets and saves the current fill mask so that the mask can be restored to its original value before exiting a graphics routine.

RETURNS If no mask is present, *_getfillmask* returns a NULL.

COMMENTS If you switch fill masks in a graphics routine, it is a good idea first to use *_getfillmask* to retrieve the current mask so that you can restore the mask to normal before returning from the routine.

SEE ALSO `_setfillmask`   To define a new fill mask

EXAMPLE Write a C program to obtain the current fill mask by using the *_getfillmask* function. Then alter the mask and verify that this has indeed happened by calling *_getfillmask* again.

```
#include <stdio.h>
#include <graph.h>
#define RED  4     /* Color number 4 is red */
/* Define a fill mask */
unsigned char fillmask[8] =
    { 1, 3, 7, 0xf, 0x1f, 0x3f, 0x7f, 0xff },
    oldmask[8];  /* Placeholder for old fill mask */
```

 Graphics Modes, Coordinates, and Attributes

```
main()
{
    unsigned char far *p_mask;
    char buffer[80];
    int i;
    short color=0, x1=0, y1=60;
/* Assuming a system with EGA, enter hi-resolution
 * graphics mode
 */
    if (_setvideomode(_ERESCOLOR) != 0)
    {
        _setcolor(RED);
        _settextposition(1,1);
        _outtext("Illustrating _getfillmask:");
/* Get current fill mask */
        p_mask = _getfillmask(oldmask);
        if (p_mask == NULL)
        {
            _settextposition(2,1);
            _outtext("No fill mask defined");
        }
/* Define a new mask */
        _setfillmask(fillmask);
        p_mask = _getfillmask(oldmask);
        sprintf(buffer,
        "Current fill mask is: %x %x %x %x %x %x %x %x",
            oldmask[0],oldmask[1],oldmask[2],oldmask[3],
            oldmask[4],oldmask[5],oldmask[6],oldmask[7]);
        _settextposition(3,1);
        _outtext(buffer);
        _settextposition(4,1);
        _outtext("Here is how it looks:");
/* Draw filled rectangle with new fill style */
        _rectangle(_GFILLINTERIOR, x1, y1,
                    x1+100, y1+60);
/* Restore original mode */
/* Give user a chance to see the result */
        _settextposition(40,1);
        _outtext("Hit any key to exit:");
        getch();
        _setvideomode(_DEFAULTMODE);
    }
    else
    {
/* Error setting mode */
        printf("Mode not supported by hardware\n");
    }
}
```

__getfillmask

__getlinestyle

COMPATIBILITY	MSC 3	MSC 4	MSC 5	QC	TC	ANSI	UNIX V
			▲	▲	getlinesettings		

PURPOSE Use *__getlinestyle* to retrieve the 16-bit mask used by the routines *__lineto* and *__rectangle* when drawing straight lines. The mask controls how the line looks.

SYNTAX
```
unsigned short far _getlinestyle(void);
```

EXAMPLE CALL
```
line_style = _getlinestyle();
```

INCLUDES
```
#include <graph.h>
```
For function declaration

DESCRIPTION The *__getlinestyle* function is used to get back the 16-bit unsigned integer that determines the appearance of lines drawn by the routines *__lineto* and *__rectangle*. The line style represented by the mask determines whether the line is solid or dashed and if dashed, what the pattern of the dashes is. The reference page on *__setlinestyle* explains how the mask is used.

COMMON USES The *__getlinestyle* function gets the current mask used by line-drawing routines and saves it before setting up a new mask. In that way, before exiting, the line style can be reset to its original value.

SEE ALSO
```
_setlinestyle
```
To change to a new line style

EXAMPLE Get the current line style and draw a line to show how it looks. Then change to a new line style, and verify that the change occurred by calling *__getlinestyle*.

```
#include <stdio.h>
#include <graph.h>
#define RED  4      /* Color number 4 is red */

main()
{
        int i;
        short y = 60, linemask = 0x3f;
        char buffer[80];
/* Enter hi-resolution graphics mode on EGA */
        if (_setvideomode(_ERESCOLOR) != 0)
        {
            _settextposition(1,1);
            _outtext("Demonstrating _getlinestyle");
/* Set up red as the current color */
            _setcolor(RED);
```

 Graphics Modes, Coordinates, and Attributes

```
/* Get current line style */
            sprintf(buffer,"Current line style: %x", _getlinestyle());
            _settextposition(2,1);
            _outtext(buffer);
            _moveto(0,y);
            _lineto(500,y);
            y += 40;
/* Select a new line style and verify by calling _getlinestyle */
            _setlinestyle(linemask);
            sprintf(buffer,"New line style: %x", _getlinestyle());
            _settextposition(6,1);
            _outtext(buffer);
            _moveto(0,y);
            _lineto(500,y);
/* Restore original mode */
/* Give user a chance to see the result */
            _settextposition(40,1);
            _outtext("Hit any key to exit:");
            getch();
            _setvideomode(_DEFAULTMODE);
        }
        else
        {
/* Error setting mode */
            printf("Specified mode not supported by hardware\n");
        }
}
```

__getlogcoord

COMPATIBILITY	MSC 3	MSC 4	MSC 5	QC	TC	ANSI	UNIX V
			▲	▲			

PURPOSE Use _getlogcoord to convert from physical coordinates to logical ones.

SYNTAX struct xycoord far _getlogcoord(short x, short y);

short x, y;   The physical x and y coordinates of the point on the screen whose
                location in the logical coordinate system is returned

EXAMPLE CALL xy_logical = _getlogcoord(x_physical, y_physical);

INCLUDES #include <graph.h>   For function declaration and definition of the structure
                                    xycoord

DESCRIPTION The *_getlogcoord* function returns the logical coordinates of the pixel whose physical location is at (*x,y*). See *_setlogcoord* for a brief description of physical and logical coordinates.

COMMON USES The drawing routines in the graphics package, such as *_moveto, _lineto, _arc, _ellipse, _pie*, and *_rectangle*, accept arguments in logical coordinates. You can use *_getlogcoord* to find the logical equivalent of a physical coordinate so that you can pass the coordinates to one of the drawing routines.

RETURNS The *_getlogcoord* function returns the logical coordinates of the specified pixel in a structure of type *xycoord*, which is declared in the header file *graph.h* as shown below.

```
struct xycoord      /* Structure for pixel coordinates */
{
    short xcoord;   /* x-coordinate */
    short ycoord;   /* y-coordinate */
};
```

SEE ALSO _getphyscoord   To convert logical coordinates to physical

EXAMPLE In a graphics mode, call *_setlogorg* to move the logical origin to the physical point (75,50). Then call *_getlogcoord* for the same physical point, and verify that the returned logical coordinates are indeed (0,0). You may also want to check that the logical coordinates of the physical point (0,0) are now (−75,−50).

```
#include <stdio.h>
#include <graph.h>
/* Yellow is 14 in EGA's default palette */
#define YELLOW 14
main()
{
    char buffer[80];
    struct xycoord logcoord;
/* Assume an EGA environment */
    if (_setvideomode(_ERESCOLOR) == 0)
    {
        printf("Not EGA environment\n");
        exit(0);
    }
    _settextposition(1,1);
    _outtext("Demonstrating _getlogcoord");
    _setlogorg(75,50);
    _setcolor(YELLOW);
    _setpixel(0,0);    /* Highlight new logical origin */
/* Verify that physical point (75,50) is logical (0,0)*/
```

 Graphics Modes, Coordinates, and Attributes

```
        logcoord = _getlogcoord(75,50);
        sprintf(buffer,"Physical point (75,50) is logical \
(%d,%d)", logcoord.xcoord, logcoord.ycoord);
        _settextposition(2,1);
        _outtext(buffer);
/* Also, physical (0,0) is at logical (-75,-50) */
        logcoord = _getlogcoord(0,0);
        sprintf(buffer,"Physical point (0,0) is logical \
(%d,%d)", logcoord.xcoord, logcoord.ycoord);
        _settextposition(3,1);
        _outtext(buffer);
/* Wait for user to hit a key, then reset everything */
        _settextposition(25,1);
        _outtext("Hit any key to reset mode and exit:");
        getch();
        _setvideomode(_DEFAULTMODE);
}
```

__getphyscoord

COMPATIBILITY	MSC 3	MSC 4	MSC 5	QC	TC	ANSI	UNIX V
			▲	▲			

PURPOSE Use _getphyscoord to convert from logical coordinates to physical ones.

SYNTAX `struct xycoord far _getphyscoord(short x, short y);`

`short x, y;` The logical x and y coordinates of the point on the screen whose location in the physical coordinate system is returned

EXAMPLE CALL `xy_physical = _getphyscoord(x_logical, y_logical);`

INCLUDES `#include <graph.h>` For function declaration and definition of the structure *xycoord*

DESCRIPTION The _getphyscoord function returns the physical coordinates of the pixel that is at the point (x,y) in the logical coordinate system.
   The physical coordinate axes (with the origin at the upper left corner, the x-axis extending to the right and the y-axis going down) are fixed on the display screen, whereas the origin of the logical coordinate system can be moved around by calling _setlogorg.

COMMON USES The drawing routines _moveto, _lineto, _arc, _ellipse, _pie, and _rectangle accept arguments in logical coordinates. The origin of the logical coordinate system is, however, specified in physical coordinates. If you want to set the origin of the logical coordinate system to the upper left corner of a rectangle, you first have to get the physical coordinate of that point by using _getphyscoord.

RETURNS   The _getphyscoord function returns the physical coordinates of the specified pixel in a structure of type *xycoord*, which is declared in the header file *graph.h* as shown below.

```
struct xycoord          /* Structure for pixel coordinates */
{
    short xcoord;       /* x-coordinate */
    short ycoord;       /* y-coordinate */
};
```

SEE ALSO   _getlogcoord   To convert physical coordinates to logical

EXAMPLE   If you have display hardware that can support graphics, set the video mode to graphics and relocate the logical origin to the physical point (75,50) by calling _setlogorg. Then call _getphyscoord for the logical origin (0,0), and verify that the returned logical coordinates are indeed (75,50).

```
#include <stdio.h>
#include <graph.h>
/* Yellow is 14 in EGA's default palette */
#define YELLOW 14
main()
{
    char buffer[80];
    struct xycoord physcoord;
/* Assume an EGA environment */
    if (_setvideomode(_ERESCOLOR) == 0)
    {
        printf("Not EGA environment\n");
        exit(0);
    }
    _settextposition(1,1);
    _outtext("Demonstrating _getphyscoord");
    _setlogorg(75,50);
    _setcolor(YELLOW);
    _setpixel(0,0); /* Highlight new logical origin */
/* Verify that logical origin is physical (75,50)    */
    physcoord = _getphyscoord(0,0);
    sprintf(buffer,"Logical (0,0) is physical (%d,%d)",
            physcoord.xcoord, physcoord.ycoord);
    _settextposition(2,1);
    _outtext(buffer);
    _settextposition(3,1);
    _outtext("It should be (75,50)");
```

 Graphics Modes, Coordinates, and Attributes

```
/* Wait for user to hit a key, then reset everything */
    _settextposition(25,1);
    _outtext("Hit any key to reset mode and exit:");
    getch();
    _setvideomode(_DEFAULTMODE);
}
```

__getvideoconfig

COMPATIBILITY	MSC 3	MSC 4	MSC 5	QC	TC	ANSI	UNIX V
			▲	▲	detectgraph		

PURPOSE Use _getvideoconfig to get information about the current graphics environment. Values of parameters such as maximum number of pixels along x and y directions, number of colors, are returned in a structure of type *videoconfig*, which is defined in the file *graph.h*. When writing a graphics application, you can call _getvideoconfig to determine, for example, the number of columns and rows of text that the monitor can support in its text mode.

SYNTAX
```
struct videoconfig far * far _getvideoconfig(struct
                                    videoconfig far *gr_info);
```

```
struct videoconfig far *gr_info;
```
Pointer to structure that holds the information about the graphics environment

EXAMPLE CALL `_getvideoconfig(&gr_info);`

INCLUDES `#include <graph.h>` For function declaration and definition of the structure of type *videoconfig*

DESCRIPTION The _getvideoconfig function returns information about the graphics environment in a structure of type *videoconfig*. The C declaration shown below describes the layout of this structure and identifies the pieces of information returned by _getvideoconfig.

```
struct videoconfig {
    short numxpixels;    /* number of pixels along X axis   */
    short numypixels;    /* number of pixels along Y axis   */
    short numtextcols;   /* number of text columns available */
    short numtextrows;   /* number of text rows available   */
    short numcolors;     /* number of actual colors         */
    short bitsperpixel;  /* number of bits per pixel        */
    short numvideopages; /* number of available video pages */
    short mode;          /* current video mode              */
    short adapter;       /* active display adapter          */
```

```
    short monitor;      /* active display monitor          */
    short memory;       /* adapter video memory in K bytes */

};
```

You are responsible for declaring this structure in your program (so that storage is allocated for the structure) and for providing a 32-bit far pointer to the structure as the argument *gr_info*.

For most of the fields in the structure, their meaning is obvious from the comments in the declaration of the structure. The value of the fields *adapter*, *mode*, and *monitor* can be intrepreted by comparing each with the mnemonic constants shown in Table 17-1 and in Tables 17-8 and 17-9 below.

Table 17-8. *Interpreting Adapter Value*

Adapter	Interpretation
_MDPA	Monochrome Display Adapter
_CGA	Color Graphics Adapter
_EGA	Enhanced Graphics Adapter
_MCGA	MultiColor Graphics Array
_VGA	Video Graphics Array
_HGC	Hercules Graphics Card

Table 17-9. *Interpreting Monitor Value*

Monitor	Interpretation
_MONO	Monochrome monitor
_COLOR	Color monitor (or Enhanced monitor in CGA mode)
_ENHCOLOR	Enhanced color monitor
_ANALOG	Analog monitor

COMMON USES This function is useful when writing a robust graphics application program. By using *_getvideoconfig* you can get several crucial details about the graphics card and the monitor and use this information to automatically configure your application. Otherwise, your program has to ask the user to enter the information in some way or, worse, you have to assume default values for them.

RETURNS The return value is the pointer to the structure of type *videoconfig* that contains the return information. This is the pointer you supplied in the argument *gr_info*.

SEE ALSO _setvideomode   To select a particular video mode

Graphics Modes, Coordinates, and Attributes

EXAMPLE   Use _getvideoconfig to determine the current display adapter and monitor present on the PC.

```c
#include <stdio.h>
#include <graph.h>
main()
{
    struct videoconfig gr_info, far *p_gr;
/* Get the current video configuration. */
    p_gr = _getvideoconfig(&gr_info);
    printf("This PC has:\n");
/* You can access the structure using the returned
 * pointer
 */
    switch(p_gr->adapter)
    {
      case _MDPA: printf("Monochrome Display Adapter");
                break;
      case _CGA:  printf("Color Graphics Adapter");
                break;
      case _EGA:  printf("Enhanced Graphics Adapter");
                break;
      case _MCGA: printf("Multicolor Graphics Array");
                break;
      case _VGA:  printf("Video Graphics Array");
                break;
    }
    printf(" and ");
/* Or, you can access the structure directly */
    switch(gr_info.monitor)
    {
      case _MONO:     printf("Monochrome Monitor\n");
                    break;
      case _COLOR:    printf(
    "Color Monitor (or Enhanced monitor in CGA mode)\n");
                    break;
      case _ENHCOLOR: printf("Enhanced Color Monitor\n");
                    break;
      case _ANALOG:   printf("Analog Monitor\n");
                    break;
    }
}
```

_getvideoconfig

__remapallpalette

COMPATIBILITY	MSC 3	MSC 4	MSC 5	QC	TC	ANSI	UNIX V
			▲	▲	setallpalette		

PURPOSE Use _remapallpalette in an EGA or VGA environment to redefine how the values that a pixel can take are associated with colors displayed on the screen. Thus, this function redefines the entire EGA or VGA palette. Once the pixel values are redefined, all existing text and graphics will change to the new colors immediately.

SYNTAX `short far _remapallpalette(long far *colors);`

`long far *color;`   Array of colors to be assigned sequentially to the pixel values (use predefined constants)

EXAMPLE CALL `_remapallpalette(&new_color_table);`

INCLUDES `#include <graph.h>`   For function declaration and the definition of color constants

DESCRIPTION Applicable only in EGA and VGA environments, the _remapallpalette associates the colors specified in the array of long integers *colors* with pixel values. The colors are assigned to the pixel values sequentially, starting with the pixel value 0 and continuing to the maximum value a pixel can take in that graphics mode. Thus, the array of long integers must have at least as many elements as the number of colors that can be simultaneously displayed on the hardware in the current graphics mode. For example, on the 16-color graphics mode on the VGA or the EGA, there must be 16 colors in the array specified by the argument *colors*.

The Microsoft C 5.1 graphics library expects the colors stored in the long integer array *colors* to be of a specific form (see the tutorial section). A set of predefined constants for the colors (see Table 17-2) appears in the header file *graph.h*. Their use is illustrated in the example below.

COMMON USES The _remapallpalette and its companion _remappalette functions are useful on EGA and VGA systems for designing user interfaces that can take advantage of the ability to quickly swap colors. For example, you can highlight selected menu items by redefining the displayed color from one that is subdued to one that really catches the eye.

RETURNS If the hardware is EGA or VGA, the _remapallpalette function returns a 0. Otherwise, it returns a −1 indicating an error.

SEE ALSO `_remappalette`   To redefine a single pixel value

EXAMPLE If you have EGA or VGA hardware, set the display to a graphics mode. Display 16 rectangles, each filled with a color from the current palette, to illustrate the

 Graphics Modes, Coordinates, and Attributes

meaning of each pixel value in the default palette (black for 0, blue for 1, and so on). When the user hits a key, call _remapallpalette_ to redefine the entire palette. Exchange the positions of cyan and black, and red and blue. The background immediately becomes cyan (because pixel value 0 is always background) and the red rectangle swaps places with the blue one.

```
#include <stdio.h>
#include <graph.h>
/* Define new color map using defined constants from
 * graph.h. Notice that we have swapped red with blue
 * and cyan with black. So the background will become
 * cyan now.
 */
long newcolormap[] =
    {_CYAN, _RED, _GREEN, _BLACK, _BLUE, _MAGENTA,
     _BROWN, _WHITE, _GRAY, _LIGHTBLUE, _LIGHTGREEN,
     _LIGHTCYAN, _LIGHTRED, _LIGHTMAGENTA,
     _LIGHTYELLOW, _BRIGHTWHITE};
main()
{
    int i;
    short color=0, x1=0, y1=60, x2=100, y2=70;
/* Enter hi-resolution graphics mode on EGA */
    if (_setvideomode(_ERESCOLOR) == 0)
    {
/* Error setting mode */
        printf("Not EGA hardware\n");
        exit(0);
    }
/* Display rectangles filled with colors from current
 * palette
 */
    _settextposition(1,1);
    _outtext(
"Remapping the color palette using _remappalette");
/* Draw the filled rectangles */
    for (i=1; i<=8; i++)
    {
        color = 2*i-1;
        _setcolor(color);
        _rectangle(_GFILLINTERIOR, x1, y1, x2, y2);
        _setcolor(color+1);
        _rectangle(_GFILLINTERIOR,
                   x1+150, y1, x2+150, y2);
        y1 += 20;
        y2 += 20;
    }
/* Now remap entire palette -- swap red with blue, cyan
```

_remapallpalette

```
      * with black
      */
        _settextposition(3,1);
        _outtext(
          "Hit any key to remap the entire palette:");
        getch();
/* Display changes immediately */
        _remapallpalette(newcolormap);
/* Restore original mode */
/* Give user a chance to see the result */
        _settextposition(24,1);
        _outtext("Hit any key to exit:");
        getch();
        _setvideomode(_DEFAULTMODE);
  }
```

__remappalette

COMPATIBILITY	MSC 3	MSC 4	MSC 5	QC	TC	ANSI	UNIX V
			▲	▲	setpalette		

PURPOSE Use *_remappalette* in an EGA or VGA environment to redefine how a specific value contained in a pixel is associated with a color displayed on the screen. Thus this function redefines a single pixel value in EGA or VGA palette. For example, since a pixel value of 0 always signifies background, you can change the background color by calling *_remappalette* to redefine color number 0 (see the example below).

SYNTAX `long far _remappalette(short pixel_value, long color);`

`short pixel_value;`   Pixel value to be redefined

`long color;`   Color to be associated with the pixel value (use predefined constants)

EXAMPLE CALL `_remappalette(0, _CYAN);   /* Alter pixel value 0 to cyan */`

INCLUDES `#include <graph.h>`   For function declaration and the definition of color constants

DESCRIPTION The *_remappalette* function, available only in EGA and VGA environments, associates the color specified in the long integer argument *color* with the pixel value *pixel_value*. The maximum possible value of the argument *pixel_value* depends on the number of colors that can be simultaneously displayed in the current graphics mode. For example, on the 16-color graphics mode on the VGA or the EGA, the pixel value can be from 0 to 15.

The Microsoft C 5.1 graphics library requires the color given in *color* to

Graphics Modes, Coordinates, and Attributes

be of a specific form. Each color is defined by three bytes: the least significant byte contains the intensity of the red component, the next byte has the intensity of green, and the most significant byte is for the intensity of blue. A set of predefined constants (see Table 17-2) are given in the header file *graph.h*.

When a pixel value is redefined, existing text and graphics that are using the pixel value show the new color immediately.

COMMON USES The *_remappalette* and its companion *_remapallpalette* are useful on EGA and VGA systems for special effects.

RETURNS If the hardware is EGA or VGA, the *_remappalette* function returns a long integer containing the previous color associated with the redefined pixel value. If the hardware is of the wrong type, *_remappalette* returns a −1, indicating an error.

SEE ALSO _remapallpalette To redefine all possible pixel values in the current palette

EXAMPLE If you have either EGA or VGA hardware, set the display to a graphics mode. Set the text color to 1 and display some text. Now change the background and the text colors by redefining pixel values 0 and 1 by calling *_remappalette*.

```
#include <stdio.h>
#include <graph.h>
#define BLUE 1  /* Blue is 1 in EGA's default palette */
/* Define array of colors using defined constants from
 * graph.h
 */
long colors[] =
    {_BLACK, _BLUE, _GREEN, _CYAN, _RED, _MAGENTA,
     _BROWN, _WHITE, _GRAY, _LIGHTBLUE, _LIGHTGREEN,
     _LIGHTCYAN, _LIGHTRED, _LIGHTMAGENTA, _LIGHTYELLOW,
     _BRIGHTWHITE};
main()
{
    char buffer[80];
    int i=0;
/* Assume an EGA environment */
    if (_setvideomode(_ERESCOLOR) == 0)
    {
        printf("Not EGA environment\n");
        exit(0);
    }
    _settextcolor(1);
    _settextposition(1,1);
    _outtext("Demonstrating _remappalette");
/* Loop through several colors for pixel
 * values 0 and 1
 */
```

_remappalette

```
        _settextposition(2,1);
        _outtext("Hit any key to go on, 'q' to exit");
        while(1)
        {
            if (getch() == 'q')
            {
/* Reset environment */
                _setvideomode(_DEFAULTMODE);
                exit(0);
            }
/* Alter pixel value 0 and 1 */
            _remappalette(0, colors[i%16]);
            _remappalette(1, colors[(i+2)%16]);
/* Select next color from array */
            i++;
        }
}
```

__selectpalette

COMPATIBILITY	MSC 3	MSC 4	MSC 5	QC	TC	ANSI	UNIX V
			▲	▲			

PURPOSE Use the _selectpalette function to activate one of up to four predefined palettes when using the CGA or the EGA in _MRES4COLOR and _MRESNOCOLOR video modes (see the tutorial section).

SYNTAX `short far _selectpalette(short palette_number);`

`short palette_number;`   Palette number being selected

EXAMPLE CALL `_selectpalette(0);`   `/* Select CGA palette 0 */`

INCLUDES `#include <graph.h>`   For function declaration

DESCRIPTION Applicable only in the _MRES4COLOR and _MRESNOCOLOR video modes, the _selectpalette function selects the predefined palette number specified in the argument *palette_number* as the current palette from which colors are displayed. When a new palette is selected, all text and graphics change to the colors in that palette immediately.

The video modes _MRES4COLOR and _MRESNOCOLOR are supported by the CGA and the EGA. Use _MRES4COLOR with color displays. It provides four palettes, each with four colors (color number 0 in each palette is the background color and can be separately selected). Colors 1 through 3 of these four palettes are shown in Table 17-4. Use _MRESNOCOLOR with

Graphics Modes, Coordinates, and Attributes

monochrome displays to produce shades of gray. When used with color displays this mode also allows a set of palettes. With an IBM EGA and an enhanced color display, both _MRES4COLOR and _MRESNOCOLOR modes provide the same palettes as the ones shown in Table 17-4. The palettes may differ on EGA clones, however, because of the differences in emulating the CGA modes in the EGA ROM.

RETURNS The _selectpalette_ function returns the previous palette number.

SEE ALSO _setvideomode   To set the display hardware to a specific mode

EXAMPLE If you have either CGA or EGA hardware, set the display to the graphics mode _MRES4COLOR. Display three rectangles each filled with colors 1 through 3 from palette 0. Now cycle through the palettes by calling _selectpalette_, letting the user see the color selections from each palette displayed on the screen. Exit when the user hits a 'q'.

```
#include <stdio.h>
#include <graph.h>
main()
{
        int i;
        short palette=0;
        short x1=0, y1=60, x2=100, y2=70;
/* Enter medium resolution graphics in EGA (emulating CGA) */
        if (_setvideomode(_MRES4COLOR) == 0)
        {
            printf("Not appropriate hardware\n"); /* Error setting
mode */
            exit(0);
        }
/* Display rectangles filled with colors from current palette */
        _settextposition(1,1);
        _outtext("Color palettes using _selectpalette");
        _selectpalette(0);              /* Use palette 0 first */
        for (i=1; i<=3; i++)  /* Draw three filled rectangles */
        {
            _setcolor(i);
            _rectangle(_GFILLINTERIOR, x1, y1, x2, y2);
            y1 += 20;
            y2 += 20;
        }
/* Let user go through the palettes and see the effect */
        _settextposition(3,1);
        _outtext("Hit 'q' to exit, else change palette:");
        while(1)
        {
            if(getch() == 'q')
```

_selectpalette

```
                  {
                        _setvideomode(_DEFAULTMODE);    /* Restore mode */
                        exit(0);
                  }
                  palette++;
                  _selectpalette(palette % 4);   /* Palettes in 0 to 3 */
            }
      }
```

__setactivepage

COMPATIBILITY	MSC 3	MSC 4	MSC 5	QC	TC	ANSI	UNIX V
			▲	▲	setactivepage		

PURPOSE Use the *_setactivepage* function in EGA or VGA graphics modes and in the text modes to select the current page or portion of display memory where graphics and text operations are performed. This function only works when the adapter has enough video memory to support multiple pages.

SYNTAX `short far _setactivepage(short page_number);`

`short page_number;` The page number to be used for all further text and graphics operations

EXAMPLE CALL `_setactivepage(1);`

INCLUDES `#include <graph.h>` For function declaration

DESCRIPTION The *_setactivepage* function selects the page specified in the argument *page_number* as the current active page. This determines the section of video memory where text and graphics operations will be performed.

In this context, a page is a chunk of storage in the video memory that can hold the contents of a screenful in the current video mode. For example, if the video adapter has enough memory to hold eight screensful of text, you can have eight pages in the text mode. In the graphics mode, on the other hand, the same adapter might have only enough memory for two screensful, giving two graphics pages. While most adapters provide for multiple pages in text modes, only EGA and VGA with 256 K of video memory support two pages in the high-resolution graphics modes.

Just as the current active page determines the portion of video memory where results of text and graphics operations are stored, the current "visual" page determines the portion of video memory that is actually mapped to the display screen. Use *_setvisualpage* to select the page being displayed. By default, page 0 is used as both active and visual page.

Graphics Modes, Coordinates, and Attributes

The number of video pages available in the current mode can be determined by calling _getvideoconfig.

COMMON USES Provided you have enough video memory for multiple pages, the _setactivepage function is useful for preparing a page in display memory while another is shown to the user. This can speed up the display or allow for smoother animation.

RETURNS The _setactivepage function returns the page number of the previous active page. If it fails, it returns a negative value.

SEE ALSO _setvisualpage   To select the page being displayed

EXAMPLE If you have an EGA with 256 K of graphics memory, you can have two graphics pages, each capable of storing one 640×350, 16-color display screen. Set the adapter to the high-resolution graphics mode. Then draw a red rectangle on page 0, and while this is displayed, use _setactivepage to select page 1 and draw a yellow ellipse on the page. Next, let the user flip through the two pages (use the _setvisualpage function).

```
#include <stdio.h>
#include <graph.h>
#define RED     4
#define YELLOW 14
main()
{
    int i;
    short page = 0;
/* Assuming EGA with 256 KB graphics memory, enter
 * high-resolution mode
 */
    if (_setvideomode(_ERESCOLOR) == 0)
    {
/* Error setting mode */
        printf("Not appropriate hardware\n");
        exit(0);
    }
/* Default active page is page 0. Draw a red rectangle
 * in page 0.
 */
    _settextposition(1,1);
    _outtext("This is page 0");
    _setcolor(RED);
    _rectangle(_GFILLINTERIOR, 20, 50, 120, 100);
/* Now set active page to 1 and draw an ellipse there*/
    if(_setactivepage(1) < 0)
    {
        _setvideomode(_DEFAULTMODE);
```

_setactivepage

```
                    printf("Cannot support multiple pages\n");
                    exit(0);
        }
/* Draw a yellow ellipse on this page */
    _settextposition(1,1);
    _outtext("This is page 1");
    _setcolor(YELLOW);
    _ellipse(_GFILLINTERIOR, 20, 50, 120, 100);
    _setactivepage(0);
/* Let user alternate between the two pages and see the
 * effect
 */
    while(1)
    {
        _settextposition(3,1);
        _outtext(
    "Hit 'q' to exit, any other key to change page:");

        if(getch() == 'q')
        {
/* Restore mode */
            _setvideomode(_DEFAULTMODE);
            exit(0);
        }
        page++;
/* Select the other page as the visual page */
/* Page number must be between 0 and 1       */
        _setvisualpage(page & 1);
        _setactivepage(page & 1);
    }
}
```

__setbkcolor

COMPATIBILITY	MSC 3	MSC 4	MSC 5	QC	TC	ANSI	UNIX V
			▲	▲	setbkcolor		

PURPOSE Use the _setbkcolor function to select a new background color.

SYNTAX long far _setbkcolor(long color);

long color;   New color value

EXAMPLE CALL
```
_setbkcolor(4L);    /* Red background in text mode    */
_setbkcolor(_RED); /* Red background in graphics mode */
```

Graphics Modes, Coordinates, and Attributes

INCLUDES   #include <graph.h>   For function declaration and definition of color constants

DESCRIPTION   The _setbkcolor function is used to set the current background color to the value given in the long integer argument *color*. In the graphics mode the change is visible immediately. In other modes, it is necessary to clear the screen (see _clearscreen) to see the new background color. The method of specifying the color depends on the video mode.

In text modes, the background color is specified by a number from the current palette. In the EGA, for example, color number 4 in the default palette is red. So when the EGA is in text mode, a call of the form _setbkcolor(4L) followed by a call to _clearscreen sets the screen to red (see the example below). The method of specifying the new background color is different in graphics modes. In this case, a predefined mnemonic constant specifies the color. These constants are defined in *graph.h*, and listed in Table 17-2. Each color consists of 3 bytes. These bytes, from the least significant (rightmost) to the most significant (leftmost), represent the intensity of the red, green, and blue components of that color. Microsoft's graphics library takes care of displaying the background color properly for your graphics environment.

COMMON USES   The _setbkcolor function sets a new background color. In text modes, this color is also used by the _clearscreen function to clear the screen and fill it with the background color.

RETURNS   The _setbkcolor function returns a long integer that has the value of the previous background color.

COMMENTS   When the video adapter is in a graphics mode, the pixels in the graphics memory that are supposed to have the background color always contain zeroes—so the background color number is 0. But this pixel value is mapped to a specific color via the current palette. Some hardware, such as EGA and VGA, allows remapping of palettes, meaning that although black is the default color associated with a pixel value of zero, you could set any color to correspond to a zero pixel value. So during EGA and VGA graphics, you can change the background color by using the _remappalette function to redefine the meaning of a zero pixel value. See the description of _remappalette for an explanation of remapping of palettes. The entire palette can be remapped by _remapallpalette.

SEE ALSO   _getbkcolor   To retrieve the value of the current background color

_remappalette   Another way of altering background color in EGA and VGA
environments

_selectpalette   To set background color in the _MRES4COLOR and
_MRESNOCOLR video modes (see _setvideomode)

EXAMPLE   In EGA's text mode, call _setbkcolor to set the background to red (color number 4 in the default palette). Call *_clearscreen* after setting the background color so that you can see the effect.

```
#include <stdio.h>
#include <graph.h>
/* Need a "long" constant for _setbkcolor */
#define RED 4L
main()
{
/* Set background color to red */
    _setbkcolor(RED);
    _clearscreen(_GCLEARSCREEN);
/* The screen should be red now */
    printf(
"Use the DOS command MODE CO80 to reset display\n");
}
```

Assuming an EGA environment, enter the high-resolution graphics mode and change the background color to blue by calling *_setbkcolor*.

```
#include <stdio.h>
#include <graph.h>

main()
{
  long lastcolor;
    char buffer[80];
/* Enter hi-resolution graphics mode on EGA */
    if (_setvideomode(_ERESCOLOR) != 0)
    {
/* First set background to _RED */
        _setbkcolor(_RED);
        _settextposition(1,1);
        _outtext("Hit a key to continue");
        getch();          /* Read a key -- to pause */
/* Now set background to _BLUE and get last color   */
        lastcolor = _setbkcolor(_BLUE);
        _settextposition(1,1);
        _outtext("Demonstrating _setbkcolor\n");
/* Report previous value so that we can check against
 * table in graph.h
 */
        sprintf(buffer,"Previous background color was: \
%d", lastcolor);
        _settextposition(2,1);
        _outtext(buffer);
```

 Graphics Modes, Coordinates, and Attributes

```
/* Restore original mode */
/* Give user a chance to see the result */
        _settextposition(40,1);
        _outtext("Hit any key to exit:");
        getch();
        _setvideomode(_DEFAULTMODE);
    }
    else

    {
/* Error setting mode */
        printf("Mode not supported by hardware\n");
    }
}
```

__setcliprgn

COMPATIBILITY	MSC 3	MSC 4	MSC 5	QC	TC	ANSI	UNIX V
			▲	▲			

PURPOSE Use _setcliprgn to define a rectangular region of the screen as the clipping region for graphics (i.e., any graphics falling outside this region will be cut off).

SYNTAX `void far _setcliprgn(short x1, short y1, short x2, short y2);`

`short x1, y1;`   Upper left corner of clipping region in physical coordinates

`short x2, y2;`   Lower right corner of clipping region in physical coordinates

EXAMPLE CALL `_setcliprgn(100, 50, 300, 150);`

INCLUDES `#include <graph.h>`   For function declaration

DESCRIPTION The _setcliprgn function defines an area of the screen as the clipping region for all graphics operations. The area is specified in terms of the physical coordinates (see the tutorial section) of the upper left hand corner (*x1, y1*) and that of the lower right corner (*x2, y2*). Unlike _setviewport, the _setcliprgn function leaves the logical coordinate system unchanged.

COMMON USES The _setcliprgn function can be used to ensure that graphics output is confined to a fixed area of the screen.

COMMENTS The _setviewport function also defines a clipping region for graphics. In ad-

dition to this, *_setviewport* also moves the origin of the logical coordinate
system to the upper left corner of the clipping rectangle.

Use *_textwindow* to limit text output to a predefined area.

SEE ALSO

_setlogorg   To define a new logical origin

_setviewport   To define a clipping region and relocate the origin of the logical
                       coordinate system at the same time

_settextwindow   Analogous operation for text output

EXAMPLE   Put your graphics hardware into an appropriate mode, define a clipping region, and draw a filled ellipse to illustrate the clipping. Remember, unlike
_setviewport, *_setcliprgn* does not alter the origin of the logical coordinate
system.

```
#include <stdio.h>
#include <graph.h>
#define RED  4  /* For defining the current color */
main()
{
    if (_setvideomode(_ERESCOLOR) == 0)
    {
        printf("EGA hi-res mode not supported\n");
        exit(0);
    }
    _settextposition(1,1);
    _outtext("Demonstration of _setcliprgn:");
    _setcolor(RED); /* Set current color to red    */
/* Dashed lines for boundary */
    _setlinestyle(0xf0f);
/* A 200 x 200 clip region */
    _setcliprgn(0, 100, 200, 300);
/* Show boundary of region, compare with example
 * for_setviewport
 */
    _rectangle(_GBORDER,0,100,200,300);
/* Now draw an ellipse filled with current color    */
    _ellipse(_GFILLINTERIOR, 50, 150, 450, 550);
/* NOTE: when tested, ellipse didn't get filled!    */
/* Return to default mode when user strikes any key */
    _settextposition(4,1);
    _outtext(
      "Press any key to return to original mode:");
    getch();  /* A do-nothing read */
    _setvideomode(_DEFAULTMODE);
}
```

 Graphics Modes, Coordinates, and Attributes

__setcolor

COMPATIBILITY	MSC 3	MSC 4	MSC 5	QC	TC	ANSI	UNIX V
			▲	▲	setcolor		

PURPOSE Use _setcolor to select the default color to be used by all future calls to the drawing functions _arc, _ellipse, _lineto, _pie, _rectangle, and _setpixel.

SYNTAX `short far _setcolor(short color);`

`short color;`   Selected color number

EXAMPLE CALL `_setcolor(4);`

INCLUDES `#include <graph.h>`   For function declaration and definition of mode names

DESCRIPTION The _setcolor routine sets up the current color to the color number specified in the argument color. This color number is used as the default color by the _arc, _ellipse, _lineto, _pie, _rectangle, and _setpixel routines. The actual color displayed depends on the current palette.

Until a color has been set, these routines use the highest color number in the current palette (see _selectpalette and _remapallpalette to set the color palette).

There is no return value, but if the color number color specifies is out of the range of values allowed by the current palette, _setcolor sets the current color to the highest numbered color in the palette.

SEE ALSO `_remapallpalette`   To set up a color palette

`_selectpalette`   To use a predefined palette

EXAMPLE For a system with an EGA and an enhanced color monitor, write a C program that displays 16 rectangles, each filled with 1 color out of the 16 available for display. The lower 8 rectangles will be intensified versions of the upper 8.

```
#include <stdio.h>
#include <graph.h>
main()
{
    int i;
    short color=0, x1=0, y1=40, x2=100, y2=50;
/* Enter hi-resolution graphics mode on EGA */
    if (_setvideomode(_ERESCOLOR) != 0)
    {

/* Error setting mode */
```

```
        printf("Mode not supported by hardware\n");
        exit(0);
    }
    _settextposition(1,1);
    _outtext(
    "16 colors in 640x350 color graphics mode");
/* Draw a filled rectangle */
    for (i=1; i<=8; i++)
    {
        color = 2*i-1;
        _setcolor(color);
        _rectangle(_GFILLINTERIOR, x1, y1, x2, y2);
        _setcolor(color+1);
        _rectangle(_GFILLINTERIOR,
                        x1+150, y1, x2+150, y2);
        y1 += 20;
        y2 += 20;
    }
/* Restore original mode */
/* Give user a chance to see the result */
    _settextposition(2,1);
    _outtext("Hit any key to exit:");
    getch();
    _setvideomode(_DEFAULTMODE);
}
```

__setfillmask

COMPATIBILITY	MSC 3	MSC 4	MSC 5	QC	TC	ANSI	UNIX V
			▲	▲	setfillpattern		

PURPOSE Use _setfillmask to define a pattern that will be used as a mask by the _floodfill, _rectangle, _ellipse, and _pie routines, which fill an area with the current color. Until you define a fill mask, a solid fill pattern is used.

SYNTAX void far _setfillmask(unsigned char far *fillmask);

unsigned char far *fillmask;   8×8 bit pattern that determines how the filled area looks

EXAMPLE CALL unsigned char far mask1[] = {1, 3, 7, 0xf, 0x1f, 0x3f, 0x7f, 0xff};
_setfillmask(maks1);

INCLUDES #include <graph.h>   For function declaration

 Graphics Modes, Coordinates, and Attributes

DESCRIPTION The _setfillmask function defines an 8×8 pattern of bits as the current mask to be used by the routines _floodfill, _rectangle, _ellipse, and _pie.

The fill pattern is specified by the argument *fillmask*, which is a far pointer to an array of eight characters. Since each character has 8 bits, you can think of this array of bits as a model of an area on the screen, 8 pixels wide and 8 pixels tall, with the first character representing the the first row of the area. When filling an 8×8 area using the mask, those pixels that correspond to 0 bits are left untouched while the rest are filled with the current color. For areas larger than 8×8 pixels, the fill operation uses the mask on successive 8×8 blocks until the entire screen is covered. Thus a solid fill is specified when all eight characters contain the value FFh. This is the default value of the fill style in the graphics package. See the example below on how to specify other fill masks using this method.

COMMON USES This function is used to select different fill styles so that objects, such as slices of a pie chart, can be distinguished from one another.

COMMENTS If you switch fill masks in a graphics routine, it is a good idea first to retrieve the current mask with _getfillmask so that you can restore the style to normal before returning from the routine.

SEE ALSO _getfillmask   To determine the current fill mask

EXAMPLE Write a C program to illustrate some of the fill styles that can be created using the _setfillmask function. Since this is a self-contained program, there is no need to save and restore the old fill mask.

```c
#include <stdio.h>
#include <graph.h>
#define RED 4      /* Color number 4 is red */
/* Define the fill style masks */
unsigned char fillmask[4][8] =
{
/* First mask */
    1, 3, 7, 0xf, 0x1f, 0x3f, 0x7f, 0xff,
/* Mask 2    */
    0xf0, 0xf0, 0xf0, 0xf0, 0xf, 0xf, 0xf, 0xf,
/* Mask 3    */
    0xcc, 0x33, 0xcc, 0x33, 0xcc, 0x33, 0xcc, 0x33,
/* Mask 4    */
    0xc3, 0xc3, 0xc, 0xc, 0x30, 0x30, 0xc3, 0xc3
};
main()
{
    int i;
    short color=0, x1=0, y1=40;
/* Enter hi-resolution graphics mode on EGA */
```

__setfillmask

```
        if (_setvideomode(_ERESCOLOR) != 0)
        {
            _setcolor(RED);
            _settextposition(1,1);
            _outtext("Illustrating different fill styles:");
/* Draw filled rectangle with different fill styles */
            for (i=1; i<=2; i++)
            {
                _setfillmask(fillmask[2*i-2]);
                _rectangle(_GFILLINTERIOR,
                           x1, y1, x1+100, y1+60);
                _setfillmask(fillmask[2*i-1]);
                _rectangle(_GFILLINTERIOR,
                           x1+150, y1, x1+250, y1+60);
                y1 += 100;
            }
/* Restore original video mode         */
/* Give user a chance to see the result */
            _settextposition(40,1);
            _outtext("Hit any key to exit:");
            getch();
            _setvideomode(_DEFAULTMODE);
        }
        else
        {
/* Error setting mode */
            printf("Mode not supported by hardware\n");
        }
}
```

__setlinestyle

COMPATIBILITY	MSC 3	MSC 4	MSC 5	QC	TC	ANSI	UNIX V
			▲	▲	setlinestyle		

PURPOSE Use _setlinestyle to define a 16-bit mask that controls how dashed lines look. The mask is used by the routines _lineto and _rectangle.

SYNTAX `void far _setlinestyle(unsigned short linemask);`

`unsigned short linemask;`　　Bit pattern that determines how the line looks

EXAMPLE CALL `_setlinestyle(0x3ff);`

INCLUDES `#include <graph.h>`　　For function declaration

Graphics Modes, Coordinates, and Attributes

DESCRIPTION The _setlinestyle function is used to define the style of lines to be drawn by the routines _lineto and _rectangle. The style determines whether the line is solid or dashed and, if dashed, determines the pattern of the dashes.

The 16-bit argument *linemask* specifies the pattern to be repeated when drawing a line. Think of this mask as one representing a line segment 16 pixels long. If a bit in *linemask* is a 1, the corresponding pixel in that line gets painted with the current color (see _setcolor). If a bit is 0, the corresponding pixel is untouched. Note that a value of FFh for *linemask* means a solid line. This is the default value of the line style in the graphics package. The example below shows how to specify other line styles with this method.

COMMON USES This function is used to select different line styles so that overlapping graphs can be distinguished from one another.

COMMENTS If you switch line styles in a graphics routine, it is a good idea first to retrieve the current style using _getlinestyle so that you can restore the style to normal before returning from the routine.

SEE ALSO _getlinestyle   To determine the current line style

EXAMPLE Write a C program to illustrate some of the line styles that can be created using the _setlinestyle function. Since this is a self-contained program, there is no need to save and restore the old line style.

```
#include <stdio.h>
#include <graph.h>
#define RED  4      /* Color number 4 is red */
/* Define the line style masks */
short linemask[16] =
{1, 3, 7, 0xf, 0x1f, 0x3f, 0x7f, 0xff,
 0x1ff, 0x3ff, 0x7ff, 0xfff, 0x1fff, 0x3fff, 0x7fff,
 0xffff};
main()
{
    int i;
    short y = 30;
/* Enter hi-resolution graphics mode on EGA */
    if (_setvideomode(_ERESCOLOR) != 0)
    {
        _settextposition(1,1);
        _outtext("Demonstrating different line styles:");
/* Set up red as the current color */
        _setcolor(RED);
        for (i=0; i<16; i++)
        {
/* Select a line style from the array of style masks */
            _setlinestyle(linemask[i]);
            _moveto(0,y);
```

_setlinestyle

```
                _lineto(500,y);
                y += 10;
            }
/* Restore original mode */
/* Give user a chance to see the result */
            _settextposition(40,1);
            _outtext("Hit any key to exit:");
            getch();
            _setvideomode(_DEFAULTMODE);
        }
        else
        {
/* Error setting mode */
            printf("Mode not supported by hardware\n");
        }
    }
```

__setlogorg

COMPATIBILITY	MSC 3	MSC 4	MSC 5	QC	TC	ANSI	UNIX V
			▲	▲			

PURPOSE Use _setlogorg to move the origin (the point 0,0) of the logical coordinate system used for graphics to a specific physical pixel location on the display screen.

SYNTAX `struct xycoord far _setlogorg(short x, short y);`

`short x, y;`   The physical x and y coordinates of the point on the screen that becomes the new origin of the logical coordinate system

EXAMPLE CALL `_setlogorg(100, 100);`

INCLUDES `#include <graph.h>`   For function declaration and definition of the structure *xycoord*

DESCRIPTION The _setlogorg function sets the origin of the logical coordinate system to the physical point (x,y). From then on, the point (0,0) in logical coordinates corresponds to the pixel at (x,y).

The graphics library maintains two coordinate systems: one physical and the other logical (see Figure 17-2). The physical coordinate axes are fixed, with the origin (0,0) at the upper left corner of the screen, with the x-axis extending horizontally to the right and the y-axis going downwards. The logical coordinate system's x and y axes are parallel to their physical counterparts. Its default origin corresponds to the physical coordinates (0,0) but with

Graphics Modes, Coordinates, and Attributes

_setlogorg the origin can be relocated to any physical point. This allows you to translate or shift objects on the screen.

COMMON USES The *_setlogorg* function is used for translations (shifts) of graphical objects. For example, to draw two identical rectangles, one translated from the other, you draw the first rectangle, use *_setlogorg* to move the logical origin, and repeat the call to draw the next rectangle (see the example below).

RETURNS The *_setlogorg* function returns the coordinates of the previous logical origin in a structure of type *xycoord*, which is declared as shown below in the header file *graph.h*.

```
struct xycoord       /* Structure for pixel coordinates */
{
    short xcoord;    /* x-coordinate */
    short ycoord;    /* y-coordinate */
};
```

SEE ALSO

_setviewport   To define a limited area of the screen as the clipping region and move the logical origin to the upper left corner of this region

_getlogcoord   To convert physical coordinates to logical

_getphyscoord   To convert logical coordinates to physical

EXAMPLE If you have graphics capability, set the adapter to a graphics mode. Draw two identical filled rectangles, one shifted diagonally from the other by some amount. Use two calls to *_rectangle* with a call to *_setlogorg* in between to achieve the shift.

```
#include <stdio.h>
#include <graph.h>
#define BLUE 1 /* In EGA's default palette, BLUE is 1 */
#define RED  4 /* and RED is 4                        */
main()
{
/* Assume an EGA environment */
    if (_setvideomode(_ERESCOLOR) == 0)
    {
        printf("Not EGA environment\n");
        exit(0);
    }
    _settextposition(1,1);
    _outtext("Shift rectangles with _setlogorg");
/* Set current color to RED and draw filled rectangle */
    _setcolor(RED);
    _rectangle(_GFILLINTERIOR,10,40,110,90);
/* Now set new logical origin and make identical call */
```

```
      _setlogorg(70,30);
      _setcolor(BLUE);
      _rectangle(_GFILLINTERIOR,10,40,110,90);

/* Wait for user to hit a key, then reset everything */
      _settextposition(25,1);
      _outtext("Hit any key to reset mode and exit:");
      getch();
      _setvideomode(_DEFAULTMODE);
}
```

__setvideomode

COMPATIBILITY	MSC 3	MSC 4	MSC 5	QC	TC	ANSI	UNIX V
			▲	▲	setgraphmode		

PURPOSE Use _setvideomode to set a display mode appropriate for a certain combination of adapter and display. For example, if you have an EGA with an enhanced color monitor you can select a 640×350 pixel graphics mode with up to 16 colors.

SYNTAX `short far _setvideomode(short mode);`

`short mode;`   Selected mode

EXAMPLE CALL `_setvideomode(_HRES16COLOR); /* 640 x 200, 16 color mode */`

INCLUDES `#include <graph.h>`   For function declaration and definition of mode names

DESCRIPTION The _setvideomode function sets up the graphics hardware to work in the mode specified in the argument *mode*. The value specified for the mode can be any one of the constants shown in Table 17-1 and defined in the include file *graph.h*.

COMMON USES This function is used to set up the graphics environment in an application program. For example, for graphics operation, you first choose a mode appropriate for your hardware, call _setvideomode to enter this mode, and proceed with the graphics operations.

RETURNS The return value is nonzero if everything went well. If the specified mode is not supported by the hardware configuration, _setvideomode returns a zero.

COMMENTS In a graphics program, setting the mode is one of the first things you do. In many cases you will want to use the highest resolution mode supported by the installed graphics hardware. Before exiting from the graphics application,

Graphics Modes, Coordinates, and Attributes

you should return back to the original mode by using _setvideomode_ again
with the mode constant __DEFAULTMODE.

SEE ALSO   _getvideoconfig   To determine the hardware configuration

EXAMPLE   If you have an EGA with an enhanced color monitor, write a C program using
setvideomode to set up the hardware for 640×350 graphics and perform
some sample graphics operations. Then restore everything to normal and
exit.

```
#include <stdio.h>
#include <graph.h>
#define RED 4      /* Color number 4 is red */
main()
{
/* Enter hi-resolution graphics mode on EGA */
    if (_setvideomode(_ERESCOLOR) != 0)
    {
        _settextposition(1,1);
        _outtext("Now in 640x350 color graphics mode");
/* Draw a filled rectangle */
        _setcolor(RED);
        if(_rectangle(_GFILLINTERIOR,
                    200, 100, 400, 200) == 0)
        {
            _settextposition(2,1);
            _outtext("Error drawing filled rectangle!");
        }
/* Restore original mode */
/* Give user a chance to see the result */
        _settextposition(2,1);
        _outtext("Hit any key to exit:");
        getch();
        _setvideomode(_DEFAULTMODE);
    }
    else
    {
/* Error setting mode */
        printf("Mode not supported by hardware\n");
    }
}
```

__setvideomode

__setviewport

COMPATIBILITY	MSC 3	MSC 4	MSC 5	QC	TC	ANSI	UNIX V
			▲	▲	setviewport		

PURPOSE Use __setviewport_ to define a rectangular region of the screen as the clipping region for graphics (i.e., anything outside this region will be cut off). You can get the same effect by calling __setcliprgn_, but __setviewport_ also sets the origin of the logical coordinate system (see the tutorial section) at the upper left corner of the viewport.

SYNTAX `void far _setviewport(short x1, short y1, short x2, short y2);`

`short x1, y1;`   Upper left corner of clipping region in physical coordinates

`short x2, y2;`   Lower right corner of clipping region in physical coordinates

EXAMPLE CALL `_setviewport(150, 50, 350, 150);`

INCLUDES `#include <graph.h>`   For function declaration

DESCRIPTION The __setviewport_ function defines an area of the screen (the "viewport") as the current clipping region for all graphics operations. The area is specified in terms of the physical coordinates of the upper left hand corner ($x1$, $y1$) and that of the lower right corner ($x2$, $y2$). After setting the clipping region, __setviewport_ also moves the origin of the logical coordinates to the upper left corner of the viewport.

COMMON USES The __setviewport_ function maintains multiple "virtual" graphics screens, each with its own coordinate system.

COMMENTS The effect of __setviewport_ is identical to that of calling __setcliprgn_ to define the clipping region, followed by a call to __setlogorg_ to move the logical origin to the upper left corner of the clipping region.

SEE ALSO `_setlogorg`   To define a new logical origin

`_setcliprgn`   To define a limited area of the screen as the region beyond which all graphics output will be clipped

`_settextwindow`   Analogous operation for text output

EXAMPLE If you have an EGA environment, put the EGA into a graphics mode, call __setviewport_ to define a viewport, and draw a filled ellipse in it. Then define a second viewport and repeat the same call to __ellipse_. Each ellipse appears in its own viewport and each is clipped according to the size of the viewport.

Graphics Modes, Coordinates, and Attributes

This illustrates the idea of using viewports to maintain multiple virtual graphics screens.

```c
#include <stdio.h>
#include <graph.h>
#define RED  4        /* Red is 4 in default palette */
main()
{
    if (_setvideomode(_ERESCOLOR) == 0)
    {
        printf("EGA hi-res mode not supported\n");
        exit(0);
    }
    _settextposition(1,1);
    _outtext(
    "Demonstration of _setviewport with 2 viewports");
/* Set current color to red    */
    _setcolor(RED);
/* Dashed lines for boundaries */
    _setlinestyle(0xf0f);
/* Set a 200 x 200 viewport */
    _setviewport(0,100, 200, 300);
/* Show boundary of viewport */
    _rectangle(_GBORDER,0,0,200,200);
/* Now draw an ellipse, remember the bounding rectangle
 * is specified in logical coordinates and the origin
 * is at upper left corner of viewport.
 */
    _ellipse(_GFILLINTERIOR, 50, 50, 250, 250);
/* Now set another viewport, and redraw same ellipse */
/* This is a 150 x 150 viewport                      */
    _setviewport(240,100,390,250);
/* Again show boundary of the viewport */
    _rectangle(_GBORDER, 0,0,150,150);
    _setfillmask(NULL);
/* Draw the same ellipse again. (NOTE: When tested,
 * this ellipse didn't get filled! Is it a bug?)
 */
    _ellipse(_GFILLINTERIOR, 50, 50, 250, 250);

/* Return to default mode when user strikes any key */
    _settextposition(4,1);
    _outtext(
      "Press any key to return to original settings:");
    getch();  /* A do-nothing read */
    _setvideomode(_DEFAULTMODE);
}
```

__setviewport

__setvisualpage

COMPATIBILITY	MSC 3	MSC 4	MSC 5	QC	TC	ANSI	UNIX V
			▲	▲	setvisualpage		

PURPOSE Use the _setvisualpage function in EGA or VGA graphics modes and in the text modes to select the current page or the portion of display memory that is mapped to the screen and displayed. This function only works when the adapter has enough video memory to support multiple pages.

SYNTAX short far _setvisualpage(short page_number);

short page_number;   The page number being displayed

EXAMPLE CALL _setvisualpage(1);

INCLUDES #include <graph.h>   For function declaration

DESCRIPTION The _setvisualpage function selects the page specified in the argument *page _number* as the current page being displayed on the screen, which is the portion of video memory that is used for the memory-mapped display operation. See the description of the function _setactivepage for more details on pages and on setting the active page for current text and graphics output.

The page where text and graphics output is stored is selected by the _setactivepage function and this need not be the same as the page currently being displayed. By default, page 0 is used as both visual and active page.

The number of video pages available in the current mode can be determined by calling _getvideoconfig.

COMMON USES The _setvisualpage function is used together with its counterpart _setactivepage to prepare complex graphics on one page while the user is viewing what was drawn earlier on another page. This provides for fast updating of the display and can be used for smoother animation.

RETURNS The _setvisualpage function returns the page number of the previous visual page. If it is not possible to have multiple pages or if the page number is beyond the valid range, _setvisualpage returns a negative value.

SEE ALSO _setactivepage   To select the page for current text and graphics output

EXAMPLE If you have hardware with enough memory to display multiple text pages, display a message to the user to wait while you prepare the other pages. Let the user select a page to look at, and make that page visible by calling _setvisualpage.

```
#include <stdio.h>
#include <graph.h>
```

 Graphics Modes, Coordinates, and Attributes

```c
#define YELLOW      14
#define BLINKING_RED 20
main()
{
    struct videoconfig config;
    char buffer[80];
    short page = 0;
/* Assuming EGA with 256 KB graphics memory, we can
 * have 8 text pages
 */
    _clearscreen(_GCLEARSCREEN);  /* Clear the screen */
    _getvideoconfig(&config);
/* Default visual page is page 0. Display a message on
 * this page
 */
    _settextposition(1,1);
    sprintf(buffer,
    "This is page 0. There are %d pages possible.\n",
            config.numvideopages);
    _outtext(buffer);
    _settextcolor(BLINKING_RED);
    _outtext("...Wait while the other pages are being \
prepared...");
    for(page = 1; page < config.numvideopages; page++)
    {
        _setactivepage(page);
        _settextcolor(page);
        _settextposition(1,1);
        sprintf(buffer,
    "Page: %d. Drawn in color number %d\n", page, page);
        _outtext(buffer);
        _settextcolor(YELLOW);
        sprintf(buffer,
        "Hit 'q' to exit or other key to go to page %d",
                    (page+1) % config.numvideopages);
        _outtext(buffer);
    }
    _settextcolor(YELLOW);
    _settextposition(2,1);
    _setactivepage(0);
/* Let user cycle through the pages and see the effect*/
    _settextposition(3,1);
    _outtext(
    "Hit 'q' to exit, any other key to go to page 1:");
    while(1)
    {
        if(getch() == 'q')
        {
```

__setvisualpage

```
/* Restore mode */
        _setvideomode(_DEFAULTMODE);
        exit(0);
    }
    page++;
/* Select the other page as the visual page */
    _setvisualpage(page % config.numvideopages);
    }
}
```

 Graphics Modes, Coordinates, and Attributes

Chapter **18 *Drawing and Animation***

Introduction

The Microsoft C 5.1 graphics library includes a set of routines to draw basic shapes and manipulate color bit-mapped images. The library currently has provisions for drawing arcs, ellipses, pie wedges, and rectangles, each optionally filled with the current color using the current fill mask (see the tutorial in Chapter 17). The image manipulation routines from the library are capable of saving a rectangular area of the screen in a buffer and restoring the image from the buffer at a specified screen coordinate. The image manipulation functions can be used to achieve "animation," the process of creating the visual effect of motion of an object on the screen. The drawing routines are the building blocks for graphics applications. With the basic shapes and the ability to draw pixels of any color, you can draw quite complicated images on the screen. This chapter describes the use of the basic drawing routines.

Notes on Drawing and Animation

Fourteen drawing and image manipulation routines are in the Microsoft C library. Table 18-1 explains the purpose of each routine and Table 18-2 categorizes them by task. Before using these drawing routines you set the adapter to a graphics mode using _setvideomode (see Chapter 17 for modes).

PARAMETERS AND ATTRIBUTES THAT AFFECT DRAWING
All the drawing routines expect logical coordinates, which we explained in the tutorial in Chapter 17. You set the origin of the logical coordinate system anywhere on the screen by using _setlogorg.

The current position, current color, line style, and fill mask are some of the parameters of the Microsoft C graphics model that affect the drawing routines. The graphics model and parameters are described in the tutorial in Chapter 17.

Table 18-1. *Drawing and Animation Routines*

Routine	Purpose
_arc	Draw an elliptic arc.
_clearscreen	Clear the screen and fill it with the current background color.
_ellipse	Draw an ellipse (optionally filled).
_floodfill	Fill an area of screen with the current color.
_getcurrentposition	Get the logical coordinates of the current graphics position.
_getimage	Save a screen image in off-screen memory.
_getpixel	Return the value of a specific pixel.
_imagesize	Return size of memory (in bytes) needed to save a particular rectangular region of screen.
_lineto	Draw a line in current color and using current line style from current graphics position to a specified point.
_moveto	Set current graphics position to a specified point.
_pie	Draw a wedge cut from an ellipse and optionally filled with current color using the current fill mask.
_putimage	Restore an image from off-screen memory and display it on the screen in a specified manner.
_rectangle	Draw a rectangle (optionally filled).
_setpixel	Set a pixel to a specific value.

Table 18-2. *Drawing and Animation Routines by Task*

Task	Routines
Clear a selected area of the screen.	_clearscreen
Draw a single point.	_getcurrentposition, _getpixel, _setpixel
Draw a straight line.	_lineto, _moveto
Draw basic shapes.	_arc, _ellipse, _pie, _rectangle
Fill a region with color.	_floodfill
Save and restore images.	_getimage, _imagesize, _putimage

DRAWING A SINGLE POINT

A basic operation in graphics is to set an arbitrary point on the screen to a selected color. This involves setting the current color and setting the selected point to the current color. You can do this in Microsoft C 5.1 by the code

```
_setcolor(1);   /* Normally color number 1 is blue */
_setpixel(100,50);  /* Turn pixel to current color */
```

which will set the point at logical (100,50) to blue.

You can also "clear" a point, which means that you set that point to the background color. In the graphics modes, color number 0 is always the background color. Thus the point (100,50) can be reset to background by

```
_setcolor(0);
_setpixel(100,50);
```

DRAWING LINES Drawing lines is another capability of the graphics library. The _lineto_ function draws a line from the current position to the specified point and updates the current position when it is done. It uses the current color to set the color of the line and the current line style to determine the appearance of the line. For example,

```
/* Draw a dashed line from (10,10) to (100,100) */
   _setcolor(4);     /* 4 is normally red      */
   _setlinestyle(0xff00); /* Dashed line       */
   _moveto(10,10);  /* First move to (10,10) */
   _lineto(100,100);    /* Then draw          */
```

draws a red dashed line from the logical point (10,10) to the point (100,100). At the end of the drawing the current point will be (100,100) and another call such as _lineto(200,100)_ will draw a line joining (100,100) to (200,100).

LINE STYLE In the line-drawing example, we used _setlinestyle_ to set up a dashed line style. The argument to _setlinestyle_ is a 16-bit mask that specifies the pattern to be repeated when drawing a line. Think of this mask as representing a line segment 16 pixels long. If a bit in the mask is a 1, the corresponding pixel in that line gets painted with the current color (see _setcolor_). If a bit is 0, the corresponding pixel is untouched. Note that a value of FFh for *linemask* means a solid line. This is the default value of the line style in the graphics package.

BASIC SHAPES The rectangle, ellipse, arc, and wedge (called the "pie") are the four basic shapes supported in the graphics library. The ellipse forms the basis of the arc and the pie because these two shapes are parts of an ellipse (see Figure 18-1).

Rectangle

The rectangle is specified by the logical (x,y) coordinates of its upper left hand and lower right hand corner. It can be drawn optionally filled with the current color or with a border in the current color and current line style. For example, you can draw a 20×20 rectangle with the upper left corner located at (10, 30) and filled in the current color by

```
_rectangle(_GFILLINTERIOR, 10,30,30,50);
```

The first argument _GFILLINTERIOR is the fill flag which, in this case, asks the rectangle to be filled. A fill flag of _GBORDER means only a border will be drawn.

Ellipse, Arc, and Pie

As shown in Figure 18-1, the specification of the arc, the ellipse, and the pie involves the concept of the "bounding rectangle," which is the smallest rec-

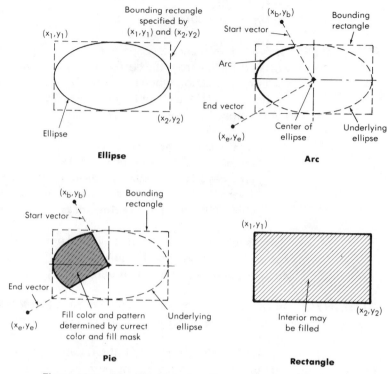

Figure 18-1. *Specifications for ellipse, arc, pie, and rectangle*

tangle that completely encloses the figure being drawn. Since the arc and the pie are both parts of an ellipse, in all cases you have to specify the bounding rectangle of an ellipse. Both the bounding rectangle and the basic rectangle shape are specified by the logical coordinates of their upper left hand and lower right hand corners.

For the arc as well as the pie, the elliptic segment is drawn as follows. A line is drawn from the center of the ellipse (of which the arc or the pie is a part) to a point specified as the beginning point. The *_pie* and the *_arc* functions begin drawing the curved edge at the point where that line intersects the ellipse. The functions trace over the underlying ellipse, using the current color, in a counter-clockwise direction until reaching the point where a line drawn from the center to a specified end point cuts the ellipse (see Figure 18-1). Curved lines are always drawn in a solid line style. Thus the ellipse and the pie can only have a solid boundary. They can, however, be filled in the interior like the rectangle.

ASPECT RATIO If your application has to produce a truthful rendition of all geometric figures, you must take into account the "aspect ratio" of the monitor, which is the ratio of the number of pixels along a vertical line on the screen to that along a horizontal line of the same length. You multiply the vertical (y-axis) dimensions of the objects by the *aspect ratio* for a properly proportioned drawing. You can compute the aspect ratio using the formula:

$$\text{aspect ratio} = (\text{width\_of\_screen}/\text{height\_of\_screen})$$
$$* (\text{number\_of\_ypixels}/\text{number\_of\_xpixels})$$

The width and height of the screen have to be supplied by you, but the number of pixels along x and y directions can be determined by calling _getvideoconfig. For example, here is how you can compute the aspect ratio of a screen that is 10 inches wide and 6.5 inches tall:

```
#include <graph.h>
   :

   :
struct videoconfig v_config;
double aspect_ratio;
   :
_getvideoconfig(&v_info);
aspect_ratio = (double)
            (10 * v_info.numypixels) / (6.5 * v_info.numxpixels);
```

FILLING AN AREA WITH A COLOR

You can use _floodfill to fill an area with a boundary. The filling begins at a point inside the area and spreads in all directions until _floodfill encounters a specified boundary color. Thus it is important to have a solid boundary for _floodfill to work correctly.

When filling an area, _floodfill also applies a mask that is defined by the _setfillmask routine. The fill mask is also used when filling shapes such as the rectangle, the ellipse, and the pie. Here is an example of filling an area:

```
unsigned char far mask[] =
{0x0f, 0x0f, 0x0f, 0x0f, 0xf0, 0xf0, 0xf0, 0xf0};
   :
_setfillmask(mask); /* Set up fill mask    */
_setcolor(4);       /* Set border color    */
_rectangle(_GBORDER, 10, 10, 110, 110);
_setcolor(1);       /* Set new fill color  */
_floodfill(50, 50, 4);  /* Stop at color 4 */
```

We first set up a fill mask and draw a rectangle with a border in color number 4 (red). Then we switch the current color to color number 1 (blue) and call _floodfill to fill the rectangle.

FILL MASK

The _setfillmask function is used to define an 8×8 pattern of bits as the current mask to be used by the routines _floodfill, _rectangle, _ellipse, and _pie to fill an area with the current color.

The fill pattern is specified by a far pointer to an array of 8 characters. Each character has 8 bits, so you can think of this 8×8 array of bits as a model of an area on the screen, 8 pixels wide and 8 pixels high, with the first character representing the first row of the area. When using the mask to fill an 8×8 area, those pixels that correspond to 0 bits are untouched while the rest are filled with the current color. For areas larger than 8×8 pixels, the fill operation is done by using the mask on successive 8×8 blocks until the entire screen is covered. A solid fill is specified when all 8 characters contain the value FFh, the default value of the fill style in the graphics package. See Figure 18-1 for an illustration of the concept.

IMAGE SAVE AND RE-STORE

The graphics library also includes provisions for saving a graphics image (*_getimage*) in a memory buffer, re-storing the image (*_putimage*), and determining the size of memory needed to store an image (*_imagesize*).

Saving an image is straightforward. You call *_getimage* with the coordinates of the upper left and lower right corners of a rectangle on the screen and the address of the buffer where you want to save the image in that area of the screen. You can use *malloc* to allocate the buffer before saving the image. When doing so, you need the size of the image, which can be found by calling *_imagesize* with the same rectangle as input. For example, you can save a 20×20 rectangular image by

```
char far *buffer;
   :
buffer = (char far *) malloc((size_t)_imagesize(0,0,20,20);
_getimage(0,0,20,20, buffer);
```

The image can be re-stored elsewhere on the screen by calling *_putimage*. You only need to specify the point on the screen where the upper left hand corner of the saved image will be placed. For example, we can recreate the saved image at (100,100) by

```
_putimage(100,100, buffer, _GPSET);
```

As you can see, re-storing the image involves specifying how the image is to be reconstructed on the screen. In the example above, the constant _GPSET specifies that the pixel values in the image should be copied into the pixels in the new area. Other options include using logical OR, AND, or exclusive OR with existing pixel values. The reference pages on *_putimage* further explain the meaning of this argument.

ANIMATION USING _GETIMAGE AND _PUTIMAGE

The ability to save and restore images can be exploited to make an object appear to move on the display screen. To achieve this effect, you first draw the object and save it once into a buffer. After that you re-store it again at the *old* location with the last argument of *_putimage* set to _GXOR. This exclusive OR operation clears out the old image. Now you can use *_putimage* at the new location and re-store it again with the _GXOR option. Repeating this in a loop makes the image appear to move around in the screen. Here is how the loop might look:

```
/* Draw image once */
        _putimage(x,y,image,_GXOR);
/* Perform some animation */
        while(!kbhit())
```

```
        {
/* First erase at last position */
        _putimage(x,y,image,_GXOR);
        x +=10;
        y += 5;
        if(x >= numxpixels) x = 0;
        if(y >= numxpixels) y = 0;
/* Redraw at new position */
        _putimage(x,y,image,_GXOR);
        }
```

In this example, the image is drawn and saved in the buffer named *image*. Then the *while* animates the figure until the user presses a key. The example in the reference pages on *_putimage* shows a complete animation program.

ANIMATION BY FLIPPING VIDEO PAGE

If your graphics adapter has enough memory to support at least two pages in graphics mode, you can use the *_setactivepage* and the *_setvisualpage* functions (see Chapter 17 for a discussion of video pages) to perform some animation. The *_setactivepage* sets the area of video memory to which all graphics go. The page being displayed is set by *_setvisualpage*. The idea is to draw the next stage of an image on the active page while the user is watching the current visual page and then swap the two pages. Now you can clear out the old image and prepare the next frame of animation and repeat the cycle to achieve the effect of movement.

The EGA with 256 K of video memory can support two pages of graphics and this can be exploited for animation. See the example in the reference pages on *_setactivepage* for an example that shows the swapping of graphics pages on an EGA.

__arc

COMPATIBILITY	MSC 3	MSC 4	MSC 5	QC	TC	ANSI	UNIX V
			▲	▲	arc		

PURPOSE Use *__arc* to draw a segment of an ellipse using the current color. The method of specifying the arc is described below.

SYNTAX
```
short far _arc(short x1, short y1, short x2, short y2,
               short xb, short yb, short xe, short ye);
```

short x1, y1; Coordinates of upper left corner of bounding rectangle of the ellipse to which the arc belongs

short x2, y2; Coordinates of lower right corner of bounding rectangle of the ellipse to which the arc belongs

short xb, yb; Arc begins at the point where a line drawn from the center of the bounding rectangle to (xb, yb) cuts the ellipse

short xe, ye; Arc ends at the point where a line drawn from the center of the bounding rectangle to (xe, ye) cuts the ellipse

EXAMPLE CALL `_arc(100, 50, 250, 100, 0, 50, 250, 100);`

INCLUDES `#include <graph.h>` For function declaration

DESCRIPTION The *__arc* function draws a segment of an ellipse defined in terms of the bounding rectangle whose upper left corner is (*x1, y1*) and whose lower right corner is (*x2, y2*). The bounding rectangle has its sides parallel to the coordinate axes.

As shown in Figure 18-1, the segment of the ellipse to be drawn is determined as follows. A line is drawn from the center of the ellipse to the point (*xb, yb*). The *__arc* function begins drawing at the point where that line intersects the ellipse. The routine traces over the underlying elliptical outline, using the current color, in the *counter-clockwise* direction until it comes to the point where a line drawn from the center to (*xe, ye*) cuts the ellipse. Unlike the *__lineto* function, *__arc* uses solid line style exclusively and it does not update the current position after drawing the arc.

COMMON USES This function is useful in constructing line drawings that include curved sections. Several arcs can be pieced together to form a curved section.

RETURNS The return value is nonzero if everything went well. If there is an error, *__arc* returns a zero.

COMMENTS It is somewhat complicated to specify the arc to be drawn. For example, in

Drawing and Animation

most applications we know the beginning and end points of the curved line segment. These coordinates can be used directly as the arguments *xb, yb* and *xe, ye*. The complicated part is to specify the bounding rectangle for the ellipse of which the yet-to-be-drawn arc is a segment.

SEE ALSO   _setcolor   To set the current color

EXAMPLE   Write a C program to illustrate how arcs can be drawn using _*arc*. Show the bounding rectangle and the lines that determine the beginning and the end point of the arc being drawn.

```c
#include <stdio.h>
#include <graph.h>
#define BLUE  1
#define GREEN 2
#define RED   4        /* Color number 4 is red */

main()
{
             /* bounding rectangle */
     short x1=100, y1=50, x2=250, y2=100,
             /* begin, end points  */
             xb=0, yb=50, xe=250, ye=100;
/* Enter hi-resolution graphics mode on EGA */
     if (_setvideomode(_ERESCOLOR) != 0)
     {
         _settextposition(1,1);
         _outtext("Demonstrating _arc");
         _settextposition(2,1);
         _outtext(
"Drawn counterclockwise from blue line to green");
/* Set up red as the current color */
         _setcolor(RED);
/* Select a dashed line style for the lines */
         _setlinestyle(0xff);
/* Draw the bounding rectangle -- with a border*/
         _rectangle(_GBORDER, x1, y1, x2, y2);
/* Draw the arc next */
         _arc(x1, y1, x2, y2, xb, yb, xe, ye);
/* Now show the line that determines the beginning of
 * the arc
 */
         _setcolor(BLUE);
/* Move to the center of the bounding rectangle */
         _moveto((x1+x2)/2, (y1+y2)/2);
         _lineto(xb, yb);
/* Next show the line that determines the end point of
 * the arc
```

_arc

```
        */
                _setcolor(GREEN);
                _moveto((x1+x2)/2, (y1+y2)/2);
                _lineto(xe, ye);


/* Restore original mode */
/* Give user a chance to see the result */
                _settextposition(40,1);
                _outtext("Hit any key to exit:");
                getch();
                _setvideomode(_DEFAULTMODE);
            }
            else
            {
/* Error setting mode */
                printf("Mode not supported by hardware\n");
            }
        }
```

__clearscreen

COMPATIBILITY	MSC 3	MSC 4	MSC 5	QC	TC	ANSI	UNIX V
			▲	▲	cleardevice		
					clearviewport		
					clrscr		

PURPOSE Use *_clearscreen* to clear an area of the screen and fill it with the current background color.

SYNTAX void far _clearscreen(short area);

short area;　　Constant indicating area to be cleared

EXAMPLE CALL _clearscreen(_GCLEARSCREEN); /* Clear the entire screen */

INCLUDES #include <graph.h>　　For function declaration and definition of names for area

DESCRIPTION The *_clearscreen* function clears out an area of the screen and fills that area with the background color. The background color may be altered by calling *_setbkcolor*. The area to be cleared is indicated by the parameter *area*, which should be set to one of the constants shown in Table 18-3. These constants are defined in the include file *graph.h*.

COMMON USES The *_clearscreen* function can be used with *_GWINDOW* as the argument to create pop-up menus.

 Drawing and Animation

Table 18-3. *Interpreting Area Constants*

Constant	Interpretation
_GCLEARSCREEN	Entire screen is cleared and filled
_GVIEWPORT	Only current viewport is cleared and filled (see _ *setviewporty*)
_GWINDOW	Only current text window is cleared and filled (see _ *settextwindow*)

SEE ALSO   _setbkcolor   To change the current background color

_setviewport   To define a limited area of the screen as a viewport

_settextwindow   To define a window within which text is output

EXAMPLE   From a text mode, define a window for text by calling _*settextwindow*. Next set a new background color by calling _*setbkcolor*. Now call _*clearscreen* to clear the text window and fill it with the new background color.

```
#include <stdio.h>
#include <graph.h>
/* Need a "long" constant for _setbkcolor   */
#define RED 4L
main()
{
/* Specify a text window using coordinates of upper
 * left and lower right corners
 */
    _settextwindow(10,10,15,70);
    _setbkcolor(RED);  /* Set background color to red */
    _clearscreen(_GWINDOW);      /* clear text window */

/* Once a text window is defined all text positions are
 * relative to upper left corner of the window. This
 * can be used for pop-up menus.
 */
    _settextposition(1,10);     /* Display a message */
    _outtext("_clearscreen on a text window");
}
```

_clearscreen

__ellipse

COMPATIBILITY	MSC 3	MSC 4	MSC 5	QC	TC	ANSI	UNIX V
			▲	▲	ellipse		

PURPOSE Use __ellipse to draw a filled or bordered ellipse that you specify by the corners of the bounding rectangle.

SYNTAX
```
short far _ellipse(short flag, short x1, short y1,
                        short x2, short y2);
```

`short flag;`   To fill or to draw a border

`short x1, y1;`   Coordinates of upper left corner of rectangle circumscribing the ellipse

`short x2, y2;`   Coordinates of lower right corner of rectangle circumscribing the ellipse

EXAMPLE CALL `_ellipse(_GFILLINTERIOR, 100, 100, 200, 300);`

INCLUDES `#include <graph.h>`   For function declaration and definition of fill flag constants

DESCRIPTION The __ellipse function draws an ellipse described in terms of a bounding rectangle whose sides are parallel to the coordinate axes (see Figure 18-1). The rectangle is specified by its upper left corner $x1, y1$ and lower right corner $x2, y2$. (See the tutorial section for an explanation of the coordinate system used.) The ellipse is centered at the mid-point of the rectangle. Note that nothing is drawn if the bounding rectangle coordinates describe a single point or just a horizontal or vertical line (i.e., when either $x1 = x2$ or $y1 = y2$ or both).

The argument *flag* indicates whether the ellipse is filled or drawn with a border. The value specified for *flag* can be either of the constants, defined in the include file *graph.h*, and shown in Table 18-4.

Before calling __ellipse, use __setcolor to select the fill color and __setfillmask to select a fill pattern. The line style of the border is always solid.

COMMON USES This function can be used as a primitive object for building more complex graphical objects.

RETURNS The return value is nonzero if everything went well. Otherwise, __ellipse returns a zero.

COMMENTS If you want an ellipse with a border color different from that used to fill the interior, you can first draw the ellipse with a border, select a new color, and then fill the ellipse by calling the __floodfill function.

 Drawing and Animation

Table 18-4. *Interpreting the Fill Flag*

Flag Constant	Interpretation
_GFILLINTERIOR	Fills the ellipse using the current color (see _setcolor). If a fill mask has been defined, the filling is done as if by painting over a stencil made out of a repeated pattern specified by the fill mask, with 1s being "holes" in the stencil (meaning the color passes through). See _setfillmask for more details.
_GBORDER	Only the outline of the ellipse is shown with solid lines drawn in the current color (contrast this with the border drawn by _rectangle).

SEE ALSO   _setcolor   To set the current color

_setfillmask   To set the current fill mask

_floodfill   To fill a bordered ellipse with color

EXAMPLE   Using a graphics mode appropriate for your graphics hardware, write a C program to draw two ellipses, one bordered and one filled, on the screen.

```
#include <stdio.h>
#include <graph.h>
#define BLUE 1    /* Color number 1 is blue */
#define RED  4     /* Color number 4 is red */
main()
{
/* Enter hi-resolution graphics mode on EGA */
    if (_setvideomode(_ERESCOLOR) != 0)
    {
/* Draw a filled rectangle */
        _settextposition(1,1);
        _outtext("A bordered ellipse:");
        _setlinestyle(0xff);
        _lineto(600,10);
        _setcolor(BLUE);
        _ellipse(_GBORDER, 0, 50, 150, 100);
/* Draw a filled ellipse */
        _settextposition(10,1);
        _outtext("A filled ellipse:");
        _setcolor(RED);
        _ellipse(_GFILLINTERIOR, 0, 150, 150, 200);

/* Restore original mode */
/* Give user a chance to see the result */
        _settextposition(20,1);
        _outtext("Hit any key to exit:");
        getch();
```

_ellipse

```
        _setvideomode(_DEFAULTMODE);
    }
    else
    {
/* Error setting mode */
        printf("Mode not supported by hardware\n");
    }
}
```

__floodfill

COMPATIBILITY	MSC 3	MSC 4	MSC 5	QC	TC	ANSI	UNIX V
			▲	▲	floodfill		

PURPOSE Use the *_floodfill* function to fill an area of the screen with the current color (see *_setcolor*) using the current fill mask (see *_setfillmask*).

SYNTAX `short far _floodfill(short x, short y, short boundary_color);`

`short x, y;` Position of starting point in logical coordinates

`short boundary_color;` Color number of the boundary at which filling should stop

EXAMPLE CALL `_floodfill(25, 75, 4);`

INCLUDES `#include <graph.h>` For function declaration

DESCRIPTION The *_floodfill* function uses a well-known graphics algorithm of the same name to fill either the inside or the outside of a solid curve whose color is given in the argument *boundary_color*. The fill operation begins at the point whose logical coordinates are specified provided in the arguments *x* and *y*.

The region that gets filled depends on the starting "seed" point. If this point is inside the curve, the inside is filled. If it is outside, the region outside the curve gets filled. If you specify a point exactly on the boundary, the fill is not done. The filling begins at the seed point and spreads in all directions until *_floodfill* encounters a pixel of a border color that must be different from the fill color to prevent the whole screen from being filled).

RETURNS The *_floodfill* function returns a nonzero value if the fill is successful. If there is an error, it returns a zero. The causes of error include specifying a seed point that lies on the boundary or outside the current clipping region (see *_setcliprgn*).

 Drawing and Animation

COMMENTS Since the filling algorithm colors all pixels on each row of pixels until it meets a pixel of color *boundary_color*, it is important to have a solid boundary for a proper fill. (In the example, we attempt to fill a rectangle with a boundary drawn in dashed line style).

SEE ALSO `_setcolor`   To define the current color

`_setfillmask`   To define a pattern for the fill

EXAMPLES If you have an EGA with enhanced color monitor, use the *_floodfill* function to fill a red rectangle with blue color. Draw the rectangle by calling *_rectangle*.

```
#include <stdio.h>
#include <graph.h>
#define BLUE 1     /* Color number 1 is blue  */
#define RED  4     /* Color number 4 is red   */

main()
{

    int i;
    char buffer[80];
    struct xycoord lastpos;
/* Enter hi-resolution graphics mode on EGA */
    if (_setvideomode(_ERESCOLOR) != 0)
    {
        _settextposition(1,1);
        _outtext("Demonstrating _floodfill:");
/* First draw a rectangle with a red border.
 * use a solid line style.
 */
        _setlinestyle(0xffff);
        _setcolor(RED);
        _rectangle(_GBORDER, 0, 50, 100, 100);
/* Now use _floodfill to fill the interior with blue*/
        _setcolor(BLUE);
        _floodfill(25, 75, RED);
/* Restore original mode */
/* Give user a chance to see the result */
        _settextposition(20,1);
        _outtext("Hit any key to exit:");
        getch();
        _setvideomode(_DEFAULTMODE);
    }
    else
    {
```

_floodfill

```
/* Error setting mode */
        printf("Mode not supported by hardware\n");
    }
}
```

If the boundary of a region being filled is not solid, the _floodfill_ function leaks colors through the holes in the boundary. Demonstrate this effect by drawing a rectangle with a boundary in dashed line style and attempting to fill its inside.

```
#include <stdio.h>
#include <graph.h>
#define BLUE 1     /* Color number 1 is blue */
#define RED  4     /* Color number 4 is red  */

main()
{
    int i;
    char buffer[80];
    struct xycoord lastpos;
/* Enter hi-resolution graphics mode on EGA */
    if (_setvideomode(_ERESCOLOR) != 0)
    {
        _settextposition(1,1);
        _outtext("_floodfill needs solid boundary");
/* First draw a rectangle with a blue border.
 * use a solid line style.
 */
        _setlinestyle(0xf0f0);
        _setcolor(BLUE);
        _rectangle(_GBORDER, 0, 50, 100, 100);
/* Now use _floodfill to fill the interior with red */
        _setcolor(RED);
        _floodfill(25, 50, BLUE);
/* Restore original mode */
/* Give user a chance to see the result */
        _settextposition(20,1);
        _outtext("Hit any key to exit:");
        getch();
        _setvideomode(_DEFAULTMODE);
    }
    else
    {
/* Error setting mode */
        printf("Mode not supported by hardware\n");
    }
}
```

 Drawing and Animation

__getcurrentposition

COMPATIBILITY	MSC 3	MSC 4	MSC 5	QC	TC	ANSI	UNIX V
			▲	▲	getx, gety		

PURPOSE Use _getcurrentposition to obtain the logical coordinates of the current graphics position, which is maintained internally by the graphics library routines.

SYNTAX `struct xycoord far _getcurrentposition(void);`

EXAMPLE CALL `curpos = _getcurrentposition();`

INCLUDES `#include <graph.h>`   For function declaration and definition of the structure *xycoord*

DESCRIPTION The _getcurrentposition function returns the logical coordinates of the current graphics position. This point is used by the function _lineto as the starting point of the line it draws. A new current position can be specified by calling _moveto and updated by the drawing routines _arc and _lineto.

An analogous concept is the current text position set by _settextposition and used during text output by _outtext.

RETURNS The _getcurrentposition function returns the logical coordinates of the current graphics position in a structure of type *xycoord*, which is declared as shown below in the header file *graph.h*.

```
struct xycoord       /* Structure for pixel coordinates */
{
    short xcoord;    /* x-coordinate */
    short ycoord;    /* y-coordinate */
};
```

SEE ALSO _moveto   To change the current graphics position

_lineto   Uses and updates current position

EXAMPLE Suppose you want to draw a line with a rectangle attached to the end point of the line. If you didn't know the coordinates of the end point, you could still draw the rectangle at the right place by calling _getcurrentposition after the line has been drawn.

```
#include <stdio.h>
#include <graph.h>
/* Yellow is 14 in EGA's default palette */
#define YELLOW 14
main()
```

```
{
    char buffer[80];
    struct xycoord current;
/* Assume an EGA environment */
    if (_setvideomode(_ERESCOLOR) == 0)
    {
        printf("Not EGA environment\n");
        exit(0);
    }
    _settextposition(1,1);
    _outtext("Demonstrating _getcurrentposition");
    _setcolor(YELLOW);
/* Draw a line from (50,40) to (150,90) */
    _moveto(50,40);
    _lineto(150,90);
/* Now draw a 20 by 20 rectangle with the upper left
 * corner at the end of the line we just drew. Suppose
 * we don't know the coordinates of the end point.
 * Let's first get it.
 */
    current = _getcurrentposition();
/* Draw rectangle using coordinates just retrieved */
    _rectangle(_GBORDER,current.xcoord, current.ycoord,
               current.xcoord+20, current.ycoord+20);
/* Current graphics position will still be the end
 * point of the line
 */
    current = _getcurrentposition();
    sprintf(buffer,"Current graphics position = \
(%d,%d)", current.xcoord, current.ycoord);
    _settextposition(2,1);
    _outtext(buffer);
/* Wait for user to hit a key, then reset everything */
    _settextposition(25,1);
    _outtext("Hit any key to reset mode and exit:");
    getch();
    _setvideomode(_DEFAULTMODE);
}
```

Drawing and Animation

__getimage

COMPATIBILITY	MSC 3	MSC 4	MSC 5	QC	TC	ANSI	UNIX V
			▲	▲	getimage		

PURPOSE Use the _getimage function to save a rectangular screen image in a buffer. You must allocate sufficient storage for the buffer and provide the buffer's address to _getimage.

SYNTAX
```
void far _getimage(short x1, short y1, short x2, short y2,
                   char far *image_buffer);
```

short x1, y1;   Upper left corner of rectangular boundary of screen image to be saved

short x2, y2;   Lower right corner of rectangular boundary of screen image to be saved

char far *image_buffer;   Buffer where image is to be stored

EXAMPLE CALL `_getimage(50,50,100,100,image); /* Save the image */`

INCLUDES `#include <graph.h>`   For function declaration

DESCRIPTION The _getimage function saves the pixels corresponding to a rectangular region of the screen into the buffer whose address is provided in the argument *image_buffer*. The screen image to be saved is specified by the rectangle whose upper left corner is ($x1, y1$) and lower right corner is ($x2, y2$).

Enough storage must be allocated to hold the image. The minimum number of bytes necessary to save an image can be determined by calling the function _imagesize.

COMMON USES The _getimage function is used in conjunction with _putimage to save and restore screen images. You can, for example, use the _getimage function to draw an object once, save it, and reproduce it at several locations on the screen with _putimage. Additionally, erasing the old image before displaying the new one enables you to make an image appear to move on the screen.

SEE ALSO _imagesize   To determine number of bytes necessary to save a screen image

_putimage   To display a stored image

EXAMPLE In a graphics mode, draw some graphical objects and save them in memory by calling _getimage. Now clear the screen and use _putimage to reproduce the objects several times on the screen.

```
#include <stdio.h>
#include <malloc.h>
```

```
#include <graph.h>
#define RED     4
#define YELLOW 14
main()
{
    char far *image;
    char buffer[80];
    unsigned numbytes;
/* Assume EGA. Put it in high-res graphics mode */
    if (_setvideomode(_ERESCOLOR) == 0)
    {
/* Error setting mode */
        printf("Not EGA hardware\n");
        exit(0);
    }
/* Draw some graphical objects to save */
    _setcolor(RED);
    _rectangle(_GBORDER,50,50,90,90);
    _setcolor(YELLOW);
    _ellipse(_GFILLINTERIOR,60,60,100,100);
/* Determine storage needed for entire screen and
 * display result
 */
    numbytes = (unsigned int)_imagesize(50,50,100,100);
    sprintf(buffer, "To save 51 x 51 image using \
_getimage, we need %u bytes of memory.", numbytes);
    _settextposition(1,1);
    _outtext(buffer);

/* Allocate buffer for image */
    if ((image = (char far *) malloc(numbytes)) ==
        (char far *)NULL)
    {
        _setvideomode(_DEFAULTMODE);
        printf("Not enough memory for image storage\n");
        exit(0);
    }
    _getimage(50,50,100,100,image); /* Save the image */
    _settextposition(2,2);
    _outtext("Image saved. Hit any key to continue");
    getch();
/* Now clear screen and draw saved image at several
 * screen locations
 */
    _clearscreen(_GCLEARSCREEN);
    _setbkcolor(_CYAN); /* Change the background color*/
    _settextposition(1,1);
    _outtext("Demonstrating _getimage and _putimage");
```

Drawing and Animation

```
        _putimage(80,80,image,_GXOR);
        _putimage(150,20,image,_GPSET);
        _putimage(300,200,image,_GPRESET);
    /* Once user hits any key, reset mode and exit */
        _settextposition(24,1);
        _outtext("Hit any key to exit:");
        getch();
        _setvideomode(_DEFAULTMODE);    /* Restore mode */
    }
```

__getpixel

COMPATIBILITY	MSC 3	MSC 4	MSC 5	QC	TC	ANSI	UNIX V
			▲	▲	getpixel		

PURPOSE Use the *_getpixel* function to retrieve the pixel value of a certain pixel whose location is specified in logical coordinates.

SYNTAX `short far _getpixel(short x, short y);`

`short x, y;`   The logical x and y coordinates of the pixel whose value is returned

EXAMPLE CALL `pix_value = _getpixel(100, 150);`

INCLUDES `#include <graph.h>`   For function declaration

DESCRIPTION The *_getpixel* function first checks to see if the pixel specified by the logical coordinates (*x,y*) lies within the current clipping region or viewport. If it does, *_getpixel* returns the *pixel value* contained in the video memory location corresponding to the pixel coordinate (*x,y*).

COMMON USES The *_getpixel* function is used to perform operations such as turning all red pixels to blue. You can use *_setcolor* and *_setpixel* to go through the pixels, checking the value of each and changing those containing red to blue. (See the example below.)

RETURNS If the pixel is inside the clipping region, *_getpixel* returns the current pixel value. Otherwise, it returns a −1 to indicate failure.

SEE ALSO `_getcliprgn, _getviewport`   To define a limited area of the screen as clipping region for graphics output

`_setpixel`   To set a pixel to current color

EXAMPLE In a graphics mode, draw a small red rectangle. Examine a larger rectangular area and use _getpixel to find all the red pixels. Turn each red pixel to blue. Since a 0 value indicates a background pixel, you can also turn each pixel containing a 0 to another color.

```
#include <stdio.h>
#include <graph.h>
#define BLUE 1      /* Blue is color number 1 in EGA */
#define RED  4      /* Red is color number 4 in EGA  */
main()
{
    short x, y, color;
/* Assume an EGA environment */
    if (_setvideomode(_ERESCOLOR) == 0)
    {
        printf("Not EGA environment\n");
        exit(0);
    }
    _settextposition(1,1);
    _outtext("Changing colors using _getpixel with \
_setpixel");
/* Draw a red bordered rectangle */
    _setcolor(RED);
    _rectangle(_GBORDER, 70,50,130,80);
    _settextposition(2,1);
    _outtext("Hit any key to turn red into blue:");
    getch();
/* Go over a rectangular region and change red to blue*/
    for(x=50; x<150; x++)
    {
        for(y=40; y<90; y++)
        {
            if(_getpixel(x,y) == 0)
            {                        /* it's  background */
                _setcolor(RED);
                _setpixel(x,y);  /* turn pixel red   */
                continue;        /* skip next check..*/
            }
            if(_getpixel(x,y) == RED)
            {                        /* it's  a red pixel */
                _setcolor(BLUE);
                _setpixel(x,y);  /* turn pixel blue   */
            }
        }
    }
/* Wait for user to hit a key, then reset everything */
        _settextposition(25,1);
        _outtext("Hit any key to reset mode and exit:");
```

 Drawing and Animation

```
            getch();
            _setvideomode(_DEFAULTMODE);
        }
```

__imagesize

COMPATIBILITY	MSC 3	MSC 4	MSC 5	QC	TC	ANSI	UNIX V
			▲	▲	imagesize		

PURPOSE Use the _imagesize function to determine the number of bytes necessary to store a rectangular region of the screen. Call _imagesize before allocating memory to store an image or before storing the image with _getimage.

SYNTAX `long far _imagesize(short x1, short y1, short x2, short y2);`

`short x1, y1;` Upper left corner of rectangular boundary of image

`short x2, y2;` Lower right corner of rectangular boundary of image

EXAMPLE CALL `bytes_needed = _imagesize(min_x, min_y, max_x, max_y);`

INCLUDES `#include <graph.h>` For function declaration

DESCRIPTION The _imagesize function computes the number of bytes necessary to store the screen image within the rectangular region specified by the upper left corner by (x1, y1) and the lower right corner (x2, y2). This is the minimum amount of storage that the function _getimage needs in order to save that rectangular region of screen.

The formula used to compute the number of bytes necessary to store the image is illustrated by the following C code fragment:

```
    long    imagesize;          /* Size in bytes       */
    struct videoconfig config;  /* For bits-per-pixel  */
        .
        .
        .
    xwidth = abs(x1 - x2) + 1;  /* x width in pixels   */
    ywidth = abs(y1 - y2) + 1;  /* y width in pixels   */
    _getvideoconfig(&config);   /* get bits-per-pixel  */
/* Storage in bytes needed to save image using
 * _getimage
 */
    imagesize = 4 + ((long)((xwidth*config.bitsperpixel
                              + 7)/8) * (long)ywidth);
```

COMMON USES The _getimage and _putimage functions in Microsoft C 5.1 provide the capability to save and re-store screen images enabling movement or animation of images on the screen.

When saving an image, you must provide a buffer of adequate size. The _imagesize function allows you to determine the buffer size, taking into account the number of bits of storage needed in the current video mode.

RETURNS The _imagesize function returns a long integer containing the number of bytes needed to store the specified rectangular screen image.

SEE ALSO

_getimage   To save an image in memory (needs storage uffer)

_putimage   To display a stored image

EXAMPLE If you have an EGA, set it in the 640×350, 16-color video mode. Then call _imagesize to determine the amount of storage _getimage will need to save the entire display area in memory.

```
#include <stdio.h>
#include <graph.h>
main()
{
    struct videoconfig config;
    char buffer[80];
    long numbytes;
/* Assume EGA. Put it in high-res graphics mode */
    if (_setvideomode(_ERESCOLOR) == 0)
    {
/* Error setting mode */
        printf("Not EGA hardware\n");
        exit(0);
    }
/* Get the maximum number of pixel on screen    */
    _getvideoconfig(&config);
/* Determine storage needed for entire screen and
 * display result
 */
    numbytes = _imagesize(0, 0, config.numxpixels-1,
                                config.numypixels-1);
    sprintf(buffer, "To save %d x %d image using \
_getimage, we need %ld bytes of memory.",
    config.numxpixels, config.numypixels, numbytes);
    _settextposition(1,1);
    _outtext(buffer);
/* Once user hits any key, reset mode and exit */
    _settextposition(24,1);
    _outtext("Hit any key to exit:");
    getch();
```

 Drawing and Animation

```
        _setvideomode(_DEFAULTMODE);   /* Restore mode */
}
```

__lineto

COMPATIBILITY	MSC 3	MSC 4	MSC 5	QC	TC	ANSI	UNIX V
			▲	▲	lineto		

PURPOSE Use _lineto to draw a line from the current position to a new point using the current color and the current line style.

SYNTAX `short far _lineto(short x, short y);`

`short x, y;`   Logical coordinates of point to which line is drawn

EXAMPLE CALL `_lineto(next_x, next_y);`

INCLUDES `#include <graph.h>`   For function declaration

DESCRIPTION The _lineto function joins the current position to the point whose logical coordinates are specified by the short integer arguments *x* and *y*. The line is drawn using the current color (set by _setcolor) and the current line style (defined by _setlinestyle). The end point of the line becomes the new current position. (See the tutorial section of Chapter 17 for an explanation of the physical and logical coordinate systems.

COMMON USES The _lineto function provides the basic capability, present in any graphics package, of drawing a line between two points. The _lineto function together with _moveto, enables you to draw the most complex line drawings.

RETURNS The _lineto function returns a nonzero value if the line is drawn successfully. Otherwise it returns a zero.

SEE ALSO `_moveto`   To move to a new point without drawing

EXAMPLE Use _lineto with _moveto to draw a graph showing a sin(x) function against x.

```
#include <stdio.h>
#include <math.h>
#include <graph.h>

#define RED    4     /* Color number 4 is RED    */
#define TWOPI  6.283 /* Approximate value of 2 Pi */
#define MAXPNT 100   /* Points on the sinusoid    */
```

```
    main()
    {
        struct videoconfig config;
        short i, x, y, oldx, oldy, midpoint;
        double xd, yd, ampl;
/* Enter hi-resolution graphics mode on EGA */
        if (_setvideomode(_ERESCOLOR) == 0)
        {
/* Error setting mode */
            printf("Mode not supported by hardware\n");
            exit(0);
        }
/* Get current configuration */
        _getvideoconfig(&config);
        midpoint = config.numypixels/2 - 1;
        ampl = (double)midpoint - 30.;
/* Let the logical origin be halfway down the screen */
        _setlogorg(0, midpoint);
/* Move to logical origin */
        _moveto(0,0);
        _settextposition(1,1);
        _outtext(
"Demonstrating _lineto with a plot of sin(x) vs x");
        _setcolor(RED);

        for (i=0; i<=MAXPNT; i++)
        {
            yd = ampl *
                sin(TWOPI * ((double)i)/((double)MAXPNT));
            xd = ((double)config.numxpixels/2.0 - 1.)*
                (double)i / (double)MAXPNT;
            x  = (short)xd;
/* Negate y so that y axis is positive upwards     */
            y  = - (short)yd;
/* Draw a line to the new point by calling _lineto */
            _lineto(x,y);
        }
/* Restore original mode */
/* Give user a chance to see the result            */
        _settextposition(40,1);
        _outtext("Hit any key to exit:");
        getch();
        _setvideomode(_DEFAULTMODE);
    }
```

Drawing and Animation

__moveto

COMPATIBILITY	MSC 3	MSC 4	MSC 5	QC	TC	ANSI	UNIX V
			▲	▲	moveto		

PURPOSE Use __moveto to change the current position maintained by the graphics routines.

SYNTAX `struct xycoord far _moveto(short x, short y);`

`short x, y;`   New position in logical coordinates

EXAMPLE CALL `_moveto(10, 20);`

INCLUDES `#include <graph.h>`   For function declaration and definition of the structure *xycoord*

DESCRIPTION The __moveto function changes the current position that is maintained internally by the graphics routines. The current position is used by the __lineto routine as the starting point for any line it draws. The logical coordinates of this point are specified by the short integer arguments x and y. See the tutorial section of Chapter 17 for an explanation of the physical and logical coordinate systems.

COMMON USES This function is one of the basic capabilities present in a graphics package. If you think in terms of drawing on a piece of paper with a pen, calling __moveto is analogous to lifting the pen and moving to a new point on the paper.

RETURNS The __moveto function returns the previous graphics position's x and y coordinates in a structure of type *xycoord*, defined in *graph.h* as shown below.

```
struct xycoord
{
    short xcoord;    /* Logical x coordinate */
    short ycoord;    /* Logical y coordinate */
};
```

SEE ALSO `_lineto`   To draw a line to another point

EXAMPLE Use __moveto with __lineto to draw a few disjointed line segments.

```
#include <stdio.h>
#include <graph.h>
#define RED  4    /* Color number 4 is red */

main()
```

```
      {
          int i;
          char buffer[80];
          struct xycoord lastpos;
/* Enter hi-resolution graphics mode on EGA */
          if (_setvideomode(_ERESCOLOR) != 0)
          {
              _settextposition(1,1);
              _outtext("Demonstrating _moveto");
/* Set up red as the current color */
              _setcolor(RED);
/* Move to beginning of a line segment and draw a line*/
              _moveto(0,40);
              _lineto(100,40);
/* Now move to the beginning of next line segment. Show
 * how to use the returned structure
 */
              lastpos = _moveto(150,40);
              sprintf(buffer,"Last position was: (%d, %d)",
                      lastpos.xcoord, lastpos.ycoord);
              _settextposition(5,1);
              _outtext(buffer);
/* Restore original mode */
/* Give user a chance to see the result */
              _settextposition(40,1);
              _outtext("Hit any key to exit:");
              getch();
              _setvideomode(_DEFAULTMODE);
          }
          else
          {
/* Error setting mode */
              printf("Mode not supported by hardware\n");
          }
      }
```

_pie

COMPATIBILITY	MSC 3	MSC 4	MSC 5	QC	TC	ANSI	UNIX V
			▲	▲	pieslice		

PURPOSE Use _pie to draw a filled or bordered wedge whose boundary consists of a segment of an ellipse and lines joining the center of the ellipse to the beginning and the end points of the segment. See below for information on specifying the shape of the *pie*.

  Drawing and Animation

SYNTAX
```
short far _pie(short flag, short x1, short y1, short x2,
               short y2, short xb, short yb, short xe, short ye);
```

`short flag;`   Indicates whether to fill or just draw a border

`short x1, y1;`   Coordinates of upper left corner of bounding rectangle of the ellipse to which the curved edge of the pie belongs

`short x2, y2;`   Coordinates of lower right corner of bounding rectangle of the ellipse to which the curved edge of the pie belongs

`short xb, yb;`   The curved edge of the pie begins at the point where a line drawn from the center of the bounding rectangle to (*xb, yb*) cuts the ellipse

`short xe, ye;`   The curved edge of the pie ends at the point where a line drawn from the center of the bounding rectangle to (*xe, ye*) cuts the ellipse

EXAMPLE CALL `_pie(_GFILLINTERIOR, 0, 150, 150, 200, 0, 150, 0, 200);`

INCLUDES `#include <graph.h>`   For function declaration

DESCRIPTION The _pie function draws a segment of the ellipse defined in terms of a bounding rectangle whose upper left corner is (*x1, y1*) and whose lower right corner (*x2, y2*). Then it constructs a wedge by joining the end points of the segment to the center of the ellipse. Depending on the value of the argument *flag*, the pie is either filled with the current color using the current fill pattern or only a border is drawn in the current color. Use _setcolor to select the color and _setfillmask to choose a fill pattern.

The curved edge of the pie is drawn as follows (see Figure 18-1). A line is drawn from the center of the ellipse to the point (*xb, yb*). The _pie function begins drawing the curved edge at the point where that line intersects the ellipse. The function traces over the underlying ellipse, using the current color, in a counter-clockwise direction until it comes to the point where a line drawn from the center to (*xe, ye*) cuts the ellipse.

The argument *flag* indicates whether the ellipse pie is to be filled or drawn with a border. The value specified for *flag* can be either of the _GFILLINTERIOR or _GBORDER constants, defined in the include file *graph.h*, and listed in Table 18-4.

COMMON USES This function is useful in programs that prepare "pie charts" for business graphics.

RETURNS The return value is nonzero if everything went well, otherwise _pie returns a zero.

SEE ALSO `_setcolor`   To set the current color

`_setfillmask`   To set the current fill pattern

_pie

EXAMPLE Write a C program to illustrate how a wedge is drawn with _pie. Draw two pieces of pie: one with a border only, the other filled using a fill pattern.

```c
#include <stdio.h>
#include <graph.h>
#define BLUE 1     /* Color number 1 is blue */
#define RED  4     /* Color number 4 is red */
unsigned char fmask[8]=
{ 0xf0, 0xf0, 0xf0, 0xf0, 0xf, 0xf, 0xf, 0xf };

main()
{
/* Enter hi-resolution graphics mode on EGA */
    if (_setvideomode(_ERESCOLOR) != 0)
    {
/* Draw a bordered pie --
 * Note that line style does not affect border
 */
        _settextposition(1,1);
        _outtext("A bordered pie:");
        _setcolor(BLUE);
        _pie(_GBORDER, 0, 50, 150, 100, 0, 100, 0, 50);
/* Draw a filled pie-shaped wedge --
 * this one complements the earlier pie
 */
        _settextposition(10,1);
        _outtext("A filled piece to match:");
        _setcolor(RED);
        _setfillmask(fmask);
        _pie(_GFILLINTERIOR,
             0, 150, 150, 200, 0, 150, 0, 200);

/* Restore original mode */
/* Give user a chance to see the result */
        _settextposition(20,1);
        _outtext("Hit any key to exit:");

        getch();
        _setvideomode(_DEFAULTMODE);
    }
    else
    {
/* Error setting mode */
        printf("Mode not supported by hardware\n");
    }
}
```

 Drawing and Animation

__putimage

COMPATIBILITY	MSC 3	MSC 4	MSC 5	QC	TC	ANSI	UNIX V
			▲	▲	putimage		

PURPOSE Use the _putimage function to display a rectangular screen image saved in a buffer by _getimage.

SYNTAX
```
void far _putimage(short x1, short y1, char far *image_buffer,
                   short action);
```

short x1, y1;   Logical coordinates of point on screen where the upper left corner of the rectangular image will be placed

char far *image_buffer;   Buffer where image has been saved

short action;   Command to _putimage instructing it to redraw the saved image in a particular manner

EXAMPLE CALL `_putimage(100, 200, image, _GXOR);`

INCLUDES `#include <graph.h>`   For function declaration and definition of action constants

DESCRIPTION The _putimage function redraws the image of a rectangular region of the screen saved earlier by _getimage in the buffer whose address is specified in the argument *image_buffer*. The saved image is drawn with the upper left corner at the point whose logical coordinates are (*x1, y1*). The size of the rectangular region need not be specified because this information is saved with the image.

The manner in which the image is redrawn depends on the value of the argument *action*. This argument should be one of the constants defined in the file *graph.h* and shown, along with their meanings, in Table 18-5.

COMMON USES The _putimage function is used to redraw screen images saved by _getimage. For example, you can draw an object, save it by calling _getimage, and move it around the screen with _putimage, in effect performing animation.

SEE ALSO
_imagesize   To determine number of bytes necessary to save a screen image

_putimage   To display a stored image

EXAMPLE In a graphics mode, draw some graphical objects and save them in memory by calling _getimage. Now clear the screen and use _putimage to animate the object on the screen.

```
#include <stdio.h>
#include <malloc.h>
#include <graph.h>
#define YELLOW 14
main()
{
    char far *image;
    char buffer[80];
    short x=0, y=0;
    unsigned numbytes, c = 0;
/* Assume EGA. Put it in high-resolution graphics mode */
    if (_setvideomode(_ERESCOLOR) == 0)
    {
/* Error setting mode */
        printf("Not EGA hardware\n");
        exit(0);
    }
/* Draw some graphical objects to save */
    _setcolor(YELLOW);
    _ellipse(_GFILLINTERIOR,0,0,10,10);
    _moveto(5,10);
    _lineto(5,20);
    _lineto(0,30);
    _moveto(10,30);
    _lineto(5,20);
    _moveto(0,15);
    _lineto(0,10);
    _lineto(10,15);
/* Determine storage needed for entire screen and
 * display result
 */
        numbytes = (unsigned int)_imagesize(0,0,10,30);
/* Allocate buffer for image */
        if ((image = (char far *) malloc(numbytes)) ==
            (char far *)NULL)
        {
            _setvideomode(_DEFAULTMODE);
            printf(
              "Not enough memory for image storage\n");
            exit(0);
        }
        _getimage(x,y,10,30,image); /* Save the image */
/* Now clear screen and draw saved image at several
 * screen locations
 */
        _clearscreen(_GCLEARSCREEN);
        _settextposition(1,1);
        _outtext(
```

 Drawing and Animation

```
              "Demonstrating animation with _putimage");
         _setlogorg(320,175);
         _putimage(x,y,image,_GXOR);
         _settextposition(24,1);
         _outtext(
           "q = exit, h=left, j=down, k=up, l=right");
/* Perform some animation */
         while(c != 'q')
         {
              c = getch();
/* First erase at last position */
              _putimage(x,y,image,_GXOR);
              switch(c)
              {
                  case 'h': x -= 2; /* 2 pixels left */
                          break;
                  case 'l': x += 2; /* 2 pixels right */
                          break;
                  case 'j': y += 2; /* 2 pixels down */
                          break;
                  case 'k': y -= 2; /* 2 pixels up   */
                          break;
              }
/* Redraw at new position */
              _putimage(x,y,image,_GXOR);
         }
/* Restore mode when done */
         _setvideomode(_DEFAULTMODE);
}
```

Table 18-5. *Interpreting Action Constants for* _putimage

Constants	Interpretation
_GAND	The image is drawn by performing a logical AND of the existing pixel value with the one from the saved image.
_GOR	The pixel values from the saved image are logically ORed with the existing pixel values in the area where the image is being drawn.
_GPRESET	Each bit in each pixel of the saved image is logically inverted, then these values are transferred to the screen, overwriting the existing image. For example, the areas of a saved EGA screen that were yellow (pixel value 14 = 1110 in binary) become blue (pixel value 1 = 0001 in binary).
_GPSET	The saved image is drawn at the specified area, overwriting any existing image.
_GXOR	Each pixel from the saved image is exclusive-ORed with the current pixels in the area where the image is being drawn. Very useful in animation because exclusive OR of an image with itself erases the image. Thus the background can be restored with this action command.

_putimage

__rectangle

PURPOSE   Use __rectangle to draw a filled or a bordered rectangle (see the tutorial section on specifying coordinates). Before calling __rectangle, use __setcolor to select the fill color, __setfillmask to select a fill pattern, and __setlinestyle to select a solid or a dashed line for the border.

SYNTAX
```
short far _rectangle(short flag, short x1, short y1,
                                 short x2, short y2);
```

`short flag;`   To fill or to draw a border only

`short x1, y1;`   Coordinates of upper left corner

`short x2, y2;`   Coordinates of lower right corner

EXAMPLE CALL   `_rectangle(_GBORDER, 100, 110, 250, 200);`

INCLUDES   `#include <graph.h>`   For function declaration and definition of fill flag constants

DESCRIPTION   The __rectangle function draws a rectangle specified by its upper left corner (*x1, y1*) and its lower right corner (*x2, y2*). The *x* coordinates go from left to right, and the *y* coordinates go from top to bottom with (0,0) at the upper left corner of the screen.

The argument *flag* indicates whether the rectangle is filled or drawn with a border. The value specified for *flag* can be either of the __GFILL-INTERIOR or __GBORDER constants, defined in the include file *graph.h*, and listed in Table 18-4.

COMMON USES   This function can be used as the basis of a graphics window program because filled or bordered rectangular regions are the building blocks for drawing "windows."

RETURNS   The return value is nonzero if everything went well. If there is an error (for example, when the coordinates of the upper left and lower right corners do not define a rectangle), __rectangle returns a zero.

COMMENTS   If you want a rectangle with a border color different from that used to fill the interior, you can first draw the rectangle with a border, then select a new color, and fill it by calling the __floodfill function. When you use this approach, the line style for the border must be solid. If the border is a dashed line, __floodfill leaks colors through the holes in the border.

 Drawing and Animation

SEE ALSO   _setcolor   To set the current color

_setlinestyle   To set the current line style

_setfillmask   To set the current fill mask

_floodfill   To fill a bordered rectangle with color

EXAMPLE   Using a graphics mode appropriate for your graphics hardware, write a C program to draw two rectangles, one bordered and one filled, on the screen.

```c
#include <stdio.h>
#include <graph.h>
#define BLUE 1     /* Color number 1 is blue */
#define RED  4     /* Color number 4 is red */
main()
{
/* Enter hi-resolution graphics mode on EGA */
    if (_setvideomode(_ERESCOLOR) == 0)
    {
/* Error setting mode */
        printf("Mode not supported by hardware\n");
        exit(0);
    }
/* Draw a filled rectangle */
    _settextposition(1,1);
    _outtext("A bordered rectangle:");
    _setcolor(BLUE);
    _rectangle(_GBORDER, 0, 50, 100, 100);
/* Draw a filled rectangle */
    _settextposition(10,1);
    _outtext("A filled rectangle:");
    _setcolor(RED);
    _rectangle(_GFILLINTERIOR, 0, 150, 100, 200);

/* Restore original mode */
/* Give user a chance to see the result */
    _settextposition(20,1);
    _outtext("Hit any key to exit:");
    getch();
    _setvideomode(_DEFAULTMODE);
}
```

_rectangle

__setpixel

COMPATIBILITY	MSC 3	MSC 4	MSC 5	QC	TC	ANSI	UNIX V
			▲	▲	setpixel		

PURPOSE Use the _setpixel function to set a specific pixel to the current color. The location of the pixel is given in logical coordinates.

SYNTAX `short far _setpixel(short x, short y);`

`short x, y;` The logical x and y coordinates of the pixel to be set to current color

EXAMPLE CALL `_setpixel(120, 95);`

INCLUDES `#include <graph.h>` For function declaration

DESCRIPTION The _setpixel function first checks to see if the pixel specified by the logical coordinates (*x,y*) lies within the current clipping region or viewport. If it does, _setpixel fills the pixel with the current color.

COMMON USES The _setpixel function can be used for drawing complicated graphics images with multiple colors.

RETURNS If the pixel is inside the clipping region and _setpixel succeeds, it returns the previous pixel value. Otherwise, it returns a −1 to indicate failure.

SEE ALSO `_setcliprgn, _setviewport` To define a limited area of the screen as the clipping region for graphics output

`_getpixel` To determine the current value of a pixel

EXAMPLE In a graphics mode appropriate for your hardware, use _setpixel to draw a rectangle filled with many different colored pixels.

```
#include <stdio.h>
#include <graph.h>

main()
{
    short x, y, color;
/* Assume an EGA environment */
    if (_setvideomode(_ERESCOLOR) == 0)
    {
        printf("Not EGA environment\n");
        exit(0);
    }
    _settextposition(1,1);
```

 Drawing and Animation

```
        _outtext("Multicolored rectangle using _setpixel");
/* Go over a rectangular region and fill pixels with
 * color
 */
    color = 0; /* Initialize to first color in palette*/
    for(x=50; x<150; x++)
    {
        for(y=40; y<90; y++)
        {
            _setcolor(color);
            _setpixel(x,y);         /* Set pixel to color*/
        }
        color++;                    /* Go to next color  */
       if(color > 15)
            color=0;                /* Color in 0-15  */
    }
/* Wait for user to hit a key, then reset everything  */
    _settextposition(25,1);
    _outtext("Hit any key to reset mode and exit:");
    getch();
    _setvideomode(_DEFAULTMODE);
}
```

__setpixel

Introduction

Text is an essential part of graphics. For example, if you prepare a bar graph or a pie chart, you have to annotate the graph so that the user can understand the meaning of the plots. The Microsoft C 5.1 graphics library includes seven routines to control text output. You can use these routines to position text anywhere in the screen, select a text color, and even have the text confined within a window, among other functions.

Notes on Mixing Graphics and Text

Table 19-1 lists the routines available for text output and for controlling the appearance of text on the screen. Table 19-2 categorizes these routines by task. The text output routines work in both graphics and text modes.

Table 19-1. *Text Output Routines*

Routine	Description
_gettextcolor	Returns current text color.
_gettextposition	Returns current text position.
_settextposition	Sets the text position where subsequent text output will begin.
_outtext	Outputs text to screen at current text position.
_settextcolor	Sets the text color to be used in future text outputs.
_settextwindow	Defines a scrolling text display window.
_wrapon	Toggles an internal flag that enables or disables wrapping of a line of text that extends beyond the window. When disabled, the line is truncated at the boundary of the window.

Table 19-2. *Text Output Routines by Task*

Task	Routines
Output text	_outtext
Control text color	_gettextcolor, _settextcolor
Position text on the screen	_gettextposition, _settextposition
Set up a window	_settextwindow
Control line wrapping	_wrapon

TEXT OUTPUT
The C library features such routines as *printf* and *cprintf* to print formatted text on the screen. These routines work in the graphics programs as well, but they do not use the current text color in the Microsoft C graphics model. For this, the graphics library provides the *_outtext* routine, which outputs text using color in both text and graphics modes.

The *_outtext* routine, however, does not have a formatting capability, but you can still print formatted text with the help of the string printing routine, *sprintf*. You first prepare the formatted string and then pass that string to *_outtext* for printing. Here is an example

```
char string[80];
double result;
    :
sprintf(string, "The result is: %.2f", result);
_outtext(string);
```

that prints the string using the current text color at the current text position, which is updated as each character is output.

TEXT COLOR
You can set the current text color by calling *_settextcolor*. A companion function, *_gettextcolor*, lets you query the graphics package for the current text color so you can save the text color before changing it. After your application, you can reset the color to the saved value. You specify the color with a color number. For example,

```
_settextcolor(14);  /* 14 is normally yellow */
_outtext(string);
```

prints the string in yellow. In text modes _TEXTC40 and _TEXTC80 the color numbers can go beyond the maximum allowed in the palette. The CGA, EGA, and VGA offer a 16-color text mode. In this mode, colors from 0 through 15 are as defined in the palette (see Chapter 17), but color numbers 16 through 31 are also allowed. These generate blinking text using the same colors as those in the 0 through 15 range.

Use the *_getvideoconfig* function (see Chapter 17) to select text colors and backgrounds that are appropriate for your adapter and monitor combination. This is important because a color combination that works well on a CGA may become invisible on the MDA. (There is no color on the monochrome adapter, so the specified values map to text attributes such as underline, blink, and reverse.)

TEXT WINDOW AND POSITION

The text position is another parameter maintained internally by the Microsoft C graphics library. Text position is always specified in the (row, column) format, even in graphics modes. Use _settextposition_ to set the text position and _gettextposition_ to find the current value.

All text positions are relative to the upper left corner of a rectangular area known as the "text window." The default window is the entire screen, but you can define a smaller window by calling _settextwindow_. For example, the code

```
_settextwindow(10,10,15,70);   /* Define a text window*/
_clearscreen(_GWINDOW);        /* Clear out text window  */
_settextposition(2,30);
_outtext("Hello!");
```

defines a rectangular text window, 5 rows by 60 columns, with the upper left corner at row and column coordinates (10,10). The call to _clearscreen_ clears out the text window only. Then _settextposition_ moves the current text position to the second row and the thirtieth column in the text window (which translates to the twelfth row and fortieth column on the display screen) and _outtext_ prints the message.

Text windows can be used to implement pop-up menus or message windows.

LINE WRAP

When a long line of text is printed using _outtext_, the entire line may not fit within the width of the text window. You can set a flag using the function _wrapon_ to control whether the line is truncated at the boundary of the window or automatically wrapped around to the next line. The call _wrapon_ _(_GWRAPON)_ turns wrapping on. Use the argument _GWRAPOFF to turn wrapping off.

__gettextcolor

COMPATIBILITY	MSC 3	MSC 4	MSC 5	QC	TC	ANSI	UNIX V
			▲	▲	gettextinfo		

PURPOSE Use the __gettextcolor_ function to get the value of the current text color parameter (see __settextcolor_ for interpretation of the value). Also, note that only __outtext_ uses this text color value; other C routines such as *printf* are not affected.

SYNTAX `short far _gettextcolor(void);`

EXAMPLE CALL `txt_color_now = _gettextcolor();`

INCLUDES `#include <graph.h>`   For function declaration

DESCRIPTION The __gettextcolor_ function returns the value of the current text color parameter maintained internally by the graphics package. This color is only used by __outtext_ to determine the color of the text it displays. The standard C library routine for text output, *printf*, does not use this color.

COMMON USES The __gettextcolor_ function allows you to save the current text color before changing it. By doing so, you can restore the color to its original value before exiting from your routine.

RETURNS The __gettextcolor_ function returns a short integer containing the current value of the text color parameter.

SEE ALSO `_settextcolor`   To set the current text color to a new value

EXAMPLE In text mode, set the color to a specific value by calling __settextcolor_. Then call __gettextcolor_ to verify that the current color is what you expect it to be. Also display a string to show the color.

```
#include <stdio.h>
#include <graph.h>
#define RED 4       /* Text color 4 means red */
main()
{
    char buffer[80];
    short color;
/* Assume we are already in text mode */
    _clearscreen(_GCLEARSCREEN);        /* Clear screen */
    _gettextposition(1,1);    /* set up text position */
    _settextcolor(RED);           /* Set text color to RED */
    color = _gettextcolor();      /* Get current color */
    sprintf(buffer,"_gettextcolor says: current color \
```

Combining Graphics and Text

```
                 = %2d\n", color);        /* Display the current color */
                   _outtext(buffer);
                   _outtext("The value should be 4\n");
                 }
```

__gettextposition

COMPATIBILITY	MSC 3	MSC 4	MSC 5	QC	TC	ANSI	UNIX V
			▲	▲	wherex, wherey		

PURPOSE Use _gettextposition_ to retrieve the current text position in a structure of type *rccoord* that contains the current row and column where text output appears if you call the output function _outtext_ or any other standard C output routine such as *printf*.

SYNTAX `struct rccoord far _gettextposition(void);`

EXAMPLE CALL `row_col_pos = _gettextposition();`

INCLUDES `#include <graph.h>`   For function declaration and definition of the structure *rccoord*

DESCRIPTION The _gettextposition_ function returns the current text position which is maintained internally by the graphics package. The current row and column are returned in the structure *rccoord*. This is the position where text appears if you call the graphics library function _outtext_ or standard C I/O routines such as *printf*.

COMMON USES The _gettextposition_ function can be used to save the current text position before changing it for the specific purposes of your routine. That way, the saved value can be used to reset the text position to its original value before exiting your routine.

RETURNS The _gettextposition_ function returns a structure of type *rccoord* containing the row and column defining the current text position. This structure, shown below, is declared in the include file *graph.h*.

```
struct rccoord      /* Structure for text position    */
{
        short row;  /* row number of text position     */
        short col;  /* column number of text position */
};
```

COMMENTS The _settextposition_ function also returns the last text position in the form of a *rccoord* structure, but you have to move to a new position (calling _settextposition_ implies this) to find out the current row and column position.

You can get this information in a more straightforward manner by calling
_gettextposition.

SEE ALSO   _settextposition   To change current text position

EXAMPLE   In a text mode, move to a specific text position by calling *_settextposition*.
Verify that *_gettextposition* returns the same location. Display a sample text
string showing the results obtained from *_gettextposition* at that location.

```
#include <stdio.h>
#include <graph.h>
main()
{
/* Assume we are already in text mode */
    struct rccoord curpos;
    short row = 1;
    char c=0, buffer[80];
    _clearscreen(_GCLEARSCREEN);     /* Clear screen */
    _settextposition(1,1);
    _outtext("1234567.. This is row 1");
    _settextposition(2,2);
    curpos = _gettextposition(); /* get new position */
    sprintf(buffer, "This string begins at (%d,%d)",
            curpos.row, curpos.col);
    _outtext(buffer);
}
```

_outtext

COMPATIBILITY	MSC 3	MSC 4	MSC 5	QC	TC	ANSI	UNIX V
			▲	▲	outtext		

PURPOSE   Use the *_outtext* function to display null-terminated C strings (arrays of characters that end with a byte containing zero) at the current text position (see
_settextposition) using the current text color (see *_settextcolor*). To display
formatted strings, first prepare output in a buffer by calling *sprintf*, and then
display the buffer by calling *_outtext* with the buffer address as the argument
(see the example below).

SYNTAX   void far _outtext(char far *buffer);

char far *buffer;   Pointer to character buffer that holds the null-terminated string
to be printed by *_outtext*

INCLUDES   #include <graph.h>   For function declaration

 Combining Graphics and Text

DESCRIPTION   The *_outtext* function displays on the screen the string whose address is specified in the argument *buffer*. The text output begins at the current text position and uses the current text color. These parameters can be set by calling the graphics library routines *_settextposition* and *_settextcolor*. The text output always occurs in the current page (a portion of video memory that can hold one screenful of text), which is set by calling *_setactivepe*.

   After displaying the string, *_outtext* updates the current text position to the screen location next to the last character printed. If a text window is defined by calling *_settextwindow*, text display is confined to this window. If a line spills beyond the window, it is either wrapped around or clipped according to an internal flag set by the function *_wrapon*.

COMMON USES   The *_outtext* function is used extensively for displaying text in both text and graphics modes. Its ability to display text in various colors is especially handy in designing text-oriented user interfaces that use color to highlight output.

COMMENTS   You will often want to display formatted text, for example, text that includes the ASCII representation of an integer value. Note that *_outtext* is not capable of any formatting. So, in these cases, you should first prepare the formatted string by calling *sprintf* and then display the string using *_outtext*.

SEE ALSO   _setactivepage   To set the block of video memory (page) where text is actually entered

   _settextcolor   To change the current text color

   _settextposition   To set the row and column coordinates where text output will begin

   _settextwindow   To define a window within which text is output

   _wrapon   Control whether text that extends beyond the display region gets wrapped or clipped

EXAMPLE   Suppose you are in a text mode. Define a window for text by calling *_settextwindow*. Make the window stand out by setting a new background color with *_setbkcolor* and calling *_clearscreen* to clear the text window and fill it with the new background color. Select an appropriate text color and display some text by using *_outtext*.

```
#include <stdio.h>
#include <graph.h>
/* Need a "long" constant for _setbkcolor  */
#define RED    4L
/* Text color number 14 is yellow            */
#define YELLOW 14
main()
{
```

_outtext

```
        char buffer[80];        /* Buffer for text string */
/* Assume we are already in text mode                      */
        _clearscreen(_GCLEARSCREEN);    /* Clear screen    */
        _settextwindow(10,10,15,70);/* Define text window*/
        _setbkcolor(RED); /* Set background color to red */
        _clearscreen(_GWINDOW);        /* clear text window */

/* Once a text window is defined all text positions are
 * relative to upper left corner of the window. Notice
 * that this can be used for pop-up menus
 */
        _settextposition(1,10); /* Set text position     */
        _settextcolor(YELLOW);  /* Set text color        */
        _outtext("_outtext in a text window\n");
/* We'll be in the next line because of the '\n'           */
/*  Prepare a formatted string and display it             */
        sprintf(buffer,
    "This line begins at = (%d,%d) and in color = %d\n",
    (_gettextposition()).row,  /* position is  returned */
    (_gettextposition()).col,  /* in a structure        */
    _gettextcolor());
        _outtext(buffer);
}
```

__settextcolor

COMPATIBILITY	MSC 3	MSC 4	MSC 5	QC	TC	ANSI	UNIX V
			▲	▲	textcolor		

PURPOSE Use the __settextcolor_ function to set the current text color parameter, a short integer value that is used as the attribute for each text character. The mapping of this "attribute value" to a specific color is determined by the current palette. The graphics library allows text color values in the range 0 to 31. The values 0 to 15 produce normal colors (see Table 17-3) while the rest (16 through 31) generate similar colors but with blinking text. As you can see, text color values are not restricted to the range of color numbers available in the current palette (current color and background color in text mode have this restriction). Note that only __outtext_ uses this text color value, other C routines such as *printf* are not affected.

SYNTAX `short far _settextcolor(short color);`

`short color;`   Text color parameter

EXAMPLE CALL `_settextcolor(1);`

 Combining Graphics and Text

INCLUDES   `#include <graph.h>`   For function declaration

DESCRIPTION   The _*settextcolor* function sets the current text color parameter maintained internally by the graphics package. In text mode, each character displayed requires 2 bytes of storage; one holds the ASCII value, the other has an attribute which is the color parameter specified in the argument *color*. This argument can take any value between 0 and 31. The first 16 numbers, 0 to 15, produce text with normal color. The mapping of the value to the color is shown in Table 17-3.

   The last 16 values, 16 through 31, display text that is blinking with the color corresponding to the value obtained by subtracting 16. This is the color in which text will appear if you call the graphics library function _*outtext*.

COMMON USES   The _*settextcolor* function enables you to use different text colors as a means of highlighting your output.

RETURNS   The _*settextcolor* function returns the previous value of the text color parameter.

SEE ALSO   `_gettextcolor`   To retrieve the current text color

EXAMPLE   Assuming that the display environment is already in a text mode, generate a screenful of text showing each text color. Use _*settextcolor* to set the color and _*outtext* to display the strings. Show the first 16 colors on the left half of the screen and the corresponding blinking colors on the right half.

```
#include <stdio.h>
#include <graph.h>
main()
{
    char buffer[80];
    short i, color, lastcolor;
/* Assume we are already in text mode */
    _clearscreen(_GCLEARSCREEN);      /* Clear screen */
/* Set up initial text position */
    _settextposition(1,1);
/* Display the first 16 colors  */
    for (i=0; i<16; i++)
    {
/* Set a text color and show what the return value is*/
        lastcolor = _settextcolor(i);
        sprintf(buffer,"Current color = %2d, \
last value= %2d\n", i, lastcolor);
        _outtext(buffer);        /* Display the string */
    }
/* Display the next 16 colors on right half of screen */
    for (i=16; i<32; i++)
    {
```

__settextcolor

```
/* Set a text color and show what the return value is */
        lastcolor = _settextcolor(i);
        sprintf(buffer,"Current color = %2d, \
last value= %2d\n", i, lastcolor);
        _settextposition(i-15, 40);
        _outtext(buffer);        /* Display the string */
    }
}
```

__settextposition

COMPATIBILITY	MSC 3	MSC 4	MSC 5	QC	TC	ANSI	UNIX V
			▲	▲	gotoxy		

PURPOSE Use *_settextposition* to move the current text position to a specific row and column in both text and graphics modes. The text output function *_outtext* as well as standard C output routines such as *printf* begins displaying text from this position.

SYNTAX `struct rccoord far _settextposition(short row, short column);`

`short row, column;`   Row and column where new text output will begin

EXAMPLE CALL `_settextposition(24, 1);`

INCLUDES `#include <graph.h>`   For function declaration and definition of the structure *rccoord*

DESCRIPTION The *_settextposition* function changes the current text position maintained internally by the graphics package to the row and column specified in the arguments *row, column*. This position becomes the starting point for all future text outputs from such routines as *_outtext, printf,* and other console I/O routines.

The upper left corner of the screen in text mode corresponds to row 1 and column 1. The maximum row and column numbers allowable can be determined by calling *_getvideoconfig* in the text mode.

Text output can be limited to a smaller region by calling *_settextwindow* to define a window. After calling *_textwindow*, all row and column references are considered relative to the upper left corner of the window (see *_settextwindow*).

COMMON USES The *_settextposition* function can position text output at arbitrary locations on the screen.

RETURNS The *_settextposition* function returns a structure of type *rccoord*, which contains the row and column of the last text position (the cursor's location

Combining Graphics and Text

before _*settextposition* was called). This structure is defined in the include file *graph.h* and is shown below.

```
struct rccoord     /* Structure for text position   */
{
    short row;     /* row number of text position    */
    short col;     /* column number of text position */
};
```

The last position returned in this structure can be used to save and restore the old text position.

SEE ALSO　_gettextposition　　　To get current text position in a structure of type *rccoord*

　　　　　　　_outtext　　　To display text starting at current text position

EXAMPLE　Suppose you are in a text mode on a color display. Define a position for text by calling _*settextposition*. Prepare a string containing the previous text position returned by _*settext* and display it by calling _*outtext*. When you hit a key, the program should advance to the next row and display the same information again. Exit when the user hits a 'q'.

```
#include <stdio.h>
#include <graph.h>
main()
{
    struct rccoord lastpos;
    short row = 1;
    char c=0, buffer[80];
    _clearscreen(_GCLEARSCREEN);      /* Clear screen */
/* Keep on displaying text until user hits 'q'        */
    while(1)
    {
/* Set new position */
        lastpos = _settextposition(row,1);
        sprintf(buffer, "Hit 'q' to exit. Last \
position = (%d,%d)", lastpos.row, lastpos.col);
        _outtext(buffer);
        c = getch();
        if(c == 'q' || c == 'Q')
        {
            _setvideomode(_DEFAULTMODE); /* reset mode*/
            exit(0);
        }
        row++;                        /* Advance to next row */
    }
}
```

__settextposition

__settextwindow

COMPATIBILITY	MSC 3	MSC 4	MSC 5	QC	TC	ANSI	UNIX V
			▲	▲	window		

PURPOSE
Use _settextwindow to define a window in terms of row and column coordinates (see the tutorial section) for scrolled text output. You can define a new background color for text (see _setbkcolor) and clear the text window to give it a different background color from the rest. Similar windows for graphics can be defined by calling the _setviewport function.

SYNTAX
```
void far _settextwindow(short r1, short c1, short r2, short c2);
```

short r1, c1;   Upper left corner of text window in row and olumn coordinates

short r2, c2;   Lower right corner of text window in row and column coordinates

EXAMPLE CALL
```
_settextwindow(10, 10, 16, 70);
```

INCLUDES
```
#include <graph.h>
```
For function declaration

DESCRIPTION
The _settextwindow function defines an area of the screen (a text window) as the current display window for text output. The window is specified in terms of the row and column (row 1, column 1 corresponds to the upper left corner of the screen) coordinates of the upper left hand corner (*x1, y1*) and that of the lower right corner (*x2, y2*).

Once the text window is defined, all row and column references are relative to the upper left corner of the window (see the example below).

COMMON USES
The _settextwindow function can be used to design pop-up menus.

SEE ALSO
_setbkcolor   To change the background color

_settextposition   To set location where text is output next

_outtext   To display text

EXAMPLE
Suppose you are in a text mode on a color display. Define a window for text by calling _settextwindow. Set a new background color by calling _setbkcolor and call _clearscreen to clear the text window and fill it with the new background color. Let the user type lines of text into the window to show the effect of scrolling in the window.

```
#include <stdio.h>
#include <graph.h>
/* Need a "long" constant for _setbkcolor  */
#define RED 4L
```

 Combining Graphics and Text

```
main()
{
    unsigned i=0;
    char c=0, buffer[80];
    _clearscreen(_GCLEARSCREEN); /* Clear screen */
    _settextwindow(10,10,15,70);
    _setbkcolor(RED);            /* Set background color to red */
    _clearscreen(_GWINDOW);      /* clear text window */

/* Once a text window is defined all text positions are
 * relative to upper left corner of the window. This
 * can be used for pop-up menus
 */
    _settextposition(1,1);       /* Display a message */
    _outtext("Scrolling in a text window\n");
/* Let user see the effect of scrolling */
    while(1)
    {
/* Notice the use of a buffer and sprintf to print a
 * formatted string with _outtext
 */
        sprintf(buffer,
            "Hit 'q' to exit. -- else scroll %d\n",i);
        _outtext(buffer);
        c = getch();
        if(c == 'q' || c == 'Q')
        {
            _setvideomode(_DEFAULTMODE); /* reset mode*/
            exit(0);
        }
        i++;
    }
}
```

__wrapon

COMPATIBILITY	MSC 3	MSC 4	MSC 5	QC	TC	ANSI	UNIX V
			▲	▲			

PURPOSE Use the _wrapon function to control whether text being output by _outtext is clipped or wrapped to the next line when the text string extends beyond the current text window. The default setting is to wrap long lines.

SYNTAX short far _wrapon(short flag);

short flag;   Turn wrapping on or off

EXAMPLE CALL `_wrapon(_GWRAPOFF);`

INCLUDES `#include <graph.h>`   For function declaration and definition of constants for the flag

DESCRIPTION The *_wrapon* function copies the argument *flag* into an internal flag in the graphics package used by the text output routine *_outtext* to decide how to handle a line of text that extends beyond the edge of the current text window. The setting of the flag can take one of two defined values shown below. The interpretation of each value is also shown. Table 19-3 shows these constants, which are defined in the include file *graph.h*.

Table 19-3. *Constants Used by* __wrapon

Constant	Interpretation
_GWRAPOFF	Long lines are truncated at the edge of text window.
_GWRAPON	Lines extending beyond the text window get wrapped to a new line.

RETURNS The *_wrapon* function returns a short integer containing the value of the *flag* before the current call.

COMMENTS The wrapping is done by character, not by word. You have to write your own routines to break lines at word boundaries.

SEE ALSO `_settextwindow`   To define a window within which text is output

`_outtext`   To display a text string

EXAMPLE In a text mode, define a window for text by calling *_settextwindow*. Fill the window with a new color to make it distinguishable from the rest by setting a new background color with *_setbkcolor* and calling *_clearscreen* to clear the text window. Select an appropriate text color and demonstrate the effects of calling *_wrapon*.

```
#include <stdio.h>
#include <graph.h>
/* Need a "long" constant for _setbkcolor  */
#define RED    4L
/* Text color number 14 is yellow          */
#define YELLOW 14
main()
{
/* Assume we are already in text mode                */
    _clearscreen(_GCLEARSCREEN);    /* Clear screen */

    _settextwindow(5,30,20,50); /* Define text window*/
```

 Combining Graphics and Text

```
/* Set background color to red                    */
    _setbkcolor(RED);
    _clearscreen(_GWINDOW); /* clear out text window */


/* Once a text window is defined, all text positions
 * are relative to the upper left corner of the window.
 */
    _settextposition(1,1);        /* Set text position  */
/* Show the effect of default setting first          */
    _outtext("As you can see, default is WRAP ON\n");


    _settextcolor(YELLOW);        /* Set text color    */
/* Turn wrapping off and show the results -- truncated
 * line
 */
    _wrapon(_GWRAPOFF);
    _outtext("This line extends beyond the edge.\n");
    _outtext("That was WRAP OFF.\n\n");
/* Turn wrapping back on and see line being wrapped  */
    _wrapon(_GWRAPON);
    _outtext("Now it's WRAP ON:\n");
    _outtext("This line extends beyond the edge.\n");
}
```

__wrapon

Index

Programming in C, Revised Edition
Stephen G. Kochan

This timely revision provides complete coverage of the C language, including all language features and over 90 program examples. The comprehensive tutorial approach teaches the beginner how to write, compile, and execute programs and teaches the experienced programmer how to write applications using features unique to C. It is written in a clear instructive style and is ideally suited for classroom use or as a self-study guide.

Topics covered include:

■ Introduction and Fundamentals
■ Writing a Program in C
■ Variables, Constants, Data Types, and Arithmetic Expressions
■ Program Looping
■ Making Decisions
■ Arrays
■ Functions
■ Structures
■ Character Strings
■ Pointers
■ Operations on Bits
■ The Preprocessor
■ Working with Larger Programs
■ Input and Output
■ Miscellaneous and Advanced Features
■ Appendices: Language Summary, ANSI Standard C, Common Programming Mistakes, The UNIX C Library, Compiling Programs under UNIX, The Program LINT, The ASCII Character Set

464 Pages, 7½ x 9¾, Softbound
ISBN: 0-672-48420-X
No. 48420, $24.95

Programming in ANSI C
Stephen G. Kochan

This comprehensive programming guide is the newest title in the Hayden Books C Library, written by the series editor Stephen G. Kochan. A tutorial in nature, the book teaches the beginner how to write, compile and execute programs even with no previous experience with C.

The book details such C essentials as program looping, decision making, arrays, functions, structures, character strings, bit operations, and enumerated data types. Examples are complete with step-by-step explanations of each procedure and routine involved as well as end-of-chapter exercises, making it ideally suited for classroom use.

Topics covered include:

■ Introduction and Fundamentals
■ Writing a Program in ANSI C
■ Variables, Data Types, and Arithmetic Expressions
■ Program Looping
■ Making Decisions
■ Arrays, Functions, Structures
■ Character Strings, Pointers
■ Operations on Bits
■ The Preprocessor
■ More on Data Types
■ Working with Larger Programs
■ Input and Output
■ Miscellaneous Features and Topics
■ Appendices: ANSI C Language Summary, The UNIX C Library, Compiling Programs Under UNIX, The Program LINT, The ASCII Character Set

450 Pages, 7½ x 9¾, Softbound
ISBN: 0-672-48408-0
No. 48408, $24.95

Advanced C: Tips and Techniques
Paul L. Anderson and Gail C. Anderson

If you have a working knowledge of the C language and want to enhance your programming skills, the examples and techniques found in this new book are just what you need. It is an in-depth look at the C programming language with special emphasis on portability, execution efficiency, and application techniques.

With entire chapters devoted to special areas of C such as debugging techniques, C's run-time environment, and a memory object allocator, the book contains detailed explanations and examples that will show you how to speed up your C programs. Techniques for creating and deciphering expressions, moving data, and coding expressions that execute predictably are included as well as end-of-chapter exercises that help you learn what has been explained.

Topics covered include:

■ C Refresher
■ The Run-Time Environment
■ Bits of C
■ There's No Such Thing as an Array
■ A Closer Look at C
■ C Debugging Techniques
■ A Memory Object Allocator
■ Appendices: Portable C Under UNIX System V, Microsoft C Under XENIX, Microsoft C Under DOS, Turbo C Under DOS

325 Pages, 7½ x 9¾, Softbound
ISBN: 0-672-48417-X
No. 48417, $24.95

Topics in C Programming
Stephen G. Kochan and Patrick H. Wood

Here is the most advanced and comprehensive coverage of the maturing C market. This sequel to *Programming in C* describes in detail some of the most difficult concepts in the C language—structures and pointers. It also explores the standard C library and standard I/O library, dynamic memory allocation, linked lists, tree structures, and dispatch tables.

Experienced C programmers can examine the UNIX System Interface through discussions on controlling processes, pipes, and terminal I/O. *Topics in C Programming* also explains how to write terminal-independent programs, how to debug C programs and analyze their performance, and how to use "make" for automatic generation of a programming system.

Topics covered include:

■ Structures and Pointers
■ The Standard C Library
■ The Standard I/O Library
■ UNIX System Interface
■ Writing Terminal-Independent Programs with the "curses" Library
■ Debug and Performance Analysis of C Programs
■ Generating Program Systems with "make"

528 Pages, 7½ x 9¾, Softbound
ISBN: 0-672-46290-7
No. 46290, $24.95

Visit your local book retailer, use the order form provided, or call 800-428-SAMS.

Microsoft C Functions   by Subject